# ADAM SMITH

## V

## Lectures on Jurisprudence

THE GLASGOW EDITION OF THE WORKS AND
CORRESPONDENCE OF ADAM SMITH

*Commissioned by the University of Glasgow to celebrate the bicentenary of
the Wealth of Nations*

I

THE THEORY OF MORAL SENTIMENTS
*Edited by* D. D. RAPHAEL *and* A. L. MACFIE

II

AN INQUIRY INTO THE NATURE AND CAUSES
OF THE WEALTH OF NATIONS
*Edited by* R. H. CAMPBELL *and* A. S. SKINNER; *textual editor* W. B. TODD

III

ESSAYS ON PHILOSOPHICAL SUBJECTS
(and Miscellaneous Pieces)
*Edited by* W. P. D. WIGHTMAN

IV

LECTURES ON RHETORIC AND BELLES LETTRES
*Edited by* J. C. BRYCE
This volume includes the *Considerations concerning the
First Formation of Languages*

V

LECTURES ON JURISPRUDENCE
*Edited by* R. L. MEEK, D. D. RAPHAEL, *and* P. G. STEIN
This volume includes two reports of Smith's course together with
the 'Early Draft' of part of *The Wealth of Nations*

VI

CORRESPONDENCE OF ADAM SMITH
*Edited by* E. C. MOSSNER *and* I. S. ROSS

*Associated volumes:*

ESSAYS ON ADAM SMITH
*Edited by* A. S. SKINNER *and* T. WILSON

LIFE OF ADAM SMITH
*By* I. S. ROSS

*The Glasgow Edition of the Works and Correspondence of Adam Smith and
the associated volumes are published in hardcover by Oxford University
Press. The six titles of the Glasgow Edition, but not the associated volumes,
are being published in softcover by Liberty Fund.*

# ADAM SMITH
# Lectures on Jurisprudence

EDITED BY

## R. L. MEEK
## D. D. RAPHAEL
AND
## P. G. STEIN

Liberty Fund

This book is published by Liberty Fund, Inc., a foundation established to encourage study of the ideal of a society of free and responsible individuals.

The cuneiform inscription that serves as our logo and as the design motif for our endpapers is the earliest-known written appearance of the word "freedom" (*amagi*), or "liberty." It is taken from a clay document written about 2300 B.C. in the Sumerian city-state of Lagash.

This Liberty Fund edition of 1982 is an exact photographic reproduction of the edition published by Oxford University Press in 1978.

Liberty Fund, Inc.
11301 North Meridian Street
Carmel, Indiana 46032
libertyfund.org

This reprint has been authorized by the Oxford University Press.

**Library of Congress Cataloging in Publication Data**

Smith, Adam, 1723–1790.
Lectures on jurisprudence.

Reprint. Originally published: Oxford: Clarendon Press, 1978.
(The Glasgow edition of the works and correspondence
of Adam Smith; 5)
Includes bibliographical references and indexes.
1. Jurisprudence. I. Meek, Ronald L.
II. Raphael, D. D. (David Daiches), 1916–
III. Stein, Peter, 1926–
IV. Title.
V. Series: Smith, Adam, 1723–1790. Works. 1976; 5.
AC7.S59   1976a   vol. 5   330.15'3S   81-23689
[K230.S6]   [340.1]   AACR2
ISBN 0-86597-011-4 (pbk.)

20   21   22   23   24   P   13   12   11   10   9

This book is printed on paper that is acid-free and meets the requirements of the American National Standard for Permanence of Paper for Printed Library Materials, Z39.48–1992. ⊚

Cover design by JMH Corporation, Indianapolis, Indiana.
Printed and bound by Sheridan Books, Inc., Chelsea, Michigan

# Contents

# Abbreviations

## A. WORKS INCLUDED IN THE GLASGOW EDITION

| | |
|---|---|
| Corr. | *Correspondence* |
| ED | 'Early Draft' of Part of *The Wealth of Nations*, Register House, Edinburgh |
| FA, FB | Two fragments on the division of labour, Buchan Papers, Glasgow University Library |
| Imitative Arts | 'Of the Nature of that Imitation which takes place in what are called the Imitative Arts' (in *Essays on Philosophical Subjects*) |
| LJ(A) | *Lectures on Jurisprudence*: Report of 1762–3, Glasgow University Library |
| LJ(B) | *Lectures on Jurisprudence*: Report dated 1766, Glasgow University Library |
| LRBL | *Lectures on Rhetoric and Belles Lettres* |
| Stewart | Dugald Stewart, 'Account of the Life and Writings of Adam Smith, LL.D.' (in *Essays on Philosophical Subjects*) |
| TMS | *The Theory of Moral Sentiments* |
| WN | *The Wealth of Nations* |

## B. OTHER WORKS

| | |
|---|---|
| A.P.S. | *The Acts of the Parliaments of Scotland 1124–1707*, ed. T. Thomson and C. Innes, 12 vol. (1814–75) |
| Anderson Notes | From John Anderson's Commonplace Book, vol. i, Andersonian Library, University of Strathclyde |
| C. | Code of Justinian |
| C. Th. | Code of Theodosius |
| Cocceius | *Samuelis L. B. de Cocceii . . . Introductio ad Henrici L. B. de Cocceii . . . Grotium illustratum, continens dissertationes proemiales XII* (1748) |
| D. | Digest of Justinian |
| Dalrymple | Sir John Dalrymple, *An Essay towards a General History of Feudal Property in Great Britain* (1757; 4th edn., 1759) |
| Erskine | John Erskine, *The Principles of the Law of Scotland* (1754) |
| Grotius | Hugo Grotius, *De Jure Belli ac Pacis libri tres* (1625) |
| Hale | Sir Matthew Hale, *The History of the Pleas of the Crown*, 2 vol. (1736) |
| Harris | Joseph Harris, *An Essay upon Money and Coins*, Parts I and II (1757–8) |
| Hawkins | William Hawkins, *A Treatise of the Pleas of the Crown*, 2 vol. (1716) |
| Heineccius | Johann Gottlieb Heineccius, *Antiquitatum Romanarum jurisprudentiam illustrantium Syntagma* (1719; 6th edn., 1742) |

| | |
|---|---|
| Hume, *Essays* | David Hume, *Essays, Moral, Political, and Literary*, ed. T. H. Green and T. H. Grose, 2 vol. (1875; new edn., 1889) |
| Hume, *History*, I and II | David Hume, *The History of England, from . . . Julius Caesar to the accession of Henry VII*, 2 vol. (1762) |
| *History*, III and IV | David Hume, *The History of England under the House of Tudor*, 2 vol. (1759) |
| Hutcheson, *M.P.* | Francis Hutcheson, *A Short Introduction to Moral Philosophy* (1747), being English translation of *Philosophiae Moralis Institutio Compendiaria* (1742) |
| *System* | Francis Hutcheson, *A System of Moral Philosophy*, 2 vol. (1755) |
| *Inst.* | Institutes of Justinian |
| Kames, *Essays* | Henry Home, Lord Kames, *Essays upon several subjects concerning British Antiquities* (1747) |
| *Law Tracts* | Henry Home, Lord Kames, *Historical Law-Tracts*, 2 vol. (1758) |
| Locke, *Civil Government* | John Locke, *Second Treatise, of Civil Government* (1690) |
| M'Douall | Andrew M'Douall, Lord Bankton, *An Institute of the Laws of Scotland in Civil Rights*, 3 vol. (1751–3) |
| Mandeville | Bernard Mandeville, *The Fable of the Bees*, Part I (1714), Part II (1729), ed. F. B. Kaye, 2 vol. (1924) |
| Montesquieu | C. L. de Secondat, Baron de Montesquieu, *De l'esprit des lois* (1748) |
| Pufendorf | Samuel von Pufendorf, *De Jure Naturae et Gentium libri octo* (1672) |
| Rae | John Rae, *Life of Adam Smith* (1895) |
| Scott | William Robert Scott, *Adam Smith as Student and Professor* (1937) |
| Stair | James Dalrymple, Viscount Stair, *The Institutions of the Law of Scotland* (1681) |

# Introduction

## 1. Adam Smith's Lectures at Glasgow University

ADAM SMITH was elected to the Chair of Logic at Glasgow University on 9 January 1751, and admitted to the office on 16 January. He does not appear to have started lecturing at the University, however, until the beginning of the next academic session, in October 1751, when he embarked upon his first—and only—course of lectures to the Logic class.

In the well-known account of Smith's lectures at Glasgow which John Millar supplied to Dugald Stewart, this Logic course of 1751–2 is described as follows:

> In the Professorship of Logic, to which Mr Smith was appointed on his first introduction into this University, he soon saw the necessity of departing widely from the plan that had been followed by his predecessors, and of directing the attention of his pupils to studies of a more interesting and useful nature than the logic and metaphysics of the schools. Accordingly, after exhibiting a general view of the powers of the mind, and explaining so much of the ancient logic as was requisite to gratify curiosity with respect to an artificial method of reasoning, which had once occupied the universal attention of the learned, he dedicated all the rest of his time to the delivery of a system of rhetoric and belles lettres.[1]

This 'system of rhetoric and belles lettres', we may surmise, was based on the lectures on this subject which Smith had given at Edinburgh before coming to Glasgow, and was probably very similar to the course which he was later to deliver as a supplement to his Moral Philosophy course, and of which a student's report has come down to us.[2] Concerning the content of the preliminary part of the Logic course, however—that in which Smith exhibited 'a general view of the powers of the mind' and explained 'so much of the ancient logic as was requisite'—we know no more than Millar here tells us.

In the 1751–2 session, Smith not only gave this course to his Logic class but also helped out in the teaching of the Moral Philosophy class. Thomas Craigie, the then Professor of Moral Philosophy, had fallen ill, and at a University Meeting held on 11 September 1751 it was agreed that in his absence the teaching of the Moral Philosophy class should be shared out according to the following arrangement:

The Professor of Divinity, Mr. Rosse, Mr. Moor having in presence of the

---

[1] Stewart, I.16. The original version of Stewart's 'Account of the Life and Writings of Adam Smith', in which these remarks of Millar's were incorporated, was read by Stewart to the Royal Society of Edinburgh on 21 January and 18 March 1793.

[2] See below, pp. 4, 9, 11, and 15–17.

meeting, and Mr. Smith by his letter voluntarily agreed to give their assistance in the teaching both the publick and private classe in the following manner viz: the Professor undertakes to teach the Theologia Naturalis, and the first book of Mr. Hutchesons Ethicks, and Mr. Smith the other two books de Jurisprudentia Naturali et Politicis, and Mr. Rosse and Mr. Moor to teach the hour allotted for the private classe, the meeting unanimouslie agreed to the said proposals . . .[3]

About the actual content of these lectures of Smith's on 'natural jurisprudence and politics'[4] we know nothing, although we do know that according to the testimony of Smith himself a number of the opinions put forward in them had already been the subjects of lectures he had read at Edinburgh in the previous winter, and that they were to continue to be the 'constant subjects' of his lectures after 1751–2.[5]

In November 1751 Craigie died, and a few months later Smith was translated from his Chair of Logic to the now vacant Chair of Moral Philosophy. He was elected on 22 April 1752, and admitted on 29 April. His first full course of lectures to the Moral Philosophy class, therefore, was delivered in the 1752–3 session. He continued lecturing to the Moral Philosophy class until he left Glasgow, about the middle of January 1764,[6] to take up the position of tutor to the young Duke of Buccleuch.

[3] Minutes of University Meeting of 11 September 1751 (Glasgow University Archives).

[4] In the letter from Smith mentioned in the extract just quoted (Corr., Letter 9 addressed to William Cullen, dated 3 Sept. 1751), Smith wrote: 'I shall, with great pleasure, do what I can to relieve him [Professor Craigie] of the burden of his class. You mention natural jurisprudence and politics as the parts of his lectures which it would be most agreeable for me to take upon me to teach. I shall very willingly undertake both.'

[5] See Stewart, IV.25. Stewart is referring here to a document drawn up by Smith in 1755 which apparently contained 'a pretty long enumeration . . . of certain leading principles, both political and literary, to which he was anxious to establish his exclusive right; in order to prevent the possibility of some rival claims which he thought he had reason to apprehend'. From this document Stewart quotes (apparently verbatim) the following statement by Smith: 'A great part of the opinions enumerated in this paper is treated of at length in some lectures which I have still by me, and which were written in the hand of a clerk who left my service six years ago. They have all of them been the constant subjects of my lectures since I first taught Mr Craigie's class, the first winter I spent in Glasgow, down to this day, without any considerable variation. They had all of them been the subjects of lectures which I read at Edinburgh the winter before I left it, and I can adduce innumerable witnesses, both from that place and from this, who will ascertain them sufficiently to be mine.'

[6] The exact date on which Smith left Glasgow is not known. The fact that he was probably going to leave the University was publicly announced for the first time at a Dean of Faculty's Meeting on 8 November 1763. Two months later, at a Faculty Meeting on 9 January 1764, Smith stated that 'he was soon to leave this place' and that 'he had returned to the students all the fees he had received this session'. The previous Faculty Meeting (at which Smith had also been present) was held on 4 January 1764, so it may reasonably be assumed that his last lecture to the Moral Philosophy class (at which, according to Tytler's account, the fees were returned) was delivered at some time during the period between these two Faculty Meetings. The last meeting at Glasgow University which Smith attended in his capacity as a member of the teaching staff was a University Meeting on 10 January 1764, and all the indications are that he left Glasgow within a few days of this date. Cf. Rae, 169–70; Scott, 97; and A. F. Tytler, *Memoirs of the Life and Writings of Lord Kames* (2nd edn., Edinburgh, 1814). i.272–3.

In order to obtain an over-all view of the content of Smith's course in Moral Philosophy it is still necessary to go back to the account of it given by John Millar:

About a year after his appointment to the Professorship of Logic, Mr Smith was elected to the chair of Moral Philosophy. His course of lectures on this subject was divided into four parts. The first contained Natural Theology; in which he considered the proofs of the being and attributes of God, and those principles of the human mind upon which religion is founded. The second comprehended Ethics, strictly so called, and consisted chiefly of the doctrines which he afterwards published in his Theory of Moral Sentiments. In the third part, he treated at more length of that branch of morality which relates to *justice*, and which, being susceptible of precise and accurate rules, is for that reason capable of a full and particular explanation.

Upon this subject he followed the plan that seems to be suggested by Montesquieu; endeavouring to trace the gradual progress of jurisprudence, both public and private, from the rudest to the most refined ages, and to point out the effects of those arts which contribute to subsistence, and to the accumulation of property, in producing correspondent improvements or alterations in law and government. This important branch of his labours he also intended to give to the public; but this intention, which is mentioned in the conclusion of The Theory of Moral Sentiments, he did not live to fulfil.

In the last part of his lectures, he examined those political regulations which are founded, not upon the principle of *justice*, but that of *expediency*, and which are calculated to increase the riches, the power, and the prosperity of a State. Under this view, he considered the political institutions relating to commerce, to finances, to ecclesiastical and military establishments. What he delivered on these subjects contained the substance of the work he afterwards published under the title of An Inquiry into the Nature and Causes of the Wealth of Nations.[7]

So far as it goes, this account would seem to be accurate and perceptive, but there is one point of some importance which it does not make clear. What Millar describes in the passage just quoted is the course of lectures given by Smith, in his capacity as Professor of Moral Philosophy, to what was called the 'public' class in that subject. But Professors of Moral Philosophy at Glasgow also normally gave a supplementary course of lectures, on a different subject, to what was called the 'private' class.[8] The subjects upon which they lectured in this supplementary course, we are told,[9] were not 'necessarily connected' with those of their 'public' lectures, but were 'yet so much connected with the immediate duty of their profession, as to be very useful to those who attended them'. Hutcheson, for

[7] Stewart, I.18–20.

[8] Cf. Rae, 51; David Murray, *Memories of the Old College of Glasgow* (Glasgow, 1927), 516; and *Discourses on Theological & Literary Subjects, by the late Rev. Archibald Arthur . . . with an Account of some Particulars of his Life and Character, by William Richardson* (Glasgow, 1803), 514–15.

[9] By William Richardson, loc. cit.

example, had employed these additional hours in 'explaining and illus-
trating the works of Arrian, Antoninus, and other Greek philosophers', and
Reid was later to appropriate them to 'a further illustration of those doc-
trines which he afterwards published in his philosophical essays'. Adam
Smith employed them in delivering, once again, a course of lectures on
Rhetoric and Belles Lettres. A student's report of Smith's 'private'
Rhetoric course, as it was delivered in the 1762–3 session, was discovered in
Aberdeen in 1958 by the late Professor John M. Lothian,[10] and a newly
edited transcript of this manuscript will be published in volume iv of the
present edition of Smith's *Works and Correspondence*.

Turning back now to Millar's account of Smith's 'public' course in
Moral Philosophy, we see that this course is described as having been
divided into four parts. About the content of the first of these ('Natural
Theology') we know nothing whatever, and about the second ('Ethics,
strictly so called') we know little more than Millar here tells us—viz., that
it consisted chiefly of the doctrines of TMS.[11] About the third and fourth
parts, however—at any rate in the form which they assumed in Smith's
lectures during his last years at Glasgow[12]—we now know a great deal
more, thanks to the discovery of the two reports of his lectures on Jurisprudence which it is the main purpose of this volume to present.

The term 'Jurisprudence', it should perhaps be explained, was normally
used by Smith in a sense broad enough to encompass not only the third
part of the Moral Philosophy course as Millar described it ('that branch of
morality which relates to *justice*'), but also the fourth part ('those political
regulations which are founded, not upon the principle of *justice*, but that of
*expediency*'). In one of the two reports 'Jurisprudence' is defined as 'the
theory of the rules by which civil governments ought to be directed',[13]
and in the other as 'the theory of the general principles of law and government'.[14] Now the main objects of every system of law, in Smith's view, are
the maintenance of *justice*, the provision of *police* in order to promote
opulence, the raising of *revenue*, and the establishment of *arms* for the
defence of the state. These four, then, could be regarded as the main
branches or divisions of 'Jurisprudence' as so defined; and this is the way

[10] See John M. Lothian (ed.), *Lectures on Rhetoric and Belles Lettres delivered . . . by
Adam Smith* (1963).

[11] What appears to be part of one of Smith's lectures on ethics is reprinted and discussed
in Appendix II of the Glasgow edition of TMS. The Introduction, 1(*a*), to that volume
considers further evidence about the character of these lectures.

[12] Little direct information is available about the form which they assumed during
Smith's *first* years at Glasgow. A certain amount can be conjectured, however, from the
Anderson Notes. For the full text of these notes, and a commentary establishing their
connection with Smith's lectures, see R. L. Meek, 'New Light on Adam Smith's Glasgow
Lectures on Jurisprudence' (*History of Political Economy*, vol. 8, Winter 1976).

[13] Below, p. 5.

[14] Below, p. 398. Cf. TMS VII.iv.37.

in which the subject is in fact divided up in both the reports. Clearly the treatment of *justice* in the reports relates to the third part of Smith's Moral Philosophy course as Millar described it, and the treatment of *police*, *revenue*, and *arms* relates to the fourth and final part of it.

## 2. *The Two Reports of Smith's Jurisprudence Lectures*

The first of the two reports relates to Smith's Jurisprudence lectures in the 1762–3 session, and the second, in all probability, to the lectures given in the 1763–4 session. Hereafter these reports will usually be referred to as LJ(A) and LJ(B) respectively. It will be convenient to begin here with a description of LJ(B), which was the first of the two reports to be discovered and which will already be familiar to a large number of readers in the version published many years ago by Professor Edwin Cannan. A re-edited version of it is published below, under the title 'Report dated 1766'.

In 1895, Cannan's attention was drawn to the existence, in the hands of an Edinburgh advocate, of a bound manuscript which according to the title-page consisted of 'JURIS PRUDENCE or Notes from the Lectures on Justice, Police, Revenue, and Arms delivered in the University of Glasgow by Adam Smith Professor of Moral Philosophy'. In the edition of this manuscript which Cannan brought out in 1896,[15] he described its main physical characteristics as follows:

[The] manuscript . . . forms an octavo book 9 in. high, 7½ in. broad and 1⅛ in. thick. It has a substantial calf binding, the sides of which, however, have completely parted company with the back . . . On the back there is some gilt-cross-hatching and the word JURIS PRUDENCE (thus divided between two lines) in gilt letters on a red label. There are in all 192 leaves. Two of these are fly-leaves of dissimilar paper and have their fellows pasted on the insides of the cover, front and back. The rest all consist of paper of homogeneous character, water-marked 'L.V. Gerrevink.'

The manuscript is written on both sides of the paper in a rectangular space formed by four red ink lines previously ruled, which leave a margin of about three-quarters of an inch. Besides the fly-leaves there are three blank leaves at the end and two at the beginning.

There is nothing to show conclusively whether the writing was first executed on separate sheets subsequently bound up, or in a blank note-book afterwards rebound, or in the book as it appears at present.[16]

This was a careful and accurate description of the document, and not very much needs to be added to it today. The back of the binding was repaired in 1897, and the volume was rebound again (and the spine re-lettered) in 1969. As a result of these operations the two original end-papers

[15] Edwin Cannan (ed.), *Lectures on Justice, Police, Revenue and Arms, delivered in the University of Glasgow by Adam Smith* (Oxford, 1896).
[16] Ibid., xv–xvi.

and one if not both of the two original fly-leaves have disappeared.[17] Discounting these, there are two blank leaves at the beginning of the volume; then one leaf on the recto of which the title is written; then 179 leaves (with the pages numbered consecutively from 1 to 358) on which the main text is written; then one leaf containing no writing (but with the usual margins ruled); then four leaves, with the pages unnumbered, on which the index is written (taking up seven of the eight pages); then finally three blank leaves—making a total of 190 leaves in all. The new binding is very tight, and full particulars of the format of the volume could not be obtained without taking it apart.

Cannan had no doubt that this document, as suggested on its title-page, did in fact owe its origin to notes of Adam Smith's lectures on Jurisprudence at Glasgow University. The close correspondence between the text of the document and Millar's description of the third and fourth parts of Smith's Moral Philosophy course, together with the existence of many parallel passages in WN,[18] put this in Cannan's opinion beyond question; and his judgement in this respect has been abundantly confirmed by everything that has happened in the field of Smith scholarship since his day— not least by the recent discovery of LJ(A).

The title-page of LJ(B) bears the date 'MDCCLXVI' (whereas Adam Smith left Glasgow in January 1764); the handwriting is ornate and elaborate; there are very few abbreviations; and some of the mistakes that are to be found would seem to have been more probably caused by misreading than by mishearing. These considerations led Cannan to the conclusion— once again abundantly justified—that the manuscript was a fair copy made (presumably in 1766) by a professional copyist, and not the original notes taken at the lectures.[19] The only question which worried Cannan in this connection was whether the copyist had copied directly from the original lecture-notes or from a rewritten version of these notes made later by the original note-taker. The scarcity of abbreviations, the relatively small number of obvious blunders, and the comparatively smooth flow of the English, strongly suggested the latter. Cannan was worried, however, by the facts (a) that the copyist had clearly taken great pains to make his pages correspond with the pages from which he was copying (presumably because the index already existed), and (b) that the amounts of material contained in a page were very unequal. These two facts taken together suggested to

[17] One of the leaves at the beginning of the book looks as if it *may* have been the original fly-leaf, but a letter has been mounted on it and it is difficult to be sure about this.

[18] Cannan, op. cit., xxxv–ix.

[19] Ibid., xvii–xviii. W. R. Scott, in an article printed as Appendix V to the 2nd edn. of James Bonar's *Catalogue of the Library of Adam Smith* (London, 1932), deduced from the remnants of a book-plate which was formerly pasted inside the front cover that the volume originally belonged to Alexander Murray of Murrayfield—for whom, Scott surmised, the copy was made.

Cannan that it was at least possible that the copyist had copied directly from the original lecture-notes rather than from a rewritten version of them.[20] In actual fact, however, the degree of inequality in the amount of material in a page is not quite as great as Cannan suggests, and certainly no greater than one would reasonably expect to find in a student's rewritten version of his lecture-notes.[21] It seems very probable, then, that the copy was in fact made from a rewritten version.

The question of the purpose for which this rewritten version was made, however, is a rather more difficult one. Was it made by the original note-taker for his own use, or was it made (whether by him or by someone else at another remove) for sale? In those days, we know, 'manuscript copies of a popular professor's lectures, transcribed from his students' notebooks, were often kept for sale in the booksellers' shops.'[22] An interesting comparison may be made here between LJ(A)—a rewritten version almost certainly made by the original note-taker for his own use and *not* for sale—and LJ(B). LJ(A), although so far as it goes it is much fuller than LJ(B), is very much less polished, in the sense that it contains many more abbreviations, grammatical and spelling errors, blank spaces, etc. LJ(A), again, faithfully reproduces many of the summaries of previous lectures which Smith seems normally to have given at the beginning of each new one, and often notes the specific date on which the relevant lecture was delivered—features which are completely lacking in LJ(B). Nor is there in LJ(A) anything like the elaborate (and on the whole accurate) index which appears at the end of LJ(B). Considerations such as these, although not conclusive, do suggest the possibility that the rewritten version from which LJ(B) was copied had been prepared for sale, and therefore also the possibility that there were two or three steps between the original lecture-notes and the manuscript of LJ(B) itself. But what really matters, of course, is the *reliability* of the document: does it or does it not give a reasonably accurate report of what was actually said in the lectures at which the original notes were taken? Now that we have another set of notes to compare it with, we can answer this question with a fairly unqualified affirmative. LJ(B) is not quite as accurate and reliable as Cannan believed it to be; but if we make due allowance for its more summary character it is probably not much inferior to LJ(A) as a record of what may be assumed actually to have been said in the lectures.[23]

In which session, then, were the lectures delivered from which LJ(B) was ultimately derived?[24] Cannan, in his perceptive comments on this

---

[20] Cannan, op. cit., xviii–xix.
[21] It is certainly no greater than that found in LJ(A) and in the report of the Rhetoric lectures. [22] Rae, 64.
[23] The beginning of LJ(B), which repeats almost verbatim some phrases from the end of TMS, appears to be a highly accurate record.
[24] We are assuming that these lectures were all of a piece—i.e. that the original notes

question,[25] declined to lay too much weight on the frequent references to the Seven Years War as 'the late' or 'the last' war, on the perfectly valid ground that 'it would be natural after the conclusion of peace for the reporter or the transcriber to alter "the war" or "the present war" into "the late war" '. The reference to the ransom of the crew of the Litchfield,[26] however, which took place in April 1760, clearly meant that it was almost certain that the lectures were not delivered before 1761–2. They could conceivably have been delivered *in* that session, but Cannan thought it more probable that they were delivered 'either in the portion of the academical session of 1763–4 which preceded Adam Smith's departure, or in the session of 1762–3 . . .'

More light can now be thrown on this question as a result of the discovery of LJ(A), which relates without any doubt (since many of the lectures are specifically dated) to the 1762–3 session. The crucial point here is that in LJ(A) the order of treatment of the main subjects is radically different from that in LJ(B). 'The civilians', Smith is reported in LJ(B) as saying,[27]

begin with considering government and then treat of property and other rights. Others who have written on this subject begin with the latter and then consider family and civil government. There are several advantages peculiar to each of these methods, tho' that of the civil law seems upon the whole preferable.

In LJ(B), then, Smith adopts the method of 'the civilians', beginning with government and then going on to deal with 'property and other rights'. In LJ(A), by way of contrast, he adopts the method of the 'others who have written on this subject', beginning with 'property and other rights' and then going on to deal with 'family and civil government'. LJ(B), therefore, cannot possibly relate to the same year as LJ(A), whence it follows (given the decisive Litchfield reference) that it must relate either to 1761–2 or to 1763–4. And it can now fairly readily be shown that it is very unlikely to relate to 1761–2. There is a reference in LJ(B) to Florida being 'put into our hands';[28] and a comparison of the passage in which this reference occurs with the corresponding passage (a much more extensive one) in LJ(A)[29] shows that it must refer to the cession of Florida at the end of the Seven Years War by the Treaty of Paris in February 1763. This event, therefore, could not have been remarked upon in the 1761–2 session; and it thus seems almost certain that LJ(B) relates to 1763–4.

Cannan, when speaking of the possibility that LJ(B) might relate to 1763–4, seemed to suggest that if this were so the lectures from which the notes were taken would have had to be delivered in the portion of that

of them were all taken down in one and the same session. We have found no evidence which suggests the contrary.

[25] Op. cit., xix–xx.  [26] Below, p. 432.  [27] Below, p. 401.
[28] Below, p. 435.  [29] Below, p. 324.

session which 'preceded Adam Smith's departure' from Glasgow.[30] But this is surely to take the words 'delivered . . . by Adam Smith' on the title-page of LJ(B) much too literally. After Smith left Glasgow, his 'usual course of lectures' was carried on by one Thomas Young, with whom (at any rate according to Tytler's account) Smith left 'the notes from which he had been in use to deliver his prelections'.[31] Assuming, as would seem probable, that Young was in fact furnished by Smith with these notes and that he kept fairly closely to them in his lectures, it would have been perfectly possible for a student to take down, in the 1763-4 session, a set of lecture-notes from which a document possessing all the characteristics of LJ(B) could quite plausibly be derived.

We turn now to LJ(A), an edited version of which is published for the first time below, under the title 'Report of 1762-3'. 'At various dates in the autumn of 1958', wrote the discoverer of the document, the late Professor John M. Lothian, 'remnants of what had once been the considerable country-house library of Whitehaugh were dispersed by auction in Aberdeen.' In the eighteenth century Whitehaugh belonged to the Leith and later the Forbes-Leith families. Among a number of Whitehaugh books and papers purchased by Professor Lothian at various dates at these sales were two sets of lecture-notes, apparently made by students. One of these (hereafter called LRBL) clearly related to Smith's lectures on Rhetoric and Belles Lettres, as delivered in the 1762-3 session. The other set, upon closer examination, proved to relate to Smith's lectures on Jurisprudence, as delivered in the same session.[32]

The manuscript of LJ(A) is in six volumes, each measuring approximately 120 × 195 mm., bound in a contemporary binding of quarter calf with marbled paper sides and vellum tips. On the spine of each volume its

[30] Above, p. *8*. Cf. Scott, 319.

[31] Tytler, op. cit., i.272. Not very much is known about Thomas Young. At a Dean of Faculty's Meeting on 26 June 1762 we find his name heading a list of six students of Divinity which was to be presented to the Barons of Exchequer with a view to the selection of one of them 'to study Divinity three years upon King Williams mortification from the 10th October next'. At a University Meeting on 24 June 1763 'a presentation was given in and read from the Barons of Exchequer in favour of Mr. Thomas Young to study Theology three years commencing at Martinmass last'. The decision to appoint Young to carry on Smith's Moral Philosophy course was taken at the Faculty Meeting on 9 January 1764 to which reference has already been made in note 6 above. According to the minutes, 'the Meeting desired Dr. Smiths advice in the choice of a proper person to teach in his absence and he recommended Mr. Thomas Young, student of Divinity who was agreed to'. Young was a candidate for the Moral Philosophy Chair which Smith vacated, and was supported by Black and Millar. Black reported to Smith on 23 January 1764 that 'T. Young performs admirably well and is much respected by the students'; and Millar, in similar vein, reported to him on 2 February 1764 that Young 'has taught the class hitherto with great and universal applause; and by all accounts discovers an ease and fluency in speaking, which, I own, I scarce expected'. See Scott, 256-7; also Corr., Letter 79 from Joseph Black, dated 23 Jan. 1764, and Letter 80 from John Millar, dated 2 Feb. 1764. Young did not obtain the Chair (which was given to Thomas Reid), and nothing is known of his later career.

[32] John M. Lothian, op. cit., xi-xii.

number—'Vol. 1', 'Vol. 2', etc.—has been inscribed in gilt letters on a red label. The make-up of the volumes is as follows:

*Volume i*: This volume begins with a gathering of 4 sheets (i.e. 8 leaves and 16 pages) watermarked 'C. & I. Honig'. The first leaf is pasted to the inside front cover as an end-paper; the second forms a fly-leaf; both these are blank. The recto page of the third leaf contains a list of contents of vol. i (only partially completed); the verso page of the third leaf and the remaining five leaves of the gathering are blank. There follow 170 leaves (three of which have been left blank), watermarked 'L.V. Gerrevink', upon which the notes have been written. The volume finishes with a fly-leaf and an end-paper, both blank.

*Volume ii*: This volume begins with an end-paper and a fly-leaf, both blank. There follow 181 leaves (one of which has been left blank), watermarked 'L.V. Gerrevink', upon which the notes have been written. The volume finishes with a fly-leaf and an end-paper, both blank.

*Volume iii*: This volume begins with an end-paper and a fly-leaf, both blank. There follow 150 leaves (the last two and one other of which have been left blank), watermarked 'L.V. Gerrevink', upon which the notes have been written. Then comes a gathering of 8 sheets (i.e. 16 leaves and 32 pages), watermarked 'C. & I. Honig', all of which are blank. The volume finishes with a fly-leaf and an end-paper, both blank.

*Volume iv*: This volume begins with an end-paper and a fly-leaf, both blank. There follow 179 leaves (none of which have been left blank), watermarked 'L.V. Gerrevink', upon which the notes have been written. The volume finishes with a fly-leaf and an end-paper, both blank.

*Volume v*: This volume begins with an end-paper and a fly-leaf, both blank. There follow 151 leaves (the last two of which have been left blank), watermarked 'L.V. Gerrevink', upon which the notes have been written. The volume finishes with a fly-leaf and an end-paper, both blank.

*Volume vi*: This volume begins with an end-paper and a fly-leaf, both blank. There follow 172 leaves (the last of which has been left blank), watermarked 'L.V. Gerrevink', upon which the notes have been written. Then comes a gathering of 8 sheets (i.e. 16 leaves and 32 pages), watermarked 'C. & I. Honig', all of which are blank. The volume finishes with a fly-leaf and an end-paper, both blank.

The presence of the blank leaves watermarked 'C. & I. Honig' at the beginning of vol. i and at the end of vols. iii and vi, we believe, can be accounted for fairly simply. So far as vol. i is concerned, the reporter would seem to have instructed the binder to insert a few blank leaves at the beginning so as to leave space for a list of contents: the list was duly started, but left incomplete. So far as vols. iii and vi are concerned, all the indications are that the reporter still had some relevant material to write up when he took these volumes to be bound, and therefore instructed the binder to insert some blank leaves at the end so that he could include this material when the volume came back from binding. Once again, however, the reporter apparently did not get round to using the blank leaves as he had planned.

The format of the volumes makes it clear that the reporter wrote the notes on loose sheets of paper folded up into gatherings, which were later bound up into the six volumes. Almost all of these gatherings—all except four, in fact—consist of two sheets of paper placed together and folded once, making four leaves (i.e. eight pages) per gathering. Each gathering was numbered in the top left-hand corner of its first page before being bound. The writing of the main text almost always appears only on the recto pages of the volume, the verso pages being either left blank or used for comments, illustrations, corrections, and various other kinds of supplementary material.

The handwriting of the manuscript varies considerably in size, character, and legibility from one place to another—to such an extent, indeed, as to give the impression, at least at first sight, that several different hands have contributed to its composition. Upon closer investigation, however, it appears more likely that at any rate the great majority of these variations owe their origin to differences in the pen or ink used, in the speed of writing, and in the amount which the reporter tried to get into the page. It seems probable, in fact, that the whole of the main text on the recto pages of LJ(A), and all or almost all of the supplementary material on the verso pages,[33] was written by one and the same hand. This hand seems very similar to that in which the main text of LRBL is written;[34] and this fact, particularly when taken together with certain striking similarities in the structure of the volumes,[35] strongly suggests that both LJ(A) and the main text of LRBL were written by the same person.

The main text of LJ(A) appears to us to have been written serially, soon after (but not during) the lectures concerned, on the basis of very full notes taken down in class, probably at least partly in shorthand.[36] After having

[33] There are a few corrections and collations on the verso pages of vol. i which may possibly be in a second hand, although this is by no means certain. Such cases are rarely if ever to be found in the later volumes.

[34] We speak here only of the 'main text' of LRBL, rather than of the MS. as a whole, because in this MS. a large number of corrections and collations were in fact made, without any doubt at all, by a second hand.

[35] Cf. the description of LJ(A) given above with that of the MS. of LRBL given in the Appendix (by T. I. Rae) to John M. Lothian, op. cit., 195. Another possibly significant similarity is that the average number of pages of MS. devoted to a lecture is almost the same in both cases—roughly 15.5 in LJ(A) and 15.3 in LRBL. The bindings of the two MSS., it is true, do differ in certain respects, but even here the differences are not very significant, and according to the opinion of the Glasgow University binder both of them could quite possibly have come from the same bindery.

[36] Our suggestion that the original notes were probably taken down at least partly in shorthand is based mainly on the sheer *length* of the reports of a large number of the specifically dated lectures. Take, for example, the reports of the lectures delivered on 5, 6, and 7 April 1763 (below, pp. 355–74), which occupy respectively 18, 20, and 16½ pages of the MS. There is little padding in these reports; they contain a great deal of quite

been written up in the form of a more or less verbatim report, the notes were corrected and supplemented in various ways shortly to be described. We do not have the impression, however, that the report was prepared with a view to sale: it has all the hallmarks of a set of working notes prepared, primarily for his own use, by a reasonably intelligent and conscientious student.

The question of the origin and function of the supplementary material on the verso pages is not at all an easy one, and there seems to be no single or simple answer to it. Most, if not all, of these verso notes appear to be written in the same hand as the main text; but the appreciable variations in pen, ink, letter size, etc. often make it difficult to be sure about this (particularly in the first volume of the MS., where the verso notes are very numerous), and it is at least possible that a few of them may have been written by another hand—that of a fellow student, or a later owner, or perhaps the original owner at a later date. Our over-all impression, however, is that at any rate the great majority of the verso notes were in fact made by the original owner, and made fairly soon after the text on the recto pages was written. Some of these notes, we think, may have been explanatory glosses added from memory, or perhaps as a result of private reading. Others were very probably the result of collation with at least one other set of notes. And others still, we feel, may possibly have been added as a result of the reporter's attendance at Smith's daily 'examination' session—at which, we are told, lecturers had the opportunity of 'explaining more clearly any part of the lecture which may not have been fully understood', and at which Smith apparently delivered many 'incidental and digressive illustrations, and even discussions'.[37] Some of the longer verso notes in LJ(A) have a distinctly digressive quality,[38] and may quite possibly have had this origin.[39]

intricate detail; and there is every reason to think that they are on the whole reliable and accurate accounts of what Smith actually said. It is difficult to believe that these reports could have been as full and accurate as this if the original notes had been taken down entirely in longhand.

[37] Our authority here is once again William Richardson in his *Life of Arthur* (op. cit., 507-8). The complete statement reads as follows: 'The professors of Ethics, or Moral Philosophy, in the University of Glasgow, employ two hours every day in instructing their pupils. In the first of these, they deliver lectures; and devote the second, after a proper interval, to regular and stated examinations. Such examinations are reckoned of great utility to those who study, as tending to insure their attention, to ascertain their proficiency, and give the teacher an opportunity of explaining more clearly any part of the lecture which may not have been fully understood. Those who received instruction from Dr. Smith, will recollect, with much satisfaction, many of those incidental and digressive illustrations, and even discussions, not only in morality, but in criticism, which were delivered by him with animated and extemporaneous eloquence, as they were suggested in the course of question and answer. They occurred likewise, with much display of learning and knowledge, in his occasional explanations of those philosophical works of Cicero, which are also a very useful and important subject of examination in the class of Moral Philosophy.'

[38] See, for example, the verso notes reproduced on pp. 20-1, 128-9, and 153-4 below.

[39] It would appear, however, from a statement made by Thomas Reid (quoted below, p. *14*), that it would be unusual for a student to attend the Moral Philosophy lectures, the

The frequency of the verso notes begins to decline after the first volume, with a particularly sharp fall occurring about two-thirds of the way through the third volume. In the first volume, there are verso notes on 64 leaves (out of 170); in the second volume, on 44 leaves (out of 181); in the third volume, on 20 leaves (out of 150), with only one note in the last 50 leaves; in the fourth, on 14 leaves (out of 179); in the fifth, on 5 leaves (out of 151); and in the sixth, on 5 leaves (out of 172). Hand in hand with this decline in the frequency of the verso notes goes a decline in their average length: in the last three volumes the great majority of the notes are very short (there being in fact only three which are more than six lines long), and most of them appear more likely to be glosses added from memory than anything else. There are various possible explanations of these characteristics of the MS., but since no one explanation appears to be more probable than any other there would seem to be little value in speculating about them.

Only one other point about LJ(A) needs to be made at this juncture. Although the treatment of individual topics is usually much more extensive in LJ(A) than in LJ(B), the actual range of subjects covered is more extensive in LJ(B) than in LJ(A). Of particular importance here is the fact that whereas LJ(B) continues right through to the end of the course, LJ(A) stops short about two-thirds of the way through the 'police' section of Smith's lectures. The most likely explanation of this is that LJ(A) originally included a seventh volume which somehow became separated from the others and has not yet come to light; but there are obviously other possible explanations—e.g. that the reporter ceased attending the course at this point.

### 3. *Adam Smith's Lecture Timetable in 1762–3*

The fact that a large number of the lectures in LJ(A), and all (or almost all) of the lectures in LRBL, were specifically dated by the reporter, means that it is possible up to a point to reconstruct Smith's lecture timetable for the 1762–3 session. Where the dates are missing, of course, guesses have to be made, and the conclusions sometimes become very conjectural. The exercise seems well worth carrying out, however: it is of some interest in itself, and it provides us with certain information which will be useful when we turn, in the next section of this Introduction, to the problems involved in the collation of LJ(A) and LJ(B).

In Thomas Reid's *Statistical Account of the University of Glasgow*, which was apparently drawn up about 1794, the following remarks appear under the heading '*Time of Lecturing, &c.*':

The annual session for teaching, in the university, begins, in the ordinary

---

Rhetoric lectures, *and* the daily examination session in one and the same academic year. But the writer of LJ(A) may of course have collated his notes with those of another student who *did* attend the examination session.

*curriculum,*[40] on the tenth of October; and ends, in some of the classes, about the middle of May, and in others continues to the tenth of June . . .

During this period, the business of the College continues without interruption.[41] The Professors of Humanity, or Latin, and of Greek, lecture and examine their students, receive and correct exercises, three hours every day, and four hours for two days every week; the Professors of Logic, Moral Philosophy, and Natural Philosophy, two hours every day, and three hours during a part of the session; excepting on Saturdays, when, on account of a general meeting of the public students, there is only one lecture given.[42]

At any rate in the early 1790s, then, it was the normal practice in the teaching of Moral Philosophy at Glasgow for the Professor of that subject to 'lecture and examine' his students for 'two hours every day, and three hours during a part of the session'.[43] The question we must now ask is whether this was also the normal practice thirty years earlier, during the last two or three years of Smith's period in Glasgow, and if so how the hours concerned were divided up in his particular case.

Curiously enough, it is once again Thomas Reid who provides the crucial piece of evidence here, in the shape of a letter he wrote to a friend on 14 November 1764, a month or so after the beginning of the session in which he took over the Moral Philosophy Chair from Smith. In this letter he describes his lecture timetable as follows:

I must launch forth in the morning, so as to be at the College . . . half an hour after seven, when I speak for an hour, without interruption, to an audience of about a hundred. At eleven I examine for an hour upon my morning prelection; but my audience is little more than a third part of what it was in the morning. In a week or two, I must, for three days in the week, have a second prelection at twelve, upon a different subject, where my audience will be made up of those who hear me in the morning, but do not attend at eleven. My hearers commonly attend my class two years at least. The first session they attend the morning prelection, and the hour of examination at eleven; the second and subsequent years they attend the two prelections, but not the hour of examination.[44]

There is no suggestion in this letter (or, so far as we are aware, anywhere else) that Reid's accession to the Moral Philosophy Chair was marked by

---

[40] According to Reid's account, 'what is called the *curriculum,* or ordinary course of public education, comprehends at present five branches—the Latin and Greek languages, Logic, Moral Philosophy, and Natural Philosophy. These branches are understood to require the study of five separate sessions.' See *The Works of Thomas Reid,* ed. Sir William Hamilton (Edinburgh, 1846), 732.

[41] In other words there were no terminal vacations as there are today. There were, however, holidays on a number of specific days during the session. Cf. David Murray, *Memories of the Old College of Glasgow,* 461–2.

[42] *The Works of Thomas Reid,* 773–4.

[43] Reid describes this as the daily programme 'excepting on Saturdays, when . . . there is only one lecture given'. Whatever the situation may have been in the 1790s, there is no evidence that Smith ever lectured on a Saturday in 1762–3.

[44] *The Works of Thomas Reid,* 39.

any change of practice so far as the lecturing arrangements were concerned; and all the indications are that Smith, at any rate in his last years at Glasgow, had followed the same routine: a lecture from 7.30 to 8.30 each morning (except Saturday); an 'examination' on this 'morning prelection' from 11 a.m. to noon; and in addition, on certain days during a part of the session, a 'second prelection . . . upon a different subject' from noon to 1 p.m. Smith's 'morning prelection' at 7.30 was of course his 'public' lecture on Moral Philosophy; the 'examination' at 11 a.m. (at which, as we already know from Richardson's account,[45] Smith delivered many 'incidental and digressive illustrations') related directly to this 'morning prelection'; and his 'second prelection . . . upon a different subject' at noon was his 'private' lecture on Rhetoric and Belles Lettres.

In our attempt to reconstruct Smith's actual lecture timetable in 1762–3 it will be convenient to begin with the Rhetoric course, since its reconstruction involves far fewer difficulties than does that of the Jurisprudence course. The first lecture in the Rhetoric notes is headed 'Lecture 2$^d$' and dated Friday, 19 November. From the '2$^d$' in the heading, and from the fact that the argument of this lecture appears to start in midstream, we may reasonably assume that at some time before 19 November Smith had already given a preliminary lecture in the Rhetoric course, which for some reason or other was not reported in this set of notes. Judging from the subsequent pattern of lecture-dates, it would seem probable that this preliminary lecture was given on Wednesday, 17 November. Starting with this latter date, then, the timetable of Smith's Rhetoric course in 1762–3 would appear to have been as follows:[46]

| Number of Lecture | Date of Lecture |
|---|---|
| [1] | [Wednesday, 17 November 1762] |
| 2 | Friday, 19 November 1762 |
| 3 | Monday, 22 November 1762 |
| 4 | Wednesday, 24 November 1762 |
| 4[47] | Friday, 26 November 1762 |
| 5 | Monday, 29 November 1762 |
| 6 | Wednesday, 1 December 1762 |
| 7 | Friday, 3 December 1762 |

[45] Above, p. *12*, note 37.

[46] The 'Number of Lecture' in the first column is the ordinal number actually ascribed to each lecture by the reporter, except in the case of the first and the last lecture where the number is conjectural (this being indicated by enclosing it in square brackets). The 'Date of Lecture' in the second column is the date actually ascribed to each lecture by the reporter, with the dates of the first and the last lecture being enclosed in square brackets to indicate their conjectural character. The course is divided up on a week-by-week basis, with a ruled line being inserted under the last lecture given in each particular week.

[47] The student has incorrectly ascribed the number '4' to two successive lectures.

| Number of Lecture | Date of Lecture |
|---|---|
| 8 | Monday, 6 December 1762[48] |
|  |  |
| 9 | Monday, 13 December 1762 |
| 10 | Wednesday, 15 December 1762 |
| 11 | Friday, 17 December 1762 |
|  |  |
| 12 | Monday, 20 December 1762 |
| 13 | Wednesday, 22 December 1762 |
| 14 | Friday, 24 December 1762 |
|  |  |
| 15 | Monday, 27[49] December 1762[50] |
|  |  |
| 16 | Wednesday, 5 January 1763 |
| 17 | Friday, 7 January 1763 |
|  |  |
| 18 | Monday, 10 January 1763 |
| 19 | Wednesday, 12 January 1763 |
| 20 | Friday, 14 January 1763[51] |
|  |  |
| 21 | Monday, 17 January 1763 |
| 22 | Friday, 21 January 1763 |
|  |  |
| 23 | Monday, 24 January 1763 |
| 24 | Wednesday, 26 January 1763[52] |
|  |  |
| 25 | Monday, 31 January 1763 |
| 26 | Friday, 4 February 1763 |
|  |  |
| 27 | Monday, 7 February 1763[53] |

[48] The argument of lecture 9 appears to follow on logically from that of lecture 8. It would therefore seem probable that Smith did not lecture on Rhetoric on either the Wednesday or the Friday in the week beginning Monday, 6 December.

[49] In the MS. '26'—an obvious error.

[50] There is no obvious break in continuity between lecture 15 and lecture 16, which suggests that Smith did not lecture on Rhetoric during the period between Monday, 27 December 1762 and Wednesday, 5 January 1763. It should be noted, however, that although he may not have lectured *on Rhetoric* during this period, it seems fairly clear from LJ(A) that he did lecture *on Jurisprudence* during this period, probably on three occasions. See below, p. *18*.

[51] From this point onwards, the 'normal' number of lectures given per week in the Rhetoric course would seem to have been reduced from three to two, the Wednesday lecture usually being the one cut out.

[52] In this week, apparently by way of exception, the second Rhetoric lecture was given on Wednesday rather than on Friday. A *possible* reason is that Smith transferred the lecture from Friday to Wednesday because the Friday concerned (the last Friday in January) was a holiday.

[53] The argument of lecture 28 seems to follow on logically from that of lecture 27. Smith lectured on Jurisprudence on Friday, 11 February 1763, but it seems probable that for some reason the Rhetoric lecture scheduled for that date was cancelled.

| Number of Lecture | Date of Lecture |
|---|---|
| 28 | Monday, 14 February 1763 |
| 29 | Friday, 18 February 1763[54] |

| [30] | [Monday, 21 February 1763] |

Smith's Rhetoric course in 1762–3, then, started in the third week in November—round about the same time, it would seem, as Reid's course in the 'different subject' two years later[55]—and *probably* finished towards the end of February.[56] In so far as a normal pattern is discernible, it would seem to be one involving the delivery of three lectures per week up to the middle of January, and two per week thereafter. This may help to explain the apparent contradiction between Reid's statement that three lectures per week were devoted to the 'different subject'[57] and Richardson's statement that only two were so devoted.[58]

Let us turn now to the Jurisprudence course, the timetable for which is more difficult to reconstruct because the specific lecture-dates noted by the student are fewer and farther between, particularly in the first part of the course. The difficulties start right at the beginning. The first Jurisprudence lecture is dated Friday, 24 December 1762,[59] but no further specific lecture-dates appear until p. 90 of the MS. of the first volume, where a new lecture is dated Thursday, 6 January 1763. The problem is to work out (*a*) how many lectures were given *between* 24 December and 6 January; (*b*) where exactly each of them began and ended; and (*c*) on which of the available lecturing days they were given.

Some assistance can be obtained here from the MS. itself, by trying to detect in it what we may call 'conjectural breaks'—i.e. points at which it seems plausible to assume, from the presence of a conspicuous space, a change of ink or pen, an unusually large number of dashes, a summary of an earlier argument, or some other indication, that one lecture may have ended and another begun. For example, there would seem to be a 'conjectural break' of this type round about the middle of p. 9 of the MS.,

[54] The reporter's notes under this date-heading are unusually extensive, and it seems likely that they in fact summarized the subject-matter of two lectures rather than one. We may therefore plausibly conjecture that the last lecture in the Rhetoric course (or, more strictly speaking, the last lecture in that course which is reported in this set of notes) was given on Monday, 21 February 1763.

[55] In the letter cited on p. *14* above, which is dated 14 November 1764, Reid says that the course in the 'different subject' is due to commence 'in a week or two'.

[56] We do not know for certain that it finished in February. It is at least possible that it went on longer, but that the remaining lectures were not reported in the set of notes which has come down to us.

[57] Above, p. *14*.

[58] William Richardson, op. cit., 514.

[59] From October to December Smith will have lectured on Natural Theology and Ethics. Stewart (III.1) tells us that after the publication of TMS Smith dealt with Ethics much more briefly than before.

suggesting that a new lecture began at this point—a lecture delivered, presumably, on Monday, 27 December 1762, which was the next available lecturing day.[60]

The material in the notes from this first conjectural break to the next specific lecture-date (Thursday, 6 January 1763, on p. 90 of the MS.) occupies 81 MS. pages. The average length of the notes of later (specifically dated) lectures is roughly 15–16 MS. pages per lecture. It may thus be surmised that the material on pp. 9–90 of the MS. was derived from a total of five lectures—a surmise which is supported by the fact that four plausible conjectural breaks (on pp. 23, 40, 53, and 68) can be detected in the MS. between p. 9 and p. 90. So far as the actual dates of the intervening lectures are concerned, we are rather more in the dark. We know that Smith lectured on Rhetoric on Wednesday, 5 January 1763, so we may perhaps assume that on this date he lectured on Jurisprudence as well. We also know that he did *not* lecture on Rhetoric on Monday, 3 January 1763, so we may perhaps assume that on this date he did not lecture on Jurisprudence either, possibly because it was a holiday. We may also assume that he did not lecture at all on Friday, 31 December 1762, which would certainly have been a holiday.[61] But this still leaves us with more available lecturing days than we have lectures to fit into them, so we must necessarily fall back up to a point on guesswork.

All these factors being taken into account, the best guesses we can perhaps hazard about the dates of Smith's Jurisprudence lectures from Friday, 24 December 1762 to Thursday, 6 January 1763, and about the specific points in the MS. at which these dates should be inserted, are as follows:[62]

| *Volume and Page of MS. on which Lecture Begins* | *Date of Lecture* |
|---|---|
| i.1 | Friday, 24 December 1762 |
| | |
| [i.9] | [Monday, 27 December 1762] |
| [i.23] | [Tuesday, 28 December 1762] |
| [i.40] | [Wednesday, 29 December 1762] |
| | |
| [i.53] | [Tuesday, 4 January 1763] |
| [i.68] | [Wednesday, 5 January 1763] |
| i.90 | Thursday, 6 January 1763 |

[60] Smith lectured on Rhetoric on Monday, 27 December 1762, so we may reasonably assume that he also lectured on Jurisprudence on that day.

[61] Christmas Day and New Year's Day were also holidays, but in 1762–3 they fell on Saturday, when Moral Philosophy lectures were not given anyway.

[62] As before, numbers and dates in square brackets are conjectural; those without square brackets are as given by the reporter.

The timetable for the week beginning Monday, 3 January 1763 may then be (conjecturally) completed by adding

[i.104]                                    [Friday, 7 January 1763]

<hr>

We may now proceed on a similar basis (but relegating the 'working' to footnotes) to reconstruct Smith's lecture timetable for the remainder of the Jurisprudence course up to the point where the reporter's notes break off. The result is as follows:

| *Volume and Page of MS.*<br>*on which Lecture Begins* | *Date of Lecture* |
| --- | --- |
| i.115 | Monday, 10 January 1763 |
| [i.129] | [Wednesday, 12 January 1763] |
| [i.143] | [Thursday, 13 January 1763] |
| [i.146] | [Friday, 14 January 1763][63] |
| | |
| ii.1 | Monday, 17 January 1763 |
| [ii.13] | [Tuesday, 18 January 1763] |
| [ii.26] | [Wednesday, 19 January 1763] |
| [ii.41] | [Thursday, 20 January 1763] |
| ii.56 | Friday, 21 January 1763[64] |
| | |
| [ii.71] | [Monday, 24 January 1763] |
| ii.87 | Wednesday, 26 January 1763[65] |

[63] The timetable for this week is very conjectural indeed. The only *certain* date is Monday, 10 January 1763; but we do know that Smith lectured on Rhetoric on Wednesday, 12 January and Friday, 14 January 1763. and we have therefore assumed that he also lectured on Jurisprudence on those two days. The main difficulty is that there is not really enough material in the MS.—even taking into account the possible implications of the mysterious note on p. 145 and the gap of 3½ pages in the MS. which follows it—to represent the summaries of a full five days' lecturing. It rather looks as if either Tuesday's or Thursday's lecture was cancelled: we have assumed, at a venture, that it was in fact Tuesday's. P. 146 of the MS. (the point at which we have assumed that the lecture on Friday, 14 January 1763 began) does seem to mark a real 'break', since at this point Smith embarks upon a summary of 'some of the last lectures'—something which he seems normally to have done only at the beginning of a new lecture.

[64] There is a certain element of conjecture in our ascription of the three mid-week dates to specific points in the MS., but everything fits in and on the whole the ascription seems fairly plausible.

[65] Apart from the certain dates of Wednesday, 26 January 1763 and Thursday, 3 February 1763, the timetables for this week and the next are very conjectural indeed. The first difficulty is that there are only thirty-one pages of MS. between the beginning of the lecture on Friday, 21 January 1763 and the beginning of that on Wednesday, 26 January 1763—not enough to represent a full three days' lecturing. We have dealt with this by assuming that Smith lectured on Jurisprudence on Monday, 24 January 1763 (when we know that he lectured on Rhetoric), but that for some reason the Jurisprudence lecture scheduled for Tuesday, 25 January 1763 was not in fact delivered. The second difficulty is that there are only fifty-seven pages of MS. between the beginning of the lecture on Wednesday, 26 January 1763 and the beginning of that on Thursday, 3 February 1763—

| Volume and Page of MS. on which Lecture Begins | Date of Lecture |
|---|---|
| [ii.105] | [Monday, 31 January 1763] |
| [ii.121] | [Tuesday, 1 February 1763] |
| [ii.131] | [Wednesday, 2 February 1763] |
| ii.144 | Thursday, 3 February 1763 |
| [ii.162] | [Friday, 4 February 1763] |
| | |
| iii.1 | Monday, 7 February 1763[66] |
| iii.6 | Tuesday, 8 February 1763 |
| [iii.23][67] | [Wednesday, 9 February 1763] |
| iii.48 | Thursday, 10 February 1763 |
| iii.65 | Friday, 11 February 1763 |
| | |
| iii.76 | Monday, 14 February 1763 |
| iii.87 | Tuesday, 15 February 1763 |
| iii.105 | Wednesday, 16 February 1763[68] |
| [iii.131] | [Thursday, 17 February 1763] } [69] |
| — | [Friday, 18 February 1763] } |

not nearly enough to represent a full six days' lecturing. There are, it is true, several longish gaps in this section of the MS. of LJ(A), but a comparison with LJ(B) suggests that there was not in fact all that much which the reporter failed to get down. The most plausible conjectural breaks in these fifty-seven pages are on pp. 105, 121, and 131 of the MS. If we assume that there were in fact three lectures between Wednesday, 26 January 1763 and Thursday, 3 February 1763; that one of these was given on Monday, 31 January 1763 (when we know that Smith lectured on Rhetoric); and that Friday, 28 January 1763 was a holiday (as the last Friday in January apparently then was), then the three lectures must have been given *either* on Thursday, Monday, and Tuesday, *or* on Thursday, Monday, and Wednesday, *or* on Monday, Tuesday, and Wednesday. In the timetable in the text we have opted for the third of these alternatives, but we would not claim that it is really much more plausible than either of the other two.

[66] The small amount of material in the MS. notes relating to this lecture, coupled with the fact that they appear to end in mid sentence and are followed by a blank page, suggests that the student either left the lecture early or for some other reason failed to get notes of the rest of it down. A comparison with LJ(B), which at this point contains some passages of which there is no counterpart in LJ(A), tends to confirm this hypothesis. Cf. below, p. *28*, note 10.

[67] It is not at all certain that the break in fact came at this point, but all things considered it seems to be the most likely place.

[68] The most likely point of conclusion to the notes of the lecture of Wednesday, 16 February 1763, we have assumed, is at the foot of p. 130 of the MS., where several dashes appear. This would make it a very long set of notes for a single lecture, but there is one other case (Tuesday, 29 March 1763) where the report of a *dated* lecture is of similar length.

[69] The report of the lecture which we have dated (conjecturally) Thursday, 17 February 1763 is cut off abruptly in mid sentence, at the end of vol. iii of the MS., and the discussion of the acquisition of slaves which is being dealt with is never completed. Nor is there any counterpart in LJ(A) of the discussion of servants, guardian and ward, and domestic offences which in LJ(B) follows the treatment of the acquisition of slaves. All the indications are that the same order of treatment was in fact followed by Smith in 1762-3, but that the

| *Volume and Page of MS. on which Lecture Begins* | *Date of Lecture* |
|---|---|
| iv.1 | Monday, 21 February 1763 |
| iv.19 | Tuesday, 22 February 1763 |
| iv.41 | Wednesday, 23 February 1763 |
| iv.60 | Thursday, 24 February 1763[70] |
| | |
| iv.74 | Monday, 28 February 1763 |
| iv.91 | Tuesday, 1 March 1763 |
| iv.104 | Wednesday, 2 March 1763 |
| iv.121 | Thursday, 3 March 1763 |
| iv.134 | Friday, 4 March 1763 |
| | |
| iv.149 | Monday, 7 March 1763 |
| iv.164 | Tuesday, 8 March 1763 |
| v.1 | Wednesday, 9 March 1763 |
| v.15 | Thursday, 10 March 1763 |
| v.31 | Friday, 11 March 1763 |
| | |
| v.44 | Monday, 14 March 1763 |
| v.58 | Tuesday, 15 March 1763 |
| v.72 | Wednesday, 16 March 1763 |
| v.84 | [Thursday, 17 March 1763][71] |
| | |
| v.99 | Monday, 21 March 1763 |
| v.111 | Tuesday, 22 March 1763 |
| v.127 | Wednesday, 23 March 1763 |
| v.140 | Thursday, 24 March 1763[72] |

student for some reason failed to get, or to write up, any notes of this material. Certainly, at any rate, he took some pains to make room at the end of vol. iii for a substantial quantity of additional notes. The third and fourth leaves of the final gathering in the volume have been left blank, and, as already noted above (p. *10*), sixteen extra leaves have been inserted, probably by the binder at the student's request. The final gathering of vol. iii is numbered 126, and the first gathering in vol. iv is numbered 129. In the light of all these circumstances, it seems reasonable to assume that Smith did in fact lecture on servants, guardian and ward, etc., in 1763, and that this lecture was given on Friday, 18 February, when we know that he lectured on Rhetoric. Cf. below, pp. *29–30*, notes 19 and 20.

[70] There is no trace of any lecture having been given on Friday, 25 February 1763, which, being the last Friday in February, was in all probability a holiday.

[71] In the actual date-heading on p. 84 of the MS., the day of the week appears as 'Friday', and the figure for the day of the month looks like an '18' which has been altered to a '17'. It appears that the penultimate Friday in March may have been a holiday (see David Murray, op. cit., 462), so we have assumed that the lecture was in fact delivered on Thursday, 17 March 1763.

[72] There is no sign of the student's having missed a lecture at this point. Friday's lecture was probably cancelled.

| Volume and Page of MS. on which Lecture Begins | Date of Lecture |
|---|---|
| vi.1 | Monday, 28 March 1763 |
| vi.24 | Tuesday, 29 March 1763 |
| vi.50 | Wednesday, 30 March 1763[73] |
| | |
| vi.63 | Tuesday, 5 April 1763 |
| vi.81 | Wednesday, 6 April 1763 |
| vi.101 | Thursday, 7 April 1763 |
| vi.117 | Friday, 8 April 1763 |
| | |
| — | [Monday, 11 April 1763][74] |
| vi.135 | Tuesday, 12 April 1763 |
| vi.155 | Wednesday, 13 April 1763 |

At the end of vol. vi of the MS., sixteen pages later, the student's report ends, and there is no way of reconstructing Smith's lecture timetable for the remainder of the Jurisprudence course. It seems reasonable to assume, however, that the pattern which is fairly consistently revealed in the lectures up to this point was continued until the course was concluded at or near the end of the session.

## 4. *The Collation of LJ(A) and LJ(B)*

As we have seen,[75] LJ(A) owes its origin to Adam Smith's Jurisprudence course as it was delivered in 1762–3, and LJ(B), in all probability, to that course as it was delivered in 1763–4. The collation of two sets of student's notes relating to the same course of lectures as it was delivered in two successive sessions would not normally involve any special difficulties. In the present case, however, there are certain complications, arising out of three features of the documents which we have already noted above.

In the first place, although the difference in the *content* of the actual lectures (taking them as a whole) may not have been very great as between the two sessions concerned, there was, as we have seen,[76] an appreciable difference in the *order* in which the main subjects of the lectures were presented. In LJ(A) the order of treatment is property and other rights, domestic law, government, police; whereas in LJ(B) it is government, domestic law, property and other rights, police.

In the second place, there is a difference in the *origin* of the reports.

---

[73] There is no trace of any lecture having been given on Thursday, 31 March, Friday, 1 April, or Monday, 4 April 1763. Since Easter Day in 1763 fell on 3 April, it seems probable that the Thursday, Friday, and Monday were holidays.

[74] As shown below (p. *31*, note 40, and p. 380, note 53), it seems very likely that quite a large amount of material (relating to a lecture which Smith must have given on this date) was omitted from vol. vi, probably by accident.

[75] Above, pp. 7–9.                          [76] Above, p. *8*.

LJ(A), if our view of it is correct, is a rewritten version of notes of Smith's lectures taken down (probably for the most part in shorthand) by a student in class, and was intended primarily as a working document for use by the student himself. The notes are relatively extensive, and the student has usually (although not always) taken some care to fill in gaps, correct errors, and add supplementary material. LJ(B), by way of contrast, would seem to be a fair copy, made by a professional copyist, of a much more summary report of Smith's lectures—for the most part owing its origin, one may perhaps conjecture, to *longhand* notes taken down in class.[77]

In the third place, there is a difference in the *range of subjects* covered in the reports, which is generally speaking more complete in LJ(B) than in LJ(A). On several occasions the writer of LJ(A), either because he has missed a lecture or for some other reason, fails to report Smith's discussion of a particular subject which *is* duly reported upon in LJ(B). And, much more importantly, LJ(A) as we have seen[78] stops short about two-thirds of the way through the 'police' section of Smith's lectures, whereas LJ(B) continues right through to the end of the course.

These considerations have largely dictated the particular method of collation which we have adopted below. What we have done is to take the subject-matter of LJ(B) as the starting-point, dividing it up in the first instance in accordance with the successive sectional headings supplied by Cannan in his edition of LJ(B), and then refining and extending these headings in a number of cases where further subdivision makes the task of collation easier. The particular pages of the MS. of LJ(B) on which these topics are dealt with are noted in the second column; and side by side with these, in the third column, we have noted the pages of the manuscript of LJ(A) on which parallel passages dealing with the same topics are to be found. In cases where there seem to us to be significant differences in the treatment of a topic as between the two texts, these differences are described in a note in the 'Notes on the Collation' which appear at the end of this section of the Introduction, a reference to the appropriate note being given in the fourth column of the collation itself. In the other cases, where there is no note-reference in the fourth column, it may be assumed that the two texts deal with the topic concerned in *roughly* the same manner—i.e. that even if (as is generally the case) the treatment in LJ(A) is more extensive than it is in LJ(B), both texts broadly speaking make much the same points in much the same order.

[77] On the other hand, the close similarity which is quite often to be observed between the *actual words* used in LJ(B) and in corresponding passages in TMS and WN suggests a degree of accuracy in the original lecture-notes which might be regarded as inconsistent with this hypothesis about the origin of LJ(B)—unless, of course, we assume that Smith (or Young) was dictating at the particular points concerned. Another possibility is that LJ(B) is a copy of a summary (perhaps made for sale) of what was originally a much longer set of notes. [78] Above, p. *13*.

## NOTES ON THE COLLATION

(1) There is no counterpart in LJ(A) of the remarks about works on natural jurisprudence which are reported on pp. 1–4 of LJ(B). One possible explanation of this, of course, is that in 1762 Smith did not in fact make any such remarks at the beginning of his Jurisprudence lectures. Another possible explanation is that he did do so, but that the student, regarding them merely as a kind of historical prolegomenon, did not think fit to include them in his report of Smith's lectures proper. A relevant indication here, perhaps, is that (as we have already seen above) there appears to be a fairly definite 'conjectural break' half way down p. 9 of the MS., which means that the reporter's notes of the lecture concerned occupy not much more than half the average space occupied by his notes of subsequent lectures.

There is another point of interest in this connection. Georg Sacke, in an article published in *Zeitschrift für Nationalökonomie* in 1939 (Bd. IX, pp. 351–6), has drawn attention to the fact that the celebrated Russian jurist S. E. Desnitsky, who had been a student at Glasgow University from 1761 to 1767, gave a lecture at Moscow University on 30 June 1768 in which there is a long passage corresponding almost word for word with Smith's remarks about works on natural jurisprudence as reported on pp. 1–4 of LJ(B). Desnitsky may well have been making use either of a set of lecture-notes identical with that from which LJ(B) was copied, or (as appears from his inclusion of some statements, not to be found in LJ(B), about Richard Cumberland, author of a seventeenth-century treatise on natural law) of a very close variant of it.

(2) There is no counterpart in LJ(A) of the last five sentences on p. 11 of LJ(B), in which Smith makes the important statement that 'property and civil government very much depend on one another', and proceeds to consider the two possible methods of presenting the subject of Jurisprudence.

(3) In LJ(A), these two topics are discussed near the *end* of the government section, in the context of the problem of the extent of the limits to the power of the sovereign. In LJ(B), they are discussed at the *beginning* of the government section; the order in which they are treated is reversed; and the context in which they appear is a much wider one. Another matter which perhaps deserves comment is that whereas in LJ(B) there is a fair amount of emphasis on the point that 'superior wealth' contributes to 'confer authority', this point is mentioned in LJ(A) only in passing, in a summary of the previous lecture (vol. v, p. 129).

(4) Both texts deal with roughly the same points under this heading, but the order in which they are dealt with is rather different. LJ(A) is generally much more extensive in its treatment than LJ(B), and contains many more historical illustrations of the points made.

(5) There is no trace *on pp. 95–99* of LJ(A) of the point made on pp. 45–46 of LJ(B) about the difference between military government in Rome and in Asia. There is, however, an extended discussion of this point at the end of the summary of the lecture concerned which Smith apparently gave at the beginning of his next lecture (see LJ(A), pp. 107–109).

(6) The passages on pp. 109–113 of LJ(A) contain certain points of which there is little or no trace in the corresponding section of LJ(B).

(7) The treatment of this topic in LJ(A) is much more extensive than it is in LJ(B). See, for example, the discussion on pp. 167–170 of vol. iv of LJ(A) of 'the situation and circumstances of England', and compare the very brief reference to this on p. 62 of LJ(B). It is also worth noting, perhaps, that there is no reference in LJ(B) to the *dangers* to liberty (as distinct from the 'securities'), whereas the dangers are specifically referred to on three occasions in LJ(A). See LJ(A), vol. iv, p. 179, and vol. v, pp. 5 and 12.

(8) The two texts make roughly the same points under this head, but they do not always make them in quite the same order.

(9) In LJ(A), on pp. 114–124 and 127–132, there is a discussion of the doctrine of an original contract and the principles of utility and authority. As already stated in note (3) above, the corresponding passages in LJ(B) appear at the *beginning* of the government section rather than near the *end* of it. There is a reference back to these passages on p. 93 of LJ(B).

(10) There is no counterpart in LJ(A) of the passages dealing with fidelity and infidelity on pp. 102–105 of LJ(B). The indications (cf. above, p. 20, note 66) are that the LJ(A) reporter either left the relevant lecture early or for some other reason failed to get the latter part of it down, so that there is no record in his notes of Smith's discussion of fidelity and infidelity. He would also seem to have missed the first part of Smith's discussion of the next topic, marriage and divorce, corresponding to pp. 105–106 of LJ(B). A report of a summary by Smith of some of the missing parts (but not of his discussion of fidelity and infidelity) will be found on pp. 6–7 of vol. iii of LJ(A).

(11) Subject to the qualification in note (10), both texts make roughly the same points, but do not always make them in quite the same order. In places, particularly round about the middle of the section, it is difficult to keep track of the correspondences.

(12) LJ(A) includes, on pp. 48–52, a report of a summary by Smith of all his previous lectures about the different types of marriage. This summary would seem to correspond to a passage on pp. 117–118 of LJ(B).

(13) Both texts make roughly the same points in roughly the same order, but towards the end, judging from the gaps in the MS., the LJ(A) reporter had difficulty in getting down all the points concerning the differences between the Scots and the English law. The very short summary in LJ(B) is of little help here.

(14) Both texts make roughly the same points, but they do not always make them in quite the same order. The summing-up on pp. 65–66 of LJ(A) is in effect a

short summary of *all* the preceding lectures on the family. The computations reported on p. 123 of LJ(B) were apparently not included in the relevant lecture in 1762–3: see the footnote on p. 64 of LJ(A).

(15) Both texts make roughly the same points in the same order, but there are some differences. In particular, the Pollio story and the Ovid citations which appear on pp. 92–93 and 100 of LJ(A) do not appear in LJ(B) until the following section (pp. 135 and 136).

(16) Some of the emphases are different as between the two texts. In particular, in LJ(B) the Pollio story (see note (15) above) is used to illustrate the readiness of the monarch to be influenced in the slave's favour rather than (as in LJ(A)) as an illustration of how badly the slaves were treated. See also the penultimate sentence of note (18) below.

(17) There are some quite substantial differences between the two texts here. Both LJ(A) and LJ(B) begin with the same point—that slavery is not only bad for the slave but is also economically disadvantageous. After this, however, the two texts begin to diverge. LJ(B) goes on to discuss the case of the colliers and salters, in order to demonstrate once again that 'slavery is a disadvantage'. LJ(A), by way of contrast, does not bring the colliers and salters into the picture until pp. 126–130, after the question of the abolition of slavery has been dealt with. LJ(B), after dealing with the colliers and salters, proceeds to discuss the point that slavery 'diminishes the number of free men'. LJ(A), however, does not discuss this point until later, on pp. 134–141. On pp. 131–134 of LJ(A) there is a discussion of the point that slavery is 'very detrimentall to population' of which there is no distinct counterpart in LJ(B).

(18) In this section, LJ(B) embarks immediately upon a discussion of the transition from *adscripti glebae* to tenants by steelbow. The corresponding part of LJ(A) begins with a longish discussion (on pp. 114–117) of the reasons why the abolition of slavery has been very limited in most parts of the world. The main emphasis in the discussion in LJ(A) is partly on man's alleged 'love of domination and tyrannizing' and partly on the fact that the abolition of slavery would be hurtful to the slave-owners. This discussion would appear to be, in effect, an elaboration of two themes which are briefly announced in LJ(B) on p. 134. After this, the points made by LJ(A) in the following pages, and the general drift of the argument, are much the same as they are in LJ(B), but the order in which the points are dealt with is often different.

(19) There are some marked differences between the two texts here. LJ(B) begins by listing the five methods of acquiring slaves, and in the course of its discussion of the fifth method considers the state of affairs in ancient Rome where many citizens had no means of subsistence except 'what they received from candidates for their votes'. It then goes on to talk about slavery in the West Indies. LJ(A) discusses the payment of money for votes in ancient Rome on pp. 141–144, *before* getting on to the methods of acquiring slaves, and in the context of a different problem—that of the reasons for the people's demand at that time for an abolition of debts. LJ(A)'s discussion of the methods of acquiring

slaves is relatively short, and is cut off in mid sentence (at the end of vol. iii) with a reference to the West Indies. Cf. above, pp. *20–1*, note 69.

(20) There is no counterpart in LJ(A) of the discussion of these three topics in LJ(B). The indications are that Smith did in fact lecture on them in 1762–3, but that the student for some reason failed to get, or to write up, any notes of the lectures. Cf. above, pp. *20–1*, note 69.

(21) Both texts begin by listing the five ways of acquiring property (LJ(A) on pp. 25–26, and LJ(B) on p. 149), and then proceed to outline the four stages theory —i.e. the theory that society normally tends to develop through four successive stages based on hunting, pasturage, agriculture, and commerce (LJ(A) on pp. 27–35, and LJ(B) on pp. 149–150). But whereas in LJ(B) the context of this outline of the four stages theory is the way in which the laws *of occupation* vary as one stage succeeds another, in LJ(A) the context appears to be a rather more general one— the way in which the laws and regulations with regard to *acquisition of property in general* vary as one stage succeeds another. After this, both texts deal with roughly the same points in the same order, but the discussion in LJ(A) is much more extensive than it is in LJ(B).

(22) Both texts deal with roughly the same points in the same order, but LJ(A) brings out more clearly than LJ(B) the 'four stages' framework of the discussion.

(23) LJ(A) goes into much more detail than LJ(B), and it is not always easy to keep track of the correspondences.

(24) In both texts the general theme is the same, but LJ(A) goes into so much more detail than LJ(B) that the correspondences appear rather sporadic.

(25) Both texts deal with roughly the same points in the same order, but the treatment in LJ(A) is much more extensive and it is by no means easy to keep track of the correspondences. No counterpart can be found in LJ(A) of some of the passages on pp. 163–164 of LJ(B): it seems likely, judging from the mysterious note on p. 145 of LJ(A) and the 3½ blank pages which follow it, that the student for some reason failed to get a part of the relevant lecture down. The account in LJ(A) includes near the end (pp. 146–147) a summary of some of Smith's earlier lectures on the subject.

(26) Although the two texts deal with roughly the same points in the same order, LJ(A) becomes much more detailed at the end than LJ(B).

(27) Both texts deal with roughly the same points, but the order of treatment is a little different (e.g. in the case of the discussion of inventions), and there is little trace in LJ(B) of the interesting discussion of thirlage, etc., on pp. 37–41 of LJ(A).

(28) The general tenor of the argument is the same in both texts, but the order in which certain points are dealt with is different and the treatment in LJ(A) is much more extensive, so that it is not easy to keep track of the correspondences. In addition, LJ(A) contains (on pp. 56 ff.) a very extended summary in which a number of points in earlier lectures are elaborated; and LJ(A) also contains discussions of at least three points (the role of the clergy, the effect of the rise of commerce, and *culpa*) of which there is little trace in LJ(B).

(29) Although the general tenor of the argument is the same in both texts, the illustrations employed are not always the same, and there is no trace in LJ(A) of the point about bankruptcy discussed on p. 181 of LJ(B).

(30) Both texts deal with roughly the same points in the same order, but towards the end LJ(A)'s treatment of some points is much more extensive than LJ(B)'s.

(31) There is no counterpart in LJ(A) of the passage dealing with bonds on p. 192 of LJ(B). The fact that there is a gap in the MS. of LJ(A) at about this point suggests that for some reason the reporter did not get the relevant material down. Otherwise, the points dealt with are roughly the same in both texts, and with one or two exceptions they appear in roughly the same order.

(32) Both texts deal with roughly the same points, but the order of treatment is not always the same, particularly towards the end.

(33) LJ(A) includes, on pp. 24–27, a summary of the main points of the previous lecture.

(34) Details of some of the calculations which appear in LJ(A) are omitted, or drastically summarized, in LJ(B), and on some occasions the figures employed differ as between the two texts.

(35) Both texts deal with roughly the same points, and more or less in the same order—except that the points about the 'law by Sesostratis' on pp. 218–219 of LJ(B) have their counterpart in LJ(A) much later (on pp. 54–55), in the course of a summary of the previous lecture.

(36) The main points dealt with in LJ(B) under this heading do not have their counterpart in LJ(A) until later in the story. The parallel passages in LJ(A) in fact occur at the beginning of a new lecture (apparently as a kind of afterthought on Smith's part), at a point in the course where he has in the previous lecture already embarked upon the next topic, the price of commodities.

(37) Both texts deal with roughly the same points in the same order, but in LJ(A) there is a break in continuity (see previous note). LJ(A) includes a summary of the previous lecture.

(38) LJ(A) includes a summary of the previous lecture.

(39) Both texts deal with roughly the same points, but not always in quite the same order. LJ(A) contains a summary of the previous lecture.

(40) The discussion of circulation, banks, and paper money on pp. 127–132 of LJ(A) breaks off suddenly at the foot of p. 132, at a point in the argument roughly corresponding to the end of the sentence 'That this has a tendency . . . opulence of the country' near the foot of p. 246 of LJ(B). There is no counterpart in LJ(A) of any of the material which appears in LJ(B) between this point and the point on p. 253 where a new paragraph begins. It is at the latter point that LJ(A) takes up the argument again, at the top of p. 133 of the MS., and from there to p. 146 the points covered in LJ(A) are roughly the same as those covered in LJ(B) from p. 253 to p. 256 (except that LJ(A) includes a long statistical discussion of which there

are only faint echoes in LJ(B)). For a possible explanation of the omission from LJ(A) of what was evidently a large amount of material, see p. 380, note 53, below.

(41) Both texts deal with roughly the same points, but not always in quite the same order. LJ(A) contains a summary of the previous lecture.

(42) Both texts deal with roughly the same topics in the same order, up to the point near the foot of p. 268 of LJ(B) where the last sentence on that page begins. At a point corresponding to this LJ(A) ceases.

## 5. *Some Particular Aspects of the Report of 1762–3*

We do not regard it as any part of our purpose, in this Introduction, to present our personal views and interpretations of the actual thought of Adam Smith, as it is reported in the documents we have edited. Since LJ(A) is published here for the first time, however, it might be considered appropriate for us briefly to list some of the ways in which, in our opinion, the discovery of this document may enable new light to be thrown on the development of Smith's ideas during the crucial Glasgow period.

Let us begin with three general considerations, arising from the fact that the treatment of individual topics is usually much more extensive in LJ(A) than it is in LJ(B). This fact means, first, that in quite a large number of places (some but not all of which are specifically referred to in our editorial footnotes) where the text of LJ(B) is unclear or corrupt, Smith's real meaning can now be ascertained by looking at the corresponding passage in LJ(A). It means, second, that in certain places (e.g. the section on occupation and that on contract) where the additional material in LJ(A) is very extensive indeed, some of the major emphases are altered—to such an extent, on occasion, as to make it appear at first sight that a quite different story is being told. And it means, third, that in some places we have been able to go farther than Cannan in our detection of the probable sources upon which Smith drew—not, we hasten to say, because Cannan's editorial work was in any way unscholarly, but simply because there happens to be more material in LJ(A) than in LJ(B), and therefore more clues as to sources. For example, whereas Smith's use of Montesquieu is clear from LJ(B), his dependence on Hume's *History* and *Essays* is more pronounced in LJ(A).

Turning now, more specifically, to vols. i–v of LJ(A), one of the most important points which emerges from them concerns the relation between the way in which Smith dealt with the latter part of the Moral Philosophy course in his Glasgow lectures, and the way in which Francis Hutcheson, Smith's teacher, had dealt with it in *his* Glasgow lectures some time before. After the discovery of LJ(B), a number of scholars (notably Cannan and Scott) drew attention to certain interesting parallels between Hutcheson's treatment of the subject and Smith's. If we now compare Hutcheson's treatment with that of Smith *as reported in LJ(A)* the parallels become more striking, since the order of treatment of the main subjects in LJ(A) is much closer to Hutcheson's than the order of treatment in LJ(B).[79] Another point of almost equal importance is that Smith's use of the four stages theory as a kind of conceptual framework within which much of the discussion is set, and his conscious acceptance of the more general 'environmental' or 'materialist' approach which underlay the four stages theory, are more clearly evident in LJ(A) than they are in LJ(B).[80]

There are various other points of a less general nature which emerge from a comparison between vols. i–v of LJ(A) and the corresponding sections of LJ(B). Of these, we may select four of the more interesting ones as examples. First, LJ(A) elaborates Smith's explanation of the natural right to property by occupation, given very summarily in LJ(B).[81] The account follows Smith's theory of the impartial spectator in TMS and is evidently intended to be an alternative to a celebrated argument of Locke. Second, it is perhaps significant that in LJ(A) the *dangers* to liberty implicit in certain features of 'the situation and circumstances of England' are referred to, whereas in LJ(B), broadly speaking, it is only the *safeguards* which are mentioned.[82] Third, as has already been stated above,[83] there is no distinct counterpart in LJ(B) of the interesting discussion in LJ(A) of the fact that slavery is 'very detrimentall to population'. On the other hand, LJ(B) contains a paragraph about the status in Britain of Negroes who had been slaves in America, an addition apparently prompted by an important court judgement of 1762.[84] Fourth, the discussion of exclusive privileges in LJ(A) contains some important passages, of which there is virtually no counterpart in LJ(B), where Smith in effect generalizes the idea that institutions which are harmful to society today may very well in their origin have been convenient and in a sense necessary to society.[85]

Turning now to vol. vi of LJ(A), which contains the report of Smith's lectures on 'police', this does not appear, at any rate at first sight, to cast quite as much new light on Smith's economic thought as we might perhaps have hoped. LJ(A), after all, stops short about two-thirds of the way through the 'police' section, so that LJ(B) is still our sole source of information concerning the remaining part of this section.[86] LJ(A), again, does not in most of this section (so far as it goes) contain as much additional

[79] Cf. R. L. Meek, 'New Light on Adam Smith's Glasgow Lectures on Jurisprudence', 452–3 and 461–2.
[80] Cf. R. L. Meek, *Social Science and the Ignoble Savage* (Cambridge, 1976), 116 ff.
[81] Below, pp. 16–17 and 459.
[82] Cf. above, p. *28*, note 7.
[83] p. *29*, note 17.
[84] Below, p. 456.
[85] Below, pp. 85–6. This section also contains, on p. 86, a brief discussion of 'the separation of trades' which heralds the later discussion of the division of labour in vol. vi.
[86] And also, of course, concerning the whole of the 'revenue' and 'arms' sections.

material—as compared with that in LJ(B)—as it does in the 'justice' section. And last but not least, at a crucial point where the text of LJ(B) obviously embodies a serious misinterpretation of Smith's argument, the LJ(A) reporter, as if with a design to thwart us, has omitted to include a report of the relevant part of the lectures.[87]

Yet when one looks into the matter a little more closely, certain quite interesting points do emerge. For example, it is perhaps significant that there is no trace in LJ(A) of the statement in LJ(B) that 'labour, not money, is the true measure of value'.[88] The more extensive treatment in LJ(A) of the effects of the prohibition on the export of bullion makes Smith's reliance on Hume's theory of specie-flow adjustment clearer than it is in LJ(B).[89] The inclusion in LJ(A) of the sentence beginning 'In what manner then . . .' at the end of Smith's account of the relatively poor position of peasants and labourers in the modern state[90] may perhaps be regarded as giving an emphasis to these passages rather different from that in LJ(B). The treatment of the division of labour in LJ(A) provides some suggestive evidence relating to the development of Smith's ideas on this subject.[91] And the inclusion in LJ(A) of a number of detailed calculations of the cost of production of a pin (which are either omitted or summarized very briefly in LJ(B)) makes the burden of Smith's argument much clearer.

Another point which emerges is perhaps of sufficient importance to deserve a paragraph to itself. A number of scholars, basing themselves on LJ(B), have argued that in Smith's Glasgow lectures capital and the accumulation of capital did not yet play anything like the central role which they were later to do in WN; that the concept of profit on capital as a basic category of class income was still missing; and that the concept of a normal *rate* of profit on capital was also missing. Now that we have another, and more extensive, report of Smith's Glasgow lectures to turn to, it is possible that these judgements may require *some*—although perhaps not very much—modification. In relation to the question of the role of capital, scholars interested in this problem will probably see some significance in a passage where Smith tries to calculate the value of 'the stock of the whole kingdom'.[92] In relation to the question of the concept of profit as a category of class income, they may wish to refer to a passage where he talks of the capacity of industry, when improved, to 'give considerable profit of the great men'.[93] And in relation to the question of the rate of profit, they will certainly be interested in a passage where Smith says that the price of a commodity must be sufficient to repay the costs of education and the apprentice fee 'not only in principall but with the interest and profit which

[87] Above, p. *31*, note 40.　　　　　　　　　　[88] Below, p. 503.
[89] Below, pp. 385-9.　　　　　　　　　　　　　[90] Below, p. 341.
[91] Cf. R. L. Meek and A. S. Skinner, 'The Development of Adam Smith's Ideas on the Division of Labour' (*Economic Journal*, vol. 83, Dec. 1973).
[92] Below, pp. 381-3.　　　　　　　　　　　　[93] Below, p. 343.

I might have made of it',[94] and also perhaps in another where he describes what happens in a competitive market when a trade is 'overprofitable'.[95]

## 6. *The Principles Adopted in the Transcription of the Texts*

The preparation of LJ(A) and LJ(B) for publication has involved a number of serious difficulties, arising in large part from the particular way in which LJ(A) appears to have been originally compiled.

As stated above,[96] the main text on the recto pages of LJ(A) would seem to have been written serially, soon after (but not during) the lectures concerned, on the basis of very full notes taken down in class, probably in shorthand. The reporter evidently took some care, when writing up the notes, to ensure that they were as accurate as possible a representation of what Smith had actually said. But the *degree* of the reporter's care varied appreciably from place to place; and since the notes were intended merely as working notes he was not overmuch concerned with legibility, grammar, and the niceties of spelling, punctuation, capitalization, and paragraphing. The handwriting varies from perfectly legible copper-plate to a hurried scrawl which is very difficult to decipher, and there is a large number of abbreviations, overwritings, deletions, and interlineations. The spelling is often careless and wildly inconsistent; punctuation and capitalization are usually very arbitrary; and paragraphing is minimal.

The editors of LJ(A) were thus faced right at the outset with a difficult problem: to what extent, if at all, should these ubiquitous imperfections be cleaned up in the interests of readability? On the one hand, it could be argued that the published text should be in effect the editors' reconstruction of what Smith might be presumed actually to have said in the lectures concerned—which would mean, of course, that the published text would deviate appreciably from the reporter's imperfect notes. On the other hand, it could be argued that the text should properly be no more than a reproduction, as exact as possible, of the reporter's manuscript notes as they stood, with all their manifest blemishes.

In the end, we decided that some kind of compromise between these two extreme views would have to be arrived at. The adoption of the first method would have allowed too much room for the editors' own subjective judgements, and would have largely deprived the reader of the opportunity to make up his own mind about the exact circumstances in which LJ(A) originated. The second method, as a number of experiments eventually showed, would have necessitated an impossibly extensive apparatus of footnotes, and would have succeeded only in making the text in many places virtually unreadable.

An important constraint here was that the principles adopted in transcribing LJ(A) should as far as possible be the same as those adopted in

---

[94] Below, p. 357.        [95] Below, p. 363.        [96] p. *11*.

transcribing LJ(B), in order that the comparison of the two documents should be facilitated. LJ(B), generally speaking, is much more readable as it stands than LJ(A): there are very few corrections and additions; the writing is almost always perfectly legible; and spelling and paragraphing are on the whole quite rational and consistent. The capitalization, however, is just as arbitrary in LJ(B) as it is in LJ(A); and the punctuation, although less arbitrary, would often hamper the reader if left unaltered.

The basis of the set of principles eventually arrived at was the drawing of a distinction between two more or less separate groups of imperfections in the manuscripts—first, those which it was thought could justifiably be corrected in the published text without (in normal cases) any specific footnote reference; and, second, those others which it was felt ought to be allowed to remain in the published text, either with or without a specific footnote reference. After much experimentation, we decided to place in the first group (*a*) punctuation and capitalization, which we felt should up to a certain point be modernized; (*b*) straightforward overwritings and interlineations, which we decided need not (in normal cases) be specifically noted; and (*c*) contractions, most (but not all) of which we thought should be spelt out. In the second group, we decided to place all the remaining imperfections—notably spelling errors, omissions, inadequate paragraphing, deletions, replacements, etc.—feeling that these should be allowed to remain in the text, with specific footnote references (or other indications) wherever necessary. This distinction was, and was bound to be, to some extent arbitrary,[97] but experience showed that it offered the best basis for a text which would satisfy as fully as possible the demands both of the general reader and of the Smith scholar.

Another and related set of decisions had then to be made concerning the number and character of the symbols and conventions to be used in the critical apparatus. From the nature of the case, it was clear that this apparatus would inevitably have to be somewhat complex; and the editors were therefore very conscious of the fact that unless they made a special effort to reduce the number of symbols and conventions to the absolute minimum it might be very difficult for readers—specialist as well as non-specialist—to find their way through the text. Three basic decisions were accordingly made:

(a) The main symbolic apparatus should consist of three different types of

[97] For example, it is obvious that no clear logical line can be drawn between overwritings (at any rate those of a more radical kind) and replacements. To note all the overwritings in LJ(A), however, would have been a virtually impossible task: there are literally hundreds of them, many of which are uncertain or illegible and most of which are of little importance. Many of the replacements in LJ(A), on the other hand, are of much greater importance, representing as they do attempts by the reporter to alter his original formulations so as to make them more consonant with what Smith actually said, or to improve the flow of the argument.

brackets—*square brackets* [ ] for superfluous words or letters; *angle brackets* ⟨ ⟩ for words or letters supplied to rectify omissions; and *braces* { } for the verso notes in LJ(A).[98]

(b) A set of conventions, as simple as possible, should be adopted for the keying-in of footnote references to deletions, replacements, illegible words, and doubtful readings.

(c) There should be only two categories of footnotes—textual and editorial, indicated respectively by italic letters and by arabic numerals in roman type. The footnotes themselves should throughout be in plain English, unencumbered by any further symbols for the reader to memorize.

These three basic decisions were eventually crystallized in a number of specific principles relating to the presentation of the text and the critical apparatus, the most important of which are the following:

## i. *Numbering of Pages*

At the beginning of vol. i of the original MS. of LJ(A), the recto pages upon which the main text is written have been numbered by the reporter 1, 3, 5, 7, etc. up to 39, when this numbering ceases. The first pages of the gatherings on which the report is written are also numbered. All these numbers have been ignored in our text, and in the case of each volume *the recto pages upon which writing appears* have been numbered 1, 2, 3, 4, etc. right through to the end of the volume concerned. Thus each volume is numbered separately, and the verso pages (together with any blank recto pages) are left unnumbered.[99] In the text, the point at which one (recto) page of a particular volume of the MS. ends and the next page begins is marked by the insertion of a vertical rule in the text and the placing of the relevant page number (in ordinary arabic figures) in the margin. For example, 23 in the margin indicates that at the point in the line level with this number where a vertical rule is inserted, p. 22 of the MS. ends and p. 23 begins.[100] If one or two words at the end of one page of the MS. are repeated at the beginning of the next, as frequently happens in LJ(A), the repetition is as it were credited to the next. At the point where one volume of LJ(A) ends and another volume begins (but only at that point), the number of the new volume is also stated. For example, iii.1 in the margin indicates that at the point in the line level with this number where a vertical rule is inserted, vol. ii of the MS. ends and vol. iii begins.

In the case of LJ(B) the position is less complex, since the main text is

---

[98] *Square brackets* are also used to enclose certain manuscript page numbers, and are sometimes employed in footnotes for other (self-explanatory) purposes. In LJ(B), where the main text is written on both the recto and the verso pages of the MS., *braces* merely reproduce braces used in the text as a form of brackets.

[99] The page containing the incomplete table of contents at the beginning of vol. i has also been left unnumbered.

[100] For the conventions relating to the pagination of the notes on the verso pages of LJ(A), see p. *42* below.

written on both the recto and the verso pages of the MS.; all the material is contained in one volume; and the pages of the MS. (although not of the index), *whether writing appears on them or not,* have all been numbered successively by the copyist. These page numbers are those which are referred to in our text. The conventions adopted for indicating where one page ends and another begins are the same (*mutatis mutandis*) as those adopted in the case of LJ(A). The few cases in which words at the end of one page are repeated at the beginning of the next, however, are specifically noted.

In our footnotes to the texts, page references to LJ(A) and LJ(B), if the number is not preceded by 'p.', are to pages *of the MSS.* If the number *is* preceded by 'p.' it refers to a page *of this edition.*

## ii. *Punctuation*

As indicated above, the punctuation in LJ(A) is often arbitrary and irrational (or non-existent); and that in LJ(B) is not much better. In the interests of readability, therefore, the punctuation in both texts has to a certain extent been cleaned up. In particular, full points have normally been inserted between sentences where they are lacking in the MSS., and in a large number of cases where a sentence requires more (or less) breaking-up for full comprehensibility, semicolons or commas have been inserted (or deleted). We have not attempted to secure *complete* rationality or consistency in punctuation, however; and in a few cases where the interpretation of a particular passage may depend upon the punctuation no alterations have been made.

## iii. *Capitalization*

The profusion of capital letters in both MSS. raises a special problem. Not only are capital letters used very frequently, but they are also used very inconsistently; and in a great number of cases it is quite uncertain whether or not a capital letter was in fact intended. In the interests of readability, therefore, a more modern system of capitalization has been employed, and an attempt made to secure a reasonable degree of consistency both within and between each of the two texts. In a few cases where the use of a capital letter in the MS. can reasonably be regarded as serving some special purpose (e.g. the emphasis of a key word, or of a new concept on the occasion of its first introduction) we have retained it.

## iv. *Straightforward Overwritings and Interlineations*

In very many cases in LJ(A), and occasionally in LJ(B), a word (or series of words) has been changed to another simply by overwriting: e.g. the scribe has begun by writing 'then' and has changed it to 'there' (the correct word) by overwriting 'there' in the space occupied by 'then'. As stated above,[101] in many of these cases the overwritten word is illegible, and since to note them all would have meant a tremendous expansion of the apparatus of footnotes and greatly hindered readability, they have not in fact been specifically indicated in the text, except where some special point is involved. Similarly, straightforward interlineations—i.e. those clearly intended to form part of the text and not involving the replacement of deleted words—have also not been specifically indicated, except where some special point is involved.

### v. *Contractions*

The contractions used in the MS. of LJ(A) for the words 'the', 'against', 'with', 'that', 'than', 'neither', 'either', 'betwixt', 'which', and 'brother' are not reproduced in the text, all these words being spelt out. So far as other contracted words (in both MSS.) are concerned, the general rule adopted is that all contractions which are raised, and all those above which a contraction symbol is placed, are spelt out, with the exception of '1st', '2nd', etc., which are reproduced in the text exactly as they appear in the MS. 'Mr', 'Dr', and 'Sr' are rendered as 'Mr.', 'Dr.', and 'Sir'. All ampersands are spelt out, and '&c.' (or '&ca.') is rendered as 'etc.' (or 'etca.'). The different signs used for the pound sterling are all rendered as '£'. All other contracted words, monetary symbols, measures, numbers, etc. are reproduced in the text exactly as they appear in the MS.

### vi. *Spelling Errors, Omissions, etc.*

The spelling in the MSS. has normally been retained in the text, even when it is clearly wrong, and no attempt has been made to secure consistency. When the spelling of a word in the MS. is doubtful, the spelling used in the text is that which is normally used elsewhere in the MS., or (in cases where this criterion cannot be applied) the correct modern spelling. Similarly, grammatical errors, unconscious omissions or repetitions of words, etc. in both MSS. have normally been reproduced in the text.

Where such errors, omissions, etc. seem likely to interfere seriously with readability, however, the following devices are used:

(a) Words or letters in the MS. which quite clearly ought not to be there are enclosed in square brackets. Example:
*MS.*: the spirit of the of the Roman Law
*Text*: the spirit of the [of the] Roman Law

(b) Words or letters which quite clearly ought to be in the MS., but are not, are inserted and enclosed in angle brackets. Example:
*MS.*: this vioated the constitution
*Text*: this vio⟨l⟩ated the constitution

[101] p. *36*, note.

(c) In cases where a word (or words) is obviously omitted from the MS., and a reasonable guess can be made of what was intended, the probable word (or words) omitted is inserted in the text, preceded by a question mark and enclosed in angle brackets. Example:

*MS.*: the laws of Scotland and were different
*Text*: the laws of Scotland and ⟨?England⟩ were different

(d) In cases where a word (or words) is obviously omitted from the MS., but a reasonable guess cannot be made of what was intended, a pair of angle brackets enclosing a question mark is inserted in the text. Example:

*MS.*: when the king was he summoned his
*Text*: when the king was ⟨?⟩ he summoned his

(e) In cases which cannot be dealt with by the above devices, a footnote is normally inserted indicating what was probably intended.

## vii. *Paragraphing*

The paragraphing in LJ(A) is minimal, and often very conjectural, if only because the first lines of new paragraphs are not indented. Sometimes the beginning of a new paragraph is marked in the MS. by a dash (or series of dashes) immediately following the preceding sentence; but such dashes, unfortunately, also frequently occur at the end of a sentence which is obviously *not* intended to be the last in a paragraph.[102] Sometimes a change in ink and/or the style of the handwriting in the MS., coupled with a change in the subject-matter, indicates that a new paragraph was probably intended. In the text, new paragraphs have normally been formed *only* in those cases where the indication in the MS. is reasonably unambiguous, or where the absence of a new paragraph would interfere seriously with readability.

The paragraphing in LJ(B) is reasonably clear and rational, and with very few exceptions has simply been reproduced in our text.

When a new paragraph starts on a new page, the vertical rule indicating the change of page is inserted at the beginning of the new paragraph and not at the end of the preceding paragraph.

## viii. *Deletions, Replacements, etc.*

(a) Where a word (or words) in a line is deleted, and not replaced by an interlined word (or words), a footnote reference is keyed in at the end of the word immediately preceding the deletion. Example:

*MS.*: from what ~~he~~ had for a long time
*Text*: from what[a] had for a long time

---

[a] 'he' deleted

[102] Dashes occurring in the middle of a paragraph are normally reproduced in the text; single dashes occurring at what is construed as the end of a paragraph are normally omitted. When several dashes occur at the end of a paragraph, however, they are normally reproduced, since they may indicate a break of some kind (e.g. the end of a lecture).

(b) Where a word (or words) at the beginning of a new paragraph is deleted, and not replaced by an interlined word (or words), a footnote reference is keyed in at the beginning of the first word of the paragraph. Example:

*MS.*: ~~Thus~~ Contracts, when they were first
*Text*: [b]Contracts, when they were first

---

[b] 'Thus' deleted

(c) Where a word (or words) in a line is deleted, and replaced by a word interlined above it, a footnote reference is keyed in at the end of the replacing word. Example:

confers
*MS.*: the balance of property ~~has~~ so small a
*Text*: the balance of property confers[c] so small a

---

[c] Replaces 'has'

(d) Where a word (or words) in a line is deleted, and replaced by several words interlined above it, a footnote reference is keyed in at the end of the last of the replacing words. Example:

about their land
*MS.*: ~~with~~ themselves and multiply their
*Text*: about their land[d] themselves and multiply their

---

[d] The last three words replace 'with'

ix. *Doubtful Readings, Illegible Words, Blanks in MS., etc.*

The footnotes 'Reading doubtful', 'Reading of last two words doubtful', etc., indicate that the editors are more than usually dubious about the reading of the word or words concerned which they have given in the text. The relevant footnote references are keyed in at the end of the word or words.

In cases of complete illegibility, a blank space of approximately the same length as the illegible word or words is left in the text, a footnote reference is keyed in at the beginning of the following word, and an appropriate footnote inserted. If the editors wish merely to note the illegibility, without making any comment, the footnote is a textual one, indicated by an italic letter and in most cases reading simply 'Illegible word'. If the editors wish not only to note the illegibility but also to make a comment, the footnote is an editorial one, indicated by an arabic numeral in roman type.

When a blank space has been left in the MS., a similar procedure is normally adopted.[103] A space of roughly the same length as the space in the MS. is left in the text, a footnote reference is keyed in at the beginning of the following word, and an appropriate footnote inserted. This footnote is

---

[103] In some cases, however (e.g. where a large part of a page, or a number of pages, has been left blank), a note of this fact is inserted in the text in italics.

a textual one if the editors wish merely to note that a blank space has been left in the MS. at this point, and an editorial one if they wish also to make a comment.

In cases where the degree of illegibility is such that the number of illegible words cannot be exactly ascertained, an attempt is made in the relevant footnote to give an approximate indication of the number of words concerned—e.g. 'Two or three illegible words'. Cases in which it appears possible that it is only *part* of a word which is illegible are not separately delineated—e.g. the footnote 'Illegible word deleted' must be taken to include the possibility that it is only part of a word which has been deleted at the relevant point in the MS.

## x. *Treatment of the Verso Notes in LJ(A)*

The verso notes in LJ(A) are incorporated in the main text, at what appears to be the appropriate place, within braces. It is to be assumed, in the absence of any indication to the contrary, that the note concerned is written on the verso of the previous (recto) page. Thus if a passage appears within braces on (recto) page 28, and no contrary indication is given, it can be taken that in the MS. it is written on the verso of (recto) page 27. If a verso note continues on to the next verso page, as sometimes happens, an indication of this is given in square brackets at the appropriate point. Thus if a passage in braces appears on (recto) page 64 of the text, and at a certain point in this passage the indication [v.64] appears, this denotes the fact that the note in question, although starting on the verso of (recto) page 63, is carried over at the indicated point to the verso of (recto) page 64.

## xi. *Cross-references*

In view of the fact that a detailed collation of LJ(A) and LJ(B) has been included in this Introduction, cross-references between the two documents have been provided only in special cases. The scope of our cross-references to other works of Smith has also been deliberately restricted, in the light of a general policy decision by the Board of Editors of the Glasgow edition to the effect that in each of the volumes of Smith's works cross-references should normally be provided only to work of an earlier date. One of the results of this policy is that in the present volume there are virtually no references forward to WN. In WN itself, however, there are very many references back to the documents published in the present volume,[104] to which readers are referred for the relation between Smith's earlier and later ideas in the relevant fields.

[104] WN also contains a number of references back to the Anderson Notes, in the version presented in the article referred to above, p. 4, note 12.

# Acknowledgements

THE editors gratefully acknowledge the help on particular points of Professor J. A. Boyle, Mr. J. A. Crook, Dr. J. Diggle, Professor A. D. Fitton Brown, Professor M. C. Meston, Mrs. Dorothy Owen, Dr. J. Riley-Smith, Mr. A. S. Skinner, and Mr. D. E. C. Yale. They are also grateful to Amax Inc. of Greenwich, Connecticut, for their generous contribution to the publication costs of this volume.

D. D. R. and P. G. S. wish it to be known that the main part of the editorial burden in relation to the present volume has been carried by R. L. M.

The editors have made extensive use of the invaluable notes provided by Edwin Cannan for his edition of LJ(B) in 1896.

R. L. M.
D. D. R.
P. G. S.

# LECTURES ON JURISPRUDENCE

---

## REPORT OF 1762-3

# CONTENTS

## VOL. 1

### Note

The above is a reproduction of the incomplete list of contents which appears on the recto page of the third leaf of vol. i (see Introduction, p. *10* above). The page numbers are those entered by the reporter himself, and relate to the numbering scheme he adopted for the first 39 pages of the MS. (see Introduction, p. *37*). The verso page of the third leaf, and the five following leaves, are blank.

## Of Jurisprudence.

Jurisprudence is the theory of the rules by which civil governments ought to be directed.

It attempts to shew the foundation of the different systems of government[a] in different countries and to shew how far they are founded in reason.

We will find that there are four things which will be the design of every government:[b]

$1^{st}$ The first and chief design of every system of government is to maintain justice; to prevent the members of a society from incroaching on one anothers property, or siezing what is not their own. The design here is to give each one the secure and peacable possession of his own property. {The end proposed by justice is the maintaining men in what are called their perfect rights.}[c] When this end, which we may call the internall peace, or

2 peace within doors, is | secured, the government will next be desirous of promoting[d] the opulence of the state. This produces what we call police. Whatever regulations are made with respect to the trade, commerce, agriculture, manufactures of the country are considered as belonging to the police.

When Mr.        [1] resigned the office of        [2] of Paris to Mr. D'Argenson, he told him that the king required three things of him who held that office,[e] that he should take care of $1^{st}$, the clean⟨n⟩ess or neteté; $2^d$, the *aisance*, ease or security; and $3^{dly}$, *bon marché* or cheapness of provisions.— The $1^{st}$ of these is two mean and trifling a subject to be treated of in a system of jurisprudence. The $2^d$ is of two sorts, first that which provides for the security of the inhabitants against fires, or other such accidents.

3 | This also is of too[f] trifling a nature to be reckoned a branch of jurisprudence. The other branch is that which provides against any injuries that may be done by other persons to the inhabitants; and this end is accomplished either by guards and patroles that prevent the commission of such crimes

---

[a] Replaces 'laws'    [b] 'The' deleted    [c] This interpolation is written on the verso of 1    [d] Replaces 'providing for'    [e] '$1^{st}$' deleted    [f] 'small imp' deleted

---

[1] Blank in MS. See next note.

[2] Blank in MS. Baron Bielfeld, *Institutions politiques* (1760), I.7 (*De la Police*), 1: 'Le premier Président du Harlay en recevant M. d'Argenson à la Charge de Lieutenant-Général de Police de la Ville de Paris lui adressa ces paroles qui méritent d'être remarquées: *Le Roi, monsieur, vous demande sûreté, netteté, bon marché.*' Marc René de Voyer, Comte d'Argenson, took up this office in 1677. Cf. vi.1–2 below.

as it were *a priori*, or by the constitution of statutes for the punishment of transgressors and the encouragement of those who discover the offenders and bring them to justice.—The 2ᵈ part may be called the justice of police, and as it is connected in that manner with the former part of jurisprudence, we shall consider it under that head. The 3ᵈ part of police is bon marché or the cheapness of provisions, and the having the market well supplied with

4 all sorts of com|modities. This must include not only the promoting a free communication betwixt the town and the country, the internall commerce as we may call it, but also on the plenty or opulence of the neighbouring<sup>g</sup> country.

This is the most important branch of police and is what we shall consider when we come to treat of police; and in handling it we shall consider the different regulations that have subsisted in different countries and how far they have answered the intentions of the governments that constituted them; and this we shall ⟨?⟩ to ancient as well as modern times.

3ᵈ As the government can not be supported without some expence, though the state was very opulent, it would next be considered in what manner this

5 expence should be | born. In all cases it is evident that this burthen at last must lye on the industrious part of the people. Whether 1ˢᵗ, it be born by the rents of what are called demesne lands, viz those that belong to the crown or the governing part of the nation. This as it abridges the possession of the subjects must be considered as a burthen on them. Or 2ᵈˡʸ, it may be supplied by a tax on the lands possessed by the subjects. These though not rents of the crown are a deducement from the rents of the possessor. Or lastly, if it be raised by customs, on manufactures, imports and such like, where it is immediately levied from the people. In all cases therefore the expenses of the government must be defrayed by the people. The summ

6 | levied to defray these expenses is what we call the revenue of the government. In treating of that branch of jurisprudence<sup>h</sup> which relates to government, we shall consider the different methods which have been taken to raise the sum necessary for the expense of the state in different countries, and how far they are adapted to do this with the least loss or hindrance to the industry of the people, which ought to be the chief thing in view. For it will also be shewn that the same summ may be raised in some ways which would mightily discourage the industry and improvement of the country and in others which would have those bad effects in a much less proportion.

4 Besides these 3 considerations of the security of property, the police, and the revenue of the kingdom or state, it must also be necessary to have some

7 means of | protecting the state from foreign injuries. Tho' the<sup>i</sup> peace within doors be never so firmly established, yet if there be no security from injuries from without the property of individualls can not be secure. The

<sup>g</sup> 'in th' deleted     <sup>h</sup> Replaces 'government'     <sup>i</sup> 'internall' deleted

danger to them on this head is no less to be feard than from those of their own society; and not only is the security of private persons in danger but the very being[j] of the state. It is therefore requisite that an armed force should be maintained,[k] as well to defend the state against externall injuries as to obtain satisfaction for any that have been committed. In treating of this subject we shall consider the various species of armed forces that have been in use in antient and modern states; the different sorts of militias and
8 train'd bands; and observe | how far they were suited to the different natures of the governments.

This naturally leads us to consider in the 4th place the laws of peace ⟨and⟩ war, the jura belli et pacis. That is, the different regulations that subsist betwixt different independent states, with respect both to the mutual intercourse betwixt them in time of peace and what priviledges may be granted them, and to the[l] effects of the success in war and what is permitted as lawful in the time that war is waged betwixt different nations. We shall under this head compare those laws of war that subsisted in antient times with those now in force and shew how far the latter are superior in moderation and humanity; and also[m] point out the causes of the gradual restrictions that have been made on the laws of war in the refinement of
9 society. | We shall also on this head shew how these regulations vary according as the independent states are of a republican, or monarchicall or aristocraticall form; which will lead us to consider the various priviledges granted to strangers in different countries, as aliens,

etc.

✻

The first and chief design of all civill governments, is, as I observed, to preserve justice amongst the members of the state and prevent all incroachments on the individualls in it, from others of the same society.— {That is, to maintain each individual in his perfect rights.} Justice is vio⟨l⟩ated whenever one is deprived of what he had a right to and could justly demand from others,[n] or rather, when we do him an injury or hurt without a cause. Let us consider then in how many ways     *Injuries a*
10 violated, that is, in how many respects a man may | be i     *man can*
may be injured as a man; 2[dly], as a member of a family     *recieve*
citizen or member of a state. Every injury that can be done a man may be reduced to some of these, and in all of these he may be injured without being affected when considered in any of the other views.—When one attempts to kill an other he does him an injury as a man; when a man is deprived of his wife or she is ill treated he is injured as a husband; or when he is deprived of his son, or his son does not act with proper regard to him,

---

[j] 'and ex' deleted    [k] Illegible word deleted    [l] The last three words replace 'and what customs'    [m] Replaces 'lastly'    [n] 'which is' deleted

he is injured as a father, and member of a family.—If one behaves[o] disrespectfully and without due honour to one that is dignified with an office or title, this is an injury done as a citizen, as his pre-eminence is founded on a civil constitution. If one who has no just right assumes any title of nobility, this is an injury both to his equalls in taking upon him the
11 character of one of rank superior | to them, and to his superiors in assuming to have himself reckon'd as their equal when he is their inferior; and the injury here proceeds as from the quality of a citizen or member of a state in which he is considered.[p] In each of these examples the injury is peculiar to the quality in which the person is considered [in]. The injury done to one as a father could not affect him merely as a man, nor could that which is done to him as a member of a state be competent to him as a man or member of a family, but intirely proceeds from his state as a citizen.

———— ———— ————

We shall consider in the first place those rights that belong to a man as a man, as they are generally most simple and easily understood, and generally can be considered without respect to any other[q] condition.
12 | A man merely as a man may be injured in three respects, either 1st, in his person; or 2dly, in his reputation; or 3dly, in his estate. 1st A man may be injured in his person two ways also, either 1st, by killing, wounding, or maiming him, or any way hurting his body, or secondly by restraining his liberty.—These rights correspond to what Puffendorff call⟨s⟩ naturall rights as those which respect a man as a member of a family or of a state do to those which they call adventious.[3]—Amongst these natural rights[r] which they define to be jura, *quae omnem actum humanum antecedunt*, vel, *quae ex nullo actu humano proficiscuntur*, they reckon up jus ad vitam, ad corpus, liberi commercii, a right of trafficking with those who are willing to deal with him, jus connubiorum, etc., and lastly jus sincerae aestimationis, or a right to an unspoiled character, to what he possesses—in all about
13 a dozen. Now these may all be reduced to the | three above mentioned. Those which affect his body may all be reduced to the first[s] class of those respecting his person; the right to free commerce, and the right to freedom in marriage, etc. when infringed are all evidently incroachments on the right one has to the free use of his person and in a word to do what he has a mind when it does not prove detrimentall to any other person.[t]

A man is injured in his reputation when one endeavours to bring his

[o] Replaces 'does not pay the' [p] 'And' deleted [q] The last two words replace an illegible word [r] 'they reckon up the' deleted [s] Replaces 'which, we said, second' [t] 'The' deleted

[3] The distinction between natural and adventitious rights is from Hutcheson, *M.P.*, II.4.2 (cf. *System*, I.293): 'The former sort nature itself has given to each one, without any human grant or institution. The adventitious depend upon some human deed or institution.' Pufendorf, III.4.3, distinguished natural (*connatae*) and adventitious *obligations*.

character below what is the common standard amongst men. If one calls another a fool, a knave, or a rogue he injures him in his reputation, as he does not then give him that share of good fame which is common to almost
14 all men, to perhaps 99 of 100. | But, again, if one calls another an honest good natured man, tho perhaps he deserved a much higher character, he can not complain of any injury being done him, as that is the character due to the generality of men. We may here observe the distinction which Mr. Hutchinson, after Baron Puffendorf, has made of rights.[4] He divides them into *jura perfecta* and *imperfecta*, i.e. perfect and imperfe⟨c⟩t rights.— Perfect rights are those which we have a title to demand and if refused to compel an other to perform. What they call imperfect rights are those which correspond to those duties which[u] ought to be performed to us by others but which we have no title to compel them to perform; they having it intirely in their power to perform them or not. Thus[v] a man of bright
15 parts or remarkable learning is deserving of | praise, but we have no power to compel any one to give it him. A beggar[w] is an object of our charity and may be said to have a right to demand it; but when we use the word right in this way it is not in a proper but a metaphoricall sense. The common[x] way in which we[y] understand the word right, is the same as what we have called a perfect right, and is that which relates to commutative justice. Imperfect rights, again, refer to distributive justice. The former are the[z] rights which we are to consider, the latter not belonging properly to jurisprudence, but rather to a system of moralls as they do not fall under the jurisdiction of the laws.[5] We are therefore in what follows to confine ourselves entirely to the perfect rights and what is called commutative
16 | justice. — — —

The last particular in which a man may be injured is his estate.

Now what is it we call ones estate. It is either 1st, what he has ⟨?in his⟩ immediate possession, not only what he has about his own person as his cloaths, etc., but whatever he has a claim to and can take possession of in whatever place or condition he finds it. {A man has a real right to whatever *vindicari potest a quocunque possessore*.[6]} Or 2[dly], what is due to him either by loan or by contract of whatever sort, as sales, etc. The first is what we call real rights or a right to a particular thing. The 2[d] is called a personall right or a right against a particular person. {Jura personalia,

---

[u] The last five words replace an illegible word     [v] 'the' deleted     [w] 'has a ri' deleted     [x] Replaces 'prope'     [y] Replaces 'it is'     [z] 'only' deleted

---

[4] Pufendorf, I.1.19; I.7.7; Hutcheson, *Inquiry concerning Moral Good and Evil* (1725), VII.6; *M.P.*, II.2.3; II.4.2 (cf. *System*, I.303).
[5] In TMS VII.ii.1.10 Smith distinguishes commutative and distributive justice without referring to perfect and imperfect rights, but in effect his distinction there comes to the same thing as here.
[6] 'Can be claimed from any possessor whatsoever'.

sunt jura ad certam tantum personam competentia, ad certam rem
servitu      7 vel valorem.⁸}

{A personal[a] right may sometimes be constituted against a certain thing,
but then it [is] only extends to that thing when in the possession of a
certain person. Thus e.g. if a man sells another a horse, but the horse is not
delivered, the buyer has a personal right against the seller. He can demand
the horse from the seller at any time. But if the owner sells him a 2ᵈ time to
another man who gets possession of him [v.16] bonâ fide, the first purchaser can not claim him from the 2ᵈ to whom he has been delivered, tho
he may have an action against the seller for damages. But the case is quite
different when the byer has got the horse delivered; thus if after he had
been delivered the byer had desired the seller to keep him for a short time
and he sold him again to another purchaser, the former can claim him from
the 2ᵈ altho he be a possessor bona fide.}

We shall first consider the real rights; they are four of them as they are
enumerated in the civill law. Dominium, Servitus, Pignus, Haereditas.
17 Dominium, or the full right of | property. By this a man has the sole[b] claim
to a subject, exclusive of all others, but can use it himself as he thinks fit,
and if he pleases abuse or destroy it. By this right if any subject be lost or
abstracted from the right owner he can claim it from any possessor, and
tho perhaps that possessor came jus⟨t⟩ly by it, yet he can not claim any
restitution but must restore it to the owner. He may indeed[c] if he can find
the means obtain restitution from him who by wrong means first possessed
it. Property is to be considered as an exclusive right by which we can
hinder any other person from using in any shape what we possess in this
manner. A man for instance who possesses a farm of land can hinder any
other not only from intermedling with any of the products but from walk-
18 ing across his field. 'Tis from the relaxation or | yielding up some part of
this exclusive right[d] in favours of a particular person that the right of
servitudes has arose.

The 2ᵈ species of real rights therefore is servitudes. These are precisely
the giving up some part of the full right of property. As if a mans farm lies
betwixt me and the publick road or any market town, I may by agreement
or by law (as we shall hereafterwards observe⟨⟩) obtain a servitude (that is,
relaxation of his exclusive right) by which I am allowed to travel on horse
or foot or drive carriages thro' his farm.

{All sort of claims on another mans property is to be considered as a
relaxation of the exclusive right of property, whether they be constituted as

---

[a] Replaces 'real'     [b] Replaces 'only'     [c] Replaces an illegible word     [d] 'that the' deleted

7 Blank in MS. The ending 'tem' has been omitted from the word 'servitutem'.
8 'Personal rights are rights available only against a particular person, in respect of a particular thing, servitude or value': Hutcheson, *M.P.*, II.5.1.

a security for some claim against the dominus serviens, or whether they be constituted without any such design. The first are what we call *pledge*, *mortgage*, or *hypothec*. The others are denominated servitudes. Thus the servitus tigni ingrediendi[9] is a relaxation of the exclusive right by which a man can hinder any one from making any use of his wall that can be any way detrimentall.}

As a man may have an opportunity of letting out his money but is not assured of its being on good security, he may take some part of the property of the person who owes the debt. By this means pledges or mortgages came
19 | to be established. There is not here any proper acquisition, as in the former case, the mortgaged subject being considered as of equal value with the debt for which it is pledged, but he has property in it so far that the debt not being paid he can claim payment from the pledge.

4.[th] If we consider the right which an heir has before his accession to the estate of his father we shall find that it is a real right, tho different from that of property. The heir has the exclusive right to the inheritance. No one can meddle with it in any shape untill he has refused it, and he can obtain restitution for anything that it may have suffered from others as well as [to the] all the accessions that may have been added to it. And as soon as he has
20 consented to enter to the inheritance | he[e] becomes full and complete proprieter of it.

{If therefore we account the right of inheritance to be a real right, as it certainly is, all other exclusive priviledges will for the same reason be accounted real rights, as the right of monopolies, which is a priviledge constituted intirely by the civil law, the right of an author to his book, the right an inventer of a machine or medicine has to the sole vending or making of that machine or drug. These often make the greatest ⟨?part⟩ and sometimes the whole of ones estate, and they are all creatures of the civil law in each country. There are severall others that have their origin in naturall reason, as the right one has to hunt down the game he has started and such like; but the most considerable of all the exclusive priviledges that are founded in nature is succession, which as we shall shew hereafter is altogether agreable to the constitution of nature.}[f]

We may observe that not only property but all other exclusive rights are real rights. Thus the property one has in a book he has written or a machine he has invented, which continues by patent in this country for 14 years, is actually a real right. During that time he can claim restitution, or shew for damages from any one who prints his book or copies his machine, so that he may be considered as having a real right to it.

[e] 'may' deleted        [f] The last fourteen words of this passage are written at the foot
of 20

---

[9] Reading of last word doubtful. *Servitus tigni immittendi*, the right to insert a beam in a neighbour's wall.

21    | We come now to the personall rights, which we will find proceed from
three sources: 1$^{st}$, Contract; 2$^{d}$,$^g$ what is called quasi ex contractu, which is
called now from Quasi Contract, or more properly the right of Restitution; 3$^{d}$—$^{10}$

1$^{st}$ Personall rights may proceed from contract. The origin of this right is
the expectation raisen in him to whom the promise was made that the
promiser will perform what he has undertaken. Thus if one promises to
give an other five pounds, this naturally creates an expectation that he will
receive five pounds from him at the time promised; and here the promiser
must be bound to make up to him any$^h$ loss he has suffered by this expectation.

2$^{dly}$ *Quasi ex contractu.* This is no more as we observed already but the
right of restitution.—If one finds any subject, as ⟨a⟩ watch, which is the
property of an other, he is bound to restore this watch to the right owner
22 whenever he | can discover him, and this without any claim to the contrary.

But if,$^i$ for example, one imagines his father owed my father *five pounds*,
and I imagined that there was such a debt, and receive payment of this
supposed debt.—After, the other discovers that the summ had been paid
and produces his discharge. Here if the money has been spent, he can not
have a real claim against me for the money. There is no particular five
pounds which he can demand of me. But nevertheless I am bound to make
restitution of five pounds to him. They say, *est res aliena* in patrimonio,
there is something in my patrimony which is the property of another. In
the same ⟨?way⟩, whenever I am benefitted by the property of another in
a manner to which I have no just claim, I am bound to make restitution
23 quantum ex re aliena locu|pletior factus sum;$^{11}$ and this not only when the
subject exists but even after it has been consumed. {Hence arise many
actions mentioned in the civil law, as that called condictio$^j$indebiti, and the
actio negotiorum gestorum, as when one in the absence of the owner
repairs the house to prevent it from going to ruins, he has an action neg.
gest.; though he had not any of his money, yet he was benefitted, and has
the possession of what was bought by his money, and is bound to make
restitution of what he has laid out on his house.}

3$^{dly}$ Ex delicto. Whatever reason there is for ones restoring what he has
come by, that was the property of another, taking it to be his own, there is
as strong if not stronger reasons for his being bound to make up any damage
another has received from him. The injury is here more sensibly felt and

---

$^g$ 'from' deleted    $^h$ Reading doubtful    $^i$ 'perhaps' deleted    $^j$ Replaces
'actio'

---

$^{10}$ A short blank space follows '3$^{d}$—' at the end of the line. The third source of personal
rights which Smith considers is delict, or delinquency.
$^{11}$ 'To the extent that I have been enriched out of another's property'.

affects us more as the wilfull transgression or criminall negligence of the person who has injured us adds greatly to the uneasiness[k] for the damage sustained. {We think one has injured us more who wilfully did us an injury than one who only did not perform some promise.} Hence arise the severall claims against another for damage sustaind whether it be from negligence which they say is ex culpa, or from wilfull injury, ex dolo. These are the several personall rights.

24    The first thing that comes to be considered in treating of rights is | the originall or foundation from whence they arise.

Now we may observe that the original of the greatest part of what are called natural rights {or those which are competent to a man merely as a man} need not be explained. That a man has received an injury when he is wounded or hurt any way is evident to reason, without any explanation; and the same may be said of the injury done one when his liberty is any way restrain'd; any one will at first perceive that there is an injury done in this case. That on⟨e⟩ is injured when he is defamed, and his good name hurt amongst men, needs not be proved by any great discussion. One of the chief studies of a mans life is to obtain a good name, to rise above those about and render himself some way their superiors. When therefore one is thrown back not only to a level, but even degraded below the common sort of men, he receives one of the most affecting and atrocious injuries that

25    possibly can be inflicted | on him.—The only case where the origin of naturall rights is not altogether plain, is in that of property. It does not at first appear evident that, e.g. any thing[l] which may suit another as well or perhaps better than it does me, should belong to me exclusively of all others barely because I have got it into my power; as for instance, that an apple, which no doubt may be as agreable and as usefull to an other as it is to me, should be altogether appropriated to me and all others excluded from it merely because I had pulled it of the tree.

We fill[12] find that there are five causes from whence property may have its occasion. 1st, Occupation, by which we get any thing into our power that was not the property of another before.—2dly, Tradition, by which

26    property is voluntarily transferred[13] | from one to an other. 3dly, Accession,

---

[k] Reading doubtful        [l] The last two words replace 'an apple'

---

[12] *Sic.* No doubt 'will' was intended.

[13] At the foot of the opposite page—i.e. the verso of (recto) 24—the following words are written upside down: 'We come now to the personall rights. These we will find will proceed from 5 sources. 1st Occupation ['or the right' deleted] by which one has a right to the'. After 'personall rights' there is a hieroglyphic apparently referring to the words 'vide page 31', which are written in the margin to the left of the passage (looking at it the right way up); and in the top left-hand corner of the page (again looking at the passage the right way up) the figure '6' has been written and deleted. What happened, apparently, was that the student began transcribing his notes of Smith's discussion of personal rights

by which the property of any part that adheres to a subject and seems to be of small consequences as compared to it, or to be a part of it, goes to the proprieter of the principall, as the milk or young of beasts.—4$^{thly}$, Prescription or Usucapio, by which a thing that has been for a long time out of the right owners possession and in the possession of an other, passes in right to the latter.—5$^{thly}$, Succession, by which the nearest of kin or the testamentary heir has a right of property to what was left him by the testator.—Of these in order.[14]

## 1$^{st}$ OF OCCUPATION

Before we consider exactly this or any of the other methods by which
27 property is acquired it will be proper to observe that the regulations | concerning them must vary considerably according to the state or age$^m$ society is in at that time. There are four distinct states which mankind pass thro:—1$^{st}$, the Age of Hunters; 2$^{dly}$, the Age of Shepherds; 3$^{dly}$, the Age of Agriculture; and 4$^{thly}$, the Age of Commerce.

If we should suppose 10 or 12 persons of different sexes settled in an uninhabited island, the first method they would fall upon for their sustenance would be to support themselves by the wild fruits and wild animalls which the country afforded. Their sole business would be hunting the wild beasts or catching the fishes. The pulling of a wild fruit can hardly be called an imployment. The only thing amongst them which deserved the appel-
28 lation of a business would be the chase. This is the age of$^n$ hunters. | In process of time, as their numbers multiplied, they would find the chase too precarious for their support. They would be necessitated to contrive some other method whereby to support themselves. At first perhaps they would

---

$^m$ 'of' deleted        $^n$ The last two words replace 'chase'

---

at the top of the first page of a new gathering—the sixth in the series. He wrote the number '6' in the top left-hand corner to indicate the commencement of this new gathering; and when he had finished writing the first sentence—'We come now to the personall rights.'— he inserted the words 'vide page 31' in the margin as a reference back to the earlier page of the MS. on which the distinction between real and personal rights was first made (p. 31 in the student's numbering; 16 in our renumbering). Proceeding with his transcription, he made an error, mixing up his notes about the three sources of personal rights with those about the five sources of property rights. After writing a few words about occupation he realized his error, and in order to mend matters deleted the figure '6', turned the whole gathering upside down, wrote the figure '6' in the top left-hand corner of what then became the (new) first page of the sixth gathering, and began once again, writing the passage which appears on 21 of the MS.

[14] The order in which these subjects are in actual fact dealt with in what follows is Occupation, Accession, Prescription, Succession, Tradition.

try to lay up at one time when they had been successful what would support them for a considerable time. But this could go no great length.—The most naturally contrivance they would think of,[o] would be to tame some of those wild animalls they caught, and by affording them better food than what they could get elsewhere they would enduce them to continue about their land[p] themselves and multiply their kind. Hence would arise the age of shepherds. They would more probably begin first by multiplying animalls than vegetables, as less skill and observation would be required. Nothing 29 more than to know what food suited them. | We find accordingly that in almost all countries the age of shepherds preceded that of agriculture. The Tartars and Arabians subsist almost entirely by their flocks and herds. The Arabs have a little agriculture, but the Tartars none at all. The whole of the savage nations which subsist by flocks have no notion of cultivating the ground. The only instance that has the appearance of an objection to this rule is the state of the North American Indians. They, tho they have no conception of flocks and herds, have nevertheless some notion of agriculture. Their women plant a few stalks of Indian corn at the back of their huts. But this can hardly be called agriculture. This corn does not make any considerable part of their food; it serves only as a seasoning or some-30 thing to give a relish to their common | food; the flesh of those animalls they have caught in the chase.—Flocks and herds therefore are the first resource men would take themselves to when they found difficulty in subsisting by the chase.

But when a society becomes numerous they would find a difficulty in supporting themselves by herds and flocks. Then they would naturally turn themselves to the cultivation of land and the raising of such plants and trees as produced nourishment fit for them. They would observe that those seeds which fell on the dry bare soil or on the rocks seldom came to any thing, but that those[s] which entered the soil generally produced a plant and bore seed similar to that which was sown. These observations they 31 would extend to the different plants and | trees they found produced agreable and nourishing food. And by this means they would gradually advance in to the age of agriculture. As society was farther improved, the severall arts, which at first would be exercised by each individual as far as was necessary for his welfare, would be seperated; some persons would cultivate one and others others, as they severally inclined. They would exchange with one an other what they produced more than was necessary for their support, and get in exchange for them the commodities they stood in need of and did not produce themselves. This exchange of commodities extends in time not only betwixt the individualls of the same society but

[o] Numbers written above different words in this part of the sentence indicate that it was intended to read: 'The contrivance they would most naturally think of'      [p] The last three words replace 'with'

betwixt those of different nations. Thus we send to France our cloths, iron
32 work, and other trinkets and | get in exchange their wines. To Spain and
Portugall we send our superfluous corn and bring from thence the Spainish
and Portuguese wines. Thus at last the age of commerce arises. When
therefore a country is stored with all the flocks and herds it can support, the
land cultivated so as to produce all the grain and other commodities
necessary for our subsistance it can be brought to bear, or at least as much
as supports the inhabitants when the superfluous products whether of
nature or art are exported and other necessary ones brought in exchange,
such a society has done all in its power[q] towards its ease and convenience.

It is easy to see that in these severall ages of society, the laws and regu-
33 lations with regard to property must be very different.— | In Tartary,
where as we said the support of the inhabitants consist⟨s⟩ in herds and
flocks, *theft* is punished with immediate death; in North America, again,
where the age of hunters subsists, theft is not much regarded. As there is
almost no property amongst them, the only injury that can be done is the
depriving them of their game. Few laws or regulations will ⟨be⟩ requisite in
such an age of society, and these will not extend to any great length, or be
very rigorous in the punishments annexed to any infringements of property. Theft as we said is not much regarded amongst a people in this age or
state of society; there are but few opportunities of committing it, and these
too can not hurt the injured person in a considerable degree.—But when
34 flocks and herds come to be reared | property then becomes of a very
considerable extent; there are many opportunities of injuring one another
and such injuries are extremely pernicious to the sufferer. In this state
many more laws and regulations must take place; theft and robbery being[r]
easily committed, will of consequence be punished with the utmost rigour.
In the age of agriculture, they are not perhaps so much exposed to theft
and open robbery, but then there are[s] many[t] ways added in which property
may be interrupted as the subjects of it are considerably extended. The
laws[u] therefore tho perhaps not so rigorous will be of a far greater number
than amongst a nation of shepherds. In the age of commerce, as the subjects
of property are greatly increasd the laws must be proportionally multi-
35 plied. | The more improved any society is and the greater length the severall
means of supporting the inhabitants are carried, the greater will be the
number of their laws and regulations necessary to maintain justice, and
prevent infringements of the right of property.

Having premised thus much, we proceed as we proposed to consider[v]
property[w] acquired by occupation. The first thing to be attended to is how
occupation, that is, the bare possession of a subject, comes to give us an
exclusive right to the subject so acquired.—How it is that a man by pulling

---

[q] 'to extend' deleted          [r] Replaces an illegible word          [s] 'still' deleted
[t] 'more' deleted          [u] 'the laws' deleted          [v] 'how' deleted          [w] 'is' deleted

an apple[x] should be imagined to have a right to that apple and a power of excluding all others from it—and that an injury should be conceived to be done when such a subject is taken for[15] the possessor. From the system I have already explain'd,[16] you | will remember that I told you we may conceive an[y] injury was done one when an impartial spectator would be of opinion he was injured, would join with him in his concern and go along with him when he defend⟨ed⟩ the subject in his possession against any violent attack, or used force to recover what had been thus wrongfully wrested[z] out of his hands. This would be the case in the abovementioned circumstances. The spectator would justify the first possessor in defending and even in avenging himself when injured, in the manner we mentioned. The cause of this sympathy or concurrence betwixt the spectator and the possessor is, that he enters into his thoughts and concurrs in his opinion that he may form a reasonable expectation of using the fruit or whatever it is in what manner he pleases. | This expectation justifies in the mind of the spectator, the possessor[a] both when he defends himself against one who would deprive him of what he has thus acquired and when he endeavours to recover it by force.—{The spectator goes along with him in his expectation, but he can not enter into the designs of him who would take the goods from the[b] 1$^{st}$ possessor.} The reasonable expectation therefore which the first possessor furnishes is the ground on which the right of property is acquired by occupation. You may ask[c] indeed, as this apple is as fit for your use as it is for mine, what title have I to detain it from you. You may go to the forest (says one to me) and pull another. You may go as well as I, replied I. And besides it is more reasonable that you should, as I have gone already and bestowed my time and pains in procuring the fruit.[17]

Having explain'd the foundation on which occupation gives the property to the occupant, the next thing to be considered is at what time property is | conceived to begin by occupation.—Whether it be when we have got a sight of the subject, or when we have got it into our actual possession. In most cases the property in a subject is not conceived to commence till we have actually got possession of it. A hare started does not appear to be

36

37

38

---

[x] Several words (the first three of which are probably 'from a tree') have been interlined here, but then deleted       [y] The last four words replace 'an'       [z] 'from him' deleted
[a] Numbers written above different words in this part of the sentence indicate that it was intended to read: 'This expectation justifies the possessor in the mind of the spectator'
[b] Reading doubtful       [c] Replaces 'say'

---

[15] *Sic.* Presumably 'from' was intended.
[16] The system of ethics of the *Theory of Moral Sentiments*, which Smith had no doubt explained earlier in the course. Cf. TMS II.ii.1.5.
[17] Cf. Locke, *Civil Government*, §§. 27–8. But Smith's explanation of the right acquired by occupation seems to be intended as an alternative to Locke's explanation; see especially 42 below.

altogether in our power; we may have an expectation of obtaining it but still it may happen that it shall escape us. The spectator does not go along with us so far as to conceive we could be justified in demanding satisfaction for the injury done us in taking such a booty out of our power.—We see however that in this point lawyers have differed considerably. Trebatius, as Justinian informs us,[18] conceived that an animall began to be our property when ever it was wounded; that this gave us a just title to it, and that one might claim it from any possessor rei vindicatio compelere ei judicabat.[19]

39 | Other more strict lawyers, as Proculus and Sabinus, were of opinion that it did not become ours till it came into our actual possession. Frederic Barbarossa, refining still more on Trebatius doctrine, made a distinction with regard to the manner in which the wound was given.[20] If it was given with a missile weapon he judged that it did not immediately convey property; but if it was with a weapon held in ones hand, as a spear or sword, he judged that the beast, e.g. a wild boar, came[d] immediately under the property of the person who gave the wound. {It was without doubt very near being in his power and he conceived it to have been altogether.} In different countries there are different constitutions on this head. It was enacted by a law of the Lombards[21] that a hart which was wounded, if killed in 24 hours after he received the wound, should belong partly to the person who gave the wound and partly to him who killd him, as the former

40 was | conceived to have had a hand in the catching him. The part given to the wounder was I think a leg and 4 ribs. In the same manner, at this day, [in] the ships which go to the Greenland fishery share the whale that was wounded betwixt the ship who wounded and that which killed the whale.[22] If the harpoon of any ship that was at the fishing the same season be found in the fish, a certain part is alotted to that ship as having by the wound contributed to the taking of the fish. In most cases however property was conceived to commence when the subject comes into the power of the captor. — — — — —

The next thing in order which comes to be treated of is, how long and in what circumstances property continues and at what time it is supposed to be at an end.

41 | At first property was conceived to end as well as to begin with posses-

---

[d] Replaces 'became'

[18] Trebatius' opinion is given in *D.* 41.1.5.1, where the opposing view is attributed merely to *plerique*. Justinian confirmed the latter view: *Inst.* 2.1.13. Proculus and Sabinus were leaders of rival juristic schools in the first century A.D.

[19] Corrupt passage. The gist is that the owner's action was available to the wounder of the animal to compel a possessor to restore it.

[20] Gothofredus' note to *D.* 41.1.5.1 (from Radevicus, *De Gestis Friderici*, I.26), cited by Pufendorf, IV.6.10.

[21] *Lex Longobardorum*, I.22.4,6; cited by Pufendorf, loc. cit.

[22] Stair, II.1.33.

sion. They conceived that a thing was no longer ours in any way after we had lost the immediate property of it. A wild beast we had caught, when it gets out of our power is considered as ceasing to be ours. But as there is some greater connection betwixt the possessor who loses the possession of the thing he had obtained than there was*e* before he had obtain'd ⟨it⟩, property was considered to extend a little farther, and to include not only those animalls we then possessed but also those we had*f* once possessed*g* though they were then out of our hands, that is, so long as we pursued them, and had a probability of recovering them.

If I was desirous of pulling an apple and had stretched out my hand towards it, but an other who was more nimble comes and pulls it before

42 | me, an impartial spectator would conceive this was ⟨a⟩ very great breach of good manners and civility but would not suppose it an incroachment on property.—If after I had got the apple into my hand I should happen to let it fall, and an other should snatch it up, this would ⟨be⟩ still more uncivil and a very heinous affront, bordering very near on a breach of the right of property. But if one*h* should attempt ⟨to⟩ snatch it out of my hand when I had the actuall possession of it, the bystander would immediately agree that my property was incroached on, and would go along with me in recovering it or preventing the injur⟨y⟩ before hand, even suppose I should use violence for the accomplishing my design. Let us now apply this to the*i*

43 case of the hunters. When | I start a hare, I have only a probability of catching it on my side. It may possibly escape me; the bystander does not go along with me altogether in an expectation that I must catch it; many accidents may happen that may prevent my catching it. If one*j* in this case should come and take the game I had started and was in pursuit of, this would appear a great tresspass on the laws of fair hunting; I can not however jus⟨t⟩ly take satisfaction of the transgressor. The forester may in some countries impose a fine on such an offender. If after I had taken the hare or other wild beast it should chance to escape, if I continued to pursue it and kept it in my view, the spectator would more easily go along with my

44 expectations;*k* one who should prevent me in this pursuit would appear | to have tresspassed very heinously against the rules of fair hunting and to have approached very near to an infringement of the right of property. {But after it is out of my power, even tho I may possibly see it, there is no longer any connection betwixt it and me; I can have no longer*l* any claim to it any more than to any other wild animall, as there is no greater probability I should catch it.} But if he had violently or theftuously taken from me what I had actually in my possession, this would evidently be an atrocious transgression of the right of property such as might justify, in the eyes of

---

*e* The last three words replace 'and'        *f* Illegible word deleted        *g* 'and' deleted, and replaced by 'but', which has also been deleted        *h* Reading doubtful
*i* 'stat' deleted        *j* 'then' deleted        *k* 'an offend' deleted        *l* Replaces 'more'

the beholder, my endeavours to recover what I had been so wrongfully deprived of.—In this age of society therefore property would extend no farther than possession.

But when men came to think of taming these wild animalls and bringing them up about themselves, property would necessarily be extended a great deal farther. We may consider animalls to be of three sorts. 1$^{st}$, Ferae, such
45 as are always in a wild state. 2$^{dly}$, Mansuefactae, [or those] which | are those which have been tamed so as to return back to us after we have let them out of our power, and do thus habitually; tho there be others of the same sort, as stags, hares, ducks, etc. of which there are some wild and others tame. 3$^{dly}$, Mansuetae, which are such as are only to be found tame, as oxen. When men first began to rear domestick animalls, they would be all under the class of the mansuefactae, as there must have been others still wild. But even in this case it would be absolutely necessary that property should not cease immediately when possession was at an end. The proprietor could not have all those animalls$^m$ about him which he had tamed; it was necessary for the very being of any property of this sort that it
46 should continue some what farther. They considered therefore | all animalls to remain in the property of him to whom they apertaind at first, as long as they retain'd the habit of returning into his power at certain times.$^{23}$ And this continues still to be the case with regard to those animalls that are mansuetae, or what we properly call[ed] tamed.—{Hawks, stags, etc. when they no longer return into the power of their owner are supposed to cede to the occupant.} But in process of time, when some species of animalls came to be nowhere met with but in the state of mansuefactae, they lost that name and became mansuetae. A farther extention was by this means introduced into the notion of property, so as that all these animalls were esteemd to be in the property of their master as long as they could be distinguished to be his; altho they had for a long time ceased to come into his power, yet still they were considered as fully his property. This was no doubt a great extention of the notion of property. But a still greater fol-
47 lowed | on the introduction of agriculture. It seems probable that at first, after the cultivation of land, there was no private property of that sort; the fixing of their habitations and the building of cities first introduced the division of land amongst private persons.$^{24}$—The notion of property seems at first to have been confined to what was about ones person, his cloaths and any instruments he might have occasion for. This would naturally be the custom amongst hunters, whose occupation lead them to be continually changing their place of abode.—{Charlevois tells us that a

$^m$ 'that' deleted

$^{23}$ *Inst.* 2.1.15.    $^{24}$ Locke, *Civil Government*, § 38.

certain Canadian woman having a great string of      [25] which serves for
money amongst them was so extremely fond of it that she could never let it
out of her sight. One day it happened that she carried it with her to a field
where she was to reap her corn. There was no tree in her field, but one in
that of her neighbour hard by. In this tree she hung up her string. Another
woman, observing her, went and took it off. The owner of the string
demanded it from her, she refused, the matter was referred to one ⟨of the⟩
chief men of the village, who gave it as his opinion [v.47] that in strict law
the string belonged to the woman who took it off the tree, and that the
other had lost all claim of property to it by letting it out of her possession.
But that if the other woman did not incline to do very scandalous action
and get the character of excessive avarice (a[n] most reproachfull term in that
country), she ought to restore it to the owner, which she accordingly did.}

The introduction of shepherds made their habitation somewhat more
fixed but still very uncertain. The huts they put up have been by the consent of the tribe allowed to be the property of the builder. For it would not
appear at first why a hut should be the property of one after he had left it
48 more than | of another. A cave or grotto would be considered as belonging
to him who had taken possession of it as long as he continued in it; but it
would not appear that one had any right to it tomorrow night because he
had lodged there this night. The introduction of the property of houses
must have therefore been by the common consent of the severall members
of some tribe or society. Hence in time the house and the things in it
became to be considered as the property of the builder. Hence the Greek
and Latin words for property, dominium and οἰκεῖον.[26] {It is to be observed that even in the age of hunters there may be fixt habitations for
the families, but property would not be extended to what was without the
house.} But still property would not be extended to land or pasture. The
life of a shepherd requires that he should frequently change his situation,
or at least the place of his pasturing,[o] to find pasture for his cattle. The
property of the spot he built on would be conceived to end as soon as he had
49 left it, in the same manner | as the seats in a theatre or a hut on the shore
belong no longer to any person than they are possessed by him. They would
not easily conceive a subject of such extent as land is, should belong to an
object so little as a single man. It would more easily be conceived that a

---

[n] Three or four illegible words deleted      [o] Reading doubtful

---

[25] Blank in MS. The reference is to P.-F.-X. de Charlevoix, *Histoire et description
générale de la Nouvelle-France avec le Journal historique d'un voyage . . . dans l'Amérique
septentrionnale* (1744), III.275–6. The woman wore a 'collier de Porcelaine', i.e. a string of
polished shells. The word intended for the blank space in the MS. was probably 'wampum'.
[26] Smith supposes that in both languages the word for property is derived from the
word for house, *dominium* from *domus* (this is incorrect), and οἰκεῖον from οἰκία (this is
correct).

large body such as a whole nation should have property in land. Accordingly
we find that in many nations the different tribes have each their peculiar
territory on which the others dare not encroach (as the Tartars and inhabitants of the coast of Guinea). But here the property is conceived to
continue no longer in a private person than he actually poss⟨ess⟩ed the
subject. A field that had been pastured on by one man would be considered
50 to be his no longer than he actually staid on it.—Even after the | invention
of agriculture it was some time before the land was divided into particular
properties. At first the whole community cultivated a piece of ground in
common; they divided the crops produced by this piece of ground amongst
the severall inhabitants according to the numbers in each family and the
rank of the severall individualls. The inclination of any single person would
not be sufficient to constitute his property in any parcel of land if it were
but for one season; the rest of the community would cry out against him as
incroaching on and appropriating to himself what ought to be in common
amongst them all. In the same manner as any corporation or society
amongst us would not permit any of their body to set appart for his own use
51 any part of their common field or any tree in it, etc., as they ought to | reap
in common the fruit of these common'd subjects. {As a confirmation of
this, we[b] learn from Tacitus[27] that each nation who had any agriculture
amongst them cultivated some spot of ground the product of which was
divided amongst the members of the community.} The first origin of
private property would probably be mens taking themselves to fixt
habitations and living together in cities, which would probably be the case
in every improved society. The field they would cultivate when living
together in this manner would be that which lies most contiguous to them.
As their place of abode was now become fixt, it would readily appear to
them to be the easiest method[q] to make a division of the land once for all,
rather ⟨than⟩ be put to the unnecessary trouble of dividing the product
every year. In consequence of this design[r] the principall persons of such
a community, or state, if you please to denominate a set of men in this
52 condition by that honourable appellation, would divide | the common land
into seperate portions for each individuall or family. We find accordingly
that Homer[28] and Aristotle, whenever they give us an account of the
settling of any colony, the first thing they mention is the dividing of the
land. Aristotle[29] too mentions the manner in which this was done. He tells

b 'find' deleted          q 'once for all' deleted          r The last three words replace 'we
find that'

---

27 *Germania*, xxvi.
28 e.g. *Odyssey*, vi.9–10.
29 In *Politics*, VII.10 (1330[a]9 ff.), Aristotle suggests a division into public and private
land, with private land sub-divided so that each citizen has a part near the city and a part
on the frontier.

as[30] that the ground lying nearest to the new built city was divided into seperate parcells as it was most convenient for each, but that which was more remote was still allowed to remain common.[s]

One thing which strengthens the opinion that the property of land was settled by the chief magistrate posterior to the cultivation is that, in [the] this country, as soon as the crop is off the ground the cattle are no longer kept up or looked after but are turnd out on what they call the long tether; that is, they are let out to roam about as they incline. Tho this be contrary
53 to Act of Parliament[31] | yet the country people are so wedded to the[t] notion that property in land continues no longer than the crop[t] is on the ground that there is no possibility of getting them to observe it, even by the penalty which is appointed to be exacted against ⟨?⟩.

This last species of property, viz. in land, is the greatest extention it has undergone. We shall hereafter consider in what shape it has been limited in different countries.

By the severall methods above mentiond property would in time be extended to allmost every subject. Yet there are still some things which must continue common by the rules of equity. Thus, first, wild beasts can not be a subject of property; to wit those which either by their swiftness or fierceness refuse to submit themselves into mens power; these are what the Roman lawyers called ferae naturâ, and also such as have not been tamed.
54 | The tyranny of the feudal government and the inclination men have to extort all they can from their inferiours, has brought property in some measure into these subjects. By the civil law and the constitutions of most countries in ancient times, game was considered as being free to every one. And this certainly is what is most agreable to reason. For no one can have any power over an animall of this sort, nor can he claim the property of it, because it pastures on his ground just now, for perhaps the next moment it may be on another[u] mans ground. But when the feudal government was established, which was the foundation and still prevails in some measure in all the governments in Europe, the king and his nobles appropriated to themselves every thing they could, without great hazard of giving umbrage
55 to an enslaved people. Amongst other encroachments | it became the rule that wild animalls should belong only to the king and those of his lords to whom he gave the power of catching them. Accordingly in the time of Henry the 7.[th] a law was made that no one should kill game but on his own ground unless ⟨?licensed⟩ by the owners of the land;[32] another was made

---

[s] 'O' deleted        [t] 'old' deleted        [u] Reading doubtful

[30] *Sic.* No doubt 'us' was intended.
[31] The Winter Herding Act, 1686, c. 11 (A.P.S. VIII.595, c. 21) ordered heritors to cause their cattle to be herded in winter as well as in summer under penalty of half a merk for each beast found in a neighbour's ground.
[32] 11 Henry VII, c. 17 (1495).

in the time of King James 1ˢᵗ by which no one who had not 100£ a year of
land rent or a lease worth a 150£ for a long term of years asᵛ 99, or some
life rents, could kill game even on his own estate;[33] and in the time of
George the 1ˢᵗ and 2ᵈ it was madeʷ punishable by a fine of 5£ st.ˣ to have
arms or game in ones possession unless he had the rent above mention'd;[34]
and by an other statute in this reign not only the magistrate but any in-
former had a title to claim the fine.[35]—There can be no reason in equity
given for this constitution; if one did the proprieter damage he might be
56 | obliged to give him satisfaction, but when there is no danger of damage any
one might catch game as well as the proprieter of the ground. The reason
they give is that this prohibition is made to prevent the lower sort of
people from spending their time on such an unprofitable employment; but
the real reason is what we before mentioned, the delight the great take in
hunting and the great inclination they have to screw all they can out of their
hands. In the same manner the fish of the sea and rivers are naturally
common to all; but the same incroaching spirit that appropriated theʸ game
to the king and his nobles extended also to the fishes. Thus all the larger
fishes, as of greater importance, are considered as belonging only to the
57 king or his vassals to | whom he has given the right of taking them. Whales,
porpoises, sturgeons, etc. are of this sort. {These larger fish are all called
royal.} Salmon,[36] too, can not be taken unless the king has granted it by
express charter. The fish no more than the game can become the subject of
property; they are not in our power, nor can they be considered as belonging to an estate as they are often changing their place, but ought to be
common to all.—An other encroachment made on the rights of the lower
rank of people was made by the statu⟨t⟩es which enacted that what ever was
wafe, as they called it (that is, being stolen was left by the thief), should if
not claimed by the owner within a year be appropriated to the king or the
lord of the land on which it was found, and to whom the king had given the
Franchise of Wafes.[37] This extended also to all subjects that had no master:
ἀδεσποτα. In the same manner, those animalls that had strayed from their
master and were found on any mans ground were not the property of the
58 finder but of the lord of the manor. It is evident | that by the law of equity
such possessions should be restored to the right owner in the same manner

---

ᵛ Reading doubtful　　　ʷ 'capita' deleted　　　ˣ Reading doubtful　　　ʸ 'beasts'
deleted

---

[33] 1 James I, c. 27 (1603) allowed freeholders of land to the yearly value of £10 or
holders of a term of life of the yearly value of £30 to kill game.

[34] 3 George I, c. 11 (1716); 9 George I, c. 22 (1722); 31 George II, c. 42 (1758).

[35] 8 George I, c. 19 (1721).

[36] Stair, II.3.69.

[37] The privilege of taking stolen goods abandoned by the thief; see *Quoniam Attachia-
menta* (a fourteenth-century manual on court procedure, in Stair Society, vol. 11), c. 48,
sec. 14.

as any other subject, as a watch that can be known certainly to be his, which are restored whenever he can shew his property in them. The only reason that is given is that it is so constituted to make the people more careful in preventing strays and more attentive to claim them in due time; but allowing this to be the case, why should they not belong to the possessor, rather than$^z$ be given to the king or the lord of the mannor, who can have no title to them, not even prescription itself.—In like manner, unless the king had granted a proprietor of land the$^a$ Franchise of Treasur⟨e⟩ troff³⁸ he could not take to himself the treasure found in his own ground, and far less what he found on anothers. These often made a good part of the kings revenues, for tho now they are seldom met with, yet formerly in those
59 confused periods when property was very | insecure and it was dangerous to be known to have any money about one, as the laws could not assure of the possession of it, nothing was more common than for a man to bury what he had got together. At this day in Turky and the Moguls dominions every man almost has a treasure, and one of the last things he communicates to his heirs is the place where his treasure is to be found. In such times the right of treasure-troaf would be of considerable importance. The reason why the nobles and those of power established these constitutions was that the people could more easily be brought to bear with some incroachment in this way than in any other. One does not form such an attachment to a thing he has possessed for a short time (as is the case here) and has acquired by little labour as he does to what he has got by great pains and industry;
60 and so will not think himself so highly$^b$ injured in | being deprived of it.

Besides those things already mentioned there are many others that are to be considered as common to all, as they can not be lessend or impaired by use, nor can any one be injured by the use of them. Thus the air is necessary to be breathed by all, and is not rendered less fit or less in quantity for the use of others. Running water in like manner or the sea are by nature common to all.³⁹ A fountain by the way side is not the worse that one has drunk from it, nor can the proprietor of the ground hinder any one from drinking out of it. But if indeed it should be in the midst of the field, one can be hindered by the proprietor, as he could not go to it without doing him damage (unless he have a servitude against the proprietors farm, ad aquam appellendi⁴⁰⟨⟩).—In the same manner the water of rivers and the
61 navigation of them, the navigation or right of sailing | on the sea, is common

---

$^z$ The last two words replace 'and not'      $^a$ 'right' deleted      $^b$ Reading doubtful

---

³⁸ Reading doubtful. The word is spelt 'troaf' on the following page of the MS. The Franchise of Treasure Trove was the privilege of taking any precious metal which had been found hidden in the ground and whose owner was unknown.

³⁹ Cf. Hume, *Treatise of Human Nature* (1739–40), III.ii.2 (ed. Selby-Bigge, 495); *Enquiry concerning the Principles of Morals* (1751), III.i (ed. Selby-Bigge, § 145).

⁴⁰ 'To drive cattle to water'.

to all. No one is injured by such use being made of them by another; one who has ship in a certain station does not usurp the property of that spot; he only has the right to it when he possesses it; then indeed he can defend his right against any one who would displace him, but as soon as he leaves it the right cedes to the next occupant. {The sea coast in the same manner seems to be common to the whole community, and accession to it to belong to the whole body, but the king has usurped this to himself, in so much that in Lincoln shire,[41] where frequent accessions and diminutions happen, a certain person having 100 acres added by the sea could not take possession of it tho his charter comprehended all the land betwixt that coast and Denmark, because that number of acres was not specified, but the whole ceded to the king.} Tho the right of navigation is in this manner naturally common to all, yet the nations and states who lye adjacent to any river or inlet of the sea have often usurped the jurisdiction *imperium*, tho not dominium or property, over them, so that they will not allow ships to enter them without their permission.[42] The reason is because this would otherwise expose them to their enemies and strangers and let them into the heart of their country. They do not however pretend to any right to the water of these rivers, only to [the] restrict the navigation.

62 | It is only such arms of the sea which make but a small appearance compared to the land adjacent which are thus under jurisdiction, as the friths of Clyde,[c] Forth, and the Murray frith.[43] The Baltick Sea, on the other hand, tho[d] it is of a large extent, is brought under the jurisdiction of the King of Denmark, but this was not from being considered as part or appendage of the land, but had its beginning from the tribute he rais'd for the support of light houses. Both Sweden and Denmark, tho' their territories on its banks have often been much larger than they are now, never exacted any tribute on that head. In the same manner as rivers and small inlets are considered to be a part of or appendage[e] of the land, so the sea and sea-coast come in like manner to be under jurisdiction. To[44] that

63 strangers are not allowed to navigate or fish near the coast | without express permission. This is particularly the case in such parts of the sea as are near any fort and within the range of its cannon, where no ships are allowed to pass or fish without acknowledging its jurisdiction. That strangers should not be allowed to fish has some foundation in nature, as what is got in this way is often the chief[f] part of the support of a large

---

[c] Illegible word deleted     [d] 'now' deleted     [e] The last two words replace 'the property'     [f] 'foundation' deleted

---

[41] Robert Callis, *Reading on Sewers* (2nd ed., London, 1685), 47–8.
[42] Grotius, II.3.13.
[43] i.e. the Moray Firth.
[44] *Sic.* Possibly 'So' was intended.

number of the inhabitants, and they would naturally think themselves injured if strangers should in⟨ter⟩rupt them. Besides this the fish in narrow seas and rivers are not unexhaustible. The restriction however on navigation and the appropriation of rivers by the community or state through whose territories it passes go on the foundation of accession, by which the smaller things cede to the larger to which they adhere.

{Accession comes next to be treated of. These two are the originall methods of acquiring property. The others are secondary, by which it is conveyed either from the dead to the living by will or succession, or by voluntary transference amongst the living.} This method of acquiring
64  property has also undergone very considerable | alterations in the different ages of society. {In the age of hunters there was no room for accession, all property at that time consisting in the animalls they had caught.} In the age of shepherds accession could hardly extend to any thing farther than the milk and young of the animalls. They would naturally be given to the person who had tamed the animall. Tho perhaps he had not them in view, yet there would seem an impropriety in allowing the milk to any other. This as well as in many other cases goes on the impropriety that appears in it rather than any inconvenience. {It would appear ridiculous that the milk of an animall should remain common, after the animall had been tamed and appropriated by a certain person; we are naturally inclined to compleat or square ones property or any other right in the same manner as we would incline to square his land estate; we do not incline to have corners sticking into it.} Even the right of occupation seems as we said to be chiefly founded on this apparent impropriety. It is to be observed that the young of all animalls is supposed to be an accession to the mother rather than the father. The actions of[g] conceiving, bearing, bringing forth, and suckling appear to produce a much stronger connection betwixt the young and the
65  mother than the transitory act of begetting does with the | fathers. {Besides this, the young even for some time after its birth as well as the milk for ever seem to be a part and but a small part of the mother, and accordingly goes to the proprietor of the whole as a part of it.—} There is no exception to this but in the swans, where it is the rule that part of the young goes to the proprietor of the male and part goes to that of the female; the reason given is that as the male cohabits only with one female he could be of no benefit to his owner unless he got part of the young he had produced. Amongst men too the child is considered as the property of the mother unless where she is the property of the husband, and then[h] the ofspring belong to the father as an accession to the wife. This was the case in the old law in the state of wedlock and in this point is still so, but naturall children are the property of the mother and generally take her name.—{Severalls of[i] the Roman lawyers did not give the name of accession to the right the dominus of the female

***

[g] 'begetting' deleted     [h] 'she goes' deleted     [i] 'the' deleted

had to the young, they called it jus ventris;[45] but what is said above shows that it has all the circumstances necessary to constitute the right of accession.}

Tho the opportunities of accession are but very few in the age of shepherds, yet they multiply to a number almost infinite when agriculture 66 and private | property in land is introduced. Then when the land was divided by the common consent of the state, the thing they would have in view would be to give each the property of the land in order that he might raise crops on it. But it would naturally arise from his having this principall part of property that he should have the property of all the trees, stones, and minaralls also that were found in it. The reason at first might be that these could not be come at without injuring the surface. But as to minaralls, a mine in one farm might be extended to that of another proprietor without injuring the surface, and would rather serve as a drain.[j] But the connection betwixt the surface and the subterraneous parts is so great that it would soon come to be the rule that every thing betwixt the surface and to the center of the earth, if he could go so far, should be the property of the owner of the surface.—{The right that was at first conveyd to the private proprietor was realy[k] that of plowing, sowing, reaping the fruits, or of pasturing upon it. This would be more easily expressed and as well conceived by saying that he had the[l] property of the land, and the same would be the method or form of expression in sales or transference. As the surface was the thing of which the property thus came[m] to be transfered, the soil and all in it would soon be considered as appertaining to the same proprietor. Tho perhaps the soil and its contents might be at without injuring the surface, the mines serving rather as drains to carry off the superfluous moisture, yet propriety would make this be looked on as an injustice and introduce the[n] laws which now take place, viz that the whole 67 soil belongs to the proprietor of the surface.} There is this difference | also betwixt the civil and fewdal law, that by the former all mines were considered as the property of the possessor of the ground. The lands in those countries were all what we call allodial,[46] i.e.[o] held of no one, but were intirely the property of the[p] proprietor, so that the state could not limit the use he was to make of any part of his estate. But in the feudal governments, the king was considered as the dominus directus, which had then a considerable benefit attending on it. The possessor⟨s⟩ as domini utiles were

---

[j] The last seven words replace 'or he might draw a drain through'    [k] Reading doubtful    [l] 'right o' deleted    [m] Numbers written above the last two words indicate that their order was intended to be reversed    [n] Illegible word deleted    [o] Reading doubtful    [p] Illegible word deleted

---

[45] Cocceius, XII.271. The expression is not Roman.

[46] Allodial land is held in absolute ownership, whereas feudal land is 'held of' (i.e. on condition of service to) a superior.

only his tenants, as they are called, and held of him. As therefore a tenant who got a lease of a woodland was supposed, altho that was not expressly specified, to [to] have a right to the brush and underwood but not to the timber trees which were reserv'd for the proprietor, so the vassals were accounted as having a right of property to the mines of lesser value, as coal,
68 lead, tin, iron, copper, etc. but | those of silver and gold were con⟨si⟩dered as reserved by the dominus directus, that is, the king, for his own use. And thus it came to pass that one who holds of the king may work for his own account the mines of lesser value, but not the gold and silver mines unless that be expressly granted by charter. — — — —

In the same manner as the soil and other substances were considered as an accession to the surface, whatever was added by the retiring of the sea or the shifting of a river was considered*q* as belonging to the proprietor of the field next adjoining. But these accessions has*r* been differently regulated in different countries. In high countries, as Italy and the most part of Great Britain, where the coast and the banks of the rivers are very high
69 above the waters, the accessions | to the land can not be very considerable either from the sea retiring of the,*s* or from the shifting of rivers; in all such countries the accessions of this sort, as being but of little consequence in respect of the land adjacent, was considered as an accession to the property of that ground. But in flat countries as Egypt and the countries on the banks of the Ganges, and the Low Countries, the sea*t* often retire⟨s⟩ or the rivers change their course so considerably as that the tracts of ground thus added can not be considered as an accession to the neighbouring field, but is the property of the state.[47] In the fens of Lincoln shire, where the additions are by law considered as*u* accessions to the neighbouring ground, yet even here the field must be particularly specified otherwise the addition goes to the crown.
70 In all cases of this sort there is no | great difficulty in determining the proprietor of the accessions. The only case where there is any perplexity is where the accession is the property of a different person*v* from the proprietor of the subject. {As when one makes a ship of anothers wood, wine of anothers grapes, or a cup of anothers metall.} Thus when one builds a house on another mans ground, it is a question whether the house should be considered as an accession to the ground or the ground to the house. It is to be observed here that in all cases where the proprietors of the accession and principall are different, the question is not which of them shall have the sole right to both, but which shall be considered as the principall and

*q* 'to' deleted        *r* *Sic*        *s* Numbers written above the last four words indicate that they were intended to read 'retiring of the sea'        *t* 'and the rivers' deleted        *u* 'the property o' deleted        *v* Numbers written above the last two words indicate that their order was intended to be reversed

[47] Pufendorf, IV.7.12.

have the right to claim the other, giving a recompense[w] ⟨to⟩ the proprietor
of it as far as he is thereby benefitted. Thus in the case above mentioned
the matter in question is whether the house shall be considered as the
principal, and consequently the builder[x] of it will have a right to possess it
71 after paying a reasonable price | for the ground or an adequate rent, or
whether on the other hand the proprietor of the ground should have a right
to the house, paying the builder as much as he is benefitted by it (quantum
locupletior factus est[48]⟨⟩), altho' perhaps this may be greatly under the
expense laid out upon it. In this case it is determin'd by all lawyers that the
proprietor of the ground should be considered as having the right to claim
the house on the condition above mentioned. It is true the house will in
most cases be of greater value than the ground it stands upon, but the rule
which is attended to here is that no one by the deed of another should be
deprived of his property. Nemo ex alienâ actione rem suam amittat.[49] This
generall rule is suited well enough[y] to most cases, but there are some where
the determination agreable to it would appear very hard. If one should
72 draw a fine painting on the wood or canvass of another man | it would appear
hard that the painter should lose this work, which might be of great value,
because it was considered as an accession to a subject of so inconsiderable
value as the wood or canvass. Accordingly tho Proculus and         [z] who
were of the more moderate lawyers gave the right of accession to the painter,
yet the more strict ones, as Cassius and Sabinus,[50] adhered to the generall
rule,[a] saying that as the picture had not altered the wood, it was to remain[b]
the property of the former proprietor.[c][51] {The picture was not considered
as altering the substance; the board was considered to be still a board, and
the reason probably was that as their walls were all either plaster or stone
the only thing that would be hung on them of that sort would be the
pictures, which were accordingly distinguished by the name of tabulae.}
In many other cases the same difficulty would occurr, as when one made
wine or ale of an other mans grapes or barley, or if[d] he made a cup of

---

[w] The last three words replace 'indemnifying'      [x] Replaces 'owner'      [y] Numbers written above the last three words indicate that they were intended to read 'well
enough suited'      [z] Blank in MS.      [a] The last two words replace 'old law'
[b] 'in' deleted      [c] 'Paulus and after him Trebatius and Justinian' deleted      [d] Reading of last two words doubtful

---

[48] 'To the extent that he is enriched'.
[49] 'Let no one lose his own property through another's action.' Cf. Pufendorf, IV.13.6.
[50] Proculus, Cassius, and Sabinus were Roman jurists of the first century A.D. Proculus
was the leader of the Proculian school and Cassius and Sabinus both leaders of the rival
Sabinian school.
[51] There was a dispute among the jurists as to whether the picture acceded to the wood
or vice versa, referred to by Paul in *D.* 6.1.23.3 and by Gaius in *D.* 41.1.9.2, but it was not
said to be a school dispute between the Proculians and the Sabinians. Smith may be con-
fusing this dispute with that over *specificatio* (see next editorial note). Justinian decided
that the wood acceded to the picture: *Inst.* 2.1.34.

another mans silver, or a ship of his wood. The strict lawyers decreeed that
the proprietor of the substance should continue to be so even after it had
73 | assumed the new form. The others were of opinion that the specificator
should in these cases be reckon'd the proprietor of the principall part.[52] But
that they might not contradict their generall rules they said that this was
not properly a species of accession, but the substance produced was a new
thing, res nova in rerum natura, that the grapes turnd into wine were no
longer grapes, the barley was become ale and the silver a cup, and therefore
could not be claimed by the proprietor of the substance so reasonably as by
him who had as it were produced it. Paulus[53] and after him Tribonian[54] and
Justinian took what they thought a middle way, though more whimsicall
than either of the others. The rule they made was that when the subject
could be reduced into its former state it should be the property of the
74 former proprietor | but, when it could not, the substance should be con-
sidered as an accessary to the form. From this rule metalls, into whatever
curious form they were wrought, would still be[e] considered as a part of the
former proprietors[f] goods, but the ship, the wine, and the ale should be
accessions to the work[g] of the specificator.—This rule has no foundation
in reason, and has proceeded only from the small[h] connection there is
betwixt the substance and the proprieter, when it can be reduced to its
former state, more than there is when it can not, as the substance is still the
same. But in many cases this rule would not be at all agreable to reason, as
in the case of the engraving. It seems more agreable to reason that the
substance should in many of these cases be considered as an accession to
75 the form, because in this way the | proprieter of the substance might be
compleatly recompensed by having the profit of the specificator paid him;
whereas if the dominus substantiae should have the accession[i] ⟨to⟩ it, the
specificator would perhaps lose considerably by receiving only as much as
the dom. subst. was enriched by his work. This might often happen with
regard to the painting, the sculptor, etc. {This determination may show us
on what slight connection in the imagination the lawyers formed their
opinions.}

There are many other cases pretty similar to this, as when a gem is set in
another mans gold; here tho the gem is probably the most valuable, yet[j] it
was considered as an accession to it, being applied or set in it in order to be

---

[e] 'the' deleted    [f] 'possession' deleted    [g] Reading doubtful    [h] Replaces
'little'    [i] The last three words replace 'possess'    [j] At this point the words 'the
proprietor of', with 'gem' interlined between 'the' and 'proprietor', are deleted

---

[52] The Sabinians attributed ownership of the new *species* to the owner of the materials;
the Proculians attributed it to the maker: Paul in *D.* 41.1.24, *Inst.* 2.1.25. The specificator
is the maker of the new *species*. Cf. Hume, *Treatise of Human Nature*, III.ii.3 (ed.
Selby-Bigge, 513, note).
[53] Roman jurist of the early third century A.D.
[54] The principal editor of Justinian's codification.

an ornament to it. They however considered$^k$ the gem was no longer an
76 accessory to the gold than it was thus fixt in it | and that when seperated it
became the property of its former master. For this reason they contrived an
evasion of the strict law, and gave the owner$^l$ of the gem an action against
the other (ad exhibendum), that is, to get a sight of it, and then as it would
be seperated he might claim it.$^{55}$ Reason here likewise seems to be on the
side of the owner of the gem,$^m$ as he might not be sufficiently indemnified
for his gem, tho the other would be recompensed for his gold, as the whole
value of it would be gain to the possessor of the conjunct ring.

  These two make$^n$ all the originall methods of acquiring property. The
1$^{st}$ of those called derivative,$^{56}$ by which the property of a thing already in
77 the possession of some other ⟨?⟩ is Prescription | {Prescription, that is, the
right one has to any subject he has possessed a long time which otherwise
without this possession would not have been his. The origin of the introduction of this manner of acquiring property seems to be that}$^o$ after
property was extended beyond possession, and goods were$^p$ thought to
remain in the property of the former possessor longer after they were out of
his power, it was found necessary that some length of possession should
transfer the right of property, that the possessor might be assured he had
then the full right to the goods; otherwise property would be always uncertain. The foundation of this right is the attachment the possessor may be
supposed to have formed to what he has long possessed; and the detachment of the former possessers affection from what$^q$ had for a long time
been altogether out of his power.$^{57}$ {This right of prescription is in fact
derived from the same principles as that of occupation. For in the same
manner as the spectator can enter into the expectations of the 1$^{st}$ occupant
that he will have the use of the thing occupied, and think$^r$ he is injured by
those who would wrest it from him; in the same manner, the right of
prescription is derived from the opinion of the spectator that the possessor
of a long standing has a just expectation that he may use what has been
thus possessed, and that the form⟨er⟩ proprieter and has so far lost all
right to it, has no expectation of using it,$^s$ as that it would appear injurious
in him to deprive the present possessor. [v.77] That these two principles, of

$^k$ 'that' deleted      $^l$ Replaces 'master'      $^m$ The last four words replace 'specificator'      $^n$ 'up' deleted      $^o$ The words 'go to the next page' are written below this
passage      $^p$ Replaces 'began to be'      $^q$ 'he' deleted      $^r$ Reading of last two
words doubtful      $^s$ Numbers written above the last fifteen words (after 'proprieter')
indicate that they were intended to read 'has no expectation of using it, and has so far
lost all right to it'

$^{55}$ *D.* 10.4.6; *D.* 6.1.23.5. The action was for production of the gem as a distinct thing,
which required its separation from the gold.
$^{56}$ Grotius, II.3.1.
$^{57}$ Kames, *Essays upon Several Subjects in Law* (1732), IV ('Of the Doctrine of Prescription').

the attachment of the possessor and the detachment of the former proprietor, are the grounds on which this right is founded is greatly confirmed
by the different requisites that have been introduced to make possession
of a long continuance transfer the right of property.}

It is necessary that the possessor should be *bona fide*, that is, should have
an opinion that he is the lawfull proprietor[t] of the subject; if he knows that
it belongs to another the greatest length of time can not give him the
78 property of it. Be|sides this it is necessary that he should possess it justo
titulo, i.e. that he should have got possession of it in a manner by which
property can lawfully be transferred. Thus if one byes any piece of goods
in the market or elsewhere, he has a justus titulus to this and may reasonably think he has the right of property to it. But if he should find e.g. a
watch on the road and should not give publick notice that such a thing was
found, though he should possess it for 100 years, and the owner or his heirs
afterwards come to the knowledge of it, he would be obliged to restore
it. [u]— {It will seldom happen that one will think he has a right to any thing,
unless he has come by it justo titulo. But if one should be so foolish, the
possession would not give him a right to it. In many cases however any[v]
title is sufficient altho it be very slight. Amongst moveable goods no title is
required, but possession alone bona fide gives the right; and in immoveables, a seasin[58] from a writ of clare con.[59]} A land estate can not be possessed without some title. As the king was considered as the proprietor of all
lands they could not be given to another without some token for the trans-
79 ference of the right. This was | a charter or parchment. Accordingly one
can not enter to an inheritance of a land estate unless he can produce some
title he has to it. But here a very slight one will suffice as the seasing his
father had when he was served heir. {The forementioned requisites tend to
make it certain that the possessor had formed an attachment to the thing he
possessed. That it might be certain the affection of the former proprieter
had been detached from it, it is, etc.} It is also necessary that the possession
be uninterupted, and that not only in a just but even in an unjust manner.[w]
In this country the only lawfull method of interruption[x] is when the proprieter claims a right to the possession of the subject.[y] It is also requisite
that the possessor should be in such a condition as that it is in his power to
make an interruption. Contra nolentem non currit praescriptio.[60] Thus it

---

[t] Replaces 'possessor'      [u] Replaces an illegible word      [v] Replaces an illegible
word      [w] 'as either of them will hurt the bona fides possessoris' deleted      [x] 'that
was' deleted      [y] 'or' and an illegible word deleted

---

[58] English seisin, Scots sasine: feudal possession of a freehold estate in land.
[59] *Clare constat*, by which a Scots superior confirmed the title of a deceased vassal's heir.
[60] *Contra non valentem agere non currit praescriptio*: prescription does not run against
a proprietor barred by some incapacity from interrupting the possession. Stair, II.12.27;
Erskine, III.7.15.

does not run against one who is absent or any other way deprived of the power of making an interruption {as minors, mad persons, wives during their husbands life time; exiles unjustly banished, as those during the
80 usurpation of Oliver Cromwell in 1648.} | Prescription too does not take place against minors; and the possessor is obliged to continue his possession for the term of years after the pupill comes of age. It is to be observed that the nature of things does not point out any precise time at which[z] prescription is to take place, whether it be at a month, a year, 10, 20, 30, or 40, etc. years. But as it was necessary that some period should be ascertain'd which gave one the right to what he possessed, so we find that some such period has been settled in all countries. In the first periods of the Roman state, when the society had made no great advances, and property was very uncertain, the composers of the 12 Tables thought a year sufficient time for the prescription of moveables and two years in immoveables. Afterwards this period was lengthned to 3 years, and some time after to 3
81 years in moveables and 10 years for | immoveables in Italy and 20 in the provinces, which took place at last in Italy also.[61]— In like manner in the feudal governments, when the proprieters of land held it of the king by certain services they were to perform to him, as attending him in his wars and be⟨ing⟩ always at his call to his councils in peace, it was necessary that there should not be any estate but what was possessed by some one who performed these services. If therefore any proprieter should desert his estate but for one year and not perform that by which he had the right to it, and another came and possessed it and performed his part, the latter (as he had done all that was requisite to get a right) would have the full right to the estate, and on the other hand, he who had neglected his duty could have no claim. {The king might indeed claim it, as he had no charter, but the former possessor could have no claim.} But when this government came to be considerably altered, and the right to an estate did not depend
82 on personall service, it seemed unjust that | one should be turned out of his estate by so short a prescription, when the troubles and insecurity of property that had given occasion to this constitution no longer subsisted. It could not then be supposed that either of the two grounds of prescription would take place in so short a time; that either the possessor had formed any attachment to it, or that the proprieter had detached his affection from what had been so lately in his possession. From hene[62] they run into the other extreme, and property was conceived to continue long after possession had been lost; but no time was fixed at which prescription should take place. This introduced a great confusion and uncertainty in

[z] 'property' deleted

---

[61] *Inst.* 2.6pr. The periods were 10 years where both parties lived in the same province and 20 years where they lived in different provinces.
[62] *Sic.* Either 'hence' or 'here' may have been intended.

property. To remedy this Hen. II[d] enacted that no action should be raised against possession, the ground of which was farther back than the reign of
83 his grandfather Hen. I[st].[63] Henry III[d] made the same con|stitution, that they should extend only to the time of Hen. II[d].[64] Edward III[d] also to the time of Richard the 1st,[65] and afterwards to that of the 2[d]. From his time it run on till the time of Henry the[a] VIII[th], who, finding that there were few estates against which some claim could not be raised, appointed that no claim should thenceforth be valid after a prescription of 60 years, if the title was      [66] nor after 50 if it was of any other sort; nor after 30 if the possession had been begun during the claimants life.[67] In Scotland by a law of Charles the 2[d] prescription is to take place after a possession of 40 years uninterrupted.[68] The prescription of moveables in England and in Scotland was originally a year; this continues still in England; in Scotland it is now restricted to those that are called wafe. Formerly after a year and a day, proclamation being made, all lost[b] goods or such as are called adespota[69]
84 were adjudged to the kings officers | or those vassalls to whom he had given the Franchise of Wafe.[70]

The[c] terms of prescription being different, the circumstances necessary to confirm a right by a long possession are also different. In Scotland, as we observed, the term of prescription being pretty long, viz 40 years, they have not required that the possessor should be bona fide; they think that this must necessarily follow from the justus titulus and longa possessio non interrupta.—The time being so long, it can hardly happen that an estate can be prescribed in less than 50 or 60 years as some minority or other interruption[71] will take place. It has therefore been customary to strengthen the right of prescription, and most lawyers have accordingly been very favourable to it. It is likeways from this that the time is continued after the interruption and not begun afresh. By the Scots law no interruption is good
85 against the | prescription except a claim instituted by the former possessor or his heirs. Interruption by war or other externall means is of no effect.—

[a] '32 year of' is interpolated between 'the' and 'VIII[th]'      [b] Replaces 'derelict'
[c] 'various' deleted

---

[63] The date was the death of Henry I, 1 December 1135.

[64] The Statute of Merton, 20 Henry III, c. 8 (1236), fixed the date as the coronation of Henry II, 19 December 1154.

[65] The Statute of Westminster I, c. 39 (1275) fixed the date as the coronation of Richard I, 3 September 1189; no further changes were made until 1540, and none by Edward III.

[66] Blank in MS. Possibly 'droitural' (based on a claim of right rather than of possession) was intended.

[67] 32 Henry VIII, c. 2 (1540): no seisin could found a claim in a writ of right unless it was within 60 years of the date of the writ, whereas possessory actions prescribed in 30 years.

[68] Act, 1617, c. 12 (A.P.S. IV.543, c. 12) introduced positive prescription of 40 years. There were other limitation statutes in Charles II's reign.

[69] ἀδέσποτα, without a master. Cf. 57 above.

[70] See above, p. 24.

[71] Prescription did not run during the owner's minority: Stair, II.12.18.

In England, where the possession must be still longer, neither bona fides nor justus titulus is thought necessary, and every thing is contrived to shorten that time; for an estate can hardly be prescribed there in less than 70, or 90 years.—{When during the mans life time it is prescribed in 30 years, but this can never take place.} The civill law, as it allows prescription to take place in a very short time, is on the other hand favourable to the claim of the proprietor. Thus not only an interruption from him but from the incursions of an enemy, their fixing their camp on his ground, was sufficient to make an interruption. Besides this an interruption did not only[d] prevent the running of prescription for the time it took place, but made the possession prior to it of no effect and obliged the possessor to count anew[e] from the ceasing of the interruption, and this in whatever way the inter-

86 rup|tion had been made {in the same manner as by a claim being preferred in our law.} There is however one thing in the civill law extremely favourable to prescription, and that is that bona fides was only required at the beginning; but tho he could be proved afterwards to have known he was not in bona fide the prescription still took place. {Res furtivae again were not prescribed[ed] by any length of time, whereas in this country they are prescribed, after being proclaimed, in a year and a day.[72]}

The cannon law on the other ⟨hand⟩, regulating every thing according to the rules to be found in foro concientiae, do not allow prescription to take place when mala fides supervenerit, as the man must be concious he detains the goods of another.[73] The civil law again pays more regard to the frailty of human nature.

Some authors derive the right of prescription from a different origin ⟨?from⟩ that here laid down. Grotius[74] founds it on the presumed dereliction of the possessor, but when we consider that no one would willingly give up a right to a considerable estate, especially a land one ⟨?⟩. It is

87 ignorance only that will hinder one (that has it in his power) from | occupying such possession that he has a right ⟨to⟩ or his forefathers were in possession of. Baron Coceii[75] founds it on the respect paid to possession

*Gap of one-quarter of a page in MS.*

The great benefit of prescription is that it cuts off numbers of disputes.— If no land especially could be possessed that could not shew an originall

---

[d] 'des' deleted        [e] Reading doubtful

---

[72] In Scots law stolen goods could be acquired by negative prescription like other movables, and the year and a day applied only to waif goods. ('Negative prescription' is that by which a right of challenge is lost, contrasted with positive prescription, by which a new title is acquired.)

[73] Pufendorf, IV.12.3. The ecclesiastical courts were said to be 'courts of conscience', being concerned not only with man's outward behaviour.

[74] II.4.

[75] Cocceius, XII.297 ff.

title, there would be none that could be secure, for then we would be obliged to trace our right back as far as the flood.

Prescription, as shall be more fully explained hereafter,[76] takes place[s] against*f* all rights, personall as well as real. I shall only at present observe that
88 the law of nations*g* likewise prescribes that prescription | should take place amongst sovereign states or kings. The right a king has to the obedience of his subjects will prescribe for the same reason as the right to the sole use of land or other estates.*h* Long possession here forms an attachment betwixt the possessing king and his subjects and an expectation that he shall govern them; and at the same time detaches the former king from the affection and expectations of his people. Immemorial possession cuts off all claims. And should the lineal descendent of the Saxon kings whom William the Conq. expelled prove their descent, no one would imagine they would exclude the present family; or those of Charlemain or the Greek emperors exclude the French king or the Grand Turk. But to the misfortune of man-
89 kind, those who sit at the head of human | affairs, tho they regulate the disputes of their subjects, have not always the disposition to bring their own disputes to an end; but choose rather to keep up some phantasticall claims which some accidentall occasion may give them an opportunity of employing to their own and their neighbours disquiet. Such is the claim kept up by the Kg. of Sardinia after 200 years to the Isle of Cyprus, by the Venetians to Cyprus and Creetes,*i* by the kings of Great Britain to the crown of France, and by the French king to the kingdom of Navarre. The King of Prussias claim to Silesia is likewise of this sort. His fam. had by the treaty of Westphalia been above 100 years out of possession. But, says he, I ought not to be deprived of my right because my forefathers were good natured, generous, or silly enough to part with it before I was born. But
90 this | can be of no force. For then there would never be wanting some child or kinsman who could claim the estate, as some one would always appear who had not given up the right in any shape.

### Thursday 6 Jan. 1763.

Having now considered the three first*j* methods of acquiring property, I come now to the 4$^{th}$ which is sucession. By succession is meant the transference of property from the dead to the living. There are two sorts of succession, either 1$^{st}$, where the succession is directed by the law; or 2$^{dly}$, where it is by the testament or will of the deceased. The 1$^{st}$ is what I shall now consider, viz. successio ex lege.

*f* 'agains' deleted        *g* 'regulates' deleted        *h* 'The' deleted        *i* Reading doubtful        *j* Numbers written above the last two words indicate that their order was intended to be reversed

[76] ii.165–6 below.

Most writers[77] on the subject of the law of nations found this method of succession on the supposed will of the deceased. The magistrate is to consider to what person he would (if he had[k] made a will) have given the inheritance, and that to him as the most naturall[l] sucessor the estate of the deceased should be confirmed by the | publick authority. If this was realy the foundation of succession ex lege,[m] it would follow that in all countries where it has taken place testamentary succession must have preceded. For if the express will of the deceased directing how his estate should be possessed was of no effect, we can not reasonably imagine[n] that this supposed inclination should be of any, far less of greater, force. In all countries therefore succession ab intestato must have succeded testamentary succession, if this hypothesis was just. But we find on the contrary that in allmost all countries where records have been kept testamentary succession has been introduced much later than succession ab intestato. In Tartary, and the countries on the coast of Africa, there are at present certain rules by which succession is directed, tho' they have no notion of a testament. Amongst the earlier Romans, testaments were unknown; they were first introduced by the | laws of the 12 Tables.[78] Before that time one who had no heirs could not leave his estate but by a law made in the Comitia Curiata,[79] which was similar to our Acts of Parliament. In like manner we find that Solon[80] was the author of testamentary succession amongst the Athenians, and in our own country the people had been formed into a regular community for 600 years before testamentary succession took place. {Besides this of the real priority of the succession of the heir at law, to testamentary succession we are also to observe that the heir at law in allmost all countries is more favoured than the testamentary heir; and the testament is reckond null and void if a few formalities, etc. be wanting. This preference could never be made if the foundation of the succ. ab intest. was the presumed will of the testator: for his presumed will could not be in reason preferred to that which he had plainly expressed.[o] It shall likewise afterwards be shewn[81] that the right of succession ex testamento is one of the greatest extentions of property we can conceive, and consequently would not be early introduced into society.—} Since, then, succession ab intestato is always prior to the testamentary succession, contrary to what would necessarily be the case if the supposed inclination of the deceased was the foundation of it, we must look somewhere else for the foundation of succession ab intestato than in the will of the deceased.

---

[k] 'been' deleted     [l] 'heir' deleted     [m] 'the' deleted     [n] Replaces 'suppose'
[o] 'and' deleted

---

[77] e.g. Grotius, II.7.3; Pufendorf, IV.11.1; M'Douall, III.4.1.3.
[78] Heineccius, II.10.2,5.
[79] A popular assembly based on kinship groups.
[80] Montesquieu, V.5, citing Plutarch, *Life of Solon* [21].     [81] 149 ff. below.

{In the age of hunters there could be no room for succession as there was no property. Any small things as bows, quiver, etc. were buried along with the deceased; they were too inconsiderable to be left to an heir.—In the age of shepherds, when property was greatly extended, the goods the deceased had been possessed of were too valuable to be all[p] buried along with him. Some of those[q] which he might be supposed to have the greatest attachment to would be buried, as a horse, an ox, etc.; the rest would go to the other members of the family as is hereafter explain'd. Some traces of the custom of burying goods are found long after.}

The most probable account of it is this.[r][82] The children and their parents all lived together, and the goods of the father were supported by the joint labour of the whole family. | The master of the family, again, maintain'd them from this stock, which as it was maintained and procured by the labour of the whole family was also the common support of the whole. The master of the family had indeed the priviledge of alienating in his life time his stock; which[s] the others had no claim to; but at the same time he could not alienate it at his death. All the members of the family came in for an equall share in it at his death, as they had all contributed their assistance to the support of it. No distinction was made with regard to sex; sons and daughters equally gave their assistance to the master of the head of[83] the family, and for this reason were equall sharers in his possessions after his death. {So that on the whole it was the connection betwixt the children and other members of the family with the goods of the master of it, that gave rise to their succession,[t] rather than the attachment of the master of the family himself, and the supposition of his will that his goods should be left to the persons to whom he was thus attached.—The members of the family did not take possession of his goods from this supposall of his will that they should do so, but they only continued their possession in what they had given their assistance in procuring and by which they had already been supported.—This is confirmed by what immediately follows.} The rules of succession have been pretty much the same in this respect in our country and amongst the Romans; excepting one considerable difference that was | occasioned by the state of the wife in the different countries. She was considered in the character of a daughter[84] amongst the Romans

---

[p] 'together' deleted    [q] 'on' deleted    [r] 'As' deleted    [s] 'priviledge' has been interlined here and then deleted    [t] 'and' deleted

---

[82] Cocceius, XII.281.

[83] *Sic.* Probably 'the master or head of' was intended.

[84] The reference is to marriage *cum manu*, whereby the wife left the power of her own father, and consequently lost her right to succeed to a share of his estate on his death, and became subject to the authority (*manus*) of her husband, to whose estate she acquired a similar right of inheritance as that of her own daughters. This form of marriage, common in early Rome, was rare by the end of the Republic: Heineccius, III.1.5 ff.

{and came in accordingly for the same share in the inheritance as a daughter and was called by the same name, filia familias,} but is a more respectable person by the custom of this country. The reason of this shall hereafter be more fully explain'd.[85] We shall first consider the order of succession amongst the Romans. We observed that the children all shared equally in the estate of the father or master of the family. But this is only with regard to those who were in the family. A son whas[86] emancipated, and by that means seperated from the society, or one who had been given in adoption, one who was a captive, an exile, or capite deminutus, had no right to any part of the inheritance.[87] A daughter who was given in marriage, whether she had been given with a portion or not, for the same reason took no share as she was then become a member of another society. {If she survived her husband the part of his inheritance came in[u] to the stock of her father, and she, as she again made a part of his family, had a claim as before for her share.} Sons given in adoption in the same manner had no part;

95 they were already provided for by being members of another | mans family and had no occasion to receive an addition. Tho when men get the power of conveying an estate by a testament they are often more willing to give their fortunes to those who are already rich, as they are their more respectable relations, than to those who are in lower circumstances.[v] {This perhaps is not altogether just but it is what men are naturally inclined to.} Not only the immediate offspring of the deceased but also the grandchildren by a deceased son took part in the inheritance. (If the son was alive they had no claim, as he would get his share.) The reason of this was that in the more early and simple times when the demands of a family are few the sons do not, as in more luxurious times, seperate from the family of the father as soon as they are married; but they and their families continued in the same house and contributed their part to the maintaining a common stock. When therefore a father of a family died, the children who made a part of it

96 succeeded equally in it. But if it happen'd that a son had died and | left children, these, as they continued in the family, came in for the same share as the father would have had he lived. This connection betwixt the children of two brothers, as they all made a part of the same family, occasioned that marriages betwixt cousin germans should be looked upon as incestuous as well as those betwixt brothers and sisters. The foundation of the latter is that the great opportunity of intercourse betwixt them makes it necessary that all[w] hopes of union betwixt them should be cut off; and for the same

[u] The last two words replace 'returned'    [v] 'and we' deleted    [w] 'intercourse' deleted

---

[85] 110-11 below.

[86] *Sic.* Presumably 'who was' was intended.

[87] Emancipation was the voluntary release of a son from his father's power; *capitis deminutio* was the loss of either freedom, citizenship, or family status.

reason where the brothers lived in the family of their father the like prohibition would be necessary with regard to cousins. This we find is the
case; in all nations where the marriage of brothers and sisters is accounted
incestuous, that of cousins-german was originally accounted*x* so also. This
like all other customs often continues after the reason of it is at an end; it
was so amongst the Romans long after the sons lived in seperate families
97 | from their fathers. It was first altered by the people to gratify the whim of a
tribune who had taken a fancy to his cousin-german.[88]— Cousins german
were accounted as brothers somewhat farther removed. Thus Cicero calls
[calls] Quintus Cicero his brother, Quintus Cicero frater meus, natura
quidem patruelis, affectione autem germanus.[89] And it is to be observed
⟨?that the words⟩ that signify a cousin german are, as their termination
evidently shows, originally adjectives. Patruelis and consobrinus, that is,
patruelis vel consobrinus frater, a brother by an uncle or aunt.[90]— If, for
example, a master of a family dying should leave 3 grandsons by a predeceased son and, besides, two sons, the inheritance would here be
divided into 3 parts; each of the sons would have a third, and each of the
grandsons $\frac{1}{3}$ of $\frac{1}{3}$, that is, $\frac{1}{9}$ of the whole estate. This, which ⟨is⟩ called
sucessio per stirpes, to distinguish it from suc. per capita, seems to contra-
dict the generall rule, propriores excludunt remotiores. But to this is
answered, that they are indeed more remote and have less of the blood of
the master of the family, but then they are considered here not as succeding
98 by their own right | but as representing their father; hence it was also called
successio per representationem.—In the Roman commonwealth this took
place very soon, but in this country it was pretty late before it was established. This proceeded from the nature of the governments; besides
severall other reasons which we shall consider hereafter, one which would
be of considerable effect is that in this country it was established in favours
of the nephews*y* and in prejudice of the uncles,[91] in favours of*z* a boy and in
prejudice of a man; that is, in favours of the weak and in prejudice of the
strong. But on the contrary it was established amongst the Romans in
favours of the strong and in prejudice of the weak; this would certainly
make it much sooner and more easily brought about. A father of a family,
dying, leaves a son and two grandsons by a predeceased son. The grandsons, as they had been in the same possession of the fathers stock as the

---

*x* 'amon' deleted      *y* Replaces 'weak'      *z* 'the w' deleted

---

[88] Montesquieu, XXVI.14, citing Plutarch, *Quaestiones Romanae* [6; he is not in fact
said to have been a tribune]. For the modification of the rule prohibiting marriage of
first cousins, see Livy, XLII.34; Tacitus, *Annals*, XII.6.

[89] *De Finibus*, V.1; Cicero refers to his cousin Lucius Cicero as *frater noster cognatione
patruelis, amore germanus* ('my cousin by blood, my brother in affection').

[90] *Patruelis* strictly indicates a cousin by a father's brother and *consobrinus* a cousin by
a mother's sister, but the latter term was extended to cover all cousins-german.

[91] Dalrymple, 169.

son, would probably claim each an equall share in it after his death; but the uncle, on the other hand, would complain that he was by this means cut out

99 of part of | lawfull inheritance*a* by his brothers death; he had not only lost his brother⟨s⟩ but had a less share of his fathers fortune than had he lived. On this ground the uncles as the stronger party would get it established that they should have the same part as if their brothers had lived. But the contrary was the case in the feudall governments.

In the same manner as grandsons, great-grandsons, if their father and grandfather were dead, came in for their share. Grandsons and other descendents by daughters took no share, as they were not in the family, nor their mother.—After the succession of descendents was established, that of the nearest adgnates[92] was the next that followed. By this, when a [a] man who had no children died his inheritance was given to his nearest adgnate.*b* This was not so much founded in the nature of things, as the families of two brothers, etc. would be seperate and the same connection would not subsist betwixt them as betwixt a father and his immediate descendents. {But tho' it was not so much founded in the connection betwixt the heirs and the goods or the continuance of possession, yet there are severall incidents that would naturally introduce it. Thus if two brothers succeded to an inheritance, ⟨?and⟩ one of them [of them] died soon after, it would appear hard in this case that the surviving one should, by his fathers dying a*c* year or two sooner, be deprived of one half of the inheritance; this would soon produce a custom that brothers should succeed; and for the reason mentioned afterwards this would soon be extended to cousins, etc.} It was accordingly

100 introduced by a law[93] | but this, as all other[s] laws which introduce a new connection or right, as this would appear to be, was inter[re]preted in the strictest manner; so that if the nearest adgnate did not choose to accept, it was not offered to the next nearest but was immediately seized by the fisc.[94] This afterwards was extended to the agnates as far as the 7th degree of their reckoning; afterwards the praetor, who was the judge of equity, gave the offer of it in like manner to the cognates to the 7th degree also. {*d*From the inclination we naturally have to square and compleat every thing, even when by this means we stretch the originall constitution; and thus it is that all laws that found any new right become in time of extensive interpretation.} But in all cases when there was no heir the fisc. claimed the inheritance, that is, it was adjudged to the publick, which always takes to itself all goods that have no master to prevent the scramble that would be made for such

*a* 'that' deleted     *b* Illegible word deleted     *c* 'year' deleted     *d* 'But' deleted

[92] Agnates were those descended from a common ancestor exclusively through males, whereas cognates were any blood relations.
[93] The Twelve Tables: Heineccius, III.2.3.
[94] i.e. the treasury: *aerarium* in the Republic and *fiscus* in the Empire.

goods and the confusion that would ensue onᵉ this scramble. In the same manner in this country the superior, or if there be no other the king as the ultimus heres and superior of all lands, takes all inheritances that are without a representative. {It is to be observed that originally the successio per stirpes did not take place in the collateral succession. If a manᶠ dying intestate left a brother and two nephews, the brother took the whole inheritance. In the same manner nephews excluded cousins german and they again second cousins. If a man had 3 nephews by one predeceased brother, 2 by another and 1 by a third, these would each take $\frac{1}{6}$th part, as the inheritance here was given per capita; and neither succession per stirpes nor per representationem was allowed to take place. Justinian afterwards allowed that it should take place for one degree, that is, that nephews should come in with the brothers, cousins with nephews, etc. and so on.[95] The reason that [v.100] successio per stirpes was not allowed amongst collateralls was that by this means the inheritance would be reduced to such small portions as would hardly be worth accepting. A man might easily ⟨have⟩ 20 or 30 cousins german and 40, 50, or more 2ᵈ cousins.}

101    | In the earlier times, a son or any child could acquire nothing to himself as long as he made a part of the fathers family; all the produce of his labour went into the fathers stock, and when he died all that he might perhaps possess at that time fell back to the father as his own property. Emancipated sons indeed might have property of their own seperate from the fathers, but this the father at their death claimed, not as being the nearest of kin, but as being the patron, in the same manner as patrons claimed the inheritance of emancipated slaves.—Julius Caesar afterwards established in favours of his soldiers that what one acquired by serving in war should belong to them intirely without any claim on it by the father. This was called peculium castrense.[96] The same was afterwards established with regard to what they acquired by the practise of the liberall arts. These, being less connected with the father, could be more easily seperated from him, and the same holds with regard to the pec. adventi.[97]— Of all these the
102  son had the power of disposing by testament. | It was necessary therefore that as the father had not the property of these, [that] it should be establishd that he should suceed as heir at law, as the son would be supposed to incline that his father should suceed if he had no children of his own. It was therefore 1ˢᵗ established that the father on the death of his son who had no

---

*ᵉ* 'such a' deleted        *ᶠ* Replaces 'brother'

---

[95] Novel 118.

[96] Property acquired by the son during military service. It was first treated as belonging to him by Augustus, *Inst.* 2.12pr. Smith may have been misled by Heineccius, II.9.2, who refers to Julius Caesar in this connection.

[97] *Bona adventitia*, property inherited by a child from his mother, which he could keep for himself.

nearer[g] heirs should take the whole inheritance. {This was afterwards extended to grandfathers, etc.} And it is to be observed that this succession, which is called[h] successio ad scendentiam,[98] would take the preference of the collaterall succession, as the father is more nearly connected with the son than the brothers were with one another; there being[i] a step betwixt the brothers, whereas there is no intervening one betwixt the son and the father.[99] In this manner it continued till the time of Adrian, when, divorses being become very frequent, it often would happen that the husband and wife did not live together but had seperate families and seperate estates. It was therefore enacted that when a son died his fortune should be equally divided betwixt his father and mother.[1] If either of them happened to be

103  dead the | sucessio secundum lineas took place. That is, if[j] the father should dye, and leave a father and mother behind him, the one half went to the mother and the other half was equally divided betwixt them, and so on, always going to the immediate ascendents of the person who if alive would have had the inheritance. This excluded collateral heirs even when they were nearer than the ascendents.—It followed also from the frequency of divorce that as the mother had also a seperate aliment from the husband so she could leave it as she pleased; and[k] her children were considered as her heirs at law. So that at the same time that the mother came to succeed to her son, the son had also the benefit of inheriting from his mother.

Of all these three methods of succession, viz of descendents, collaterall, and of ascend[end]ents, the first would take place long before the others; it is evidently founded on the connection betwixt the heirs at law and the goods of the defunct. The other two are not indeed founded on the same

104  principle, but on the supposed will | of the testator;[2] which as we said[l] could not be the case with regard to the succession of descendents. This sort is, as we said,[3] in all countries prior to testamentary succession; the others again are always posterior to it and so might very probably take their arise from it and the supposall of the testators inclination in such cases as [as] he had made no will.

I shall now proceed to consider the order of succession which has pre-

---

[g] Reading doubtful      [h] 'direct' deleted      [i] 'but one' deleted      [j] Replaces 'when'      [k] 'the' deleted      [l] Two or three illegible words deleted

[98] i.e. *successio ascendentium*, succession of ascendants.
[99] The degree of relationship of collaterals was calculated through the common ancestor, brothers being two degrees apart, uncle and nephew three.
[1] The senatusconsultum Tertullianum, said to be of Hadrian's reign (*Inst.* 3.3.2), gave the mother a claim to her son's estate, but it was subordinated to that of the father and that of the brothers. Succession of ascendants by 'lines' was the product of Justinian's Novels 118 and 127. Earlier, Justinian had allowed the mother to share with the brothers: *C.* 6.58.14.
[2] i.e. the deceased intestate.
[3] 91 above.

vailed in modern countries. We will find here that the succession to moveables is founded on precisely the same principles and has been in most
respects the same as the order of succession in generall amongst the
Romans; and indeed during the allodiall government of Europe the succession to land estates was directed in the same manner.

We shall then consider $1^{st}$ the order of succession to moveables. The
father of the family dying, the moveable goods he had possessed were
divided into 3 equall parts. One of these was given to the wife, another was
105 | divided amongst the children {and for the same reason grandchildren by
sons who were in the family, if any were, perhaps I think took part.} The
$3^d$ part was considered as the part of the deceased; this part was at first
laid out in charitable purposes to get mass said and other things of that
sort, that they thought might tend to the quiet rest of the souls of the
deceased, {as these appeared then to be the method in which he would
incline to dispose of it.} But when these superstitious rites fell into disrepute,
and the maintenance of the children appear'd to be the most pious use it
could be applied to, this part also was given to the children, {except a little
still reserved for those pious use⟨s⟩.} This division appears evidently
founded on the same principles as the division amongst the Romans. The
family was considered as consisting of 3 parts during the husbands life time,
each of which had their share in the possessions, and this was still continued after his death, {this manner appearing to keep up in the most
proper way the communio bonorum that before subsisted — — —$^m$ and it
was this third part alone that the father, after testamentary succession was
established, could alienate by any deed at his death, altho in his lifetime he
could spend every shilling of what should have$^n$ ⟨been⟩ the common support of the family; in every case,$^o$ excepting that where the estate which had
been left him was under the care of tutors.—The wife again had not the
power of alienating any part during her husbands life, any [v.105] more
than the children, all they poss⟨ess⟩ed falling back into the common stock.
— — —} That this division also was founded on the connection of the
children with the fathers goods, and not on the connection betwixt them
and the deceased himself, will appear from this, that daughters who were
given in marriage and were by that means no part of the family, had no
106 share in the bairns-part, | as it is called in this country. In the same manner
as emancipated sons amongst the Romans, so forisfamiliated$^4$ sons who
were precisely similar to them amongst us formerly took no part in the
inheritance.—They were called so because for the convenience of both

---

$^m$ Three short dashes in the MS., presumably indicating an omission     $^n$ The last
two words replace 'was to be'     $^o$ 'unless' deleted

---

$^4$ Forisfamiliation, the Scots equivalent of emancipation, was the separation of a son
from his family when he set up house on his own.

parties they did not live in the same house with their father, but having
settled in some other place were no longer considered as a part of the
family, and this without any distinction betwixt those who had received a
portion at their removall from the family and those who had not; neither of
them had any claim to a share of their fathers inheritance. It has indeed
been establishd some time ago that a son shall not be esteemed as compleatly forisfamiliated unless he has given his father a compleat discharge
of his share of his fortune.—*p* In this case he has no claim for any share.
But if he has not given this discharge, altho he has received a portion at his
107 leaving the family, he*q* is then to bring | his portion into what is called in
England hotch-pot,[5] that is, he is to join with the bairns part of the inheritance and take his share of the whole as if he had no portion before.
Thus if an emancipated son had receivd a portion of 100£, ⟨and⟩ his
father dyes worth 1500£ leaving 3 children besides, the bairns part is 500;
to this he joins his 100£, and each of the 4 will have 150£. These statu⟨t⟩es,
as they enact that a son shall not be considered as forisfamiliated*r* unless he
has given his father a discharge,[6] show that formerly this word was of a
more strict sense and that those who had left the family, whether they had
received a portion or not, were considered as intirely forisfamiliated, and
this is what the word itself seems to imply.

In England we will find the progress of succession has been very nearly
the same.*s* [The cannon law was what*t* regulated succession amongst them
108 and this being chiefly founded on*u* the novells | of Justinian the order of
succession was the same in most respects as that established by the 18 and
19 novell.[7]— This was the legall distr] In the first periods the bishop[s], who
was the ordinary in these matters thro the greatest part of Europe, had the
distribution of every inheritance committed to his care; and as he was a
holy man and therefore not considered as capable of acting amiss, he was
not accountable to any one. But in time, when they had greatly abused this
power, giving to themselves, that is, to the church, a considerable part of
the estate in prejudice of the creditors, it was found necessary in the time of
Edward the 1.st to make the ordinary accountable ⟨to the⟩ creditors.[8] This
throwing a great deal of trouble upon them, they constituted commissaries

*p* 'But' deleted     *q* 'has still' deleted     *r* 'till' deleted     *s* The passage in
square brackets which follows has been struck through. It ends in the middle of the fourth
line on 108, and the remainder of this line is left blank.     *t* 'they' deleted
*u* 'succession' deleted

[5] In Scotland called collation.
[6] Not statutory but a common law rule in Scotland: M'Douall, III.8.1.16. The principle
of hotchpot was enacted in the English Statute of Distributions, 22 and 23 Charles II,
c. 10 (1670).
[7] Novel 118.
[8] 13 Edward I, c. 19 (Statute of Westminster II, 1285); cf. Kames, *Essays*, IV ('On
Succession or Descent'), 177.

to settle the distribution of inheritances; but these they made accountable
to themselves for their administration, and by this means they insured
109 | themselves of their share. To prevent this it was enacted that no one[v]
appointed commissaries should be accountable to the ordinary.[w] But as the
ordinary had still the power of choosing whom they pleased for their commissaries, these good bishops, who do not easily quit their power, used not
only to make an agreement with the commissary beforehand in what way
he should settle the inheritance, but even took surety for him, or made him
out of his own private fortune disburse the summs they wanted to apply to
their own uses, and left him to reimburse himself out of the inheritance,
under the pretext of those pious uses. To prevent these contrivances it was
also farther constituted that no one could be appointed a commissary but
those who were nearest of kin to the deceasd. But as there might often be
a considerable number in the same degree, as 6 or 7 brothers, 20 or 30
110 cousins, the ordinary had still an | opportunity of choosing whom he
pleased of this number; and might in the same manner make a bargain with
him beforehand. To prevent this, a constitution settling the distribution of
goods ⟨?was made⟩ pretty much in the same manner as it is in Scotland.[9]
Before this regulation, the rule by which the ordinary called the relations
to the inheritance was that establish'd by the cannon ⟨law⟩, which being
chiefly founded on the novells of Just. the method would be that appointed
in the 19 novell.

The chief difference betwixt this distribution and that settled amongst
the Romans was the great share the wife took in the inheritance. This arises
from the difference betwixt the Christian and Roman marriage. Amongst
the Romans the husband had the power of divorcing his wife on any pre-
tence he thought proper. (This was indeed afterwards restraind to certain
111 causes and the same priviledge granted to the | wife.) And divorces were
always so frequent that the wife was greatly dependent on the husband and
could not be considered as having any great connection with his goods. But
some time after Christianity was established, marriages became almost
indissoluble, as no divorce could be granted but by the spirituall court on
account of some great transgressions. This rendering divorces not easily
obtainable gave the wife a more respectable character, rendering her in a
great measure independent on the husband for her support. She was
accordingly considered as a considerable member of the family, who had the
same interest in the common stock as the master or the children; and from
this it was that the wife after the demise of her husband came in for the
same share as either of the other two parts of the family. — — — — —

---

[v] 'should be' deleted    [w] The last six words replace 'but the nearest of kin to the
deceased'

---

[9] 22 and 23 Charles II, c. 10 (1670); cf. Kames, *Essays*, 180.

Another considerable odds arose from the difference of the constitution
of the two states. — — The greater and lesser noblesse, i.e. the nobility and
112 the gentry, were the only persons who could | have any thing to suceed to,
as they indeed were the only ones who had any property. It is well known
that the tenants were then in a state of villainage or slavery, and had no
property of their own; whatever the⟨y⟩ acquired went to their masters. It is
as certain, tho' not equally known, that the burghers and traders in towns,
tho they might have some greater liberties, were also in a state of villainage.
This is evident from the charters granted them in the earliest times, in
which they have granted them the right of marrying when and whom they
incline, of giving their daughters in marriage and succeding to estates, and
other such like[x] that plainly show those who [who] had them not must have
been in a state of abject slavery; and in fact all the buroghs were absolutely
dependent on the king or some of the great men in the neighbourhood. The
only persons, then, in this state of the country, who had any thing to leave
113 behind them were the | greater and lesser noblesse. The lower people
would probably live in the same manner as the poorer sort in other
countries; the sons would not leave the house of their fathers after marriage
but [the] all their[y] families would form one society. But they could have no
weight in the establishment of succession as they had nothing to succeed to.
The noblesse, on the other hand, who were alone capable of inheritance,
were of too considerable[z] a fortune and genteel appearance to admit of two
families living in one society. That way of life would not suit with the pomp
and state they had to maintain; {nor did the grandchildren after their
fathers death return with their mother into their grandfathers family, but
continued with their mother in their fathers house.} The law of sucession,
as it must be ruled by their convenience, established succession in such a
manner that those sons who were thus forisfamiliated should take no part
of the succession, and far less[a] could successio per stirpes take place when
the parents had no right to the succession. Thus it was that the right of
114 representation did not take place at[b] those countries where | these[c] customs
prevailed. This rigour has however been softened with regard to the
forisfamiliated sons in this country, and in England their children are
allowed by order of succession to take their fathers part; this has not [yet]
been introduced in Scotland as yet tho it may probably soon be extended
to them also.

Another considerable odds that subsists betwixt the Scots law and the
civill arose from the method of succession established by the feudall law in
the succession to indivisible subjects; by the feudal constitution, as shall be
explaind hereafter, the collaterall succession is preferred to that of ascendents. And from hence they imagined that collateralls were nearer to the

inheritance than ascendents, and called them to the inheritance before ⟨?⟩ ascendents whatsoever. In this country, therefore, if a man dyes his brothers succeed him, altogether excluding his parents of either sex. In England it is otherwise. If he leaves a father, he takes the whole inheritance;
115 and if he leaves a mother, she | comes in equally with the[d] children.[10]— There is this difference also[e] betwixt the Scots and English law, that in Scotland the successio per stirpes never takes place; but in England grandsons come in for their fathers share. This difference, as well as an other that is made by the statute of distribution,[11] are borrowed from the novells of Justinian by which those statutes are generally directed [by]; the difference is that in collaterall succession representation does not take place, whereas it is allowed in England in the same manner as we mentioned that Justin. had permitted it.

### *Monday Jan. 10ᵗʰ 1763*

The method of succession therefore to all subjects, indivisible as well as divisible amongst the Romans, and to divisible subjects amongst the modern nations of Europe, for in most of them succession (ab intestato) is governed by the same laws, {There are indeed some varieties. In      [f] females are not allowed to succeed. This is said to have been the case in Athens; but it is somewhat uncertain.[12] In Rome we know females came in for the same share as males.} is intirely founded on the communio bonorum. This was the rule formerly in all the nations of Europe; the subjects of the deceased of all sorts were equally divided by the children. {The Goths, Hunns, Vandals, etc. all used that method of succession.} But now a different
116 method is introduced, | I mean the right of primogeniture. As this method of succession, so contrary to nature, to reason, and to justice, was occasioned by the nature of the feudall government, it will be proper to explain the nature and temper of this constitution or form of government, that the foundation of this right may be the more evident.

When the barbarous nations of the north overran the Roman Empire, and settled in the western parts of Europe, property came to be very unequally divided. At the same time all arts were intirely neglected. This threw a great share of power into the hands of those who possessed the greatest property. It will be evident also that the balance of property will make those who are possessed of it have a far greater superiority in power,

---

<sup>d</sup> 'rest' deleted    <sup>e</sup> 'that' deleted    <sup>f</sup> Blank in MS.

---

[10] With *her* children; 1 James II, c. 17 (1685) allowed the intestate's mother to share with *his* brothers and sisters.
[11] 22 and 23 Charles II, c. 10 (1670); 110 above.
[12] Meursius, *Themis Attica* (1685), II.13, citing Demosthenes, *Against Macartatus*.

than the same share of property will give one in a more refind and cultivated age. In these times one who is possessed of 10000£ sterling per year
117 may | be said to possess what would maintain 1000 men; if he was to
restrict himself to a moderate allowance such as is necessary to support a
man andᵍ furnish ⟨?him⟩ with food and cloathing. But we see that this is
not the way men use their money. This ten thousand pound maintains only
the man himself and a few domestic servants. The arts which are now cultivated give him an opportunity of expending his whole stock on himself. He
has architects, masons, carpenters, taylors, upholsterers, jewelors, cooks,
and other minissters of luxury, which by their various employments give
him an opportunity of laying out his whole income. He gives nothing away
gratuitously, for men are so selfish that when they have an opportunity of
laying out on their ownʰ persons what they possess, tho on things of no
value, they will never think of giving it to be bestowed on the best purposes
by those who stand in need of it.[13] Those tradesmen he employs do not
118 think themselves any way indebted to him; they | have given him their
time and labour equivalent to what they have received of him; and tho
they may reckon it a small favour that he gives them the preference in his
custom, they will not think themselves so greatly indebted to him as if they
had received a summ from him in a gratuitous manner. This manner of
laying out ones money is the chief cause that the balance of property
conferrsⁱ so small a superiority of power in modern times. A tradesmanʲ to
retain your custom may perhaps vote for you in an election, but you need
not expect that he will attend you to battle. On the other hand whenᵏ the
western parts of Europe were first possessed by the barbarous nations, arts
were in a very low state. Architecture and masonry were almost unknown;
the men of the greatest property lived in houses little better than those in
the remotest parts of this country. The other arts were all proportionably
uncultivated. It was impossible for a man in this state, then, to lay out his
119 whole fortune on | himself; the only way his[14] had to dispose of it was to
giveˡ it out to others. A man then who possessed a property equall in value
to 10,000£ at this time would be able to maintain a thousand persons. This,
as it rendered the whole of these people dependent on him, would give him
vast authority. The lands he possessed could not easily be disposed of any
other way than by parcelling them out to others; the possessors of these
farms pay'd a small rent to the possessor rather as an acknowledgement of

---

ᵍ Illegible word deleted    ʰ 'adva' deleted    ⁱ Replaces 'has'    ʲ 'may'
deleted    ᵏ Replaces 'in'    ˡ Replaces 'lay'

---

[13] Cf. TMS IV.1.10, where, however, Smith says that the rich, 'in spite of their natural
selfishness and rapacity, . . . are led by an invisible hand to make nearly the same distribution of the necessaries of life which would have been made had the earth been divided
into equal portions among all its inhabitants'. See also iii.134 ff. below.

[14] *Sic.* Presumably 'he' was intended.

their dependence than as the value of the land. This rent again he could dispose of no other way than by bestowing it on those who came to his table. The rent of the land was accordingly paid in victualls; and the term farm lands signifies properly lands which paid victuals for their rent; the word farm signifying in the old Saxon or German language victualls;[15] feu lands, feodum or feudum signifying lands that were held in another way afterwards to be explained. These farms, as the lord or great man could not consume them all himself, were eat about his house by those whom he
120 enter|tain'd, and often a great part by the very tenents who had payd them. Hospitality was then such as we can now have no notion of; the lord entertain'd ordinarily about his house for 3, 4, 5, or 6 months in the year all those who held their lands of him. {And in the same manner as the lesser lords entertain'd their vassals, so the greater ones entertained them, and the king again those who depended on him; for (as shall be hereafter explained⟨⟩) the different lords were in time dependent on each other.} We read that the great Earl of Warwick dined at his table in his different manors in the country about 30000 persons every day in the year, of his dependants; this was in the reign of Hen. 7$^{th}$[16] It is told too in commendation of the famous Thomas Becket, who lived in the time of Henry the 2$^d$, as a piece of great luxury and nicety, that he had always the floor of his hall strewed with rushes,[17] that the nobles and great men who dined with him might not dirty their cloaths as they sat on the floor. This may at the same time shew us the *immence* hospitality of those times, and the great want of all sorts of arts that was amongst them. And if they were thus barbarous in the time of
121 Henry 2$^d$ we may conjecture what must | have been in the time of Alfred or Edgar, in comparison of which those of the Henry's were polite and cultivated.—The hall of William Rufus, now called Westminster hall, is three hundred feet long and proportionably wide, and was then not reckoned too large for a dining room to him and the nobles who attended his court. As the dependents were in every respects so entirely maintain'd by these allodiall lords (as they were called) for maintainance and every thing they enjoyed, it was naturall that they should attend$^m$ him ⟨in⟩ war and defend him when injured by the other lords or their dependents. And they were constanly about him, whether in peace or in war; in peace they were entertained at his table, and in war they were his soldiers. These vassalls, in the first establishment of this government, possessed their lands during the pleasure of their lord, and might be turned out by him on neglecting their attendance in war or any other transgression, and their farm given to any

---

$^m$ 'him war' deleted

---

$^{15}$ H. Spelman, *Tenures*, cap. 7, cited by Dalrymple, 27. The modern word 'farm' is now considered to be derived from the medieval Latin *firma*, fixed payment.
$^{16}$ Hume, *History*, II.361.
$^{17}$ Ibid., I.272.

122 one the lord inclined. In this state they | continued for some time, till by
the demand of the tenants and to secure their service, the lords granted them
for lives, one or more as was agree'd. {These sort of farms that were held
for a life were called beneficia, benefices, as those that were for pleasure
were called munera. From this it is that the livings of the clergy were called
benefices, as they are settlements for life.[18]} Conrad the second, the German
emperor, was the first who introduced the perpetual tenure, which was
called feudum.[19] In his expedition into Italy, his soldiers (that is, his
tenants, for then there were no others) complained that as they were going
on a dangerous expedition into a distant country from whence it was uncertain if they should ever return, the wives and children of many of them
would be intirely ruined. To satisfy these complaints and make them easy
as to their service, he assured them that their wives and their posterity
should be certain of the possession of those lands. This custom was soon
diffused over the rest of the west. There is no mention of the word feodum
in the English law till a few years after the Norman conquest, nor in the
French till after the time of 50 or 60 years after Conrad. These periods[n] are
123 all somewhat posterior to that of the | introduction of perpetuall possession
of lands by Conrad, abovementioned, and shew that the generallity of
writers on the origin of the feudall government are mistaken when they
give out that the feus were establish'd immediately after ⟨the⟩ destruction
of the Roman Empire by the barbarians, as it was in the 5th[o] century
before these feus were introduced in Germany and some other countries,
and abou⟨t⟩[p] 500 and some more before it was established in Britain.[20]
After this time (as was hinted above) came in the distinction of the words
feudum and allodium. *Allodium* is a barbarous word of uncertain etymo-
logy,[21] signifying a farm or possession of any sort, exactly synonymous
to the Latin words *praedium* or *fundus*. But when the *feuda, feoda*, now
called fee lands from the word *feu* or *fee*, signifying a *rent* or *hire* (as a
servants fee) ⟨?⟩, those lands were denominated allodia that were free from
this burthen and were held without any rent. At the same time the words
which denoted the possession or holding of a farm were in like manner
124 | altered from *habere, possidere*, to have, to possess, to *tenere*, to hold. This
method of holding land soon spread over the most part of Europe, for such
causes as it was begun in Germany. In process of time, too, when some of
the lesser lords were incroached on by others and were not able to defend

[n] Reading doubtful     [o] The last three words replace '400 or 500'     [p] Reading
doubtful

[18] Dalrymple, 161; cf. iv.127, below.
[19] Craig, *Ius Feudale*, I.4.8.
[20] Ibid., I.7.1 ff.
[21] Cf. P. Bouquet, *Le Droit public de France, éclairci par les monumens* (1756), 32–3.
The word is considered to be from an old Germanic word *allod*, entire property.

themselves, they had no other way of obtaining assistance but from other allodiall lords of greater power. This they could not obtain without some concession, and the one they agreeed to as most common was that they should hold their lands in feu from them. {This too was a less concession than if they had subjected themselves to hold of him*q* lands as munera or beneficia. Besides in these barbarous times they are always very ready to come under contracts,*r* possibly because they have no very strict notion of the obligation they are under to keep them.} These greater lords again being afterwards in danger from others or a combination were induced as their last resource to ask assistance of the king, and obtain'd it on the same conditions, viz. that they should hold feu of him. By this means it was, that in about 500 or 600 years after the destruction of the Roman Empire all the west of Europe*s* was brought under the feudall government.

{N.B. it will be proper to read what is said of jurisdiction before the burthens the lords or superiors imposed in order to maintain their authority, as it is the end of this account.}*t*

125 | It is to be observed that*u* this form of government required that the possessors of estates should attend their lord in war, or in council in peace, so it was requisite that every estate should be filled by one who was able to perform those duties. Hence it came soon to be established that when an estate fell to a minor, the lord considered as his tutor took it up and disposed of it to some one who was capable of serving him. By this means the burthen of ward was introduced. And*v* this view of considering the lord as the tutor of all the wards of his vassalls introduced also another burthen. For as it would seem a high affront for the pupil to marry without the fathers consent, so in this case it would seem somewhat more than affront, an heinous injury, for the pupil to marry without the consent of his lord and tutor who had the sole management of him. By this pretext, and also as they gave out that no one might marry into a family that was in enmity with the lord and by that means be withdrawn from his allegiance, they

126 established | the burthen of marriage on the feudall vassalls, by which no man could marry without the consent of his superior. In the same manner as the burthen of wardenage was established, so likewise that of marriage; for as a woman could not discharge the duties of a vassall, it was necessary that the man she married should be one willing and able to perform these duties. For this reason it came also into use that no heiress*w* could marry without the consent of the superior of the estate.

As the lord had once got the estate of a minor into his power, and as there was a procedure at the lords court necessary to reinstate the pupill when he came of age, the servants of the king or lord must be satisfied for their

---

*q* 'as' deleted          *r* Replaces 'obligations'          *s* 'was extended over all' deleted
*t* This note is written at the top of the verso of 124          *u* 'as' interlined and deleted
*v* 'on' deleted          *w* Replaces 'one'

trouble, and such was their rapacity that it was necessary[x] to settle what
127 this summ should be, and this was in some places a | years, in others two
years or more years rent. This was called the burthen of[y] relief or sufferage.
Besides these it was always taken for granted that failing of heirs the
estate or feu should fall to the lord, or be escheated[22] to him.—By these
means all lands came at length to be holden primarily of the king and under
him under the superior lords, with the burthens 1st, of Hommage, that is,
being his man or servant on all demands;[z] 2[d], of Fealty or fidelity to him;
3[dly], of Knights Service, or the burthen of serving him in his battles; 4th, of
Wardenage; 5th, of Marriage; and 7th,[a] of Relief; and 8th, of Escheat.
    It is to be observed that this government was not all[23] all cut out for
maintaining civill government, or police. The king had property in the land
128 superior indeed to what the others had, but not so greatly superior | as that
they[24] had any considerable power over them. The only person who had
any command in the remoter parts of the kingdom was the superior or lord.
How then should one recover a debt at a distance, a merchant at London,
e.g. from one residing at York? Or in Scotland, how could one have any
thing restored to him at a distant place; when in neither case the king had
any standing army, nor garrisons, nor in Scotland were there any towns than
the poorest village in the Highlands. If he should send the kings messenger
they would hang him up without delay, and the king could have no redress
but by a civill war carried on betwixt him and the chieftan. The only
method was to gain the good will of the lord; he, if he inclined, might by
raising what they called the posse comitatus[25] give him restitution; if
129 not there was no remedy. By | this means it was established that all the
lords and great men[b] {The chief of the feudal ones likewise, as their
possessions were sometimes as large as the others, had often the jurisdiction in their grounds as well as the allodiall — —} who held of the king
should exercise the right of jurisdiction in their own country; allmost all
the great men had this right. Till the time of the Rebellion in '45 Mr.
Cameron of Lochiel[26] was in the common practise of exercising this
priviledge, and even hanging or        [c] any offender. Thus al the lords
held of the king by Hommage, Fealty, Knights Service, Wardenage,

[x] 'that' deleted          [y] 'hommage' deleted          [z] 'and' deleted          [a] Sic
[b] Illegible word deleted          [c] Illegible word

[22] Escheat was the reversion of land to the lord, either because the tenant died without heirs or because of some offence committed by him.
[23] Sic. Presumably 'at' was intended.
[24] Sic. Presumably 'he' was intended.
[25] The county force of men whom the sheriff could order to attend him for the purpose of keeping the peace.
[26] Donald Cameron (1695?–1748), the chief of Clan Cameron, who called out his clan in support of Prince Charles in 1745.

Marriage, Relief, and Escheat, having the same rights and that jurisdiction over their vassals.—We shall afterwards shew how the right of primogeniture ⟨?⟩.

The severall great allodial lords (and the chief of the feudall in some measure[d]) were in all respects to be considered as little princes in the kingdom. (The feudalls indeed paid a small acknowledgement to their superior, 130 and were subjects to severall burthens | but still their power was very great.) They made regulations in their territories, exercised[sed] jurisdiction on their vassals, and that frequently without any appeal to the kings courts. They had the power of carrying their vassalls to war and concluding a peace with their enemies. The law at that time (as we shall explain when we consider the origin of government) did not provide, nor indeed could it, for the safety of the subjects. Each principality, as they may very well be called, being in much the same state as the greater and lesser princes of Germany at this day, provided for its own defence; if they repulsed their enemies by their own strength so much the better; but if they could not they had no resource but to call the assistance of some of the neighbouring lords, or of the king, who was equally bound to defend his own territory, and if he was not able of himself and his vassalls he must in the same manner call the assistance of some of his allodiall lords. In this state a small property must be very insecure, as it could not defend itself and must 131 be entirely depen|dent on the assistance of some of the neighbouring great men. Nowadays, the[e] smallest property is as secure as the greatest; a single acre is as securely possessed by its owner as 10000, and as the law takes the defence of property under its protection there could not in this condition be any hazard in dividing an immoveable subject into as many parts as one inclined. But as the only security in the other case was from the strength of the possessor, small property could be in no security. If therefore an estate[f] which when united could easily defend itself against all its neighbours should be divided in the same manner as moveables were, that is, equally betwixt[g] all the brothers, it would be in no state of equallity with those to whom[h] it was before far superior.

It has always been found a most detrimentall practise, and one that tended most to weaken the kingdom, to divide it amongst the children of the deceased king. This was the practise in France during the two first 132 races of its kings. The whole kingdom was divided amongst | the sons which the preceding king had left. E.g. if a king had left two sons, each of these[i] took a half of the kingdom. But tho their territories were thus seperated, there[j] were in the dominions ⟨?of⟩ each enemies to their sovereign. The

[d] The last three words are interlined without any specific indication as to their proper placing        [e] Reading doubtful        [f] 'in land' is interlined here, but has apparently been struck out        [g] Reading doubtful        [h] The last two words replace 'that'
[i] Reading doubtful        [j] Reading doubtful

brothers, being both bredd at their fathers court, would have formed acquaintances and friendships with the noble men thro the whole kingdom. When therefore the kingdom was divided there would be a party in each court formed for the other brother. They would by all means encourage and incite him, who was naturally enough disposed, to free them from a king they did not like and take the whole kingdom to himself, which he well deserved. While this was going on in the court [of the court] of one, the same schemes would be brewing in the others dominions, the same incitements and the same encouragements of assistance would be given him. In this manner civill wars betwixt the brothers were almost unavoidable, till the whole was brought into the power of one. We see accordingly that in the times of the two first | races of French kings, after the death of a king there were frequently 5 or six different sovereigns, but in 4 or 5 years at most they were reduced to one, and this surviving king was not only the conqueror but the murtherer of his brother. The same bad[k] consequences which[l] attended the division of a kingdom amongst the sons, would attend the division of an allodiall estate. The Gordon estate, or the Douglass one, could when under one head support itself against the neighbours, the Frasers e.g., but had this estate been divided amongst 7 or 8 sons, no one of these portions could have supported itself against the neighbours, or against the designs which would be formed amongst the others, without subjecting himself to some of those powerfull neighbours, who were able to defend him against injuries and perhaps could cope with the king himself. {It is to be remarked, then, that it was not the introduction of the feudal government and military fiefs that brought in the right of primogeniture; but the independency of the great allodiall estates, and the inconveniencies attending divisions of such estates. The time indeed of the introduction of this right and that of the milit. fiefs coincide pretty nearly, as it was not till about that time [v.133] that the inconveniencies attending on the division of these lands were sufficiently experienced so as to shew the necessity of introducing a practise so contrary to nature, and which met with so many other obstacles. The allodial government, as it subsisted only for 3 or 400 years, did not afford sufficient time for this. But after the introduction of the feudal govern., altho the great fiefs were not so independent yet they were almost equally liable to those inconveniences which had begun this right amongst the allodial estates.} But notwithstanding all these inconveniencies, the right of primogeniture was[m] not established for | a considerable time after the introduction of the allodial government. But when the abovementioned inconveniencies had been for some time endured, it was found proper that the land estate should be given to one of the sons. When this was agreed on there was no doubt which of them should be preferred. The distinction that determined the choice must be something

---

[k] Reading doubtful     [l] Replaces 'that'     [m] 'long after' deleted

that could not be called in question; it could not be beauty nor wisdom, nor strength; these were all disputable; it would be[n] seniority. This could always be known without any doubt. {Besides this, in barbarous nations where literature is little cultivated and wisdom can only be got by experience, age is much more respected than when letters, conversation, and other artificiall methods of acquiring knowledge are introduced. Father is the most [is the most] honourable title one can confer on another. Brother, makes one his equall; son,[o] his inferior. Age is so much respected by some nations that the succession is not to the eldest son but the eldest of the family. Amongst the      [p] Tartars at the death of the [v.134] king, a meeting is held to choose a new one, but this is no more than to enquire which is the eldest of the royal family.} This right however was not introduced very early, and no wonder; the younger brothers would think it very hard that they should be entirely excluded from their fathers inheritance and instead of being the equalls should become his subjects and dependents. The people too would be apt to take part with them and facilitate their seizing a part to themselves. By this means it was not till the 10th or end of

135  the 9th century that[q] this right was introduced into generall | practise. We find that some of the lands in the end of the Saxons government were succeded to in this manner, {as the estate of the great allodial lords Leveric and Alric}[27] but many more continued as formerly to be divided in the manner called      [28] equally betwixt the sons. We mentioned before[29] that this was continued for 2 races of kings amongst the French. In the later reigns of the second race it was more and more adhered to, and at length was firmly established. — —

But whatever difficulties there were in the introduction of the right of primogeniture, there would be far greater in the introduction of the right of representation or succession per stirpes. {It would even be impeded by the right of primogeniture being introduced before, as on that account the injury done to the sons would appear to be far greater.} If it was hard that the eldest son should exclude his brothers, they would think it hard that their nephew should exclude them[r] after his death. That he who should naturally owe his safety and depend on them for his protection should be not only not dependent on them but, on the other hand, that they who were

136  men should be subjected and dependent on one who might often | be a minor or an infant. {They would say, that by his repre⟨se⟩nting his father

---

[n] 'the' deleted        [o] Reading doubtful        [p] Blank in MS.        [q] Reading doubtful    [r] 'still' deleted

---

[27] Leofric, Earl of Mercia (d. 1057), and Alfric, Earl of Mercia (d. about 1004).

[28] Blank in MS. Probably 'gavelkind' was intended. By this form of tenure, which was supposed to have been the general custom of England in Saxon times, the land descended to all the sons together.

[29] 131 above.

they could understand nothing but that he represented him in affinity; in age he could not represent him. His father was prefered on account of his seniority; but he had no such claim.} By these and such like motives the younger brother would be prompted to deprive[s] their elder brothers children of the right of inheritance, and by this means it was long after the introduction of primogeniture ere the right of representation took place. The succession of the collaterals[t] also was found to have its hardships as well as that by representation. {It often occasiond great disputes and contest about the succession.} It appeared hard that the minor should be deprived of the best part of his fathers inheritance because his father had died a few years before; had he survivd his brothers he would have inherited the whole without dispute. If he was of age to form any hopes, he must have formed a reasonable expectation of[u] succession to his father.—It was objected also that one in this age could not perform the necessary duties to the superior. We see accordingly that this right was introduced by slow

137 degrees and with con|siderable difficulty. The sentiments of the people were often divided betwixt those who claimed the succession on these different titles. The author of our old Scots law-book, the *Regiam Majestatem*,[30] states it as a question, which had puzzled him not a little, whether the son of the deceased father or his brother should inherit his estate. For my part, it would seem rather that his son should retain the possession,[v] and especially if he had done homage for the land to his superior. But in all cases, says he, it may be decided by single combat. The uncertainty of this right it was which gave occasion to the dispute betwixt Bruce and Baliol.[31] The latter, by our account, would have the undoubted right, being come of the eldest daughter. But in that time the opinion, as we learn from the foreign authors who mention this dispute, was rather in favours of Bruce, as being a step nearer to the common stock. And Edward 1st gave

138 sentence in favours | ⟨of⟩ Baliol merely because he had made some concessions to him that could not be obtained from Bruce, who was of a far more generous and spirited temper. It was introduced the famous betwixt[32] the houses of York and Lancaster. The claim of the house of Lancaster was founded on the right of representation; that of the house of York on the nearest step of the relation. There had been one precedent in favours of

---

[s] Replaces 'turn out'    [t] Illegible word deleted    [u] Illegible word deleted
[v] Illegible word deleted

---

[30] II.33 (Skene's numbering); Dalrymple, 172; Kames, *Essays*, 139.

[31] The Great Cause concerning the right to the throne of Scotland, 1291-2. Balliol and Bruce were descended from two sisters, Balliol being the grandson of the elder and Bruce the son of the younger. Dalrymple, 180 ff.

[32] *Sic.* Possibly something like 'introduced into the famous quarrel betwixt' was intended. Henry VI of Lancaster was descended from the third of Edward III's sons, while Richard of York was descended from both the second and fourth son (by the latter of whom he was nearer in degree to Edward than was Henry).

representation, and severalls against. In the time of the Saxons a manner of
succession prevailed which would now appear[w] very strange. The great
Alfred was the third brother[33] who succeeded, all the former[x] having left
child behind them. The Lancaster family always favoured the right of
representation, as the more instances there were of it the stronger was their
139 claim. The York family, on the other hand, being possessed | of the throne
⟨?⟨⟩ by the inclination of the people who began to doubt the right of the
Lancastrians after they had succeded 3 or 4 times by representation) did all
in their power to discourage it. However in time this method of succession
has come to be established thro all Europe. But in some places but very
late. In the German electors, the houses of Brandebourg, Brunswick, and
Hanover have receivd it but very lately. When this is established in its full
extent,[y] which soon follows after it is once generally practised, there can be
no doubt concerning the succession, as the descendent⟨s⟩ of the eldest son
exclude all others (whether the descendents be male or female in this
country), and so to the next eldest son, etc.; this is the order observed by
the royall family on the throne.—{And for the same reason there can be no
objection to collaterall representation in this case, as it can allways be
ascertain'd who is come of the eldest branch of the family, and to him or
her the whole estate goes as it is indivisible, and he excludes all others of the
same rank. But as we observd already this is otherwise in moveables, as they
are divisible subjects.} As an instance of the difficulty of introducing this
representation we may take the succession        [z] of Don Sebastian[34] to the
140 throne | of Portugal, in preference of his brothers daughters. They said in
his favours that as this right of representation was borrowed from the
Roman law, they should consider what[a] effect it had amongst them. This
was that if any one died leaving, besides his children, grandchildren by a
predeceased son, they should come in for the same share as their father
would, and in every shape should represent him. Let then, say, this child[b]
come into his place as a son; but why as an eldest; the child can represent
him in nothing but affinity; it cannot represent him in age and far less in
sex. The father was preferred to the other brothers as being elder and
superior in wisdom and age. But shall his daughter be preferred, who is
inferior not only in age, but in sex. She should be farther from the inheritance than his sisters, as they are equall to her in sex and superior in age.
This may shew the great difficulties that stood in the way of this right of[c]
representation and the great time it took to establish it.
141   In the first period of the feudall | government the succession of females

[w] Replaces 'look'       [x] Reading doubtful       [y] Two or three illegible words are
interlined here       [z] Blank in MS.       [a] Reading doubtful       [b] Replaces
'daughter'       [c] Illegible word deleted

---

[33] Actually the fourth.
[34] Posthumous child of a son of John III; succeeded his grandfather as king in 1557.

was never allowed; for they could not perform any of the services required of those who were vassalls either of the king or his nobles; they could neither serve him in the field nor in the council; and as they could not inherit so neither could their descendents by their right. {Nor could it for the same reason be allowed of in the allodial governments, as the females could neither lead the vassalls to battle nor preside in council and exercise jurisdiction. But in time*d* the military fiefs came to be considered in most respects as property, and the services of the field were not always required, but were*e* dispensed with for a certain gratuity. This gratuity, which they called          35, was often more esteemed than the performance of the actuall services, and new fiefs were given out on that condition. The lords or feudall chiefs did not now exercise the jurisdiction themselves, but by their steward. In this state of things females could succeed in every shape as well as males; they could pay the          35 and maintain a steward to exercise judgement on their tenents as well as men. From this time therefore females were admitted to the succession.} But afterwards when this sort of service was not so necessary, and the feudall government had in time rendered feudall lands nearly of the same priviledges with property, they came both to be inherited by females as well as males; and at the same time this would be extended to their descendents allied to the estate. Collateralls too by females were called after those allied by males.*f*

142    After | the introduction of female succession, fiefs (or feus) became of two sorts, masculine and feminine. The masculine are those wherein the*g* old Salic law is adhered to, and in which no females are admitted, neither are their descendents. In the feminine again females and their descendents are admitted, in defect of males. The royal family of France succeed in the manner of a masculine fief. The crown of Great-Britain, on the other hand, is a feminine fief; thus in the present royal family, the late Prince of Wales would have succeeded to his father, but on his death it fell to his son, the present king, and failing him would have gone to his next eldest brother, and so on thro them all, and failing all male issue of him, to his daughters in order.36 Then in defect of them to the Duke of Cumbe. and his issue, and in

143    defect of them to the Princess Royal and her sons and so on.*h* | Some German authors talk of a third kind which they call mixt fiefs. In these the inheritance goes to the sons in succession and then returns to the descendents of the eldest son, and so thro them. Of this sort I can find no

---

*d* The last two words replace 'when'      *e* 'allow' deleted      *f* The five lines which follow in the MS. are cancelled by a succession of oblique strokes, and are largely illegible
*g* 'whole' deleted        *h* Reading of last six words doubtful

---

35 Blank in MS. English, escuage; Scots, taxtward.
36 Frederick, Prince of Wales, eldest son of George II, predeceased his father. His son succeeded to the throne as George III in 1760. William Augustus, Duke of Cumberland (1721–65), the victor of Culloden, was Frederick's younger brother.

example in any country either in publick or private possessions. If it has ever taken place at any time it must have been only by an entail, which may establish this as well as any other foolish order of succession.

Thus it was that the rights of primogeniture and of representation and of female succession were established in the greater land estates, and now it is extended to all sorts of indivisible estates in the same manner in Scotland and England, excepting a few*i* cases to be mentioned in the next lecture.

We may observe here that though females were not at first admitted to the inheritance of the greater *allodial* and *feudal* estates, yet there were two
144 sorts of inheritances | to which they were at all times admitted. These were, I*st*, the inheritance of moveables to which they were admitted equally with males as a divisible subject which had no priviledges attending them nor any burthens imposed on them. Of this already.[37] II, sockage, or sock lands.[38] The great allodiall and feudall lords in letting out their estate gave the greatest part ⟨of⟩ it as military fiefs, for the service in war, etc. Other parts they gave either for a certain rent, or for the performance of certain works. These latter were called sock lands [lands]. Those who live in the country*j* must keep some part of their lands in their own hand for the maintenance of the family. This land they did not cultivate by their own servants, but by the tenants who held in this manner and were thence said to hold by the sock. Of this method of holding there are still many remains in this country. Those who held in this way were always men of no great possessions in property; they [they] could have formed no reasonable
145 | hopes, imagination, or expectation that he could of himself defend his possessions; for this he must depend on his master. There could be no reason here for not dividing the inheritance, as it would be as safe in the one case as in the other. And as females were at that time equally engaged in the country work as the men, there was no reason why they should be excluded, as they could do the service as well.*k* Accordingly they were always held capable of the inheritance of sock lands, to which they were admitted as heir portioners.—Here I have a blank and you etc. ∧ others have no more.[39]

*i* 'exceptions' deleted      *j* Illegible word deleted      *k* Reading of last two words doubtful

---

[37] 104 ff. above.

[38] Socage was a tenure by a certain and determinate service, in contrast with knight-service.

[39] The words after 'heir portioners.—' appear to be written with a different ink and pen, but may well be in the same handwriting as the main text of the MS. The reading given above, particularly of the words we have rendered as 'blank' and 'others', is very doubtful indeed. If the reading is correct, however, the note *may* indicate that the reporter was unable to take down what Smith said in the final part of this lecture, and therefore left the next three and one-half pages of his notes blank in the hope that one of his fellow students might be able to supply the missing material. On checking with another set of notes, however,—probably those of a friend whose notes he usually collated with his own—

*Gap of three and one-half pages in MS.*

146  | In some of the last lectures I have endeavoured to explain the different methods of succession ab intestato. These differ according as the subjects are divisible or indivisible. There are two generall methods of succession to divisible subjects; either 1$^{st}$, that where they are equally divided$^l$ amongst all the children and the wife, she being considered in the same manner as a daughter; or 2$^{dly}$, where the wife takes one third and the children two thirds amongst them, one third as their own share and the other as the successors of their father. The first is that which prevailed [in] amongst the Romans and most ancient nations. The other is that which is universally in use in all the modern states of Europe.—In like manner there are two methods of succession in indivisible subjects, viz masculine fiefs, and feminine fiefs. These were exemplified in the succession of the crowns of France and England. It was observed also that the methods of succession in Scotland and England were not altogether either in the manner of mascu-

147 line fiefs or feminine fiefs, but differed in | severall particulars from both and from one another. These differences we may observe are only to be found in the succession of collateralls or ascendents. In that of descendents there is hardly any variety; men are more explicit with regard to the latter as it is more founded in nature. But in the other their opinion is less fixed$^m$ and may be turned different ways by many different circumstances.—{And many of them are accordingly very whimsicall, as those with regard to half-blood, and the relation by the mother, and the succession of ascendents.} All these varieties betwixt the Scots and English law with regard to succession, as well as severall differences in the order of succession betwixt them and the civil law, have been already considered, and the causes which brought them about explained from the nature of the severall constitutions. There are two other methods of succession different from both these. The first is called gavelhaide.$^{40}$ This took place amongst some of the Saxon$^n$ principalities, and does so still in soccage$^o$ lands in severall parts of England. By it the inheritance was equally divided amongst the sons exclusive of the daughters, and only came to them in failure of sons. This is said to have

148 | been the law amongst the Athenians prior to the time of Solon; but the matter is not altogether certain. The other method, which is still in use in some parts of England as well as in some other countries in Europe, is

---

$^l$ Illegible word or words deleted    $^m$ Reading doubtful    $^n$ 'nations' deleted
$^o$ 'and farm' deleted

---

he found that the latter had had the same difficulty and had merely written 'etc.' and a caret in the relevant place. Further inquiries, we may surmise, elicited that other students had 'no more', and the reporter, presumably for the benefit of his friend, therefore scribbled the words which appear in the text at this point and gave it up as a bad job.

$^{40}$ *Sic.* No doubt 'gavelkind' was intended. It survived in Kent.

called burrow English;[41] by this manner of succession the youngest son inherits all that the father was possessed ⟨of⟩ at his death. The reason of this seems to be that in the farm lands, as soon as a son was come to be a man, his father got him a farm and settled him in it. In this manner it had often happened that the sons being all forisfamiliate before the death of their father, excepting the youngest, who generally staid with his father, the whole inheritance devolved on him. The judges, who must regulate their sentence by the common practise, finding it to be[p] in common use that the youngest son should succeed to all his father died possessed of, established this as the rule in the severall burrows and counties where they found this practise.

149    | We come now to treat of testamentary succession. There is no point more difficult to account for than the right we conceive men to have to dispose of their goods after their death. For at what time is it that this[q] right[42] takes place. Just at the very time that the person ceases[r] ⟨?to have⟩ the power of disposing of them; for the testamentary heir has no claim or right to any of the testators goods untill the moment that he is dead; for till that time he can not even have any reasonable expectation of his possessing them, as the testator may alter his inclination. A man during his own life may very well be conceived to have the power of disposing of his goods; the very notion of property implies that he may abuse, give away, or do what he pleases with them. In the very beginnings of property it would be[s] uncontroverted that a man might make what use he pleased of a wild beast he had caught in hunting.—But how is it that a man comes to have

150 a power of disposing as | he pleases of his goods after his death. What obligation is the community under to observe the directions he made concerning his goods now when he can have no will, nor is supposed to have any knowledge of the matter. {For what reason is it that we should prefer the person made heir in the testament to the heir at law if he has one.} The difficulty is here so great that Puffendorff[43] called in to his assistance the immortality of the soul. He says we allow the will of the deceased to take place supposing that he is still alive and wills[t] in the same manner; and that out of regard to this will[u] we allow his testament to be effectual. But we need not go so far to find a sufficient account of this.—The regard we all naturaly have to the will of a dying person seems to be sufficient to explain

---

*p* 'thus' deleted        *q* Reading doubtful        *r* 'has' deleted        *s* 'an' interlined and deleted        *t* Reading doubtful        *u* 'will' deleted

[41] Borough-English, a custom of inheritance by the youngest son, so called because it was mainly found in parts of England.

[42] At this point the student has interlined the words 'right' and 'conveyed', the former being deleted and partially overwritten by the latter, indicating perhaps that the sentence was intended to read 'For at what time is it that this right is conveyed.'

[43] IV.10.4, quoting the view of Leibniz.

it. That period is of so momentous a nature that every thing that is connected with it seems to be so also. The advices, the commands, and even
the very fooleries of the dying person have more effect on us than things of
151 the same nature would have had at any other period. | We have a great
reverence for his commands at such a time; and after his death, we do not
consider what he[v] willd, but what if he was then alive would be his will: we
think, as we say, what would be his will if he should look up from the grave
and see things going contrary to what he had enjoined. Suppose a man on
his death bed calls his friends together and entreats, beseeches, and con-
jures them to dispose of his goods in such or such a manner, {to look upon
such a friend in the same manner as they did on him or on his children,
etc.}. They would afterwards be, as it were, forced by their piety to the
de⟨ce⟩ased person to dispose of his goods as he desired; they would imagine
what he would think were he to see them disposing of them in a manner[w]
contrary to what they were so solemnly intreated. But this piety to the dead
is a pitch of humanity, a refinement on it, which we are not to expect from
a people who have not made considerable advances in civilized manners.
152 Accor|dingly we find that it is pretty late ere it is introduced in most
countries. In the first ages of Rome no testament could be made, but by
what we would call an Act of Parliament, viz a decree of the whole people
assembled in the Comitia Calata, where he adressed them thus: Velitis
jubaeatis, juveniles, etc., the will of the whole people appointing that such
an one should be accounted as his son.[44] So that it was rather an adoption
than a testament; and we are told that this was only allowed in the case
that a man had no children. It was natural for one in that condition to
desire that some of his most intimate and dearest friends should possess his
fortune and represent his family. Private testaments were not thought of till
they were introduced by the laws of the 12 Tables, which borrowed it
153 probably from the laws of the Athenians. Testaments were also | intro-
duced by Solon into Athens,[45] before his time under the laws of Draco.[46]
   In the same manner no testament could be made in England for a considerable time {for more than the fathers share, that is, ⅓ of his property if
he had a wife and children, or one half if he had no wife or no children.}
Henry 8th gave the liberty of disposing[x] of the estate by testament, and now
the whole estate may be given in that manner.[47] In Scotland, no testament

---

[v] Illegible word deleted          [w] 'so' deleted          [x] 'of ¾' deleted

---

[44] The Comitia Calata was the Comitia Curiata (above, 92) when it assembled to
approve adrogations and testaments. The presiding magistrate asked, 'Do you wish and
command, citizens?' The text substitutes 'youths' for 'citizens' (*quirites*). Heineccius,
II.10.2, citing Aulus Gellius, V.19; Kames, *Law Tracts*, I.186–7.

[45] Cf. 92 above.

[46] It seems probable that there is a lacuna in the MS. here.

[47] 32 Henry VIII, c. 1 (1540) as amended by 34 and 35 Henry VIII, c. 5 (1543) gave the
power to devise all socage land and two-thirds of that held by knight-service.

can be made with respect to an estate; it can only be disposed of by a disposition of the same sort as that by which property is transferred amongst
the living.[48]— In the savage nations of Asia and Africa testamentary
succession is unknown; the succession is intirely settled; a mans estate goes
always to his nearest male relations, without his having the power of disposing, by any deed to take place after his death, of the smallest subject. It
is not till society is considerably refined that such respect is paid to the will
of the decceased; piety to the dead (as it is called⟨⟩) is too refined a doctrine
154 for a barbarous people. | But tho' this piety to the deceased and regard to
the will of the testator inclines us to dispose of his goods[y] and obey his will
for some time after his death, yet we do not naturally imagine that this
regard is to last for ever. In a few years, often in a few months, our respect
for the will of ⟨the⟩ testator is altogether worn off. A man who died 100
years ago, his will is no more regarded than if he had never lived. We do
not naturally imagine that a man can settle how his estate shall go for any
longer time than that which immediately follows; as soon as he dies and the
heir succeeds, they are possessed by another who has the same ⟨?power⟩ of
doing with them as ⟨he⟩ pleases as the deceased had. There are therefore no
such thing as entails amongst the Romans for a long time after testamentary
succession had been introduced. The only thing that bore any resemblance
to it was the vulgar and pupillary substitution. The former was establishd
that if it should happen that an inheritance was so burthend that the man
whom he intended for his heir, who perhaps was rich,[z] might not incline to
155 accept of, | and the trouble attending it, the testator was in this case allowed
to name severall heirs in order {that he might not die without some one as
his heir, which was reckon'd discreditable}. But then this went no farther
than one succession, for if any one accepted it went intirely to him and his
heirs, the rest being altogether excluded. The other kind provided that if a
mans nearest relation or any other[49] whom he designed to institute heir was
under tutors and consequently incapable[a] of making a testament, and if
there were severalls whom he had a greater affection for than the heir at law
to this pupill, the testator was then allowed to appoint an heir to him in case
he died before the age of puberty. But in this case also it did not extend[b]
above one degree.

In time however entails were introduced amongst the Romans, and as

[y] Reading of last two words doubtful    [z] 'was rich' deleted    [a] Replaces an
illegible word or words    [b] 'to a' deleted

[48] The transferor executed a conveyance of the land, to be put into effect after his
death by an agent: Dalrymple, 130–1.
[49] Pupillary substitution was possible only where the pupil was a descendant in the
testator's power, who would, on the testator's death, become independent before reaching
the age of puberty (14 years for males), at which he would acquire capacity to make a will
for himself. Until that age his interests were looked after by a guardian (tutor). *Inst.*
2.15,16.

this was brought about by means of fideicomisses,[50] it will be necessary to explain their nature and origin. By the ancient marriages, which were performed either by confarreatio or coemptio, the wife became intirely the slave of the husband.[51] He had absolute power over her, both of death and

156 of divorce. Wives | could not at that time give any great adition to a mans fortune. They brought either nothing with them or a very small matter, as seven acres of land were accounted a large estate. The wives were accordingly not much regarded in those times. {It was also introduced that if a man lived with a woman for a year and day without being three nights absent, she became his wife in the same manner as those who had been married by the former ceremonies. She became his wife usu, and was prescribed in the same way as any other moveable.} But when the Romans became from a very poor a very wealthy people; and the women, who are in all polite and wealthy countries more regarded than they are by a poorer and more barbarous nation, came to have large fortunes which they could conferr on their husbands; they could not submitt, nor would the friends allow it, to the subjection that attended the old form of marriage. They therefore made certain concessions to one another; the husband, on consideration of the use of such large summs of money as they might sometimes receive, gave up some parts of his authority, and the woman on the other hand gave him the use of her portion during his lifetime. There articles were drawn up in a[c] writing called the instrumenta dotalia,[52] which

157 as I shall shew hereafter,[53] | like the priests form of marriage, was what chiefly made the difference betwixt[d] wives from concubines, which chiefly consists in this, that the children of the latter can not inherit and are counted no ones relations. By this marriage the husband and wife might seperate whenever they inclined; and least the wife *usû conveniret in manum*[54] she was directed to be absent from her husband three nights every year, which interrupted the prescription.

As these procedings seemed very great infringements on the ancient disciplines and severity of manners to Cato, Oppius,[55] and other such austere disciplinarians, they did all in their power to curb them by bringing the wives into their former subjection; and this they attempted by bringing

---

[c] 'pape' deleted      [d] The last four words replace 'distinguished'

---

[50] Fideicommiss was the Scots version of the Latin *fideicommissum*.

[51] *Confarreatio* (a ceremonial meal), *coemptio* (bride-purchase), and *usus* (prescription) all created marriage *cum manu*, subjecting the wife to the husband. Cf. 94 above.

[52] Dowry deeds.

[53] iii.8–9 below.

[54] 'Should contract a *manus* marriage by prescription'.

[55] M. Porcius Cato, the Elder, notorious for his severity as censor in 184 B.C. C. Oppius, tribune of the plebs in 213 B.C., carried the *lex Oppia*, which limited luxury among women. Cato tried unsuccessfully to prevent the repeal of this law in 195.

their portions to be of a less value. For this purpose the Voconian law[56] was
158 made. Some are of | opinion that after it no one could leave to a woman
above ¼ of his inheritance, but for this their can be no good reason given.
In some way or other however it is certain the property of women was
restricted; {For as women are reckoned incapable of publick offices or the
exercise of the more lu⟨crative⟩ employments, the only means by which
they can be possessed of considerable fortunes is succession, and when this
is restricted their property must of consequence be diminished.} and it is
also evident that contrary to the opinion of Perizonius[57] and others, this law
must have extended to successors ab intestato as well as testamentary
successors, otherwise it might have been evaded by dying intestate. To
evade this law, which would ⟨be⟩ very dissagreable to the rich and powerfull, they contrived that e.g. am[58] who inclin'd to leave all his fortune to a
daughter or to his sister, should appoint some friend whom he could trust
as his heir, and desire him solemnly to restore it afterwards to his daughter.
For tho they might hinder death bed deeds, the law did not extend to
donations inter vivos. This was called a fideicomiss.—For some time these
159 were not reckond absolutely binding, tho the not | performing the promise
which was often express'd in the testament was reckon'd dishonourable.
There were however many instances of their not being observed,[e] some of
which are mentioned by Cicero.—The first who made them absolutely
binding was Augustus. He, being left heir in this manner by      [59], not
only performed the fidecom. himself but made all those to be made
thereafter, or lately before, absolutely binding, and appointed the consuls
to take care of the observance of the law. This office was afterwards conferred on a pretor fideicommissarius.—This constitution in effect abrogated
the Voconian law, and so we find it is hardly ever mentiond after the time of
Augustus.

The *praetor fideicomissarius* had it assigned him as his province to take
care that the fidieicomisses were duly observed, and that the three persons
160 concerned should perform their part. These three were the fi|deicomittens,
who made the fideicomiss; the haeres fiduciarius, who was bound verbis
prec.[60] by the testament to give it to the 3ᵈ person, called the haeres
fiduciarius.[61] In these fideicomissary inheritances the heir might be bound

---

[e] 'and' deleted

---

[56] The *lex Voconia*, 168 B.C., prohibited wealthy testators from instituting women as
their heirs and from bequeathing legacies which exceeded what the heirs received.
Montesquieu, XXVII.1.

[57] Jacobus Perizonius, *Dissertationum Trias* (1679), II (*De lege Voconia feminarumque
hereditatibus*, 99 ff.).

[58] 'e.g. am' replaces 'a father'. Possibly 'e.g. a man' was intended.

[59] Blank in MS. Lentulus: *Inst.* 2.25pr and 2.23.1; Cicero, *De Finibus*, II.55,58.

[60] *Verbis precariis*, 'in words of request'.

[61] *Sic.* Presumably 'fideicommissarius' (the beneficiary) was intended.

either to restore the inheritance either at such a time in his life or he might
be desired to give at his death to such an one the sum respected.*f* By this
latter method it might be continued for a very long time after the testators
death. This was indeed restricted to 4 degrees, by a novell of Valentinian
and Severus;[62] but for som⟨e⟩ considerable time there was no restraint, viz
from the time of Trajan or thereabouts, when fideicomisses had come to
have their full force, till Valentinian. But notwithstanding this,*g* entails in
the full extent of the word never*h* were in use amongst the Romans. They
do not seem to have allowed that a man should leave his estate to Varro,
e.g., failing him and the heirs of his body to Seius, and so on thro the whole
of his children or other relations. This if it had been allowed would have
been a compleat entail. | This is however the case in most of the nations of
Europe. The German nations which overran Europe had no notion of testamentary succession; every inheritance was divided amongst the children;
the only people amongst them {after the introduction of Christianity}
who had any such idea were the clergy. They were*i* under a necessity of
understanding Latin that they might read the liturgy; they had likewise
generally read the book wherein the Roman law was contained, and had
from it, as well as the practise of the country where they had been educated,
contracted a reverence for the will of the dead. This they enculcated to
their people, as a piece of piety not to be dispensed with, and by this means
gradually brought it about that the will of the deceased with respect to his
goods or*j* heirs should be observed. As the clergy were the introducers of
testamentary succession, so they were reckond the most proper persons to
judge of it, as being best skilled; and accordingly each bishop | in his
diocese, and even every priest in his parish, had formerly the judgement of
all testamentary succession. In England indeed before the Conquest, the
bishop and the sheriff of the county, which then was the same extent with
the diocese, sat in judgement together.[63] He, according to the custome
which prevaild in his own country, took this altogether from the civil judge
and appointd the spiritual court to be the sole judge in all testamentary
matters. In the eastern parts of Europe, where the civill law was that by
which the magistrate was directed, the clergy had no concern with testaments, and        [64] expressly prohibited testaments being presented to the
bishop.—The bishop however continues to be the judge in all testamentary
matters. The making of entails came in also in some degree soon after the

161

162

*f* Reading of last five words doubtful        *g* 'they' deleted        *h* 'had' deleted
*i* Replaces 'having been'        *j* Reading doubtful

[62] In fact Justinian's Novel 159.
[63] H. Spelman, 'Of the Probate of Wills or Testaments', *English Works* (1723), II.128.
[64] Blank in MS. Perhaps a reference to the ruling of the Fourth Council of Carthage,
c. 18: *episcopus tuitionem testamentorum non suscipiat*, contained in Gratian's *Decretum*,
D.lxxxviii, c. 5.

introduction of testaments. When once the notion of the will of the deceased directing his succession for one step ⟨?⟩ it was no difficult matter to*k*
163 | suppose that it should extend farther. They however found some evasion of all entails before the statute de donis[65] was made, which appointed that all gifts of the testator should be valid in the very manner he appointed, and that no one of the heirs of entail could alienate what was entaild to him and his heirs, and that when it came to the last heir of entail it should not be alienated but fall to the crown. They have however contrived to evade this statute, which is in effect abrogated with regard to entails by what is called the statute of fine and                    [66]. In Scotland however entails that are valid in law may be made if they are done without*l* exclusive, restrictive, or irritant clauses.[67] The first of these prohibits him from leaving the inheritance to any but those specifi'd, but does not prohibit its being[68] alienated. The 2ᵈ· proh

*Gap of five or six lines in MS.*

164     | Intails made in this manner were by a statute in the time of James the 2ᵈ in 1682[69] made altogether binding, and are so at this day.—{It has been a question whether deeds of this sort made before that time are to be accounted valid or not. The most of our eminent lawyers[70] determine that they are not.—It may be a question too whether they may not even now be looked on as null at common law. An eminent lawyer says ⟨?⟩} Now there can be nothing more absurd than this custom of entails. That a man should have the power of determining what shall be done with his goods after his death is aggreable to our piety to the deceasd, and not contrary to reason. But that he should have the power of determining how they shall dispose of it, and so on in infinitum, has no foundation in this piety and is the most absurd thing in the world. There is no maxim more generally acknowledged than that the earth is the property of each generation. That the former generation should restrict them in their use of it is altogether absurd; it is

---

*k* Illegible word or words deleted     *l* Reading doubtful

---

[65] Statute of Westminster II, 13 Edward I, c. 1 (1285).

[66] Blank in MS. Entails were barred by the procedural device of Recovery (an elaborate fiction). 4 Henry VII, c. 24 (1490) provided that a fine (i.e. final concord) should in certain cases be a bar: Dalrymple, 136.

[67] Prohibitory, irritant, and resolutive clauses: Kames, *Law Tracts*, I.201 ff. Irritant clauses rendered void (*irritus*) acts done contrary to the deed's provisions; resolutive clauses took away (resolved) the rights of the offender.

[68] What appears to be a small caret at this point may have been intended to refer to an entry at the side of the page, which reads 'burthened with debts so as to ma'.

[69] In fact 1685, c. 22 (A.P.S. VIII.477, c. 26); Kames, loc. cit.; Dalrymple, 142.

[70] Kames, op. cit., 216: 'Finding entails current in England, we were, by force of imitation, led to think they might be equally effectual here; being ignorant and not adverting that in England their whole efficacy was derived from statute.'

theirs altogether as well as it was their predecessors in their day. It would
⟨be⟩ altogether absurd to suppose that our ancestors who lived 500 years
⟨ago⟩ should have had the power of disposing of all lands at this time. But
165 this | is no more than would have been the case had they had the power of
making entails; and is what we claim to ourselves over the estates of our
posterity, not only for 500$^m$ years but for ever. The difficulty is to find at
what period we are to put an end to the power we have granted a dying
person of disposing of his goods. There is no evident time at which this
should cease. And it has been this uncertainty that has introduced the
right of making intails into all the countries of Europe. The best rule seems
to be that we should permit the dying person to dispose of his goods as far
as he sees, that is, to settle how it shall be divided amongst those who are
alive at the same time with him. For these it may be conjectured he may
have contracted some affection; we may allow him reasonably then to
settle the succession amongst them. But persons who are not born he can
166 have no affection | for. The utmost stretch of our piety can not reasonably
extend to them.

This right is not only absurd in the highest degree but is also extremely
prejudiciall to the community, as it excludes lands intirely from commerce.—The interest of the state requires that lands should be as much in
commerce as any other goods. This the$^n$ power of making entails intirely
excludes. I shall hereafter shew more fully, only hinting at it now, that the
right of primogeniture and the power of making entails have been the
causes of the almost total bad husbandry that prevails in those countrys
where they are in use.—When land is in commerce and frequently changes
hands it is most likely to be well managed; those who have raised a fortune
by trade or otherwise have generally money besides what they lay out.
They are generally also men of scheme and project, so that they for the most
part have both the desire and the ability of improving. Those on the other
167 hand who possess old family estates seldom | have any money besides.$^o$
The anual luxury and expense of the family consumes the income. We see
accordingly that lands which lie near great towns, which frequently change
masters, are much better cultivated than those which lie at a distance from
them and continue long in one family.—The estate of a great family stands
very little chance of being farther improvd than it is at present. The lord
has nothing to lay out upon it and the ten[en]ants are not$^p$ in the state
which would induce them to improve. If this estate was divided into a number of small possessions each$^q$ having a seperate master, it would soon be
cultivated to a high degree. Farms set out for long leases or feus$^r$ are those
which tend most to the improvement of the country. Short ones, as leases
at pleasure, can never induce the tenent to improve, as what he lays out will

$^m$ 'but 5000' interlined and deleted     $^n$ 'right' deleted     $^o$ 'so that' deleted
$^p$ 'the' deleted     $^q$ Replaces 'all'     $^r$ Reading doubtful

not be on his own account but on an others. But even in long leases the tenent has perhaps a third part of his

*End of Volume One of MS.*

ii.1 | income, to pay as a rent. This is a great discouragement. But were all these farms converted into property, the land as being all cultivated by the masters would soon be well improved. And this would soon be the case were it not for the unnaturall right of primogeniture and this of entails, supported by nothing but the vanity of families.

*Monday January 17ᵗʰ 1763.*

I come now to the last method of acquiring property, viz voluntary transference. To this there are two things necessary: 1ˢᵗ, the will of the proprieter or transferrer, distinctly signified, that the thing should be transferred to the transferré; and IIᵈˡʸ, tradition, that is, that ⟨the⟩ thing the property of which is transferred should be put into the power of him to whom it is transferred. The will of the proprieter, without transference, can signify only that he has a design of giving the property to the other; but unless the transferre has got the subject once into his power he can not be
2 said | to have got the property of it. As occupation, by which property is originally acquired, can not take place[s] unless the subject has been brought once at least into the power of the occupant, and becomes by that means seperated from the common[t] ones, so a thing that is the property of a certain person[u] can not become the property of another unless it be given into his power.

As the will of the proprieter and tradition are both absolutely requisite, so the effects are also different when they are seperate and when they are both conjoined. The declaration of the proprieters will conveys to the transferreé (if we may be allowed the expression) a personall action against the proprieter, by which he can demand and compell him to fulfill the engagement he has come under; but does by no means give him a real right to the thing of which the proprieter made the declaration; that right is
3 acquired only when tradition is joined to the declaration of the pro|prieter. (For we are to observe that tradition [without that tradition] without a declaration [without a declaration] of the will of the proprieter can constitute no right to the thing transferred.) If e.g. a man should sell one his horse and receive[v] the price, should even show him the horse in the stable, but did not deliver him into the power of the byer, if he should afterwards sell and deliver him to an other, the first purchaser would have an action

---

[s] The last two words replace 'be supposed'    [t] 'stock' deleted    [u] The last three words replace 'another'    [v] Replaces 'agree on'

against the seller for the price and what damages he might have sustain'd, but he could not claim the horse from the 2ᵈ byer, as he had never properly been in his possession. But if after the bargain was concluded the proprieter should deliver the horse into the power of the other, and if he should only touch the reins or any other way signify his having got him in his power, but should afterwards desire[w] the proprieter to keep him for some time, and the[x] seller should in that time sell him to another, the first

4 purchaser could then claim him as his (by a real action) from | any possessor. Grotius[71] disputes the constant necessity of tradition, affirming that there are some cases where the[y] bare will of the proprieter is sufficient to transfer the property. The instances he gives are, when the property of the mortgage is transferred to the mortgagee, of the pawn to him who has it pledged, of the depositum or trust to the trusteé. In all these cases, he says, the will of the[z] proprieter without any tradition transferrs the property. But let us consider for what purpose is it that tradition is required and what end it serves;[a] for no other cause than to give the transferree the power over the subject. Now in all these cases the subject is already deliverd into the power of the person to whom the property is transferred; the pawn broker is already in possession of the pledge, the trustee of the thing trusted, etc., so that in all these tradition is unnecessary, because it has already preceded the will of the proprieter to transferr the property. He quotes also a law of the Wisigoths, a barbarous nation who settled in the south-west of France,

5 which enacts that property should thereafter begin from the time of | the delivery of[b] {a contract or writ of livery, which when writing came to be in use was taken in place of a verbal declaration.} But we find the following part of the law, which he has not quoted, that the legislator, tho willing to begin property from the declaration of the proprieters will, yet he found this not easily reconciled to all the different circumstances. For in case that the transferree should die before the tradition was made, he determines after some hesitation that the property of the subject should remain with the proprieter and his heirs; whereas if the property had been transferred from the delivery of the writ the property must have belonged intirely to the transferree and his heirs, without any connection with the former proprieter. We are to take notice also that as the laws of these nations were regulated by the clergy, they were formed on the plan of the cannon law, that is, on the novelles of Justinian, to which the cannonists chiefly adhere;[c] both of which laws, as well the imperiall as the civill, endeavour to extend

6 the effect of contracts | and obligations of all sorts much farther ⟨than⟩ they

---

[w] Replaces 'deliver'    [x] 'pro' deleted    [y] 'is' deleted    [z] Illegible word deleted    [a] The last five words are entered vertically at the side of the page    [b] 'the subject' deleted    [c] 'and' deleted

---

[71] II.8.25, citing *Lex Visigothorum*, V.2.6.

naturally do, or would have done amongst a barbarous people left to their own disc⟨r⟩etion. {The ancient Roman law plainly affirms that property is transferred only usucapionibus and traditionibus.[72]} We can easily conceive in what manner the tradition of moveable subjects should be performed,[d] as a horse, a book, etc., as these subjects can easily be put into the power of the transferree. But it is not so easy to conceive how the larger subjects, as houses or land, should be transferred by tradition, as the other can not take possession of every part of these. The way in which this has always been performed is by a symbolicall tradition; as the[e] delivery of the keys of the house and the opening of the door give the possession to the transferree. In the same manner, the keys of a granary. In this country when a crop is sold, if it be standing the delivery of a single stalk, or if it be cut down of a single sheaf, is supposed to give possession of all the stalks or all the sheaves.

7 | In the same manner the tradition of a land estate is made by the delivery of a turf and a stone; and if it be to be held by esquirage, a staf⟨f⟩ and a shield. Bacculus et parma are delivered along with it.—{In England a land estate may be transferred with⟨out⟩ the transferree's being actually upon it, by its being only pointed out at a distance; but this does not serve for a delivery unless he afterwards take possession of it.—In England also it is necessary that when one alienates an estate the new acquirer should be infeft by him in every part, if it so happen that it should not be contiguous. But in Scotland the levery of one part serves to convey the property of the whole, whether the severall parts lie in the s[h]ame shire or not. For every one in the same manor (or baronny or lordship) is supposed to know what is doing in all the different parts of it, and in the same manner all in the same shire are supposed to know what is doing in it; and for this reason also there is but one registration required. — — —}

It is to be observed here that in the first times of the feudall government, when it was in its full vigour, no vassal whether of the king or of any lord could alienate his lands without the consent of his superior, either to hold of himself,[f] or to hold of his superior in the same manner as he did. For as they held by military tenure, it was not just that they should have it in their power to alter the persons who should be his servants. It was however pretty soon introduced that the vassals could give their lands to others to hold of them, tho they were prohibited from alienating the right they had to it.—In the same manner as the vassals were prohibited from alienating the right they had to the use and profit of the land, so the superior was prohibited from alienating the property he had in the land without the consent

8 | of the possessors, whether they held by the noble tenures of military

---

[d] 'but there is some difficulty in' deleted    [e] 'proper' deleted            'by what they' is written above the last three words

---

[72] 'By long possession and delivery': *C.* 2.3.20.

service or by the ignoble ones, as soccage, which was before explain'd.[73]
For if they were of the noble sort, it would not only be hard that the master
whom he should serve was to be at anothers disposal, but also it would often
happen that his master, having been at variance with any of his neighbours,
might make peace with his enemy, who dropt his resentment against the
master but perhaps retained it against the vassall, who by this means would
often have been ruined. If they held by the ignoble tenures the 1ˢᵗ argument
is equally strong, as they held their lands[g] for ever [as]; or even altho they
held but for their own life time, as was the case in the first beginnings of the
feudall government.—There were in this manner two properties conjoined
in the feudal governmen⟨t⟩, one of which was vested in the lord and consisted in certain casualities or services which he had a title to from the
9 vassall, | and the vassal had on the other hand the benefit of the land and its
fruits, in his own property; and (as is the case of all conjunct proprieters⟨⟩)
neither of them had the power of alienating their part without the consent
of the other. When the vassal designed to alienate his property, in any part
of his possessions, he must surrender it into the hands of the superior,[h74]
either in            75 or in favorem. In the first case the land returned into
the intire property of the proprietor, who was thereafter vested both in the
domin. directum et utile. In the other case it was resigned to the superiors
in favor of some third person who was to hold it in the same manner as the
present vassall did, and to whom the superior was desired to transfer it. In
this later case if the superior should not incline to transfer it to the person
specified, it returned to the vassall in the same manner as it was before,
notwithstanding of the surrendering. The consent of the superior was at
first altogether voluntary. The 1ˢᵗ case in which he was obliged to grant his
10 consent was[i] that the estate might be sur|rendered to creditors. After this
was enacted, it might easily be brought about at any time that the superior
should be obliged to grant his consent. For the vassal who had a mind to
alienate his estate had no more to do[j] after he had received the value of the
estate than to grant a bond to that extent to the bargainneé, to whom as a
creditor adjudger the superior was obliged to grant the lands.—On the
other hand the superior came in time to have the power of alienating his
part of the[k] estate without the contour            76 of the vassal. This was
gradually introduced after the fiefs came to be considered as property and

---

*g* The last three words replace 'are proprieters'      *h* 'who' deleted      *i* 'when'
deleted      *j* 'than' deleted      *k* The last four words replace 'the'

---

[73] i.144 above.
[74] In Scotland until the rule was abolished by 20 George II, c. 50 (1747).
[75] Blank in MS. *Ad perpetuam remanentiam*: Stair, II.11.1; M'Douall, III.2.2.8.
[76] Blank in MS. Contournement: English 'attornment', the acknowledgement by the
vassal of a change of superior and of his duty of fealty to the new superior. Cf. Dalrymple,
211.

the superiority only as a small burthen, and when the vassals were not intirely dependent on the protection of their superior but were protected in their part of the property by ⟨the⟩ law of the land, whatever master they were under. In this case their contour[77] of the vassall need not be looked on as so absolutely necessary. We may observe here also that in England the

11 consent | of the superior to the alienation of the vassals land was very soon dispensed with; and it was but of late that the contournement of the vassal was not thought requisite to the superior. On the other hand in Scotland the cont      [78] of the vassal has been thought unnecessary for 300 or 400 years, whereas it was not till the end of 16 or beginning of the 17th century that the method of alienation by the purchaser claiming to be infeft by the character of a creditor adjudger ⟨?⟩; and this is the form which is in some measure still kept up.

There was[l] a method of transferring property lately[m] in use in England wherein tradition was not necessary. It was thus introduced. In the feudal government, the landholders being often called out to war and obliged to leave their estate, they found it necessary in order to preserve their estates to transfer the use of it to some persons who should possess it till they came to claim it. When this was the condition of uses, the bargainer who sold an estate might begin[79] continue the use of the estate to the

12 | bargainee but could not be considered as possessing it for him. And if he should during the time of this use sell it to another person, the bargainee would have a personall action against him for the value of estate he had had and for damages, but would have no real action for it, a quocunque possessore. But when it was declared by the statute of Uses[80] that use continued possession, tradition was no longer necessary as it the[n] possession of the former proprietor, who came then to be considered after the sale as the bargainees servant or attorney, was the same as if he had possessed it himself, and when he took actuall possession of it it was not[o] considered as if he took possession of what had been an others till that time[p] but only as a continuation of his own.—The bargainer possessing it for him from the time of the sale.

There is also another method of transferring property now in common use in England where no tradition is requisite; viz. by lease and release.

[l] Replaces 'is'      [m] Replaces 'now'      [n] Reading doubtful      [o] 'as' and an illegible letter deleted      [p] The last thirteen words are entered at the side of the page, replacing a number of words which have been struck out in the main text. After 'considered as', the words 'being before that time the property of another' have been struck out. The words 'if he took possession', interlined between 'as' and 'being', have also been struck out.

---

[77] *Sic.* See last note.
[78] Blank in MS. See last note but one.
[79] 'begin' is interlined. Possibly 'begin and' was intended.
[80] 27 Henry VIII, c. 10 (1536).

13  That is, the bargainer gives the bargainee | a lease of the estate he designs to
alienate in his favours for a certain gratuity, reserving to himself certain
burthens and services; of these he releases by a subsequent deed, wherein
he declares that he shall be free from all the burthens or duties he had
reserved to himself in the preceding lease. From that time then the bar-
gainee becomes fully proprietor of the estate. This is the method generally
in use in England,[q] or rather a method where the method by sale and use is
joined with it. For it being often inconvenient that the bargainèe should
come and take possession of the estate betwixt the making of the lease and
the release, it is now customary that the proprietor shall be supposed to
possess it for him.

Having now gone thro all the 5 different methods of acquiring property,
I come to consider the 2$^d$ species of real rights, viz.

14                        | SERVITUDES.

Servitudes are burthens or claims that one man has on the property of
another. The Romans considered servitudes as being either real or personal;
i.e. as being due by a certain person or by a certain thing. They divided
them also into servitutes urbanorum praediorum and servitutes rust. praed.
The 1$^{st}$ are those that are due by one farm in the country to another, as
servitus aquae, etc. The other such as were due by one praedium in the
town to another. It is to be observed that all servitudes were originally
personall; and this will easily appear if we consider the manner in which
they have been introduced. Thus to take a common instance, we shall
suppose that the farm of one man lies betwixt the high way or the market
town and the farm of his neighbour. Here it will be very convenient if not
highly necessary that the possessor of the former farm should have the
liberty of a road thro the farm of his neighbour. This he may obtain for a
certain gratuity from the possessor; and take his obligation to grant[r] him
15  | that liberty in time to come. This[s] would be given him not as being such
a man but as being possessor of such a farm, and would be stipulated not
only for him but for his heirs and successors likewise. And if he should
afterwards sell or dispose of his farm he would account that liberty as a part
of his possessions, and demand some reasonable compensation for it from
the purchaser as well as for the farm itself.—But let us suppose that the
proprietor of the servient farm should dispose of his farm, and that he
should according to agreement with the owner of the dom. praed.[81] take
the purchaser bound to grant him the liberty stipulated; that the farm in
this manner passes thro three or four different hands; and that the 4$^{th}$

---

[q] 'being found more con' deleted        [r] Replaces 'permit'        [s] 'he' deleted

---

[81] *Dominans praedium*, 'the dominant land' for whose benefit the servitude exists.

possessor refuses to grant him the liberty stipulated.[t] In what manner shall he compel him to perform it. He is bound indeed to the third possessor,

16 but not to him, so that the dom. prae. dom.[82] can have no action | against him. He can only come at his right by raising an action against the first possessor, to make him perform the obligation he had come under. He again might compell the 2[d], and he the third, and he the 4th; or he might raise an action against the 1st to oblige him to cede to him the obligation the 2[d] had come under, and then the 2[d] the 3[d] and so on. To prevent such a multiplicity of actions, which would often be very troublesome, it came to be enacted by[u] actio servitia, and afterwards by the[v] actio quasi servit.,[83] first that some and afterwards that the greater part of servitudes should be consider⟨ed⟩ as real rights.

There were a great number of different servitudes amongst the Romans, both urbane and rustic.[84] Amongst the latter are jus itin. act. and via jus aquaehaust. and ad aquam appellendi, etc. 2[d], jus stillicidii, tigni injiciendi, oneris ferendi, etc.[85] Most of these besides many others are in use amongst us. { The life rent or 2[dly] the use of a house or other subject, as the opera servorum, may also be considered as servitudes as soon as it is lawfull, as it certainly may be, to sell a superiority with such a burthen.} It is to be

17 observed that all feudall hold|ings[w] may be considered as servitudes and in like manner were at first personal. The vassals at first held their lands by military and other such service during pleasure or for lives,[x] and were intirely dependent on the proprietor of the land. The property was vested in him and the other had only the use of the land for the time he pleased or for the number[y] ⟨?⟩. After the feudal government was introduced and the holdings came to be[z] hereditary the dominium directum was still in the hands of the superior; the vassal, for the smallest defect of service or trespass on the property of the superior or other land which he had not in his holding, was liable to be turned out and his lands forfeited to the superior. The lands could not be alienated to another without the consent of the superior and the performance of the same services on the part of the new vassall which the former one had payd him. In the same manner the heir could not enter to an inheritance unless he performed homage and

---

[t] 'and' deleted        [u] 'the' deleted        [v] Illegible word deleted        [w] 'were at first' interlined and deleted        [x] Reading doubtful        [y] Reading doubtful
[z] 'for' deleted

---

[82] *Dominantis praedii dominus*, 'the owner of the dominant land'.

[83] The *actio Serviana* and *actio quasi-Serviana* did not enforce servitudes, but enabled a creditor holding a hypothec over property to recover the property from third persons, so making hypothecs 'real rights'. Servitudes were enforced by *actio confessoria*.

[84] *Inst.* 2.3.

[85] 'Right of way on foot, driving cattle and with vehicles, right of drawing water and of driving cattle to water, etc. 2d, [urban servitudes] right of letting rain-water drip on to another's land, of inserting a beam in another's wall, of support for one's own wall, etc.'

18 swore fealty to his superior, and if the heir | happen'd to be a minor he could not enter to the inheritance, but the whole profits of the estate during his*a* minority fell to the superior, nor could he reasume the estate unless he payd the relief, which was at first arbitrary. From this it evidently appears that the property was lodged in the superior burthen'd with a servitude to the vassal which in effect was only personall, as the holding was so precarious.—But in progress of time (by a progress we shall explain more fully explain'd*b*⟨⟩) the vassal came to be more secure in his estate; the casualties due by the vassal were converted into a*c* setled*d* rent or escuage,[86] and the relief was fixt to a certain sum, which were all of very small value compared to the value of the estate. {Which they paid either to the king or to some one who held of him, for all in time held of him either mediately or immediately.} So that here which ever of them we consider as having the dom. dire. the vassal had the profit,*e* which was burthend only by a

19 small servitude due to the superior. In the same ⟨manner⟩ | as these above mentiond, all other valuable and necessary servitudes came to be reckoned real; those that are of less value being only for pleasure are now, and were amongst the Romans, considered only as personal. We shall by and by show that this conversion begun with a sort of servitudes which of all others should have*f* last, and inde⟨e⟩d ought never to have been a real one.

All burthens on property, as they can only have taken their rise from a contract, must have originally been personall, as was said, for a contract can produce nothing but a personall right. They became real only by the intervention of the law. This holds equally with regard to the 3ᵈ species of real rights, viz

### Pledges

That is, a subject*g* which is given or pledged to an other for the security of a debt due to him. Now if this subject was to be any way abstracted so that the pawnee had it not in his power to make his payment, from whom

20 could he claim | it? If he should claim it from any possessor he would*h* refuse to restore it; as he was not the proprietor so he could have no action against the possessor; the only way was for him to demand it from the pawner, who could as proprietor claim it *a quocumque possessore.* To prevent this troublesome circuit it was established that pledges should be esteemed to constitute a real right. The difference betwixt a pawn or pledge and a hypotheque is that in the former case [that in the former case] the thing from whence the security is given is put into the hands of the pawnee, and in the other case it is allowed to remain with the pawner. This distinction

---

*a* 'inheritance' deleted    *b* *Sic*    *c* 'sma' interlined and deleted    *d* Reading doubtful    *e* Replaces 'property'    *f* 'been' deleted, probably mistakenly    *g* 'from' deleted    *h* 'not' deleted

---

[86] Annual rent paid in lieu of knight-service. Cf. i.141 above.

may be as well considered as being a division of pledges into those of moveable and small subjects and of immoveable ones.[i] Moveables when pledged are generally put into the possession of the pawnee. Thus if one wants to borrow 5 guineas he gives the lender his watch which may be worth 10,[j] and tells him that if he does not pay it he may keep that watch.

21 | Now there is nothing in such an agreement which can properly be called unlawfull, for the parties can make any agreement they incline with regard to the disposal of their own property. If they made this agreement there can be no reason why they should not stand to it. It is a well known maxim that uti contrahentes verbis nuncupaverant ita jus esto.[87] The agreement of alienating[k] the subject may be considered as a wager that {they should pay against such a time, as[l] people in low[88] circumstances are very ready as they commonly expect that they will be able to perform more than what they find is the case.}

Now in these cases, before[m] the lex commissoria,[89] if the payment was not made at the time appointed, or if there was no time specified, in a certain time after the payment had been demanded the whole pawn fell to the pawnee, to the great loss of the pawner as these pawns would often be of much greater value than the debt and interest could amount to. But it being found that this was allmost always the case, as debtors are often inclined to please themselves when the creditors do not push them, and for this ⟨?reason⟩ are generally inclined to be slow in paying the debts, it was enacted as more equitable that if the debt was not payd at the time appointd

22 or in a certain | time after it was demanded, [that] the pawn should not from that day be the pawnees but that he should be allowed to sell it at a reasonable price, and take payment of principall and interest and the costs of his suit, {the rest being restored to the pawner or his heirs.} This is the case too in Scotland; but in England the pawn brokers as they are called, but more properly the pawn-takers, as they do not deal in broking, if the pledge be not redeemed, which is often not easily done, as they take a most extravangt interest, at the day appointed or before the death of the pawner, take the whole subject pawned. So that neither the persons themselves nor

---

[i] A line reading as follows is here deleted: 'In the 1ˢᵗ case ['was' interlined] by the old Roman law'      [j] Reading doubtful      [k] Reading doubtful      [l] Reading doubtful      [m] Replaces 'by'

---

[87] 'As the contracting parties have declared in words, so let it be in law', based on Twelve Tables, VI.1: *'uti lingua nuncupassit, ita jus esto.'*

[88] Above the last three words there is written the word 'agreement', followed by what appear to be a bracket and the usual contraction for 'which'. Possibly the words after 'such a time' were intended to read something like 'an agreement which people in low circumstances are very ready to enter into, as they commonly', etc.

[89] The forfeiture clause, allowing the pledge to vest absolutely in the pawnee if the debt were not repaid on time. It was prohibited by Constantine; the text should read 'before the *lex commissoria* was prohibited'.

their heirs have any claim against him. For as the persons who enter into
such agreements, who would pawn their cloaths, etc., are not inclined that
their transactions should be known, there[90] is commonly known, as it is an
evident sign of their poverty and low circumstances ⟨?⟩. The licensce of
pawn brokers is therefore, as shall be shewn hereafter, one of the greatest
23 nuisances in the English constitution, especially | in great cities. With
regard to immoveable pledges the constitutions in Rome[n] and Scotland
are the same as with regard to moveables. An heritable bond on an estate
does not commonly bear any time at which payment shall be made, but
only that it shall be paid when demanded. Therefore in a certain time after
the demand the creditor may sell the estate, having it adjudged to him for
the principall and interest and a 5th part of what was due at the time of
demand as costs and damages. In England on the other hand if the debt was
not pay'd at the time when it was demanded, the lands or other immoveables fall immediately to the mortgager; but by the statute law all lands[o] are
redeemable for forty years, and then prescribe. But the Chancellor declared
that in this case he will allow the pawner to redeem them for twenty
years,[91] counted from the time the debt was demanded. Besides these that
are constituted by agreement there were amongst the Romans a great many
24 tacit hypotheques, | many of which are received amongst us. But all of these
have no other effect than to constitute a preferable claim to the person who
has such a hypotheque. Thus one who lets a house has no other security for
his rent than the furniture and goods of the tenent, from whic⟨h⟩ he can
take his payment preferably to any other creditor. Anciently in this country
he would have had an preferable[p] action not only againstt those goods which
were in his own hands but preferable to all others. After the cultivation of
lands by villains or slaves was not used, the most common sort ⟨of⟩ farms
were those which held by what is called steel-bow, and in French        [92].
The method was that the landlord when he set the land at the same time
gave him a plough of oxen, 5 or 6 yoke, which he was obliged to return[q] as
many and of equal value according to the judgement of some honest man.
At the end of every harvest the lord and the tenent divided the crop equally
25 | sheaf by sheaf. In this case the lord had equall property in all his goods
and crops,[r] and if he alienated any part of it without his consent, and before
he had got his payment, he could claim it as his own from any possessor.
This method of letting land, which as shall be shown hereafter is one of the
worst that have ever been in use, is now laid aside in most parts of this
country, unless some of the remoter parts, but is that which is practised

[n] Replaces 'England'        [o] The last two words replace 'they'        [p] Replaces 'exclusive'        [q] Illegible word apparently deleted        [r] Reading doubtful

[90] Reading doubtful. Possibly 'that' was intended.
[91] M. Bacon, *New Abridgement of the Law*, s.v. Mortgage, III.654.
[92] Blank in MS. Probably '*métayage*' was intended.

over more than 5/6 of France. But even after that[s] method of[t] letting land came to be laid aside, the landlord was still considered as having a property in the goods so that he could claim them if sold without his consent. This however has not long ago been restricted by a decree of the Court of Session, continued by Act of Parliament;[93] so that now the land⟨l⟩ord has only a preferable debt to all other debtors, but can not [but can not] claim the goods if alienated without his consent, especially if the purchaser be

26 bona fide, that is, had no intention | by his bargain to defraud the landlord of his rent and had entered into no such scheme with the tenant.[94] (The Romans had also many other tacit hypothecs, which are not admitted by our law. Thus if one borrow'd money with which he built a ship or a house, as there was something in this house or ship which was purchased by his money, so he was supposed to have a preferable claim[u] to that of all other debtors. But this is not now admitted.) (The lands in Italy were in the same manner cultivated either by servi, slaves which were the property of the landlord, or by coloni, which were in much the same condition as the holders by steel bow or                    [95]; and the landlord had a joint property with the colonus and consequently could ⟨?claim⟩ the goods alienated before payment without his consent.⟨⟩⟩

We come now the 4th real right, viz — — —

27                              | Exclusive Priviledges.

The four real rights treated of in the civil law are the three we have already mentioned, Property, Servitude, Pledge, and fourthly, Haereditas, or Inheritance.

It is plain that this can not be considered as a different species of real right after the heir has entered to the inheritance, for then he has the same right that the defunct had and is considered as the same person, having full property in every respect. It can be in no other case than during the time[v] betwixt the death of the last proprietor and the entrance of the heir that the inheritance can be considered as giving a new species of a real right. Now what right is it that the heir has before his entrance? No other but that of excluding all others from the possession untill he determine in whether he

---

[s] 'right' deleted        [t] 'giv' deleted        [u] Numbers written above the last two words indicate that their order was intended to be reversed        [v] 'of' deleted

---

[93] 1469, c. 37 (A.P.S. II.96, c. 12); Kames, *Law Tracts*, I. 233.

[94] In between the lines at this point there is inserted a sentence which appears to be 'Read the next parenthe. before this'. If this reading of the interlineation is correct, it presumably means that the bracketed passage beginning 'The lands in Italy', which occurs lower down on 26, should properly come before the bracketed passage which immediately follows 'with the tenent'. This interpretation is supported by the fact that the number '2' appears in the margin opposite the beginning of the latter bracketed passage, and the number '1' opposite the beginning of the former.

[95] Blank in MS. Probably '*métayage*' was once again intended.

will enter heir or not. Before this determination the other heirs who follow
28 after him can not have any claim for the | inheritance, but after his refusall
the subsequent heir has the same right as he had. If therefore inheritance
is to be considered as a real right, all other exclusive priviledges have the
same title, and appear evidently as well as it to be real rights. Some of them
are founded on[w] natural reason, and others are intirely the creatures of the
civil consti⟨tu⟩tions of states. This of inheritance is evidently founded on
natural reason and equity. There are however some others that owe their
origin to it. Thus if one who has a right to hunt starts a deer, and when he is
in pursuit another comes in and takes this deer before he [he] has given
over hopes of catching him, this 2ᵈ person appears evidently to have acted
contrary to good manners and may accordingly be punished by the forest
laws. It can not however be accounted a breach of property, as that can not
29 begin till the beast is actually brought into | the possession of the pursuer.[96]
If after that time he should take away the beast this would be considered as
a theft or a robbery.—The trespass here is plainly against the exclusive
priviledge the hunter has to the chase or pursuit of the beast he has
started.—[x] In the year 1701 an English man[ner] of war came up⟨on⟩ some
French merchantmen under convoy of a man of war, and when he was
engaging the war ship a Scots privateer came and pi⟨t⟩ched up⟨o⟩n the
merchantmen. The captain of the man of war sued the privateer before the
Scots Privy Council which then subsisted; he represented that without he
had engaged the war-ship the privateer could never have taken the mer.
men, and that if he had not come up they would inevitably have fallen into
his hands. He therefore demanded they should be restored. The Privy
30 Council agreed | and adjudged the privateer to restore them, specifying
that he had been guilty of a breach of property.[97] But if they had spoke
properly they would have said that he had been guilty of a breach of an
exclusive priviledge. For if he had broke property he would have been
sued not for restitution but have been tried as a pirate, yet ⟨?that⟩ was not
the case. The breach was of the exclusive priviledge one has to pursue and
take the ships he spies[y] and[z] chases. Had the ships been in tow of the man of
war and he cut them off in the night, this would have been piracy and a
breach of property.

The greatest part however of exclusive priviledges are the creatures of
the civil constitutions of the country. The greatest part of these are greatly

[w] 'the' deleted     [x] 'In the same manner we shall find' deleted     [y] Reading
doubtful     [z] Illegible word deleted

[96] Cf. i.38–44 above.
[97] *King's Advocate* v. *Rankine* (1677), M. 11930, of which there is an account in Stair,
II.1.33. Cf. Sir George Mackenzie's argument on the case: *num navis acquiratur iure civili
per prosecutionem sine actuali apprehensione* (*Works*, I (1716), 115).

prejudicial to society. Some indeed are harmless enough. Thus the in-
31 ventor of a new machine or | any other invention has the exclusive privi-
ledge of making and vending that invention for the space of 14 years by
the law of this country,[98] as a reward for his ingenuity, and it is probable
that this is as equall an one as could be fallen upon. For if the legislature
should appoint[a] pecuniary rewards for the inventors of new machines, etc.,
they would hardly ever be so precisely proportiond to the merit of the
invention as this is.[b] For here, if the invention be good and such as is
profitable to mankind, he will probably make a fortune by it; but if it be
of no value he also will reap no benefit. In the same manner the author of
a new book has an exclusive priviledge of[c] publishing and selling his book
for 14 years.[98a] Some inde⟨e⟩d contend that the book is an intire new pro-
32 duction of the authors and therefore ought in justice | to belong to him and
his heirs for ever, and that[d] no one should be allowed to print or sell it but
those to whom he has given leave, by the very laws of naturall reason. But
it is evident that printing is no more than a speedy way of writing. Now
suppose that a man had wrote a book and had lent it to another who took a
copy of it, and that he afterwards sold this copy to a third; would there be
here any reason to think the writer was injured. I can see none, and the
same must hold equally with regard to printing. The only benefit one
would have by writing a book, from the natural laws of reason, would be
that he would have the first of the market and may be thereby a considerable gainer. The law has however granted him an exclusive priviledge for
14 years, as an encouragement to the labours of learned men. And this is
33 perhaps as well adapted to the real value | of the work as any other, for if
the book be a valuable one the demand for it in that time will probably be a
considerable addition to his fortune. But if it is of no value the advantage he
can reap from it will be very small.—These two priviledges therefore, as
they can do no harm and may do some good, are not to be altogether
condemned. But there are few so harmless. All monopolies in particular
are extremely detrimental.—The wealth of ⟨?a⟩ state consists in the
cheapness of provisions and all other necessaries and conveniencies of life;
that is, the small proportion they bear to the money payd, considering ⟨the⟩
quantity of money which is in the state; or in other words that they should
be easily come at. Its poverty again consists in the uncomeatibleness or
difficulty with which the severall necessarys of life are procured. Now all
monopolies evidently tend to[e] promote the poverty or, which comes to the
34 same thing, | the uncomeatibleness of the thing so monopolized. Thus for

[a] Reading doubtful        [b] At the side of the page near this point is written 'Granted
him by patent'        [c] 'making' deleted        [d] Reading of last two words doubtful
[e] Illegible word deleted

[98] Statute of Monopolies, 21 James I, c. 3 (1623).
[98a] 8 Anne, c. 19 (1709).

example if one should get an exclusive priviledge of making and selling all the silk in the kingdom, he would as he had it at his own making greatly increase the price; he would perhaps lessen the quantity made to a tenth part of that now in use; and would raise the price nearly in proportion; and by this means he would make great profit at a less expense of materialls and labour than can be done when many have the same liberty. The price of the commodity is by this means raised, and the quantity of this necessary, ornament, or conveniency of life is at the same time lessend, so that it becomes doubly more uncomeatible than it was before. The same bad consequences follow from all other monopolies. The establishment of corporations and other societies who have an exclusive right is equally

35 detrimental. The severall corporations in towns | have all an exclusive priviledge of exercising that trade within the liberties of the town, {no one being allowed to take up a business but who has served an apprenticeship in the town; formerly no one but whose father had been a burgher.} Now, e.g., the corporation of butchers have the sole liberty of killing and selling all the flesh that is brought to market. Here the priviledge is not vested in the person of one man, but as the number is fixt they will readily enter into compacts to keep$^f$ up the price of the commodity and at the same time supply the market but very indifferently with flesh.—In the same manner the bakers, the brewers, the tanners, etc. have all the exclusive priviledge of exercising the severall trades.—Now$^g$ these priviledges must be of a great hurt to the community is very evident, as it makes all sorts of necessarys so much the more uncomeatible. {Besides this the goods themselves are worse; as they know none can undersell them so they keep up the price, and as they know also that no other can sell so they care not what the quality be.} This has never been doubted. But that they are hurtfull to the corporations is not so generally acknowledged. But it is no less true. If there was but one corporation in a place, the profits of that society would

36 be immense as they would be in a state the most profitable of any,$^h$ | that of bying cheap and selling dear. But as there are always a great number of such corporations where there is one, the priviledge comes to be of no value. They sell their$^i$ commodity dear, but then they bye every thing else dear also. He hinders indeed this concourse to the market of those who trade in his goods, but at the same time the others hinder the concourse which would be if the trade was free of all other traders; in which the price of every thing would be at the proper and naturall standard, for if one was not inclined to sell at a low price another would. Besides by these corporations the number of inhabitants is greatly diminished; and any who would settle in the city are hindered from so doing. By this means there are generally two or three large villages in the neighbourhood of every city. If a corporation lessens

---

$^f$ Reading doubtful    $^g$ 'that' deleted, probably mistakenly    $^h$ Reading of last
two words doubtful    $^i$ Reading of last three words doubtful

37  the number of rivalls, it also lessens the number of | customers. These shall
be more fully treated of hereafter.

I have now considered the severall real rights, not only property but
also servitudes and pledges, and shown that these were originally merely
personall rights, tho by the determination of the legislature, to prevent the
confusion this was found to produce, they were afterwards changed into
real rights. I have also endeavoured to shew that the severall feudall
duties were all properly speaking servitudes, and make by far the greatest
and most important parts of the servitudes in use in this country. That
which is commonly distinguished however by the name of servitude, is
indeed no servitude; it is[j] the obligation that the possessors of some estates
are under to grind their corn at a certain milne and no other. This they call
being thirrle to the milne, and this burthen is generally called by the
lawyers[99] the servitude of thirrleage. But it is very evident that this is no
38  servitude, but only an | exclusive priviledge. For that the severall estates in
the neighbourhood should be obliged to grind at a certain milne can not be
at all answerable to a servitude, which always implies that there is jus in re
aliena constitutum. It is an exclusive priviledge of grinding all the corn
that shall grow on a certain tract of ground. This is a priviledge that
extends over all most all the low parts of Scotland; there is hardly any estate
but what is thirlle to some milne. This in the present state of things is one
of the old constitutions which had much better been removed; and of this
sort there are many. But notwithstanding of this, it may have been very
convenient in the first constitution or settlement of milnes. A wind or a
water milne dispatches the work much easier and in less time than it could be
performed by the hands of men. When therefore some persons set up these
machines for the service of the neighbourhood, it was necessary that they
should some way ⟨?be⟩ secured in a reasonable profit; and for this end the
neighbours for a greater or less distance bound themselves and their heirs to
39  give their work | to that person; and by this means secured him in a tollerable
subsistence. But such constitutions at this day are not only altogether
useless but very detrimentall, as they discourage industry and improvement
of the arts. It is in many places a very considerable grievance and a great
burthen on the persons who are under it. And from this it probably has
been that the lawyers called it a servitude, meaning that it was a burthen.

In the same manner[k] the exclusive privileges of corporation which, as I
endeavoured to shew, are now detrimentall to the community, but ⟨?to⟩ the
individualls of each corporation may have at first been very convenient and
all most necessary. When a set of men agree'd to live together in a community, it was necessary that they should have the power of defending

---

[j] Reading of last two words doubtful      [k] 'although' deleted

[99] e.g. Mackenzie, *Institutions of the Law of Scotland*, II.9.

themselves against the incroachments of their neighbours, (that is) that they should have a jurisdiction of a certain extent, which we find ac-
40 cordingly that all cities have. | By this means a provision was made for their[l] safety, but it was also necessary to provide for their safety in prosperity. It is[m] found that society must be pretty far advanced before the different trades can all find subsistence, that is, before those trades which do not immediately procure food of some sort, as bread, flesh, etc., or even most of these, can be depended on for a subsistence. A carpenter or a weaver could not trust intirely to his work in that way; he would only take in this trade as a subsidiary one. And to this day in the remote and deserted parts of the country, a weaver or a smith, besides the exercise of his trade, cultivates a small farm and in that manner exercises two trades, that of a farmer and that of a weaver. To bring about[n] therefore the separation of trades sooner than the progress of society would naturally effect, and prevent[o] the uncertainty of all those who had taken themselves to one trade, it was found
41 necessary to give them a certainty of a comfortable subsistence.— | And for this purpose the legislature[p] determined that they should have the priviledge of exercising their seperate trades without the fear of being cut out of their livelyhood by the increase of their rivalls. That this was necessary therefore in the 1st stages of the arts to bring them to their proper perfection, appears very reasonable and is confirmed by this, that it has been the generall practise of all the nations in Europe. But as this end is now fully answered, it were much to ⟨be⟩ wished that these as well as many other[q] remains of the old jurisprudence should be removed.

---

Having now finished all I shall advance at present with regard to real rights, I proceed to consider:—

### PERSONAL RIGHTS

That is, the right one has to demand the performance of some sort of service from an other. The former or real rights are by the civillians called jura in re. These are called jura ad rem; or jura personalia; and are
42 | defined to be facultas vel jus competens in personam quo aliquid facere vel dare teneatur.[1] It is evident from this that all personall rights must take their origin from some obligation. Now obligations are of three sorts. They proceed either 1st, from contract; or 2dly, from what the civilians call quasi contract, that is, the obligation one is under[r] restore to the owner whatever of his property has come into his possession either voluntarily or otherwise; or 3dly, from some injury (or delict) he has done what is his.

---

[l] Illegible word or words deleted    [m] 'the earlier times' deleted    [n] The last two words replace 'prevent'    [o] Replaces 'stop'    [p] 'found' deleted    [q] 'parts' deleted    [r] 'to perform' deleted

---

[1] 'A power or right available against a person by which he is bound to do or give something'.

We shall first consider the obligations which arise from contract or agreement; and before we consider them, it will be proper to consider[s] what it is in[t] a contract which produces an obligation to perform the thing contracted.[2] Now it appears evident that a bare declaration of will to do such or such a thing can not produce an obligation. It means no more than that ⟨?it⟩ is the present design of the person who makes such a | declaration to do so and so; and all that is required of him to make such a declaration lawfull is sincerity, that is, that it be really his intention at that time to do as he said. If he should afterwards be induced by circumstances to alter his intention, we could not say that he had violated an obligation; we might indeed[u] if he did so on slight grounds accuse him of levity, and being easily turned and altered in his designs. The only thing that can make an obligation in this manner is an open and plain declaration that he desires the person to whom he makes the declaration to have a dependance on what he promises. The[v] words in which we commonly make such a declaration ⟨?are⟩ I promise to do so and so, you may depend upon it. The[w] expectation and dependance of the promittee that he shall obtain what was promised is hear altogether reasonable, and such as an impartial spectator would readily go along with, whereas in the former case the spectator could ⟨?not⟩ go along with him if he formed any great expectation. | If I should say that I intend to give you voluntarily £100 next new years day, but make this declaration in such a manner as plainly shews I don't intend you should depend upon it, and expressly say, 'You need not depend upon it, but this is my present design', the spectator could not here imagine that he to whom I made the promise would have any reasonable expectation; but this without doubt he would, if I should plainly declare that I meant that he should depend upon it.—We are to observe here that the injury done by the breach of a contract is the slightest possible; at least the slightest one can well account to require any satisfaction. It is a common saying, that he who does not pay me what he owes me, does me as great an injury as he who takes as much from me by theft or robbery. It is very true the loss is as great, but we do not naturally ⟨look⟩ upon the injury as at all so heinous. One never has so great dependence on what is at the mercy or depends on the good faith | of another as what depends only on his own skill. The spectator can not think he has so good a ground for expectation of the possessing it. We accordingly find that in the early periods of every society those crimes were punish'd much more severely; in those times no punishment was inflicted but on the more heinous crimes, such as murther, robbery, and

---

[s] 'in' deleted     [t] The last three words replace 'way'     [u] 'say' deleted
[v] 'generall' and an illegible word interlined above it both deleted
[w] 'reasonable' deleted

---

[2] Cf. Hutcheson, *M.P.*, II.9; *System*, II.1 ff.; Hume, *Treatise of Human Nature*, III.ii.5; Kames, *Essays on the Principles of Morality and Natural Religion* (1751), I.ii.7.

theft and other such which were breaches of the peace and disturbed the order of society. All trials in early times were carried on by the whole people assembled together; and this was not so much to inflict a punishment as to bring about a reconciliation and some recompense for the damage[x] the injured party may have sustained. Even in case of murther the chief business was to procure some concessions from the murtherer in order to attone for the injury done the friends of the deceased, and on the other part to mitigate the resentment of the friends of the murthered

46 person. When all trials | were thus carried on by the assembly of the whole people, which must have been attended with many inconveniences in calling the people from their necessary employments, none but the most important causes would[y] be brought into judgement. The injury arising from the breach of contract would not be thought of consequence enough to put the whole people to the trouble which trials then necessarily occasioned. Besides this there are[z] several reasons which greatly retard the validity of contracts, as[a] the uncertainty of language. Language at all times must be somewhat ambiguous, and it would be more so in the state of society we are talking ⟨?about⟩. This must render it very difficult to conclude with exactness the intention of the contracting parties, and determine whether it was their inclination to produce a reasonable expectation or only to signify a design which they had at that time of acting in such a

47 manner. | 2$^{dly}$, the small value of the subjects which in an early period would be the objects of contract, would make it not of great consequence whether they were binding or not; and 3$^{dly}$, the small number of occasions in which they would be requisite.—We find accordingly that in the first periods of society, and even till it had made some considerable advances, contracts were noways binding.		[3] of Damascus, an author quoted by Stobaeus (where we have many passages from him very useful with regard to the state of society in the first periods of it) tells us that among some nations in the East Indies no contract was binding, not even that of restoring a depositum, that in which the obligation seems to be strongest as the injury in the breach of it is most glaring; {and they gave as th⟨e⟩ reason, that by so doing they avoided a multitude of lawsuits which would[b] the validity of contracts follow immediately.[c]} Aristotle[4] tells us also that even as far down as his time, there were severall states in Greece where the validity of contracts was not acknowledged, and that both[d] to prevent the

---

[x] Replaces 'injury'		[y] Reading of last two words doubtful		[z] Illegible word deleted		[a] Several illegible words deleted		[b] Illegible word deleted		[c] Numbers written above the last six words indicate that they were intended to read 'immediately follow the validity of contracts'		[d] 'because' deleted

---

[3] Blank in MS. Nicolaos of Damascus, cited by Stobaeus 2, 160 (ed. Hense) (Jacoby, *Die Fragmente der griechischen Historiker*, 2A.386).

[4] *Nicomachean Ethics*, 1164$^{b}$13-15.

48 multitude of judicial proceedings, and also because, said | they, one who enters into a contract trusts to the fidelity of the person and is supposed to have trust in him. He has himself to blame therefore if he is deceived, and not the law which {does not give him redress.} We see also from our old book the Regiam Majestatem, and from Glannmores book[5] which was wrote in the time of Henry 2ᵈ, that contracts were just beginning to be regarded at that time, both in Scotland ⟨?and in England⟩. The Kings Court was then established and took notice of some of the most necessary ones. The author of the Reg. Maj. however tells us that, in matters of so small importance as contracts are, the Kings Court seldom interests itself.[6]

If we consider now the reasons why contracts were not binding, we will discover also the causes which gradually introduced their validity. The 1ˢᵗ thing I mentioned which obstructed their being allowed to be binding was the uncertainty of language; when therefore this was removd the objection could no longer have any effect. We find accordingly that the first contracts which were binding were[e] {those wherein the intention of the con-

49 tracter was plain and uncontroverted; that is, such} as were con|ceived in a certain set form of words which it was agreed expressed the design of the contracter that the other should depend on the performance of what was contracted. {That it was this reasonable expectation of the contracter to whom the promise was made which constituted the obligation appears pretty plainly from this, that for some time after these contracts were reckoned binding the breakers of them were not made liable to perform the thing contracted, but only to pay the damages he might have sustained by the dissapointment of his expectations.} These were called verborum obligationes or verbal contracts.[7] They were performed by a set form of words, called stipulationes; on both sides, the question was solemnly asked and solemnly agreed to. Thus in the settling of a dower, Annon manus causeos spondes mihi cum tua filia nomine dotis: Spondeo: Et ego accipio.—In Scotland at this time all contracts of whatever sort are equally binding; a bare promise produces an obligation at law.—This proceeded from the ecclesiasticall law. They at first introduced the custom that contracts of the sort above mentioned should be binding;[f] not only obliging them to perform the engagements but also enjoining them ecclesiasticall pennances; and even threatening them with excommuni-

50 cation, which at that time was a very | terrible punishment as it not only

*e* 'such' deleted       *f* 'denouncing' deleted

---

[5] Glanvill, *Tractatus de Legibus et Consuetudinibus Regni Angliae*, on which the Scottish *Regiam Majestatem* is largely based.

[6] *Regiam*, III.4 and III.14 (Skene's numbering) from Glanvill, op. cit., X.8 and X.18.

[7] *Inst.* 3.15: *stipulatio*, a unilateral contract formed by the promisor's unqualified acceptance of the promisee's proposition, indicated by the use of the same word, such as *spondere*, in question and answer. The text of the example which follows is corrupt.

banished them from all Christian society but also forfeited their estate to the crown. These constitutions soon rendered the contracts effectuall; and to these the ecclesiasticks soon added all contracts whatsoever. In the same manner as all other constitutions introduced by the clergy so the judgement of all matters regarding contracts was by the people, who payd them a very great veneration, devolved back upon them. This veneration however was not a blind superstitious one as we are now apt$^g$ to imagine, but a very rational one. The clergy were at that time the chief support of the peoples rights. The civill law of the country was at that time very imperfect, and the cannon or ecclesiasticall law, tho far from perfect, was much preferable to the other; and it was by this the clergy were directed. Their judgements would therefore be most equitable. The whole right of testamentary
51 succession | proceeded from them, as well as the obligation of contracts. They were ⟨the⟩ only obstacle that stood in the way of the nobles; the only thing which made them keep some tollerable decency and moderation to their inferiors. The people saw this; they saw that if that body of men were oppressed, they would be oppressed at the same time. They were therefore as jealous of their liberties as of their own, and with reason paid them a very high degree of veneration. Thus an ecclesiasticall court, which in a country where the regulations of the civill government are arrivd to a considerable perfection is one of the greatest nuisances imaginable, may be of very great benefit in a state where the civil government is baddly regulated; just in the same way as corporations may be very advantageous in a low state of the arts tho of the greatest detriment when they are carried to a considerable length.[8]
52     | After these verball obligations the next that were introduced were what are called real obligations.[9] We are to observe here that the word realis has very different significations when applied in different ways. Thus a real right is a right to a certain thing in whatever condition. A real servitude, servitus realis, is not a$^h$ servitude upon a certain thing, for all servitudes are due in that manner, but a servitude which is due to a person not as being such an one but as being the owner of such a farm; it is said to be due to such a thing. Here again a real contract is not one which gives an action for a certain thing, but one in which there has some thing been actually done. {As an other hindrance of the validity of contracts was the small value of the subjects into which they could enter, so when$^i$ property came to be very valuable they were$^j$ of too great impo⟨r⟩tance to be overlooked, as$^k$ contracts might then extend to a very great value.} These were very soon made

---

$^g$ Numbers written above the last two words indicate that their order was intended to be reversed        $^h$ The last two words replace 'a right to a'        $^i$ 'the' deleted        $^j$ The last two words replace 'and'        $^k$ Reading doubtful

---

[8] Cf. 39–40 above.                                        [9] *Inst.* 3.14.

binding, as otherwise when a part of the contract was fu⟨l⟩filled on one
side, if the other did not fulfill his part the loss would have been too con-
53 siderable. Of this sort were mutuum, a loan, | dipositum, pignus, etc.
These when[l] one part of the contract was performed became binding for
the rest. But if there had been no part[m] performed the verball agreement
was not considered.

The extension of commerce also added several contracts to those already
binding. In the first stages of commerce, when it was confined to those at
no great distance and amongst them was not very extensive, all sort of
commodities were purchased by immediate exchanges. One man gave an
other money and got wine, or gave one corn and had ⟨a⟩ horse in exchange,
in the same manner as trade is carried on at this day amongst the negroes on
the coast of Guinea. At this time no contract could be made but amongst
those who actually[n] uttered the words[o] by which the contract was compre-
54 hended. An oath can only be taken from | one who actually delivers it
from his own mouth. A written and signed oath is of no effect. Writing is
no naturall expression of our thoughts (which language is,[p]) and therefore
is more dubious and not so setled in the meaning. Oaths we may observe
are most in use amongst barbarous and uncivilized nations; as they are
there thought necessary to signify plainly the will of the person; as the
language is not fixt in its meaning; and in the state of the greatest barbarity,
an oath is thought necessary to confirm every thing that is deliverd.
Contracts (as I said) at first could be only made[q] betwixt parties who were
present; *contrahitur tantum inter praesentes non autem inter absentes.*[10]—
But when commerce was more extended, it was found necessary to extend
55 the power of making contracts. A merchant[11] | at Rome wanted to bye corn
of one at Alexandria, but this by the old constitutions he could not do
unless he had been present and delivered the money. But that trade might
go on the more easily, it came to be in use that all the more necessary
contracts were considered as binding, and that whether inter praesentes or
absentes. In this manner emptio venditio, locatio conductio, societas, and
mandatum were all considered as binding obligations. That is, a contract
of sale; one where a thing is hired for a summ of money; societas, a
contract of copartnership; and mandatum, whereby one give⟨s⟩ another a

[l] 'the' deleted        [m] 'binding' deleted        [n] 'delivered' deleted        [o] Illegible
word deleted        [p] 'and' deleted        [q] Illegible word deleted

---

[10] 'Contracts are made only between those present, not between those absent.' Formal
contracts required the presence of both parties (*Inst.* 3.19.12); consensual contracts were
based on formless agreement (*Inst.* 3.22) and so could be made by parties not present
together.

[11] At the foot of the opposite page—i.e. the verso of (recto) 53 of the MS.—the words
'punishment as it no' are written upside down. This was evidently a false start, which the
student apparently rectified in the same way as he had rectified a similar false start in vol.
i (see above, pp. 13–14 of this edition)—i.e. by turning the whole gathering upside down and
starting again. The relevant (corrected) passage begins on 50 of the MS.

commission to do so and so in his name. These as being most necessary to commerce were alltogether binding; others of less importance were never 56 made binding by the Roman law, they saying that | when those which were necessary were so, there was no great matter with regard to the others. And indeed these would be very extensive. Thus loc. conductio might include the settling a factor, etc., and so of others. These were called nominati contractus, as they had a particular name by being frequently in use; and the others which were not so much in use and had no particular name, innominati. — — —

### *Friday. January 21ˢᵗ 1763.*

In my last lecture I endeavoured to shew in what manner the obligation of contracts arises; that it arose intirely from the expectation and dependance which was excited in him to whom the contract was made. I shewed also that declaration of the will or intention of a person could not produce any obligation in the declarer, as it did not give the promittée a reasonable ground of expectation. It is the dissapointment of the person we promise to 57 which occasions | the obligation to perform it. What we have solemnly promised[r] to perform begets a greater dependance in the person we promise to than a bare declaration of our intention. But the dissapointment occasion'd by the breach of a promise depends on two causes; not only on the solemnity and certainty with which the promise is made, but also upon the importance of the thing promised. The dissapointment occasioned by the breach of a promise of little value is not so great as when it is a matter of more importance. If one promised to drink tea with me tonight and did not fullfill the engagement, I would not be so much dissapointed as if he[s] paid me a summ of money he owed me.[12] We see accordingly that all sensible men have measured the obligation one is under to perform a promise by the dissappointment the breach of it would occasion. Thus if I promised to drink tea or walk at the cross with one, and, something intervening, could not conveniently do it; tho' I had made this promise in pretty solemn 58 terms yet the matter itself is of so small importance that the dissa|pointment can not be great. If I did not fulfill it[t] I might very reasonably be thought to have acted amiss and in an ungentlemany manner; and might perhaps be thought to have put a slight affront on the person, but not such[u] an injury as would merit a very high resentment, or give a sufficient cause for a suit at law.

[r] Replaces 'declared our intention'          [s] Reading of last three words doubtful
[t] Replaces 'them'          [u] 'a dissapoin' deleted

---

[12] *Sic.* Possibly something like 'as if he promised to pay me a sum of money he owed me' was intended.

On the other hand if I had come under an engagement to pay a summ of money, as a debt, this may be of such importance to the person as may[v] if not performed dissapoint and perplex him considerably. All such contracts are therefore thought binding by every one; whereas trifling engagements, though they ought in good manners and fair gentlemany behaviour to be performd, yet the injury occasioned by the breach ot them, nor the crime of the breaker, are never looked on as so heinous.

We may observe here that the obligation to perform a promise can not proceed from the will of the person to be obliged, as some authors[13] imagine. For if that were the case a promise which one made without an intention to perform it would never be binding. If I promised to pay you £10 tomorrow, but had no intention of performing, this promise according to the doctrine abovementioned would be noways binding, as the promisor did not will that he should be under any obligation. But such promises are and have universally been acknowledged to be as binding as any others, and the reason is plain: they produce the same degree of dependance and the breach of them the same dissapointment as the others.—Nor can the obligation to fullfill a contract be probably derived from the obligation to veracity which most writers[14] on the law of nature and nations assign as the cause of this obligation; nor the crime of a breach of a promise from that of the breach of veracity. For all that veracity can extend to is either what is past or what is present. If one tells what he realy thinks to be true with regard to the past and the present state of things, this is all that the man of the greatest veracity can require of him; with regard to what is future veracity can have no effect, as knowledge does not extend to it.—Besides, it can never happen that a less crime should be | of a greater.[15] Now it is evident that the breach of a contract or promise is a much greater crime than that of the breach of veracity. If we see one whom we know makes a common custom of telling lies and making up wonderfull and amazing adventures to entertain the company with, we may justly look on this as a very low and despicable character, but we do not consider him as being guilty of a very great crime. A man of this sort may often have a very strong sense of the obligation of a contract; and we would do him a very great injury if we should conclude from this way of talking that he would pay no regard to his promise or contract.—If a man should engage to do me some considerable service, his failing in which would be a great dissappointment to me, and should in this promise act sincerely and realy have an intention

---

[v] Illegible word or words deleted

[13] Grotius, II.11.2 ff.; Stair, I.10.1 ff. For the criticism, cf. Hutcheson, *M.P.*, II.9.1; *System*, II.2–3; Hume, *Treatise of Human Nature*, III.ii.5 (ed. Selby-Bigge, 523–4).
[14] Pufendorf, III.5.5 ff.; Richard Price, *Review of the Principal Questions and Difficulties in Morals* (1758), ch. 7 (ed. Raphael, 155–6).
[15] *Sic*. Presumably something like 'the ground of a greater' was intended.

to perform, but should afterwards thro some inconvenience he found in the
61 performance [should] not fullfill his promise; if again | another should
thro levity or idleness promise me the same service tho he had no intention
to perform it, but afterwards, from a sense of the great dissapointment his
failure should give me, should alter his former design and perform his
promise: which of these two, I ask, would be the best man. The latter without doubt, who tho he promised what he did not intend to perform, yet
afterwards, reflecting on the dissapointment I must suffer, became of a
better mind. But the other man is he who adhered strictly to the truth and
had the greatest sense of honour, as he did not undertake what he had no
design of fullfilling, but being overballanced by a selfish motive broke his
obligation notwithstanding of the dissapointment he knew it would produce. We may see from this instance that sometimes the sense of honour
and veracity may be without a sense of the obligation of a promise, and
62 that on the other hand, one who is no great | observer of truth in small
matters may yet pay a great regard to the obligations of a contract, at least
to the dissapointment the breach of them would produce.

I endeavoured also to point out some reasons which would hinder contracts from sustaining action, that is, from being a subject for a judiciall
claim, and cause that constitution to be of very late introduction into most
nations. These were, 1$^{st}$, the smalness of the injury done by a breach of
promise, which I showed to be much less in the eyes of most men than the
breach of property; 2$^{dly}$, the uncertainty of language, which would make it
hard to determine whether a man barely signified his intention or made a
promise; 3$^{dly}$, the difficulty and inconvenience of$^w$ obtaining a trial of any
crime. Men are at first very shy in punishing crimes; the whole body of the
people must be assembled at every trial. This makes all judicial procedings
63 very troublesome. | It is not also$^x$ what we call civill causes that are first
brought into judgement, but criminall ones; that is, such as require force
and violence (which ⟨?we⟩ call breaches of the peace) such as disturb the
peace and order of society. Murder, robbery, larceny, and the like, which
either violently injure a man in his person or in his property.—Breaches of
contracts are in themselves done very quietly and without any open violence.
They may indeed provoke the injured person to revenge, but do not in
themselves produce great disturbance. 4$^{thly}$, to these we may add the small
value of the things which contracts could include in the early times.

I showed also that those contracts were first allowed to sustain action,
wherein the will and intention of each$^y$ party to create a dependance in the
other was indisputable; these were such as were conceived in a set form of
64 words appointed for that purpose and were called stipulationes.— | We
find too that those contracts where the will of the contracting parties was
indisputable were the first which were thought to sustain action in England

$^w$ 'tri' deleted    $^x$ Illegible word deleted    $^y$ Replaces 'the cont'

before the civill court. I mentioned that those which were confirmed by an
oath were those which the ecclesiasticall court first allowed to sustain
action; and afterwards extended this to all contracts whatsoever. But those
which the civill court first sustain'd were such as the parties entered
solemnly into in presence of the Kings Court. Of this there are some traces
to this day in the English law. What they call a recognoiscance is precisely
of the same nature. These are entered into by an indenture hoc modo[16]
wherein the terms of the agreement were wrote, and the paper being cut in
two denticulariter, the one half was formerly kept by the contrahee and the
other by the clerk of the court; but now each party has a half.—This
method ⟨is⟩ in dissuse in Scotland. We may observe that where courts are
65 | for a long time on the same footing there is much less difference[z] in the
manner of proceding from the old customs than where new courts are
instituted. Now the constitution of England has been long much the same
with regard to the courts as it is at present. The Court of Kings Bench is as
old as Edward the $1^{st}$'s time; that of the Exchequer much older; and also
that of Common Pleas is very old: these accordingly adhere in a great
measure to the old manner of proceedings. A new court, as that of the Star
Chamber instituted by Henry $8^{th}$, would pay little attention to those of
former courts, and we see accordingly that it proceeded very arbitrarily as
long as it subsisted. The constitutions of Scotland are of very late establishment. The Court of Session in its present form was created by James
66 the        [17]. A new court, ispecially a supreme one as this is in | many
causes, would instead of adhering to the proceedings of the old alter them
in many circumstances; as all new courts are supposed to be intended to
correct some defects of the old ones. We find accordingly that the English
courts have many more traces of the old proceedings than those in Scotland,
and this of recognizan⟨c⟩e amongst them. It is to be observed that after
these contracts by stipulation sustained action,[a] gratuitous contracts were
not even then allowed to sustain action unless they had what was called
a compensation,[18] that is, some just cause of entering into them. Thus if
a father promised a portion with his daughter, his being her father was a
justa causa. If an uncle promised to give a portion with his niece, this was
sustained also, quia loco parentis habetur. But if a stranger promised a
portion this was not sustained, nor others of this sort. It is without question
67 a very improper and blameable piece of conduct for | one thus to break
thro his engagement, and such as he would be justly condemned for; but

[z] Replaces 'variety'        [a] The last two words replace 'were entered into'

---

[16] A small diagram is drawn here, representing a document divided into two halves
with a wavy line illustrating *denticulariter*, 'like little teeth'.
[17] Blank in MS. It was created by James V in 1532.
[18] *Causa* in the civil law, consideration in English law.

then it seems as ungentlemanny and worthy*b* blame*c* to ensist on ones*d* making such a contract. It is to be taken notice of here that if one in this manner entered into a gratuitous contract, tho this would not sustain action, yet if he confirmed this engagement and declared his desire that he should depend upon the performance, the 1ˢᵗ contract was sustained as a justa causa for the 2ᵈ.

The same reason which made the contracts which were entered into by a solemn form of words sustain action would soon bring those which are called real contracts (which were before explained) to sustain action also, for in them all the inclination of the contracting parties to be bound is as plain as if expressed by the most solemn form of words. {At first a stipulation was required even in real contracts, but this was afterwards dispensed with, as the will of the contracters to great¹⁹ a dependance was equally evident as in those where a sollemn form of words was made use of.} In this manner, the four contractus nominati were soon allowed to
68 sustain action. | When one enters into the contract which they called mutuum, the will of the parties is altogether plain. This contract is when a thing is lent which is consumed by use, as money, wine, corn, etc. The commodatum is that where a thing is lent to be used but not consumed. The distinction here is not merely an imaginary one but produces some real difference. In the mutuum the property of the thing is transferred and the borrower is allowed to consume it, and is only bound to restore an equall quantity and quality but not the same thing; in the other he is bound not to consume or destroy th⟨e⟩ thing lent, but to restore the very individuall thing. In the first case there can be no action for damages done to the thing lent, as it is the property of the borrower, but in the 2ᵈ case there may, as he has only the use. These would very soon be allowed to sustain action, as the desire of the contracting parties is very plainly to be
69 bound to fullfill the contract or at least to create a | dependance. When these were allowed to sustain action, deposita would soon follow, where the thing put into ones custody is not to be used but only kept for the owner. Here if he uses it contrary to the agreement or consumes it, the truster would have an action against him. In the same manner in pledges, the pledge is not given away intirely to pay the debt but only as a security of payment; the agreement in this case is plain; and therefore if the pledge was appropriated by the pawnee the pawner had an action against him on the contract of pledge.

The extension of commerce introduced severall others. All contracts which were necessary for the carrying on of business after this time were

*b* 'of' deleted    *c* Numbers written above the last two words indicate that their order was intended to be reversed    *d* Reading doubtful

---

¹⁹ *Sic*. Possibly 'create' was intended.

considered as sustaining action, and that[e] whether made inter praesentes or absentes. Thus (as I said) contracts of sale, of letting and hiring, partner-
70 ship, etc., were[f] soon allowed to sustain action.— | We are to observe, however, that for some time at least these contracts were not allowd to sustain action unless a stipulation had accompanied them, either by word of mouth or one in the same manner by writing. Some solemnity is at first required to make a contract appear altogether binding.—Herodotus[20] tells us that the Scythians, when they desired to make a contract entirely bind- ing, drew blood of one another into a bowl, dip't their arrows in it, and afterwards drank it off. The Arabians had a similar custom. And Tacitus[21] tells us that the Armenians, when they made a contract, let blood of each other in the thumb and sucked out some of the blood. Sallust says it was commonly reported that Cataline and his conspirators, when they took the oath of secrecy, mixt blood with the wine they drank.[22] This report he attributes to the fear and terror of the people. But that may serve to shew that the people generally believe that such horrid ceremonies make the
71 contract which they | accompany appear the more binding, and they must make a great impression on the mind of the contracters. — — —

We may observe that those contracts which were allowed to sustain action on account of the great necessity they were of in the carrying on of commerce, at first even after this required the transmission of writings, at least in some cases. These were called contractus literales and are pretty fully explain'd in the Theodosian Code.[23] Justinian mentions them in his Institutions, but in a very confused manner.[24] This afterwards was not required, and the consent of the parties was sufficient without either tradition or any other ceremony. These were called contractus consensuales. In this manner the contracts were at first of four sorts.[g] 1st, those which were entered into by a solemn form of words, or stipulation; 2dly, real contracts; 3dly, those which were enterd into literis; and 4thly, consensuales, besides the nuda pacta which we shall take notice of immediately. After-
72 wards | they were reduced to four, even when the nuda pacta are included; the literales bein⟨g⟩ put on the same footing as the consensuales; or indeed to three, as the consensuales had intirely the same effect as those per stipulationem.[h]

---

[e] 'wither' deleted     [f] Illegible word deleted     [g] 'which bore action' deleted
[h] The next two sentences, reading as follows, are struck out: 'In England contracts are on a very different footing than they are in any other part of Europe. By the common law there is no action for the fullfilling of a contract there [several words, probably 'is no action', deleted] can be no more satisfaction obtain before these courts than what arises from the compensation of damages.'

---

[20] IV.70, but the blood was dripped into a bowl of wine. Also cited by Kames, *Law Tracts*, I.94.
[21] *Annals*, XII.47.                    [22] *Bellum Catilinae*, XXII.1.
[23] *C. Th.*, 2.27; 5.10; 11.39.                    [24] *Inst.* 3.21.

The nuda pacta, as well as those verbal contracts which had a justa causa or compensatio, were never allowed by the Romans to sustain action. But at the same time they gave an exception.[25] That is, they were sufficient to overturn an action, though they could not constitute one. Thus if I owed you an hundred pounds, and you[i] said you would not require it of me, this

73 was sufficient on a satisfactory | proof to free me from the debt; but if you had gratuitously promised to give me £100, this would not give me a claim at law for that summ. The same tenderness for the liberty of individualls which made action on contracts so late of taking place, as all such obligations are a restraint on this liberty, inclined them to free those who were under such obligations, on a very slight ground.—Among the European nations at first the common law gave no actions on contracts of any sort; the ecclesiasticall courts were the only ones which sustained them as giving action. When the civil courts came at length to allow action on contracts, it was only on such as were entered into in the form of a recognizance or a sollemn deed done in presence of the court and recorded in their books. The ecclesiasticall or cannon law[j] proceeding alltogether on the principles of honour and virtue, did not so much attend to [the] what

74 would naturally appear equitable | to a rude people, as what was the duty of a good Christian and the rules by which he ought to regulate his conduct. They accordingly gave action on every contract how slight soever.[k] The Scots law and [in] that of most other nations of Europe[l] are altogether the same with the civil law, except that the nuda pacta sustain action. If a man in this country promise any summ of money or other thing, and this can be plainly proved, he is obliged to perform. The reason of this was that these courts, as the Parliament of Paris and the Court of Session, were established long after the civil and cannon law had been in great force in those countries, and consequently borrow considerably from both of those laws. The English law was on the other hand formed into a system before the discovery of Justinians Pandects; and its courts established, and their method of proceedings pretty much fixed, before the other courts in Europe were

75 instituted, or the civil or cannon law | came to be of any great weight. It is for this reason that it borrows less from those laws than[m] the law of any other nation in Europe; and is for that reason more deserving of the attention of a speculative man than any other, as being more formed on the naturall sentiments of mankind.

On this account also it is very imperfect with regard to contracts. It was not till after the erection of the Court of Chancery and the great powers

---

[i] 'engaged' deleted     [j] Illegible word deleted     [k] 'In' deleted     [l] Two or three illegible words deleted     [m] 'any' deleted

---

[25] i.e. a defence: *D*. 2.14.7. Bare pacts alone sustained no action.

which it assumed that the English law allowed an action for the specifick performance of any contract. It allowed only of an action of damages for the breach of a contract. This indeed appears to be naturall enough in the first stages of a civill government, as the point it has in view is to redress injuries rather than make the individualls perform their engagements; that they left to their own good faith. This action for damages might in many cases be equall to the specifick performance, as where the one party in

76 contract of sale had delivered the goods and the other | had not paid the price. Where there had been a rei traditio, in deposi[s]tum especially, indeed, by a fiction of law restitution at least of the thing given might be obtaind. This was done by the action of trouver and conversion,[26] where they feigned that the thing had not come into his possession by his knowledge, but had been found and claimed in that manner; either the individuall if it existed, or the value if it had been converted to his use. But in all cases this might be evaded by the oath of the person against whom the suit was instituted. If it was but a simple contract, he might wage his law and a simple bailment was sufficient to acquit him.[27] {The same reason was given as the Grecians gave for not giving acction on contracts, viz, that as he had trusted his honesty and fidelity, why might not they be allowed to trust it now he was put to his oath.}[n] That is, his oath without any proof on his side was sufficient to free him, and no proof on the side of the pursuer was admitted. An⟨d⟩ in case there had been something delivered, the action may be voided by his oath and the concurrent testimony of six witnesses that he had either not received or had returned the thing claimed. And in

77 cases where the contract was not performed on either side there | was no action till the Court of Chancery. The method they made use of in contracts where something had been delivered was to sue for damages whenever[o] it was apprehended the defendant would wage his law; as in this case he cant swear that he has done no damage to the amount to be provd as he does not know what it is. The damages are left to the determination of the jury, which in many cases may make it equall to the specific performance, as before observed; and by this means the writ of detinue, which is that which is generally used[p] with the action of trouver and conversion, is seldom applied, but the action of damages, in all cases where it is in the least to be suspected that the defendant would wage his law. But by the Scots law

---

[n] Below this passage on the verso page there is written the word 'Bell' or 'Ball', which has possibly been deleted        [o] Reading doubtful        [p] 'against' deleted

---

[26] The form of action was 'trover and conversion'.

[27] Wager of law was a proceeding whereby a defendant discharged himself from a claim by his own oath denying it, accompanied by eleven (not six) neighbours who swore that they believed his denial to be true. It could not in fact be used in trover and conversion, but it was available in the older action of detinue; that action provided a remedy in the case of a 'simple bailment', which was the delivery of a chattel to the defendant with the plaintiff's consent. The passage in the text is confused.

action is given on all contracts. They are here on precisely the same footing
78 as | by the civil law, excepting that the nuda pacta are also allowed to
sustain action. By which means there are but two species of contracts
amongst us, viz real contracts which do not sustain action unless traditio
rei has intervened, and consensual ones which are allowed to sustain action
by the bare consent of the contracters.

There are two questions with regard to contracts which I shall just
mention here, as there will be a more proper plac[c]e afterwards for treating of them. The 1st is to what degree of diligence the contracters shall be
bound. To this purpose we must take notice of the distinction of culpa or
neglect into culpa lata, levis, and levissima, which is handled in the
Institutes[28] and was explained at length in the *Theory of Morall Sentiments*[29] and therefore need not be here repeated. The Romans considered
79 contracts as being either gratuitous or | onerous. Amongst the first were:
mutuum, commodatum, depositum, and mandatum; in these the profit is
intirely in ordinary cases on the side of the mutuarius, comm⟨o⟩daturius
and deponens, and mandans. They therefore are bound to pay even culpa
levissima and are bound to the greatest diligence; and the other person to
the smallest, and the praestandum      [30] salam. For even in the mutuum
th⟨e⟩ contract is reckond to be gratuitous, as no reward or interest is given.
And even in our law no interest is due on the loan of money unless it be
seperately mentioned. It is true an accepted bill of exchange bears interest
from the time it becomes due, but that is by a particular statute.[31] In other
cases where the[y] contract is onerous on both sides, they are bound to the
culpa levis.

Another question is, if one borrows a summ of money and before the
80 time of payment the money is called in and | a new coinage ⟨?is intro-
duced⟩ where the value of the money is altered, commonly debased,
whether the debtor will be allowed to pay his debt with the new coin or will
be obliged to pay it in the old. As for instance if one should borrow £100
and before the payment the silver should be called in and a new coinage
⟨?introduced⟩ where the same nominall value ⟨?is⟩ put on the half of the
silver debased with alloy as before, that is, that instead of near 400 ounces
the £100 should contain only about 200; the question is whether in this
case the debt is to be paid with 200 ounces debased in this way, or by 400
ounces of the old, or a real value equall to it in the new. And here the civil
law of all countries and naturall justice and equity the[32] quite contrary.[33]

---

[28] The classification does not occur in any ancient sources, though *culpa lata* is in *D.*
50.16.213.2 and 223pr, and *culpa levissima* in *D.* 9.2.44pr. Cf. 89 below.

[29] II.iii.2.8–10.

[30] Illegible word, probably 'custodiam'. '*Salam*' should be '*salvam*', and the meaning
of the phrase is the duty to keep in safe custody.

[31] 1681, c. 20 (A.P.S. VIII.352, c. 86).

[32] *Sic.* Presumably 'are' was intended.          [33] Cf. Pufendorf, V.7.6.

Justice and equity plainly require that one should restore the same value
81 as he received without regard to the nominal | value of money, and there-
fore he is to restore as much in the old coin or an equall value in the new as
he receiv'd. But the civil government in all countries have constituted the
exact contrary of this.—The reason of this conduct is as follows. The only
cause which can induce the government to make any alteration on the
value of the money {which as shall be shewn[34] is a very detrimental step}
is the difficulty of raising money. Suppose for instance that the government
should have use for and be obliged to expend above 10,000000 liv$^q$ but that
by no means whatever they could raise above 5 millions. In this what shall
they do. The only expedient they can fall on is to call in the coin and debase
the value one half. It is seldom that such great changes [as these] are made
as this; but in the year 1701 the French, being in this condition, instead of
28 caused 1$^{st}$ of all 40, then 50, and at last 60 l⟨i⟩vres$^r$ ⟨?⟩ out of the 8 oz
82 French of silver.[35] In this way with less than half the real value | they paid
all their troops, fleet, officers, and loans. But least the imposition should
be too soon felt by the creditors of the government, they ordered that all
debts should in like manner be paid by the new coin. This expedient
concealed the fraud. For there are two purposes in which we may use
money, either 1$^{st}$, in bying commodities; or 2$^{dly}$, in paying of debts.$^s$ Now
in the 1$^{st}$ method of using money, the money when debased in its real value
and raised in its nominal one half, will purchase no more than the same
quantity of silver did before, for$^t$ the value of the money is always to be
counted by the quantity of pure metall; the alloy goes for nothing, as the
labour in seperating counterballances the small additionall value. By this
means the money would soon fall to its former value with regard to all
goods. But then it is also applied to pay debts. As I shall shew hereafter,[36]
83 | it is the riches of the lower class of people that regulate the price of all
sorts of ordinary commodities, bread, beef, beer, etc. These can never rise
higher than they can afford. Now the soldiers, and all sorts of mechanicks,
being paid by the new money and consequently receiving but half their
former wages, can afford but half the price they formerly gave for the
commodities, so that here the new money would purchase as much for the
same nominal value as the old. And by this means, and also by all former
debts being paid in this manner, the value of money or coin would fluctuate

---

$^q$ Reading doubtful       $^r$ Reading doubtful       $^s$ Illegible word or words deleted
$^t$ 'tho' deleted

---

[34] vi.119 ff. below.
[35] The reference is probably to the recoinage of 1709, discussed in J.-F. Melon, *Essai
politique sur le commerce* (1734), ch. XVI (in E. Daire, ed., *Économistes financiers du XVIII$^e$
siècle* (1843), 721 ff.), and the observations on that chapter of C. Dutot, *Réflexions politiques
sur les finances et le commerce* (1738), ch. I, art. 4–6 (Daire, 797 ff.).
[36] vi.73–5 below.

betwixt the old and the new for some time. Its value in bying would only be the half; for instance, one of the new shillings would only purchase as much as an old 6ᵈ; but then a new sh. will pay as much as an old one, and

84 by these combined the value will for some time continue abou⟨t⟩ | 10 or 9ᵈ. So that by such an alteration the loss of the creditors will not be so sensible, and the money will not by this lessening of its real value and increase of its nominall lose above 1/3.

There is also another question pretty much similar to the last one. That is, ⟨if⟩ the gold should ⟨be⟩ lessend with regard to its comparative value [of it] to silver, whether one who had borrowd e.g. G.100 when they were worth 25 shillings would pay his debt by 100G. when they are brought to 21 shillings; and the answer plainly is that he would not, for he received 125 and would by this means pay only 105. For in all cases the value of gold is estimated by that of silver, and not that of silver by that of gold. Indeed if he had agreeed to pay 100 guineas in specie the case might be different. But all bonds are drawn with regard to the silver coin, so that this could seldom happen.—

_____

85    | We come now to the 2ᵈ species of obligations, viz those which arise from quasi contract, or quae quasi ex contractu nascuntur;[37] that is, the duty of restitution. The most simple sort is that which the civilians call petitio indebiti, where one thinks that he is due an other a certain sum, and that other that the former is due that summ also, and payment therefore insues; but on casting up his accounts the former finds that this summ has been paid. In what way shall ⟨he⟩ claim restitution. He can not claim it from contract, for no contract was made, nor did either expect such an accident; nor can he claim the pieces as his own, they are probably spent; and besides he fairly alienated them without any reservation. But still the other has what belongs to him; est res aliena in ejus patrimonio, and no one

86 it is presumed is inclined to be made richer by what is an others. | For this reason he is obliged to restore the money and the repetitio indebiti is given against him. In the same manner in the negotia utiliter gesta, tho my money is not in his patrimony yet there is something purchased by money. Therefore he is bound to make restitution of what I have laid out on it. This is the case when by these negotia some advantage accrues to the person for whom I act. And if there should no advantage accrue to him, yet if the negotia be utiliter and honestly done to encourage such good offices, he is bound to restitution. In the same manner it is with averaging the obligation which arises from the lex Rhodia de jactu,[38] as here the goods of

[37] *Inst.* 3.27; Hutcheson, *M.P.*, II.14; *System*, II.77.
[38] The Rhodian sea-law concerning jettison; when goods were thrown overboard to lighten a ship and so save both ship and cargo from wreck, proportionate shares of loss were borne by the owners of ship and cargo saved, so 'averaging' the loss: *D.* 14.2.1.

the others are savd by the loss of one. As well as the actions which joint
sureties or cautioners have for being indemnified by each other, for here the
others are locupletiores facti jactura ejus, qui debitum etc. solverit.[u][39] All
the actiones contrariae of the Romans go on this principal, for from the
contracti the cases in which they occur are never attended to. But in case
87 any | impensae extraordinariae, non autem[v] ordinariae, should be laid out,
the expender has an action against the proprietarius; and in the same
manner the action the tutor has against the pupil for extraordinary ex-
expenses proceeds from this, but not for ordinary. {Neither need we consider the duty of tutors as arising from quasi contract, as their duty arises
from their accepting of that office.} For in all these[w] the obligation to
indemnify the person who is at the expense is not from the contract but
from the duty of restitution, which requires *neminem locupletio*rem fieri
*aliena jactura.*[40] In all countries these actiones contrariae are given; and as
the duty of restitution is the foundation of them, so the expender may
either bring an actio contraria or an actio negotiorum gestorum against the
person whom he has served. I shall only observe farther on this head that
it may often ⟨?be⟩ that all the severall kinds of personall rights may concur
in the same cause, both that from contract, from quasi contract or resti-
88 tution, and | from delinquency. Thus if I employ one to hire a house[41] for
me, the owner may have an action against the hirer to fullfill the contract;
the hirer may have an action from quasi contract for what extraordinary
expenses he may have been at; and the owner against the rider from
delinquency if he has overrode or any way abused his horse.

I come now to consider the third species of personall rights or obligations, which is, those which arise from

## Delinquency.

That is, the right one has to be repaid the damage he has sustained ex
delicto, from the delinquency of an other. Delinquency may be of two sorts.
Either the damage may arise from the willfull injury[x] *malice propense* of the
person, or from a criminal or faulty negligence, or culpa. Negligence or
89 culpa may also be considered, as was before observed,[42] as being | of 3
sorts. Either the negligence is so great as that no man could have been
guilty of the like in his own affairs, tho this man has been in those of
another, in which case the delinquency is said to arise from culpa lata; or

---

[u] This sentence is written vertically at the side of the page          [v] 'extra' deleted
[w] 'January 26. 1763' is interlined at this point          [x] Illegible word deleted

---

[39] 'Enriched at the expense of him who has paid the debt'.
[40] The principle that 'no one ought to be enriched to the detriment of another' derives
from *D.* 50.17.206.
[41] *Sic.* Presumably 'horse' was intended.
[42] 78 above.

$2^{dly}$, it is called culpa levis, where the delinquent has been guilty of no greater negligence in the affairs of an other than he is in his own, being generally a man who was not very attentive to his affairs;[43] or lastly, from culpa levis⟨sima⟩, where the[y] negligence or culpa is no more than the most attentive man might have been guilty of.—I shall however consider in the $1^{st}$ place those which arise from dolus, or what we call malice propense, and is a willfull and designed injury done to another.

Now in all cases the measure of the punishment to be inflicted on the delinquent is the concurrence of the impartial spectator with the resentment of the injured.[44] If the injury is so great as that the spectator can go
90 along with the injured person in revenging himself by | [z] the death of the offender, this is the proper punishment, and what is to be exacted by the offended person or the magistrate in his place who acts in the character of an impartial spectator. If the spectator could not concur with the injured if his revenge led him to the death of the offender, but could go along with him if he revenged the injury by a small corporall punishment or a pecuniary fine, this is the punishment that ought here to be inflicted. In all cases a punishment appears equitable in the eyes of the rest of mankind[a] when it is such that the spectator would concur with the offended person in exacting ⟨it⟩. The revenge of the injured which prompts him to retaliate the injury on the offender is the real source of the punishment of crimes. That which Grotius and other writers[45] commonly alledge as the originall measure of punishments, viz the consideration of the publick good, will not
91 sufficiently account for the constitution of punishments. | So far, say they, as publick utility requires, so far we consent to the punishment of the criminall, and that this is the naturall intention of all punishments. But we fill[46] find the case to be otherwise. For tho in many cases the publick good may require the same degree of punishment as the just revenge of the injur'd, and such as the spectator would go along with, yet in those crimes which are punished chiefly from a view to the publick good the punishment enacted by law and that which we can readily enter into is very different. Thus some years ago the British nation took a fancy (a very whimsicall one indeed⟨)⟩ that the wealth and strength of the nation depended entirely on the flourishing of their woolen trade, and that this could not prosper[b] if the

[y] 'injur' deleted    [z] There is a large stain running down this page which renders the readings given of a number of the words more than usually doubtful    [a] The last three words replace 'unconcerned spectator'    [b] Reading doubtful

---

[43] This is *culpa levis in concreto*; more common is *culpa levis in abstracto*, failure to show the objective standard of care of the 'good head of a family'.

[44] For this doctrine, and for much of the whole paragraph, cf. TMS II.ii.3.6–11. See also Appendix II of the Glasgow edition of TMS, which includes and discusses an earlier version of Smith's views on punishment.

[45] Grotius, II.20.7–9; Pufendorf, VIII.3.9–12.

[46] *Sic.* No doubt 'will' was intended.

exportation of wool was permitted. To prevent this it was enacted that the exportation of wool should be punished with death.[47] This exportation was no crime at all, in naturall equity, and was very far from deserving so high[c] a punishment in the eyes of the people; they therefore found that | while this was the punishment they could get neither jury nor informers. No one would consent to the punishment of ⟨a⟩ thing in itself so innocent by so high a penalty.[48] They were therefore obliged to lessen the punishment to a confiscation of goods and vessel. In the same manner the military laws punish a centinell who falls asleep upon guard with death. This is intirely founded on the consideration of the publick good; and tho we may perhaps approve of the sacrificing one person for the safety of a few, yet such a punishment when it is inflicted affects us in a very different manner from that of a cruel murtherer or other atrocious criminall.

92

We may likewise observe that the revenge of the injured will regulate the punishment so as intirely to answer the three purposes which the authors above mentioned mention as the intention of all punishments. For 1$^{st}$, the resentment of the offended person leads him to correct the offender, as to make him | ⟨?feel⟩ by whom and for what he suffers. Resentment is never compleatly, nor as we think nobly gratified by poison or assassination. This has in all nations and at all times been held as unmanly, because the sufferer does not by this means feel from whom, or for what, the punishment is inflicted.—2$^{dly}$, the punishment which resentment dictates we should inflict on the offender tends sufficiently to deter either him or any other from injuring us or any other person in that manner. 3$^{dly}$, resentment also leads a man to seek redress or compensation for the injury he has received.

93

Crimes are of two sorts, either 1$^{st}$, such as are an infringement of our natural rights, and affect either our person in killing, maiming, beating, or mutilating our body, or restraining our liberty, as by wrongous imprisonment, or by hurting our reputation and good name. Or 2$^{dly}$, they affect our acquired rights, and are an attack upon our property, by robbery, theft, larceny, etc.

94

| It is to be observed that the declining to fullfill a contract has never been considered as a crime, tho a fraud always is. The judge sentences a person cited before him for having neglected to fullfill a contract, in the first place to fullfill it, and 2$^{dly}$ to make satisfaction to the other party for what damages the delay and suit may have occasioned him, but never inflicts any punishment for the intended evasion. But on the other hand one who

---

[c] Reading doubtful

[47] 13 and 14 Charles II, c. 18 (1662) made export of wool a felony (as 18 Henry VI, c. 15 had done earlier).

[48] Preamble of 7 and 8 William III, c. 28 (1696), which reduced the crime to a misdemeanour.

fraudently would bring another under a contract is very severly punished. Thus one who forges a bill or bond is in this country punish'd with death.[49]

We shall begin with those crimes which are an attack upon the person. The first and the most attrocious of these is willfull murder. For this, to be sure, the only proper punishment is the death of the offender. The resentment of the injured persons can not be satisfied by a mere simple punishment, unless there be an equality at least betwixt the sufferings of the injur'd person and the offender, (that is) unless the injury be in some 95 measure retaliated. | We find accordingly that in all civilized nations the punishment has been the death of the murderer. But amongst barbarous nations the punishment has generally been much slighter, as a pecuniary fine.—The reason of this was the weakness of government in those early periods of society, which made it very delicate of intermeddling with the affairs of individualls. The government therefore at first interposed only in the way of mediator, to prevent the ill consequences[d] which might arise from those crimes in the resentment of the friends of the slain. For what is[e] the end of punishing crimes, in the eyes of people in this state? The very same as now of punishing civil injuries, viz the preserving of the publick peace. The crimes themselves were already committed, there was no help for that; the main thing therefore the society would have in view would be to prevent the bad consequences of it. This therefore they would not attempt by a punishment, which might interrupt it. For it was not till a society was far advanced that the government took upon them to cite 96 criminalls | and pass judgement upon them.

Intercession was therefore made betwixt the parties, either by some individuall of eminent worth and consequently of authority, or by the whole society together, advising and exhorting the parties concerned to such and such measures. What then is the most reasonable thing persons thus interposing would propose to be done. They would certainly exhort the murderer to appease the friends of the slain by presents, and them to accept of such satisfaction. Pére Charlevoix[50] and de La Fulage[51] tell us that among the Iriquois and severall other of the savage nations of North America, when a person is slain by an other of the same family the society never intermeddles, but leaves it to the father or head of the family to punish or forgive it as he shall think proper. But if a person of one family is slain by one[f] of another, then they interpose and settle the presents which

---

<sup></sup>[d] Illegible word or words deleted     [e] 'it that is' deleted     [f] Replaces 'that'

[49] Sir G. Mackenzie, *Laws and Customes of Scotland in Matters Criminal* (1678), I.27. English law was less severe.

[50] P.-F.-X. de Charlevoix, *Histoire et description générale de la Nouvelle-France, avec le Journal historique d'un voyage . . . dans l'Amérique septentrionnale* (1744), III.272 ff.

[51] Presumably J. F. Lafitau, *Mœurs des sauvages amériquains, comparées aux mœurs des premiers temps* (1724), I.486–90.

are to appease the friends of the slain; and if the person is not able to furnish sufficient presents, the whole community makes a collection for
97 him, every one contributing | something to so good a design. These presents are generally divided into 60 parts, one of which goes to the mother of the slain to get her something to sit upon to mourn over her son, another to procure her a pipe of tobacco for her comfort, another part is given to the sister, to the brothers, etc., one is to clear the road of the brambles, another to cover the blood which has been spilt, as they express it; and so on.— Among the northern nations which broke into Europe in ⟨the⟩ beginning of the 5th century, society was a step farther advanced than amongst the Americans at this day. They are still in the state of hunters, the most rude and barbarous of any, whereas the others were arrived at the state of shepherds, and had even some little agriculture. The step betwixt these two is of all others the greatest in the progression of society, for by it the notion of property is ext⟨end⟩ed beyond possession, to which it is in the former state confined. When this is once established, ⟨it⟩ is a matter of no great difficulty to extend this from one subject to another, from herds and flocks to the land itself.—They had therefore got a good way before the
98 Americans; and government, | which grows up with society, had of consequence acquired greater strength. We find accordingly that it intermeddled more with those affairs; so that in the laws of all those nations there is a particular rate fixed for the attonement that shall be made for the death of persons of every rank in the state from the king to the slave, and this is called the wingild.[52] This wingild varies according to the different ranks of the persons; for as they were of higher rank their friends would be more powerfull and consequently more difficultly appeased, as they would have the greater hopes of obtaining satisfaction. For this reason the compensation or wingild of a king is much greater than that of a thain, that than that of an earl, that than ⟨that⟩ of a baron, that again greater than that of a simple free man, and this still more than that of a slave or villain.—By the Salick law,[53] when a man was not able to pay the wingild he was confined by himself in a tent, {the first time he was asked if he could pay it; if not his friends were called and each asked seperately; if none of them would pay it for him, then they were desired to pay it amongst them; and if this third time they refused, he was delivered up, etc.} and his friends were three times called together arround him and asked if they would contribute
99 to pay his fine; if they refused every time, then | he was delivered up to the friends of the slain to be put to death or treated as they had a mind. {The relations of the deceased were at firsst always the executioners, tho this is now given to the[g] public officers, as the publick now comes in the place of

_____
[g] Illegible word deleted

[52] Usually wergeld, or vergelt: Kames, *Law Tracts*, I.43 ff.
[53] *Pactus legis Salicae*, 50.

these relations.—The death of one who has murthered a near relation from accident, or his punishment from some other cause, may sooth the anger of his friends but can not gratify their revenge, as it does not come from them.—Poison or assassination by unknown persons is somewhat more satisfactory, as they know he suffers by their means. But the revenge is then only fully and nobly gratified when he is made sensible that it is by them and for their sake that he suffers.} This expiation of a crime by presents we find very universall in ancient times. There are severall instances of it in Homer. Nestor[54] tells Achilles that presents appease everyone; for presents a father forgives the death of his son.—In the description of the shield of Achilles, in one of the compartments the story represented is the friends of a slain man receiving presents from the slayer.[55] The government did not then intermeddle in those affairs; and we find that the stranger who comes on board the ship of Telemachus tells us he fled from the friends of a man whom he had slain, and not from the officers of justice.[56]

As the governments of Europe gain'd more and more strength, they thought themselves intitled to some gratuity for their trouble in interposing. As their interposition was always favourable to the criminall, in protecting him from those who would take away his life and procuring him some easier way of satisfying them, they thought them|selves well intitled to some gratification for this protection. This was called the freedom or frank-guild. And as the composition bore proportion to the power of the relations of the deceased and the danger of his punishment, so this bore proportion to the power of the protector, and was greater or less according to the dignity of the person within whose peace (that is, jurisdiction) the crime was committed. Thus the freeguild payable for a crime committed within the jurisdiction of the king, for he too had a seperate jurisdiction, was much greater than that due for a murder committed within the peace of an earl, and this than that within the peace of a baron.—By degrees the sovereigns came to consider, at least in practise, themselves as the persons chiefly injured. The addition therefore which was made to the punishment of the offenders was not to the composition or wingild due to the friends of the deceased, but to the frank-gild due to the king. This in Scotland and severall other countries came to be a considerable part of the | kings revenues, and the kings advocates (as I shall show hereafter)[57] were nothing else but officers who went about to collect these compensations due to the king which were inflicted by the judges, who *then acted as the jury, tho* now they have little more authority than to keep order and regularity. This compensation due to the king, in Scotland especially, so far exceeded that which was paid to the friends of the deceased that the criminal came to be

---

54 In fact Ajax: *Iliad*, ix.632.        55 *Iliad*, xviii.500.
56 *Odyssey*, xv.271 ff.        57 v.13–14 below.

considered as punished, not as the murtherer of the relation of such persons, but as the murtherer of the free subject of the king. The sovereigns
however in time found it more for their advantage, in order to keep peace
and harmony amongst their subjects, to substitute a capitall punishment in
the room of that frankguild which was due them. This punishment in
Scotland was never substituted in the room of the wingild, but as that due
to the king for the death of his subject. This idea took place very compleatly
102  in Scotland, where the government was very | early aristocraticall and
favourable to the kingly power. So that the relations can not of themselves,
nor without the concurrence of the kings advocate, prosecute the mur-
therers of the deceased. And as the prosecution, at least as far as it regards
the life of the murtherer, is carried on in the name of the king, so he claims
also the power of pardonning and forgiving the capitall punishment as due
to him alone. But it was found by a late decree of the Court of Session in the
case of one         , a         [58] who murthered a smuggler without sufficient
cause, that the royal pardon, tho it extended to the capital punishment,
could not however free him from what is called the assythment (the name
now given to the wingild) due to the friends of the deceased. Tho the king
could[h] pardon the capitall punishment due to himself, as any other man can
forgive debts due to himself, yet he could not pardon that satisfaction due
to the friends of the deceased, any more than he could excuse[i] them from
any other debt due to them. For it is realy and truly a debt as any other due
103  | from contract. In England, where the seeds of democracy were earlier
sown, {Capital punishment here came in place not only of the frank guild
due to the king, but also of the wingild or compensation due to the friends
of the slain.—} the relations had the power of prosecuting independent of
the crown, and capital punishment followed on this prosecution as well as
that derived from the kings authority. When therefore the king assumed
the right of pardoning, the relations of the deceased had still a prosecution
after this pardon, under the name of an appeal of blood, and the capitall
punishment which followd on this the king could not pardon. This process
still subsists but is very seldom attempted, because the legislature is very
unfavourable to it and the least informality renders it void.[59]— Thus if a
husband is murthered no one can prosecute but the widow, and failing of

---

[h] 'not' deleted        [i] Reading doubtful

---

[58] Blanks in MS. Malloch, an exciseman. That a royal pardon did not affect the action
for assythment was decided by *Keay* v. *McNeill* (1717), unreported; see Baron David
Hume, *Commentaries on the Law of Scotland re trial of crimes* (1800), II.387. In *Malloch* v.
*Fulton's relict and child* (1751), Morison's *Dictionary of Decisions*, 11774, it was decided
that cessio bonorum of the debtor's goods did not prejudice the claim of the widow and
children, which presupposed that assythment was unaffected by the pardon. In the text,
'friends of the deceased' should be 'family of the deceased'. Smith may have heard of
Malloch's case from Lord Kames, who as H. Home was Malloch's advocate.
[59] Hawkins, II.23, paras. 36 ff. and 103 ff.

her the nearest male relation, and failing of them no one. No one can prosecute for the death of his brother but the elder brother or other
104  relation of the males, | *j* and failing one step the rest can not prosecute, etc. The error in the name, time, or other circumstances all render the suit void. So that it ⟨is⟩ hardly ever attempted nowadays — — — — — —

*Gap of one and two-thirds pages in MS.*

105    | Excepting this priviledge of appeal, there is very little difference betwixt the English and Scots law with respect to murder, or indeed betwixt it and the law of most other countries. There are however some distinctions with regard to the killing of a man which are more fully observed in the English law than in any other. Murther properly signifies the killing of a man,*k* for whom the murtherer has lain in wait. Men (as I observed before) are very late of punishing even the killing of a man with death. The first attempt that was made this way in England was by Canute the Dane.[60] The resentment of the English against their new masters made it often happen that they lay in wait for the Danes and killed them on a sudden. Canute, to prevent this, made a law that any one who killed a Dane in this manner should be punished with death. The crime was also
106  denominated *murdrum*, murder. This punishment, for reasons we | shall soon advance wore out after the Norman Conquest and a composition was taken, but was not long after established with regard to the wilfull and premeditated killing of a man in whatever manner, which is what is properly to be called murder and is always punished with death. But when one 2$^{dly}$ who had no malice forethought or evill designs against the person he killed, but by some sudden provocation should thro passion kill an other, this is not considered as so great a crime, as there was no premeditated design of injuring the person; it is therefore called by the name of manslaughter, which [is] indeed is not accounted an excusable crime but a slight punishment inflicted when one claims the benefit of clergy (to be explained hereafter). {His goods are by law forfeited to the king but there is a regular process by which he may recover them and claim pardon, which is always done immediately after he pleads the benefit of clergy.} It is not however reckoned justifiable, for tho there was no premeditated intention of killing a man yet there must have been one before the action was committed. For this reason it is even esteemed felonious.*l* {These two kinds are called felonious homicide, as the punishment is capitall, for even in manslaughter sentence of death is pronounced, and the punishment is not lessend till the

---

*j* The first line on 104 of the MS., reading 'and one step failing the prosecution [illegible word]', has been deleted. The words 'and one step failing the pro', written at the top of the verso of 103, have also been deleted.          *k* 'for whom' deleted          *l* This sentence is written vertically at the side of the page

---

[60] Hale, I.35, saying that Canute penalized the township where a Dane was killed.

criminall plead the benefit of clergy.} The 3ᵈ distinction is that which they call *chance manly*,[61] that is, when one kills a man altogether thro' accident

107 without any intention of killing him either beforehand | or at the time of his comitting the action. {This is said to be per infortunium—where the killing of the man is merely a matter of accident without any design. There is also a 2ᵈ species of excusable homicide, which is that called homicidium se defendendo,[62] where after a quarrell has been begun one is brought to such a condition that ⟨he⟩ has no probable means of making his escape. This is reckoned excusable but not justifiable, as the quarrel which brought it on and the using deadly weapons is of itself criminall.—} This isᵐ reckoned excusable and is therefore not capitally punished (but as there is generally some rashness attending such accidents the killer is generally punishedⁿ by the forfeiture of his goods, to make others be more upon their guard.) {We are also to distinguish the last species of excusable homicide from that one where it is reckoned justifiable[63] to kill one in his own defence, as in the former case, viz se defendendo, a quarrell is supposed to have preceded, whereas in the other the man is reduced to this strait without any fault of his own but merely by the attack of another.} There are however two cases in [the] which the killing of a man is reckoned altogether justifiable, and is not affected with any punishment. These are the killing of a man who made resistance by any of the kings officers, going about their lawfull business and executing their office, or 2ᵈˡʸ the killing a man inᵒ defence of ones person or in that of his house and goods.ᵖ This is to be distinguished from manslaughter by there being no injury done on the part of the killer, but merely in the defence of his rights. For these no punishment is exacted. The only thing that can be called in question is the distinction betwixt these severall different sorts of homicide. Murder, strictly speaking, is where one kills another of set purpose, having lain in wait for him. But all

108 homicide which proceed⟨s⟩ | from an evil intention where there was ill will before is also accounted murder. For though the killing of a man in passion be accounted only manslaughter, yet this is always taken in the strictest sense.[64] Thus as to the provocation which will acquit one from murder, it is limited to that which proceeds from blows. Words or gestures are not reckoned to give a sufficient provocation. But at the same time the law is so far favourable to the man who kills one in this way, that if the provocation has been sufficient to provoke him to strike the person, and he has returned the blow, the killing him afterwards is looked on as manslaughter. If the persons having had a dispute should both draw and fight, the person who

---

ᵐ 'in the same manner' deleted     ⁿ The word 'uncertain' is written in the margin at this point     ᵒ 'ones own' deleted     ᵖ The last eleven words are written vertically at the side of the page

[61] Chance medly or killing *per infortunium*: Hale, I.39; Hawkins, I.29.
[62] Hale, I.40.          [63] Hawkins, I.28.          [64] Hale, I.36.

has been obliged to kill the other in this manner is only guilty of killing se
defendendo,[q] but can not be altogether justified, as the quarrel which
preceded it and[r] the fighting with deadly weapons is of itself a crime.—
But if these persons had bore a grudge to on⟨e⟩ another, tho neither of
109 them had layn in | wait for the other, yet if they drew and fought on meeting
this will be accounted murder. In like manner if two persons should fight
in the evening for a quarrell that happend in the morning, or in the morning
after having quarrelled the evening before, it will be constructed as murther. But if in the heat of the quarrel, when they had no weapons, they
should run each to his house for arms and fight immediately, it will be
accounted manslaughter only. {If after any quarrel one of the parties should
challenge the other, and he should not accept of it, but should at the same
time tell him that he was every day at such a place, the death of one of the
parties would then be considered as murder, as it is evident they designed
to evade the law by not fighting of set purpose. And all duels where time or
place are mentioned are in like manner held as productive of murder.—}
The same is found to be the law if a son should come in all[s] beat and
abused, and his father should immediately run out and come up with the
person who had abused him and kill ⟨him⟩, even tho' he had 3/4 of a mile
to run, so that he might be supposed to have cooled, yet as it was done uno
actu, without any interruption, it is interpreted only as manslaughter.—
Manslaughter is not punished with death, but with a brand in the hand, on
the pannels pleading his clergy, and confiscation as above. The origin of
110 this custom of acquitting one for manslaughter who | can read took it⟨s⟩
rise in the following manner.[65] The clergy in the earlier times, as we are all
apt to think well and commend the customs of the times we live in and
prefer them to all others, were very averse to the introduction of capitall
punishments. They said that ⟨?the⟩ mild and humane temper of the
Christian religion could not admit of such severe punishments, {as we
find by severall of the books of cannon law}; a fine or composition was all
that could be exacted by a man who had a due regard for religion, even for
the greatest crimes.—They therefore opposed with all their might all
capital punishments, ascribing that to religion which was no more than the
remains of barbarity and an evident mark of the weakness of government.
When Canute introduced capital punishments, they did all they could
to        [t] that proceeding, but all their endeavours were to no purpose.
They still however contended that the clergy could not be subjected to such
111 an unjust constitution. When therefore any one | was condemned before
the civil court, he might be claimed by the bishop, which generally was the

[q] The last four words, which are written vertically at the side of the page, replace 'of
manslaughter'        [r] The last six words are written vertically at the side of the page
[s] Possibly deleted        [t] Illegible word

[65] Hale, II.44.

case; or if not he might claim the benefit of clergy and by that means be carried before the ecclesiasticall court, which as it was of the least severity was always more agreable. Here, notwithstanding of his former sentence, he was allowed an oath of purgation, to which if he could add the oaths of 12 witnesses declaring him to be innocent in their opinion, he was acquitted. But altho he could not thus purge himself of the crime, the bishop might consider whether he was reclaimable or not; if he was thought reclaimable he was adjudged to perform certain ecclesiasticall pennances; and if he was not thought reclaimable he was confined for life.—In this manner not only the clergy themselves evaded the law, but all those who had any dependance on the church evaded the law; the man who swept the church, the door-keeper and the other servants all came in as clergy. {As every one who was any way a clergy man was freed from the punishment, it was easy for the clergy to free any one they pleased from it by making one of the lower orders of clergy, as deacons, by the first tonsure, similar to what we call preachers; [v.111] and as the clergy were then inclin'd to grant their pro-tection to any one who asked it few or none would be punished.} To

112 | restrain therefore in some measure this power of the clergy, it was estab-lished that when one claimed the benefit of clergy the Bible should be brought him, and if he could read the claim was sustained but if he could not he was rejected. Reading was then thought a sufficient test of his being a clergy man, as the chief part of their employment was to read the liturgy and none but clergy men had acquired so much learning as to be able to do this. This continued till the time of Henry the 8th, who took it away intirely with regard to murder.[66] {This benefit of clergy extended at first not only to homicide but to all felonious deeds or felonies, that is, all crimes which were under the pain of capitall punishment excepting treason, and by this means included even homicide from malice fore-thought. — — —} But notwithstanding, it still subsists with regard to manslaughter, {which is the 2ᵈ species of felonious homicide. In the ex-cusable it was never necessary.—}ᵘ and to this day it is in use that one who claims the benefit of clerg⟨y⟩ having been guilty of manslaughter, except-ing in the cases above mentioned, is acquitted, unless a small punishment of being branded in the hand. {The power of the clergy was no less in Scot-land than in England; but as this benefit of clergy was not necessary in the civil courts here, so it was intirely abolished on the expulsion of the Romish clergy. And now there is no distinction betwixt murder and manslaughter according to the Scots law, both being equally punishable with death.[67]

ᵘ 'and chance manly' deleted

---

[66] 23 Henry VIII, c. 1 (1532).
[67] Cf. TMS II.iii.2.8: 'if, by . . . imprudent action . . ., he should accidentally kill a man, he is, by the laws of many countries, particularly by the old law of Scotland, liable to the last punishment.'

[v.112] By a statute of Queen Anne[68] this priviledge of the benefit of clergy was extended even to persons who can not read, as many cases occurred where the person was not to be got off, for want of that qualification.}

    Chance manly, which is the accidentall killing of a man without any
113 design, is | reckoned altogether[v] excusable; but this as well ⟨as⟩ manslaughter is under severall restrictions. For ⟨if⟩ it is committed in the attempting some felonious action, the crime is considered in the same light as murder.[69] Thus if one in shooting tame fowls, in order to convey them away by stealth, should happen to kill a man, he is considered as a murderer altho he had no design to kill any one, as the action he was engaged in was of itself unlawfull and felonious. The same is the case with one who in breaking a warren or park in order to steal the deer or rabits[w] should happen by accident to kill the keeper. For tho neither the accidentall killing of a man, nor the breaking of a park or warren, when there was no theft committed are capital, yet as the attempt is felonious he is considered as a murtherer. {And here not only the murtherer but all who were engaged in the same undertaking will be liable to a prosecution for murder.} The stricter lawyers are even of opinion that one who has no title to hunt or carry fire arms, if he should then happen to kill a man, would be capitally
114 punished; but by the present law he | will only be liable in the penalty enacted against those who hunt or carry arms without a proper title. In the same manner, if one riding an unruly horse in the streets with a design to frighten people should by any means kill a man, he would according to the opinion of the more strict lawyers be considered as a murderer, but by mildness of the present laws would rather, I imagine, be punished in a less severe manner. {And in the same manner, in killing a man se defendendo it must be altogether evident that there was no other way of saving his life but the death of his adversary; as when he is pushed to the wall.} The 1st of the justifiable homicides, {which is to be distinguished from se defendendo by there being no previous quarrel, in which case it is only excusable,} is that which is committed by one in the defence of his person or goods or house. Thus if one should be atta⟨c⟩ked on the high way and had no probable way of escaping but by killing the robber; or if his house was attacked and in the defence of it he should happen to kill the assailant, he would be liable to no punishment. Nor would one who was without provocation attacked in the streets and had no way of escaping. But if he should
115 retire 10 or | 12 paces, not with a design to make his escape, which might have been done, but to draw his weapon, and should afterwards return to

---

    [v] The last two words replace 'in like manner'    [w] Numbers written above the words 'deer' and 'rabits' indicate that their order was intended to be reversed

---

    [68] 5 and 6 Anne, c. 6 (1706).
    [69] Hale, I.37; Hawkins, I.31.40 ff.

the charge, he will be accounted guilty of manslaughter at least.[x,y] The
other case is when a man who resists the kings officers or flies from them
is[z] killed either in the scuffle or in the pursuit by them or their attendants
⟨?this⟩ is not thought to render them any way punishable. But if he should
be killed by persons no way concerned, they will be liable to the punishment of murther. For though they have a right to apprehend and stop him,
yet they can not with any justice go the length of putting him to death as
they are not going about their proper business. There is a 3ᵈ case in which
homicide is justifiable and liable to no punishment. That is, where one has
no way to save his life but by killing another. There is but one case wherein
116 this can occur, as far as I know, which is the instance commonly | given by
authors, which is when two men after a shipwreck get upon the same plank,
and it appears evident that they can not be both saved by it; if then one of
them should push the other off the homicide would be accounted justifiable, for tho' he had here no better right to push the other off than the
other had to push him, yet he had the plea of necessity on his side as there
was no other way of saving his life. But this is of so little consequence and
so seldom occurs that the law omitts it altogether.[70]

Homicide therefore by the English law is of 3 kinds. 1ˢᵗ, felonious
homicide, which is of two species, murther from malice forethought, and
manslaughter. 2ᵈ, excusable homicide, also of two kinds, chance manly or
homicidium per infortunium, and hom. se defendendo. 3, justifiable
homicide, which is also considered as being of two sorts, either where one
kills a man in defence of his person, family, or property, or when an officer
in apprehending a criminal who makes resistance, or when one is in this
case killed by those who are giving assistance to the kings officers.[a]

There is a considerable difference betwixt justifiable homicide and
117 those which are only excusable or | pardonable by the benefit of clergy. For
if one be accused of murther and knows that he has been guilty only of
manslaughter, he can not free himself by alledging that he was only guilty
of manslaughter, but he must plead either guilty of m. or not g.,[b] be
arraigned of murder and stand his triall, and leave the circumstances of the
proof to shew his crime to have been manslaughter. And if it appears so to
the judge, or rather jury, they give in their verdict, not guilty of murther,
but guilty of manslaughter, and he may then plead the benefit of clergy. In
the same manner one who being only guilty of chance-manly or se defen. is

---

[x] The last three words replace 'murther'    [y] At this point the following sentence
is struck out: 'But he has now [illegible word] a legal process by which he can obtain his
pardon.—'         [z] Illegible word deleted    [a] At this point the following words are
struck out: 'There is this difference with regard to manslaughter peculiar to it, that the
person who is accused of ['it' deleted] murther and found guilty can no'    [b] The
reading of the last eight words, which are interlined between 'must' and 'be', is doubtful

---

[70] Hawkins, I.28.11, 17, and 26.

accused of murder, he can not plead at first guilty of chance-manly or murder se defendendo, but must plead guilty of murder or not guilty, and leave to the jury from the alleviating circumstances to bring him not guilty of murder but guilty of chance manly, on which he is dismiss'd with penalty of goods, etc. But on the other hand, if one who is guilty only of justifiable ⟨homicide⟩ is accused of murder, he need not allow himself to be arrainged of murder, but may at the first plead not guilty of murder, and

118 may | specify what sort of homicide they have been guilty of and the circumstances which shew it to be so, on which they will be immediately dismissed.

We may observe here also that not only the rationall creatures which have been the occasion of the death of a man are liable to punishment, but in allmost all nations even the animate and inanimate things which have been the occasion of so great a misfortune as the death of a man {were in a manner given up to punishment.} We naturally look upon such things as have been the occasion of the death of our friend, especially if it has been by accident, with a certain horror and aversion, as the sword or other instrument, or the ox which gored him. They were considered as horrenda et excrabilia, horrible, excrable, and devoted. Hence they were said to be deodat,[71] which signifies not only consecrated but what was to be held as unhallowed. Among the Athenians there was a court called       [72] which

119 had the triall and disposall | of all such things; and we read that an ax, which falling from the cornice of a house by accident killed a man, was solemnly condemned and carried with great pomp and thrown into the sea.[73] By the Jewish law the ox that gored was to be put to death.[74] When in this manner animate or inanimate things happen to be the occasion of a mans death, it excites in us a sort of[c] resentment or anger in our animall nature which must be appeased somehow or other;[75] a sword which accidentally killed our friend is, as we said, looked on with abhorrence; but if when it performed that deed it was in the hand of another, our resentment passes from the sword to the person who held it as the cause of the death. By the English law of deodat, what ever was the occasion[s] of a mans death was thus devoted; formerly the clergy claimed it, and now the king,

---

[c] 'animall' deleted

---

[71] Sc. deodand.

[72] Blank in MS. 'Prytaneum': Pausanias, *Description of Greece*, I.28.11, mentioning the trial of an axe.

[73] Meursius, *Themis Attica* (1685), I.17, cited by Kames, *Law Tracts*, I.13; it was a statue which fell.

[74] Exodus 21:28.

[75] In TMS II.iii.1.3, after noting that resentment and gratitude are often directed both at inanimate objects and at animals, Smith adds that the latter is less irrational than the former. 'Animals, therefore, are less improper objects of gratitude and resentment than inanimated objects. The dog that bites, the ox that gores, are both of them punished.'

as being the head of the church. If a single$^d$ horse in a$^e$ when it was standing
120 still, killed a man, or if one climbing up by the wheel fell and was | killed or
much hurt, then the wheel or the horse is deodat. But if the team be in
motion, and the man is killed by the joint force of the whole {or if one fell
from a waggon in motion}, then the whole team and waggon and all in it is
deodat. The same hel[le]d with regard to a miln-wheel. But it has lately
been determined that the goods in the waggon shall not be deodat, nor the
miln-wheel unless it be severed and set up against a wall. Not only the ox
that gores or the horse who kicks {which are in most countries put to
death}, but the horse from whom one has fallen and been killed, tho by his
own negligence, may be claimed by the king. But one who is killed by a fall
from a tree or a house, and in generall all that is called vincta et fixa, does
not render that thing deodat. It has been disputed whether a man by
falling into the sea from a ship rendered the ship deodat. This has been
determined in the negative, as sailors are by their condition exposed to such
dangers at all times and they must very frequently happen.[76]
121      | This is all I think necessary to say [to say] concerning homicide or the
killing of a man, the most atrocious injury which can be committed against
the person of a man.—We come now to another method by which men may
be injured in their persons, that is, by mutilation, demembration, beating,
bruising, etc.—With regard to all these the most antient laws of all countries
have appointed pecuniary compensation, and that from the same motives
as they appointed them for murder.—This appears to have been the practise of the barbarian ancestors of all the nations of Europe, in one generall
manner. In the laws of every one of these nations we find a particular
estimation set upon each particular member.—Thus in the [the] laws of the
Lombards[77] if one drives out 1 teeth of those$^f$ [teeth] which appear in
laughter he paid 2 shil.; if 1 of those which do not, that is a jaw tooth, 1$^{sh}$;
if 2 of the former, 4$^{sh}$; if 3, 6$^{sh}$; if two of the latter, 2$^{sh}$; if 3, 3$^{sh}$; but if he
122 smote$^g$ out any more of either sort | he paid no more but got them into the
bargain. In the same manner there was a certain price set on a blow on the
head, about 3 shill. But after they had given as many as came to 18$^{sh}$ they
paid no more, the rest being taken into the bargain; for otherwise one might
be ruined by giving an other a very hearty drubbing. In the same manner
there was a set price for the cutting off every particular finger of ones hand,
which differed also according as it was of the right or left hand; and so of
the foot; so much for a hand or arm, foot or leg, as it was right or left; so
much for an eye, a nose, or an ear. This prevailed over all Europe. It was

$^d$ Reading doubtful        $^e$ 'drawing' deleted        $^f$ Numbers written above 'teeth'
and 'of those' indicate that their order was intended to be reversed        $^g$ Reading
doubtful

[76] Hale, I.32; Hawkins, I.26.5,6.
[77] *Lex Longobardorum,* I.7.

only such members as were absolutely necessary for military service, the great business of those times, the mutilation of which were subjected to a severer punishment, as a capitall one or retaliation; and to these we may add castration.

123   The laws of all countries in their secondary state have introduced retaliation in place | of the pecuniary compensation. This was at first brought in when the delinquent was not able to pay the forfeit, in the same manner as capitall punishment for murder was introduced in place of the compensation, when the murderer or his friends were not able or would not pay the composition.—And in the same manner as[h] revenge requires that the death of the person should attone for the death of the friend, so it will require that the delinquent should be as much hurt and in the same way as the offended person. Thus the Jewish law says eye for eye and tooth for tooth,[78] and the laws of the Twelve Tables quicunque, etc. nisi pacit cum eo, detur talio.[79] Laws still posterior to these gave damages to the injured person instead of retaliation. Retaliation is without doubt a barbarous and inhuman custom, and is accordingly laid aside in most

124   civilized nations. In Scotland and England | it is quite abolished. It however still remains in some measure in Holland, particularly with regards to wounds in the face, which is a sort of maiming very common in that country. The offender is in this case brought to the scaffold, measures the wound he had made in the face of the other, and endeavours to make one in his face of the same length, breadth, and depth.—Maiming from malice forethought is death, by a particular incident which happened in the time of Ch. 2ᵈ.—[80] During a debate in the House of Commons, whether the playhouse should be kept up or not, some of the members happend to alledge in its defence that it was kept for the kings amusement. On this Sir John Coventry asked whether this was meant of the male or the female players. This so enraged the court party, as it was a rude joke tho very

125   great | affront, that at the kings desire the Duke of Monmouth, his natural son, and some others way-laid Sir John, and tho he defended himself very gallantly, yet he was at last overpowered and the assassins slit his nose and ears. This appeared ⟨so⟩ shocking to the House of Commons that they immediately made a law,[81] making it capitall for any person to ly in wait for and maim another. This law has only been once put in execution since that

---

[h] 'murder is' deleted

---

[78] Exodus 21:24, Deuteronomy 19:21.

[79] *Si membrum rupit, ni cum eo pacit, talio esto* (Tab. VIII.2). 'For the breaking of a limb, unless there is agreement (for compensation) let there be talion' (cited by Kames, *Law Tracts*, I.42).

[80] Rapin, *History of England*, tr. Tindal, II.658; Burnet, *History of His Own Time* (1753), I.397.

[81] 22 and 23 Charles II, c. 1 (1670).

time; and in that case too was considerably extended. The case was this. One Woodbairn, an attorney, lay in wait for his brother in law, attended by *i*, a smith, whom he had hired for his assistance.[82] They knocked down the man with a hedge-bill and afterwards endeavoured to dispatch him with a reaping hook; but instead of killing him they only mangled his face and nose in a most shocking manner. The⟨?y⟩ were apprehended and

126 tried | on the above mentioned statute, which from the cause of its being enacted is called to this day the Coventry Act. He plead in his defence that he had not lain in wait for him with a design to maim him but with a design to murder him, and that as an attempt to murder the brought to the last point,*j* as the firing a pistol is not punishable with death, so he could not be condemned. The jury, however, being anxious to bring him in guilty, answered to this that though he had not lain in wait with a desire to maim, yet ⟨?as⟩ the instruments he used were such as that if they did not kill they must maim he ought to be condemned, and he and his accomplice were accordingly executed. Since which time, the lying in wait for one with instruments which must either*k* kill or maim has been considered as punishable with death.

Not only maiming, mutilation, and such like are punishable injuries, but

127 even the | bringing a person into fear of them by any threat or menace, as the clenching a fist, the drawing of a sword or pistol. This is called an assault. In the same manner when one beats or bruises one, without maiming or mutilating, he is punishable for the batterie. These as they are generally concommitant come under the title of assault and batterie, and are punishable by an arbitrary fine and damages. For the law is to provide not only for the safety but also for the security of the individualls.

Another injury which may be done to a mans person is by confining him and depriving him of his liberty. No one ought in equity to be confined but a criminall; there would however be an end of all exercise of judgement if the judge were not allowed to confine one before there was full proof made of his guilt. He has therefore the power of emprisonment, but not at

128 pleasure, for a capricious emprisonment without just | foundation is accounted wrongous or false (in England) imprisonment. But the information of one witness, whether it be attended with an oath or not, common fame, or any private knowledge of the judge, is a sufficient ground and frees him from the accusation of wrongous imprisonment. But if either the judge of himself commit one with⟨out⟩ sufficient grounds or the witness give designedly a false information, the imprisonment is accounted false in

---

*i* Blank in MS.        *j* Sic        *k* Illegible word deleted

[82] *Woodburne and Coke's Case* (1722), Howell's *State Trials*, XVI.53. The 'attorney' was in fact Coke (or Cooke), who, having unsuccessfully solicited Carter, a smith, to kill one Crispe (Coke's brother-in-law), then persuaded Woodburne, a labourer, to do it in his presence.

England and wrongous in Scotland, and a very high penalty is inflicted on the judge in the 1$^{st}$ case and in the 2$^d$ on the witness. Besides this if the judge refuses to take a sufficient bail for all crimes that are bailable (tho indeed an insufficient bail is highly punishable), which extends even to manslaughter, he is accounted as having been guilty of wrongous imprisonment, which in Scotland incurrs a penalty of £6000 for a peer, 300 for a gentleman, and so on.[83]—It might however happen that notwith-
129 standing | of all these precautions an innocent person (or other) might be detain a long time. For if he was taken immediately after an assize, and was not able to procure sufficient bail, he would be confined for about 6 months till the next assize before he could be brought to a trial. In England therefore it is provided that one by being at the expense of a writ of Habeas Corpus, and paying his journey costs, may be transported to the metropolis, and trial is given in 40 days.[84] This however is still a hardship, as a poor man can not afford these expences. This too is avoided in Scotland, as there is no need for a writ of Habeas Corpus, the sheriff in each county being a competent judge even in criminall causes, and judgement must be given in 60 days, and         $^l$ it is delayed is punished with a highe⟨r⟩ penalty, being counted wrongous imprisonment, besides a compensation
130 of 100 pound Scots for every such day for a peer, | and so proportionally for others; and if the party incline he may be transported personally to the Court of Session at Edinburgh.

*Gap of three-quarters of a page in MS.*

131      | Besides this of wrongous or false imprisonment, a man may be injured in his liberty in other shapes. Thus a man who by forcible confinement or other violence done to his liberty, or any threatenings, compells another to come under an obligation to$^m$ him, injures his liberty, as all obligations bring one under a restraint. Now all such contracts or obligations which are forced from on⟨e⟩ by duresse, as it is called, that is, by bringing one into a hardship or fear of one, are void, being extorted by fear. And all fear in the parties renders the obligation they have entered into void from the beginning.—A rape, as it is a breach of the liberty of the woman and a great injury to her,$^n$ is by the law of all civilized nations punished with death, as that alone seems to be a sufficient compensation for the injury done her. In the same way a marriage which is entered into by force is void; and

---

$^l$ Illegible word          $^m$ The last six words replace a number of illegible words, which may be 'to make a contract with'          $^n$ Two or three illegible words deleted

---

[83] Act, 1701, c. 6 (A.P.S. X.272) declares all non-capital crimes bailable. Failure to grant bail incurred the penalty of wrongous imprisonment: 6,000 pounds for a nobleman, 4,000 pounds a landed gentleman, 2,000 pounds another gentleman or burgess, and 400 pounds any other person.
[84] 20 days: 31 Charles II, c. 2 (Habeas Corpus Act, 1679).

besides, the party who forced the other is liable to a capitall punishment; for as it is generally the man who compells the woman, the same injury is
132 done to her reputation as | in the case of a rape. The death of the injurious person seems here to be the only satisfactory compensation for the injury of the woman. In the same manner also the person who compelled the other involuntarily to enter into an obligation not only loses that obligation but is also liable in an arbitrary penalty. Formerly indeed an arbitrary punishment of a fine was all that was exacted for a rape, but this in more civilized countries has always been converted into a capitall punishment; and this not only with regard to the compensation due to the person but also for the fine due to the king. There are in all criminall[o] cases two ways by which the criminall may be sued, either 1$^{st}$ on an indictment in the kings name, or 2$^{dly}$ by an appeal, which is at the instance of the private prosecutor. If therefore in the case of a rape, or a marriage or obligation extorted by duresse, the person injured should give consent to it afterwards,
133 or as they call it posterior agreement, this vitiates his appeal, | but still the criminal may be she[e]wed on an indictment in the kings name.—{We are to observe here that though[p] threatenings which put the person in fear, and by this means oblige him to enter into an obligation, render such obligations null and void; yet we are to understand this only with regard to such fear as the person has no tittle to put him into, as the threatening him with any accusation or defamation; but if he should threaten him with a prosecution on the head the obligation was demanded, this as it is *malus non injustus* will not render the obligation void.} There is however none of the personall rights of mankind which it is more difficult for the government of a country to preserve intire to the subject than that of liberty of his person. It must often happen that innocent persons accused of a crime will be either obliged to find bail for their appearance; or if the crime be very heinous or the bail necessary very high, even to suffer imprisonment. This indeed is not by the law looked upon as wrongous or false imprisonment, if he be committed on due evidence or information, but is at the same time a great incroachment on the liberty of the subject. It is however unavoidable in all societies; for if no person could be put in prison or secured till the crime he was accused of be proved against him, no criminall could ever be brought to justice. If the judge was not allowed to commit a person on
134 sufficient grounds of his being guilty, it would be the same in effect as | if he was not allowed to punish a criminall. A man who is not due a debt may indeed be made to bring bail for the summ, or if it be great to suffer imprisonment, but unless the judge had it in his power to imprison for debt many debts could never be paid. And the difficulty of bringing criminalls to justice would be still greater. The liberty of the subject is indeed as well provided for in Great Britain as in any other country. For as was before

---

[o] Replaces 'capitall'                                              [p] 'all' deleted

observed, the judge if he commits wrongously on his own opinion, or the person who gives a false information, is liable in a very high penalty. $2^{dly}$, judgement may be obtaind, either by being brought personally before the supreme courts, or in Scotland before the sheriff of the county, who being a judge even in capitall causes supersedes the necessity of the *Habeas Corpus Act*, in a very short time; and $3^{dly}$, every day in which the prisoner is detaind after that time and not brought to trial is punished by a severe penalty, either on the judge who delays to call him to judgement or on the
135 officer | who delays ex⟨e⟩cuting the sentence are liable in a very high penalty.[q] There are few countries where so great provision is made for the[r] liberty of the subject; in all arbitrary governments the subjects may be put into prison at the pleasure of the monarch; a lettre de caché in France will clap any one into the Bastile, nor has he either the power of bailing himself or of bringing on his triall till the government pleases; and in most other countries in Europe there is the same power. It must however happen, notwithstanding of all these precautions, that innocent persons will sometimes undergo hardships of this sort, in every society.

The next species of personal rights are those which entitle a man to a fair character, etc. The injuries which may ⟨be⟩ done to one in this way are[s] [are] commonly divided into those which are done by some action in presence of others, that tends to make on⟨e⟩ meanly thought. These are called real affronts.
136 The $2^{d}$ are those which are com|mitted by words, these are called *verball* affronts;[85] or lastly when they are put into writing, which are called libells.

First as to reall affronts. The law has been apt to consider these rather in the sense they were taken by the old law than in that which is suitable to the customs of modern times. That is, rather as assault or batterie than as an affront; and accordingly has given but a very small satisfaction for them. And to this in a great measure may be ascribed the great frequency of duelling. A blow, or the shaking of ones fist at one, or the spitting in ones face, by the law can receive but a very small satisfaction; ten pounds is all the fine that is paid for a blow in the face. {In the Roman law the penalty for such an injury was only about 2 or 3 shillings;[86] and of the same little consequence was the recompense for all those injuries which would be reckoned the highest affronts. And by our law at this day the fine for pulling ones nose, etc. is but very little.[t] The smallness of the punishment had not [v.136] indeed the effect of introducing duels into Rome, but the different circumstances of the nations easily accounts for that.} And indeed these injuries, considered as assault and batterie, are

[q] The last seven words are clearly superfluous [r] 'secu' deleted [s] 'what' deleted [t] A new paragraph apparently begins at this point in the verso note

[85] Mackenzie, *Laws and Customes of Scotland in Matters Criminal* (1678), I.30: 'injuries are either verbal or real.'

[86] 25 asses; cf. Aulus Gellius, XX.1.13.

but very inconsiderable and are sufficiently recompensed by the penalty incurred by law. But this fine is by no means an adequate satisfaction when they are considered in the manner they are in those countries where the
137  laws[e] | of honour are received, for there they are considered as the greatest affront imaginable, and indeed are in this case very great ones. The injury does not consist in the hurt that is done, but in the necessity it puts one to, either of exposing his life in a duel, or being for ever after despised and contemned as ⟨a⟩ poor, mean-spirited, faint-hearted wretch by those of his own rank, from whose company he will be ever afterwards excluded. The small pecuniary[u] punishment is no sufficient recompense for such an affront. The same is the case with regard to many verball injuries, such as giving one the lye, or other reproachfull words, which as they are looked on at this time as sufficient cause for a duel must be very heinous injuries. {They are in themselves very unmannerly, but without the consideration of their consequence would not be the most unpardonable.} It is intirely from this new notion of honour that the injury of such affronts has arose. This owed its first origins to the judicial combat which was established by law, but has several other concomitant causes which
138  | have kept it up till this day, after the judicial combat has been 300 or 400 years in dissuse. Before that time these injuries were considered merely by the hurt they did the person, and the punishment is accordingly very small, and so inaddequate to the injury that no one will think it worth his while to sue for it.—We see that formerly those actions and words which we think the greatest affront were little thought of. Plato in his dialogues commonly introduces Socrates giving the lye to those whom he converses with, which is taken as no more than ordinary conversation. Longinus quotes, as one of the most sublime passages in all Demosthenes' writings, that where he[v] relates in the most pathetick terms the hearty drubbing the clien⟨t⟩ had got, how his adversary struck him first in one
139  place, then in another, and so thro the whole of the squabble, | dwelling on every particular and explaining it fully to his judges.[87] This passage[s] Longinus quotes as an instance of the sublime, so that it is evident it was not reckoned mean in any one to sue one before a court for such an affront and to expatiate on all the circumstances. But if one should at this time explain to the judge all the particulars of the drubbing he had got and beg him to give redress, this would appear the most ridiculous and mean behaviour possible, that he had not called the offender to account of

---

[u] Replaces 'arbitrary'      [v] 'introduces one' deleted

[87] Demosthenes, 21.72 (*Against Meidias*), cited by Longinus, *On Sublimity*, 20, but simply as an example of combined figures of speech, not 'as one of the most sublime passages . . .'. Smith has misremembered Longinus' remark a few lines earlier (end of ch. 18) that a certain passage of *Herodotus* is reckoned one of the most sublime. The reporter first wrote 'drubbing he had got' (correctly, since the assault was on Demosthenes himself) but then changed 'he' to 'the' and interlined 'clien'.

himself. For when the law do not give satisfaction somewhat adequate to the injury, men will think themselves intitled to take it at their own hand. The small punishment therefore which is incurred by these affronts according to our law is one great cause of duelling, and is to be accounted a deficientia juris. The punishment which was contrived by the court of honour in France, though it did not take effect, was much better calculated

140 to the | injury received by such an affront. Viz, as the injury done was with a design to expose the person and make him ridiculous, so the proper punishment would be to make the person who injured the other as ridiculous as he had made him, by exposing to shame in the pillory, and by imprisonment or fine, arbitrarily adapted to the circumstances of the affront.— Verball injuries are of [of] all others least easily prevented, as there is nothing so ungovernable or which is so apt to offend on a sudden as the tongue. Those[w] which are of little moment are not heeded by the law; tho some of them are punished very severely according to the strict laws of honour. The law however gives redress for the more important ones which might be of prejudice to the person. Thus if one is said by another to have been guilty of murder, adultery, or any other crime which

141 would make him liable to punishment, he may have redress before | the civill court. Or if one injures anothers title, e.g. affirms that I have no better title to the house he possesses[88] than he has, as by this means he may give me trouble by setting others to raise a claim against me, he may be called to account before the court. It is also to be observed that the truth of these calumnies, tho it may be alledged as an alleviation of the crime, can not altogether barr the prosecution, for it is not the business of any unconnected person to expose the secret faults or the secret defects of right of any one. {The punishments for these injuries are what are naturally pointed out by the revenge of the injured person. For as the injury was in exposing the person, so the punishment is an arbitrary fine, imprisonment, or pilloring.—} There are other calumnies which the civill court does not attend to, as that of incontinence, etc. The civill court does not punish these if they were realy committed; that is left to the ecclesiasti-call court; and in like manner when an accusation is brought against one of having charged another with these crimes, the prosecution must be before the ecclesiasticall court. And in general all redress for false accusa-

142 tions must be obtained before that court where the crime, if com|mitted, would be prosecuted.

Written injuries or libells, as they are more deliberate and malicious injuries than those that are spoken, often without thought, so are they more severely punishable by the law. Not only the[x] author but the writer,

---

[w] 'therefore' deleted        [x] 'writer' deleted

---

[88] *Sic*. Presumably 'I possess' was intended.

printer, or publisher or spreader of all such libells. Pillory, imprisonment, etc. are the penalties annexed to this crime, and this is even extended to those who, finding such a libell, are at pains to spread it. {But however as the libeller generally hurts his own character more than that of him whom he libells,[v] it is most prudent to despise and not to raise prosecutions on such libell, unless the accusation be particularly marked with circumstances as to make it probable, and be of such a nature as to hurt considerably the reputation of the person. For in other cases the taking notice of a libell makes the person appear more probably to be guilty than if he had despised them.} The severity of the punishment of libells and the earnestness of their prosecution depends greatly on the form of the government. In all aristocraticall governments, or where ever the nobles have great power, they are punished with the greatest severity, and even more than in absolute governments. For a libell which would not affect the king, as being too much above such scandall, would greatly irritate a lesser lord [or][z] and consequently they would prosecute the offenders with the

143 greatest rigour. There is no country in Europe | excepting the republics of Holland and Switzerland where they are less regarded than in England; libells and abusive papers are handed about here every day which would send the writers to the Bastile in France or be punished with death; and the severity is no less in most of the monarchies of Europe at this day. In old Rome, in the monarchicall and aristocraticall governments, the publishers of libells were punished with death. The law of the Twelve Tables ran thus, Qui malum carmen in alium condiderat,[a] capite plectetur.[89] This is said to have been only of those which accused one of capitall crimes, but for this there is no foundation.[b] But in the time of the democraticall government of Rome this punishment, which was a very unreasonable one, was taken away, and great freedom in this respect indulged to the people. But when the monarchicall form of government was again restored, the old punishment returned; Augustus renewed the law of the 12 Tables, and many were executed on that law in his time, and still more

144 under Tiberius.[90] | And in the time of Valentinian and Theodosius or thereabouts, this extended not only to the author and writer but even to one who found a libell and did not immediately burn it but shewed it to others.[91] In generall the freedom in this respect is a great test of the liberty of the people. In all absolute governments and arbitrary ones they are

---

[v] 'this' deleted        [z] Illegible word deleted        [a] Several illegible words deleted
[b] The last sentence is written vertically at the side of the page

---

[89] 'Whoever had composed an incantation against another shall suffer a capital penalty' (Tab. VIII.1). The exact text has to be conjectured, e.g. from Horace, *Satires*, II.1.82: *si mala condiderit in quem quis carmina, ius est iudiciumque.*
[90] Tacitus, *Annals*, I.72.
[91] *C.* 9.36.2 = *C. Th.*, 9.34.7.

altogether suppressed, but where the people enjoy more freedom they are not much regarded. Libells of the most scandalous sort indeed, but which are of no great detriment by their frequency, are every day published without being taken the least notice of. Aristocracies are of all others most jealous of them, and all[c] monarchies endeavour to suppress them, unless it be the British.

### *Thursday Febry 3ᵈ 1763*

The only injuries which can be done to a man as a man which have not been already considered are those which injure one in his estate.[d] {This may be done either by injuring him in his real or his personall estate.
145 First, of the injuries done to one in his real estate.} These may | be of two sorts, for they may either 1ˢᵗ injure him in his immoveable or 2ᵈˡʸ in his moveable possessions. Again one may be injured in his immoveable possessions either by burning and destroying his house, which by the English law is called arson; or by being forcibly dispossessed of his estate. — Fire raising, incendium or arson, when a fire is raised wilfully in an others house, is punished capitally by the Roman, English, and Scots law. The setting ones own house on fire, if it be done with design to raise fire in the adjoining, has also been thought liable to be capitally punished. It is also punishable in a less degree if it be done with intention to hurt any one or his goods who may be in it. {But the burning of a house thro negligence is not punishable.} The dispossessing one of his estate is in all cases punishable; and the dispossesser is obliged to restore the estate to the person who was turned out, by a very short and expeditious process. And in this case the civil constitution extends considerably farther than reason
146 and | nature dictate. For naturally any one who is turned out of what he justly poss⟨ess⟩es would think himself intitled to reinstate himself in the[e] possession of his property by force. But this civil governments do not allow, as dissagreable to the peace and order of society. Insomuch that one ⟨who⟩ violently takes possession of what he knows he has a right ⟨to⟩ is, as well as any other who turns one out of what he possesses, liable to be sued by an action on that head, which by a very summary process obliges him to give up the estate. And this process requires no more than the proof of the force used to dispossess him, whereas the proof of ones right to the estate is always tedious and often very doubtfull. When one has been thus reinstated in the estate he possessed, the other may then bring the proofs of his right; but violence is at all times prohibited in the taking possession of an estate.
147 It is to be observed however, that if one | who has thus violently taken possession of an estate be allowed to possess it peaceably for the space of

---

two years,[92] he can not afterwards be sued on the plea of violence, but must be allowed to continue in the possession of it untill the other make out his rights, which ⟨is⟩ as was said a much more doubtfull and tedious process.— It is to be observed also that tho it be unlawfull to take possession of ones own by violence, yet it is not unlawfull to keep[f] ones possessions by force, as that is no more than acting in his own defence.

In the moveable part of ones estate the injury may be of thre⟨e⟩ sorts, either 1ˢᵗ, theft, that is, the clandestinely conveying away anothers goods with design to apply them to his own use; 2ᵈ, robbery; and 3ᵈ, piracy, which differs from the other as the one is committed by land and the other at sea.

Theft appears naturally not to merit a very high punishment; it is a
**148** | despicable crime and such as raises our contempt rather than any high resentment.— It is however punished capitally in most countries of Europe, and has been so since the        [93] century. In England all theft which amounts to above the value of 12ᵈ is accounted grand larceny and is punish'd by death without the benefit of clergy. Thefts to a less amount than 12ᵈ are punishd by banishment, a fine, or whipping. The English law and the Scots also accounted, till the time of George 2ᵈ, no theft capitall unless the thing stole was the property of some certain person.[94] Thus it is not theft punishable to convey away pigeons at a distance from the pigeon house, nor geese or ducks when they have strayed far from the house; {nor is it theft for one who has no title to shoot wild fowl of any sort.} tho it is theft to convey them from the house or the nests. In the same manner, till a statute of George the 2ᵈ, it was not theft to kill a deer in a forest or chase, tho it was in a park or inclosure, unless the theft was committed in the night time by persons whose faces were blacked.[95] But
**149** by that | statute the killing of a deer by a person who has no right to it is punishable with death. In Scotland all sorts of theft are punishable by death, but the amount of the theft must be considerably greater than it is in England. Thefts of smaller value are punished by banishment. But there is one case wherein thefts of the smallest value are punished with death both by the Scots and English law, that is, where a house is broken open in the commission of it. The security of the individualls requires here a severer and more exact punishment than in the other cases. Burglary

---

*f* Replaces 'defend'

---

[92] In fact three years: 31 Elizabeth I, c. 11 (1589); Hawkins, I.64.8,14.

[93] Blank in MS. Probably 'twelfth' was intended; cf. the reference to Frederick I on p. 129 below.

[94] Hawkins, I.33.24–6 (English); M'Douall, II.3.12 (Scots). The reference is probably to statutes for the better protection of game by higher penalties for poaching, e.g. 10 George II, c. 32 (1737) (England) and 24 George II, c. 34 (1751) (Scotland).

[95] 9 George I, c. 22 (1722), made perpetual by 31 George II, c. 42 (1758); Hawkins, I.49.

therefore is always capitally punished. The punishment which is commonly inflicted on theft is certainly not at all proportionable to the crime. It is greatly too severe, and such as the resentment of the injured person would not require. Theft appears to be rather contemptible and despicable than fit to excite our resentment. The origin of this severe punishment arose

150 | from the nature of the allodial and feudal governments and the confusions which were then so frequent. Each allodiall lord was as it were an independent prince, who made war and peace as he inclined. Each of these lords was commonly at war or at least in enmity with all his nei⟨gh⟩bours, and all his vassals were in like manner seperate from those of the other lords and would always endeavour to carry off plunder from the lands of their neighbours. The punishment of theft was at first some pecuniary fine, or compensation. {Amongst the Romans theft was punished with the restitution of double of the thing stolen, with this distinction, that if the thief was caught with the thing stolen about him he was to restore fould,[96] and two fold if he was not caught in the fact: in the fang or not in the fang (as it is expressed in the Scots law⟨)⟩, and in the Latin writers fur manifestus et nec manifestus. It will be proper to take the more notice of this, as the reason of it does not appear to be very evident, and that which is alledged by Montesquieu,[97] tho very ingenious, does not appear to me to be the true one. He says that this law was borrowed from the Lacedemonians, who, as they traind their youth chiefly to the military art, encouraged them in theft, as it was imagined this might sharpen their wit [v.150] and skill in the stratagems of war. Theft therefore was as they suppose not ⟨?at⟩ all discouraged amongst them, but rather honoured if it was not discovered before it was finished; but when the thief was discovered it was looked on as a disgrace, as being not cleverly performed. From this custom of the Lacedemonians, the Romans, says he, borrowed their law; which though it was proper enough in the Lacedemonian government was very unfit in the Roman. But this does not appear probable in any part. For in the 1st place there is no good ground for imagining that the Lacedemonians encouraged theft. This is conjectured from some passages[g] of      [98], particularly one where he tells that there was a table kept at the publick charge for the old men of the city, but none for the younger men. They however were encouraged to pourloin for themselves what they could from the table, for the reason above assigned. This however is very different from what is properly denominated theft, which was not at all encouraged. 2dly, we do not see that theft was ever encouraged by the Romans, for the

*g* Reading doubtful

[96] *Sic.* Probably 'four fold' was intended. *Inst.* 4.1.3,5.
[97] XXIX.13.
[98] Blank in MS. Plutarch, *Life of Lycurgus*, 17–18.

fur nec manifestus was punished as well as the fur [nec] manifestus; though not so severly. The reas[v.151]on was this. Punishment is always adapted originally to the resentment of the injured person; now the resentment of a person against the thief when he is caught in the fact ⟨?is greater⟩ than when he is only discovered afterwards and the theft must be proved against him, which gives the persons resentment time to cooll. The satisfaction he requires is much greater in the former than in the latter case. We see too that there was the same odds made in the punishment of other crimes. The murderer who was caught *rubro manu* was punished much more severely} than he against whom the murder was afterwards proven.} But to prevent the abovementioned dissorders the Emperor    the  99 made a law that theft should be punished with death. From this law of his, capitall punishment first was inflicted on those who were guilty of theft; this took place at first in Germany and Italy and spread afterwards over the whole of Europe. The great facility of committing any crime, and the

151 continuall danger that thereby | arises to the individualls, always inhance the punishment. Theft was in this state of government very easily and securely committed and therefore was punished in a very severe manner.— The Scots law some time ago inflicted a punishment still more severe than on any others on those landed gentlemen who were guilty of theft. This would appear very odd at this time, but naturally followed from the manners of the times. Every clan was at enmity with all its neighbours, and each chieftan was the chief abbettor and receipt of all the thefts, robberies, and

*h* that were committed. They were the grand receipt and the chief spring of all those irregularities; it was therefore necessary that their punishment should be the more severe. It was therefore not only a capitall punishment, but this crime was allso attended with forfeiture of goods, an incapacity of inheriting, and all other parts of the punishment of petty

152 treason.[1] But tho a capitall | punishment might be in some respects proper in those times, yet it is by no means a suitable one at this time. Ignominy, fine, and imprisonment would be a far more adequate punishment.

The progress of government and the punishment of crimes is always much the same with that of society, or at least is greatly dependent on it. In the first stages of society, when government is very weak, no crimes are punished; the society has not sufficient strength to embolden it to intermeddle greatly in the affairs of individualls. The only thing they can venture upon, then, is to bring about a reconciliation and obtain some

---

*h* Illegible word

---

99 Blanks in MS. Frederick I: *Lib. Feudorum*, II.27.8, and Gothofredus' note thereto.
[1] Sir G. Mackenzie, *Laws and Customes of Scotland in Matters Criminal* (1678), I.19.12, citing Act, 1587, c. 50 (A.P.S. III.451, c. 34).

compensation from the offender to the offended. But when the society gathers greater strength, they[i] not only exact a compensation but change it into a punishment. The punishment⟨s⟩ in this stage of society are always the most severe imaginable. It is not the injuries done to individualls that a society which has lately obtaind strength sufficient to punish crimes will first take into its consideration. These it can only enter into by sympathy,
153 by putting | itself in the state of the person injured. Those which immediately affect the state are those which will first be the objects of punishment. These the whole society can enter into as they affect the whole equally. Of this sort are treason; all conspiracies against the state; and deserting the ranks in the field of battle, and all such cowardice. Tacitus[2] tells us that cowardice and treasonable practises were the only crimes punishable amongst the antient Germans, {and all such crimes were capitally punished.} When therefore the state came to take under its consideration the injuries done to particular persons, it was rather as injuries to the state than as injuries to the individualls; the punishments therefore for all crimes were in this stage of society,[j] immediately after compensation had been thrown aside, the most bloody of any and often far from being proportionable to the injuries.[k] When society made a still greater progress and the peace and good order of the community were provided for, and tranquillity firmly established, these punishments would again be mitigated
154 | and by degrees brought to bear a just proportion to the severall crimes. History affords us many instances of this. The laws of the 12 Tables, which were made about the time of the declension of compensation, punished many of the slighter crimes with death. A libell, as we observed,[3] was capitally punished. But afterwards the praetors changed these punishments into milder ones, more suited to naturall equity. In the same manner the first laws that the Athenians had after the method of compensation had been laid aside were those of Draco, the most bloody ones imaginable. Death was the punishment of the smallest as well as of the greatest crimes; so that      [4] says he punished in the same manner the stealing of a cabbage as he did sacrilege or murder. These were afterwards succeeded by the mild and equitable laws of Solon. In the same manner also in Britain allmost all crimes of moment were considered as treasonable; the killing of any person, at first[l] and afterwards the husband or the wifes killing
155 the other, robbery, and theft in some cases, as that | before mentioned, even the non payment of a debt, were considered as treasonable, and punishd accordingly. We already observed that this has been in some measure

---

[i] Replaces 'and has'      [j] 'when' deleted      [k] Illegible word deleted      [l] Numbers written above the last five words indicate that they were intended to read 'at first of any person'

---

[2] *Germania*, xii.                                                    [3] 143 above.
[4] Blank in MS. Plutarch, *Life of Solon*, 17.

taken away as with regard to theft. That regarding debt has been altogether taken away in Scotland, and is laid aside in the practise of the English law. These treasons were in generall taken away at the union of the kingdoms in Queen Annes times.[5] The first punishments after compensation is laid aside are always the most severe and are gradually mitigated to the proper pitch in the advances of society.

The 2$^d$ manner in which a man may be injured in his moveable estate is by robbery. Though theft does not excite our resentment to any great pitch, yet robbery, which forcibly takes our goods from us, will step up our resentment very much. Robbery has therefore been generally punished with death in all countries when compositions were laid aside, which was the first thing that was provided for in all criminall cases. Not only the

156 forcible carrying off ones goods by putting him in fear of his person but | all extortions by means of fear are accounted robbery. Thus if one should either make one give him a summ of money for a commodity of no value, an expedient often try'd by robbers to evade the law, or if he should make one sell his goods at a great dissadvantage, all such extortions are accounted robbery and are punished with death. But if one should oblige another to sell him his goods for a price considerably higher than what he could reasonably expect, this would not be accounted robbery as the person was not deprivd of any part of his price, but would rather be attributed to whim and caprice.[6]

Piracy is another species of robbery which likewise requires a severe punishment, and that not only from the resentment which all robberies excite in us but also from the great opportunities there are of committing it and$^m$ the great loss which may be sustained by it, as a great part of a mans property may be at once exposed, render a very high punishment absolutely necessary; and this as I said is generally a capitall one.[7]

157 | We come now to those injuries which may be done one in his personall estate. These are either, first, by fraud, whereby one cheats another out of his property in his personall estate; or 3$^{dly}$, by perjury; or 2$^{dly}$, by forgery.

The lesser frauds are generally obliged to be recompensed by the deceiver and are besides punished with a fine. There are however two species of fraud which are more severely punished; the 1$^{st}$ is with regard to bankruptcy. By the statute of bankruptcy in England, the debtor, on giving up all his substance to his creditors, is freed from all farther distress; but if he embezzles above 20£, besides his and his wifes wearing apparel, he is punished with death.[8] This law was made in the time of George 2$^d$, and many have been since executed upon it; and with great justice. For

---

$^m$ 'also' deleted

---

[5] 7 Anne, c. 21 (1708).                              [6] Hawkins, I.34.7.
[7] Hawkins, I.37.                    [8] 5 George II, c. 30 (1732); Hawkins, I.57.

though the resentment of the injured would not perhaps require so great a punishment yet there are severall circumstances which make it necessary. 158 The great benefit the person bankrupt receives | from this statute is no small agravation of his crime. But besides this, there is no fraud which is more easily committed without being discovered; one may take 1000 ways to conceal his effects; and the loss of the creditors may by this means be very great, as the best part of the effects may in this manner be very great.[n] The temptation also the debtor is under to commit this fraud and save some part of his effects make a high punishment necessary. For where ever the temptation and the opportunity are increased, the punishment must also be increased.— {For this reason, tho theft amongst the Romans was punished in most cases with the restitution of double, one half for the thing stolen and the other for retaliation, yet the stealing any of the utensils of husbandry, as plows or harrow, was punished with death; and they were deemed sacred to Ceres.[9]} The 2$^d$ sort of fraud to be here observed is one with regard to insurance. The insurance,[10] on the masters giving in an account of the value of the ship and cargo, insure her for that summ. There is an Act of Parliament[11] however which makes it death for one to give in an ⟨?account⟩ of this sort above the real value. For by that means the master, having insured his ship above the value, might take an opportunity 159 of wrecking her on some place where he might easily save | himself and crew; and by this means enrich himself to the great loss of the insurers. And as the detection of all such transactions is very difficult, and great profits might be made by it, the temptation to commit such a fraud is very great and consequently the punishment must be high.— — —

Forgery is the next thing we are to consider. Whenever written obligations came to be binding, it became absolutely necessary that all frauds of this sort should be prohibited. For otherwise one by forging an obligation might extort any sum he pleased. Forgery therefore is both by the English and Scots law [is] capitally punished; with this difference, that by the Scots law all sort of forgery whatever, without regard to the nature of the obligation, is punished with death. By the English law only those forgeries are liable to a capitall punishment which are done in the manner of those papers which draw immediate payment, as bills, India bonds, banks bonds, 160 bank notes, and all others payable at a certain time.[12]      [o] But | bonds, properly so called, conveyances of land estates, and such as do not exact any immediate payment, are not punished with death but with pillory, fine,

[n] *Sic*      [o] Blank in MS.

---

[9] The Twelve Tables, VIII.9, penalized the nocturnal cutting of and the pasturing of animals on another's crops by death and sacrifice to Ceres.
[10] *Sic.* Probably 'insurers' was intended.
[11] 4 George I, c. 12 (1717); Hawkins, I.48.
[12] 5 Elizabeth I, c. 14 (1563); Hawkins, I.70.

and imprisonment. The reason here is the same as that of insurance and bankruptcy. For here the payment of the money being to be made immediately, the discovery of the person or the recovery of the money is very precarious. Whereas in bonds and conveyances the danger can not be so great, as the subjects are not so perishable and there is longer time to examine the title.

Perjury is a crime no less dangerous.[13] For by it one may be deprived of his estate, or his life itself. The false oath of a witness may bring all that about; but this crime is not punished with death but with a very ignominious punished,[14] the loss of both his ears which are naild to the pillory, his nose, and a fine and imprisonment. There are indeed some cases where one may ⟨be⟩ executed from perjury, but then that is not as a perjurer but as a murderer, having by his false oath been the occasion of a mans suffering innocently, | and this extends to the subborner as well as other cases of perjury. Some authors inde⟨e⟩d affirm that there have been instances of persons hanged on account of perjury, but these have probably been of the sort above mentiond. Sir George McKenzie and Forbes[15] also alledge that women guilty of adultery have been hanged on the statute of perjury; but if there were any such instances it was a very wrong extention of that Act; for we are to observe that it is only affirmative perjury that is thus punishable. A promissory oath (tho it adds greatly to the solemnity of the obligation),[p] tho it may be very sincerely made, does not appear when broke to make on⟨e⟩ guilty[q] ⟨of⟩ so heinous a crime as one who willingly and knowingly affirmd what he then knew to be false. The breach of such oaths is rather to be attributed to weakness and frailty than to any malice or ill will, and this is the case with regard to adultery.—

*Gap of three lines in MS.*

162    | Before we leave the subject of personall rights, it will be proper to consider in what manner they come to an end. All reall rights come to an end in three different manners, either 1ˢᵗ, by          16; 2ᵈˡʸ, by praescription; and 3ᵈˡʸ, by voluntary transference. Personall rights of all sorts are in like manner ended in three different ways.[17]— — —

The 1ˢᵗ of these is by the performance of that which we have a right to exact. Thus one who owes me a sum of money,[r] by paying this debt frees

161

---

*p* 'does not' deleted        *q* The last three words replace 'be'        *r* Illegible word deleted

---

[13] Hawkins, I.69.
[14] *Sic.* Presumably 'punishment' was intended.
[15] Mackenzie, *Laws and Customes of Scotland in Matters Criminal*, XVIII.1,2; W. Forbes, *Institutes of the Law of Scotland*, II (1730), IV.5. Bigamy was punished as perjury under Act, 1551, c. 19 (A.P.S. II.486, c. 11).
[16] Blank in MS. Probably 'renunciation' or 'abandonment'.
[17] Hutcheson, *M.P.*, II.17.1.

himself from the obligation. It would be absurd to suppose that I can have afterwards any claim against him. In the same manner one who has been guilty of a crime frees himself from the obligation he is under to the offended person by submitting[s] himself to the punishment which is to be inflicted on that crime, whether it be required by the law of nature and equity or by the civil law of the country. If the punishment which is to be inflicted is death, the death of the person takes away the right of those 163 to whom this punishment is due; and in the same way | if the punishment be a pecuniary fine or a lesser corporall punishment or any other whatever, the right of the party to demand it, whether it be the publick or an individual, is plainly at an end when the criminall pays the fine or submitts himself to the corporall punishment. For it is evident that a right against a person must end as soon as the thing or service we have a right to is payd or performed.— — —

The 2[d] manner in which personall rights come to an end is by discharge or acquittance, and pardon.— If one owes me a debt and I, tho I have not received payment of this summ, engage by a contract not to demand payment of it but to free him from it, his obligation will certainly be taken away. He has then as good or a better claim to be free from the debt as I have to exact it. I may indeed alledge that he is bound by contract to pay me such a summ and that I am dissapointed by his nonperformance, but he has the same claim to be exempted from performance as he has a contract on that also to free him from the debt; and his claim is besides greatly preferable to mine, as the dissappointment I receive by his non-164 performance must be very small | after I have engaged not to exact it; whereas the dissapointment of the debtor may reasonably be very great after I have received an obligation to be freed from the payment of the debt. {Thus the obligation the creditor comes under by a discharge, as it is called in Scotland, or acquittance in England, must free one from the debt. The debtor has here a much more reasonable expectation of being free from it, proceeding from the discharge or acquittance, than the creditor has of payment from the bond.} In the same manner also if one is liable,[t] either by the law of equity or the civill law of the country, to suffer such or such a punishment, he will be altogether freed from this if the party who has a right to exact it agrees voluntarily that he should be so. This it is which gives the foundation to the right of pardonning. The pardon frees the criminall from the punishment, in the same manner as an acquittance frees the debtor from the debt. In the same manner also, as it is the creditor alone who can grant an acquittance, so it is only the person who has a right to exact the punishment[u] who can grant a pardon. If the punishment be due to an individuall, the individuall can grant him forgiveness; or if it be due to the community or the prince as representing

---

[s] Replaces 'subjecting'　　　　　[t] Replaces 'bound'　　　　　[u] 'that' deleted

165 them, the prince can for the same reason grant forgiveness | and pardon. Thus in England, where the relations of the deceased can prosecute the murderer on an appeal, as well as the king on information and indictment, these parties can free the person from the capitall punishment as due to them but not acquit him also from it as[v] due to the other. The private prosecutor can not stop the prosecution in the name of the crown, nor grant him acquittance from the sentence; nor does the kings pardon free him from capitall punishment on the appeal of the relations. But the relations may free him from it as[w] due to them, and the king may grant him pardon[x] and freedom from the punishment which is due to him as representing the community.

3[d], personall rights are put an end to by prescription no less than real rights. The reason too is the same in both; the person who has not exercised his right for a[y] long time is supposed not to have thought of it, or at least not to have any great dependance on it; and on the other hand one who has

166 for severall ⟨?years⟩ | not been called on may be imagined to have forgot his debt, or at least to have an expectation.[z] By the English law all bills and bonds that have a fixt day of payment prescribe in 6 years,[18] and those that have any particular priviledges, as bills of exchange, lose those priviledges after three years. By the Scots law bills and obligations which have a day of payment specified do not prescribe in six years,[19] but they lose their priviledges before that time also.       [a] Bonds which in the proper sense of the word bear no day of payment ought reasonably to take a longer time to be prescribed, as the dereliction or omissions of the creditor or the hopes of the creditor[20] that the debt is forgiven can not take place so soon where the time of payment is left to the will of the creditor. But still if the creditor has [for a long] neglected to call for principall or interest for a long tract

167 of years, it is altogether just that the bond | should prescribe. For if no interest has been stipulated, and consequently none due by the debtor, it must be presumed that such a debt is to be payed in a very short time, as few will incline to ly out of their money in that manner. The time however is by the Scots law fixt to forty years,[21] as well as in immoveable subjects. If there is interest payable and this interest is duly called for, it is evident that the creditor still has his debt in view, and the debtor can not form any expectation of being free from payment. In this case a bond will not

---

[v] Reading of last two words doubtful       [w] Reading of last two words doubtful       [x] 'of th' deleted       [y] 'a very' deleted       [z] *Sic*       [a] Blank in MS.

---

[18] 21 James I, c. 16 (1623) limited actions on bills to six years but did not apply to bonds under seal.

[19] In Scotland sexennial prescription of bills was introduced by 12 George III, c. 72, sec. 37 (1772).

[20] *Sic.* Presumably 'debtor' was intended.

[21] Act, 1469, c. 29 (A.P.S. II.95, c. 4); Act, 1474, c. 55 (A.P.S. II.107, c. 9).

prescribe at all; one may have interest paid on a bond 100 or 200 years old and be in no danger of its prescribing, for it would be unjust that he should be deprived of that which he plainly accounted as a part of his estate and depended on for a share of his yearly support. But if on the other hand he should neither call for principall or interest for 20, 30, or 40 years, it appears probable that he has altogether forgot it, as one would not readily give up

168 so great a part of his subsistence. | The bond is 20 years doubled by interest, and in 40 years there would be due 3 times the originall summ. No one would knowingly be so much out of pocket; and at the same time it would seem hard that one who had peaceably possessed a sum for so long a time should at once be called on to pay 3 times what he had received. By the strict law, however, if one should in the 39$^{th}$ year demand a years interest and obtain payment of it, neither the principall nor interest will prescribe. If in the 40$^{th}$ year he demands another and gets payment, and so on, this still saves the principall, but each year a years interest will also prescribe if not paid; thus in the 41$^{st}$ the 1$^{st}$ years, in the 42$^{d}$ the 2$^{d}$ years, and so on. This is what the strict law prescribes. But it is probable that the Court of Session, which is a court of equity as well as of strict law, would cut them off considerably faster. In the same manner as debts, so the punishment due for the commission of crimes, whether it be due to the public or to

169 individualls, ought reasonably to | prescribe in a time considerably shorter than that of a mans life time. If one has been either overlooked or has kept out of the way for a considerable time, it would be altogether unreasonable that he should be punished. We will find that it is alltogether proper that the punishment of crimes should prescribe, whether we found the reasonableness$^{b}$ of punishing crimes on that principle which I have here explaind, or on those on which Grotius and most other writers on this subject have founded it.[22] These are, the$^{c}$ correction of the offender and the bringing him to a sense of his duty; 2$^{dly}$, the deterring of others by making him an example to them; or 3$^{dly}$, the safety of the community by taking away an unworthy and dangerous member.

As to the resentment of the injured person or his relations, it is plain that this must wear away by time; one who had been guilty of a great injury against me would not raise my resentment 20 years after near so much as at the time the deed was committed, or even in a much shorter

170 time. On this principle it is plain therefore | that$^{d}$ the punishment of crimes should not extend for a very long time. If again we should found it on those principles above mentioned the case will be the same.— As to the first, the correction of the offender, this can not make the punishment due for a

---

$^{b}$ Replaces 'right'      $^{c}$ 'pu' deleted      $^{d}$ 'on' deleted

---

[22] Cf. 89–93 above. The third principle of Grotius and Pufendorf is as stated here, not as is implied on 93.

very long time, for if one had been guilty of a very atrocious crime 10, 20, or 30 years ago, if he has lived since that time peaceably and innocently and with a fair character it would appear ridiculous to say that [t]he[e] any way required to be corrected; he may in that time have become a very different person.— In the same way the safety of the community, which requires the removall of a dangerous and pernicious member out of the society, can not extend to a very great number of years. For one who had been guilty 20 years ago of a very great crime and was then a very dangerous member of society may by this time have become a very different person; if he has lived since that time a peaceable and innocent life we could never
171 think it just to remove him out of society as a | dangerous person. The other reason or foundation of punishment assigned by thes⟨e⟩ authors may at first sight appear to justify the continuance of the punishment for a much longer time than the two former. For it would appear to tend greatly to deterr others from being guilty of a heinous crime, when they saw that even a long continuance of better conduct could not free them ⟨from⟩ the punishment of their former guilt. But even this will expire after a long time; for if one should be punished in this manner for a crime he had been guilty of long before, and which was very unlike his after conduct, no one would be greatly affected by the punishment as it would ⟨?appear⟩ to be rather capricious than following necessarily from the commission of the crime. In all cases therefore the punishment of crimes will prescribe in a considerable time; in most cases this ⟨is⟩ regulated by the resentment of the person injured, tho the others will no doubt have an effect on it also.
172 In England the prosecution on appealls | expires in one year,[23] as they are entirely founded on the resentment of the private prosecutor, and are not much encouraged by the government. Treasonable practises and such like must be prosecuted within three years after the commission, otherwise the prosecution is of no effect, except in such cases as the treason was not in one single act but a continuance of treasonable practises, in which the time is considerably longer.[24] And in generall the legislature allows all crimes to expire in a certain time, which is longer or shorter according to the particular nature of the crime, unless it be some very horrid crimes where the punishment may be inflicted[f] at any distance of time whatever. We are to observe however that this only regard⟨s⟩ those cases where the criminall has not been brought to a trial nor any sentence pronounced
173 against him. For if sentence has been pronounced, and he has | afterwards made his escape, he may be executed or otherwise punished on that sentence by the strict law for forty years after. The very making his escape and

[e] 'had' deleted        [f] Replaces 'exacted'

[23] Appeals of death: Hawkins, II.23.48.
[24] 7 and 8 William III, c. 3 (1695).

evading the punishment that was justly pronounced against him is considered as a crime, which being added to the former lengthens the time of
prescription. But tho this be the regulation according to the strict law, it
will be very seldom put in practise. A very unhappy gentleman, Mr.        25
Lord Ratcliff, was executed on a sentence passed on him long before. He
had engaged in the rebellion in the 1715 and had been tried and condemned,
but made his escape to France. He resided however unmolested at London
from the year forty till the forty five, solliciting his pardon. He then joined
the rebellion at that time, and was apprehended and executed on the former
sentence. But had he remain'd quiet it is not at all probable he would have
174 been in | the least mollested, altho the forty years were not near being past.
Dr. Cameron[26] also was executed in the year 50 or 51 on the sentence
passed on him in the year 1745. The government were then not altogether
free from fear of another rebellion, and thought it necessary to take that
precaution. But had he kept out of the way for some years longer he would
probably have been altogether safe.— — —

I shall only observe farther with regard to criminall causes that there
are severall phenomena in the punishment of crimes which, as they are
easily accountible for by the principle of punishment I have laid down,
tend greatly to establish it. The attempt to committ a crime when it comes
to the last point is in every respect as punishable, tho it has not taken effect,
[as if it had] according to the principles of punishment laid down by
175 | Grotius and others, as if the crime had actually been committed; for with
regard to the guilt of the offender, there can be no difference; it is the
intention and not the effect which regulates that. The safety of the society
also would require the removing a dangerous person as well here as in the
other case; as he has given the same proof of his being so, by firing a pistoll
and running at one with a sword, as if he had actually killed him. It is
evident also that there is the same reason for making an example of him
to the deterring of others. Yet as far as I know there is no country where the
attempt to committ a crime is punished with the same severity as the
actuall committing it. The resentment of the party injured is not however
so great; and it is on this, as I have endeavoured to shew, that the punishing
of criminalls is founded. The resentment of the friends of one who had
been attacked with a design to murder him and had made his escape is not
near so great as if he had been actually murdered. In this case the grief for
176 their friend | blows up their resentment and makes them demand the
greatest rigour of punishment. In the other case their joy on the escape
of their friend sooths and lays asleep their indignation. In the same manner

[25] Blank in MS. Charles Ratcliffe, brother of the Earl of Derwentwater: Foster's
Reports, 40; Howell's *State Trials*, XVIII.430.
[26] Dr. Archibald Cameron was executed in London in 1753 on the strength of a bill of
attainder passed against him in 1746: Foster's Reports, 109; Howell's *State Trials*, XIX.
734.

one who, doing a thing in itself dangerous, if he happens to kill or hurt one, is punished much more severely than if no bad effect should follow. Thus if one by throwing a stone into the street should kill a man he would be punished as a murderer, the action being in itself[g] improper and dangerous and such as a strict police would punish, tho in most countries it would be overlooked if no bad effects had followed.[27] But in this case on those principles above mentioned he should be punished with no less rigour than when these bad effects follow. The guilt of the person is the same and requires the same correction, as there was the same danger in both cases and the effect was only accidentall. The safety of the society requires punishment rather more in the one case than in the other, and in
177 reality rather more, as the committing | such an action without any harm following may give both him and others less reluctance in the commission of such actions on future occasions than if he had been the occasion of damage by so doing.[h]— The same may be said of one who, riding an unruly horse in the street or market place with design only to frighten the people for his diversion, happens to kill a man. In both these cases we feel a much less resentment against the offender when no bad effects follow[s], than when he is the occasion of a great misfortune.—It is on the same principle that we are apt to inflict some sort of punishment on irrationall animalls and even innanimate things when they have been the occasion of the death of any person. This proceeds from a resentment blind and foolish indeed, but such as       [i] legislators have not neglected.

There are also some persons which are never esteemed liable to punish-
178 ment for any actions. Such are chil|dren, idiots, and madmen. If a child[j] say he would shoot or stab one and should actually do so, and altho this should proceed from rage and passion, he would not be esteemed liable to punishment. Yet by those principles they should be as liable as others. The danger is no less great to the community, and the examples where there may be an opportunity of committing are no less frequent, and even more so, as they have less reason to restrain them. But the insignificance and the weakness of that age both in mind and body makes them appear no proper objects of resentment; and in the same manner a madman who committs the most horrid crimes seems no object of resentment or punishment. The totall depravation and the[k] great appearance there is that their morall faculty is in them altogether obliterated puts them on a quite

---

[g] 'unju' deleted        [h] Reading of last two words doubtful        [i] Illegible word
[j] Illegible word deleted        [k] 'allmost' deleted

---

[27] Cf. TMS II.iii.2.8: 'Thus, if a person should throw a large stone over a wall into a public street without giving warning to those who might be passing by, and without regarding where it was likely to fall, he would undoubtedly deserve some chastisement. A very accurate police would punish so absurd an action, even though it had done no mischief.'

179 different footing from other men. They appear so different from | the common idea we form of men that those actions they commit do not in the least shock us. A madman is one who would knock a man on the head that he might see which way he would fall, and committ other such like actions from the most ridiculous and frivollous motives. It is the generall behaviour of a man which makes us look on those who are guilty of the most enormous crimes with abhorrence and aversion. When the crimes are not committed from such frivolous motives as those above mentioned, but from such as would have some considerable weight with any reasonable man, tho they would not influence a good man to be guilty of such horrid actions, it is then that from the resemblance such men bear to others [that] we are shocked at their actions. Thus one who murders an other to get his money becomes an object of our abhorrence and resentment, as
180 that | is a very strong motive, and tho it would not influence a good man to commit that crime, is still one of considerable weight with any reasonable ⟨?man⟩. The resemblance betwixt the motives of such men and those of others creates an abhorrence and resentment at the actions which are committed by them in a criminall manner from such reasonable motives.— — — — —

*End of Volume Two of MS.*

| *Monday Febry. 7ᵗʰ 1763*

I proposed in treating of justice to consider the rights of men on which it is founded under three heads: 1ˢᵗ, those which belong to a man as a man; 2ᵈ, those which belong to a man as a member of a family; and thirdly, those that belong to a man as a member of a society. I have now said all that I think necessary concerning the first branch of rights, under the 3 different classes of the right one has to his person, to his character, and property, and the injuries which may be done one in each of these respects.

I come now to consider the rights which belong to a man and the correspondent injuries which may be done a man as

## A Member of a Family.

There are 3 different relations in which the members of a family may stand [in] to one an other. They may be either in the relation of[l] Husband and Wife; or of Father and Son; or of Master and Servant.[28] Correspondently to
2 these | a (man) or person may ⟨be⟩ injured in as many different ways when con⟨si⟩dered as a member of a family. One may be injured either as a husband or wife; as a father or son; or as a master or servant. In order to proceed the more regularly I shall begin with the relation of husband and wife, as it is the foundation of all the rest. In considering of this there are three things to be chiefly attended to, viz 1ˢᵗ, the manner in which this union is entered into and the origin of it; 2ᵈˡʸ, the obligation or rights that are thereby acquired and the injuries corresponding to these; and 3ᵈˡʸ, the manner in which it is dissolved. Of these in order. We may observe that in all the species of animalls the inclination of the sexes towards each other is precisely proportionable to the exigencies of the young and the difficulty of their maintenance. In all quadrupeds the inclination of the sexes ceases as soon as the female is impregnated. For in them the female is of herself sufficiently qualified to provide sustenance for the young. For after the birth of the young and sometimes before it the greatest part of the
3 | food of the mother turns into milch, the proper food of the young one. So that in this case the ordinary labour of the female in providing food for herself is sufficient to provide for the maintenance of the young. In birds again who have no milch, the whole labour that is necessary to provide for the safety and maintenance of the young is an additionall one to that which the parents before required for their own support, and is such that the female would be altogether unable and unqualified to undergo. That this

---

[l] 'father and s' deleted

---

[28] Hutcheson, *M.P.*, III.1-3; *System*, II.149 ff.

connection therefore may still continue, it is wisely provided that the inclination of the sexes should still continue.[29] It is this inclination that is the bond of their union; they have not probably in view the maintenance and support of the young. In the quadrupeds, as soon as the female is impregnated the male ceases to be an object of desire to the female and he to her; but here on the contrary this still continues as long as the young require their assistance. In the human species, the maintenance of the

4 young is provided | for in the same manner. The female (the woman) indeed is furnished with milch which might perhaps enable her to support the child for some time of its infancy; but then it often happens that by the time the 1$^{st}$ child is weaned the woman has a 2$^d$, and so on. So that long before the 1$^{st}$ child is any way qualified to provide for itself there is a 2, a 3$^d$, or a 4$^{th}$ child born. This necessarily requires a degree of labour to which the woman would be altogether unequall. That therefore this additionall labour may be sustain'd, and the children supported in their helpless state, it is [was] necessary that union of the parents should be of a very long continuance. The affection of the sexes is therefore constant and does not cease on any particular occasion; and as the children, at least some of them, require the attendance of the parents pretty far in their life, this affection and love betwixt them which is the foundation of their union generally continues the greatest part of their lives (And as Mr. Smith else where observed[30] is supplied in the latter part by the habitual

5 affection and esteem that is then continued$^m$). | The long time that children are dependent on their parents and unable to subsist by themselves, which$^n$ is much longer than in any other species of animalls, is likewise productive of the most salutary effects. During all this time the child being dependent on the parents is obliged in many instances to yield its will to theirs, to bring down its passions and curb its desires to such a pitch as they$^o$ can go along with,[31] and by this means learns in its very infancy a chief and most essentiall part of education, without which being first implanted it would be in vain to attempt the instilling of any others. This is one of the most necessary lessons one can acquire. Unless one can so bring down his passions

$^m$ Reading doubtful    $^n$ Reading doubtful    $^o$ 'are' deleted

---

[29] Locke, *Civil Government*, § 79.

[30] The reference is perhaps to TMS I.ii.4.2: 'With what pleasure do we look upon a family, through the whole of which reign mutual love and esteem, where the parents and children are companions for one another, without any other difference than what is made by respectful affection on the one side, and kind indulgence on the other.' But neither here nor elsewhere in TMS does Smith say directly that sexual attraction is succeeded by habitual affection and esteem. In TMS VI.ii.1.7, writing of family affection generally, Smith says: 'What is called affection, is in reality nothing but habitual sympathy.' This passage, however, was written for edition 6, published in 1790.

[31] Cf. TMS I.i.4.7: 'The person principally concerned . . . can only hope to obtain [sympathetic affection] by lowering his passion to that pitch, in which the spectators are capable of going along with him.'

and restrain his will and so[p] accomodate it to that of others as that they can go along with him, it is impossible for him to have any peace or enjoyment in society. This lesson is learned by all children, even by those of the most profligate and wicked parents[32]

*Gap of one page in MS.*

6                        | *Tuesday February 8. 1763*

In yesterdays lecture I gave you some account of the origin of the perpetuity of marriage, and also of the power of divorce which was generally supposed to be possessed by the husband.[33] The wife amongst the Romans in the earlier times of the commonwealth was absolutely in the husbands power; the marriage was made either by the religious ceremony of confarreation which produced that effect, or else by the coemptio, a civill one by which the husband bought her as a slave, or lastly, the husband by possessing a woman constantly for a year and day prescribed her in the same manner as any moveable subject; for this was also the time in which moveables, and at first indeed immoveables, were prescribed amongst the Romans.[34] By these means she came either into the place of daughter or slave, which was in effect the same. Therefore as the master of a family had the power of chastising his [his] children or slaves, even in a capitall manner as shall be shewn hereafter, either by inflicting a punishment upon them or by
7 burning[35] | them away, so he had the same power over his wife. But as a daughter or child had not the power of leaving his fathers family and manumitting himself when he inclined, nor a slave of running away or leaving his masters house without his consent, so neither had the wife the power of leaving and seperating from her husband. Besides, as I observed before,[36] the government is at first in all nations very weak, and very delicate of intermeddling in the differences of persons of different families; they were still less inclined to intermeddle in the differences that happen'd amongst persons of the same family; on the other hand, that some sort of government might ⟨be⟩ preserved in them they strengthend the authority of the father of the family, and gave him the[q] power of disposing of his whole family as he thought proper and determining with regard to them even in capitall cases. By this means the father possessed a power over his

---

[p] Replaces an illegible word          [q] 'wh' deleted

---

[32] The word 'parents' falls at the beginning of the last line of 5. There is no full point after it, and the remainder of the line is left blank. There is evidently a lacuna in the MS. here.

[33] Most of this was presumably in the passage missing before 6.

[34] Cf. i.80–1 above.

[35] *Sic.* Presumably 'turning' was intended.          [36] ii.95,152 above.

whole family, wife, children, and slaves, which was not much less than supreme. So that tho the husband had the power of divorce, the wife had not.

8    | In time however this came to be altered, the reason of which I before hinted at. In the earlier periods of Rome, when there was but little wealth in the nation, the fortune a woman could bring to her husband or could possibly be in possession of was not so great as to entitle her to capitulate or enter upon treaty with her husband; she was content to submit herself to the power of the husband. But when the state became exceedingly rich, there[r] would be very rich[es] heiresses who brought great fortunes along with them, as happens in every country nowadays; and as Rome was much richer than this country so the wealth of the heiresses was proportionably greater. It seems to have been[s] originally in favours of such ladys that the new marriage was[t] introduced. The relations thought it hard to allow so great a fortune to go out of the family and be transferred to the husband, who acquired also a very great authority over the wife. {But as heiresses incline to take a husband [as husband] as well as other women, they, etc.} They therefore contrived a new sort of marriage in which none of the old forms, neither the religious nor civill one, were used. The

9    instrumenta dotalia which | corresponds to what we call the contract of marriage were drawn up, in which the husband was specified to have the management[u] of the wifes money, at least of the interest of it, for the mony was often consigned into some other persons hands. {The husband after this came to the wifes house and took her home with some solemnity, which was called domum deductio.} The wife however did not come into the power of her husband, nor was indissolubly join'd to him. And least she should be prescribed and by that means herself and her fortune belong intirely to her husband (as every thing of a slave did), and the whole effect of the contract be in this manner dissanulled, she was advised to seperate herself from her husband for 3 or four nights every year. This sort of marriage, tho it had none of the old solemnities, was found by the lawyers to save the ladys honour and legitimate the children.— After this time the husband and the wife came to be much more equall in their power; as the marriage was entered into merely by the consent of the parties, so it was dissolved without near so great difficulty as the marriages formerly contracted had been. The consent of both parties or even the will of one

10   ⟨?was sufficient⟩ to dissolve the | marriage. If the husband left her and cohabited with an other woman, the wife was at liberty as before the marriage. This great liberty of divorce on the smallest occasions continued from the latter part of the Republick till a short time before Justinian, when by a rescript of the Emperors Valentinian and Theodosius divorce

---

[r] Replaces 'it'    [s] 'first' deleted    [t] 'first' deleted    [u] Replaces an illegible word

was allowed only on certain conditions.[37] But Justinian restored the former unbounded liberty.[38] As this liberty was a consequence of the new form of marriage, the old forms were laid aside almost intirely; the latter one was found to be much more convenient and better adapted to the licentiousness of the times. {It was exactly similar to the condition of a man and his mistress in this country, only that the womans honour was safe and the children legitimate. The cohabitation and connexion[v] was intirely voluntary as long as it continued.} It alone therefore was used; so that Tacitus[39] tells us that when a certain office of the priesthood was to be supplied in which it was necessary that the person admitted should be born of parents married by the old forms, there were none such to be found in the city. This license of divorce was productive of the worst consequences. It tended plainly to corrupt the moralls of the women.[w]

11 The wives often | passed thro 4 or 5 different husbands, which tended to give them but very loose notions of chastity and good behaviour. And as this was frequently practised by women of the highest stations and most conspicuous rank in the whole state, the corruption could meet with no opposition. Ciceros daughter Tullia, whom her father celeb⟨r⟩ates as one of the sweetest manners, greatest virtue and chastity, and in a word as poss⟨ess⟩ed of all the female virtues, was married 1st to Piso, 2dly Crassipes, then Dollabella, and then to a 2d Piso;[40] and many other instances are to be met with in the Roman history. Hence it was that female chastity was so rarely to be met with. For tho the anecdotes and annalls of the private life of the Romans at that time have come down to us in a very imperfect manner, yet there is hardly a great man in the end of the Republick who is not a cuckold upon record. Cicero, Caesar, Pompey, Marc Antony, [Pompey,] Dollabella, etc., etc. are all reckorded in this character. Milo, a very strict sort of man, married the daughter of Sylla, and the day after

12 the marriage was celebrated | found Sallust the historian in bed with her.[41] This licence of divorce met with no interruption in the time of the emperors till the constitution of Theod. and Valentinian above mentioned, which was also abrogated by Justinian. After his time it continued probably in the eastern Empire, for [tho] Justinian tho he conquered the western and kept possession of it for some time was properly an eastern emperor, ⟨?and it⟩ continued after that[x] in full force as long as the Empire subsisted.

---

[v] Reading doubtful     [w] 'insomuch that' deleted     [x] 'at least till the introduction of Christianity' deleted

---

[37] *C.* 5.17.8.
[38] In fact he penalized those who divorced without cause, although the divorce itself was valid; cf. Montesquieu, XXVI.9.
[39] *Annals*, IV.16.
[40] Tullia was divorced from Dolabella in 46 B.C. and died the following year without any further marriage.
[41] Aulus Gellius, XVII.18; Scholiast to Horace, *Satires*, I.2.41–8.

In the western Empire it was much sooner abolished. The savage nations which issuing out from Scandinavia and other northern countries overan all the west of Europe were in that state in which the wife is greatly under the subjection of the husband. By the small remains of the laws of those nations which have come down to our hands, this seems to have been very much the case. The husband had then a very great authority over her and was allowed divorce in the same manner as formerly amongst the Romans,

13 | but the wife had no power of d⟨i⟩vorcing the husband. This was greatly strengthened by the introduction of Christianity, which was very soon received amongst them. They were then in that state which made them regard their priests not only with respect but even with superstitious veneration.—The[v] laws of most[z] countries being made by men generally are very severe on the women, who can have no remedy for this oppression. The laws however introduced by the clergy, and which were soon receivd by these barbarous and ignorant and consequently superstitious people, tended to render their condition much more equall. The first step which was taken was to curb the licence of divorce which was as we have seen very great. This was at first limited to certain[a] cases; these were the infidelity of either of the parties or the great cruelty of the husband, as[b] this will be the most common case (ob saevitiam et mortis metus⟨⟩). The effect of divorce was that the parties were considered as if they had never been

14 married, and were at liberty to take a husband or wife | after the divorce. But in some farther time no divorce was allowed. The only cases in which those who had been married were allowed to[c] marry after being divorced were in such cases as the marriage[d] would have been null from the beginning, as 1st, when the marriage was within the prohibited degrees of consanguinity, which were extended far beyond their former limits by the clergy so that it often happened that persons might ignorantly marry in a prohibited degree. These marriages were either altogether null or were indulged by a particular licence from the Pope or other clergy; and 2dly, on account of the frigidity of the husband and the incapacity of generation, not the barreness of the wife; for in these cases also the marriage was null from the beginning. {Or of a previous contract to another woman either in praesenti or in futuro in the case afterwards mentioned.} Separation was however allowed on two accounts, either on the infidelity of the parties, or ob saevitiam et mortis metum, as in these cases there would be an evident hardship in compelling them to live together. But there was however no

15 allowance of marriage on this account after seperation, | and any one who married them, and they themselves, was supposed to commit adultery. There was also another great change introduced by the constitution of the

---

[v] What appears to be the letter 'c' (perhaps standing for 'civil') is interlined here  
[z] Reading doubtful    [a] 'condi' deleted    [b] Reading doubtful    [c] 'take' deleted  
[d] Replaces 'divorce'

clergy. Before this time the infidelity of the wife was reckoned a great breach of the conjugall duties and was allowed to be punished by him, even with death, and had*e* the name of adultery given it. On the other hand the infidelity of the husband was not accounted adultery; it was called *petticatus*[42] and in this he had all freedom, being no way accountable for it. {Indeed in the times of the later marriages they would be more carefull to conceal these transgressions, as the wife had the power of divorce as well as the husband.} This according to the*f* account generally given of the punishment of adultery, viz that it was to prevent a spurious ofspring being imposed upon the husband,[43] might appear somewhat reasonable, but that as I endeavoured to shew[44] it is the jealousy of the*g* parties, which allways attends the passion of love when society is the least refined, in which the publick goes along with the injured party; and this is equally common to the husband and the wife, as it shews the allienation of the affection from the one as well as the other. The real reason is that it is men*h* who make the laws with respect to this; they generally will be inclined to curb the women as much as possible and give*i* themselves the more indulgence. The clergy were much more impartiall judges. The former legislators*j* were husbands and consequently a party concerned; but as the priests were not husbands, not being allowed to marry, they were the best qualified that could possibly be for the office of judge in this matter. They accordingly*k* set them in this respect perfectly on an equall footing. The infidelity of the husband as well as the wife was accounted adultery and might produce a separation. {And it was for some time punished not as adultery but as a perjury.} The licence of divorce was as we observed greatly curbed and put at the same time on an equall footing with regard to both. {The husband and wife were put alltogether on an equall footing in allmost all respects. This, on the principle I have endeavoured to explain, may be very equitable, as the injury to the jealousy of the woman is [v.16] no less grievous than to that of the man. But still as in allmost all contracts of marriage the husband has a considerable superiority to the wife, the injury done to his honour and love will be more grievous, as all injuries done to a superior by an inferior are more sensibly felt than those which are done to an inferior by one whom they look upon as above them.} The laws in England with regard to divorce are on the very same footing in most respects [the same] with those of the cannon law. One cannot obtain a

16 |

---

*e* Reading doubtful          *f* 'generall' deleted          *g* 'husband' deleted          *h* 'and husbands' deleted          *i* Reading doubtful          *j* Replaces 'judges'          *k* 'allowed' deleted

---

[42] Probably *peccatum* (or *peccatus*), 'sin', 'failing', was intended.
[43] Montesquieu, XXVI.8.
[44] Probably in the passage missing before 6. Cf. LJ(B) 103, below.

**17** | divorce in any way but by an Act of Parliament, which is absolute and can do any thing. But by a suit at Drs. Commons, which comes in place of the ecclesiasticall court, {In Scotland divorce is granted to the dalys⁴⁵ for infidelity by the commissaries, who come in place of the ecclesiasticall court. The clergy after the Reformation, being not confined to celibacy but allowed to be husbands themselves, were perhaps on this account[s] more indulgent. The popish clergy had before allowed a separation on this cause.—} a separation is all that can be obtaind,⁴⁶ which the clergy who made the laws on this head as strict as possible found it necessary to grant, but would not allow the liberty of a posterior marriage, as a punishment to the offenders.— — —

For some time after these regulations with regard to marriage took place there was no great ceremony required at the commencement of it; the hierologe⁴⁷ was not required till the time of Pope Innocent the iiiᵈ. Before that time, as the old forms of confarreatio and coemption were laid aside, theˡ form which they used was much the same as that of the new marriage amongst the Romans before Christianity. There was no more required than the mutuall consent of the parties, either before witnesses

**18** or not. The one asked the other if she inclined to be his wife, | and she replied yes, and I take you for my husband. The husband afterwards went and brought her home to his house, and no other form was required. Innocent afterwards required that these declarations should be made in facie ecclesiae, the manner much such as that now in use, by solemnly proclaiming the bands of marriage betwixt such and such persons. However after this was required as the only regular sort of marriage as it is at this day in all Christian countries, the other method by consent was not altogether without its effect, insomuch that a previous one by contract alone, that is, a previous irregular one, broke one made in facie ecclesiae. In this however there was a distinction. If the marriage or agreement was in praesenti, that is, if the parties agreeed to be husband and wife from the time of the agreement, *I take you for my wife* or *I marry you* and the other agree'd, this made even a subsequent marriage in facie ecclesiae of no

**19** effect, altho consummated; the parties being still ⟨?liable⟩ | to ecclesiasticall punishment, as for incontinence, for all irregular marriages.—But if it was only a promise of marriage or a contract in futuro, this if it could be provedᵐ by witnesses or by the oath of the party pursued brought marriage, and might prevent a subsequent one (especially copula interveniente)

---

ˡ Illegible word deleted     ᵐ Illegible word deleted

⁴⁵ *Sic.* Probably a scribe's error, by metathesis, for 'ladys'.
⁴⁶ Separation *a mensa et thoro* was granted by the ecclesiastical consistory courts, which sometimes sat at Doctors Commons, the college of Doctors of Civil Law.
⁴⁷ The proclamation in church: *Decretals* 4.3.c. 3 (1215); not actually essential for the validity of the marriage.

in facie ecclesiae, but if it was completed could not annull it. This was
the case in England till the late Marriage Act,[48] which makes no promise
of marriage nor any irregular one whatever of any effect. In Scotland any
marriage of whatever sort in praesenti, where the mutuall consent is
declared before any Justice of Peace or comissarie, or any other way,[n] is
sustain'd as valid. If they be in futuro, if they be said[o] by the one party
and not refused[p] by the oath of the other they are valid[q] si copula inter-
venerit and this be proved in the ordinary way, viz the birth of a child;
but the pa⟨r⟩ties are still liable to ecclesiasticall censure.— — —

20    [r]Marriage came by these means | to be almost indissolluble. There was
a very great change introduced by this means into the character and regard
which was had to the passion of love. This passion was formerly esteemed
to be a very[s] silly and ridiculous [and] one, and such as was never talked
of in a serious manner. We see that there is no poems of a serious nature
grounded on that subject either amongst the Greeks or Romans. There is
no ancient tragedy except Phaedra[49] the plot of which turns on a love story,
tho there are many on all other passions, as anger, hatred, revenge, ambi-
tion, etc. Nor does it make any figure in epic poems. The story of Dido[50]
may be called a love story, but it has no effect on the procedure of the
great events, nor is it any way connected with them. The poem indeed
rather thwarts love as betwixt Lavinia and Turnus;[51] for we can not say
that there was any love betwixt Aeneas and her as they had never seen one

21    another.— | The Iliad we may say turns upon a love story. The cause of
the Trojan war was the rape of Helen, etc., but what sort of a love story is it?
Why, the Greek chiefs combine to bring back Helen to her husband; but
he never expresses the least indignation against her for her infidelity. It is
all against Paris, who carried away his wife along with his goods. The reason
why this passion made so little a figure then in comparison of what it now
does is plainly this. The passion itself is as I said[52] of nature rather[t] ludi-
crous; the frequency and easieness of divorce made the gratification of it of
no great moment: it could be to day, it might ⟨be⟩ to morrow, and if not
this year it might ⟨be⟩ the next; and one might find another object as

[n] 'declared' deleted        [o] Reading doubtful        [p] The last two words replace
'proved'        [q] Two or three illegible words deleted        [r] 'Thus' and an illegible word
deleted        [s] Illegible word deleted        [t] 'ridiculous' deleted

[48] 26 George II, c. 33 (1753) made marriage contracts no longer enforceable in the
ecclesiastical courts.
[49] Smith may mean either or both of Euripides' *Hippolytus* and Seneca's *Phaedra*.
[50] In Virgil, *Aeneid*, iv.
[51] *Aeneid*, vii.
[52] On 20 above Smith has said that the passion of love 'was formerly esteemed' to be
silly and ridiculous, but it is probable that the present reference is to the passage missing
before 6; cf. LJ(B) 103, below. In TMS I.ii.2.1 Smith says that sexual passion, though
natural, is 'always, in some measure, ridiculous'.

agreable as the former. The choice of the person was of no very great importance, as the union might be dissolved at any time. This was the
22 case both amongst the Greeks and Romans. But | when marriage became indissoluble the matter was greatly altered. The choice of the object of this passion, which is commonly the forerunner of marriage, became a matter of the greatest importance.— The union was perpetuall and consequently the choice of the person was a matter which would have a great influence on the future happiness of the parties. From that time therefore we find that love makes the subject of all our tragedies and romances, a species of epic poems till this time. It was before considered as altogether triviall and no subject for such works.— The importance being changed, so also the figure it makes in the poeticall performance. It is become from a contemptible a respectable passion as it leads to a union of such great importance, and accordingly makes the subject of all our publick entertainments, plays, operas, etc. In those of Greece or Rome it never once appeared.

23 This is the generall account of marriage | in Rome and the European nations. Divorce amongst all rude nations is considered as in the power of the husband but not of the wife. The Romans afterwards extended this to both parties equally; and lastly the clergy took it away in all cases, unless where the marriage was null from the beginning.

I shall now proceed to consider another species of marriage very different in many respects from the former, viz that where one man is allowed to have a considerable number of wives. As in Rome and Greece, so in[u] all the modern European nations one man is confined to one wife; plurality of wives is not allowed, neither where voluntary divorce takes place or when it does not. But both in the ancient and in modern times polygamy has been allowed in many places. In all the eastern countries, particularly the East Indies, in Persia[n] and in Turky and[v] Egypt and other countries formerly, polygamy to any extent a man inclines and can afford it is allowed.— We may observe in the first place, as is very justly taken notice
24 of by Grotius,[53] that there is not[w] any | reall injustice either in voluntary divorce or in polygamy in those countries where they are allowed by the laws of the country, tho, as I shall by and by shew, they are very inconsistent with a well regulated police. For with regard to voluntary divorce, there can not be said to be any injustice done to the person who is turned away in this manner. The practise is allowed by the law, and therefore when the wives[x] enter into this agreement it is during pleasure of the husband. They agree to live together as long as he shall find it convenient;

[u] The last two words replace 'and'    [v] 'in Persia' deleted    [w] 'naturally' deleted
[x] Replaces 'persons'

[53] II.5.9.

their living together, when they continue to do so, is voluntary, and when they seperate it is on those conditions on which they came together.[y] In the same manner where polygamy is allowed, as it has been and is in many countries, there can be no injustice in taking a wife in that manner. Where voluntary divorce is allowed, the wife is taken on the condition that the husband may turn her off when he pleases, and this is known to her. In 25 the same manner when poly|gamy is allowed, the wife is taken to be one of 4, 5, 10, 20, 100 wives; this is the condition, and there can not be said to be any injury done her when she finds herself in that situation. But altho there is not any injustice in the practise of polygamy where the law permits it, yet it is productive of many bad consequences.

We shall consider 1st what will be the condition of the female part of a family in which this is practised. They, it is evident, must look upon one another with the greatest jealousy; they share his affection amongst them, and must do all that they can to supplant their rivalls. Continuall discord and enmity, the naturall consequences of rivallship, must prevail amongst them. They are rivalls and consequently enemies, and this rivallship is of a nature which generally produces the greatest enmity and most unsuffer-able discord. These in the greatest degree must therefore attend[z] polygamy with regard to the wives, from the jealousy they have to one another of 26 their husbands love. Besides this there is another cause | of continuall discord and jealousy[a] amongst them. The affection of the husband must here be greatly divided, not only amongst his wives but amongst their children; a man who has ten or twenty wives may have 50 or 100 children amongst whom his affection is divided, and consequently can not be very strong with regard to any particular one. The affection of the wives again will be entirely confined to her own children. She perhaps is the mother of 5 or 6 children; on these all her affection, all her care and concern, is bestowed. She is concerned alone for their interest and advancement. Her affection therefore to her children must be immensely stronger than the feeble and divided affection which the husband can feel for the children of any one.[54]— In all cases where there is another person equally connected as we are with an object of our affection, we measure his affection by that which we ourselves feel. When therefore the mother compares the affection 27 she feels towards | her children with that of[b] their father who stands in the same relation to them, the great disproportion there is betwixt them raises her jealousy in the greatest degree. She is concerned for the interest and advancement of her own children only, and is therefore at pains to draw[c] all

[y] 'and this holds both where the power of divorce is common to both' deleted
[z] 'the' deleted        [a] Numbers written above the words 'discord' and 'jealousy' indicate that their order was intended to be reversed        [b] Replaces 'which'        [c] Reading doubtful

[54] Montesquieu, XVI.6.

the affection of their father towards them, and looks on all the other wives and their children as her rivalls and opposers.[d] The others look also on her in the same light. The jealousy of love and that of interest both conspire to raise the discord, enmity, confusion, and disorder of such a family to the highest pitch. We are told indeed that in the seraglios of the great men of the Turks, the Persian⟨s⟩, and Mogulls there is the greatest tranquillity and the greatest humility and resignation amongst the[e] women. But this apparent tranquillity, for it is only apparent, is that which proceeds from
28 severity and hard usage. Rebellious subjects when | reduced into order are the most abject and humble of any; and unless it be in the very act of rebellion they appear to have the greatest tranquillity and submit with the utmost readyness to the will of the master. This is the very case in all these countries. As there can be only a few who are in a capacity of maintaining a vast number of wives, so there must be a great many who are utterly[f] debarred from all commerce with the other sex, unless it be in the publick stews. Many of these, to render them fit for the office they are intended, are even degraded from the rank of men and made eunuchs. Their business is to attend in these seraglios and keep the women in proper order. For this purpose they are allow'd to treat them with the utmost severity and exercise all the tyranny over them which they think proper. It is this abject subjection alone which produces the apparent tranquillity which is to be
29 found in all the seraglios of the | great men. We see accordingly that this tranquillity is only to be found with those whose wealth enables them to maintain a set of eunuchs for this purpose. In Turky there must be[g] many men of this sort residing at all the chief towns, as Smyrna, Constantinople, and Cairo; and in the east, as the riches is still greater, there is still less disturbance amongst them at Ispahan and Bdelli[55] and Agra; and as the Mogulls are still richer than the Persians, so they are the better able to maintain these masters to their wives; and the Chinese still more so. In these indeed we find very little disorder and a great deal of apparent tranquillity. But on the other hand in all the countries on the coast of the Mediterranean Sea, and in many places in Turky, where the wealth of the people is not such as can afford these servants, the utmost confusion,
30 disorder, discontent, and unhappiness is altogether | apparent.—[h]

The misery of these women must be greatly increased by other circumstances. The only companions they are allowed to have are those which of all others will be the most dissagreable. No one is allowed to see the women in these countries but the eunuchs who attend them. The jealousy of the husband debarrs[i] all other communication. The only persons they can see,

---

[d] Reading doubtful    [e] Illegible word deleted    [f] Illegible word deleted
[g] 'severall' deleted    [h] 'What' deleted    [i] Reading doubtful

---

[55] i.e. Delhi.

then, are either*j* those tyrannicall masters, which can not be very agreable, or tho it may be more so than their other companions can not be much possessed by any one, as they must be continually going from one to the other in order to preserve peace amongst them. Besides these they have none to converse with but the other wives or concubines in the*k* seraglio, whose company must always be rather dissagreable than otherwise. For
31 what harmony, friendship, or enjoyment ⟨?can there be⟩ | amongst those who are jealous of each other and rivalls in the most tender points?— The condition of the female part of these families is then without question most wretched, and exposed to the greatest envy, malice, hatred, and disorder, confusion, etc., etc., etc., etc., etc. imaginable. We will find that that of the male part is not much more desirable. Those who are degraded from the rank of men and deprived of all the opportunities of happiness are not the persons we are to consider. But we will find that even the master of this seraglio, this happy man to appearance, is not much more agreably situated. For in the 1$^{st}$ place he will be racked with the most tormenting jealousy. For tho in those countries one who keeps only one wife has never the least suspicion of her nor the least jealousy, yet when they have any great number they are sensible that in this case the women can not have great reason to be faithfull to them. They enjoy but a very small part of
32 | their affection, which must be divided amongst the whole; or if it be any way partially bestowed*l* the others are the still more dissatisfied, and his jealousy will of consequence be heightened. His affection to his children can be but very small, being divided amongst such a great number; this too is productive of the greatest discontent, as he can never satisfy any of his wives with the share of his affection he bestows on their children, which as I observed must be always greatly disproportioned to that which they expect. By this means he has no enjoyment in the exercise of the parentall affections, but a great deal of anxiety, jealousy, and vexation. He can also have but very little conjugall affection, but a greater share of jealousy than any other man has. The jealousy they entertain of their wives deprive⟨s⟩ them also of the free communication and society which is enjoyed in this country and in most others where polygamy is not allowed. It hinders
33 them | altogether from receiving one another in their houses, through fear of their getting a sight of or corrupting their women. They are jealous even of the imaginations; a Turk would take it very ill if you should ask him concerning his wife or even mention her in any shape; they must behave as if there was no such person in the world. {Even the physicians themselves are not admitted to see the women, their patients. Mr. Tourneforte[56] tells

---

*j* Reading doubtful          *k* Illegible word deleted          *l* 'bestowed' deleted

---

[56] Tournefort, *Relation d'un voyage du Levant* (1717), II.27–8; referred to in Hume, *Essays* ('Of Polygamy and Divorces'), I.235.

that being at Ispahan, where they are still more cautious and circumspect in this respect than in Turky, he was called to visit the wives of a certain great man; he was carried into a room where there were a number of scrolls put thro' the wall telling the person, etc., and he was allowed to feel their pulses thro holes in the wall, but did not see one of them.} By this means there can be no friendship or confidence in these countries betwixt the heads of families. They are by this means altogether incapacitated to enter into any associations or alliances to revenge themselves on their oppressors, and curb the extravagant power of the government and support their liberties. We see accordingly that all the countries where polygamy is received are under the most despotic and arbitrary government. Persia, Turky, the Mogulls country, and China are allso. They have no way of making any opposition, so that the government soon oppresses them and they can never again recover. And as the goverment is arbitrary

34 so | the heads of the families are entrusted with the most absolute and arbitrary authority that possibly can be. The whole of the family is at their disposall, both their wives and their eunuchs, as it would be impossible otherwise to preserve order in the state.— By this method of living it necessarily happens that a great number of persons must be intirely incapacitated to have wives and families, for in all countrys of this sort they pay a price for their wives instead of receiving a dower; and many of these are made eunuchs in order to attend on the wives of the others. But altho they had sufficient stock$^m$ to maintain their wives, yet it will still happen that the number of women will be too small; the wealth⟨y⟩ will deprive the others altogether.

It is advanced indeed in favours of polygamy by Montesquieu$^n$[57] on the authority of      $^o$ that at Bantam, the capitall of the island Java, there are 10 women born for one man; and a Dutch author[58] tells us that on the coast

35 of Guinea there are 50 | women for one man. In Europe we are certain that the proportion is very different. It is generally thought that ⟨there⟩ are about 12 women to 13 men, and others say that there are about 16 to 17, and that proportion appears certainly to be hereabouts from the bills of mortality which are kept in different parts of Europe. So that here there is a man to be lost, in war or other$^p$ hazardous labours, out of 13 or 17 before they can all have one wife. It is not probable or to be believed without good foundation that the laws of nature vary so much in other countries. We see

$^m$ Numbers written above the last two words indicate that their order was intended to be reversed      $^n$ 'and' deleted      $^o$ Blank in MS.      $^p$ Illegible word deleted

[57] XVI.4 and XXIII.12, citing *Recueil des voyages qui ont servi à l'établissement de la Compagnie des Indes Orientales* (2nd edn., 1725), I.347.
[58] W. Bosman, *New and Accurate Description of the Coast of Guinea* (1705), says (p. 211) that women remain unmarried because their number much exceeds that of the men; and also (p. 344) that men commonly have forty or fifty wives.

that the laws of nature with respect to gravity, impulse, etc. are the same in all parts of the globe; the laws of generation in other animalls are also the same in all countries, and it is not at all probable that with regard to that of men there should be so wide a difference in the eastern and the northern parts. We are told that at Macao, the capitall of Japan, when the
36 inhabitants were | numbered there were found about 11 women to 9 men.[59] This indeed would be a disproportion to the prejudice of the women, but would not be sufficien⟨t⟩ to establish polygamy as there would not then be two wives, far less 30 or 40, to one man without cutting out a great number. This fact we are indeed pretty well assured of, as it was found so on a publick numbering of the people. But then it does not even establish that there was so great a disproportion as it appears to do. For we are to consider that as this was the capitall of the country, in which the head man of their religion resided who alone had 500 or 600 wives, and many other rich men who would no doubt have considerable numbers, there would be collected here a number of women which might well be supposed to make this disproportion, altho in the other parts of the country they were born in the same proportion as in Europe, which is very probable.
37 | This is the only fact which is well attested, for we have never heard of any bills of mortality being kept in those countries of which this is related. The two facts above mentioned on which Montesquieu ground⟨s⟩ this argument are not at all well ascertaind. They are taken on the authority of two Dutch skippers, the one of whom was about a year on the coast of Guinea trading from one place to an other, and in this way he might from what appeared to him have wanted to believe that $W^n:M^n::50:1$. The other was about 2 or 3 months at Bantam, and the greatest part of that time on ship board, so that in that capitall they might have appeared to be as $10:1$. {If this was realy the case it would be altogether proper that polygamy should take place. The inconveniencies above mentioned would follow, but for that there would be no remedy as the thing would be necessary where such a law of nature took place.}

It is ascerted also as an argument in favours of polygamy[60] that in the warmer climates the women loose there beauty much sooner than they do in this country, and that at the time when their beauty [and] would render
38 them fit to be the object of affection[q] | their weakness and youth render them all together unfit for being the objects of his confidence and proper to be put on an equall ⟨?footing⟩, as this time is past before the other

---

[q] At this point the words 'confidence and on an equall footing with men they' are deleted. The word 'affection' in the text is interlined above the first of these deleted words.

[59] Montesquieu, XVI.4 and XXIII.12, citing E. Kaempfer [*History of Japan*, tr. J. G. Scheuchzer, I (1727), 199] who gives figures of 182,072 males to 223,573 females in the emperor's capital (which was known as Miaco or Meaco) about 1675.
[60] By Montesquieu, XVI.2.

comes. And on the other hand when their sense and experience would render ⟨them⟩ fit for this, their want of beauty and incapacity of bearing children counterballance it. They tell us that the women in those countries ripen much sooner than in the northern ones, that they are fit for marriage by 7 or 8 and leaveʳ bearing children in 20ᵗʰ or thereabouts. Now this fact is not better ascertained than the former. We are told indeed that they have children by 11 or 12 years of age, and so would many women in this country as well as in the southern ones. It is said thatˢ Mahomet married his wife       ⁶¹ at 5 and lived with her at 8. But this has probably been no more than the rape of an infant, which areᵗ but too common in more northern climates. On the other hand there is no certainty that they

39 | cease to bear children nearly so soon as is alledged. We find that Cleopatra, an Aegyptian, at the age of 36 when the women are past the prime of their beauty even in this country, had charms enough to retain Antony, a man generally very fickle, so as to bring on a separation with Octavia and his ruin; and about a year before this she had born a child.       ⁶² queen of Naples had a child when she was 56; this indeed was reckoned a wonder there, and so it would here. And as the thing was so extrao⟨r⟩dinary, and the child to heir the crown, she got a tent erected in the middle of the street and was brought to bed in the presence of the people, that there might be no suspicion of fraud. But altho it was realy the case that the time in which a woman was capable of bearing children and being a proper companion for a man was limited to betwixt twelve and 20, this

40 would not at all require the | establishment of polygamy. It might indeed require voluntary divorce, that the husband, after the woman was incapable of being a proper companion for him, should have it in his power to put her away and take another, but it could never require that he should have more than one who were fit wives at the same time. But the strongest argument of any against the aforementioned opinion that the women are born in greater numbers than the men in the eastern countries, is the constant importation of women into Constantinople, Smyrna,ᵘ Agra, and other towns, from Georgia, Circassia, and other countries of Asia where polygamy is not allowed, or not practised in such extent. And as this is continually going on, it shews that altho a vast number of men are deprived of their wives, yet even by this there are not enough to supply the seraglios.

41 The conquests of barbarous and savage nations is what has given | rise to this in all nations where it is practised. It is very common in most savage nations for the leaders and chief men to have 2 or 3 wives. When such a

---

ʳ Reading doubtful          ˢ 'the' deleted          ᵗ Illegible word or words deleted
ᵘ 'Agra an' deleted

⁶¹ Blank in MS. Cadhisja, according to Montesquieu (XVI.2), but in fact it was Ayesha, whom Mahomet married at six years.
⁶² Blank in MS. Constantia: Villani, in Muratori, *Rer. Ital. Scriptores*, XIII.140B.

nation conquers an other the savages will be very apt to indulge themselves in their brutall appetites, and at[v] this time[w] the leaders and other chief men have it in their power to take 10 or 20 wives instead of 2, and by this means polygamy has been introduced by the savage nations into all countries where it is to be found. The Tartars, a savage nation, have overrun all Asia severall times and Persia above 12 times. The conquest of the Turks, who are properly Tartars, with some Moors, introduced it into Greece.— — —

Polygamy is prejudiciall to the liberty of the subject, not only as it prevents all associations and friendship amongst the heads of families by the jealousy it occasions, but also by the absolutely preventing the existence
42 of a hereditary nobi|lity. When a man who is placed in an eminent station leaves behind him but three or four children, these may be all in a capacity to maintain their fathers dignity, or at[x] least one, where the right of primogeniture takes place, may fill his fathers place in most respects. Those who were connected with the father can easily and naturally continue their affection to the son. The persons who are connected with those we esteem come into their place in our affectio⟨n⟩, and this when they are but few in number may extend to the whole, or be greatly fixed on one who comes into his place. But where polygamy takes place the children may be so many that the connection with the father makes but little impression on us, our affection being divided amongst so great a number that[y] it will hardly be productive of any effect. Nor is there here any one distinguished amongs⟨t⟩ the children of different wives, and so great a number, above the rest. When a bashaw dies, therefore, his children are no more regarded
43 than those of the meanest person, | and they themselves often fall back into the lowest stations.[z] There is not the least regard paid to one on the account of his being come of one who had possessed that dignity; if one of these raises himself to the offices of the state, the respect that is held him proceeds intirely from that new station. There is accordingly no family that is considered as noble or any way distinguished from the rest exceppt the royal family; a haereditary nobility[a] is never heard of amongst them. Now we will find that it is this which chieffly supports the liberty and freedom of the people. It is absolutely necessary that there should be some persons who are some way distinguished above the rest and who can make head against the oppressions of the king, or head the people when they are in danger of being oppressed by foreign invaders. Both these ends we see
44 have been answered by the nobility in France and England. | But in those countries where there is no nobility the people have no head to attach themselves to. The whole defense of such a country against a foreign invader must be made by the standing army, but if it be once beat the

---

[v] Replaces 'by'      [w] Replaces 'means'      [x] Reading of last two words doubtful
[y] Reading doubtful    [z] 'themselves' deleted   [a] 'nobility' deleted

people can never after make any opposition. We see accordingly that Alexander by two victories made himself master of the greatest part of Asia then known. The same had been done by Cyrus before him. The two great conquerors Tamerlane and Cengis-Kan obtaind their empires by two or three victories. The people here after their first defeat had no persons whom they could pitch on for their leaders. The divisions and disorders which afterwards arose proceeded from the conquerors, and not from any struggles of the conquered. The empires of Tamerlane and Cengis-Kan were split immediately after their deaths, but it was amongst the

45  Tartar chief⟨s⟩ | who accompanied him. The empire of Alexander was in like man⟨n⟩er soon divided, not by the disputes or discontents of the Persians or other nations whom he had conquered, but by the rivalship of his captains. The empire of the caliphs was in like manner split in a short time after the death of Mahome[n]t, not by the efforts of the effeminate and dastardly people whom he had conquered, but by the rivalship of the savage Arabians. They have neither power to resist the invaders after the 1ˢᵗ defeat, nor can they have any way to shake off the yoke when they are once subjected to the dominion of an absolute monarch, as those generally must be who govern these people. On the other hand where there is a nobility, tho the country be conquer⟨ed⟩ and over run by foreign troops yet they can make repeated attempts to recover there liberty; we see accordingly that tho France has been severall times over run by the English

46  they have as often shaken off the yoke. | Germany is every 10ᵗʰ or 12ᵗʰ year almost totally possessed by the troops of foreign states, but no city ever[b] remains with the conquerors. Hungary has been often conquered by the Turks, but was never long in their possession as they had heads to join themselves to in their attempts for liberty.— Besides all these inconveniencies it must certainly be detrimentall to the population of the country. For[c] there must be a great number who have no wives; now there would certainly be a much greater probability of a great number of children being born when the women were divided equally than when they were confined to a few. 100 women married to as many men would in all probability have many more children than when they were all belonging to one man. This may possibly be the reason why Persia, and the countries of Gre⟨e⟩ce, and those on the African coast, which were formerly very populous, are now

47  but very thinly inhabited. There are indeed some countries | where polygamy has been admitted which are still remarkably populous. The countries on the banks of the Nile and the Ganges, and besides these China, all are[d] instances of this. But then the populousness of a country is no sign that all the regulations tend to produce that end. For there may be other circumstancces which more than counterballance that hindrance. These countries

---

[b] Reading doubtful        [c] 'as' deleted        [d] Numbers written above the last two words indicate that their order was intended to be reversed

are all remarkably fruitful. The banks of the Nile and the Ganges are overflowed by those rivers, and yield immense crops, 3 or 4 in a year. This as there must be plenty of food and subsistance for man must, for reasons I will afterwards explain, promote population, as the number of men is proportion'd to the quantity of subsistence. This is also the case with regard to*e* China, and there may also be other reasons with which we are unnacquainted. We see too, on the other hand, that regulations that tend to population do not always produce that effect. Thus the law of marriage
48 in Scotland evidently appears from | the reasons already mentioned to tend to population, yet it has not the effect, being counterballanced by the other obstacles, as the barreness of the country and difficulty of subsistence.*f*

*Thursday. Febry. 10ᵗʰ 1763.*

In the two or three former lectures I gave you some account of the different sorts of marriage that are or have been in use in different parts of the world. There are in generall four sorts of marriage: either 1ˢᵗ, polygamy is allowed, where every man is allowed to have as many wives as he inclines and is able to maintain. Or every man is confined to one wife; this, which we may call *monogamy*, is of 3 sorts: either the husband has the power of divorce; or 2ᵈˡʸ, both the husband and wife have this power; or 3ᵈˡʸ, the power of divorce is not granted to either of the parties but is lodged in the hands of the civil magistrate, who can grant a divorce on hearing the circumstances of the case. I shewed ye also that polygamy was*g* on many accounts much inferior to monogamy of every sort. With
49 regard to the | wives it produces the greatest misery, as jealousy of every sort, discord, and enmity must inevitably attend it. The children also must be greatly neglected in every shape and lead but a very wretched life. The servants must all be slaves and entirely under the power of their master. With regard to the man himself, to whose happiness or rather pleasure the good of all the rest seems to be sacrificed, he also has no great enjoyment. He is racked by the most tormenting jealousy and has little enjoyment from the affections of his family or the intercourse of other men. It is detrimentall also to population, and besides is very hurtfull to the liberty of the people. We will find also that of all the species of monogamy above mentioned that which is established in this country is by much preferable. The disadvantages which attend the 2ᵈ species, where the husband and wife can seperate on the pleasure of either, must evidently produce the worst effects. I shewed allready what great licentiousness and dissoluteness of manners this produced in Rome during the latter periods of the Commonwealth

*e* Illegible word interlined      *f* 'The sc' deleted      *g* 'detrimental' deleted

50 and those which followed. It must[h] produce | very little confidence or trust in the parties, as they have the power of seperating themselves and are continually in fear of being dismissed by the other party. The children must in this case be under very great dissadvantages; it is always found that a stepmother is[i] no proper person to take care of the children. She has not only far less affection than the mother, but has commonly a jealousy and ill will towards them as rivalls to her and her ofspring. This can never happen in the present state of marriage but on the death of the mother, or divorce, which can seldom happen, whereas the liberty of divorce gives occasion to it frequently during her life. We see that there were few of the great men of Rome, after the latter periods of the Republick, who had not two or three wives in succession, and in this state the children must lead a very uncomfortable life. The 1st species, where the husband has the sole power of divorce, may be considerably preferable, as the expectation of a separation, tho it must considerably influence both parties, does not give such uncertainty and instability to their conduct as when both have this power. The method of marriage now in use avoids all those inconveniencies, as the union is here indissoluble and must therefore give occasion to none

51 of those | evills above mentioned. The knot indeed[j] may perhaps be too straitly tied in some cases. It has been very justly thought proper that the infidelity (of the wife at least⟨⟩) should give occasion to a divorce. That injury is such that there can be no harmony or agreement, but continuall distrus⟨t⟩ and animosity amongst the parties. Now for the same account all injuries which excite the same resentment and hatred, and which render the union equally uncomfortable, ought to produce a[k] divorce as well as the others. But however it is better the knot should be too strait than too loose.

These four species of marriage comprehend all those that have been ever in use as far as I know. The power of divorce was never lodged in the hand of the woman alone, as she is considered as the inferior, tho in this point she has been put on an equality. Where polygamy takes place the power of divorce is always vested in the husband. The wives are altogether the slaves of the husband, and are in the same manner bought for a summ of money. They are therefore intirely at his disposall and can be turned away when ever he inclines. This is the case in all countries where polygamy

52 takes place, for, as far as I can learn, the laws respecting marriage | differ very little in the severall countries where it has been receivd.

It may be proper to consider here what concern and interest the husband and wife have in the effects[l] of each other according to these different sorts of marriage. Where polygamy takes place the wife has not the smallest concern in the affairs of her husband or the management of the family.

---

[h] 'also' deleted    [i] Illegible word deleted    [j] 'indeed' deleted    [k] 'separat' deleted    [l] Reading doubtful

That is intirely entrusted to the eunuchs, who are absolutely necessary where this marriage is used. The wife is intirely the slave of the husband, and has no more interest in his affairs than any other slave.— In that species of marriage where the husband has the power of divorce, which was that used in the first ages of Rome, and amongst all the nations of Europe in early times, before the introduction of Christianity, the whole estate of the wife whether real or personall becomes intirely the property of the husband, and the wife has no longer any power over it either[m] during her life nor at her death. She is considered in the same light as a daughter or filia familias; she had no more connection with the estate of the husband

53 than she had, and at her death[63] | got the same share of the fathers fortune, without any regard to the fortune she brought along with her. In the new marriage of the Romans, which as I said before[63a] was introduced in favour of heiresses, the case was altogether different. The husband had here no property in the goods of the wife. The whole of her estate was to return to her on the death of the husband, or to her relations if she died before the husband, or before a divorce. The husband had indeed the *dominium dotis*, but this was in effect no more than the administration of the estate: i.e. if it was a land estate he lifted the rents; if it was a summ of money or personall estate he had the interest of it; if it was consigned into another persons hands, or if he had the use of it, he gave security for the restitution of the principall. The dower on the death of the husband, or divorce, returned to the wife, and at the death of the husband she got besides any settlement he had made upon her; or if there was none such she came in as a daughter,[64] besides the carrying away her portion. The separate interests

54 which would often arise from this sort of | mariage would render the union of the parties very uncertain, and the society much less agreable than when they have one common interest, which is allmost allways the case by the sort of marriage in use in this country. The wife here has a middle rank in the family betwixt that which she had in the old and in the new method of marriage amongst the Romans. The law of most countries in Europe is much the same on this head, but there are severall considerable differences with regard to the Scots and English law. The law with regard to land estates in[n] England is that[o] the husband draws all the rents of them during his life.[p] After his death they return to the relations of the wife, unless they have had children.— But both by the English and Scots law[q]

---

[m] Reading doubtful      [n] 'the' deleted      [o] The last three words replace 'nearly the same in both'. The words 'Chattles Reall' are written vertically in the margin at this point.      [p] The following words are deleted at this point: 'If they are disposed of during the wifes life time the price becomes intirely the husbands; but if he does not sell them'      [q] The words 'and with her consent', written vertically in the margin at about this point, are deleted

---

[63] i.e. *his* death.          [63a] 8–9 above.          [64] i.e. on her father's death.

there is allowed what is called the courtesy of England and Scotland, by which[r] the husband who has had a living child by his wife has the liferent of the estate. It is considered that if the child had lived the father would
55 have been his guardian by the common | law, and this continues for the fathers life time; this is granted by the courtesy of Scot. and Eng. when ever there has been a child born who has been heard to cry, as this child would have heired the estate.[s] What is called the chattles reall, which includes not only land property but all mortgages, servitudes, or what ever is due from a land estate {is so far the property of the husband that he may dispose of them by his own authority, and in that case the money he gets for them is intirely his; but if he does not dispose of them they go to the heirs of the wife.} The chattles personall are all bills and other debts, all the moveables of the wife, jewels, plate, etc.; these are intirely the husband

*Gap of two lines in MS.*

But bonds properly so called are on the same footing with the chattles real; that is, if the husband exacts them the money belongs intirely to him, but if not they go to the heirs of the woman, unless the contract specify other-
56 wise.[t] It is also provided that if | the wife has not been provided by the contract, she shall have her[u] the third part of the husbands personal estate {which in England contains all debts of whatever sorts, bills, etc., as well as the moveables; besides which she has what is called the dower, which is a third part of the land estate during her life.} This is given by the laws of most nations. The Scots law does not give the husband such power over the wifes fortune, nor the wife over the husbands. For here tho the husband may sell the chattles real or draw payment of a bond, yet the wife or her executors may make him give up the money he has so got, but this can⟨n⟩ot go to their heirs. The part of the moveable or personall estate which she gets is the third as in England, but does not comprehend the debts or bills, only the bygone rents of his estates.

*Gap of about eight lines in MS.*

57      | This is the regulations with regard to the estates after the death of the parties. With regard to them during their lifetime, the wife is not supposed to be capable of entering into any contract or coming under any obligation whatever, either respecting her own or her husbands fortune, unless for such things as are necessary for furnishing the house; for she is considered to have the management of the family under the husband as his servant.

[r] 'a' deleted      [s] 'And this is the case with regard to all' deleted      [t] At this point the following sentence is deleted: 'Choses manly on the other hand belong alltogether to the husband; and under this is included all the moveables of the wife, jewels, plate, etc.; these are alltogether at his disposall.'      [u] 'dower which' and two or three illegible words deleted

If one sends his servant to market or to the shop of any particular person, and once or twice pays the goods he has taken up in his name, he is concluded to be obliged to pay those he afterwards takes up unless he signify his design to the contrary. It is the same with respect to the wife: she is conceived to have the business of furnishing the family, and what debts she contracts in that manner he is conceived to be bound to pay. But in Scotland if he finds her extravagant he may by a public intimation declare that he will not pay such debts as she contracts, and by this means interdict

58 | her from meddling in his affairs. In England there is no such interdiction by any publick deed, but one may give this intimation by letter or otherwise to any particular persons. As she is [is]$^v$ conceived to be$^w$ under$^x$ her husbands influence, so$^y$ no sale of her estate is valid unless she come into court and declare her inclination that it should be so, and unless this be done she may claim restitution,

*Gap of about seven lines in MS.*

I shall only observe farther on this head of marriage some few things with regard to those persons who are prohibited to marry together, and whose marriages are looked upon as incestuous. {These are betwixt those who are connected in certain degrees of affinity and consanguinity.} First, with regard to ascendents and descen⟨den⟩ts, their marriages are always prohibited by the civil and cannon laws, that is, a man can not marry his

59 daughter, granddaughter, and | so on, nor his mother, grandmother, etc. in infinitum. With regard to the marriage of the mother and the son, this is of all the others the most contrary to nature, the most shocking and abominable. For here the affection which the son ought to feel towards a mother is very different from that which a husband ought to have towards a mother;$^{65}$ and that of a mother is in like manner very different from that of a wife. A son is considered as an inferior to his mother and under her$^z$ command, which idea is altogether inconsistent with that of a husband and wife, where the husband is conceivd to have the superiority. The marriage of the father with the daughter is also very shocking and contrary to nature, but not altogether so much so as that of the son with the mother. The affection of a father is without doubt very different from that of a husband, and that of a daughter from that of a wife. A father is considered as the guardian and tutor of his daughter, who is to educate her in all sort of virtues and instill into her the purest moralls and the chastest affections. Now this notion is altogether inconsistent with that of a lover, a seducer,

60 for there is | always some seduction necessary to persuade one to be a wife.

$^v$ 'not' deleted        $^w$ 'able to come' deleted        $^x$ 'any contract' deleted        $^y$ 'in Scotland' deleted        $^z$ Illegible word deleted

$^{65}$ *Sic.* Presumably 'wife' was intended.

{Add to this that nothing could more tend[a] to disturb the quiet and peace of the families than the allowing of such marriages. The mother would look on her daughter in a very dissagreable and even a jealous light when there was the least prospect that she might some time fill her place in the marriage bed, and in the same manner the father could not behold his son with pleasure when he thought there was a possibility of his taking his place as the husband of his wife.} But then there is not the same contrariety betwixt their condition in other respects. The father is the superior and the daughter the inferior, and this still continues in the husband and wife; whereas the mother is the superior and the son the inferior, which is altogether contrary to the idea of husband and wife, where the husband is always considered as the superior. Besides this, before the son is fit for marriage the mother is often past child bearing; whereas this is not the case always with respect to the father and the daughter. We see accordingly that tho the marriage of mothers and sons has been prohibited in every country {except from the delirium of superstition, from which the magi, out of veneration to Semiramis,[66] allowed that practise}, yet that of fathers and daughters has been tollerated amongst some barbarous nations. The famous Attila, the conqueror of the Romans, married his daughter        [67], and there are other instances of the like. {The case is the same in all respects with regard to more distant ascendents.} Marriage of brothers and sisters is in most countries prohibited. The constant intercourse betwixt them who generally are bred up together, and the many opportunities as well as
61  the great | incitements this[b] connection would give them, made it absolutely necessary to put an insuperable barr to their union. There could be no other means to prevent their corruption in such a near and close connection.— Besides if it were not for this barr marriages would never be made out of the family. A man would never incline to take a wife from a family where there were brothers, as he might be pretty well assured of her being allready corrupted. That ⟨?this⟩ is the real reason of the prohibition of marriage betwixt brothers and sisters will be greatly confirm'd by this observation, that where there is the same danger of corruption the prohi-⟨bi⟩tion is still farther extended and the marriage reckoned incestuous. At Rome[c] in the early periods the sons[d] lived after marriage in their fathers family, and consequently their children, that is, the cousins german, lived in the same intimacy and familiarity as brothers and sisters do in other countries; they were accordingly called brothers ⟨?and sisters⟩. For this
62  reason, as there was the | same danger of corruption, so the marriage of

---

[a] Numbers written above the last two words indicate that their order was intended to be reversed        [b] Illegible word deleted        [c] 'where' deleted        [d] Replaces 'brothers'

---

[66] Montesquieu, XXVI.14.
[67] Blank in MS. Esca: Montesquieu, loc. cit.

cousins german was prohibited and accounted incestuous. On the other hand at Athens the marriage of brothers and sisters consanguinean, tho not of those who were uterine, was allowed and often practised.[68] The womens and the mens appartments were there[e] altogether seperated, and no communication allowd betwixt them. The jealousy was so great that, tho they allowed a son to go into his mothers appartments with freedom, yet they did not allow the stepson to go into his mother in laws; they did not place the same confidence here as in the other case. The brothers therefor, as they never saw their sisters consanguinean and never went into their appartments, as they always staid with their mother,[f] and had consequently no opportunity of corrupting them, were always allowed at Athens to marry those sisters. But as they were allowed freely to enter into their mothers appartment and saw by that means their sisters,[69] there was the same necessity of preventing their corruption as in other countries.

63    With regard to | the marriage of uncles and nieces, and nephews and aunts, there is the same reason for the prohi⟨bi⟩tion of it as of the marriage of fathers and daughters, or sons and mothers. The uncles and aunts are considered as a sort of parents who have superiority and authority over their nephews and nieces. The affections betwixt them are very different from that of husband and wife.[g] But in the same manner as the marriage of the son with the mother is more shocking than that of the father and daughter, the aunt is naturally considered as a superior to the nephew, whereas when she becomes his wife she comes into the station of an inferior; whereas the uncle is always considered in the light of a superior to his niece. {And the disproportion of age affects these less then the former, as in that of parents and children.} We see for this reason the marriage of nephews an⟨d⟩ aunts has never been allowed, tho that of nieces and uncles has been in many countries. At Athens as the uncles never saw their nieces as they did never go into their brothers houses, at least into the womens appartment, there was no danger of their corrupting them. They were

64    therefore very common there. The story which is the foundation | of one of Lysias orations,[70] which I will perhaps read in the other lecture,[71] proceeded from a marriage of this sort. We see also that the Roman Catholicks frequently get indulgences to marry their nieces (from the Pope) tho they never do to marry aunts; these marriages are never allowed in Protestant countries.

With regard to the marriages of remoter collateralls, there was no prohibition beyond the 4th degree in any case unless where they were

---

[e] Reading doubtful    [f] 'were allowed' deleted    [g] There is a reference here to an unfinished and partially deleted note on v.62 which seems to read 'And there is a'

---

[68] Montesquieu, V.5.                              [69] Sc. uterine.
[70] Oration XXXII (*Against Diogeiton*).
[71] i.e. in one of the lectures in the course on Rhetoric.

parentum et liberorum loco; that is, the brothers or sisters of immediate
ascenden⟨t⟩s, as uncles and nieces, grand-uncles and grandnieces, etc.;
and in this prohibition the cannon law agrees with the civil. But besides
this they extend their prohibition to the 7th degree of their computation,[72]
that is, to 7th cousins according to ours. By this they had considerable
imoluments, as people might often rashly and ignorently marry such distant
relations, and were then obliged either to seperate or get out a dispensa-
65 tion. This has been taken away in this country | and all Protestant ones at
the Reformation, and we now observe those regulations in most respects
which are delivered in the 18 and 20th chapters of Leviticus. It is to be
observed also that by the civil and other laws the same degrees of affinity
are prohibited as of consanguinity, as these persons have somewhat of
the same relation. The sister of my wife is as it were my sister, and so in
other cases.

### Friday February 11th 1763.

I have now explained in the four preceding lectures the origin of the
perpetuity of marriage, and the injury that is conceived to be done by the
infidelity of either party, and why this injury is conceived to be more
grievous when committed by the wife against the husband than e contra.
I have explain'd also the 4 severall sorts of marriage, the great inconveniencies of polygamy, and made also a comparison betwixt the other 3 sorts. I
have shewed also the interest which the wife had in the husbands possessions in these severall sorts; that in the old marriage, where she was in
66 manu mariti, she was considered only as | his servant, and had no more
management during his life than as considered in that capacity; and that
in the new marriage, where the powe⟨r⟩ of divorce was common, she had
very little power over her fortune; that in the present marriage the wife
was in a middle way betwixt the two; as well as the differences betwixt
the English and Scots law; and lastly the degrees of consanguinity and
affinity in which marriage is reckoned incestuous and is accordingly
prohibited.

We may here observe that the prohibitions which are in force in this
country with regard to consanguinity, and are borrowed from the law of
Moses, are alltogether agreable to nature and reason. It is altogether
necessary that the marriage of the mother and the son should be prohibited;
the contrary would be shocking and abominable. The marriage of the

---

[72] There is a reference here to a footnote written at the bottom of 64 which reads as
follows: 'The computations of the cannon and civil law being explaind in Heinec. need not
be here repeated.' Cf. Heineccius, *Elementa juris civilis secundum ordinem Institutionum*,
§§ 153 ff.; above, i.102. Canon law computation was based on the number of steps to the
common ancestor, sixth cousins being in the seventh degree.

daughter and the father, of the uncle and the niece, and aunt and nephew, are also prohibited as being naturally shocking and contrary to reason. The marriage of brothers and sisters is also prohibited with great reason and according to naturall        [73]. But some of the prohibitions with regard
67 to the marriage of persons connected by affinity appears to | be rather an ordinance of a well regulated police than to be pointed out as naturally and originally improper. There are three points which may be observed with regard to this: 1st, that the passage of Leviticus[74] from which this prohibition is collected is rather overstreatched; 2dly, that there are severall well regulated polices where this ⟨is⟩ allowed, with some reason; and 3dly, that it is however a better regulation of police to forbid them.— 1st, the passage in Levit. from which this is collected is 'Thou shalt not marry the sister of thy wife *least it vex her.*' Now the reason here assigned, *least it vex her*, plainly shews that this proceeded from the customs of the Jews, who allowed of a plurality of wives, and that here it was forbade to marry two sisters at the same time, least they should be jealous of and ill will each other. And it must be a considerable extension of this to make it be a rule in those countries where it is not allowed to have two wives at the same time, but only one after another. 2dly, there are severall countries under no bad regulations where there is no hindrance of these marriages. In the East Indies in particular they are not only allow'd but considered as the
68 most proper of any, and are accordingly very common. | They consider that the sister of the childrens mother is likely to make a better mother in law than any other person; that she is more nearly connected with them and has already something of a parentall affection.[75] And in this there is indeed some justice. But we will find perhaps, 3dly, that it is rather more suitable, and a sign of a better regulated police, that they should be prohibited. For tho there is not the same danger of corruption, as the sister of the wife does not before the marriage live in the same house with the husband as his own sister does, yet this prohibition greatly facilitates the sisters living in the house with her sister and her husband. The inseperable barr that is put[h] to the union of those persons by the law of the country makes all connections of that sort be looked on as abominable and shocking; they are considered as brother and sister, and are accordingly brothers and sisters in law. By this means the house of the married sister is made a certain refuge and shelter for the unmarried sister. As no one but a mad
69 man would be jealous of the brother of his wife, | so by this constitution no one but a mad woman would be jealous of her husband with her sister,

[h] Reading doubtful

---

[73] Blank in MS. Possibly 'law' was intended.
[74] 18:18: 'Neither shalt thou take a wife to her sister, to vex her, to uncover her nakedness, beside the other in her life time.'
[75] Montesquieu, XXVI.14 fin.

unless ⟨he⟩ be a very brutal man, as all intercourse of that sort is looked on as shocking. It may perhaps be true that the sister would make a better mother in law to the children. Yet they perhaps would be still better taken care of if the sister of the mother could live in the house of their father without scandall[i] tho not as his wife. This she can by the above constitution do very well; and in this case they will probably be very well taken care of, as she considers them as her sisters children without looking on them as the rivalls of her own.

I shall only observe farther with regard to marriage what are the effects of the want of it. The great effect of marriage is that the children are looked on as legitimate and inherit from their father.— On the other hand those children who are not born in lawfull wedlock are not capable of inheriting. They are called spurii, nothi, sine patre nati, etc. These and all other 70 | illegitimate children are conceiv'd to have no relations either by the father or mothers side. Their father is thought to be uncertain, even although he should acknowledge them; and tho the mother is certain yet they are not allowed to succeed her; and on the other hand as they are not supposed to be capable of receiving any thing by inheritance so they are not allowed to make a testament, at least in some countries. These disadvantages of illegitimacy may in some respects be taken away in Scotland by letters of legitimation issued by the king.[76] The effect of these however is only to render the person capable of testing; this however is not used in England. The bastard in both countries, as he was conceived to have no relations, so his goods fell back to the community, and as the king in Scotland and England is the representative of the community in these matters, and ultimus haeres of every one, so he succeded to the fortunes which illegitimate children may have acquired.[77] In Scotland it seems it was thought 71 that where the king was the heir | there was no power to cut him out of his right by testament. (This, viz the succession of the king, indeed is the case in all countries only in case the person have no children; for if he has married and has children they succeed as in other cases ⟨?and his widow⟩ has her tierce of the moveables and the third of his land estate if he has any; and if he has a wife only, she will have the liferent as before of her dower and the half of the moveables;[78] {and if a child has been[j] born tho it be dead, that is, there was inheritable blood of the marriage, the estates

[i] Reading doubtful      [j] The last two words replace 'be not'

---

[76] Erskine, III.10.3.
[77] The words 'If they have no ch' are written vertically in the margin at about this point, but may possibly have been deleted. The king acquired only if the bastard died childless.
[78] Terce was a life-rent of one-third of the husband's heritage (land). The bastard's widow had terce, together with her *ius relictae*, which was one-third or one-half of his movables, according as there were children or not; 'tierce' should be 'third' and 'dower' should be 'terce'.

go to the nearest of kin, but this is not allowed if the child be not born at the parents death; it is considered as a res non existens, contrary to the practise of the civill law which accounts children unborn as giving the same rights as those which are born in the time of the father.}) In England on the other hand this notion was never receiv'd, so that there is there no occasion for any such letters; and if they were to be issu'd they would give the person no right which he had not before. But in Scotland they are necessary to give those[k] who are illegitimate the power of testing. The inheritance is supposed to be due to the king, and therefore if he does not give up his right to it the person can not give it away to any other; and the kings letters will be fully sufficient to do this. But tho they make him capable of leaving by will, they will not make him capable of succeding ab intestato to any of his relations. Tho the king can dispose of what is his own, yet he can not give one the power of depriving another of his right.

72 The heir at | law, that is, the nearest of the legitimate relations, would in this case be injur'd, and this the king has in this country no power to do. There is however ⟨?a means⟩ by which in most countries bastards may be made legitimate even with regard to the power of inheriting, viz by subsiquent marriage. That is, if one marries a woman who before lived with him as a concubine, the children born ⟨?before⟩ the marriage are supposed to be legitimate and the stain of their blood is conceived to be washed off; which is indeed but a mere fiction as no subsequent deed can alter the manner of their origin. This manner of legitimation was introduced by the later emperors, and from them borrowed by the cannonists and so spread over the greatest part of Europe. The Romans had severall methods of legitimation besides this.[79] As they allowed of adoption of the sons whose fathers were alive, so those who were sui juris were adrogated.[80] If therefore a naturall son, who [was] as he was reckoned to have no father was sui juris, submitted himself to the patria potestas of his real father, he was

73 reckond to have the same rights with regard to him | as any other who was adrogated. The rescript of the prince[81] also legitimated them in every respect.— 4th, if a father presented his son to the parish court or curia, and the son subjected[l] himself to be liable to the office of decurio, a parish office of a very troublesome nature, he was said to be legitimated per curiae dationem.[82] But this as well as that per adrogationem served only to

---

[k] Reading doubtful        [l] Reading doubtful

---

[79] Heineccius, I.10.23 ff.

[80] A legitimate son became *sui iuris* (not subject to paternal power) either because his father had died or because he had been emancipated. Adoption, being the transfer of a son from the power of one father to that of another, was a purely private transaction. Adrogation, involving the subjection of an independent person to the power of another, was subject to the approval of the popular assembly. Cf. i.152 above.

[81] i.e. the emperor.

[82] *Per oblationem curiae* ('by favour of the court').

make him capable of succession with regard to the father and some offices of which he was otherwise incapable; and this was also the effect of another method, viz that by which the later emperors allowed, viz that a father should by testament legitimate his children. The legitimatio per subsequens matrimonium was at first introduced by the later emperors, Anastasius, Xeno,[83] etc., but not with design that it should be perpetuall. They ordained that all those who should marry their concubines before a certain time should by that means legitimate their children; and so far was it from being designed to be perpetuall that it was intended to encourage them to

74 marry rather than to keep concubines. Justinian however | made it perpetuall; and from his novells,[84] which are generally followed by the cannonists with respect to marriage, the cannonists transcribed it into their law. {The cannonists however introduced some restriction with regard to this which seem not to have been acknowledged by the civill law, as that adulterous bastards, that is, such as were born by a concubine when one or both of the parties was married, could not be legitimate by their marrying on the death of the former wife or husband.} The cannon law, as it was at one time or other in force in all countries of Europe, spread this custom over the whole and it has been accordingly universally receivd, excepting England. The clergy at the time this was introduced into other countries had rendered themselves very odious to the nobility by joinin[in]g with King John and        [85] in their designs against the people. So that when this law was proposed they replied nolumus veteres leges Angliae mutari.[86] It has been intirely receivd in Scotland. The ecclesiasticall court however receivd this custom, and accounted all those legitimate whose parents had married together;[m] and as the civil courts did not acknowledge it there have arose several niceities which are unknown in other countries. If one marries a woman who has bore him children before, those born after are without ⟨?doubt⟩ lawfull[n] and may succeed him; but those who were born

75 before are not by the civill or common laws[o] | accounted legitimated. These are called speciall and all others generall bastards. These however do not by the English law succeed in preference of the younger sons[p] born after the marriage. He is therefore called the mulier        [87], corrupted from the French        [87]. {Robert III.[d] succeeded to Robert II.[d], tho he was

---

[m] Reading doubtful        [n] Reading of last four words in MS. doubtful        [o] Reading doubtful        [p] 'after' deleted

---

[83] In fact Constantine, recorded by Zeno, *C.* 5.27.5; Anastasius, *C.* 5.27.6.
[84] Novel 89.
[85] Blank in MS. Possibly Henry III was intended.
[86] Statute of Merton, 20 Henry III, c. 9 (1236).
[87] Blanks in MS. Mulier puisne, legitimate issue preferred before an elder brother born out of wedlock, known as bastard eigne.

born of Eleanor More[88] who was within the prohibited degrees, before the dispensation came from the Pope.} But if the eld⟨?er⟩ speciall bastard, or bastard enné, gets possession of the estate and is not disturbed by his brothers, and his children are allowd to succeed, they cannot be turned out by the heirs of the mu        [87]. Speciall bastards also are allowed to be clergymen, as they are not reckoned bastards by the ecclesiasticall law, but generall bastards, who are so by both laws, are not. An Act of Parliament however can legitimate any one. The predecessor of Henry the        [q], by whom he came to the crown, was a bastard who had been legitimated.[89] Other dissadvantages attend bastards in some countries, as they are not capable of publick offices.

76                    | *Monday. Febry. 14ᵗʰ 1763.*

After having taken notice of the 4 different sorts of marriage and the different consequences which followed them, I made some observations concerning the effects of marriage, the chief of which respects the children, as it is the marriage of the parents which gives the children the power of inheriting, etc., and the want of it which makes the children of a concubine incapable of it. We may observe here that ⟨it⟩ is these incapacities which attend the want of marriage which alone maintain monogamy in any country. We see that in all countries where polygamy takes place there are no such incapacities attending the children of a concubine. Where a man has a number of women about him, it matters but little whether he gives them the honourable title of wife or not; there can be but very little difference in the situation of any of his women. The incapacities attending on illegitimacy are the only thing which prevents the introduction of poly-
77 gamy into any country. For if the children were allowed to suc|ceed, the conveniencies, at least the apparent ones, which attend the want of marriage would soon cause it ⟨to⟩ be laid aside. In the first place, the liberty of separation; 2ᵈˡʸ, the having it in his power to take another wife; and 3ᵈˡʸ, the having the wife absolutely under his power. It is not generally the desire of possessing a womans fortune that makes one submit himself to

    [q] Blank in MS.

---

    [88] Elizabeth Mure, mistress of King Robert II of Scotland, was married to him *c.* 1347 by papal dispensation, thereby legitimating their children, including the future King Robert III, born *c.* 1340. Canon law widened the prohibited degrees well beyond those of Leviticus; 64 above.
    [89] Henry VII derived his claim to the throne from his mother's great-grandfather, John of Gaunt. The bastard 'predecessor' (ancestor) was John Beaufort, son of John of Gaunt and Catherine Swynford, whose children, born before their marriage, were legitimated by Act of Parliament.

the restraints of marriage, as that might be had without them; nor is ⟨it⟩ that he may leave her a share of his fortune: a voluntary deed could answer that end; nor is it that they may live together, as they could do that without it; but it is that he may have children who should succeed to his fortune and represent him in the state; and if children out of wedlock were equally capable of this men would not confine themselves by it, but would live with their women during pleasure only and not confine themselves to one. Polygamy would in this manner be very soon introduced.

78 | We come now to consider the second[r] relation which arises from the connections in a family, viz the authority of a father over his children. This we find in all early societies was altogether absolute. There are many reasons which would make this very naturall, which have been already hinted at in treating of marriage. We may observe also that in the early and more rude periods of society men were not conceived to be bound to aliment their children (or maintain them). It was not then supposed that one was bound to do any thing for those who did not do their part to their own maintenance. As now men are only bound not to hurt one another and to act fairly and justly in their dealings, but are not compelled to any acts of benevolence, which are left intirely to his own good will, so in the ruder times this was extended to the nearest relations, and the obligation they were under to do for one another was supposed to be binding only 79 by their inclination; and all kindnesses betwixt | them were reckon'd as acts of benevolence and not as what they were bound in justice to perform. If a son is taken by pirates, or any other set of men, as the barbarous nations on the coast of the Mediterranean sea, who will either in all probability put him to death or reduce him to slavery, we do not look on the father as bound to ransom according to the rules of justice, but only as a great sign of inhumanity and hardheartedness. This was extended at first much farther, and a parent was considered as at liberty either to maintain and educate his children or to leave them at the mercy of the weather and the wild beasts. When therefore he was at the trouble and expense of maintaining a person whom he might without injustice have neglected, that person would appear to be under the greatest obligations to him; which, joind with the other causes before mention'd, produced in early times a great and sovereign authority in the father of the family. The practise of exposing children we see was practised in most early nations.[90] The Roman law indeed prohibited ⟨?it⟩ pretty early, and these prohibitions were afterwards repeated; but they do not appear to have 80 | been in any considerable degree effectuall. For we find that long after the first of them the exposing of children was extremely common, in so

---

[r] Replaces 'third'

---

[90] Cf. TMS V.2.15. For Roman law, *C.* 8.51.2 (A.D. 374).

much that a pillar in the city was, from the children which were often laid down at it, denominated *columna lactaria*;[91] and indeed it does not appear to have been ever thoroughly and effectually prohibited till the establishment of Christianity in the Roman Empire. We see also that it was allowed by law at Athens and many other of the Grecian states, particularly *Lacedaemon*. The missionaries tell us that ⟨it⟩ is practised very frequently in China,[92] and indeed it is so in most countries where polygamy takes place. The women are there, too, remarkably prolifick. They had a notion, it seems, that it was much more humane to put them to death by drowning them than to allow them to lie exposed to the greatest dangers. There were therefore women who made a practise of going about from house to house every morning and receiving the children, which they carried and thro*[s]*

81 into the river, in the same manner as we would send a parcell | of puppies or kittons to be drowned. The fathers make a great merit of their conduct on this occasion. They converted to Christianity two of these women, and took their promise that they should bring them to be baptised before they drowned them. And in this they glory as having saved a vast number of souls. It seems these pious fathers did not consider that it was contrary to the principples of the Christian religion to put a child to death either before or after it was baptised. The power of the father over his children was at first, in Rome, altogether absolute. His authority extended to three different heads: 1$^{st}$, he had the power of life and death over his children; 2$^{dly}$, that of selling him; and 3$^{dly}$, that every thing which was acquired by him was to belong to the father, he being considered as incapable of property. But these powers seem to have been pretty soon mitigated, in the same manner as that which the husband had over his wife. The laws of Romulus gave the father an unlimited power over his children, but this

82 was soon abriged. Numa made a | law by which the fathers were forbidden to sell their sons after their marriage.[93] And although the 12 Tables revived the law of Romulus without any restriction, and expressly gave the father the power of selling his sons three times, yet it is probable this extended only to those which were unmarried, for*[t]* when a man takes a wife from another family he becomes bound to her for his labour and work. She has a claim upon him as well as his fathers family. She and the children claim his attention, so that it would be very hard that the son should be seperated from her and sold to be the slave of another man. The authority of the father over the life of the son, which seems at first sight so excessive, appears to have been very soon brought to a moderate and proper pitch. In

---

*[s]* *Sic.* No doubt 'threw' was intended.     *[t]* Almost a whole line of illegible words is deleted at this point. The word 'severall' has been overwritten at the beginning of the line.

---

[91] Paulus Diaconus, *Epitoma Festi* (Lindsay, 118M).
[92] Montesquieu, XXIII.16.
[93] Dionysius of Halicarnassus, *Roman Antiquities*, II.27, cited by Heineccius, I.9.6.

the same manner as when one marries a woman her relations are apt to take concern in the treatment she receives, and not allow him to exercise more rigour than was just in the punishment of her offences, so there were persons who would keep the exercise of the fathers authority over the

83 children within due limits and not allow of greater severity | than was proper. The other relations, the uncles, etc., would often look on the son somewhat in the same light as a father and be anxious for his being justly dealt with. An uncle might have a nephew whom he designed to institute his heir. The fathers authority was by this means far from being an arbitrary one, as we are apt to conceive it, but was in effect no more than the power of preventing the magistrate in the punishment of those crimes which were punishable by law, and this he did not by his own private authority but with and by the consent of the other relations. We see that as early as the time of Valerius Corvus[94] the publick took concern in the conduct of the fathers to their children. He was called before the praetors for sending him out to the country to work with the slaves and not giving him proper education, as the story is told in Ciceros Offices. When therefore the publick took cognizance of so small an offence against the parentall duty, it is not probable it would pass by the arbitrary punishment of crimes

84 which were not liable to a publick[u] | correction. The son too was supposed to be incapable of having any property; whatever he had from his father was supposed to be recallible at pleasure, and whatever he got from others came to him. In this too the power of the fathers seems to have been pretty soon restricted. It is probable that in the early times it was extended to those sons only who were not married. When a man takes a wife he has her and his family to maintain. The children indeed are not under his patria potestas but under that of their grandfather, but the wife and they were to be supported by him. We see that the father even in the early times of the Commonwealth was not allowed to dissinherit his children but on certain accompts. For the 12 Tables declared pater familias uti legassit de re sua tutelave suae rei ita jus esto;[95] yet there were many cases in which the passing over or exheredating the children rendered the testament invalid. And when the father could not deprive the son of his inheritance, they

85 would not probably allow | him to make him destitute in his life | time. We see also that as early as the time of Marcianus[96] an order was made by which

---

[u] Illegible word deleted

---

[94] In fact Lucius Manlius: Cicero, *De Officiis*, III.112; cf. Valerius Maximus, V.4.3 and VI.9.1.

[95] Tab. V.3: *uti legassit super pecunia tutelave suae rei, ita ius esto* (*Epitome Ulpiani*, XI.14): 'as one shall have made bequests concerning his property or the guardianship of his estate, so shall the law be.'

[96] D. 23.2.19, where the jurist Marcianus cites the *lex Julia* of Augustus' time and legislation of Severus and Caracalla.

the praetor was empowered to compell those parents who did not permit their children to marry, when they had a suitable offer, not only to allow them, but also to grant them a portion agreable to their rank. To what purpose would this have served, if the parent had had the power to recall it whenever he inclined. It is well known that Julius Caeser gave them the peculium castrense, and the emperors some time after the pecu. quasi castrense; and some time after they were allowed also to have the property of all that came to them from strangers or by their mother, reserving only the usufruct to the father. Upon the whole the power of the fathers, tho very considerable, does not appear to have been so unbounded as we are apt to imagine.

The power of the fathers amongst our barbarous ancestors which over-
86 | threw the Roman Empire in the west of Europe was at first also very great, but was gradually mitigated and reduced to the present form.— One of the great differences betwixt the state of the fathers in Rome and in this country, and all other Christian ones, is that the father is bound to provide for and aliment his children. The exposing of a child is in this country accounted[v] the same[w] with the murdering of one, which is punished in the same way as any other murther. The children are in like manner bound to maintain their parents if they should happen to become destitute and unable to maintain themselves. The power of the father over them is also greatly abriged; it extends now no farther than the parentalis castigatio, or a moderate correction. This they have over their younger children who live in the family; but if they have taken up a separate family of their own he has no power at all over them, tho they are without doubt allways bound
87 | to give them all due respect and filiall piety. The only thing in which the father differs from other relations is that he is a preferable one to all others. If his son during his minority falls heir to any relation or has a fortune left him, the father becomes his guardian and manager without being appointed, and that without being bound to give security or caution for the faithfull performance of his office, as all others are. The naturall affection he bears his children is conceived to be a strong enough tie upon him without any other.

### Tuesday. February 15th 1763.

The rights which arise[x] from the relations which may subsist in a family are as I observed before of 3 sorts: they belong either to a person as being husband or wife; 2dly, as father or son; and lastly, as master or servants. I have already considered the two former, and come now to consider the third relation which subsists in a family, viz that of master and servant.

[v] Replaces 'on'      [w] 'footing' deleted      [x] Reading doubtful

88 | The same reasons which established the authority of the father of the family over the other members of it hold in a great measure with respect to the servants. The head of the family is the person on whom the others are all naturally in a great measure dependent for their support and defence. The government in most early periods of society, when it is in a very weakly condition, is necessitated to establish jurisdictions in the different parts of the country; they can find no other method which will be sufficient to keep the subjects in due subjection and in any[y] tollerable order. The same thing will incline them to commit great authority over the other members[z] of the family into the hands of the head of it, and to strengthen his power over them, as they can discover no other method of bringing them under the authority of any sort of government. This gives the head of the family always a very great power over the other members of it in

89 all early times. | The other members however have some[a] connections which may probably mitigate this authority considerably. When one takes a wife, she is generally connected with a father or a brother or some other near relation of equall power and authority in the state; she has these to complain to if she be hardly used by her husband; and they will take care that he inflicts no punishment upon her greater than her deserts. The husband therefore, when he sat in judgement on his wife, took her relations into council with him, and the punishment which was inflicted was agreed on by the joint consent of the whole. The children were in like manner guarded against the too great severity of the father by the interposition of the other relations who thought themselves concerned for their safety and honour. But the servants had no such persons who would or could have any influence with their masters to mitigate their punishment. They had either no relations near them, or none who were of power and conse-

90 quence any way equall to that of their master. No | restraint therefore was ever put to the authority of the masters over[b] their servants, who became therefore slaves[c] under the absolute and arbitrary power of their master.— Their condition was therefore very grievous in many different ways.

1st, with regard to their lives, they were at the mercy of the master, who might do with them as he pleased. His authority was not like that of a father over his children, which[d] only executed by the private will of the father the sentence which the laws of the country would have given, but was altogether arbitrary; he might put a slave to death on the smallest transgression, or the slightest neglect of his commands, and no fault was to be found with him. 2[dly], as his life, so was his liberty at the sole disposall of his master; and indeed properly speaking he had no liberty at all, as his master might employ him at the most severe and insupportable work

---

[y] Reading of last two words doubtful    [z] 'of the head' deleted    [a] 'means' deleted    [b] Replaces 'of'    [c] Replaces 'absolutely'    [d] Illegible word deleted

without his having any resource. But as the master had the sole right to his work and labour, so had he the power of disposing of it and transferring him to another master perhaps still more severe than himself. He under-
91 went | in this manner the most severe and grievous tasks imaginable, without having the prospect or even the possibility of being freed from it but by the great good will or the caprice of his master.— — —

3<sup>dly</sup>, he was incapable of<sup>e</sup> having any property. The fruit of all his labours, which were exacted in the most rigorous manner, went to his master. He was allowed nothing more than was barely necessary for his maintenance, as a horse or other work animall. And if by the most parsimonious life he had saved anything from this scrimp allowance, this could be called in by the master at pleasure. Not only the fruits of his labour, but whatever came any how to him, was immediately the property of his master. He might indeed make any lucrative agreement, as the stipulating for himself a summ of money to be paid against such a day, but this money did not belong to himself but to his master; whatever money was left him in a legacy all was<sup>f</sup> claimed by his master. He could enter into no contract without either the
92 express or the tacit consent of his | master. If he should engage to perform certain services or pay any money to one, these could not [bind] be<sup>g</sup> binding as       <sup>h</sup> would accrue to his master from hence. By the consent of his master however he could enter into any contract, which by that means became binding on his master; or if he had not expressed his consent, but had before acted in such a way as that his consent would be presumed. Thus if a master set up his slave in a shop, all contracts of sale or others which regarded the management of the business were binding on the master to the amount of the peculium he had entrusted him with.[97] The condition of the slaves was therefore in all these respects most miserable. Their masters had no restraint put on their cruelty, and the hardest usage was commonly practised on them; their lives were taken away on the slightest occasion. We are told that Augustus once manumitted all the slaves of V       [98] Pollio with whom he supped. A slave bringing in a dish happened to break it. The slave fell at Augustus feet and requested him,
93 not to get his pardon of his master, for | death he thought was inevitable, but that he would request his master that after he was crucified, which was the common punishment inflicted on slaves, he should not hack his body into pieces and throw it to feed the fish in his ponds, which was it seems his common way of treating them. Augustus was so shocked at the story that he ordered him to manumitt not only that slave but all the others he had

---

<sup>e</sup> Illegible word deleted    <sup>f</sup> Numbers written above the last two words indicate that their order was intended to be reversed    <sup>g</sup> Interlined    <sup>h</sup> Illegible word

[97] *Inst.* 4.7.1–4.
[98] Blank in MS. Vedius Pollio. Seneca, *De Ira*, III.40 and Dio Cassius, *History*, LIV.23 both have the story, but neither says that all the slaves were manumitted.

about his house; which though it was not perhaps a punishment adequate to the crime, yet would be a very considerable fine. A man who would entertain Augustus at that time would have at least 8000[99] or 1000 slaves, and if we estimate these at the ordinary price of a slave in the American colonies or on the coast of Africa[n], that is, about 50 or 40£ each, this would amount to a fine of £40000 or 50000.— They were used in every shape with the greatest severity. They had nothing which could bind them to have any affection for their master, and the most severe discipline was necessary to keep them to their work.

94    | [i]By this we may see what a miserable life the slaves must have led; their life and their property intirely at the mercy of another, and their liberty, if they could be said to have any, at his disposall also. But besides these hardships which are commonly taken notice of by writers, they laboured under severall others which are not so generally attended to. They were, in the 1st place, reckoned incapable of marriage. We are told that the male and female slaves lived together in contubernium, which is generally supposed to denote the same thing with regard to the slaves as matrimonium with regard to the free persons. But ⟨it⟩ is very plain that there must have been a great difference. For no union betwixt them could have been of a long continuance from the very nature of their condition.— First of all, that which creates the obligation to fidelity in the wife was altogether wanting[j] when a male and female slave cohabited together. When a man takes a wife she comes to be altogether under his protection; she owes her safety and maintenance {especially in the lower ranks} intirely to her husband, and from this dependance it is that she is thought

95    to be bound to be faithfull and | constant to him. But a female slave who cohabits with the male one has no such obligation; she is not maintaind by his labour, nor defended by him, nor any way supported; all this, as far as she enjoys it, she has from her master, who will take care of every thing which may enable her to perform her work the better. As therefore she has no particular obligation to him, so she was not conceivd to be bound to fidelity to him. For this reason we see that the corrupting a female slave who lived in contubernio with a male one was not looked on as any way reprehensible or injurious. It was no injury to the master, nor was it any to the slave as he had no claim to her fidelity. The female slaves will therefore always live in a state of prostitution, which we see is the case in the West Indian colonies; and this alone may shew how destructive it is to population, as a state of prostitution is always detrimentall to population. Many other things render their cohabitation precarious. The duration of it does not depend on themselves but on their master. If he thinks that they

[i] 'But besides these mos' deleted    [j] 'in the' deleted

[99] *Sic.* No doubt '800' was intended.

do not labour so well together, he may send ⟨them⟩ to different parts of
96 his farm, or he | may sell either of them at his pleasure. Or if he thinks he
has not the profit he might have by the slaves the female would bear him,
he may take her from her present mate and give her to another. The slave
is in this manner deprived of all the comforts and can have but very little
of the parentall affections of a parent. Tho he be satisfied that they were
begotten by him, he knows too that they were not supported nor maintained
by him, nor any way protected, which as I said before[1] is that which alone
constitutes the parentall and filial affections. The slaves at Rome were
likewise under an other hardship which is not known by our legall slaves
at this time. They are indeed otherwise in much the same condition. The
slaves were then not only altogether dependent on others for their lives
and property and deprived of their liberty and cut out of the consolations
of marriage, for we may justly say they had no wives, but had as we may say
no god. Slaves were admitted to no religious society and were reckond
profane.[k] I observed before[2] that superstitious fears and terrors increase
97 | always with the precariousness and uncertainty of the[l] manner of life
people are engaged in, and that without any regard to their religion. Game-
sters,[m] who are generally a most profligate, irreligious, and profane set of
men and almost entirely devoid of[n] religion, are generally most remarkably
superstitious; they have a great opinion of a run of luck, etc. Jesters,[o] who
are generally not the most religious, are more superstitious than any other
set of men whatever; the continuall uncertainty they are in necessarily
occasions this. Slaves were of all others the most dependent and uncertain
of their subsistence. Their lives, their liberty, and property were intirely at
the mercy of the caprice and whim of another.— It was therefore very hard
that they who stood most in need of some consolation in this way should
be intirely debarred from all religious societies, {which might at least sooth
their superstitious dreads}. The gods then were alltogether locall or tute-
lary; they did not conceive any god that was equally favourable to the
prayers of all. Each city had its peculiar deities. Minerva presided over
98 Athens; Rome was under the protection of Mars and Jupiter who dwelt | in
the Capitoll. These were supposed to favour only their particular people.
What had Jupiter who dwelt in the Capitoll to do with a slave who came
from Syria or Cappadocia. Besides, the deities then could never be addressed empty handed; who ever had any request to ask of them must introduce it with a present. This also intirely debarred the slaves from religious
offices as they had nothing of their own to offer; all they possessed was

---

[k] 'and' deleted            [l] 'subsistance' deleted        [m] Replaces an illegible word
[n] 'superstition' deleted   [o] Reading doubtful

---

[1] 4 above.
[2] Apparently not in the Report as we have it; 13 above refers to superstition as a consequence of ignorance. Cf. LJ(B) 133, below.

their masters.— Their masters prayed for their thriving and multiplying in the same manner as for their cattle. 　　　　　　*p teneris sic aequies alumnis.*[3] The only slaves who were supposed to be under the protection of any god were those which belonged to the priests and ministered in the temples; these were esteemed to be under the countenance and favour of the god whom they thus served. This it was which made all religions which taught the being of one supreme and universall god, who presided over all, be so greedily receivd by this order of men. Even the Jewish religion, which is of all others least adapted to make conquests, was

99 | greedily receivd by them. This religion is not at all calculated for conquest, but by those very reasons is admirably adapted for defence. The proselytes, as they are not of the seed of Abraham, can never be, nor their posterity, entitled to the same promises as the seed of Abraham, of whom they say the Messiah is to be born. They have many other hindrances, as the restrictions from eating certain foods which men generally do it,[4] as strangled,[5] pork, etc.; these inconveniences make it that we never here now of any converts to Judaism, but at the same time there are very few who desert the Jewish faith. Notwithstanding of these obstructions, as the proselytes of the gate and of the temple, etc. were admitted to some part of the religious worship, and the religion was that of one supreme god common to slaves and freemen, the progress it made at Rome was very rapid. Tacitus[6] and

　　　　　*q* tells us that a great part hominum servilis et libertinae conditionis were greatly addicted to the Jewish religion. When the Christian religion was spread abroad, which put all men on an equality without any of these

100 foolish restrictions with regard to meats, the progress | it made amongst these folks was most astonishing. The case was the same with respect to all those who taught the being of one supreme god, as that of Zoroaster and of Mahomet. As the slaves were in this manner in such a subjected condition, we find they were treated with the greatest harshness and their labour exacted with the utmost rigour. And this without being reckoned contradictory to good moralls.—The slave who was used for the porter w[h]as chained in his cell near the gate, as we would chain a great dog.*r* Catullus[7] mentions in some of his elegies how happy he was when he heard the rattling of the chains of the porter of his mistresses house. If the slave was

---

*p* Blank in MS.　　　　*q* Blank in MS.　　　　*r* 'Juve' deleted

---

[3] Probably Horace, *Odes*, III.18.3,4: *abeasque parvis aequus alumnis* ('look kindly on my little nurslings as you depart').

[4] *Sic.* Probably 'eat' was intended.

[5] i.e. presumably the flesh of animals that have been strangled. Cf. Acts 15:20.

[6] Probably *Annals*, II.85, where 4,000 *libertini generis* are said to be *ea superstitione infecta*.

[7] In fact Ovid, *Amores*, I.6, cited by Hume, 'Of the Populousness of Ancient Nations', in *Essays*, I.386. Hume also quotes 'the ancient poet, *Janitoris tintinnire impedimenta audio*' (Afranius, *Comicorum Romanorum fragm.* 392).

a runnaway, but his work requird that he should go about, he had a great log of wood chain'd to him. The slaves who wrought in the country were kept all night in cells underground, but a few in each that they might not break loose, and when they were carried to work they were coupled two and two together, and in that manner they wrought. Nothing was more common then[s] to turn out the old or diseased slaves to die, as we would a dying

101 | horse. Cato, who was a man of the most severe virtue and the strictest observer of the morall rules then in fashion, used frequently to do this and confessed it without any shame; and this he would not have done if it had been contrary to the practise of the times.[8] In the same man⟨n⟩er as it is common near a great city to have a place where they put dying cattle, so there was an island in the Tiber into which they[t] used to turn the slaves who were about to dye, and we are told it was white all over with their bones.

We are apt to imagine that slavery is entirely abolished at this time, without considering that this is the case in only a small part of Europe; not remembering that all over Moscovy and all the eastern parts of Europe, and the whole of Asia, that is, from Bohemia to the Indian Ocean, all over Africa, and the greatest part of America, it is still in use. It is indeed all-most impossible that it should ever be totally or generally abolished. In a republican government it will scarcely ever happen that it should be

102 abolished. The persons who make all the laws | in that country are persons who have slaves themselves. These will never make any laws mitigating their usage; whatever laws are made with regard to slaves are[u] intended to strengthen the authority of the masters and reduce the slaves to a more absolute subjection. The profit of the masters was increased when they got greater power over their slaves. The authority of the masters over the slaves is therefore unbounded in all republican governments. And as the service which is exacted of them is so great, and their masters so rigorous, they require the strictest discipline to keep them in order. In all countries where slavery takes place ⟨?we see⟩ that the number of free men is very inconsiderable in comparison of that of the slaves. A Roman of a middling fortune would have 500 or 600 slaves in the house about him, and in the country some thousands under the direction of 5 or 6 freemen who exer-cised the most tyrannicall authority over them, in the same manner as the negroe slaves are in the sugar colonies. The greatest rigour is necessary

103 to make them be in safety. | They were therefore used with the utmost severity. It was a customary thing for the master to give the slaves a whip-ping every evening, as they do in the West Indies in the morning. Seneca

---

[s] *Sic.* Probably 'than' was intended.        [t] Replaces 'wh'        [u] 'ad' deleted

---

[8] Plutarch, *Life of Cato*, 4, cited by Hume, *Essays*, I.386.

complains (in his De Beneficiis),[9] when declaiming on the vices of the times, that he was waked at midnight by the cries of the slaves, whom the master chastised then instead of in the evening; it is not the thing, but the bad hours, of which he complains. The state was in continuall hazard from their insurrections; the servile war was chiefly owing to them, and requ⟨i⟩red the skill of the ablest generalls to quell it. This made still greater severity necessary. The freedom of the free was the cause of the great oppression of the slaves. No country ever gave greater freedom to the free-men than Rome; so that a free man could not be put to death for any crime whereas a slave could for the smallest. The slaves who were in the house or on the road with their master, whether they had fled or not, where he was murthered were frequently all put to death.[10]     [11] tells us that

104  a man[v] being murtherd in his house, all his | slaves to the number of 400 were carrying to execution; on which the mob rose. The Senate was called, and one of the severer[w] senators who adhered to the old principles stood up and told them that there could be no safety for any one if this example was not made, that the slaves might see that the greatest attention was to be paid to their master, etc. In the same manner Carthage, Tyre, Lacede-mon, etc. were all in danger from their slaves. In a monarchicall govern-ment there is some greater probability of the hardships being taken off. The king can not be injured by this; the subjects are his slaves whatever happen; on the contrary it may tend to strengthen his authority by weaken-ing that of his nobles. He is as it were somewhat more of an impartiall judge, and by this means his compassion may move him to slacken the rigour of the authority of the masters. We see accordingly that no absolute

105  monarchy was ever in danger from the ⟨?slaves⟩, | neither the Mogulls country, Persia modern or ancient, nor Turky, etc. ever were.


### Wednesday February 16th 1763

We may observe here that the state of slavery is a much more tollerable one in a [a] poor and barbarous people than in a rich and polished one. There are severall things which naturally tend to produce this effect. 1st, in a wealthy and opulent country where slavery is tollerated their number is always very great, and far greater than that of the freemen. Their wealth enables them to maintain immense numbers. A wealthy noble man would have 1000 or perhaps severall 1000s We are told that Trebellius,[12] a man

---

[v] Reading doubtful     [w] Reading doubtful

[9] In fact Seneca, *Epistles*, 122, cited by Hume, *Essays*, I.387.
[10] Senatusconsultum Silanianum, cited by Montesquieu, XV.15.
[11] Blank in MS. Tacitus, *Annals*, XIV.43, cited by Hume, *Essays*, I.392.
[12] In fact Tigellius: Horace, *Satires*, I.2.3 ff. and I.3.11–12.

who was reckoned one of the most sober and least expensive at that time, that some times he had 200 and some times but 10 slaves, according as his work required. From whence we may see, by the manner in which it is told, that 10 slaves was as few or fewer than any one who pretended to the character of a gentleman would keep at that time. The slaves in this manner were generally at least ten times as numerous as the free men. They were
106 |consequently a very formidable body, and would keep the state in continuall terror. In a poor country on the other hand the wealth of the inhabitants can not put it in their power to maintain a great many slaves; there will be few that can come the length of 10 or 12; many will have but 2 or 3, and the far greatest part none at all. The number of slaves therefore in this country would be less or very little greater than that of the freemen, and consequently would not put them in any terror. In rich countries therefore, as they will be in continuall fear of their slaves, so will they treat them with the greatest severity and take every method to keep them under. We see accordingly that at Rome, where the riches was immense and the people in continual dread of their slaves, of which there were a prodigious number, far greater than that of the free men, the slaves were treated with the utmost severity, and were put to death on the smallest transgression. Amongst the old Germans and others, as Tacitus[13] tells, they were used
107 with the greatest humanity. He says a man would kill his | slave their in no other way than he did his enemy, that is, he would kill him in a fit of passion, but not thro caprice or for any small transgression. We see in the same manner the slaves in the American colonies on the continent are treated with great humanity and used in a very gentle manner. Their masters are not at all rich, and consequently can not afford to keep any great number and are in no terror concerning ⟨?them⟩. In the West Indian sugar islands, where they are strictly used, their numbers are very great. The sugar trade as every one knows is much more profitable than the cultivation of corn, in which the planters of North America are chiefly employed, and who as they have thereby but very moderate fortunes keep but few slaves. But the sugar trade being the most profitable of any, and many persons often raising themselves immense fortunes in a very short time, they can well afford to keep a multitude of slaves; their numbers therefore far exceed the number of freemen. This keeps them in continuall dread of them, and the greatest rigour and severity is consequently exercised upon them. They are put to death in prodigious numbers on the least
108 appearance of insurrection. | Any one who appears to make the least disturbance is immediately hanged up; and this not in the common way with a rope, but with an iron collar such as they use for the dogs,[x] in which

---

[x] Reading doubtful

---

[13] *Germania*, xxv.

they will hang 6 or 7 days till they die of hunger. Besides the dread the freemen are in of the slaves in a rich country, there are other things which will make them be treated with much greater severity. In a poor country there can be no great difference betwixt the master and the slave in any respect. They will eat at the same table, work together, and be cloathed in the same manner, and will be alike in every other particular. In a rich country the disproportion betwixt them will be prodigious in all these respects. This dis⟨pro⟩portion will make the rich men much more sevr[14] to their slaves than the poorer ones. A man of great fortune, a nobleman, is much farther removed from the condition of his servant than a farmer. The farmer generally works along with his servant; they eat together, and[y] are little different. The disproportion betwixt them, the condition of the nobleman and his servant, is so great that he will hardly look on him as being

109 of the same kind; he thinks he has little title | even to the ordinary enjoyments of life, and feels but little for his misfortunes. The farmer on the other hand considers his servant as almost on an equall with himself, and is therefore the more capable of feeling with him. Those persons most excite our compassion and are most apt to affect our sympathy who most resemble ourselves, and the greater the difference the less we are affected by them. {The same will be the case with slaves.} The old Romans during their simple and rude state treated their slaves in a very different manner from what they did when more advanced in riches and refinement. In those early times, which are generally accounted the virtuous as well as the simple times of Rome, there was no great number of slaves, and those which there were[z] ⟨?were⟩ treated with the greatest humanity.[15] Their number was not sufficient to make them jealous of them, and they[16] was also much less disproportion in their manner of life. They wrought, they eat[a] altogether[ther]; so far were they from looking on them as creatures of little value and below their regard that they put the greatest confidence in them; they looked on them as faithfull friends, in whom they would find sincer⟨e⟩ affection. {The slaves were treated much in the same way as the children

110 of the family.} So far re|moved were they from the[b] cruelty of their posterity, who would feed their fish with the bodies of their slaves. The Germans had very little distinction from their slaves; idem Cattus,[17] idem victus; they had the same dress and the same manner of living, and they were accordingly very humane to them. In the same manner a North-

*(margin note: relates to 184)*

---

[y] Illegible word deleted        [z] Illegible word deleted        [a] 'and' deleted        [b] 'savage' deleted

---

[14] *Sic.* No doubt 'severe' was intended.
[15] Montesquieu, XV.15.
[16] *Sic.* No doubt 'there' was intended.
[17] i.e. a German. The Catti (or Chatti), often mentioned in Tacitus, were one of the most important tribes of the Germans. The meaning is, 'like master, like man'.

American planter, as he is often at the same work and engaged in the same labour, [he] looks on his slave as his friend and partner, and treats him with the greatest kindness; when the rich and proud West Indian who is far above the employment of the slave in every point gives him the hardest usage. It is not the barbarity of the North Americans but merely their poverty which makes them thus familiar, and of consequence as I have shew⟨n⟩ humane. The more society is improved the greater is the misery of a slavish condition; they are treated much better in the rude periods of mankind than in the more improved. Opulence and refinement tend greatly to increase their misery. The more arbitrary the government is in like manner the slaves are in the better condition, and the freer the people the more miserable are the slaves; in a democracy they are more miserable than in any other. | The greater ⟨the⟩ freedom of the free, the more intollerable is the slavery of the slaves. Opulence and freedom, the two greatest blessings men can possess, tend greatly to the misery of this body of men, which in most countries where slavery is allowed makes by far the greatest part. A humane man would wish therefore if slavery has to be generally established that these greatest blessing⟨s⟩, being incompatible with the happiness of the greatest part of mankind, were never to take place.

It is evident that the state of slavery must be very unhappy to the slave himself. This I need hardly prove, tho some writers have called it in question. But it will not be difficult to shew that it is so to the masters. That is, that the cultivation of land by slaves is not so advantageous as by free tenents; that the advantage gained by the labours [slaves] of the slaves, if we deduce their originall cost and the expence of their maintenanc⟨e⟩, will not be as great as that which is gaind from free tenents. In the antient governments where slaves were the sole cultivators of the land the method was to assign them a piece of ground to cultivate, all the produce of which belong'd to their master, except what he allowed to them for their main-

112 tenance. | We find that this part which was over that which was necessary for the maintenance of the cultivators in the fruitfull countries of Greece and Italy was about $\frac{1}{8}$ part of the produce, whereas in Scotland and England where the rents are high the tenant pays $\frac{1}{3}$ part for the rent. The cultivation of the lands of Greece and Italy must evidently from thence have been very bad, when they produced only $\frac{1}{8}$ part more than was necessary to maintain the cultivators, altho the soil be exceedingly fruitfull and the climate very favourable; whereas the barren and cold countries of Scot. and Eng. afford 2ce as much to the landlord and must[c] consequently the land produces about       [d] much as it did before. The reason of the loss in cultivating land in this manner other than by free tenants will be very evident. The slave or villain who cultivated the land cultivated it entirely for his master; whatever it produced over and above his maintenance

[c] *Sic*      [d] Blank in MS.

belonged to the landlord; he had therefore no inducement to be at any great expense or trouble in manuring or tilling the land; if he made it produce what was sufficient for his own maintenance this was all that he
113 was | anxious about. The overseeer perhaps by a hearty drubbing or other hard usage might make him exert himself a little farther, so as to produce from the farm a small portion for the landlord; but this would not be very great, and accordingly we see that a farm which yielded[e] ⅛ part of the produce to the master was reckoned to [to] be tollerably well cultivated. On the other hand as the free tenant pays a stated rent to the master, whatever he makes the farm produce above that rent is intirely his own property, and the master can not exact as he could from the ancient villains or slaves exact, any part they have saved above the rent,[f] what they had saved out of the part allowed for their maintenance. This gives them much greater spirit and alacrity for their work; they will then be at expense to manure and improve their land, and will soon bring it to that degree of cultivation as to be able to pay ⅓ part to their masters and nevertheless have a much better as well as a more certain livelyhood out of the remaining two thirds; and whatever they produce above that, which is supposed to be about ⅓ of the produce, is altogether their own. Such a manner of
114 cultivation is therefore far | preferable to that by slaves, not only to the servants[g] but even to the master.— Notwithstanding of these superior [of] advantages it is not likely that slavery should be ever abolished, and it was owing to some peculiar circumstances that it has been abolished in the small corner of the world in which it now is. In a democraticall government it is hardly [hardly] possible that it ever should, as the legislators are here[h] persons who are each masters of slaves; they therefore will never incline to part with so valuable a part of their property; and tho as I have here shewn their real interest would lead them to set free their slaves and culti- vate their lands by free servants or tenents, yet the love of domination and authority and the pleasure men take in having every ⟨thing⟩ done by their express orders, rather than to condescend to bargain and treat with those whom they look upon as their inferiors and are inclined to use in a haughty way; this love of domination and tyrannizing, I say, will make it impossible for the slaves in a free country ever to recover their liberty.— In a monar- chicall and absolute government their condition will possibly be a good
115 deal better; the monarch | here being the sole judge and ruler, and not being affected by the easing the condition of the slaves, may probably incline to mitigate their condition; and this we see has been done in all arbitrary governments in a considerable degree. The condition of the slaves under the absolute government of the emperors was much more tollerable

---

*e* 'which' deleted    *f* Numbers written above the last eighteen words indicate that they were intended to read: 'any part they have saved above the rent, as he could from the ancient villains or slaves exact'    *g* Replaces 'master'    *h* 'the' deleted

than under the free one of the Republick. But although the authority of the sovereign may go a considerable way in the mitigating of the condition of slaves, yet it never has ⟨and⟩ can never proceed so far as to abolish slavery altogether. In all countries where slavery takes place[s] the greatest part of the riches of the subjects consists in slaves. If he is possessed of a land estate the whole management of it is carried on by the slaves; without them there can be nothing done; they work and till the ground, and practise every thing else that is necessary to the cultivation of the land or the support of their master. A man of a considerable estate would have some thousands of slaves upon it, and the meaner sort in proportion, but allmost every one if the country be tollerably wealthy will have[i] some slaves; and

116 in them the greatest part | of their wealth will consist. In the same manner we see at this time the great stock of a West India planter consists in the slaves he has in his plantation. To abolish slavery therefore would be to deprive the far greater part of the subjects, and the nobles in particular, of the chief and most valuable part of their substance. This they would never submit to, and a generall insurrection would ensue. For no single man ever had or possibly could have power sufficient to enable him to strip his subjects in that manner. If he set a slave at liberty this was robbing his master of the whole value of him. This therefore could never take place. This institution therefore of slavery, which has taken place in the beginning of every society, has hardly any possibility of being abolished. The government in the first stages of society is as I said[18] very weak, and can not interpose much in the affairs of individualls. Government is far advanced before the legislative power can appoint judges at pleasure, as is now the

117 case in Britain where the king can ap|point any one a judge he pleases who is a lawyer by profession, and for the lower judiciall offices any one he pleases. This could not be done in an early society. The people would not submit themselves in that manner. The government therefore would find it necessary to take advantage of the superiority and authority of certain persons who were respected in the country and put the judicial power into their hands. Jurisdictions were in this manner established, and the same cause made it necessary to strengthen the hands of all private masters of families. Slavery therefore has been universall in the beginnings of society, and the love of dominion and authority over others will probably make it perpetuall. The circumstances which have made slavery be abolished in the corner of Europe in which it now is are peculiar to it, and which happening to concurr at the same time have brought about that change.[j]

The government of Europe was at that time feudall. The power of the

118 great lords consisted in their vassalls and their | villains. The whole of the land at this time was (as was before mentioned) cultivated by villains or

---

[i] 'a considerable number' deleted       [j] 'I' deleted

[18] Above, ii.95,152; iii.7.

slaves in the same manner as by the slaves in the ancient governments of
Rome and Greece. There were two thing⟨s⟩ which brought about their
freedom. In the first place, the church and the clergy were at that time
a very powerfull set of men in all the countries of the west of Europe. The
clergy have allways more weigh⟨t⟩ and authority over the lower and more
laborious part of mankind than over the rich and the powerfull. There
authority[k] therefore was at this time chiefly over these villains or slaves.
They saw then or thought they ⟨?did⟩ that it would tend greatly to aggrandize the power of ⟨the⟩ church, that these people over whom they had the
greatest influence were set at liberty and rendered independent of their
masters. They therefore promoted greatly the emancipation of the villains,
and discouraged as much as lay in their power the authority of the great
men over them.— The kings interest tended also to promote the same
thing. The power of the nobles, which often was dangerous to their
119 authority, consisted in the dependance of their | vassals, and theirs again
of their vassals or villains. The slaves when numerous and in a rich and
free country, as they become an object of dread and terror to the body of the
people are never trusted with arms, as they are there[l] the naturall enemies
of the governing part; but in a poor country and one under arbitrary government, especially in rude times, they are no object of terror to the government or great people; they[m] accordingly made the chief body of the
soldier⟨s⟩[n] in these times, and in them the power of their superiors consisted. The kings interest also led him on this account to lessen the authority of the nobles and their vassalls over their villains. The kings courts on
this account were very favourable to all claims of the villains, and on every
occasion endeavoured to lessen the authority of the landlord over them.
They gave particular favour to the speciall villains, as they were called.
These were such as having got some substanc⟨e⟩ by some means or other,
agreed to hold a piece of land of the lord of the manor and pay him in the
120 manner that | the others did, during the pleasure of their master. The words
that were used in this bargain were that they should hold *according to the
custom of the manor*. The court took advantage of this expression for the
benefit of the dependents and interpreted them thus: that as the lords did
not commonly or customarily turn them out unless for some great offence,
so they made their agreement to be that they were to continue in possession
for ever, unless on any such transgressions or offences as were punishable
by law. In this manner they became from being speciall villains to be copy-
holders.[o] The landholders were[p] in this manner restricted in their authority
over their villains by two of the most powerfull members of the state. The

---

[k] 'and' is interlined at this point, but has possibly been deleted    [l] Reading doubtful    [m] 'were' deleted    [n] Replaces 'people'    [o] Above 'copy-holders' the
word 'no' is interlined, and in the margin near this point the following is written vertically: 'N.B. I doubt this is not altogether as Mr. Smith deld it.'    [p] Replaces 'being'

clergy, a body at that time very powerfull, thought it their interest to encourage the villains, and the authority of the king, the head of the state,
coincided with theirs. They in this manner agreeing rendered the authority
of the masters of the villains but very inconsiderable, if compared to what
121  it had | been some time before. They saw too perhaps that their lands were
but very ill cultivated when under the management of these villains. They
therefore thought it would be more for their own advantage to emancipate
their villains and enter into an agreement with them with regard to the
cultivation of their lands. In this manner slavery came to be abolished; for
at this time the villains were the only sort of slaves.[q] Our ancestors were
then a rough, manly people who had no sort of domestic luxury or effemi-
nacy; their whole slaves were then employed in the cultivation of the land.
When therefore[r] villainage was abollished slavery was so also. The great
power of the clergy thus concurring with that of the king set the slaves at
liberty. But it was absolutely necessary both that the authority of the king
and of the clergy should be great. Where ever any one of these was wanting,
122  slavery still continues. In Scotland, England, | the authority of the king
and of the church have been both very great; slavery has of consequence
been abolished; the ⟨?same⟩ has been the case in France, Spain, etc. But
in the elective kingdom of Poland, the elective empire of Germany, and
the kingdom of Bohemia, which was elective till the House of Austria got
possession of it, slavery still continues;[s] they have the adscripti glebae solo
advincti,[19] as they call them, on the same footing as the old villains in this
country. For in all these countries the authority of the king could never be
very considerable; for all elective kings as I shall shew more fully afterwards
have much less power than those who are hereditary. On the other hand
tho zars of Moscovy have very great power, yet slavery is still in use, as the
authority of the Greek church tho very considerable has never been nearly
so great as that of the Romish church was in the other countries of
Europe; as we see from the accounts of that country even before the time
of Peter the Great.

The villains being thus emancipated had no stock wherewith they could
123  undertake the | cultivation of a farm.— Tenents holding by steel-bow,
or mettierés[t] as they are called in France, were the first species of free
tenents who followed on the abolition of villainage. The landlord agreed to
furnish them with every thing necessary for their work, as they had nothing
of their own. He gave them oxen, which they were to restore at the end of
their lease, which was generally at the end of the year, ad arbitrium boni
viri, equall in number and value to those they had received; he gave them

---

[q] Illegible word or words deleted        [r] 'the' deleted        [s] 'which' deleted
[t] Reading doubtful; presumably a mis-spelling of *métayers*

---

[19] 'Registered with the land, attached to the soil'.

all other necessaries; with these they cultivated the land, and had for their labour a part of the produce. The agreement was that they should divide the produce at years end; the farmer took one sheaf and the landlord another and in this manner they divided equally the whole produce. 'Twas in this manner the tenents by steel bow were the first which followed on the villains. This manner, tho as I shall hereafter shew the worst of any by free tenents, was yet greatly preferable to that by slaves. Whatever the slave by culture made the farm produce above what was necessary for his main-

124 tenance belonged to the master, | and if he had from his part saved a little his master could recall it at pleasure. He had by this means no temptation to any extraordinary exertion of labour. But the farmer by steel-bow was equally profited by a great produce as the landlord; he had so many sheaves more, as well as the landlord, than when the crop was indifferent. His interest therefore[u] as well as that of the landlord ⟨?⟩. But still it was a great discouragement that when he had bestowed an extraordinary expense or labour on the farm the landlord, who had done nothing more than he did in any other year, should carry off the half of the profits. All such defalcations from the produce of industry must greatly retard any efforts of the farmer. Tythes are for this reason, as shall also be more fully explaind, very detrimentall to the industry of the farmer, as the parson without any labour of his takes the 10th part of all the farm produced by the additionall industry of the farmer.— When these farmers by steel bow had

125 by hard labour and great parsimony got together | in 10 or 20 years as much as would enable them to stock a farm, they would then[v] make an offer to their master that they should stock the farm themselves and maintain this stock, and instead of his having the uncertain produce of the harvest, which might vary with the season, he should have a yearly gratuity, on condition that he should not be removed at pleasure but should hold his farm for a term of years. This proposall would not only be agreable to the farmer but also to the landlord. He would be very willing to change the half of the product of the farm, which might vary with ⟨the⟩ season, into a certain some[20] proportionable to that which he got one year with another. And from this it is that the half of the product was generally reckond to be the proportion of the rent. This way of farming would tend much more to promote industry than the former. The farmer here is certain that all which he can raise from the farm above the stated rent will be his own, and therefore has a great inducement to exert his activity

126 upon it. This stated rent where | land is high rated is about $\frac{1}{3}$ of the produce, and this as I said[21] is greatly more than what was paid out of a farm when

---

[u] 'required' deleted          [v] Illegible word deleted

---

[20] *Sic.* Presumably 'sum' was intended.          [21] 112 above.

cultivated by slaves; and the part which the farmer has is also much greater.

There is one instance, and that one which we are best acquainted with, which shows very plainly the dissadvantage of the culture or work of any sort being carried on by slaves when compared with that carried on by free and hired[w] men. That is the colliers and salters, which are the only vestiges of slavery which remain amongst us. Tho these are in far better condition than the servi or villani formerly, yet the labour carried on by them is very expensive.— They are far more easy in many points than those antient slaves. In the first place, their lives are under the protection of the laws of the land, as well as those of other subjects. A master of a coal or salt work can not kill his slave at pleasure as the Romans could, and is as liable for such a murder as for any other.— Their property is also safe, for they do not, as the old slaves, work | intirely for their master, deducing only what is necessary for their support, but are paid for the work they do in the same manner as other labourers; and whatever they acquire in this manner is intirely their own and can not be siezed by their master. They can be sold, it is true, but then it is only in a certain manner. When the work is sold all the colliers or salters which belong to it are sold allong with it. They in this respect resemble the villani or adscripti glebae in Germany, which always go along with the land they cultivate but can not be sold seperate. The colliers in the same manner are adscripti[x] operi; they are sold allong with the work, but can not be sold or given away singly.[22] They have also the liberty of marriage, for as they are not seperated from one another the⟨y⟩ may marry and live together as other labourers. They have also the free exercise of religion, which the nature of it makes free to all. But we are not to imagine the temper of the Christian religion is necessarily contrary to slavery. The masters | in our colonies are Christians, and yet slavery is allowed amongst them. The Constan⟨t⟩inopolitan emperors were very jealous[y] Chrristians, and yet never thought of abolishing slavery. There are also many Christian countries where slavery is tollerated at this time.— The colliers in this manner have a great many of the priviledges of free men; their lives are under the protection of the laws as others; their property is also insured to them; and their liberty is not alltogether taken away. They have the benefit of marriage and the exercise of religion. So that they are no way restricted[z] more than other men, excepting that they are bound to exercise a certain business and in a certain place. And this has been the case with many other persons who thought themselves free. Many nations in the East Indies who account themselves altogether free

127

128

---

[w] Reading of last three words doubtful          [x] 'glebae' deleted          [y] Reading doubtful          [z] 'in thei' deleted

---

[22] Erskine, I.7.39.

are bound to exercise the trade or profession of their father. The old
Aegyptians, who never thought themselves in any respect slaves, were
after the time of Sesostris[23] obliged in like manner to adhere to ⟨the⟩
129 exercise of their forefathers business. Yet altho | they differ in so small a
degree from free men, their labour is much higher. The price of the work
done by day labourers in time of peace when workmen are not scarce is
very moderate in this country; I mean of such labours whose art[24] requires
no art but mere labour. Those which require even some degree of art are
but very low. A weaver, e.g., will ask from 8$^d$ to 9$^d$ per day; and others
which require no art, that is, such as are acquired without great instruction
by a short practise, as that of a plowman, ditcher, etc., which every strong
man who lives in the country acquires without serving an apprenticeship,
these earn from 8$^d$ to 5$^d$ per day. 6$^d$ is the mean rate. A collier on the other
hand, whose work is mere labour such as any man who can handle the
pick will learn by a very short practise, earn⟨s⟩ at the rate of 2$^{sh}$, 2$^{sh}$6$^d$, or
3$^{sh}$ per day. This immoderate price of labour in these works would soon
fall if the masters of them would set their colliers and salters at liberty,
and open the work to all free men, who are now deterred from ever entering
130 into one as it is a rule that one who works a year and day in the coal | pit
becomes a slave as the rest and may be claimed by the owner, unless he
has bargain'd not to take advantage of this. But this the masters of coal
works will never agree to. The love of domination and authority over
others, which I am afraid is naturall to mankind, a certain desire of having
others below one, and the pleasure it gives one to have some persons$^a$ whom
he can order to do his work rather than be obliged to persuade others to
bargain with him, will for ever hinder this from taking place. This work
indeed, being somewhat more dissagreable and more hazardous than others
of the same sort, they might perhaps require wages somewhat higher, but
this would not come above 8$^d$ or 9$^d$; so that a collier has now about 4
times the wages he would have were the work open to all men. But notwithstanding of this high wages we see the colliers frequently run off
from the works in this country to those about Newcastle, where they will
not earn above 13$^d$ or 14$^d$ a day as the work is open; but we never saw
any come from Newcastle here.— — —
131      | There are severall other inconveniencies arising from the institution
of slavery, which I shall take notice of in treating of police.[25] I shall only
observe one or two remarkable ones. 1$^{st}$, that it is very detrimentall to

$^a$ 'by' deleted

---

[23] Dicaearchus, fragm. 7 (Müller, *Fr. Hist. Gr.*, 2.235), says Sesostris enacted that all
occupations should be hereditary. Aristotle, *Politics*, 1329$^b$2–4, reports a tradition that
Sesostris enacted a separation of military and farming classes.
[24] *Sic.* Possibly 'exercise' was intended.
[25] Cf. LJ(B) 290–1, 299–300, below.

population. As it is for the labour of the slaves that the masters desire to have them, so it is chiefly male slaves which they procure as they are most able to sustain a great degree of hard labour. The women are not of such strength, and are therefore not much coveted. They are never desired for propagating, for as it is always much cheaper to bye an ox or a horse out of a poor country where maintenance is cheap than to rear them in a rich one, so is it much cheaper to bye a slave from a poor country than to rear them at home. We see accordingly that there were very few *vernae*, as they called them, in Rome;[26] the far greater part were brought from Syria, Scythia, Cappadocia, or other poor countries. We are told that at the isle of Delos, which lay in the course betwixt Rome and these different countries, there

132  have been sold in one day on account of | the Romans above 10000 slaves at market time;[27] and we may see from thence what a prodigious annual import of them there must have been at that time. There is also a prodigious number, tho not so great as the former, annually carried from the coast of Africa to the severall European colonies in America and the West Indian islands. Of these there is but a very small part women. Demosthenes[28] in one of his orations, giving a catalogue of the fortune his father left him, tells us he left him fifty male slaves and 2 female ones, so that here the proportion is as $1:25$. Nor is there many more in the West India sugar islands. It must necessarily happen from the nature of things that these women will live in a state of prostitution, a state of all others the least proper for propagation; so that there is no great probability that there will be many children born of them. But if it should happen that there were some born, as must necessarily happen sometimes, there is no great prospect of their being reared up to maturity.— A child is a very delicate plant, one that requires

133  a great deal | of care and attendance, and attention in the rearing.— It is generally reckond that the half of mankind die before 5 years of age. But this is the case only with the meaner and poorer sort, whose children are neglected and exposed to many hardships from the inclemencies of the weather and other dangers. The better sort, who can afford attendance and attention to their children, seldom lose near so many. Few women of midd⟨l⟩ing[b] rank who have born 8 children have lost 4 by the time they are 5 years old, and frequently none of them at all. It is therefore neglect alone that is the cause of this great mortality. And what children are so likely to be neglected as those of slaves, who are themselves despised and neglected by all. Tho therefore some children be born, few of these will be reared. It is found that by all thes⟨e⟩ concurrent reasons the stock of slaves

[b] Replaces 'tollerable'

[26] Hume, *Essays*, I.389. *Vernae* were slaves born in the master's house.
[27] Strabo, XIV.668, cited by Hume, *Essays*, I.389.
[28] Demosthenes, *Against Aphobus*, I.9–10, cited by Hume, *Essays*, I.391; all fifty-two slaves were males.

in the West Indies would be exhausted alltogether in 5 or 6 years, so that in each year they must import about $\frac{1}{5}$ or $\frac{1}{6}$ of the whole;[29] a proportion
134 | which we find in no other state of men.

I shall only observe farther on this head that slavery remarkably diminishes the number of freemen. That it must diminish the number of freemen is altogether evident, as a great part of the free will become slaves. But it does this in a most astonishing proportion and such as one can hardly conceive.

A man according to the ordinary computation may make a shift to support himself and perhaps a wife and family on 10 pounds a year. When therefore we look on a man of an overgrown or large estate, we are apt to conceive of him at first sight as a monster who destroys what might afford subsistence for a vast number of the human species. And in this light our forefathers did consider them, and took all methods to prevent their arising.— A man who has an estate of £10,000 per ann. has what might afford a subsistence to 1,000 men and their families; but this, supposing
135 him to be a mean man who gives | nothing away and has no generosity, he consumes on himself and 4 or 5 servants.[30] We look on this man as a pest to society, as a monster, a great fish who devours up all the lesser ones; for it is all one whether one destroys the persons themselves or that which ought to afford them their maintenance. A man who consumes 10,000 pounds appears to destroy what ought to give maintenance to 1000 men. He therefore appears to be the most destructive member of society we can possibly conceive.— But if we observe[c] this man we will find that he is no way prejudiciall to society but rather of advantage to it. In the 1st place, he eats no more than what any other man does; he has not a larger stomach than any ordinary plowman;[31] all the odds is that his is better chosen and culld out from the heap. As to his cloaths, he may indeed seem to consume more of these. He has indeed a great many suits and is at a great expense for cloaths, but then he does not consume these all at once. In reality he does not consume so much as an ordinary plowman. His cloaths are of
136 greater | variety, it is true, but then he wears them very little; he is hardly ever out of his chair unless it be to take a walk in a fine day. He never exposes them to be spoiled by the weather or rubbed[d] and torn by hard labour. After he has done with them they are fit for many different purposes; whereas the plowman who has his cloaths continually exposed to all sorts of destruction wears considerably more; his cloaths when he has

---

[c] Replaces an illegible word    [d] Reading doubtful

---

[29] Hume, *Essays*, I.390, note: 'It is computed in the West Indies, that a stock of slaves grow worse five per cent every year, unless new slaves be bought to recruit them.'
[30] Cf. i.116–17 above.
[31] Cf. TMS IV.1.10: 'The capacity of his stomach bears no proportion to the immensity of his desires, and will receive no more than that of the meanest peasant.'

done with them are fit for nothing but to be thrown on the dung hill to manure the land. This man therefore, as he consumes hardly any more, nay perhaps not so much as another, all the odds is that what he consumes is culled with nicety and care. And as the flower when the finest part is taken from it is almost as good as before, so what this man leaves is not much less fit for the maintenance of men than it was before. Let us suppose that he has this rent paid in kind (for there can be no odds in that), and that one man pays him 1000 measures of wheat, another as many of barley,
137 another as many oxen, as many sheep, | another as many measures of wine, and anothe⟨r⟩ of oil. Now of all of these he consumes but a very small part. That part is indeed chosen with great nicety and care; the rest he gives away to those who[e] cull out this part for him. This part which he consumes is wrought up by labour so as to be worth immensely more than what it was before, or what the part which would support a man was naturally worth. This part here is changed from 10£ value to be worth 10000, so that it is wrought up to 1000 times its value. In the same manner those who receive the rest of his goods will perhaps spend 5 or 600£, so that there what is consumed by them is wrought up to above 100 times its value. Others again below these consume what costs them 200 or three hundered pound; others again 50 or 60, and so down to those who consume but about 10£ or less in the year. The produce of his estate is by this means wrought up to be worth altogether 1000 times its originall value. It will not however support more men than before; the rich man has not that effect. But he gives occasion to a greatly[f] of work and manufacturing, such
138 as is necessary | to raise so much in its value. It would therefore be of no advantage to the state in the present state of things to prevent the growth of such large fortunes. For tho an agrarian law would render all on an equality, which has indeed something very agreable in it, yet a people who are all on an equality will necessar⟨il⟩y be very poor and unable to defend themselves in any pressing occasion. They have nothing saved[g] which can give them relief in time of need. But when goods are manufactured, a very small quantity of them will procure an immense one of the unmanufactured produce of an other country. Half a ships loading of cambricks or broad cloath will procure in Russia as much unmanufactured flax as will load a whole fleet. The higher the manufacture is carried the greater will be the quantity it will procure. A man can carry as much of the finer Brussels lace in his pocket as will get him at Riga or Petersburgh as much flax or hemp as will load a ship. A poor country of the sort above mentiond will be entirely ruined by a famine; they have nothing within
139 themselves and have no way of procuring | from others. If they be obliged even in time of plenty to send an army out of their own country they have great difficulty in procuring them subsistence. But in a country where

---

[e] Two or three illegible words deleted     [f] *Sic*     [g] Reading doubtful

manufactures are carried on a small part of this manufactured produce will bring a great quantity of unmanufactured, which may supply their present necessities or employ their industry so as to procure more in futurity. So that in the present state of things a man of a great fortune is rather of advantage than dissadvantage to the state, providing that there is a graduall descent of fortunes betwixt these great ones and others of the least and lowest fortune. For it will be shewn hereafter[32] that one who leaps over the heads of all his country men is of real detriment to the community. This i⟨s⟩ not the case in England, where we have fortunes gradually descending from £40,000 to 2 or 300.— — — — —

But altho in this present condition it would be very unnecessary and even detrimentall to crush all such overgrown fortunes, yet in the ancient times the case was very different. The wisest men were always of opinion that these overgrown fortunes were very detrimentall to the interest of the

140 community. They looked on these wealthy men | as the objects of their dread and aversion, as so many monsters who consumed what should have supported a great number of free citizens. Their fears we will find were well grounded. A man, e.g., who possessed an estate of £10,000 per annum then actually destroyed not only the maintenance of 10000[33] but of 6,000 free citizens. For we are to consider that the lands were then intirely cultivated by slaves; there was no such thing as free tenents. A man who was possessed of 10,000 occupied then not only the ground which produced to the value of £30000, as he would in the present state of affairs, but what yielded to the value of 60000. Five sixths of this was consumed by the slaves who cultivated it, so that here the greatest part of the produce was bestow'd on the slaves. The remaining part also was not as at present distributed amongst free citizens [(as at present)] who wrought to the rich man and raised up what he consumed to the value of what he laid out, but on his own slaves or those of other rich men. The rich men then set up their slaves in all the different trades they had occasion for; one was a mason, another a carpenter, another a shop-keeper, another a brewer or a baker,

141 etc. These were always employed to | do his work; and if it happened that a rich man had occasion for a workman in a trade which was exercised by none of his own slaves, he would rather oblige another rich man who was his friend by employing his slave than employ a poor citizen, as we see Cicero employd Cyrus,[34] the slave of his rich friend, as his architect. So that the whole produce of the estates of the rich was consumed by the master and his slaves. We see from this the reason of what otherwise, as it is intirely different from the customs of our times, appears to us allmost

---

[32] 144 below.  [33] *Sic.* Probably '1000' was intended.

[34] Cicero's architect Cyrus (*Ad Atticum*, II.3.2; *Ad Quintum Fratrem*, II.2.2) was probably not a slave. Smith probably confuses him with Eros, a slave accountant of his rich friend Atticus, whom Cicero employed to look after his financial affairs (e.g. *Ad Att.*, XII.7.1; XII.21.4; XIII.2a.1).

unintelligible. We are told by Aristotle[h][35] and Cicero[36] that the two sources of all seditions at Athens and at Rome were the demands of the people for an agrarian law or an abolition of debts. This was no doubt a demand of the taking away so much of ones property and giving it to those to whom it did not belong. We never hear of any such demands as these at this time. What is the reason of this? Are the people of our country at this time more honestly inclined than they were formerly? We can not pretend that they

142 are. But | their circumstances are very different. The poor now never owe any thing as no one will trust them. But at Rome every poor citizen was deep in debt, and the case was the same at Athens. The poor people now who have neither a land estate nor any fortune in money can gain a livelyhood by working as a servant to a farmer in the country, or by[i] working to any tradesman whose business they understand. But at Rome the whole business was engrossed by the slaves, and the poor citizens who had neither an estate in land nor a fortune in money were in a very miserable condition; there was no business to which they could apply themselves with any hopes of success. The only means of support they had was either from the generall largesses which were made to them, or by the money they got for their votes at elections. But as the candidates would have been ruined by the purchasing the votes of the whole people at every

143 election, they fell | upon an expedient to prevent this. They lent them a considerable summ, a good deal more than what they gave for a vote, at a very high interest, ordinarily about 12 p cent and often higher, even up to 30 or 40 p cent. This soon ran up to a very great amount such as they had no hopes of being able to pay. The creditors were in this manner sure of their votes without any new largess, as they had already a debt upon them which they could not pay, and no other could out bid them, as to gain their vote he must pay off their debt, and as this had by interest come to a great amount there was no one who would be able to pay it off. By this means the poorer citizens were deprived of their only means of subsistence. It is a rule generally observed that no one can be obliged to sell his goods when he is not willing. Bun[37] in time of necessity the people will break thro all laws. In a famine it often happens that they will break open granaries[38]

144 and force | the owners to sell at what they think a reasonable price. In the same manner it is generally observed as a rule of justice that the property of any thing can not be wrested[j] out of the proprietors hands, nor can debts be taken away against the creditors inclination. But when the Roman

[h] Replaces 'Demosthenes'        [i] Illegible word deleted        [j] Reading doubtful

---

[35] Not in Aristotle (W. L. Newman, *Politics of Aristotle*, IV.335); cf. Plato, *Republic*, VIII.565E; Demosthenes, *Against Timocrates*, 149, and *On the Treaty with Alexander*, 15.
[36] *De Officiis*, II.78.
[37] *Sic.* No doubt 'But' was intended.
[38] Cf. Hume, *Enquiry concerning the Principles of Morals*, III.i (ed. Selby-Bigge, § 147).

people found the whole property taken from them by a few citizens, and the whole of the money in the empire ingrossed also, and themselves in this manner reduced to the greatest poverty, it need not be wondered at that they desired laws which prevent these inconveniencies.— We may see from this that slavery amongst its inconveniencies has this bad consequence, that[k] it renders rich and wealthy men of large properties of great and real detriment, which otherwise are rather of service as they promote trade and commerce.

I shall now observe the different methods in which slaves might[l] be
145 acquired in those countries where it has been in use.— | The 1st, captives taken in war. These are considered as belonging entirely to the captor in all countries where slavery takes place. When the conqueror has got his enemy into his power there is then no one to protect him; his life and all he has he owes to the mercy of his conqueror if he inclines to spare him. He is reckoned to belong intirely to the conqueror, in recompence for his delivery, and as there was no one to protect him. This seems to have been the originall introduction of slaves, and was universally received amongs⟨t⟩ all the early nations, and continues still in many countries. We are told by Tacitus that in the two battles of          [39] betwixt the armies of Galba and Vittellius, and the latter an⟨d⟩ Vespasian, there were no prisoners made on either side; for as they were their country men they could not become slaves, and for this reason no quarter was given.[40]—As the captives had no person who could protect or defend them, so their children were in as
146 helpless a condition. They therefore became slaves | as well as their fathers, which makes 2d method of acquiring slaves, which comprehends all those who are born of slaves.— 3d method is when criminalls are adjudged to slavery. Slavery is a punishment often inflicted on criminalls in those countries as any other, and those who are condemned to it are either given over to the person injured or else they were considered as belonging to the publick. 4th is that by which insolvent debtors were adjudged[m] or given over to their creditors. These 4, as well as the 5th, are all admitted in every country where slavery takes place at this day, in Turky, Persie, and in Russia, they make all the prisoners they take in their wars with the Turks slaves in the same manner as the Romans did their prisoners, tho they do not of those whom they take from their fellow Christians. They admit also of all the others. 5th method is that by which a free citizen becomes a slave
147 by selling himself to a master. | But as the person and all that he hath becomes his masters from the moment the bargain begins, such bargains

---

[k] 'those' deleted     [l] Replaces 'may'     [m] 'by' deleted

---

[39] Blank in MS. The missing word is 'Bedriacum'. See next editorial note.
[40] *Histories*, II.44 on the battles of Bedriacum, the first between Otho and Vitellius and the second between Vitellius and the forces of Vespasian; cf. Plutarch, *Life of Otho*, 14.

would be altogether ilusory and the slave would receive no benefit from the      [n]. But the case where this generally happens is where an insolvent debtor does not incline that he should become the slave of his creditor, but chooses rather to belong to some other person. This person on paying his debts gets him for his slave.— These are all the methods.— I shall only observe farther with regard to slavery, in confirmation of what I asserted, that it was the weakness of government that gave rise to it; that this was entirely the case with regard to the West Indian and at

*End of Volume Three of MS.*

[n] Illegible word

iv.1 | *Monday Febry. 21st 1762*[o]

In the beginning of these lectures I divided justice into 3 parts: 1st, that which respects a man, merely as a man; 2d, that which regards a man as a member of a family; and 3dly, those rights which belong to a man as a member of community or society of men. I have already considered the two first of these divisions, and come now to the 3d division.

In order to consider more distinctly those rights which belong to a man as a member of a society or community or state, it will be necessary to consider the severall forms of government which are in use in different societies and the manner in which they have arose. The forms of government, tho they may be infinitely varied, may be reduced to 3 generall classes, or distinct forms. The 1st is that wherein the power of making laws and regulations, of trying causes or appointing judges, and of making peace or war, are all vested in one person. This is called a *monarchicall government.*
2 | The sovereign power in a state consists[p] of 3 parts. The first is the legislative, or the power of making laws. The 2d is the judicial, which is also evident from the word; it is that of trying causes and passing judgement or of settling other judges. The third, which is[q] the power of making peace or war, is called by Mr. Locke[41] the foederal power and by Baron Montesquieu[42] the executive power, and I shall call it barely the *power of making peace or war*. These in a monarchicall government are all possessed by the *monarch*; he can make what laws he inclines, pass judgement by himself or others as he thinks proper, and make peace or war at his own good pleasure.— — The other forms of government may be all considered as republican; in which the severall powers above mentioned belonging to government are not committed to one single person but to a greater number.— This may be of two sorts—either—1st, an aristocracy. In this form
3 of government | the sovereign power in all its parts is not in the hands of a single person but is possessed by a *certain rank or order of men* distinct from the body of the people, by *the nobles* or *men of rank*. These, in the same manner as the prince in a monarchicall government, may make laws, judge causes, and ⟨make⟩ peace and war at their own pleasure. Or 2dly, a republican government may be a *democracy*, in which these severall parts are not confined to any particular person or any rank of nobility in the state, but is exercised by the *whole body of the people* conjunctly. All these forms

[o] *Sic*  [p] The last six words replace 'government consists'  [q] 'called' deleted

[41] *Civil Government*, ch. XII: 'Of the Legislative, Executive, and Federative Power of the Commonwealth.'
[42] XI.6.

of government may be varied in many different ways, but all the different forms of government may be reduced to one or other of these.— But before I enter on these particularly, it will be proper to explain the origins of government, what I take to be the originall form of it, and how the severall governments which now subsist have sprung from it, and how this origi-

4 nal government arose and at what period | of society.— In the age of hunters there can be very little government of any sort, but what there is will be of the democraticall kind. A nation of this sort consists of a number of independent families, no otherwise connected than as they live together in the same town or village and speak the same language. With regard to the judicial power, this in these nations as far as it extends is possessed by the community as one body. The affairs of private families, as long*r* as they concern only the members of one family, are left to the determination of *the members of that* family. Disputes betwixt others can in this state but rarely occur, but if they do, and are of such a nature as would be apt to disturb the community, the whole community then interferes to make up the difference; which is ordinarily all the length they go, never daring to inflict what is properly called punishment. The design of their inter-meddling is to preserve the public quiet and the safety of the individualls;

5 they therefore endeavour to bring about a reconcile|ment betwixt the parties at variance. This is the case amongst the savage nations of America, as we are informed by Father Charlevoix[43] and Monsieur Laffitau[44] who give us the most distinct account of the manners of those nations. They tell us also that if one has committed any very heinous crime against another, they will sometimes put him to death; but this is not in a judicial way, but thro' the resentment or indignation the crime has raised in each individuall. In such cases the whole body of the people lie in wait for him and kill him by an assassination in the same manner as they would an enemy. A very common method in these cases is to invite him to a feast and have some 3 or 4 persons appointed before hand who dispatch him. The power of making peace and war in such nations belongs to the whole people. A treaty of peace amongst them is no more than an agreement to cease

6 hostilities against each other, and to | make such an agreement compleat it is necessary that the consent of every individuall in the society should be obtaind, every one thinking he has a title to continue hostilities till he has obtained sufficient satisfaction. And in the same manner an injury done to any individuall is sufficient to make him commence hostilities against the injurious person, which will commonly bring on a generall

*r* Replaces 'far'

[43] P.-F.-X. de Charlevoix, *Histoire et description générale de la Nouvelle-France, avec le Journal historique d'un voyage . . . dans l'Amérique septentrionnale* (1744), III.271 ff.
[44] J. F. Lafitau, *Mœurs des sauvages amériquains, comparées aux mœurs des premiers temps* (1724), I.490 ff.

quarrell. The legislative power can hardly subsist in such a state; there could be occasion but for very few regulations, and no individuall would think himself bound to submit to such regulations as were made by others, even where the whole community was concerned.— The whole of the government[s] in this state, as far as there is any, is democraticall. There may indeed be some persons in this state who have a superior weight and influence with the rest of the members; but this does not derogate from the democraticall form, as such persons will[t] only have this influence by their

7 superior wisdom, valour, or | such like qualifications, and over those only who incline of themselves to be directed by him. In the same manner as in every club or assembly where the whole members are on an equall footing there is generally some person whose counsil is more followed than any others, and who has generally a considerable influence in all debates, and is as it were the king of the company.

The age of shepherds is that where government properly first commences. And it is at this time too that men become in any considerable degree dependent on others. The appropriation of flocks and herds renders subsistence by hunting very uncertain and pr⟨e⟩carious. Those animalls which are most adapted for the use of man, as oxen, sheep, horses, camels, etc. which are also the most numerous, are no longer common but are the property of certain individualls. The distinctions of rich and poor then arise. Those who have not any possessions in flocks and herds can find[u] no way of maintaining themselves but by procuring it from the rich. The rich

8 | therefore, as they maintain and support those of the poorer sort out of the large possessions which they have in herds and flocks, require their service and dependance. And in this manner every wealthy man comes to have a considerable number of the poorer sort depending and attending upon him. And in this period of society the inequality of fortune makes a greater odds in the power and influence of the rich over the poor than in any other. For when luxury and effeminacy have once got a footing in a country, one may expend in different manners a very large fortune without creating one single dependent; his taylor, his          [v], his cook, etc. have each a share of it, but as they all give him their work in recompense for what he bestows on them, and that not out of necessity, they do not look upon themselves as any ⟨?way⟩ dependent on him. They may reckon that they are obliged to him, but not one of them would go so far as to

9 fight for him. But | in the early periods, when arts and manufactures are not known and there is hardly any luxury amongst mankind, the rich man has no way of spending the produce of his estate but by giving it away to others, and[w] these become in this manner dependent on him. The patriarchs we see were all a sort of independent princes who had their dependents

---

[s] Replaces 'supreme authority'      [t] Illegible word deleted      [u] 'of the' deleted
[v] Illegible word          [w] 'as' deleted

and followers[x] attending them, being maintain'd by the produce of the flocks and herds which were committed to their care. Over these they would naturally have considerable power, and would be the only judges[y] amongst the people about them. — —

{The authority of the rich men would in this manner soon come to be very great; let us therefore consider its progress.} In this way of life there are many more opportunities of dispute betwixt the different persons of a tribe or nation than amongst a nation of hunters. Property is then introduced, and many disputes on that head must inevitably occur. Let us suppose then a nation of shepherds living together in a village or town. {We will find that the form of government which would take place here will also be democraticall. Let us therefore consider the severall parts of the supreme power, and we will find they are all in the hands of the body of the people. 1st, with regard to the judiciall power,} the way they would most readily think of, and which the severall individualls would most readily agree to, of accomodating any such differences as might arise would be to
10 refer them to the assembly of the whole | people. There would no doubt as I said above be many more disputes in this stage of society than in that of hunters, but not near so great a number as there afterwards are[z] in the farther advances of society. For the great sources of debate, and which give ground to the far greater part of lawsui[sui]ts,[a] were not known in the earlier periods of society. The most of those which now employ the courts arise either 1[st], from some question concerning the meaning of the will of a deceased person; this they at that time had not, for as I observed before[45] no testaments were allowed or thought of in the first periods of society; or 2[dly], from marriage settlements: these also are unknown in the early periods of society; or 3[dly], from voluntary contracts, which do not sustain action nor are they supported by the community at this time. The business therefore would not be very great; nor would the inhabitants be so much engaged as not to have leisure to attend these meetings.— But as in every society there is some persons who take the lead and are[b] of influence over the others, so there would without question be some persons of eminence
11 who would have some influence over the[m] | deliberations of the others. The rich men who have large possessions in flocks and herds would as I observed[46] have many dependents who would follow their council and direction, and in this manner they would have the greatest influence over the people.— As these persons would be the most eminent among the old people, so would their sons be amongst the younger one⟨s⟩, as their fathers eminence would convey respect to their character, and as they would be

---

[x] 'who' deleted    [y] Illegible word deleted    [z] Reading doubtful    [a] Reading doubtful    [b] Reading doubtful

---

[45] i.91–2 above.                                        [46] 8 above.

thus respected in their fathers life time they would naturally fill his place after his death. If there were two sons the authority would be divided amongst them, as well as the estate. And tho nothing can be more in convenient than a government thus split when the king or monarch comes to be of considerable authority, yet it is not attended with the same in convenience in these periods. We see that at the time of the Trojan wars there were severall nations who were led on by different chiefs. Sarpedon and Glaucus led on the Cretans, Diomedes and Idomeneus the Beotians, Menestheus and 5 others the people of Attica.[47] It generally happened

12 indeed that some one | was more respected than the others, as we see these Grecian leaders were in the same order as those of each country here are mentioned. The authority therefore of these chief men in this state would soon become hereditary, and when in the farther advances of society they would find thes⟨e⟩ inconveniences attending on these divided, the right of primogeniture and the other regulations of succession would be brought in ⟨in⟩ the manner I mentioned when treating on that subject.[48] But this was not an infringement of the democraticall form of government, as these persons had not any authority more than was acquired by their private influence. The community would also have it in their power to punish in some manner any heinous offences.[c] They may perhaps sometimes assassinate any of these, in the manner I mentioned before[49] with regard to the North Americans, and they would have it also in their power to punish them by turning from out of the society. The members of any club have it in their power to turn out any member, and so also have the members of

13 such a community. This, tho it would be no great grievance on | the first commencement of a society when the members had formed no connections or friendships with each other, would be a very great one when they had lived together some time and perhaps been born and educated in the society. When they were turned out they would have no friends, no acquaintances else where; commerce does not then take place, so that they would have no opportunity of communication with others. They would be banished from all their friends and connections. So that this would be one of the most severe punishments that could be inflicted.[d]

With regard to the executive power, or that of making peace and war, this also as far as it would extend would be in the same hands as the former.

[c] The words 'Cape of Good Hope', followed by the letters 'Hot' which have been deleted, appear on v.11 at about this point, with no indication as to the part of the text to which they are intended to refer      [d] 'What would make' deleted

[47] Sarpedon and Glaucus were commanders of the Lycian contingent before Troy (*Iliad*, ii.876); Idomeneus commanded the Cretans (*Iliad*, ii.645); Diomedes and Sthenelus commanded the Argives (*Iliad*, ii.564 ff.); Menestheus commanded the Athenians (*Iliad*, ii.552); the Boeotians had five chiefs (*Iliad*, ii.494).
[48] ii.116 ff. above.      [49] 5 above.

Wars betwixt nations of this sort are generally undertaken on a sudden, and decided by one or two set skirmishes. The whole people would rush out when they were attack'd, or make an incursion on their neighbours in a body. Their leaders would not be any regular commanders; their army
14 | would* be rather an unruly band than a disciplined body. Those who appeard most valiant an⟨d⟩ courageous would lead on the others. Tacitus tells us of the Germans, Reges ex nobilitate duces ex virtute sumant. Nec regibus infinitas et libera potestas, et duces exemplo potius quam imperio si prompti, si conspicui; si ante aciem agant, admiratione praesunt, etc., etc.[50] The power of these leaders continues no longer than they were in the war, and indeed was then little more than that of leading to battle. The tribes or nations at this time of society are but very small, and their wars for that reason can not be of any long duration. We may see of what importance a few members were reckoned, when we are told that the men of Schechem were so desirous of receiving Isaac and a few attendants that the whole people consented to undergo a very painfull operation.[51] The legislative is never met with amongst people in this state of society. Laws and regulations are the product of more refind manners and improved
15 government, and are never found | till it is considerably advanced.

When mankind have made some farther advances, the determination of causes becomes an affair of more difficulty and labour. Arts and manufactures are then cultivated, and the people are by this means less able ⟨to⟩ spare their time and attendance at the tryalls. Besides this the causes of dispute also multiply. Testaments come to be in use, contracts of marriage, etc. gradually come in, so that on the one hand the business is increased and on the other hand the people has less time to spare. So that one of two things must happen: either the causes or disputes must lie undetermined, or some persons must be appointed who shall judge in these matters. The 1st of this alternative can never be allowed, as confusion and quarrels must inevitably follow on it. The latter therefore is always taken. A certain number of men are chosen by the body of the people, whose business it is to attend on the causes and settle all disputes. The chief and leading men of the nation will necessarily make a part of this council. Their authority will
16 still | continue, and they will become a sort of head or president in the court. His authority in this station will grow very fast; much faster than in proportion to the advances made by the society. For in all thes⟨e⟩ early

* 'consist' deleted

---

[50] Tacitus, *Germania*, vii: 'They pick their kings for noble birth, their military commanders for bravery. The kings do not enjoy unlimited or arbitrary power, and the commanders rely on example rather than on authority, on their men's admiration for their conspicuous activity and for fighting ahead of their troops.' Read *sumunt* for *sumant*; *infinita aut* for *infinitas et*.

[51] Genesis 34.

countries the custom is altogether contrary to that now in use. The rich now make presents to the poor, but in ⟨the⟩ beginnings of society the rich rec⟨e⟩ive presents from their dependents. They will never enter on the consideration of a cause without a gratuity. No one can have access to the Mogul unless he have a present in his hand, and so in all other rude and barbarous nations. A Tartar prince can not be spoke to without you open his ears by a gift. As this will soon increase their riches, so the number of their dependents and their power must increase proportionably, and their influence on the council will also be increased. This number is originally pretty large in all countries. They dont think it safe to trust themselves and their property in the hands of a few persons, but think they are much
17 safer when they are under the management of a considerable body. | The sovereign court of Athens[52] consisted of 500 persons. The affairs and debates relating to peace and war are originally very simple and soon determined, but when the affairs of the state multiply, and any extraordinary provision is to be made, this is a matter of too tedious a nature to be determined by the whole people, who can not detach themselves so long from their private affairs as these matters would require. It here again becomes absolutely necessary for the safety of the state either to give the management of these affairs [either] to the same court as that to which the determination of private[f] causes was before committed, or to appoint a new one. This latter they never think of. The power therefore of providing for the safety of the state and all necessary conveniencies for it generally accompanies the former.[g] The senatoriall[h] power at Rome extended to these things; they had the care of the revenue, of the walls of the city, etc. They seem to have been a council taken to assist the king in his judiciall and executive capacity.
18 The judiciall capacity was indeed | seperated at Rome from the kingly power as early as the time of Tullus, under whom we hear of duumviri[i] rerum capitalium, etc.[53] Tacitus tells of the kings council,[j] concilium simull et autoritas, adsunt.[54] The people however still retain'd in most countries the power of appeal to themselves in all matters of moment. This was[k] the case at Rome, and after it had been laid aside it was resumed again. Tacitus says also, De minoribus rebus, principes[l] consultant, de majoribus omnes. Ita tamen ut ea quoque quorum penes plebem arbitrium est, apud principes pertractentur,[55] {and this also must add greatly to the power of the

[f] Replaces 'civill'  [g] 'But' deleted  [h] Reading doubtful  [i] Reading doubtful
[j] Illegible word deleted  [k] 'soon' deleted  [l] Replaces 'reges'

---

[52] The Boule.
[53] Presumably a reference to the *duoviri perduellionis* appointed by Tullus Hostilius to deal with cases of treason: Livy, I.26.
[54] *Germania*, xii: *consilium simul et auctoritas adsunt* ('contributing advice together with authority').
[55] *Germania*, xi: 'Minor matters the chiefs discuss, major matters everyone; but in those matters where the decision lies with the people the chiefs consider them first.'

rulers.} The executive and judiciall powers are in this manner in the hands of the people, who trust them in some measure to a court of a few persons. The legislative power makes but a very small figure during all this time. Its progress we shall next consider

*Gap of three lines in MS.*

19                    | *Tuesday. February 22ᵈ 1763*

In the foregoing lecture I endeavoured to explain to you the origin and something of the progress of government. How it arose, not as some writers[56] imagine from any consent or agreement of a$^m$ number of persons to submit themselves to such or such regulations, but from the natural progress which men make in society.— I shewed that in the age of hunters there was nothing which could deserve the name of government. There was in this case no occasion for any laws or regulations, property not extending at this time beyond possession. The little of order which was preserved amongst men in this state was by the interposition of the whole community to accommodate such differences as threatend to disturb the peace of the state. But this was not as judges, but merely to bring about an accommodation and agreement betwixt the parties at variance. The executive power or that of making peace and war was also equally in the hands of the whole people, and each individuall had the same power$^n$ as an other. They do not conceive that they have power to force any of the particular persons to engage in war at their pleasure. If two or three families

20    | did not incline to go out to war and commit hostilities against their neighbours, the others were not conceived to have any right to compel them. And in the same way if after the community has made peace with their neighbours a few families should still continue to commit hostilities and make incursions with their scalping parties on their neighbours, the community does not pretend to have any authority to punish them or compel them to submit to the generall agreement. But there is here one difference. Men are generally much more hot and eager when they engage in war than when they make peace. They are for this reason more enraged against those who do not join in the common wars of the country than those who continue hostilities after the generall peace or make incursions without the consent of the others. For this reason it frequently happens that the body of the nation will lye in wait for one who thus denies to join in the common cause, and assassinate him. Tho the other is without doubt

---

$^m$ Reading doubtful          $^n$ Reading doubtful

---

[56] Theorists who believe in a historical social contract; cf. v.114 below.

21 more dangerous to the state | and will often bring on the ruin of the whole, yet ⟨he⟩ is not so apt to raise their resentment. But when any one is put to death for that injury to the community, it is not as by the authority the people have over the individualls but in the same way as they would put an enemy to death, thro resentment.— I should also ⟨?say⟩ that the age of shepherds is that where government first commences. Property makes it absolutely necessary. When once it has been agreed that a cow or a sheep shall belong to a certain person not only when actually in his possession but where ever it may have strayed, it is absolutely necessary that the hand of government should be continually held up and the community assert° their power to preserve the property of the individualls. The chase can no longer be depended on for the support of any one. All the animalls fit for the support of man are in a great measure appropriated. Certain individualls become very rich in flocks and herds, possessed of many cattle and sheep, while others have not one single animall. One will have a stock sufficient to

22 maintain himself and 50 or 60 besides | himself, when others have not any thing whereon to subsist themselves. In the age^p of the hunters a few temporary exertions of the authority of the community will be sufficient for the few occasions of dispute which can occur. Property, the grand fund of all dispute, is not then known. The individualls may sometimes quarrel where there is no interest of either in question, as school boys will, and perhaps kill one another; but this will but rarely happen, and when it does may be made up with the friends of the injured person, as I showed before,[57] by the interposition of the community. But here when in the manner above mentioned some have^q great wealth and others nothing, it is necessary that the arm of authority should be continually stretched forth, and permanent laws or regulations made which may ascertain[58] the property of the rich from the inroads of the poor, who would otherwise continually make incroachments upon it, and settle in what the infringement of this property consists and in what cases they will be liable to punishment.[59] Laws and

23 government may^r be considered in this | and indeed in every case as a combination of the rich to oppress the poor, and preserve to themselves the inequality of the goods which would otherwise be soon destroyed by the attacks of the poor, who if not hindered by the government would soon reduce the others to an equality with themselves by open violence. The government and laws hinder the poor from ever acquiring the wealth by violence which they would otherwise exert on the rich; they tell them they must either continue poor or acquire wealth in the same manner as they

° Reading doubtful     ^p Replaces 'arm'     ^q 'a' deleted     ^r 'here' deleted

[57] 4 above.
[58] The word 'ascertain' is apparently used here in the now obsolete sense of 'secure'.
[59] Cf. Locke, *Civil Government*, § 94: 'Government has no other end but the preservation of property'.

have done.— Settled laws therefore, or agreements concerning property, will soon be made after the commencement of the age of shepherds. The whole of the administration of these rules and settling of all disputes will as I mentioned in the last lecture[60] naturally be left to the generall assembly of the whole people. This alone seems[s] has authority and weight sufficient,

24 or figures enough in the eyes of the men, to claim the determi|nation of any disputes in this respect; therefore the government is entirely democraticall. The community has also here a great opportunity of authority and influence over the individualls; as every club or society has a title to say to the severall members of it, Either submit to the regulations we make or get you about your business, so the community may say to the individualls who are members of it, Either make your behaviour agreable to our laws and rules or depart from amongst us. This will be a very grievous punishment after the society has been some time formed and the members born and bred up in it, as they will then have no other acquaintances or know where to retire to. This authority they may very readily exercise but will not for some considerable time venture any farther.— The executive power or that of making peace and war will also be intirely in the hands of the body of the people. They will have the regulation both of the pre-

25 parations for the defence of the state | and the determination in what cases war shall be made, etc. But altho the power of the government with regard to the private affairs of individualls under disputes betwixt them was for some time considerably restricted, yet with regard to all public matters their authority was soon after the settlement of shepherds in all countries pretty absolute. The affairs of private persons do not much concern the state; they concern it so far as that it is their interest to prevent disputes from running very high, but then this does not strike immediately at the community. But all those which concern the state directly and immediately will be taken under their[t] consideration with much more exactness, and their authority would be more exerted in preventing every thing that tended to the detriment of the community than in the former case. They therefore are much more severe in the prevention of them. I observed

26 before[61] that it was not those crimes which | appear the most heinous to individualls which were first liable to what is properly called punishment after compensation had begun to be laid aside, but thos which immediately struck at the wellfare of the community. These are two in number, viz treachery and cowardice. Treasonable practises or joining with the enemy must undoubtedly appear very heinous, as it tends immediately to the ruin of the state and is accordingly punished most severely. Cowardice in a common soldier is still liable to punishment, but is not considered as

---

[s] 'to' deleted        [t] Illegible word deleted

---

[60] 9–10 above.                                              [61] ii.152–3 above.

treachery as the running away of one man can have little effect on the fate of the battle. But in a party of hunters or shepherds consisting often of twelve men only, the desertion of one may be the ruin of the whole body and has all the effects of treachery. This therefore is punished as treachery by all early nations. The Germans punished these crimes with death in the manner mentioned by Tacitus chap. 12.[62] They punished no other crimes

27 however but theft and robbery, which were punished | by a pecuniary fine. The Tartars in like manner punish no other crimes but these two, and theft and murther; the latter by a pecuniary fine or composition and the other by death. A severe punishment was absolutely necessary as their way of life exposes them much to it. Tho perhaps if the man was able to give it a compensation would be receivd, but then poor persons are those who most commonly commit this crime. There are many things in the modern governments which shew that the government was at some time or other in a very weakly condition with regard to the triall of private causes.— In this country when one comes before the court he is asked how he inclines to be tried; to this he can give now but one answer, viz By God and my country. But formerly he might have given many others. He might have referred it to the judiciall combat and demanded that it should be determined by the

28 strength of | his arm. This plainly was avoiding a submission of his cause to his country, and a demand that it should be determind by the method any one trusts[u] to in the first ages before government is established. They however have gained here a considerable point. They say to them when they are offered this, which was called the judiciall combat, which they said was trusting their cause to God, that they must not[v] disturb the country by gathering their dependants together and fighting in a body, but decide by their own private arm. Thus the great end they had in view is considerably answered. That which would otherwise have provd a sort of a rebellion is decided by a single duel. The trial by boiling water and the ordial trial in like manner are all signs of the weak authority of the court, which could not oblige those who came before it to stand to its judgement. They however answered one great end as they put a speedy end to the dispute. We would

29 be apt to imagine that in the triall by boiling water every one would | be brought in guilty. The way was that the person accused should put his hand into a kettle of boiling water and take something from the bottom of it.[w] {The hand was then wrapt up and sealed, and three[x] days afterwards it was unloosed and if no scar appeard the person was acquitted.} But the skins of persons who are much abroad or much amongst water, as our ancestors

---

[u] Reading doubtful    [v] Illegible word deleted    [w] Two or three illegible words are interlined here and deleted    [x] Reading doubtful

---

[62] *Germania*, xii. Traitors and deserters were hanged on trees, cowards were drowned in bogs. Cf. Montesquieu, VI.18.

were, the skin becomes hard and callous so that boiling water will not hurt
them.[63] {A man opened a red hot oyster.} So that very few were brought in
guilty. And the same happend in that where they held a piece[y] of hot iron
in their hand, or in the ordial trial. All these were no more than committing
the issue of the cause to chance, as it were to a throw of the dice, rather
than to the judgement of the country.— They were however very long kept,
which shews the weakness of the government with respect to these matters.
The judicial combat extended not only to criminall causes when the one
party had beat or hurt or affronted an other, but even to civill ones. A
dispute concerning the right of an estate was often decided by it. This has
now worn into desuetude in England. There was however one demanded
as late as Queen Elizabeths time[64] with regard to a crim. cause, and one in
30 King Chas. I[st] time[65] to decide | a criminall one; but they were prevented.
There is however no express statute or Act of Parliament or even a rule of
court (similar to our acts *of sederunt*) against it. It has gone into disuse
gradually in the same way as villainage. They are both laid aside but no one
can tell at what precise time.— But tho the government was late of exercising the greatest authority in private causes, yet in those which immediately concerned the community the authority of the generall assembly
of the people became soon very powerfull. And as all matters relating to
peace and war, the providing provisions for an army, etc., were of great
importance, these were all determined by this generall assembly, and that
without any great liberty of dissenting in the hands of any individualls,
who were obliged to conform to the determination of the body of the people.
— I showed you also[66] in what manner a chieftan naturally arose in this
31 state of society. In all these assemblys, whether | for judging in private
causes or publick ones and in the executive part, ⟨?some one⟩ would take
the lead by his superior power and influence or other means in which he
would excell others[z] in this mobbish assembly. When[a] it was for the reasons
explained yesterday[67] found necessary to establish a court for the determination of causes, to ease the people of that burthen, this man would
naturally be a member of it and continue in it to have his superior influence. The same would be the case when a court was established to take
off the hands of the people the less important parts of the executive power,
that is, to give a sort of senatorial power to the court, who determined every
thing necessary to the safety of the city and the peace and war with their
neighbours for some certain length. They had the power of levying armies,

[y] Reading doubtful       [z] Several illegible words deleted       [a] Illegible word deleted

[63] Montesquieu, XXVIII.17.
[64] *Lowe* v. *Paramour* (1571), a criminal case: Dyer's Reports, 301.
[65] *Claxton* v. *Lilburn* (1638), a civil case, described in H. C. Lea, *Superstition and Force*
(3rd edn., 1878), 213–14. Trial by battle was abolished by 59 George III, c. 46 (1819).
[66] 7 ff. above.                    [67] 15–16 above.

providing subsistence for them, taking care of the walls of the city if it had any, receiving ambassadors, and holding all sorts of deliberations whatever. In these courts the leading man would soon become a kind of president;

32 | he would first give his opinion on every question or ask that of others, and those whom he thus preferred before the rest would be looked on as some way of greater importance and weight than the others. This is the very method Tacitus[68] mentions was in use in the assemblies of the Germans. I mentioned also[69] how the authority of this chieftan was naturally[b] hereditary {and went at first to his children in common who made a sort of joint chieftains, and how this was afterwards altered to be either the eldest sons property or the eldest relations.} In all barbarous nations no one can have an audience of the chief man without a present. This is the custom amongst the Mogulls, the Tartars, and all the nations of Africa and America. And our Saxon kings, and even some of the first of the Norman race, never performed any of the common offices of humanity without they had receivd a present before hand. In this time the great all received presents from the poorer sort as a token of their submission to them, intirely contrary to the modern practise where to receive a present is a sign of depen-

33 dance and inferiority, as it brings the receiver under an obligation to | the donor. But in the early times the⟨y⟩ did not conceive any obligation to arise from the receiving a favour; they considered it merely as an acknowledgement of authority and submission. This made a considerable part of the revenues of the kings in all early governments. The chief man or president, receiving these gratuities as an addition to his stock, already great and which he cultivated in the same way as the others, would soon become very powerfull, and have extraordinary influence in all the courts. They would appear to be his councils; {His authority would naturally increase very greatly from the naturall disposition of men. One whom we have been accustomed to obey comes in some things [comes] to expect our submission, and we are in the same manner disposed to pay him respect and deference.} and a state of this sort to a careless observer would appear to be monarchicall. {But the king, as they would call him, has properly no power but only weight and authority.} But tho all matters of less importance would be referred to the courts and their president, as the trialls of private causes and the preparations and deliberations for war, yet these in the last resort would be[c] brought befor⟨e⟩ the general assembly. The condemning of a

34 criminall, etc., as is the case in | Tartary and was so in old Germany, ⟨and⟩ is so at the Cape of Good Hope, the finall declaration of war,[d] or concluding a definitive treaty of peace, would be referred to the whole body.

---

[b] Reading doubtful          [c] Illegible word deleted          [d] Replaces 'peace

[68] *Germania*, xi.          [69] 11–12 above.

The body of the people in this manner transferrs*e* to the courts a part of the judicial and*f* executive power, or what we may call the senatoriall power. The judicial power gradually rises from being at first merely an interposition as a friend without any legall authority, which however will be of considerable effect if this third person have a great influence with both parties, to be, $2^{dly}$, a power resembling that of an arbiter to decide the causes referred to them and inflict some gentle penalty. They then venture on some thing as a punishment for atrocious crimes, as expelling the person from the society, and lastly it comes to be that of a free judiciall authority with which the magistrates are vested, the arise of which from the com-

35 positions has been already explained. | With regard to laws and the legislative power, there is properly nothing of that sort in this period[s]. There must indeed be some sort of law as soon as property in flocks commences, but this would be but very short and ⟨?have⟩ few distinctions in it, so that every man would understand it without any written or regular law. It would be no other than what the necessity of the state required. Written and formall laws are a very great refinement of government, and such as we never meet with but in the latest*g* periods of it. It is a sign of great authority in the government to be able to make regulations which shall bind ⟨them⟩-selves, their posterity, and even persons who are unwilling. This then is the state of government from the age of hunters thro all the time of shepherds, and even when something of agriculture is practised, that is, till the appropriation of lands.— I shall only observe farther on this head some things relating to the state of those countries where this is the state of the govern-

36 ment, particularly | with regard to two great nations who have been merely shepherds as far back as we can trace them and still are so without the least of agriculture. These are all the nations north of Mount Caucasus thro all Asia, that is, all the whole body of Tartars, and $2^{dly}$, of the Arabians.

In the age of hunters it is impossible for a very great number to live together. As game is their only support they would soon exhaust all that was within their reach. Thirty or forty families would be the most that could live together, that is, about 140 or 150 persons. These might live by the chase in the country about them. They would also naturally form themselves into these villages, agreeing to live near together for their mutuall security. In the same manner tho they could not conveniently enlarge their village, yet severall sets or tribes of this sort would agree to

37 settle their villages as near as they could conveniently, | that they might be at hand to give on⟨e⟩ another assistance and protection against the common enemy. In the same manner as there would be some men in each village who would preside in the affairs of it, so there would be some one who would have a superior influence over the other chiefs and become in this manner

---

*e* The words 'frees itself off' are interlined at this point          *f* 'senatori' deleted
*g* Replaces 'rudest'

a chief of chiefs, or king of kings. As the affairs of each family would be determined by the members of it, of a village by the members of it, so would the affairs of the community[h] or association of villages by the members of the whole directed by their president, and the chief president receiving[i] the lead in all these would appear a sort of sovereign. This is the case in Africa, Asia, and America; every nation consists of an association of different tribes or villages. In the age of shepherds these societies or villages may be somewhat larger than in that of hunters. But still they can not be very large, as the country about would soon be eat up by their
38 | flocks and herds. So that the ground for 4 or 5 miles about will not be able to maintain the flocks of above 1000 people, and we never find that the villages amount to a greater number in any country of shepherds.[j] These may in like manner combine together under their different heads to support one another against the attacks of others. We see that the Grecian nations were in this man⟨n⟩er led on by Agamemnon.— There is however one great difference betwixt men in the one state and in the other. The hunters can not form any very great schemes, nor can their expeditions be very formidable. It is impossible that 200 hunters could live together for a fortnight. They could not find subsistence by the chase when in so large a body, nor have they provisions to carry with them. ⟨N⟩or if they had by some means or other provided as much as would support them could they transport it, as they have no carriages. The party must therefore carry its provisions or subsist by hunting during the time of their expedition, so that it will be impossible for any considerable number to make any expedition.
39 | A scalping party seldom consists of above ten or twelve. So that there can be no great danger from such a nation. And the great astonishment our colonies in Am. are in on account of these expeditions[k] proceeds intirely from their unacquaintedness with arms, for tho they might plague them and hurt some of the back settlements they could never injure the body of the people.[70] The case is the same with respect to shepherds as long as we suppose them stationary; but if we suppose them moving from one place to another, 4 or 5 miles every day, we can set no bounds to the number which might enter into such an expedition. If then one clan of Tartars (for instance) should, setting out on an expedition, defeat another, they would necessarily become possessed of every thing which before belonged to the

[h] Two illegible words deleted    [i] Reading doubtful    [j] An illegible word has been interlined above 'shepherds' and apparently deleted    [k] 'they would' deleted

[70] Cf. William Douglass, *A Summary . . . of the First Planting, Progressive Improvements, and Present State of the British Settlements in North-America* (London, reprinted, 1755), I.191: 'Upon good enquiry it will be found, that our properly speaking Indian wars have not been so frequent, so tedious, and so desolating, as is commonly represented in too strong a light. . . . In our northern parts, the Indians generally appear in small skulking parties with yellings, shoutings, and antick postures, instead of trumpets and drums; . . . The Indians are not wanderers like the Tartars, but are ramblers . . .'

vanquished; for in this state when they make any expedition of this sort
wives, children, and flocks and every thing is carried along with them, so
that when they are vanquished they will lose their all. The far greater part
40 therefore will follow these | and join themselves to the victor, tho some
perhaps might still adhere to the vanquishd chief. If this combined army
should be in the same manner successfull against a 2ᵈ, a 3ᵈ, and [and] a 4ᵗʰ
tribe, they would soon become very powerfull, and might in time subdue
all the nations of their country about them and become in this means
immensely powerfull. So that tho a country possessed by shepherds is
never extremely populous yet immense armies may be collected together
which would be an even¹ match for any of its neighbours. This has happend 2ᶜᵉ or 3ᶜᵉ with regard to Tartary. Tamerlane, having conquered all
Tartary, invaded and over ran all Asia with above 1,000,000 of men, a body
alltogether invincible. And Cengis Kan with still greater numbers, having
conquered all the barbarous nations about the source of the Indus, over
ran all the neighbouring countries. The Arabs were in the same way united
under Mahomet, whose successors        ⁷¹ and Omer over ran the neighbouring countries, who could not resist their immense power.


41                    | *Wednesday. Febry. 23ᵈ 1763*

In the last lecture I endeavoured to explain to you more fully that form
of government which naturally arises amongst mankind as they advance in
society, and in what manner it gradually proceeded.

With regard to the internall police of such a state, there can be nothing
more simple and easily comprehended. We have at the head of it the chief,
or chieftan, who has in all matters an influence superior to that of any other
person. This chief is distinguished from the rest by two things: 1ˢᵗ, by his
superior wealth; and 2ᵈˡʸ, by his family descent, being generally the son or
very near relation of the late chief. Superiority of wealth gives one in this
age a greater influence and authority than the same disproportion does at
any other time. One who possessed flocks and herds which could by their
produce support a hundred men had no other way of disposing of it than by
supporting a hundred men out of it. Manufacturing of the produce of the
42 | earth was not then introduced. They were consumed in the same rough
state as nature brought them. Or perhaps when arts were a little improved
they might consume a part of their estate, yet this could not extend near so
far as at present.— The descent from the great families who had been in
possession of this chief dignity in the state is likewise another source of

---

¹ Reading doubtful

---

⁷¹ Blank in MS. The first two Caliphs were Abu Bakr and Omer.

authority. In the age of hunters there can be no hereditary nobility or respect to families. Families can then be noways respectable; one who has distinguished himself by his exploits in war and signalized himself as a leader will have considerable respect and honour. This will in some measure descend to the son by his connection with his father. But if he be noways remarkable or distinguished as a leader, his son will not be esteemed a whit the more because he was come of such or such a great man, as

43 military glory and famous atchievements are the only thing which | can give one weight in a country of this sort. But in the age of shepherds descent gives one more respect and authority than perhaps in any other stage of society whatever. In this stage, as property is introduced, one can be eminent not only for his superior abilities and renowned exploits but also on account of his wealth and the estate he has derived from his fore-fathers. This continues the respect paid to the father down to the son and so on, for ever perhaps.[m] We see many instances of the vast respect paid to descent amongst the Tartars and Arabs. Every one of these can trace themselves, at least they pretend to do so, as far back as Abraham. The Tartarian history[72] which was published some time ago in English, being translated from the French into which it was translated from the Swedish of                [n], who being taken prisoner when attending Charles 12th of Sweden in his expeditions was carried into Siberia ⟨and⟩ met with and translated it into Arabic with very sensible notes, may furnish us with a very good example of this. The whole of that work, which was wrote by

44                [o], a very great conqueror as well as a consi|derable writer, is taken up with genealogies. It is just such an account as we should expect to meet with in the history of one of the clans in the remoter parts of this country. It gives us an account of the descent of the great men of the family, rectifying the mistakes which had formerly been made in these matters, and the severall exploits they committed in a very brief manner. This prince, who was a descendent of the famous Cengis Kan himself, being taken prisoner when very young by the Persians was educated and very well instructed in the sciences by                [p], the Sultan of Persia, and making his escape to his countrymen was received with the greatest joy; and the nearest relation who in his absence had taken the government of the hurd upon him resigned it with the greatest readyness, than which there

[m] Numbers written above the last three words indicate that they were intended to read 'perhaps for ever'      [n] Blank in MS.      [o] Blank in MS.      [p] Blank in MS.

---

[72] The *Shajarat al Atrak*, written in Chaghatai Turkish by Abu'l-Ghasi Bahadur Khan, Khan of Khiva from 1643 to 1663 and a descendant of Gengis Khan. It was translated, probably into German, by Philip John von Strahlenberg, a Swedish officer who was for thirteen years a prisoner of war among the Tartars. A French translation, *Histoire généa-logique des Tartares*, was published in Leyden in 1726, and an English version appeared in 1730. For 'into Arabic' read 'from Turkish'.

can be no greater token of respect to families. We see that the Jews, who
were originally a tribe of Arabs, paid the greatest respect to genealogies
45 and were at great pains to preserve them. There is one thing | which will
tend greatly to increase the respect for families in this stage of society more
perhaps than in any other, ⟨?which⟩ is that they will be all of very great
antiquity. A family which [which] had been once raised to dignity and
wealth could hardly ever be deprived of it, unless the nation was conquered, in which case all would be lost. But if this does not happen there
is hardly any way in which he could reduce his fortune; he knows easily
how many dependents his flocks and herds will maintain without incroaching on the stock. He has no way of expending it on luxuries as afterwards. Perhaps a man might lay out on himself at this time as much as
would maintain 30 men, so that one who could have maintaind 100 will
only maintain 70; but he could not as now spend a fortune which would
maintain 1000 on himself in luxuries and curiosities. They might*q* then
give one sort of rough produce for a smaller quantity of another, but not
46 1000 lib of unmanufacturd | naturall productions for a few ounces of stuff
nicely tricked up, as one now does of beef, bread, etc. So that it was not
possible for one to spend a great estate, as one may very easily do in the
present state of affairs. There lustre therefore continues uniform and in
most cases encreases, so that the old families must be very respectable; and
for this reason long descents are much counted*r* here, more so than in any
other state of society, as in other cases the upstart families, that is, those
who have been but lately raised to dignity, are*s* often of as great influence,
but these will be but seldom met with. We see that there is in man a great
propensity to continue his regard towards those which are nearly connected
with him whom we have formerly respected. The sons and particularly
the eldest son commonly attract this regard, as they seem most naturally
to come in the place of the father; and accordingly in most nations have
been continu'd in their fathers dignity. In most elective kingdoms, which as
47 I shall hereafter | shew[73] you was the case of all kingdoms at first, we find
the son generally preferred to any other. There are some states indeed
where this has been expressly forbidden, as at Venice where there is a law
forbidding the son of the deceased doge to be chosen in his room. But this
sufficiently shews that there is such a naturall inclination amongst men,
otherwise no such law would have been found necessary.— Besides this
chieftan who presides in the assembly, the whole power of the government
is lodged in the body of the people. They have the whole of the judicial
and executive power committed to them.— There is one great difference
betwixt these people and those in any other state of society, that is, in their

---

*q* Replaces 'could not'        *r* Reading doubtful        *s* 'generall' deleted

---

[73] 67–8 below.

way of making war and peace. These nations generally have no fixt habitations. The Tartars live in a sort of waggons, or rather houses set upon wheels; their country is altogether plain and void of wood or stones to interrupt them; not a tree nor hill over the whole country, so that they have nothing to interrupt them in their progress. A people in this state have no
48 attachment to their particular spot where ⟨they⟩ | have taken up their habitation. Their whole property is then easily carried about with them. But when the society have made some farther steps in improvement, the amor patriae, the love of the soil, naturally arises. Those who have property in land will never think of deserting it as they can not possibly transport it with them. In the same way others, tho they have not land property, have nevertheless valuable property in goods and furniture, which it is very troublesome to transport even from house to house; and to remove from one part of the country to another would require the equipage of a regiment. Though Scotland be no rich country nor well cultivated, yet the inhabitants will never think of leaving it to seek new seats. The Tartars on the other hand [the Tartars] have all their property in what is properly to be called moveables,*t* that is, in herds and flocks. These they can transport without much inconvenience, and their families ar⟨e⟩ transported in
49 waggons covered | with a sort of felt which they use in those countries. They therefore will be very little attacched to any particular spot; where ever they find pasture for their cattle, there they will fix their habitation for the time. A people of this sort will frequently leave their country to seek for new seats where they may have better pasture, and remove in whole bodies or great colonies. Thus the Helvetii (as we are told by Caesar[74]) who inhabited the country now possessed by the Swiss, and were the most warlike nation of Gaul, thought it hard that they who were the best warriors and most warlike nation of the country should have the worst territories; they therefore left their country and would probably have over run all Gaul had they not been stopped by Caesars army. In the same manner the Cimbri and Teutones at different times made attacks on Greece, Italy, and Gaul;
50 they were indeed repulsed in them all, but | made frequent attempts of this sort. The severall nations in Germany have all been in this state, though they are now removed out of it. I shall however refer the account of th⟨e⟩ revolutions brought about by them, and the settling of the severall kingdoms and states which has arose from this, for another lecture.[75] {In the same manner the Lombards, who came originally from about the Palus Maeotis,[76] settled first in a body on the north of the Danube where they

---

*t* 'property' deleted

---

[74] *De Bello Gallico*, I.2 ff.                    [75] 114 ff. below.
[76] The ancient name of the Sea of Azov.

had a territory assigned them by the Romans. However when they had exhausted that fine country they passed over to the south side of the river. There again they had a territory assigned them. But some time after on *u* being discontented sent inviting them into Italy*v* and sent presents of the fruits of the country, which soon induced them to quit their country;[77] and they accordingly poss⟨ess⟩ed themselves of it for 400 or 500 years.} They were in the very same state as the modern Tartars, only that they had a little agriculture. I mentioned in yesterdays lecture[78] how formidable a nation of this sort may be when united under one leader, and that they may often produce great revolutions, and instanced the two great nations of shepherds, viz the Tartars and the Arabs. Now [of] this the Tartars will happen far more frequen⟨t⟩ly among*w* than among the Arabs. The former have no obstacles of any sort in their country, no mountains or rough ground, no barriers of woods; they have indeed some of the largest rivers in the world, but these a Tartar party, as they are all excellent horsemen, will
51 | swim over tho half a mile broad. {Nor have the⟨y⟩ any stone to raise fortifications, nor even wood, insomuch that they are obliged to burn cow dung during their long and severe winter.} The lord of a hurd therefore who has been victorious over another has nothing to obstruct his progress to attack another; one battle decides the dispute, as they are all ruind by the first defeat which deprived them of their property all at once.*x* We see accordingly that the Tartars have been severall times united under one head; Cengis Kan and Tamerlane, from being the lords or leaders of very small clans, rose thro many hardships and defeats in their youth to be sovereigns of all Tartary, and over ran even the most part of the neighbouring nations. Tamerlane extended his empire from the Indus to Smyrna, over all Persia, Indostan, and Asia Minor, part of China, and carried an army even into Siberia. The country again inhabited by the Arabs is full of mountains, rocks, and fastnesses which rend⟨er⟩ it allmost innaccessible to an enemy. The severall tribes are allmost intirely seperated from each
52 other; and it will cost severall | battles and a great deal of bloodshed to conquer any one; so that the greatest perseverance will be necessary to*y* conquer any great number of hurds and turn them out of their fastnesses. We see accordingly that they were never united under one head but by Mahomet, and then indeed they over ran the adjacent countries with a fury

*u* Blank in MS.        *v* 'where they' deleted        *w* Numbers written above the last eight words indicate that they were intended to read 'will happen far more frequently among the Tartars'        *x* The last three words replace 'as well as their'        *y* Illegible word deleted

---

[77] The Lombards entered Italy in A.D. 568, allegedly at the invitation of Narses, who had been slighted by the Emperor Justin II.
[78] 40 above.

as irresistable as that of the Tartars under their leaders. Besides these incursions in quest of new territories they often make others merely in quest of spoil, and return again to their own country, which they never think of doing when they make a generall move. They will often send out a party to over run and plunder which will return again in a few years. The expedition of the Vandalls into Italy under Attila[79] seems to have been of this sort. After they had staid in it for about twenty years and plundered the

53  whole country, they returned to their country loaded with | booty. A polished nation never undertakes any such expeditions. It never makes war but with a design to enlarge or protect its territory; but these people make war either with design to leave their own habitations in search of better, or to carry off booty. As the Tartars have been always a nation of shepherds, which they will always be from the nature of their country, which is dry and high raised above the sea, with few rivers tho some very large ones, and the weather and the air is too cold for the produce of any grain, and as they are for the reasons already mentiond easily united under one head, so we find that more of the great revolutions in the world have arose from them than any other nation in the world. If we look back into the first periods of profane history of which we have any distinct account, we find Cyrus with his Persians over running Media; this nation appears undoubtedly to have been a Tartar nation; they were all horsemen, as the Tartars are, and ⟨in⟩ every shape resembled them. The Medes too, who possessed those coun-

54  tries before them, appear | to have been Tartars originally, from the account given of them by Herodotus[80] and Justin.[81] That fore mentioned author,[82] talking of the invasion of Greece by the Thessalians and Scythians, says that nothing hindered them from over running and conquering the whole of Europe and Asia but their want of union. Had they been united, no human force, says he, could have withstood them. After Cyrus time Cyaxaris,[83] who again raised up an empire in Persia, seems to have been a Tartar prince. The Parthians, who afterwards over ran that country, were without doubt a Tartarian nation; and made a noble stand against the Roman arms. After this time Cengis Kan, whose conquest we have already mentioned, arose amongst the same nation; an⟨d⟩ 2 or 300 years after, Tamerlane of the same country made still greater revolutions. But previous to these the Huns made very great commotions in the affairs of

[79] A conflation of the Huns' expedition under Attila in A.D. 452 and the Vandals' expedition under Gaiseric in A.D. 455.

[80] I.96 ff.

[81] Justinus, *Epitoma Historiarum Philippicarum*, XLI–XLII.

[82] Presumably the reference is to Herodotus, but neither he nor Justinus says what is reported here. The reporter may have conflated and confused two or three remarks about Herodotus. See next note.

[83] Cyaxares was king of Media 634–594 B.C., at the time of the Scythian invasion of Asia but *before* the time of Cyrus, founder of the Persian empire. Probably Darius, king of Persia 521–485, was intended here.

the world. We are told they were originally a nation inhabiting to the east[84]
55 of the Chinese Wall, who being expelled by the Chinese traversed | the
country till they came to the Palus Maeotis and the Euxine Sea. This they
thought was the bound of the world and therefore made no attempts to
settle[z] beyond it. But 200 or 300 years after, discovering that there was
still land to the west of these lakes or seas, they soon agreed, as people in
this state are very fickle, to leave the country they possessed and pass over.
This they accordingly did, and drove out the Ostrogoths, who in their turn
drove out the Wisigoths; for a people of this sort, as they will leave their
country on account of seeking a better, so they will when defeat⟨ed⟩ by the
enemy, in case they be not intirely ruin'd as it often happens that they are.
The Wisigoths in their turn, under the different leaders Theodoric and
Aleric, over ran all Italy and Gaul[a] and continued there till they were
repelled by Charlemagne.—

   If we should suppose that a nation of this sort was settled in country
56 naturally defended against invasions, | capable of maintaining themselves
against their enemies, in such a country a regular form of government
would soon take place. But this can never be the case in Tartary, as the
country is unfit by its dryness and cold for agriculture, and has no fastnesses
nor materialls for constructing them; nor can it be in Arabia, where agriculture is debarred by the ruggedness and steepness of the country, which
is a combination of hills without any intermediate valleys, or if there are
any they are all filled with sand. But we see that this happened in other
more fertile and secure countries pretty early. The first inhabitants of
Greece, as we find by the accounts of the historians, were much of the
same sort with the Tartars. Thus renowned warriors of antiquity, as
Hercules, Theseus, etc. are celebrated for just such actions and expeditions
as make up the history of a Tartar chief. We see also that they resembled
57 them in this also that they made frequent | demigrations.[b] The Heraclidae,
who were the followers or clan of Hercules, settled first of all in the great
island of Euboea, and from there[c] went out and settled at Mycenae          [85]
and Sparta. These severall countries, being continually exposed to the
inroads of their neighbours, did not soon alter their way of life. We see that
at the Trojan war the expedition was not undertaken with a view to conquest but in revenge of goods that were carried off; and that when the city
was taken each returned to his home with his share of the spoil. All the
disputes mentioned to have happened by him[86] were concerning some

---

[z] Illegible word deleted          [a] Reading doubtful; replaces an illegible word
[b] *Sic*      [c] 'sent' deleted

---

[84] A mistake for 'north'; cf. LJ(B) 30, below.
[85] Blank in MS. Messenia, Argos, and Sparta.                    [86] Homer.

women, or oxen, cattle, or sheep or goats. Attica was the country which first began to be civilized and put into a regular form of government. The sea surrounded on two sides of the triangle and a ridge of high mountains 58 on the third. It had therefore little to fear from enemies by land; | the sea was the only means by which they could easily be attacked. They therefore at first built none of their villages near the sea. As the country was so much securer than the others, people flocked into it from all hands, tho it was rather the poorest of all the Grecian countries. But the rovers from the sea might still invade them in the night. The only method they had to secure themselves was to have some place of strength to drive their cattle and other goods into, upon an invasion.[d] This was the advice given by Theseus; he advised them to live together in one place that they might be at hand to assist one another and might have a place to protect their cattle in. The city of Athens was therefore built and fortified under the acropolis or citadell. When this was done he abolished the jurisdiction⟨s⟩ which were enjoyed by the leaders of the severall villages, as these mostly resided in the 59 great city; and by this means in⟨?creased⟩ | his own power as well as diminished that of his people and became a sort of monarchy, or as it was afterwards called a tyranny. But in a small country the revenue of the chief man can not so far exceed that of the other great men as to render his power of great duration. Many rivalls in wealth and authority would start up against ⟨him⟩. Theseus himself was even turned out of the kingly power by Menestheus.[87] This Demophoon recovered,[e] and it continu'd in the hands of the family for some time, but this was afterwards exchanged for the government by archons. These were at first for 10 years,[f] but were also 2[g] in number which lessened their power, and afterwards 5;[h] they were at length chosen anually.[88] These continued for some considerable time, but were at last abolished and the magistracy laid open to those who were of power enough to obtain them. This was the case in all the states of Greece; they became in this manner from monarchys or nearly so to what we would 60 | call democracys, as the legislative power altogether, and the other two in the last resort, were in the determination of the generall assembly, but were called by them aristocraceyes with great propriety, ὑπο των ἀριστων, as there were always men of power and authority who influenced the people as they inclined.

---

[d] Reading doubtful          [e] 'it' deleted          [f] The last two words replace 'life
[g] Reading doubtful          [h] Reading doubtful

---

[87] Plutarch, *Life of Theseus*, 32–3. Demophon was the son of Theseus.

[88] There were originally three archons, elected for life. Their period of tenure was later limited to ten years and eventually to one year. Their number was increased from three to nine, and in 487 B.C. simple election was succeeded by a system of choosing the archons by lot from elected candidates.

*Thursday February 24ᵗʰ 1763.*

In the last lecture I endeavoured to shew in what manner those governments[i] which ⟨?were⟩ originally Tartarian ones or under chiefs in the same
manner as the Tartars, came from thence to settle in towns and become republican {in many parts of Greece, and the same was the case in Italy, Gaul,
etc.} We may easily conceive that a people of this sort, settled in a country
where they lived in pretty great ease and security and in a soil capable of
yielding them good returns for cultivation, would not only improve the
earth but also make considerable advances in the severall arts and sciences
and manufactures, providing they had an opportunity of exporting their
61 sumptuous produce and fruits of their labour. | Both these circumstances
are absolutely necessary to bring about this improvement in the arts of life
amongst a people in this state. The soil must be improveable, otherwise
there can be nothing from whence they might draw that which they
should work up and improve. That must be the foundation of their labour
and industry. It is no less necessary that they should have an easy method
of transporting their sumptuous produce into foreign countries and
neighbouring states. When they have an opportunity of this, then they will
exert their utmost industry in their severall businesses; but if their be no
such opportunity of commerce, and consequently no opportunity of
increasing their wealth by industry in any considerable degree, there is
little likelihood that they should ever cultivate arts to any great degree, or
produce more sumptuous produce than will be consumed within the
country itself; and this will never be wrought up to such perfection as
62 when there are greater spurs to industry. Tartary and Araby labour | under
both these difficulties. For in the first place their soil is very poor and such
as will hardly admit of culture of any sort, the one on account of its dryness
and hardness, the other on account of its steep and uneven surface. So that
in them there is no room for cu⟨l⟩ture; the soil itself debarrs them. Neither
have they any opportunity of commerce, if it should happen that they
should make any advances in arts and sciences. They are deprivd in most
places of the benefit of water carriage, more than any other nation in the
world; and in some places where they would have an opportunity of it,
the land carriage which would be necessary before it, debarrs them no less
than the other. In these countries therefore little or no advances can be
expected, nor have any yet been made. But in Greece all the necessary
circumstances[j] for the improvement of the arts concurred. The severall
parts were seperated from each other by mountains and other barriers, no
63 less than Arabia, but is[k] far more | adapted to culture. They would there-
fore have many inducements to cultivate the arts and make improvements

---

[i] 'became' deleted        [j] Numbers written above the last two words indicate that their
order was intended to be reversed        [k] *Sic*

in society. The lands would be divided and well improved and the country would acquire considerable wealth. And as a nation in this way would be vastly more wealthy than their neighbours, having more of what Homer calls κοιμηλια,[89] that is, good⟨s⟩ stored up, they would be very apt to be attacked and plundered by their neighbouring nations, who would often set out on piraticall expeditions from their country. We find that at the time of the Trojan war such expeditions were very frequently undertaken, nor were pirates then looked on as any way disshonourable. We see that in the Odyssey, Ulysses, who very seldom gives a true account of himself, is often asked whether he was a merchant or a pirate.[90] The account he generally gives of himself was that he was a pirate. We see too that this was a much more honourable character than that of a merchant, which was allways
64 looked on with | great contempt by them. A pirate is a military man who acquires his livelyhood by warlike exploits, whereas a merchant is a peaceable one who has no ocasion for military skill and would not be much esteemed in a nation consisting of warriors chiefly.[l] {The severall clans, as we may call them, would plunder on one another in the same way as the clans did in this country and in every country where they are established; and if the people without the consent of the chief should make any incursions they would always be protected by him.} They would naturally therefore take some precautions against these robbers and pirates, both by land and sea, for they might in the night time be attacked by a set of pirates from the sea as well as land robbers. We see that none of their hamlets were built near the sea; but as this would not secure them against others, they would be necessitated to have some fortifications to secure themselves, their cattle, and other goods. This would be much more easily accomplished by the fortifying of one large place, in which they might reside altogether, than by fortifying each particular hamlet. This was accordingly done and all the principall persons removed into it. This we
65 find was the case in all the states of Greece, in each of which we | find some great city. The neighbouring country was but thinly inhabited; the houses in it were but poor; they had no country houses of any consequence, but only sheds and hovels for their cattle. The rich people who had much substance, or inclined to live somewhat more comfortably or elegantly than others, would all shelter themselves in this city. And hither too they would drive in their cattle in time of danger, as we are informed by Thucidides[91]

---

[l] Numbers written above the last three words indicate that they were intended to read 'chiefly of warriors'

---

[89] κειμήλια; e.g. *Iliad*, vi.47; *Odyssey*, iv.613.

[90] Only once, in fact, *Odyssey*, ix.253–5, but the same question is asked of his son, Telemachus, in *Odyssey*, iii.72–4. Smith's statement that pirates were not then thought dishonourable, as may be seen from Homer, is an echo of Thucydides, I.5.1–2.

[91] II.13 ff.

was done in the beginnings of the Peloponesian[m] war, and in many others; and indeed we have the best account which is to be had of the ancient state of Greece from the beginning of his work, and from Homer. I shewed you also in the last lecture[92] in what manner those governments which were at first under the chieftans and governed in the manner of a clan, became in time to be a republican govt in all the states which were originally in that form. The great men of the country would as I have already mentioned

66 leave | the villages in which they had presided to live in the city. The authority of the chief would not be at all agreable to them if it came to be any way excessive, nor would they be so much below him as to be greatly under his power. The revenue which would be derived from a small kingdom would not be sufficient to give the king or lord of it very great superiority over the nobles or other great men. Three or four of them combini⟨n⟩g would be able to wrest the authority and management of the state out of his hands. Kings nowadays still maintain their authority altho they have their nobles living at court about them, but it is becaus⟨e⟩ their revenue is far superior to that of the nobles, and because the nobility have easier access to all posts of honour and profit than they could have if they were more laid[n] open, as then upstarts of parts might interfere with them. We see that the government of all citys is republican, managed by a town

67 councill. | In the same manner the nobles,[o] the chief men of the state, would endeavour to reduce the state into their power. They therefore in most countries began to reduce the power of the state into their own hands from those of the chief. This was done by degrees at Athens, and the government laid open to the people by slow degrees. {And in about 200 years after the Trojan war, when all Greece was under single leaders or a few chieftans, the states were all become aristocracies.} There[p] does not seem to have been any law at first obliging[q] the people to choose their magistrates from the nobles, but this however they always did, as they would be most inclined to favour those who had supported and protected them and whom they had in some measure been accustomed to obey. The governments in this manner became aristocraticall, from that of the kingly sort. But in fact there seems to have been a considerable degree of the democraticall form under what were generally reckoned monarchies. For we see that the people had the sole power of making laws, and even the last

68 determi|nation of all affairs with regard to peace or war. {And they had the power of choosing all magistrates, insomuch that the authors say that Theseus, by calling the people to live in a city together, laid the foundations

[m] Replaces 'Trojan'          [n] Numbers written above the last two words indicate that their order was intended to be reversed          [o] 'or lords' deleted          [p] 'government' deleted          [q] Reading doubtful

[92] 59–60 above.

of the democracy.[93]} The king, as he was called, was no more than a leading man who had superior influence in their deliberations. The nobles coming in his place had in the same manner the lead in all affairs, and were accordingly chosen into all the magistracies. This was what the ancients called an aristocracy, tho from the priviledges above mentioned which were possessed by the people we should be apt to term them democracies. They gave the name of democracies to those governments where the people had the same access to the magistraci⟨e⟩s and offices of state as the nobles. But of these we have none at this time in Europe. They were succh as Genoa, Milan, Venice, etc. were formerly. The people of all these countries voluntarily resigned the power into the hands of the nobles[s], and they alone have since had the administration of affairs. We find nothing similar to
69 this[94] in any of the ancient republicks. | The institution of slavery seems to have been the cause of this difference. In the modern republicks every person is free, and the poorer sort are all employed in some necessary occupation. They would therefore find it a very great inconvenience to be obliged to assemble together and debate concerning publick affairs or tryalls of causes. Their loss would be much greater than could possibly be made up to them by any means [could be made up], as they could have but little prospect of advancing to offices. But in the ancient states the mechanick arts were exercised only by the slaves. The freemen were mostly rich, or if they were not rich they were at least idle-men, as they could have no business to apply themselves to. They therefore would find no inconvenience in being called to the publick affairs. Besides this, the vast difference betwixt a freeman of the lowest rank and a slave was so great
70 that it made that amongst the freemen them|selves not perceptible; whereas nowadays the difference betwixt the freemen is not much less than[r] betwixt the free and the slaves formerly. Liberalitas, ἐλευθερια, species liberalis, signify no more than the behaviour and appearance of a gentleman. For the distinction betwixt free and slaves made the same as betwixt the vulgare and the people of fashion or gentlemen. These therefore being few in number, and having no other employment, would easily attend on all trialls or courts, and might have besides som⟨e⟩ probability of rising.— But in the modern commonwealths this was a burden on the common people, without any hopes of rewards. They therefore have all given it up. The Venetians resigned this power to the councill of 1000 chosen for that purpose out of the best families, who have still retaind it. The same has happened at Genoa, and in the United Provinces, where the whole people

---

[r] 'amongst' deleted

---

[93] Thucydides, II.15; Plutarch, *Life of Theseus*, 24–5.
[94] A short arithmetical calculation—probably related to the personal accounts of the student, and certainly not related in any way to the text of the lectures—has been written on the verso of 67 at about this point, and apparently deleted.

had at first equall access to the magistracies, but finding it altogether
71 troublesome | resign'd it to the town council, who still continue to be
possessed of it, and have the power of choosing their own members on a
vacancy.—The aristocraticall government in the manner above mentioned
took place after the government by a chief and the people under his direction was abolished. The nobles became jealous of his power[d] and at
length deprivd him of it. Tho it happend sometimes that previous to this
change the chief oppressed the nobles and people, as at Rome, Corinth,
and other places; but in all of them the authority was at length taken out of
his hands.—We see that this was the case in Gaul, where the people at
Caesars time were under the aristocraticall form of government, and in
Spain, where the government was that sort of an aristocracy in which the
nobles only have access to the magistracies. Of all the countries which have
undergone this change in the form of government,[s] Rome is that of which
72 we have the distinctest account, and of the graduall advance of the | demo-
cracy which followed hear as well as at Athens. The nobles at first in both
had the sole government committed to them, as they only had the power of
being chosen into the magistracies; at least they only[t] were ever chosen.
The A⟨t⟩henian magistracies were also confind at first to the highest class.
But as the power of the nobles declined very fast when either commerce or
luxury were introduced, the people strug⟨g⟩led for liberty, which was
beginning even in the time of the decemviri, as an express law made some
time before was introduced into the 12 Tables making the patricians alone
capable of being elected.[95] The constitution of the Comitia Centuriata had
in effect before given the two first classes the sole power in all debates (as is
well known), and these Tables made the aristocracy still more firm by many
laws. One I mentioned already concerning libells[96] was peculiarly adapted
to the aristocraticall form of government. But the power of the nobles and
their influence over the people soon decreased on the introduction of
73 wea⟨l⟩th and luxury. And it probably would be still ⟨?⟩ | in that case in the
Roman state than it would now. One who spends 10000£ on himself and
domestick luxury does not indeed form any dependents, nor would he have
3 men that would follow him in case he should rebell, ⟨?but he⟩ would
nevertheless have the votes in the election of those he favour with his
custom. But in Rome, where all the luxury was supported by slaves who
had no weight in the state, the luxury of the nobility destroyed all their
power. They therefore made many demands of a share in the power of the
government. They at length obtain tribunes[97] who were to support their
interest in all cases. These for their own sakes as well as that of the people

---

[s] 'we find' deleted        [t] 'could' deleted

---

[95] i.e. elected consuls.                              [96] ii.142–3 above.
[97] Tribunes of the plebeians were established in 494 B.C. Livy, II.33.

strove to have the magistracies⁹⁸ communicated with them. This they at
last obtained; but for severall years afterward there was not one plebeian
magistrate chosen, as the patricians, tho divided amongst themselves, all
combind against the plebeians, and the plebeians, being accustomed to
obey them and look upon them as their superiors, were more inclind to
vote for them than to give their vote to enstall*ᵘ* their equalls over their
74 heads. The tribunes however still persevered, | and at last attained to their
wish by procuring a law,⁹⁹ to which the people readily consented, that the
half of all magistrates, 2 consuls, 6 military tribunes, 8*ᵛ* praetors, etc.
should be chosen from the people; from which time they were anually
elected in that manner. The Athenians¹ were allowed by Solon to choose
magistrates out of the three higher classes, and afterwards by Aristides out
of any class. The Greeks² as I said seem to have been in much the same
state as the Greeks a little after the Trojan war, and the Spaniards as they
were before the time of the Persian expedition.— — —

### *Monday Febry. 28. 1763.*

In some of my last lectures I have explain'd how ⟨government⟩ arises
and what progress it makes in the state of hunters and shepherds. I showed
how that at first there was properly no government at all, that this arose
first amongst a nation of shepherds, and that these in certain circumstances
75 would | naturally unite themselves and form a city, which at first was under
the government of a chief, but afterwards became in the ordinary and
naturall progress of things [became] an aristocracy and afterwards a democracy. I shall now shew in what manner and from what causes these states
necessarily come to an end. They at first, as I shewed you already, and as
was the case at Athens, Sparta, and*ʷ* all the other states of Greece, consisted of a large city which, as Athens, would contain perhaps 100,000
persons with a very small territory arround it. This was the originall form
of all these republicks.—Now here one of two things must happen: either,
1ˢᵗ, the state must always continue in this state of a large city in the midst

*ᵘ* Reading doubtful          *ᵛ* Reading doubtful          *ʷ* Reading of last four words
doubtful

⁹⁸ Particularly the consulship which was reserved to patricians. In 445 B.C. a *lex Canu-
leia* provided that in any year the Senate could substitute for the two consuls military
tribunes (usually six in number) with consular power, and plebeians were eligible for
election as military tribunes. Livy, IV.1 ff.
⁹⁹ The *leges Liciniae Sextiae* of 367 B.C. abolished the military tribunes with consular
power and provided that one of the two consuls must thereafter be a plebeian, and that the
ten keepers of the oracles should be half patrician and half plebeian. The first praetorship
was established at the same time, the number growing to six by 197 B.C. Both patricians
and plebeians were eligible for election. Livy, VI.34 ff.
¹ Solon restricted the office of archon to members of the highest or two highest property
classes; it was opened to the third class in 457 B.C. after the death of Aristides. Cf. Potter,
*Archaeologia Graeca* (7th edn., 1751), 14, 16.
² *Sic.* Probably 'Venetians' was intended. Cf. 70–1 above.

of a small republick; or 2$^{dly}$, it must extend its territory and conquer some of the adjacent states, for it is already so small that it can hardly be dim⟨in⟩ished without the totall ruin of the state. I shall first consider what
76 will be the fate of one of the first sort, which we may call a defen|sive republick, of which the severall states of Greece will serve for examples; and 2$^{dly}$, what will be the fate of a conquering republick, of which Rome will serve us for an example, and Carthage also; for as I shall shew by and by Carthage would have shared the same fate as Rome had it not [have] been overrun by the latter.

We are therefore to consider, 1$^{st}$, what will be the fate of a defensive[x] state which continues to maintain its small territory. In the first place, it must necessarily happen that as a state of this sort advances in arts and improvements in society, [that] its power and strength must be greatly dimin[s]ished. As the arts and improvements and consequently the easieness of procuring livelyhood increase, it is true, the city will become more populous, that is, its number of inhabitants will increase, but the soldiers will be greatly less. The number of people will be greater, but the number of fighting people will be very small, so that the improvement of arts and manufactures which, as I shew more fully hereafter than I have hitherto
77 done, must necess|arily happen in every state of this sort, will greatly weaken its strength; tho not[y] equally in every state, for the reasons I shall explain by and by.—In a nation of shepherds every one without distinction goes to war. This was the case amongst the Children of Israel, and is so at present amongs⟨t⟩ the Arabians and Tartars. Amongst the Calmucks and some other nations the women fight as well as the men. They are, as being weaker, not so good soldiers, but they have their horse, their bows and arrows as well as the men. In a state which is a little more refined than this the men *only* go to war, but then the whole of the men, whether they be shepherds or a nation in the form of a small agrarian state, where the greatest and richest men, those who are at the head of affairs, have not above 10 or 11 acres, as was the case with Regulus, Cincinnatus, and others at the time of their greatest glory. Such persons can all go out to war as easily as
78 the shepherds. In this state the campaigns were only sum|mer ones. The⟨y⟩ continued but three or four months in the middle of the summer, after the spring and before the harvest work. They could easily be absent in the intermediate time, as the corn grows and the crop comes on, if the season favours, as well as if they were at home. A shepherds flock feeds tho he is not with it. Nothing therefore detains them. This was the case with the Peloponesians at the time of the Pelop. war, and had been so some time before at Athens, as Lysias[3] mentions in the oration where he exorts them

---

[x] Replaces 'conquering'        [y] 'always' deleted

---

[3] *Funeral Oration*, 50 (the victory was at Megara).

to imitate the brave actions of their forefathers, who, when all those fit for service had gone to Megaera and the old men and boys had been left with the women, as was customary, to defend the walls, they, when the enemy was spoiling the country, rallied out and gain'd a great victory. But this advice we dont see that they followed. So that a state of this sort could send out all those of the military age, which are generally counted to be 1 in 4, or

79 25 in 100. Of the 100, 50 or the half | are women; of the other 50 men, the half is reckoned to be below 16 or above 45 or 55, the longest term of the military age.—But in a state where arts, manufactures, and handicrafts are brought to perfection this is not the case. They can not dispense with the labourers in this manner without the total loss of business and the destruction of the state. Every hour a smith or a weaver is absent from his loom or the anvill[z] his work is at a stop, which is not the case with the flocks of a shepherd or the fields of the husbandman. Trade, commerce, can not go on, and they therefore will not go out to the wars.—As one in 4 can go out in the former case, so not above 1 in 100 in those who are polished and cultivate the arts. This is the computation commonly made with regard to Britain and Holland and others, but ⟨it⟩ is probably too large. For here as before 50 are women, 25 above and below the military age, so that there must be one out of 25 go to the war, and this does not appear to have been

80 the case even in this war,[4] which has exhausted the country more | than any one since the time of Edw^d 1^st. This is the computation with regard to the most parts of Germany, and Baron        [5], Minister to the King of Prussia, affirms that not above 1 in two hundred can go without detriment to the country. That country is not so much improved in arts as Britain, and consequen⟨t⟩ly could better spare. But as the other is too large, so this is I believe too small with regard to our country. From this we see that at first a small state, as Athens, might be very well able to defend itself. It contained perhaps 100,000 inhabitants or more; of these 25 or 30000 would be of the military age, so that it could furnish an army of considerable strength even at this day amongst more powerfull states, as they did at Marathon, Cheronea, etc., 10,000 or 20000. But when the whole people comes to be employed in peacefull and laborious arts, 1 out of 100 only can go, that is, about 1000, which would be no more than a poor city guard and could do

81 nothing against an enemy; nor even 4 or 5000. | So that the very duration of the state and the improvements naturally going on at that time, every one applying himself to some usefull art, and commerce, the attendant on all these, necessarily undo the strength and cause the power to vanish of

---

[z] Numbers written above the words 'loom' and 'anvill' indicate that their order was intended to be reversed

---

[4] Cf. LJ(B) 38, below, and see Introduction, p. *8*.
[5] Blank in MS. Baron Bielfeld, *Institutions politiques* (1760), I.16.4.

such a state till it be swallowed up by some neighbouring state.—Britain, tho highly advanced in arts and commerce, can nevertheless furnish great armies. The British Isles are computed to contain[a] about 15,000000, so that if one out of 100 goes to war this will make an army of 150000, which is about the number of ⟨the⟩ standing army raised in this country during the war, altho there were near 500000 in battle ray;[b] and I suspect also that this computation is two low, as those of other countries of Europe are too high, for this is the same as it was in Charles 2[d] time, since which the country is greatly improved and consequently the number of men, tho not in the same proportion as I shall shew hereafter.—Thus it must happen that the improvement of arts and commerce must make a[c] great declension in the force and power of the republick in all cases. But this does not hold equally

82 | of all. There is a difference betwixt those countries where slavery takes place and those where it does not, in favours of the former, and this is perhaps the only advantage which attends the institution of slavery.[d] In all countries where slavery takes place, they are the only persons (as I shewed already)[6] who carry on arts and trades of all sorts. The masters indeed had the direction of it, but were no more than overseeers, as they never wrought themselves. And we see that those lawgivers, as Solon, who encouraged trade and commerce, and obliged every one to cause ⟨his⟩ son ⟨to⟩ be as we say [be] bound apprentice to some trade, were anxious that they should not work themselves. They considered, and I believe with justice, that every sort of constant labour hurt the shape[e] and rendered him less fit for military exercises, which made the chief view of all lawgivers at that time. (We can know a taylor by his gate.) At Sparta there were no trades at all, and at Athens no free man was engaged in any. The freemen therefore could still go out to battle and leave the superintendence of their slaves to the old

83 men and the women. Thus at the battle of Chironea[7] | they had 9000 or ten thousand men, tho they had long before made great progress in arts and sciences. But in the Italian republicks, as soon as arts, etc. were improvd, there was an intire decradation and loss of courage in the whole state. This we may ascribe as the cause of th⟨e⟩ quick decay of Florence, Milan, etc. This naturally must happen, for no state can impose any very great and intollerable hardships, as the military service would be, in a refined state. Formerly it was not reckoned any hardship to serve in the field. The men of the best fashion served in battle. Those who are now knights were dragoons, and the other gentlemen or esquires were foot soldiers; and

[a] Replaces 'furnish'    [b] Reading of last two words doubtful    [c] Illegible word deleted    [d] 'Not right, I think' is written in the margin of the MS. beside this sentence    [e] Reading doubtful

[6] Presumably 69 above, though the statement there refers only to 'the ancient states', not 'all countries'. Cf. iii.140 ff. above.
[7] Chaeronea, 338 B.C., when Philip of Macedon defeated the Athenians and Thebans.

these, though of better fashion often than most of us here, thought it no hardship to serve 3 or 4 months in the year on their own expenses. The case we see was the same at Rome. Men of fashion then lived at the same ease and with no greater luxury in the field than at home, where they were generally employed in hunting. They fared as well, slept as soft abroad as at home, and had no particular business at home to engage them. Whereas nowadays, or whenever luxuyr*ᶠ* comes in after commerce and arts, nothing

84 but the most | urgent necessity, something which threat⟨en⟩ed the state with immediate ruin, could now induce men to leave their business and engage in war as a common soldier. The only people who could go out to war in this state would be the very lowest and worthlesest of the people. And these too could never be trusted, nor would they engage in any services with spirit, unless formed into what we call a standing army and brought under military discipline. Gentlemen will fight out of regard to their honour and love to their country; but it is fear only and respect of the officers which causes the lower sort, the common soldiers, to fight. Thus then when arts were improved, those who in the early times of the state had alone been trusted would not now go out, and those who before had never engaged in battle were the only persons who made up the armies, as the proletarii or lowest class did in the later periods of Rome. The armies are diminished in number but still more in force. This effect commerce and arts had on all the states of Greece. We see Demosthenes[8] urging them to

85 go out | to battle themselves, instead of their mercenaries which their army then consisted of; nor of these were there any considerable number. Whenever therefore arts and commerce engage the citizens, either as artizans or as master trades men, the strength and force of the city must be very much diminished.

2^dly, there is an other improvement which greatly diminishes the strength and security of such a state; I mean the improvement of the military art. The taking of cities was at fir⟨s⟩t a prodigious operation which employed a very long time, and was never accomplished but by     *ᵍ* stratagem or blockade, as was the case at the Trojan war. A small town with a strong wall could hold out very well against its enemies. They had no way to take it with any probability but by a blockade, and it would be very difficult to*ʰ* get any sufficient number of men to engage in such a tedious operation. Thus Athens held out for 2 years even after it had lost its navall force.[9] But when the method of attack, as now in use, by warlike engines

86 came to be | use⟨d⟩, and the ordering of zig-zag approaches was known,

---

*ᶠ Sic*       *ᵍ Illegible word, possibly deleted*       *ʰ 'do this' deleted*

---

[8] *Third Olynthiac*, 36.
[9] Presumably the reference is to the end of the Peloponnesian War in 404 B.C., but the interval was in fact less than one year.

the taking of a city was not near so uncertain. A skilful engineer can guess within 1 week or two what time a place will surrender; and if the army be somewhat more numerous and the attack properly carri'd on, the taking of it is certain. The besiegers in this case have the advantage. From the time of the expulsion of the chieftans to the Peloponesian war, that is, during the glory of Gre⟨e⟩ce, no city was taken without a blockade; Athens, Plaetea, and Syracuse were all attacked but in this manner, nor had they any other idea of a siege. But when battering rams, balistas, catapultas, and the regular methods of approach, and all the other branches of the military art were brought to some considerable perfection by Philip, who was a very great engineer, improvd by Alexand⟨er⟩, and still more by Demetrius
87 Poliorcites,[10] who took many cities in much shorter ⟨time⟩ | than was ever done before, every state of this kind held its liberty by a precarious tenure. A siege of 8[i] weeks, or two or 3 months, was a certain means of bringing it into subjection; tho these were not probably of such effect as our cannon (as        [j] contends⟨⟩) yet they facilitated the attacks very much, so that a place which would stand out now 5 or 6 weeks would then hold out perhaps 10 or 12. All states of this sort would therefore naturally come to ruin, its power being diminished by the introduction of arts and commerce, and its territory,[k] and even its very being, being held on a very slender tack after the military art was brought to tollerable perfection, as it had nothing to hope for when once defeated in the field.

We come now to consider what is like to be the fate of a conquering state, such as that of Rome, or Carthage, which, tho the catastrophe was prevented by the more speedy ruin brought on it by the Romans, yet before this [it] had extended its conquests over all the coast of Africa, over all
88 Spain, etc. These also must hold | by a very precarious tenure; not indeed that they are in danger from externall enemies,[l] but as their liberty is in danger by its own subjects. For when arts and[m] luxury have in the naturall progress of things been introduced into the state, and considerable improvements have been made in these, the rich and the better sort of people will no longer ingage in the service. The lower ranks make up the armies. Before the time of Marius[11] the whole of the Roman armies was composed of the better sort, of people of fashion and honour. But he accep[e]ted of freed men and all others of the lower class, and put them into the form of what is called a standing army under a sort of discipline; and of these all the armies at Rome from this time, as they had done at Carthage, consisted.

---

[i] Reading doubtful    [j] Blank in MS.    [k] Illegible word deleted    [l] Replaces 'violence'    [m] 'progress and' deleted

---

[10] Demetrius Poliorcetes ('the Besieger'), 336–283 B.C. Cf. Plutarch, *Life of Demetrius*.
[11] C. Marius (157–86 B.C.), rival of L. Cornelius Sulla (138–78), reformed the Roman army so as to make it a professional force instead of a militia.

They were composed of freed men, or liberti, of run-a-way slaves, deserters, or the lowest of the mob. An army of this sort, serving under a commander for severall years, and being engaged in[n] [in] war for severall years, would become very much dependent upon him. They would owe
89 to him their rank in | the army, and all indeed that they were worth in the world. If this generall then should be affronted at home, or any ⟨?way⟩ discontented, ⟨he⟩ would naturally ask redress from his army, who, as they would in this case be men of no principle, would as readily agree to assist him in all his undertakings; and if he succeed the government is at an end, as he can bring the whole under his power. From the first establishment of this custom, this allways happened whenever the case above mentioned occurred. Sylla took offence at the haughty and imperious conduct of Marius, at the head of his army of the sort above mentiond, and expelled him; but[o] Cinna[12] and others of his followers afterward[p] raised commotions in his favours, and at last he, after being successfull against Mithridates, returnd with great glory. Sylla being affronted at the treatment he had met with, he applied to his army, returned home, and after 10 or 12 battles
90 became perpetuall Dictator, and then overthrew the government. | But out of an innate magnanimity, which he possessed perhaps more than any other man, along with all his other qualities, he resigned his authority, and the republican form continued 30 or 40 years after, till the same thing happened under Caesar. Pompey was in the same condition as Marius; he had been successfull in the Sertorian war in Spain, against the pirates, and against the servile warriors, and against Mithridates and Tigranes, and came home with glory and admiration and was without question the head man in the state; of which authority he would not probably have made the same use as Caesar. He, being a bankrupt above 10,000000, got himself at the head of an army, with which in the 9 years he commanded it he conquered both the Gauls.[13] This gave him the highest reputation; the Gauls were to the Romans what the French are to us, the oldest and most formidable enemy. This eclipsed the glory of Pompey, and raised his jealousy
91 so [so] that he would not allow the people to | grant his demand of being elected consull in his absence. This affronted Caesar; he had recourse to his army who willingly joind him, and by repeated victories he became Dictator for ever. The remains of the same victorious army afterwards set Antony and Augustus, and at last Augustus alone, on the throne. And the same will be the case in all conquering republicks where ever a mercenary army at the disposall of the generall is in use.

[n] 'severall' deleted        [o] Reading doubtful        [p] The following words are deleted at this point: 'were allso expelled. This affronted Marius but'

---

[12] Cinna was consul in 87 B.C. and enforced the return of Marius from exile.
[13] Caesar campaigned in Cisalpine and Transalpine Gaul between 58 and 49 B.C.

*Tuesday March 1ˢᵗ*

In my last lecture I endeavoured to shew you how the republican governments naturally came to lose their strength and be ruind and that, 1ˢᵗ, with regard to the defensive ones. Here improvement in arts and cultivation unfit the people from going to war, so that the streng⟨th⟩ is greatly diminished and it falls a sacrifice to some of its neighbours. This was the case of most of the republicks of Greece. Athens in its later time could not send out the 5ᵗʰ part of what it formerly did. Besides this the improvement 92 of arts also weakens the security | as, as far as we yet know, the besiegers are more capable of taking the advantage than the besieged. The art of attack can be, as far as yet has been thought of, carried higher than that of defense. Thebes we see fell a sacrifice to Alexander on this account,[14] tho it was still but little advanced in the arts and could send out the greatest part of its men to war. Thus all defensive states at length fall a sacrifice to their neighbours.—I mentioned also what must naturally be the fate of a conquering republick. Of this sort we have an example in Rome. Athens too would have fournished us with an other example, had it not been for one particular constitution in which it differed from Rome. This was that the Athenians were very chary and scrupulous in admitting any one into the freedom of their city, and even when they admitted some great men and kings it was only to some of the priviledges of a citizen, as that of being free from imposts and customs at the port of Athens. Whereas the Romans were continually adding new members to the city, taking 1000ˢ and 10000ˢ by the slump from other countries. The reason of this was that the 93 | citizenship of Athens was attended with some profit and made a small livelyhood to him, and for that reason was a defalcation from the fortunes of the rest of the citizens, who would therefore never consent to the admission of new members, whereas at Rome the citizenship was not attended with any emoluments, and therefore they were not so chary of admitting others to the same rights. Athens accordingly never increased in its power so as to be able greatly to extend its conquests. But Rome increased vastly in power and opulence, which at last brought the common wealth to ruin. When the armies are fighting abroad the conquering state enjoys great peace and tranquillity at home. This length of peace and quiet gives great room for the cultivation of the arts, and opulence which follows on it. Commerce too will naturally introduce itself, tho' not, as now, particularly studied and a theory laid down. The industry of the individualls will necessarily occasion it. The wealth which this introduces, joined to that which is brought in by the conquest of other nations, naturally occasions the same diminution of strength as in a defensive republick. The better

---

[14] In 336 B.C., having revolted on the death of Philip of Macedon, father of Alexander the Great.

94 sort no longer engage in the service, and the army becomes a me⟨r⟩cenary one | and of the lowest people. These when the generall becomes dissatisfied naturally follow him as the person to whom they have been most indebted. The armies become more under the power of the generalls than of the people. This we see has been dreaded in all republicks. In the republick of Great Britain, as it was called, the Parliament soon grew jealous of their generall and leader Cromwell; they thought he ruled with too high a hand, and took measures to reduce him; they ordered him to disband his army, etc. He then applied to his army, not openly as those generalls Marius, Sulla, and Caesar, as he was a man of a much less generous temper, but in an indirect, canting way; they gave him their aid, reduced the Parliament into order, and established him protector, or monarch rather, of the republick. Of all the republicks we know, Rome alone made any extensive conquests, and became thus in danger from its armies under the victorious leaders. But the same thing was feared and must have happend at Carthage had the project of Hanniball succeeded, and he made himself master of Italy. His brother was at the head of a great army in

95 Spain, who had conquered that country | when servine*q* under him, and had he joined to this another victorious army from Italy, and had the party of Hanno,[15] as they probably would, got him to be affronted in the Senate, these two armies would probably have enslaved their country. The scanty allowances he had plainly show how jealous they were of him, nor does it appear that they ever intended his project should succeed. Aristocraticall lords are of all others most jealous of those who are any way distinguished in the state; and perhaps they would choose rather to be conquered by a for[e]eign enemy than by one of their own body. They have no ill will at the one as they hav⟨e⟩ at the other; they would be grievd to see their equall raised above them. The same jealousy the Athenians had against their generall Alcibiades. Thucidides[16] indeed justifies him from having had any bad design; and so far indeed we may say of all these generalls that they had not the subversion of the government in their view at first. But the temptation when offered is such as few men would be able to resist.

96 We can't pretend to determine what will be the form of government | in a defensive republick which has been over-run by its neighbours. This depends on the caprice of the conquerors, who may do as they please. It will commonly be of the same sort with that of the conquerors. Thus Athens established a democraticall government in the countries it subdued; Sparta again an*r* aristocracy, as that of 30 tyrants at Athens, as that which

*q Sic*        *r* 'democracy' deleted

[15] Leader of the aristocratic party at Carthage and chief adversary of the family of Hannibal.
[16] VI.28–9, 61.

most suited their customs, and we see too that those[s] ⟨?who⟩ the one sort favoured[t] of government were of the Athenian party and *e contra*. The Romans more politickally (as I shall shew hereafter⟨⟩)[17] reduced their conquests into the form of a province.—But there is only one form of government which can take place in a republick subdued by one of its own members. The action of subduing ones country, and (the army) the instrument by which it was performed, necessarily determine it to be a military monarchy. The army which conquered the country continues to be kept up as necessary to keep the people in awe. The Roman monarchs who succeded the Repub. were distinguished by [by] the name of *imperatores*, which was originally a title conferred by the army on successfull generalls. The government of Rome after this was entirely a government of soldiers. The army made the emperors, the army supported him in his authority and

97 executed his orders. The private affairs | of individualls continued to be decided in the same manner and in the same courts as before. The emperor had no interest he could obtain by altering those forms, and on the other hand the people would more readily submit to his authority when they were allowed to continue. But the whole of the executive and the far greater part of the legislative power he took into his own hands. The Senate, the praetors, and all the other magistrates became to have no authority of their own but were intirely his creatures. War and peace, taxes, tributes, etc. he determind without comptroll by the power of his army; but right and wrong were as equitably determin'd as they ever had before. In the same way we see that Cromwell by an army of about 10,000 men kept the whole country in awe and disposed of every thing as he pleased, more arbitrarily than they had ever been before, but left the course of justice betwixt man and man as before, and indeed made severall improvements. Both these here mentioned were military governments, but very different from those of Turky and the east. A system of laws had been introduced beforehand. This it was

98 not his interest to alter. He therefore left the | disputes concerning private property to be decided by the old rules, and even made severall improvements. He 1st changed[u] feudall holdings into sockage lands,[18] took away the *Navigation Act*;[19] and we see accordingly that the first thing done after the Restoration of Ch. 2[d] was to make a statute[20] in the 12th or 1st year confirming many of the regulations made by Cromwell. A new goverment

---

[s] 'of' deleted        [t] Numbers written above the last four words indicate that they were intended to read 'favoured the one sort'        [u] 'military' deleted

---

[17] 99 ff. below.
[18] Act of 24 Feb. 1645/6 (*Acts and Ordinances of the Interregnum* (1911), I.833) converted tenures by knight-service into common soccage. It was confirmed by Act of 27 Nov. 1656 (*Acts and Ordinances*, II.1043).
[19] Act of 9 Oct. 1651 (*Acts and Ordinances*, II.559).
[20] 12 Charles II, c. 24 (1660), i.e. twelfth year from the death of his father in 1649 (and his own proclamation as king in Scotland) and first from his Restoration in 1660.

always makes good laws, as it is their inte⟨r⟩est that the state should in its private affairs be under salutary regulations. Julius Caesar[21] we are told had the same project of amending, not of altering, the laws. And justice ⟨in⟩ private affairs was never better administered than under the emperors, and the worst of the empe⟨r⟩ors, Nero and Domitian.[22] Tho their cruelty made them often act with great barbarity, their interest lead them to improve the laws and keep up very strict discipline. The oppressions of the governors of provinces had never before been so thoroughly prevented during the republican form. Thus a military government admitts of regulations, admitts of laws, and tho the proceedings are very violent and arbitrary with

99  regard to the election of emperors and in the punishment | of all offenders against his dignity, who were punished without any triall, or by what was worse than none, a sham trial which was a mockery of justice. But in every other thing it was his interest that justice should be well administered. And this was the case in the Roman Empire from the time of Julius Caesar to that of the ruin of the Empire. But this government, as all others, seems to have a certain and fixed end which concludes it.—For the improvement of arts necessarily takes place here; this, tho it has many great advantages, renders the people unwilling to go to war. We see that foreign mercenaries have been in use in all such rich and opulent states; the Dutch never go to war but by an army of foreign mercenaries, whose officers are all foreigners also, for their no one can be spared from his work. This was the case of the Roman Empire. The provinces were all rich and had a considerable degree of commerce, the city was rich and luxurious, and the whole people unwilling to go to war. Besides, the publick revenues would have been greatly diminished, as it, in all commercial nations, is levied by tax or excise on

100 different manufactures. | It was then no longer the interest of the government to press its subjects to go to war. It becomes much more convenient to recruit their armys from the barbarous nations about it, both because they will accept of less pay, being poorer and not accustomed to high living as the subjects of the Empire are, and 2$^{\text{dly}}$, as it is not detrimentall to industry. This therefore becomes the policy of all governments in this state. The Romans recruited there armies from Britain, Scythia, and all the northern parts of Europe. This was at first no more than recruiting, having$^v$ got liberty for that purpose from the chief (as the Dutch had in Scotland).[23] But they found it afterwards still more easy to make a slump bargain with the chief to lead out a certain number of men, which he should maintain for a certain summ paid by them, and the command of

$^v$ Reading doubtful

---

[21] Suetonius, *Life of Julius Caesar*, 44.

[22] Suetonius, *Life of Nero*, 15; *Life of Domitian*, 8.

[23] Until the beginning of the Seven Years War: 29 George II, c. 17 (1756).

them is given to him, as he will be better able to raise a considerable number and to lead them out to battle. Whenever this chief becomes offended with the government, in the same manner as the great generalls of the Republick took possession of the command of the state and turnd it into a monarchy, so will he turn his forces against them and take possession for himself of whatever province he happens to be in. And in this
101 manner it was that all | the Roman provinces were taken possession of by the generalls who commanded in them at different times. In this manner it was that Clovis got possession of Gaul, and the Saxons of Britain. The generallity of writers mistake the account of this story.—The case was, as we are informed by the best writers, that Aeseius,[24] being pressed very hard in Gaul by the Germans and northern Scythian nations, told the Britains that they must provide for their own defence against the Scots and Picts, two nations who as we see from the poems of Ossian were much in the same state as the Americans, tho they dont appear to have had the custom of roasting men alive. The Roman army had before defended themselves by means of the wall they had built and in which they had always kept a garrison; but the army being withdrawn, the Britains or rather Roman colony, not inclining to leave the cultivation of their lands in which they had made a considerable progress, could not easily protect themselves. They generally tell us that Aeseius gave them their liberty. But this is not probable: for 1st, no government would ever give liberty to a province they
102 could possibly maintain; nor in the | 2d place, would they have taken it as any favour, as they had been a province for about 4 or 500 years, under the protection of the Roman army. They would not therefore think it any favour to be desired to provide for their own defence, that the government could give them no farther assistance, any more than a county in England or the colonies in America would to be deserted by Britain and left to defend themselves against the savages. This was what Aeseius did; he told them they must be at the trouble to defend themselves, as the army was necessary in Gaul, a province of more importance.[25] They not inclining to leave there work agree'd to bring over the Saxons, who came at first over[w] under Hengist and Ho      [26]. They soon expelled the Scots and Picts (who had before made many incursions and depradations), being a much more formidable nation, but finding that they had the whole country under their power sent over for others, who soon subdued the Britains and established the Saxon Heptarchy under the different chiefs. And in the

[w] Numbers written above the last three words indicate that they were intended to read 'over at first'

---

[24] Aetius, the *patricius* or first minister in Rome in the mid fifth century A.D.
[25] Hume, *History*, I.10.
[26] Blank in MS. Horsa: Hume, *History*, I.13.

103 same manner all the other provinces were usurped by those who had | formerly been their defenders. The others indeed who lay more contiguous to the heart of the Roman Empire were often attacked by them; but the Saxons were never disturbed. This however was the first settlement of the severall provinces. Such was the fate of the western empire. The eastern Empire fell[x] by the incersions of the Turks and Arabs.

In this manner the great security, and opulence, and progress of arts and commerce which takes place in a military government of some standing makes it both difficult and prejudicial to the state for the people to go to war themselves.[27] They begin therefore first to recruit amongst the barbarians, and afterwards to make a bargain with the chiefs. This was the policy of the Roman emperors from the time of Caracalla and still more from that of Dioclesian, Arcadius, and Honorius. From this time all the great men were chieftans of some barbarous nation. The patricians, which were formerly the men of old noble families, were no longer of that sort.

104 The patricius | was no other than the emperors Prime Minister, in which office some of these barbarous chieftans served him as well as in that[y] office of generall of his forces. These often would not submit to his orders, but rebelled from his authority and set up for themselves. Stilico,[28] Aeseius, and all the other great defenders or betrayers of the Empire were of this sort. Stilico we know betrayed it; and Aeseias indeed is said to have been always faithfull, but was nevertheless greatly suspected and was accordingly put to death by order of      [29], who was himself murthered afterwards by a defender and friend of Ae⟨se⟩ias.

### Wednesday. March 2[d] 1763.

In the last lecture I gave you some account of the government which takes place in a[z] great and powerfull republick when it is subdued by one of its own subjects, such as that of the Roman emperors, that which would soon have been the case at Carthage, which had very large territories on the coast of Africa and Spain, had it not been interrupted by the Roman arms.

105 It actually | took place in the great and powerfull republick of Syracuse, whose great general Dyonysius      [30] reduced it under his own power; and happend too in the British republick under Cromwell. This form is no other than that of a military monarchy. The manner in which it is attained to and the instrument which procures it make it still necessary to exercise the authority over the people by a military force. The greatest part of the

<hr>

[x] 'a sacri' deleted      [y] Reading doubtful      [z] 'gre' deleted

---

[27] Hume, 'Of Commerce', *Essays*, I.290.
[28] Flavius Stilicho, Roman general under the emperors Theodosius I and Honorius, was suspected by the latter of treason and was assassinated in A.D. 408.
[29] Blank in MS. Valentinian III, in A.D. 454.
[30] Blank in MS. The elder.

supreme power comes to be lodged in the hands of the emperor. The executive power and that of making peace and war was entirely in their hands; and the legislative power was so in effect allso, for they soon took the power of making laws from the body of the people to whom it originally belonged and gave it to the Senate. They, being intirely the creatures of the prince, were entirely directed by him, and the laws were in effect of his making. And we find that after the end of the reign of Augustus all the regulations or statutes were not what was properly called laws, that is, decrees of the

106 whole body of the people, | but senatus consulta,[31] as the senatus consultum Orphitianum, s.c. Tertul., etc. The emperor had also the power of appointing all magistrates and officers, of which they very soon deprived the people. The judiciall power came also at last in the last resort to the emperor. The people were at first the judges of all causes. The Senate had properly no judiciall authority. They had what is properly called a senatoriall power; they determind all the necessary previous steps[a] to peace and war, as levying armies, imposing taxes, and providing for the safety and convenience of the state. But the emperors took also the judiciall power from the people and gave it to the Senate, who as I said being intirely his creatures put it also, as well as the legislative, into his power. And we see also that about the time of Marcus, or Honorious and Arcadius, the laws were made by the emperors themselves, that is, the edicta et rescripta

107 principum had the same effect | as a law, and of such the Codex[32] is chiefly composed. The military power was that which put all his orders in execution. These governments were indeed military, but not of the same kind with those of Turky and the east. Tho in the R. Empire the nobles and great men who were obnoxious to the government were often, as we see from Tacitus and Suetonius, massacred in great numbers, yet those who lived at a distance from the court were under a mild government, and lived more peaceably and happily than they did under the Republick, as the governors were more frequently called to an account, and the people could always appeal; and in a word the ancient form of government as to private justice was still allowed to subsist. Whereas in the others there is no regulations or laws at all to direct the administration of justice. The difference is that the monarchy in the one case was formed by those who had lived under the laws in the ancient state, and when they founded the

108 new one it was not for their interest to abolish those | laws of whose salutary effects they themselves had been sensible. But[b] the others, in the

---

[a] Reading doubtful          [b] 'in' deleted

---

[31] i.e. resolutions of the Senate only and not of the Comitia or popular assembly. The Orphitianum (A.D. 178) and the Tertullianum (in Hadrian's reign) both dealt with succession between mother and child.

[32] That part of Justinian's *Corpus Juris Civilis* which contained imperial legislation. Imperial edicts and rescripts were in fact common from the second century A.D. onwards.

eastern countries, were all established by Tartarian or Arabian chiefs. The present Sultans, Grand Seignors, Mogulls, and Emperors of China are all of Tartarian descent. These had no knowledge of the benefit of laws; they therefore never thought of continuing the old or of establishing new ones. Their own authority was altogether absolute; the magistrates or bashaws they appointed under them naturally obtained the same power over those who were under their jurisdiction. They had not been accustomed to receive any restraint themselves, nor did they think of imposing any. The bashaws and every inferior magistrate have sovereign power in their own part of the empire. The people live<sup>c</sup> in a most miserable condition, having their lives and property at the mercy of judges of the lowest order, not much better than a pitifull Justice of Peace or sheriff.—They can indeed be called to account by the emperor, but the people have no way of complain-

109 ing. There is in this manner no laws | or settled method of administring justice. The caliphs who succeded Mahomet had indeed some better regulations with regard to the administration of justice; but they, falling on that account into peaceable industry and commerce, cared not to go out to war themselves and took the expedient ordinary in such cases: they called in the Turkamans to protect their country. This Tartar nation in the same manner, and others of their employment, in a short time overthrew the empire of the caliphs and made way for the Ottoman family into Europe. In the last the lecture before[33] I took notice of the manner in which defensive republicks come to ruin, and I observed also that the institution of slavery made those where it took place fail, but not so soon as the others, and indeed intirely alters the nature of the government. There was<sup>d</sup> not amongst all the republicks of Europe any one which was properly a demo-cracy. In some indeed of the smaller ones the people had the power of choosing the magistrates. But there is none where the body of the people

110 had the power of making peace and war, choosing magistrates, | levying taxes, and enacting laws in the last resort, which makes what is properly called a democracy. There were indeed some states who injoyed these rights for some time, but the people have always resigned that power into the hands of the great. The Venetians resigned their power for ever into the hands of the then magistrates, which gave occasion to the Venetian nobility. In a state where slavery takes place all the arts are exercised by slaves; the freemen are all idle and at liberty to attend the publick assem-blys. Whereas where no such constitution is allowd the freemen are all engaged in some trade, from whence they can not be seperated without great loss to the state as well as the individualls. I shewed also[34] that trade

---

<sup>c</sup> Reading doubtful          <sup>d</sup> Replaces 'is'

[33] Numbers written above the last five words appear to indicate that they were intended to read 'the lecture before the last'. Cf. 76–87 above.
[34] 82 above.

and commerce tend much more to enervate and weaken the military strength
of the state where there are no slaves than where there are. Slavery has not
been allowed in any of the modern republicks. The people therefore became
unfit to be burthened with the publick business, and gave up this power into
111 the hands of a few. Commerce and industry soon rendered | them very
rich. The Italian republick had in their hands at that time the most
profitable branccches of trade. They had the whole of the silk manufacture,
a very profitable one, and the greatest part of the linnen trade. Their
situation also gave them an opportunity of having the whole of the East
Indian trade that came into Europe pass thro their hands. The Cape of
Good Hope was not then discovered; the goods brought from the East
Indies were conveyed up the Red Sea, from thence into the Nile, and by
that means to Alexandria, where they were brought up by the Venetian
and Genoese merchants chiefly, and by them dispersed thro Europe.
Milan too, tho no sea port, had great commerc⟨e⟩. It was the centre of the
trade betwixt the other tns, and had besides the greatest share of the silk
trade, which all centered in it. The trade and manufactures in these
commonwea⟨l⟩ths soon intirely ingrossed the people, who had no time to
go to war, or their business would be ruin'd; these therefore, as well as the
other states, had recourse to mercenary troops; tho they were never very
112 powerfull nor*e* made any conquests, | they had occasion for troops for the
defense against other nations. They therefore engaged the chiefs of the
German, Helvetian, or other barbarous nations near the head of Italy to
defend their country, for which they paid very high subsidies. The dukes
of Milan, particularly        *f*, paid subsidies to allmost every prince in
Europe. We may allways judge of the wea⟨l⟩th of a nation when a war
breaks out by observing which of them pays subsidies to its allies. The
Empress Queen[35] and the King of Prussia never pay subsidies; their
extensive dominions make them powerfull, but their countries are not
rich. France pays large subsidies to its allies; Britain allmost maintains her
allies; Holland does the same when engaged in war; Spain and Portugall,
tho they have not commerce, yet derive great riches from their mines and
other rich products of their colonies, and accordingly pay some small
subsidies. The Italian republicks in the same manner paid subsidies to
some of the neighbouring chiefs who engaged to bring 10,000 or 5000
horse, which were then chiefly in request, for their protection. Every small
113 state had some of | these in their pay. This in*g* soon brought on their ruin.
For as soon as these generalls were any way affronted he turned the army
against them, who having nothing to defend themselves by, their only
resource then acting against them, always fell under his power. In this

*e* 'made great' deleted        *f* Blank in MS.        *g* 'the' deleted

---

[35] Presumably the Empress of Russia (Catherine II at this date) is intended.

manner　　　　*h* de Fero made himself master of Fero,　　　*i* de　　　*j*
of Milan,[36] and after him　　　*k* who was called in by his successors in his
turn compelled　　　*l* to give him his only daughter in marriage and settle
his dukedome upon him. The family of Medici in the same manner got
possession of Florence, tho not in so direct and open a manner.

I have now gone thro all the forms of government which have existed in
the world, as far as we have any account, except those that are now in
force in Europe. I have given you some account of the sort of government,
if it may be call'd so, which takes place in the age of[m] hunters; that imperfect and rude sort which takes place amongst shepherds; how these
form into states under a chief, which become at last republican, being at
first aristocraticall and afterwards democratical, of which there are two
114　sorts, either where slavery | is established or where it is not; and of the
military governments which arise from the conquest of a republick; and of
that which takes place after the conquest of savage nations. I shall therefore
proceed now to give you an account of the origin and constitution of these
severall governments. These as well as the others have taken their rise from
the same Tartarian species of government.

The German and other[n] northern nations which over ran the Roman
provinces in Europe were in the same form of government as the Tartars
still are, but somewhat more improv'd; they had the knowledge of agriculture and of property in land, which they have not. The first thing therefore which they set about after they had got possession of any kingdom, as
Britain, France, etc., was to make a division of the lands. In this division of
the lands the king or leader would have a very great share; the nobles or
other chieftans who attended him, and had each their seperate dependents,
had also their shares, less considerably[n] than those of the king but still very
115　considerable. | These they would give out to others, either for military
service or for a certain rent or for both. In this manner the allodiall
government of Europe, distinguished from the feudall, arose out of the
ruins of the Roman provinces. The feudall government arose[o] about 400
years afterwards, about the 9th century. In the allodiall government, the
lords held their lands of no one, but possessed them as their own property.
The burthens of wardenage, relief, etc. were not then known, and were
introduced long after. Besides these the old inhabitants of the country
possessed a good part of it. The Saxons indeed seem to have intirely ex-

*h* Blank in MS.　　　*i* Blank in MS.　　　Blank in MS.　　　*k* Blank in MS.
*l* Blank in MS.　　　*m* 'shepherds' deleted　　　*n* Numbers written above the last two
words indicate that their order was intended to be reversed　　　*o* Illegible word deleted

[36] Gian Galeazzo Visconti became first Duke of Milan in 1395; Francesco Sforza
married the natural daughter of Filippo Maria, the last Visconti Duke, and himself became
Duke in 1450. 'Fero' is perhaps Ferrara, ruled by the Este family.

terminated the inhabitants of England,[p37] or put them to the sword. They certainly did not admit them into their society, for tho their is a considerable mixture of the Saxon and Norman language in the Scots and English dialects, as those latter conquerors did not exterminate the inhabitants in

116 the same manner, yet there is no mixture | of the Erse or Welsh in either of them. The conquerors in other countries did not proceed with the same severity. The Franks in Gaul, we see, permitted the old inhabitants to continue. We see in their laws mention made both of the Franks and the Gauls. A man who killed a Gaul, or a Roman as they called him, was to pay for his composition 100 shillings, but for a Frank 300, and generaly the composition is tripled in that manner.[38] These allodiall lords, possessing great territories and having great wealth in rents of the produce itself, came to have a great number of dependents as they possessed the whole or the greatest part of the lands of the kingdom. This inequality of property would, in a country where agriculture and division of land was introduced but arts were not practisd, introduce still greater dependance[q] than amongst shepherds, tho there too it is very great. For amongst the shepherds one who had got possession of flocks or herds had them maintain'd by the

117 produce of the land, tho' he did not | pay any thing for it. But when[r] the lands were all appropriated, tho one had property in cattle it could be of no service to him unless he got liberty to pasture them from some of these great lords. Now at this time there was no arts practised by them. These people being[s] rough and wil[l]d[t] had no discipline amongst them; the country was infested by robbers and banditti, so that the cities soon became deserted, for unless their be a free communication betwixt the country and the town to carry out the manufactures and import provisions no town can subsist. The inhabitants were therefore dispersed, and settled themselves under the different lords.—Another accident, which happend a little before establishment of the feudall government[u] and tended to ruin the commerce of allmost all the western parts of Europe, was the depredations of the Normans and Danes, a rough nation who originally inhabitted the isles and peninsulas of the Baltick Sea and set out frequently on piraticall expeditions,

118 pillaging all the | maritime countries. They made frequent incursions, and frequently pillaged and at last conquered England; and tho our historians give us but an imperfect account of them, yet we find by our old ballads and poems that they made very frequent incursions. They also plundered all the coast of France, and at last conquered Normandy.—The lords

[p] Replaces 'Britain'      [q] Replaces 'inequality'      [r] 'agricult' deleted      [s] 'a' deleted      [t] 'people' deleted      [u] 'which' deleted

---

[37] Hume, *History*, I.401: 'The Saxons, who conquered England, as they exterminated the antient inhabitants . . .'
[38] *Pactus legis Salicae*, 41, provides for a penalty of 100 solidi for the homicide of a 'Roman' and of 200 solidi for that of a Frank: Montesquieu, XXVIII.3 and XXX.25.

therefore had a great number of dependents; some of these held lands of them as tenents, and others were retaind about the house and maintaind by the lord. These were[v] a set of idle-gentlemen who did not work but consumed the produce of the estate. Of these, which they called H          [w] villains, a lord would amount to 1000 or more. These two different parties in his dominions put it in the power of the lord to preserve good order amongst them. His tenents naturally hated those idle fellows who eat up the fruits of their labours at their ease, and were allways ready to give their assistance to curb the insolence of his retainers; they again were no less
119   ready to give their assistance to bring the tenents into | proper order. The king also found it absolutely necessary to grant the power of jurisdiction to these lords; for as he had no standing army there could be no other way of bringing the subjects to obey[x] rules. A debt could not be taken up, nor an offender punished, any other way. A kings officer would have been laughed at or massacred. This jurisdiction extended not only to those who were their immediate vassalls and dependents, but to all the free and independent men who held of no one (of which there were a considerable number) within certain limits. Besides the power he had of punishing and amerciating, he had also severall of those rights which we now reckon regalia. He had the power of coining money within his jurisdiction, and also of making by laws and statutes {Those which are now called manors in England were formerly allodiall lordships, which afterwards became barronnies and are now called by that name. In these there are still severall regulations with regard to succession and the holding of land alltogether peculiar to themselves.} which were of effect as far as his authority extended, both which would be very necessary at that time. The[y] chief members[z] of the state therefore were the king and these lords. But as there would be[a] a continuall jarring of interests betwixt these two parts of the state, it was necessary to
120   have some middle power betwixt them; | this was attempted to be made out of the other freemen of the severall counties ⟨?by⟩ severall regulations. Every county was divided into so many tythings, as they were called. These were supposed to contain about 10 families. Every man was obliged to enter himself as a member of some tything, and the severall members of it were accountable for the others and obliged to produce the members who had committed any offence, or if they could not do it, to pay his composition. Ten of these tythings made an hundred, and as each of the tythings were accountable for and had authority over the seve⟨r⟩all members, so had the hundred over all its members. Besides those there were also tr⟨i⟩vings, or trifings, which contained the third part of a county; but the particular office at this court is not well known.—Besides all these was a sort of supreme court in each county which was called the Wightenogema;

---

[v] 'just' deleted     [w] Blank in MS. Probably 'Hommes'.     [x] Illegible word deleted
[y] 'state therefore was' deleted     [z] Replaces an illegible word     [a] Replaces 'make'

in this the first member was the sheriff or officer sent to govern it and
121 regulate the affairs of it by the king. Next the bishops of the | county, and
the abbots, and even the abesses, for as I said the women of all barbarous
nations are intrusted with a considerable share in all their deliberations.
Then the great allodiall lords, of which there might be 3 or 4 in a county;
and lastly the wights or wise men, the senes, senatores, or patres; these were
chosen out of each trithing, hundered, or even tything, and from them the
court was called the Wightenogema, or the council of the wise men. To this
court were accountable not only the severall tythings but the hundreds and
even the trivings. — — —

### *Thursday. March. 3ᵈ 1763 [176]*

In my last lecture I begun to explain to you the nature of that government which the severall barbarous nations which over run Europe established in it after the expulsion of the Romans. This as I shewed was the
allodial government properly so called. We may observe with regard to it,
that it was made as nearly the same as was possible with that which they had
lived under in their own country. In that state the affairs of each hamlet or
122 small | district are decided by the severall members of it; any disputes
betwixt [of] those of different small districts by the members of larger ones;
and the affairs of the whole nation, or disputes betwixt members of the
different large divisions, by the assembly of the whole nation and their
leader or chief. The government which was established by the Saxons in
Britain, the Franks in Gaul, and the Burgundians and Wisigoths in the
south of France, were all of this sort.—The first court they established was
that of the decennry.ᵇ A barbarous nation are very jealous of each individual and oblige him to join with some decennry, and require that this
court should be accountable for the behaviour of each of the members of it,
and these passed judgement on all affairs within it. 10 of the deceneries
made a hundred; which decided the affairs of those who were [members of]
different the members ofᶜ decennries, which could not be tried in either of
them; and to it also lay an appeal to any one who was dissatisfied with the
judgement of his decenery. The whole of these within a county, meeting
together, formed the county meeting, which decided the affairs of the
different hundreds or appeals from any one. From this county also their lay
123 an appeal to the Kings Court, but this was | allowed only in two cases: the
1ˢᵗ was in case of a denial of justice, when the county court would not take
the cause into consideration; and 2ᵈˡʸ, long and unnecessary delay of
judgement, when they did not refuse absolutely to try the cause, but only
delayed it afterwards, which came to the same thing. This court seems to

---

ᵇ 'The' deleted        ᶜ Numbers written above the last four words indicate that they
were intended to read 'the members of different'

have been the same with that of the *Wittenogemot*. In it the king presided; next was the alderman or earl who was judge or president of the county and of all its affairs. Then there came the bishops and abbots and abbesses (as I mentioned already);[39] then the severall great allodial lords; and lastly the wi(ghts)tes or wise men. This form of government appears to be very natural and orderly. Nothing could be more naturall than that the affairs of the individualls should be decided by his neighbours. This made the decennry of 10 families or thereabouts, and that if he was not satisfied with this he should appeal to the greater assembly. And if a dispute happend betwixt the members of 2 different lesser assemblies this affair should be decided by both together; but as there was no regular assembly of that number the affa⟨i⟩r was left to the next greater one which had a right of trying causes. That from these again the county court determined all
124 appeals. And if an injury had been done to any one by a person | of a different county, as the peace of that county only had been broke in which the action was done, the affair was given over to its determination, whether it was the county to which the offender or the injured belonged; and[d] if this court delayed or refused judgement, the affair might be lodged before the Kings Court, which was the same with the Witten-ogemot.

This was the government which the Anglo Saxons meant to have established in Britain. But the power of the great lords soon destroyed the order and harmony of its severall parts.—These nations as I mentioned had no commerce of their own. Their lawless and freebooting manner of life also destroyed all the commerce and industry of the former inhabitants, who were obliged to leave the cities and seek possessions and protection in the lands of the several lords. These had no other way of consuming the product of their lands but by giving them out to persons who for that reason became their dependents. They were still but little advanced beyond the state of shepherds, and as they had property in land already established
125 those[e] who had got flocks or herds | could reap no benefit from them unless they got lands from these lords. This made the number of their dependents still greater than at any other time of society. The large territories which the Saxons gave to their great lords in this manner procured them immense numbers of dependents. These besides their military service generally paid a small rent, commonly in kind; or if it was in money, this money could be exchanged for nothing but the coarse and rough produce of the earth. This also he could consume no other way but by giving it out to his retainers and dependents. Thus one lord would have had 1000 about his house, and 5000 perhaps settled as tenents on his estate, who all were ready and engaged to follow him in arms to battle. He could therefore with ease, and no one else,

---

[d] 'from' deleted        [e] 'dependents' deleted

[39] 121 above. Cf. Hume, *History*, I.143–4.

keep pe[e]ace within those territories. His power was greater frequently than that of the county court itself, as the half or a third of the county was altogether under his direction. William of      *f*, who came over with W<sup>m</sup>
126 the Conqueror, got the whole of the county | of Chester for his share.[40] The only method by which one could obtain justice or payment of any debt which he had*g* to demand from one within the limits of his power was to apply to this lord; he easily could procure him satisfaction; but the king himself could not without involving himself in a war about a matter of little consequence. These lords therefore had great jurisdictions independent of all the courts, whose order was thereby intirely destroyed. This disorder increased in the same manner as their power, and at last it came to be generally apprehended that the great lord of a county was hereditary alderman or earl of the county, as he alone could execute that office with ease and could have hindered all others. In the same manner the chief lord in every hundred, etc. came to preside in it. And all these lords became judges, possess'd of large estates which they possessed*h* altogether free, without those burthens introduced by the*i* feudall government which I shall mention immediately. As they were always at war with each other and
127 often with the king, their whole power | depended on the service of their retainers and tenents; but the greatest part consisted in their tenents, who held their lands at first during pleasure, in which time they were called *munera* or presents. When therefore they had occasion to demand any extraordinary service of these tenents (either the lords or the king) they promised them the possession of their lands for a longer term of years. In this manner the munera became at first to be held for the life of the tenent, in which case they were called *beneficia*. Then in progress of time they were held for the life time of the tenent and of his son, and so on till they came to be altogether hereditary, in which state they were called *feuda*.[41] But in all these different forms, the ground on which they were held was that of military service, for which reason they capitulated for themselves that if the heir by age or otherwise ⟨?was⟩ incapable of performing those duties he should take him into his protection, and the lands also into his hands, and give them over to another, or procure by their means another, who would
128 perform those services which were required, viz | service in war and attendance in council. In this manner arose the emolument of wardenship. In the same manner came in the emolument of marriage, as soon as females were allowed to inherit; for then it became necessary that the lord should have it in his power to give her a husband who would perform those

*f* Blank in MS.        *g* Reading of last two words doubtful        *h* Replaces 'held'
*i* 'other' deleted

[40] Hume, *History*, I.405: 'He [the Conqueror] gave for instance to Hugh de Abrincis, his sister's son, the whole county of Chester.'
[41] Dalrymple, 161; i.122 above.

services in a suitable manner. And in some countries this took place even with regard to males, as the pupill was conceived to be accountable to the lord as his tutor in all cases for his marriage, and was liable to fine and amercement in case he marri'd without his consent.—3<sup>dly</sup>, as every person who held these lands was conceived to hold them for military service, so no one even of age was allowed to take possession of the estate at first. The lord took ⟨it⟩ into his own hands, which was called the right or emolument of primur seisin.⁴² And again when a pupil came of age, which was at first at 14, as the⟨y⟩ then could serve in war, afterwards when the armour became heavy at 18, and when still heavier at 21. In both these cases he had

129   ½, one, or two years | rent, according to the custom of the place, to give to the lord as a present before he was admitted to the possession of it; for nothing, not even the common acts of justice, were ever performd without a gratuity. These make the great characteristicks of the feudall holdings.

They had besides this another more accidentall emolument, viz that of escheat, derived from the French eschouter, to fall. If the family became extinct, then it escheated or fell to the lord, and the same was the case if the tenent refused service in war or attendance in council, or if he refused that he was his vassal or any way denied his authority. For these considerations the king gave up all his demesne lands, and the great allodiall lords their estates, to be held as feuda, which before had been held as munera. A tenent who held a feu was very near as good as property. He held it for himself and his heirs for ever. The lord had the dominium directum, but he had the dominium utile which ⟨?was⟩ the principal and most beneficial part of property. He became then considerable more independent than he had been before, tho he was still dependent, and considerably inferior to

130   allodial lands.—Allodium signifyed at first an estate in | land, fundus in general, when all land was free from any burthens. But after another sort of land was introduced, to wit, the feudall lands, it denoted those which were possessed in the old manner and signify'd free<sup>j</sup> land, whereas feudum denoted those lands which were held by the feudall burthens.—In the manner here mentioned all the munera which were already become beneficia, and all these inferior possessions, came to be held in the feudall manner.

When any of the great allodial lords was in danger of being oppressed by his neighbours, he called for protection from the king against them. This he could not obtain without some consideration he should perform to him. A rude and barbarous people who do not see far are very ready to make concessions for a temporary advantage. They therefore generally agreed to

<sup>j</sup> Reading doubtful

---

⁴² Prima seisin, the lord's right to possess the land on the death of the vassal, until payment of a relief by his successor.

hold of the king in the feudall manner, retaining all his jurisdictions and authority entired,[k] being subject only to the feudall casualties. In this manner the allodial[l] possessions as well as the munera and beneficia came to be feudall. This had come in before with regard to the inferior or allodiall
131 lordships. A small one of | this sort, situated betwixt two great ones, saw no better method to obtain protection and prevent his being swallowed up than to submit himself to the feudall holding. He would not consent to become a munera[m] possessor, as that made him hold precariously from having been altogether independent, he had ⟨no⟩ other method but to hold feudally; and this he would readily agree to, as he and his heirs were still secure of the possession, with the burthen only of those services and some other casualties, as that of *talliage*,[43] or a contribution to pay his lords ransom when taken prisoner, a present to make a dower for his daughter, and another to help to make his son a knight. Those services secured his protection, and in this manner the inferior allodial lords came to hold of the great ones, and these again of the king; and the whole thus held of him either mediately or immediately, and the king was conceived to have the dominium directum of all the lands in the kingdom.—But till within a[n] hundred and fifty years ago their were still some allodial lands, and the maxim nulle terre sans seigneur is but of late invention.—We will find
132 a great confirmation of this account of the feudall government | from Spelman,[44] tho he himself does not seem to have understood it and thought it arose immediately after the settlement of the Saxons and other German nations. Bouquet[45] has explaind it extremely well. He observes that there was hardly any feudall land in Britain before the conquest by William the Conqueror. The terms of the modern law were all introduced at that time[s] and were intirely unknown before. The Saxon law used, to denote the allodiall lands, the words *possidere, habere*. Our phraseology of tenere, etc. came about that time allong with the feudall law properly so called, when every one held either mediately or immediately of the king, who had the dom. dir. of the whole, and his tenents of whatever sort, noble or ignoble, the domin. utile. We may observe here also another mistake of the generallity of the writers on this subject. They seem to think that this change of the allodiall into feudall lands was an usurpation of the nobles, as they, according to their opinion, changed a precarious into a certain possession,
133 who took an opportunity | in the troublesome times to[o] nestle[p] and fix

[k] Reading doubtful     [l] 'holdings' deleted     [m] Reading doubtful     [n] Replaces 'these'     [o] 'settle them' deleted     [p] Reading doubtful

[43] Tallage: a money tax or tribute.
[44] H. Spelman, 'The Original Growth, Propagation and Condition of Feuds and Tenures by Knight-Service in England', *English Works* (1723), II.1 ff.
[45] Pierre Bouquet, *Le Droit public de France, éclairci par les monumens de l'antiquité* (Paris, 1756), 239 ff., gives the general argument without reference to Britain.

themselves in their estates. But this is altogether a mistake, and was on the other hand an augmentation of the ks power, as we find that there were many allodial lords before that time who were free from all burthens, as is shewn by Bouquet,[46] which were hereditary and had many of the regalia and jurisdictions: they had: 1$^{st}$, t                              ; 2,                              ; 3,                              [47]; 4$^{th}$, the power of making laws; and 5$^{thly}$, that of coining money. But the strongest proof of any is that$^q$ William the Conqueror, who was a very politick$^r$ prince$^s$ and ⟨k⟩new$^t$ what would aggrandize his own power, changed all at once the allodiall into the feudall government. He by an act of power obliged all the Normans and any of the Saxons whom he permitted to continue to hold of him in the feudall manner. Malcom Keanmoir, who was also a sagacius prince, changed them in Scotland in the same manner. From then the power of the king was as we evidently see greatly increased, and the goverment administerd in an orderly manner; the times after the conquest appear clear and enlightend

134 compared with those of the Saxon race. And the | same may be observed in France, where during the 2 first races, viz the Merovingian and the Carlovingian races, the greatest disorder and confusion overspreads every thing till the time of Hugh Cappe;[48] from thence justice and order begin to be established.

### Friday. March. 4$^{th}$ 1763.—

In my last lecture I endeavoured to explain to you the manner in which the allodiall form of goverment came to be changed into the feudall form. This change happend in the whole of Europe about the 9, 10, and 11$^{st}$ centuries. The lands were at first only munera; these were afterwards held as beneficia, and at last as feuda. The Germans, when carried out of their country by Conrad, in expeditions into Italy, complaind that there families would be ruin'd if they should not return, and Conrad,[49] to induce them to serve him with the greater willingness, promised them that their lands should be possessed by their sons and afterwards by their grandsons,$^u$ and failing them by their brothers and other relations; so that they at last became hereditary feus. This was in the end of the 11$^{th}$ or beginning of the

135 twelfth century. For as I shall | shew by and by, the progress of law and

---

$^q$ 'Malco' deleted        $^r$ 'and we' interlined above 'politick' with omission mark after 'prince'        $^s$ 'changed' deleted        $^t$ Reading doubtful        $^u$ Replaces 'grandfathers'

---

[46] *Le Droit public*, 258 ff., gives as the prerogatives of allodiality: the right of making laws, the right of life and death, the right of coining money, taking cognizance of false measures, the right of safe-conduct, raising of troops, raising of taxes, the rights over roads, game, and forests.

[47] Blanks in MS. The three missing powers are detailed at 136 below.

[48] Hugh Capet (died 996).

[49] Conrad II's *edictum de beneficiis* in 1037. Cf. i.122 above.

government was slower in Germany than in most other parts of Europe. If, before this time, any allodiall lord had wanted the assistance of the king or one who was more powerfull than himself, he would resign his lands to him and consent to hold them as munera or beneficia. But when lands came to hold by perpetuall tenure, they would rather take them in that manner. They[v] when in any danger or in want of protection held them feudally, which transaction was done in this manner: they resigned their lands intirely into the hands of the king, who afterwards gave them [them] back with a charter in which they were bound to military service with the three talliages or        [w] as mentioned in the last lect.,[50] to ransom the lord, etc. And in this manner all the allod. lands became feudall, and the different burthens of it were soon introduced. Sometimes for the present of a small piece of land they received from the king, they consented to hold both it and their other lands feudally.                        [51] of Scotland, by giving out
136 his demesne lands in feu, obtaind that all the other lands | of the great lords should be held feudally of him also; and in this the same form was used. They surrendered their lands to him and receivd them back with a charter binding them to the military service and other burthens. And in these feudall casualties the whole difference betwixt the feudall and the allodiall forms consisted; in the time of a minority, the rents of the estate did not as formerly go to the relations but to the king, and so in other cases. And on the other hand the feudall lords were more immediately under the protection of the king than when they were allodiall ones. He was bound to protect them, and this it was his interest to perform, as they were his vassals from whom he might expect to reap considerable benefit. The feudall jurisdictions still containd all that the allodiall ones did.[52] They had 1st, the power of deciding all matters respecting property within their baronry, earldome, or other jurisdiction; 2[dly], of determining all disputes concerning freehold land or        [x] and of succession; 3[dly], the power of life and death; 4[thly], that of making by laws for their own domain; and
137 lastly, | that of coining money; and allmost all the regalia which are considered as marks of sovereignty; being only subject in some measure to a lord still greater. The aristocraticall part of the feudall constitution was a good deal weakend by this, as they became greatly more dependent on the king, and were obliged from this time to manage and coax him to obtain those favours they might want of him; and we see accordingly that the kings in all countries favoured the feudall tenures.

In my last ⟨lecture⟩ I explained the form of government which took

---

[v] 'then' deleted        [w] Blank in MS.        [x] Blank in MS.

---

[50] 131 above.
[51] Blank in MS. Malcolm Canmore: Kames, *Essays*, 11 ff.
[52] Bouquet, op. cit., 296 ff.

place when the lands were allodiall. I shall now consider those which came in when they held in the feudall manner.—In the first place we may observe that the feudall govenment took away every thing which was popular in the allodial form; of which sort [there were] there are$^y$ many traces. The decennries were alltogether popular, and so were the hundreds and the

138 county courts. The$^z$ Kings Court was also in a great measure popular, | for tho the lords and earls were there in council, yet the wites chosen from the people sat there [also] in judgement also. But as I already observed the power of the allodial great lords in a great measure ⟨?prevented⟩ the free operation of this manner of government; so that at last the presidents or aldermen of the county court were not chosen by it or appointed by the king as they were at first, but the great lord or baron in the county became hereditary earl or president in it.—The feudall government however put an entire conclusion to all these courts; and all the lands fell under the immediate jurisdiction of the lords or of the king, who administred judgement in them either by himse⟨l⟩f or by judges sent for that purpose. In the council of the king none were allowed to sit but those great lords who held immediately of him. These were all called to a *colloquium* or conference with him; the word parliamentum did not come to be used for some time after. To these colloquia none were called but those who held in capite$^{53}$ of the

139 king. These were considered as companions or | comites of the king, and his attendants, and were peers or pares, equalls of each other. Nothing of importance with regard to the state was done by the king without their advice and consent, and any thing done without it could be of no effect as their power was such that they could easily have prevented the execution of it. Without their consent and advice$^a$ no laws or rules respecting the country could be made. These who composed the Kings Court were in this manner pares curiae regis, convivii, comites, socii regis. In the same manner those who made up the barons court were pares curiae baronis, convivii, socii, comites baronis. With these he consulted concerning all matters relating to the baronry.—They had all become his vassals voluntarily. They considered the expression that was in their charters of their being free and gratuitous deeds of the king or lord as a form, and it was in fact no more as they had promised him service in return for protection. They were all armed and ⟨?had⟩ a court of their own, composed of their

140 vavassores, so that without their consent nothing | could be done. Nor could they again without that of their vavassores. No regulations with respect to the country, no determinations with respect to peace or war,

---

$^y$ Reading doubtful        $^z$ 'county' deleted        $^a$ The numbers '1' and '2' are written above 'consent' and 'advice' respectively. Presumably the numbers are the wrong way round, and it was intended that the order of the two words should be reversed.

---

$^{53}$ i.e. tenants in chief holding their land directly from the king.

could be made or could possibly have been effectuall without the advice and consent of these lords. This made the government become altogether aristocraticall; the king as chief at the head of it, the lords, and their vassalls.— All those who held by military service of the king, whether it was immediately or thro a descent by intervening mean or middle lords, of which there were sometimes 5 or 6 betwixt the lowest vassall and the sovereign, all these as long as they held by military service were considered as holding by a noble tenure and had certain priviledges common to them all. 1$^{st}$, they could not be turned out of the possession of their lands on any pretext by their superior [with] without the consent of all their peers, and far less could they be put to death. Each of these would find it to be his interest that the others should get entire justice, as the same might soon have been his own case. Nothing could be done to a lord without a fair trial and

141 sentence pronounced against him before the pares | curiae regis. Nor could any thing be done or any proceeding undertook against the barons vassalls; they could not be turned out of their estates or deprived of their lives without a triall in curia baronis, before his peers, pares curiae baronis. Their maxim was that nothing could be done to a man without a trial before his peers. This still remains in some measure.

Besides these, which were honourable and noble tenures, there were two other classes of men, which were reckoned ignoble and contemptible.[54]— The 1$^{st}$ of these is the villains or slaves who ploughed and tilld the ground. These were reckoned incapable of property; they were bought and sold allong with the land estate. They were however in a much better condition than the slaves in ancient Greece or Rome. For if the master killed his villain he was liable to a fine;[b] or if he beat him so as that he died within a day he was also liable to a fine; these, tho small priviledges, were very considerable and shewd great superiority of condition if compared with

142 that of the old slaves. They had besides severall other priviledges, as | that they could be sold only along with the estate, so that they had the benefit of a marriage in which they were securd by the[c] clergy, who took care that they should not be separated from their wives. It was also a rule that if the lord used him unjustly, or did not plead his cause and appear for him in court when he was accused, and it was found that he had been innocent in this case, he was free. They were slaves in many things but had priviledges superior to those of other constitutions, as monarchicall governments are allways more gentle than republican to this order.

The 2$^{d}$ ignoble class was that of the burghers. These were at first slaves or villains who belonged to a certain lord or master to whom they paid a summ of money for the liberty of trading. They lived in small towns or

---

[b] 'in other cases indeed' deleted        [c] 'king' deleted

---

[54] Hume, *History*, I.404.

villages for the convenience of trading, but in but very small numbers. York
at the time of W^m Conqueror containd only about 300 houses, which might
be about 2000 persons. Trades men naturally choose to live in towns, as
they have there a market for their goods and an opportunity of bying those
143  | which they stand in need of; whereas if they stay in the country, there must
be a great loss of time in providing their tools,^d etc. and going to sell their
commodities. But at this time there was little encouragement for manufactures. The lawless and disorderly state of the country rendered communication dangerous, and besides there was little demand for any of the
produce of the mechanick. There were therefore but few of them in the
country and very small towns. The tradesman or merchant in a country in
that state would be altogether helpless. They^e were generally slaves of some
lord, or if they were poor freemen they became dependents either on the
king or on some great lord, according as their lands lay most contiguous
and were best able to afford them protection and liberty. By this means
they were very little better than villains or slaves of these great men.—The
king however, being jealous of the power of the nobles, found it to be his
interest to weaken their power and therefore ⟨re⟩leased^f all their villains,
and those more especially who were least dependant and could be most
144  easily | freed from their authority. These burghers were such, and were
therefore greatly encouraged by them, and we find accordingly that all the
burghers and freeed sort of slaves who lived in the villages or towns, which
any villain became who left his master and lived in one of these towns for a
year without being claimd, had the liberty of marrying whom they pleased,
of free trade, etc., without any toll.^55 They were afterwards formed into
corporations holding in capite of the king, having a jurisdiction and territory for which they paid a certain rent. At first this was taken up from every
individual, but afterwards the community farmed it, which made the
burthen much easier than when it was exacted without distinction by the
kings officers. In this manner these small towns became free and able to
protect themselves, as they had a stout^g stone wall about the town and kept
a constant watch and ward, which was one part of the duty of a burgher,
and were always ready for arms and battle to defend themselves against the
145  attempts of the | lords, who frequently disturbed them and often plundered
their towns.—During the time in which the burrghs were emancipating
themselves and coming into a state considerably better than that of the
villainage, another great change was going on. But still^h after this change
the burghers were looked on as a more contemptible sort of men, insomuch
that if the king or any nobleman married his ward to the son or daughter of

---

^d Reading doubtful          ^e 'had therefore' deleted          ^f Reading doubtful
^g Reading doubtful      ^h Reading doubtful

---

^55 Glanvill, *Tractatus de Legibus et Consuetudinibus Regni Angliae*, V.5.

a burgher even this was reckoned a disparagement, and they were declared
to be free from their wardship.

The feudall aristocracy at the same time came to decline. Feudall
property was originally, as I said, not much inferior to allodiall and was
confined to a few great men; but like all others, property came to pass thro
different hands. These (great lords or all who held of the king) had at first
a tittle to sit in Parliament with the king, and nothing was done in it
without their consent and advice as they only were capable of having
146 influence | in the kingdom.—At the time of W^m the Conquerror, the whole
land of England was, as we learn from^i        ^j, possessed by about 700 [h]
who held immediately of the king;⁵⁶ of these probably only 3 or 400 could
attend at the court, so that the assembly would not be so numerous as our
present House of Commons, which consists of about 500.—But in time the
lands came to be divided; parts were given off to second sons or other
relations, and the number of knights who held of the king by military
service became too numerous. In this case it was impossible for them all to
attend at the three different times of Michaelmass, Christian-mass,⁵⁷ and
Easter; and the very expence of these journeys would have ruined some of
them. Many persons now came to hold of the king by nights^k service. For
this reason Henry 3^d and Edward the 1^st of England, and Ja's 1^st of
Scotland desired these lesser lords to choose a representative out of each
147 | county to sit in the Great Council and give his advice and consent to the
determinations of the great body of the nobles.⁵⁸ These lesser lords were^l
possessed ⟨?of⟩ about a half perhaps of the lands in the kingdom; their
power therefore, tho less than that of the greater lords, was very considerable, so that their consent to all laws, taxes, or generall regulations was
absolutely necessary. They were all likewise baronis comites and pares
curiae regis, so that they were intitled to sit in the same court and council
with the others.—The burghers being also free as to marry, to trade, they
having also a walled town and paying only a small rent for the liberty of
trade, came to be considered as free. This rent was generally^m farm'd by a
slump rent which continued the same for ever from the lord, and this rent
continued still the same after the cities were vastly increased. It was then
also not levied by poll, which is always reckoned an uneasy way, but by
tolls on fairs and markets, which tho attended with some dissadvantages is
148 | nevertheless much preferable to the others. The burghers were also
allowed to send deputies to the court, from the similitude of their^n state to
that of the others, as the idea then was that all those who held in capite of

---

^i 'from' deleted    ^j Blank in MS.    ^k *Sic*    ^l Reading doubtful    ^m Illegible
word deleted    ^n 'more' deleted

⁵⁶ Dalrymple, 262; Hume, *History*, I.407.
⁵⁷ *Sic*. No doubt 'Christmas' was intended. Cf. Hume, *History*, I.410.
⁵⁸ Hume, *History*, II.88.

the king had a tittle to send represent⟨at⟩ives to Parliament. Tho the burghers themselves singly were not pares curiae regis, comites, etc. yet the whole corporation was. These did not indeed sit in the same court, but there consent and advice was necessary in all affairs relating to the public duties*o* and particularly the levying of taxes. This had in all countries been very grievous to them, and generally was heaviest on those who could least bear*p* ⟨?it⟩, as those who were stronger heaved off the load from their shoulders till at last it fell on them who ⟨?tho⟩ they could not bear it easily were obliged to submit, and this is the case*q* in all such circum. They therefore were greatly concerned*r* in all these matters. The same progress happened in the rest of Europe, as in Spain with*s* Philip the Handsom.

149        | *Monday. March. 7.*[th] *1763*—

In the last lecture I explaind to you the nature of that government which came in after the introduction of the feudall tenures. The whole business of the natiom*t* came immediately and directly before either the Kings Court or that of some of his barons. The democraticall part of the constitution was now altogether abolished; all the courts*u* of the people were now laid aside; and the inferior persons who formerly had a share in the sovereign court of the nation were now no longer admitted into the great court of the king. The only persons who*v* were admitted as members of it were those who held immediately of him.—As in the Grecian states the government*w* was at first a republican monarchy, that is, an aristocracy with a king at its head, so likewise was the government of Europe a democracy headed by a king, which however was greatly disturbed by the nobles even in the allodial government, and intirely subverted as soon as the feudall government was introduced thro all Europe excepting England. The only reason

150   why they did not in Europe as well as in Greece intirely destroy | the kingly power was the difference of the territory the nations possessed, which was not as in Greece a small territory of the size of a large county, with one large city in the midst of it in which all the great men were collected, but a large country thro which they were scattered, so that they had no such opportunity to meet and unite their joint strength against him. All they could do was to overthrow the democraticall part of the constitution and establish an aristocraticall monarchy. This was done in every country excepting England, where the democraticall courts subsisted long after and usually did business; and at this day the county court, tho it has not been used of a long time, is nevertheless still permitted by law. They ordinarily did business in all smaller causes, the greater, of felony and

---

*o* Reading doubtful     *p* Reading doubtful     *q* Reading of last two words doubtful     *r* Reading doubtful     *s* Reading doubtful     *t* *Sic*     *u* Reading doubtful
*v* 'held of him' deleted     *w* 'which' deleted

treason, being taken from them by the *Magna Charta* {the great foundation of the aristocraticall government}, till the institution of Justices of Peace,[59] who dispatch those affairs with much greater readiness and facility. The great court of the king was composed of those who held immediately of

151 him.—The kingdom was considered as one great fief, | the business of which was to be managed by those who held of that fief; every thing concerning the property or lives of any of these was to be considered in a court of the lords, his paramonts or peers; and in the same manner the business of the barons court was to be managed by those who possessed his fief.

I showed you also how the representatives which now make up the House of Commons came first to be called. The king was very jealous of the power of his[x] nobles, who frequently raised great disturbances and turned out many of the kings, John, Henry      [60] ⟨? and⟩ took the power for some time out of the hands of the others.[y] The king therefore took every method to lessen their power, and for this purpose as I mentioned he strengthened the hands of their villains as well as the vassals, and took every method to render them more independent, and also by supporting and strength⟨en⟩ing the burrows, which they did by allowing them to be formed into a corporation,

152 to defend themselves by a wall and guard, | to have the trial of certain small causes within their own limits in which they had a considerable jurisdictory power. In this manner they came to be very considerable, having perhaps two or 3oo men, which was then a formidable body as they were all trained to arms.—The reason that occasioned the kings calling his lords together was that their consent to all steps respecting the government was absolutely necessary, otherwise their power would have prevented the execution of it. The same reason held with regard to the burrows, as he could not raise those subsidies which he wanted to bear the expense of government without their consent. At first they were sollicited by emissaries sent by the king, who stipulated certain subsidies from them. This however was soon found to be very troublesome. They were therefore desired to send representatives to court as well as the barons, who might give their advice and consent to all the necessary regulations relating to the subsidies and other

153 expences of the | government.—The king as well as the nobles changed the knights service which was due by those who possessed his demain lands into what they called an escuage or scutage. When any one did not incline to go to war in person, he was bound to pay a certain some of money such as would be sufficient to get one to supply his place in the army, or that of his dependents. This was generally preferred to knights service; for those men of power and influence were generally very troublesome and unruly.

---

[x] 'vassals' deleted        [y] Reading doubtful

---

[59] 34 Edward III, c. 1 (1361).
[60] Blank in MS. Henry III. Cf. Kames, 'Constitution of Parliament', *Essays*, 28 ff.

Whereas when they paid money, this would enable them to procure other
soldiers as good as they, who also, being mercenary, would be more under
discipline and command. This escuage furnished a considerable pt. of the
kings revenue. The rest of it consisted entirely of 1$^{st}$, the feudall emoluments already enumerated; 2$^{dly}$, compositions, fines, and amercements for
crimes; 3$^{dly}$, all bona nullius, as wafes, strays, and treasure trouffe; 4$^{thly}$,

154  swans, royall fishes, and the great beasts of the chase.— | We are to observe
that all these necessarily diminished at the same time that the expense and
demands of the government encreased, so that supplie[ie]s, subsidies,
auxilia, became absolutely necessary. The people we see were always most
free from their severall burthens when the profits arising from them to the
state were most necessary for its support. We see accordingly that those
which are most favourable to liberty are those of martiall, conquering,
military kings. Edward the 1$^{st}$ and Henry the 4$^{th}$, the two most warlike of
the English kings, granted greater immunities to the people than any others.
There are severall reasons for this, as 1$^{st}$, they of all others depended most
on the goodwill and favour of their people; they therefore court it greatly
by all sorts of concessions which may induce them to join in their enter-
prizes. Peaceable kings, who have no such occasion for great services or
expensive expedition⟨s⟩, [and] therefore less courted their love and favour.
2$^{dly}$, it soon became a rule with the people that they$^z$ should grant no
subsidies till their requests were first granted. No subsidies therefore

155  | could be obtain'd without the grant of some priviledge or immunity
granted to certain members or bodies in the nation. His necessity obliged
him to grant these; and martiall princes are most liable to come into this
condition. These two ⟨?reasons⟩ made martiall princes always grant great
priviledges to their subjects. Philip Augustus of France gave great privileges to the people. Representatives in Parliament were first granted by
Edward 1$^{st}$, and the priviledges were greatly increased under Edwd. 3$^d$.
The House of York also, who were allways doubtful of their tittle to the
crown, seem to have made it a rule never to demand any subsidie or other
grant from the people without having previously granted some immunities
as a bribe.

The representatives of the burrows, as I said, always sat in a seperate
court from the others, being consulted chiefly with regard to those matters
which concernd the revenue. The representatives of the knights of the
shires, as their principalls had done before, sat in the same court with the
nobles. But when they multiplied greatly they became in process of time

156  so | insignificant that it could no longer be thought proper that they should
sit in the same court with the nobles; they were seperated from them and
joined to the burrow representatives. It however from this time became a
rule that no aid or subsidy could be granted which did not proceed at first

$^z$ 'should grant no' deleted

from the House of Commons; they had generally directions from their principals not to grant any subsidies till the peculiar grievances of that county, etc. were redressed; besides it is to be remembered that the Commons paid the far greater share of all subsidies; if the nobles paid 15, they 10;[61] if 8, 6; and so on. The nobility had now also come to be very numerous, and there were many whose fortunes were altogether insignificant. Their number and their fortunes would not allow them to assemble all at once. The king therefore called them some times to Parliament by letter, and sometimes did not, as he thought proper. These became distinguished from the rest, being barons[a] by writ. No one would now incline to go

157 unless summoned by the king, which letters or patent came in time | to be the mark of nobility. Originally one was noble by his tenure only; who ever possessed land of the king in capite was considered as such. But those only afterwards were considered such who were selected and pitched on by the king and called by these patents to court. This came by degrees to be considered as the mark of nobility. The other by tenure is now entirely laid aside. The lordship one possessed was what[b] formerly conferred the dignity of a lord upon one who possessed it. Whereas now one may be created a peer who is not possessed of the place he takes his title from, and even tho he is not possessed of any property in land at all.[62]

The power of the nobles however declind in the feudall governments from the same causes as everywhere else, viz, from the introduction of arts, commerce, and luxury.—Their power consisted in the number of their retainers and tenents. The number of their retainers and even of their dependents was owing to their plain and hospitable way of living. Richard Nevil,[63] who was sirnamed King        [c] from the great share he had in the

158 commotion at that time in favours of        and        [d] | an Earl of Warwick is said to have maintaind every day at his table in his different manors about 30000 men. He seems indeed to have been by far the greatest baron who has appeared in England since the time of W$^m$ the Conqueror.—But when elegance in dress, building, and gardening, cookery, etc. was introduced, it was no difficult matter to spend a fortune even as great as that of Warwicks, and by this means he would lose all his retainers except a few menial servants who could give him no influence. His influence over his tenents also came to be greatly diminished. The tenents were originally (as they were in the Highlands till very lately⟨)⟩ all tenents at will, who had very advantageous leases. The proprietor gave out some piece of land to some

---

[a] Reading doubtful        [b] Reading doubtful        [c] Blank in MS.        [d] Blanks in MS.

---

[61] Presumably a mistake for 'if the subsidy was 15, they paid 10'.

[62] Kames, 'Honour: Dignity', *Essays*, 86 ff.

[63] Richard Neville, known as the Kingmaker in the Wars of the Roses, became Earl of Warwick in 1449; Hume, *History*, II.361-2. Cf. i.120 above.

friend or relation for 100£, which produced perhaps to him 200. He again subset this to 100 for 40<sup>shs</sup> each, when they had to the value of 4 or 5 pounds; and in generall the rent was only about half of the profit. These intirely subsisted and depended on him as well as his retainers; they called him their master, which is the term still in use in this country, and would

159 readily attend him to battle on whom | their all depended. When luxury came in, this gave him an opportunity of spending a great deal and he therefore was at pains to extort and squeze high rents from them. This ruind his power over them. They would then tell him that they could not pay such a rent on a precarious chance of possession, but would consent to it if he would give them long possessions of them; which being convenient for both is readily agreed to; and they became still more independent when in the time of Henry 2<sup>d</sup> these leases came to sustain action at law contra quemcumque possessorem. Thus they lost a man for 10 or 5 sh., which they spent in follies and luxury. The power of the lords in this manner went out, and as this generally happened before the power of the commons had come to any great pitch, an absolute government generally followed. This was the case in England during the Tudor family. The nobles were then destroyed. They had been massacred by Edward 4<sup>th</sup> in his battles with Henry the 6<sup>th</sup>; afterwards in various insurrections and disputes for

160 | the crown.—The same thing happen'd in Scotland, with this difference, that the declension of one family here served only to raise an other; as the fall of the Cummin,s[64] made way for the Douglass,s, as they had not those arts which they had in England and which gave an [an] opportunity of spending his whole estate on himself. The Tudors accordingly were absolute. They imprisoned any one at will; which liberty destroys the freedom of the people altogether, as imprisonment will compell one to agree to any thing. The Parliaments had then no power, but were alltogether ruled by them, King Henry 8<sup>th</sup> and Queen Elizabeth. Freedom of speech was then a crime. A member happend to oppose a bill which Henry wanted to be passed. Henry called him asside, and putting his hand on his head told him, Man, I'm informed you opposed the bill; if you do so I will take off your head. This promise, as he generally stood by all of this sort, made the man alter his design.[65] And in the same manner the fall of the

161 nobles, having left no rivall to the | kings power, established an absolute government.—In order that the inequality of property should have the effect above mentiond, there must be a graduall declension and subordinate degrees of wealth. Thirty thousand pounds may at present be spent on domestick luxury, as their are intermediate steps of 25, 20, 15, 10000, and 1000, 100£ betwixt this and the lowest class, thro all which the progress of arts, manufactures, and industry can easily pass. But when property goes on in the progression by great leaps or jumps, the arts, commerce, and

---

[64] i.e. the Comyns.                          [65] Hume, *History*, III.128 note.

luxury can not creep after them. When this inequality goes on slowly, the arts follow, so as that one who spent 50 can spend a hundred, and goes still farther and farther; the luxury then easily traces the same course as the property. The case is otherwise with*e* great leaps, as nothing fills up the intervalls, so that luxury cannot keep pace. This is the case with sovereigns in most countries, as in Britain; the Civill Lis[is]t consists of about*f* £300,000, 30*g* times as great as the free mony of any estate, deducing taxes and public burthens, so that the luxury arts even*h* employed on a       *i* can

162 not | affect him so much that he will not be able to form many dependents and pensioners, as well as different offices as those of excise, custom, etc. Besides which he has the disposal of about three millions for the ordinary demands of the government. He cannot possibly spend all this, but divides it amongst different officers who become his dependents and followers. For these reasons the sovereigns have become absolute, as during the Tudors in England, after Henry 4*ths* in France, and also in Spain.—In other countries the arts and luxury have produced the very opposite effect, in establishing the aristocracy more firmly. After the time of Charlemagne, before the feudall government which first introduced order and regularity into Europe was introduced, the emperors of Germany had become elective; their authority therefore was much less than of a hereditary one. He is then an upstart [from]*j* from others who had as good a title; his elevation is galling and uneasy to them who had been before his equalls or nearly so. They therefore are very confident against him; nor are they affeard of the*k*

163 | resentment of his children, as they will not have any power mor⟨e⟩ than others. The nobility therefore opposed the emperor and at length overthrew his power. Germany is a large country, vastly larger than Britain and considerably larger than France, tho not so well peopled.—Large estates must therefore fall into the hands of single persons. In the great scramble of human society every ⟨?one⟩ scrambles to get as much as he can and keep what he has got. As in a mob, where 100*l* pounds are throw⟨n⟩ about in shillings, he will be a lucky man who should get 20*sh*, but if £1000 were thrown about, the same person would be probably able to collect by his strength 100, as he had more opportunities of taking from those about him. So in Germany, as the country is larger and ⟨?there is⟩ more to be scrambled for, one would get much more than in Scotland or England. The greatest estates in this country are altogether frivolous when compared to those of the Count Palatine, Marquis of Brandeburgh now*m* King of Prussia.

164 These and many others are now | altogether absolute. The introduction of luxury and arts affected the inferior people, but could not affect them, as their estates are worth some hundred thousand pound per annum.

---

*e* Reading doubtful          *f* Illegible figures deleted          *g* Reading doubtful
*h* Reading doubtful          *i* Illegible word     *j* Reading doubtful          *k* Reading of
last six words doubtful          *l* Reading doubtful          *m* Reading doubtful

They have therefore still a great number of dependents who follow them to battle, and their authority is often in their own dominions altogether absolute.

*Tuesday. March. 8!ᵗʰ 1763 ——*

In the last lecture I observd how the nobility necessarily fell to ruin as soon as luxury and arts were introduced. Their fall everywhere gave occasion to the absolute power of the king. This was the case even in England. The Tudors are now universally allowed to have been absolute princes. The Parliament at that time, instead of apposing and checking the measures they took to gain and support their absolute power, authorized and supported them. Henry the 7ᵗʰ was altogether an absolute monarch, and Henry the 8ᵗʰ still more so; Edward the 6ᵗʰ had no less power, which still if possible increased under Elizabeth. She indeed was much more mild and gentle in her conduct than her sister Mary, who was of all the English
165 sovereigns | the most absolute. In France their fall occasioned the absolute power of the sovereign which continues to this day.—The nobility came to ruin before any system of liberty was established. The luxury which followd on the arts ruind their power, who before had the only power to resist or stop the great sway he had in the nation; when they therefore were taken away nothing remaind to appose them. We see too that this has always been the case; the power of the nobles has ⁿ allways been brought to ruin before a system of liberty has been established, and this indeed must always be the case. For the nobility are the greatest opposers and oppressors of liberty that we can imagine. They hurt the liberty of the people even more than an absolute monarch. In an absolute government, as that of the Tudors, the greatest part of the nation, who were in the remote parts of the kingdom, had nothing to fear, nor were in any great danger of being
166 appressed by the sovereign, who | was terrible to those only who were near at hand to the seat of his court. Whereas every one is in danger from a petty lords, who had the chief power in the whole kingdom. The people therefore never can have security in person or estate till the nobility have been greatly crushed. Thus therefore the government became absolute, in France, Spain, Portugal, and in England after the fall of the great nobility.

The ruin of the feudall government which followed on arts and luxury had a very different effect in Germany; it occasioned the increase of the power and absolute authority of the great nobles or princes of the empire, and not of the emperor. Their estates were, for the reasons already explain'd, so much greater than those of the others below them that luxury could not surmount the great leap which there was necessary to get at them. They could not possible by any personall luxury consume all their

---

ⁿ Replaces 'must'

revenues; they therefore contrived to have a great number of retainers and
167 dependents, and have accordingly become absolute. | It had also for some
time before been the policy of the nobles to elect those for emperors who
had no, or very small, estates of their own, so that their power could not be
very great nor much to be feared. But when they elected Chas. V^th, who
had at that time the whole Spanish dominions, a very large estate in
Germany, and large possessions in Italy also, they being put on their
guard by the Elector of Saxony capitulated and treatied with him that he
should act in such and such a manner, giving up a considerable part of the
imperiall dignity. This had not before been necessary, but is still continued
on the death of every emperor of that family in which it has still continued,
and this capitulation generally deprives them of allmost any influence
merely deriv'd from their character as emperor. The princes have in this
manner become very absolute in their own dominions.

The absolute power of the sovereigns has continu'd ever since its
168 establishment in France, Spain, etc. In England alone | a different govern-
ment has been established from the naturall course of things.—The
situation and circumstances of England have been altogether different.^o It
was united at length^p with Scotland. The dominions were then entirely
surrounded by the sea, which was on all hands a boundary from its
neighbours. No foreign invasion was therefore much to be dreaded. We
see that (excepting some troops brought over in rebellions and very im-
politicly as a defence to the kingdom) there has been no foreign invasion
since the time of Henry 3^d. And        ^q himself was brought over by
       ^r to support him in his disputes with Henry.[66] The Scots however
frequently made incursions upon them, and had they still continued
seperate it is probable the English would never have recovered their
liberty. The Union however put them out of the danger of invasions. They
were therefore under no necessity of keeping up a standing army; they did
not see any use or necessity for it.—In other countries, as the feudall
militia and that of a regular one which followd it wore out, they were under
169 a necessity of establishing a | standing army for their defense against their
neighbours. The arts and improvement of sciences puts the^s better sort in
such a condition^t that^u they will not incline to serve in war. Luxury
hinders some and necessary business others. So that the very meanest sort

---

^o Illegible word or words deleted      ^p Numbers written above the last three words
indicate that they were intended to read 'at length united'          ^q Blank in MS.
^r Blank in MS.        ^s Illegible word deleted        ^t 'on' deleted        ^u 'hand and'
deleted

---

[66] The future French king Louis VIII invaded England at the end of King John's reign
and was in England when Henry III became king. There may be confusion with Louis IX
of France (St. Louis) who never came to England but was appealed to as mediator in the
dispute between Simon de Montfort's baronial party and Henry III in 1264.

only go to the wars. The better sort of mechanicks could not get a sufficient compensation for the loss of their time. An army composed of gentlemen has occasion for very little discipline; their sence of honour and character will make them do their duty. But when the army comes to be compos'd of [of] the very meanest of people, they must be formed into a standing army and a military discipline must be established; that is, the soldiers must$^v$ be put in such a condition as to fear their officers, who are still gentlemen, more than the enemy; in this case they will fight but not otherwise: they will follow them rather than flie from the enemy. This institution has therefore taken place in all countries where arts and luxury are established. We see in

170 France that Henry the fourth kept up generally a standing | army of betwixt 20 and 30,000 men; this, tho small in comparison of what they now keep up, was reckoned a great force, and it was thought that if France could in time of peace maintain that number of men it would be able to give law to Europe; and we see it was in fact very powerfull. But Britain had no neighbours which it could fear, being then thought superior to all$^w$ Europe besides. The revenues of the king being very scanty, and the demesnes lands, the chief support of the kings, being sold, he had no more money than was necessary to maintain the dignity and grandeur of a court. From all these, it was thought unnecessary as well as inconvenient and useless to establish a standing army. The States of France, the Diet of Sweden and Poland, and the Lords and Commons in England had the power of making what laws and regulations and imposing what taxes they pleased; the Tudors we see overruled all their debates, and if they had had a standing army they would have been able to have done what he pleased. But as the sovereign had no standing army he was obliged to$^x$ call his Parliament.

171 | This was the case in the time of the Stewart reign. Another thing ⟨?which⟩ also contributed to the diminution of the kings authority, and to render him still more weak, was that Elizabeth in the end of her reign, forseeing that she was to have no sucessors of her own family, was at great pains to gain the love of the nation, which she had generally done, and never inclined to lay on taxes which would she knew be complaind of; but she chose rather to sell the demesne lands, which were in her time alltogether alienated.[67] James 1$^{st}$ and Charles had in this manner no revenue, nor had they a standing army by which they could extort any money or have other influence with the people. They were therefore obliged to call the Parliament to obtain their consent. The Commons were now far from being insignificant, as at first, but had now great property, equall perhaps or greater than that of the nobles, and looked on themselves, as representing so powerfull a body, as on an equality with the peers themselves. They

$^v$ 'still' deleted      $^w$ Reading doubtful      $^x$ 'consult' deleted

[67] Hume, *History*, IV.729.

172 were, and I believe not without reason con|sidering the state of the king-
dom, very sparing and indeed nigardly in their allowances. Nor did they
ever grant even these pinched shares[y] [of] with[z]out taking away some part
of the royall prerogatives. In this manner in Jas 1[st] time, as well as in the
beginning of Charles 1[st], they took from the sovereign the liberty of taking
up loans and all sorts of taxes whatsoever without consent of Parliament.
They established their own liberty of speech, which had never before been
secured, and obliged him to communicate with them all debates concerning peace and war, and all state affairs. Many other such incroachments
were at this time made on the power of the sovereign, the necessities of his
condition oblidging him to accept of what conditions they pleased to gain
a small subsidy. At last an attempt to alter the form of worship in Scotland
(a very impolitick step⟨⟩) raised a rebellion in this country. The Scots army
marched into England. The king had no military force to resist them, nor
money to procure one. He applied to Parliament but found they were of

173 the same | sentiments as the Scots, being puritans at heart as well as they;
so that they would grant him no supplies. He was therefore obliged to
capitulate with them; but at last, not agreeing to their demands, they took
off his head. At the Restoration a step was taken which in the hands of more
vigorous princes might have established an absolute authority over the
people. A revenue of 1,200,000 was settled upon the king; this, had it been
employed in the support of an army, might have maintaind one which
would have kept in awe the whole kingdom. The King of Prussia maintains
a vast army on not much larger[a] funds, and Cromwell with less had just
before kept the whole kingdom in subjection. But the extravagant and
luxurious turn of Charles made him choose rather to employ it in the
pursuit of his pleasures, so that he became as necessitous and dependent on
Parliament as any of the preceding monarchs had been. James, being still
more extravagant both in his expenses and all his proceedings, was turned
out of his kingdom and a new family brought over. They, being altogether

174 |strangers and upstarts in the kingdom, were obliged to court the Parliament
more than ever and to submit to what conditions they pleased to impose;
and many were imposed which the weakest prince of the Stewart family
would not have agreed to. All this they were obliged to submit to in order to
obtain a very moderate supply. The kings revenues are made up of the
Civill List, the regular taxes imposed every year, and the extraordinary
ones which are granted from year to year. The Civill List amounts in this
reign to 800,000; in the last reign it was somewhat more; and in the
preceding reign it amountd to about 700, which was somewhat greater
than that in the two reigns preceding it. This summ is set appart for
maintain⟨in⟩g .the kings household and supporting the dignity of the

---

[y] Reading of last two words doubtful     [z] 'to the' deleted     [a] The last three
words replace 'much smaller'

crown, but might in the hands of more vigorous or ambitious princes give
the king more authority than the constitution of the kingdom designed he
should have. The other part which arises from the great[b] taxes laid on the
subjects, viz that on malt and that on land, which[c] varies from 2 to four
175 shillings | in the pound. These amount ordinarilly to something above
300,000£. They are set appart for maintain⟨in⟩g the marine and land forces,
the fleet and army, for which they generally suffice in time of peace, extraordinary supplies being granted in the time of war. The 3ᵈ part of the
revenue is the funds mortgaged to pay the debts contracted in the present
reigns. The creditors requird some security for this money. For this
purpose fixed taxes have been introduced, and the revenue arising from
them mortgaged for their payment. With ⟨?this⟩ the king can not meddle.
It is paid into the offices of the exchequer where it is perfectly secure. The
auditor and other officers of the exchequer are accountable for ⟨it⟩ to
Parliament and must give in their discharges to it, none of which will be
received except they be from the publick creditors appointed by Parliament. This part of the revenue can therefore give him no authority but as
it gives him the disposall of some very profitable places. It strengthens also
176 his interest against that of the Stuart family as these[d] | creditors would, on
their introduction, be cut out of both principall and interest. It is levied
indeed by his officers but never comes into his hands, but goes (as I said⟨⟩)
first to the exchequer and then to the creditors. There is generally a
surplus in these taxes above what is necessary to pay the creditors interest
to whom it is appropriated. This goes, being unnapropriated, into what is
called the unappropriated or sinking fund; this the king can never come at.
It is under the immediate direction and care of the auditors and other
officers of the exchequer, who, as they are officers for life with very high
salaries and are generally the first men in the kingdom, will not risque for
any consideration the loosing of those offices by granting the use of it for
other purposes than those to which it has been alotted. The Civill List is
established indeed at the beginning of every reign, but gives[e] in the present
management no authority, as it is all expended on the luxury and magnifi-
177 cence of the court and the household of the king. | The other part[f] which
is[g] revenue, viz that raised from land, excise, and customs, is alotted[h] for
the fleets and the army and is granted from year to year. The mortgaged
taxes are necessarily perpetuall; the Civill List for the life of the king; and
the other part is occasionall,[i] which would therefore fall if the Parliament
was not called. The funds for the support of the armies and fleets also
depends on the grant of the Parliament; so that the whole of the govern-

---

[b] 'reve' deleted     [c] 'amounts to' deleted     [d] Reading doubtful     [e] Reading
doubtful     [f] The following words are deleted at this point: 'which is collected for the
maintenance of the standing army and fleet is raised from year'     [g] 'a standing'
deleted     [h] Reading doubtful     [i] Reading doubtful

ment must be at an end if the Parliament was not regularly called. So far is
the king from being able to govern the kingdom without the assistance of
Parliament for 15 or 16 years, as Chas. 1ˢᵗ did, that he could not without
giving offence to the whole nation by a step which would shock every one,
maintain the government for one year without them, as he has no power of
178 levying supplies. In this manner a system of | liberty has been established
in England before the standing army was introduced; which as it was not
the case in other countries, so it has not been ever establishd in them. The
standing armies in useʲ in those countries put it into the power of the king
to over rule the Senate, Diet, or other supreme or highest court of the
nation.—The supreme power in legislation is here divided betwixt the king,
Lords, and Commons. A law may begin in either House and be passed by
the other. The king cant however interfere after the debate is begun and
tell them that he dissaproves of such or such a debate, tho he may recom-
mend one to their consideration before it has been consider'd. Money bills
however can not begin anywhere but from the Commons. The Lords
indeed have disputed this priviledge, but we see it has been possessed by
the Commons for above 100 years. The Lords can only either assent to it
simpliciter or refuse it simpliciter, but can not alter or add to it in any shape.
The king has in all cases the power only of putting his assent or negative
179 | to a bill, and the denying any bill that has passed both Houses, being
altogether unpopular, has gone into dissuse. The king has always given his
assent to every bill since Wᵐ 3ᵈˢ time. Charles 2ᵈ was so sensible of it
being altogether disagreable to the people that he never attempted it, tho
he often used methods very low and mean, as the stalingᵏ of a bill, etc.; the
umbrage this would give, he thought, was less than that of plainly refusing
it. The Civill List and the standing army are the only things which can any
way endanger the liberty of the subjects. The Civill List is so considerable
that in the hands of designing, vigorous, and ambitious princes it might
give them an influence far superior to that which the dependance of a few
officers about the palace can bestow. But customs of this sort are very
difficultly changed by any prince.—The standing army might also without
doubt be turned against the nation if the king had attained great influence
with it. But there is one security here also. Many of the persons of chief
rank and station in the army have also large estates of their own and are
members of

*End of Volume Four of MS.*

v.1 | the House of Commons. They have in this manner an influence and power
altogether independent of the king. It would never be their interest to join
with the king in any design to inslave the nation, as no consideration he

ʲ Reading doubtful        ᵏ Reading doubtful

could bestow on them will be able to turn their interest to his side. So that however mercenary we should suppose them, those at least may be depended on who have a seat in the Parliament or offices depending on it.

*Wednesday. March. 9<sup>th</sup> 1763.*

In yesterdays lecture I explaind to you how a system of liberty came to be established in Britain after the fall of the nobles, not indeed immediately after it but about 100 years after the race of the Tudors had become extinct and the Stewarts came to the throne. There were two great causes which contributed to bring about this change.—The 1<sup>st</sup> and chief was the situation of the kingdom, which made a standing army be thought unnecessary. The want of this made it impossible for the king to establish laws or levy taxes without the assistance of the Parliament. The kingdom had indeed been ruled by Chas 1<sup>st</sup> for 16 years by proclamations and edicts; these
2 under Henry the eights time also had very nearly tho not | altogether the authority of an Act of Parliament, and were sufficient to keep the people in awe. Dissobedience to them would have been highly punishable, but this was not then the case. The other cause which had a considerable effect also was that the ancient and ordinary revenues of the crown had been more dissipated*ˡ* in Britain than in any other country. The remains of the ancient demesnes lands had been intirely alienated by Elizabeth, who, seeing she was to have no issue, becoming careless in what condition her successor should receive the government, engratiated herself with ⟨the⟩ people by decreasing the expences of the govt., particularly in the end of her reign in the war against Spain, by the money procured by the sale of these lands, as is particularly explaind by Ld Bolingbroke.⁶⁸ In this manner a greater defalcation of the revenues of the crown had been tried here than any where else. As the king also had no standing armies he could of himself raise no taxes or subsidies, and was altogether dependent on Parliament. The House of Commons had also the ascendency over the House of Lords as*ᵐ*
3 at this time. The number of voices | in that House was much greater; they consist of about 500 members, whereas the Lords are not much above 200; and of these 500 there are perhaps 200 possessed of as great property or greater than the Lords. But besides this personall influence, they had a still greater one as being the representatives of the whole body ⟨of⟩ the people both in the burrows and the country, and in this light as it were the weight of the whole people. The nation in generall also trusts them much more

---

*ˡ* Reading doubtful          *ᵐ* Reading doubtful

---

⁶⁸ *Remarks on the History of England,* Letters 13 and 14 (*Works* (1841), 369 ff.) for general praise of Elizabeth's economy; for the sale of demesne lands, Hume, *History,* IV.729.

than the nobles. The nobles, it may be feared, will have respect to the aggrandizing of their families and fortunes as it is from them that they derive their influence. The Commons on the other hand must have a respect to the voice of the people and the good will of their constituents, which they must endeavour to maintain as their authority depends on it; they therefore have the compounded weight[n] of their own weight and that of the people also.[o] They have also a considerable influence from the old custom that all money bills should take their rise from them; and money bills
4 now | make the greatest and most important part of any. The members of the House of Commons are also much more accustomed to debate and deliberation than the Lords, so that on the whole the far greater part of the bills take their origin from them, and generally pass of course before the Lords. The Lords would now have hardly any business were it not for the Scots appeals, at which there are ordinarily not above 4 or 5 present,[p] unless it were on deliberations on the concluding of a peace or other such important transaction. In all other cases the Commons have by far the greatest and most considerable share. The Commons also endeavoured to establish a custom which would have put all bills on the same footing with money bills, and given the Lords no more power than that which the king has, viz that of assenting to or refusing a bill without altering it. This they attempted by what they called a tack, that is, a clause join'd to a money bill in which some thing of a different nature was included, and saying that this was a money bill they[q] demanded that the Lords should have only the power of refusing etc. it as a money bill. But this they never would agree to,
5 as every law would have | been put into the form of a money bill.

Liberty thus established has been since confirmed by many Acts of Parliament and clauses of Acts. The system of government now supposes a system of liberty as a foundation. Every one would be shocked at any attempt to alter this system, and such a change would be attended with the greatest difficulties. The chief danger is from the Civill List and the standing army (as above).[69] One security for liberty is that all judges hold their office[r]s for life and are intirely independent of the king. Every one therefore is tried by a free and independent judge, who are als⟨o⟩ accountable[r] for their conduct. Nothing therefore will influ⟨en⟩ce them to act unfairly to the subject, and endang⟨er⟩ the loss of a profitable office and their reputation also; nothing the king could bestow would be an equivalent. The judge and jury have no dependance on the crown.—The sheriffs indeed in many counties of England as well as in Scotland are appointed by the king, but

---

[n] Numbers written above the last two words indicate that their order was intended to be reversed     [o] 'are generally the body from which all laws begin' deleted     [p] Illegible word deleted     [q] Illegible word deleted     [r] Replaces 'independent'

---

[69] iv.179 above.

this office is also for life, and is not attended with great dignity and no
6 profit,ˢ so that many pay a fine of 500£ to be excused from it. | The dis-
posall of it can give no influence to the king, nor can he greatly over rule
them, orᵗ act contrary to law and justice. One who levied any tax which was
not authorised by Parliament may be tried of robbery, and that too in the
way of appeal, which the king can not pardon, tho he can those on indict-
ment or information. So that no one will readily be influenced by the king,
his protection or orders not being able to screen one from justice. Another
article which secures the liberty of the subjects is the power which the
Commons have of impeaching the kings ministers of mal-administration,
and that tho it had not visibly encroached on liberty. This power still
remains, tho it has not been exercised since the time of William 3ᵈ. This
priviledge as well as many others favourable to liberty we owe to that
tyrannical prince, Henry 8ᵗʰ. The ordinary method which they took to get
free of any of his ministers of whom he had become jealous was to get him
impeached by his servile House of Commons, and from this time they have
7 still retaind it. The king can not pardon an | appeal, that is, a prosecution
at the instance of a private person; he has that power only with regard to
indictments, that is, when the grand jury finds the bill to be true, or what
we call the relevancie, and afterwards delegates the particular case to the
committee or lesser jury. These he can pardon as well as ordinary infor-
mations, but not appeals; nor for the same reason can he pardon impeach-
ments, as they are at the interest of another body.—The fear of disgrace
and loss of reputation, as well as this of capitall punishment, from which they
can not appeal or be pardoned, serves to intimidate the ministers from
attempting any ⟨?⟩ against the commonwealth, and secures the liberty of
the subjects and establishes those great rights which they have now
obtained. The *Habeas Corpus* Act⁷⁰ is also a great security against oppression, as by it any one can procure triall at Westminster within 40 days who
can afford to transport himself thither. Before this Act the Privy Councill
could put any one they pleased into prison and detain him at pleasure
without bringing himᵘ to triall. Now no one can be imprisoned anywhere
but in the county gaol or the nearest to it where the crime is said to have
8 been committed; he cant be sent out of Britain to Jersey, | Guernsey, or the
plantations, that is, alway⟨s⟩ within the extent of the Hab. Corp. Act.—
This sufficiently secures the liberty of the people; for tho many could not
afford the expense, yet it is not such who will be in greatest danger from the
king. The rich and powerfull are most obnoxious to his displeasure; tis
rich and not poor folk who are sent to the Bastile in France. No judge can
oppose the Habeas Corpus Act; infamy and a high penalty are the punish-

ˢ *Sic*        ᵗ Reading doubtful        ᵘ 'self' deleted

⁷⁰ 31 Charles II, c. 2 (1679). The period is 20 days. Cf. ii.129 above.

ment which attend it. No influence of the king could ever induce them to make any such attem⟨p⟩t. And so strict is this Act that in the time of rebellions or other exigencies of the state, when it is necessary to imprison[v] without such speedy triall, it is commonly taken off for 6 months. But it will never be allowed to be reppealed, as that would destroy in a great measure the liberty of the subject.

The frequency of the elections is also a great security for the liberty of the people, as the representative must be carefull to serve his country, at
9 least his constituents, otherwise he will be in danger of | losing his place at the next elections. In an absolute government favours are bestowed and all publick offices conferred on the favourites of the king. But in a country like this publick favours are generally bestowed on the active, bustling, important men; such are most bold to demand any favour for their constituents, and are in this manner naturally more distinguished than the others; and it is not a bad way that power should be conferred on those who have naturally the greatest influence. The more frequent these elections are, the more dependent are the representatives. It was for this reason that the Parliaments were changed after the war ⟨of⟩ 1715 from trienniall to septenniall ones,[71] as it makes them less dependent on their constituents and diminishes the democraticall part of the government. The voice of the people for the same reason is of less importance towards the beginning of a Parliament than towards the end, as they are then nearer the time of their next election. The minister therefore generally contrives to get any im-
10 portant business, as the making of a peace | and such like, done in the beginning of Parliament, as if it were near the end an opposite party might raise a faction which would be very troublesome.—The method of elections is also an other security peculiar to England. The elections of members for the burrows were formerly on the same footing in England as they are in Scotland; they were in the hands of the aldermen and common councill men. But before Ch. 1s[w] times there were some burrows where the elections were in the whole body of the people, and in the Parliament of 1642, who were very democraticall, it was orderd that all elections should be in the hands either of the freemen of the burrow or of every inhabitant of it, every one as they say who has a boiling pot. This manner is altogether democraticall. It is impossible ⟨?but⟩ that the person chosen should be one whose character is agreable, at least in the town where he is chosen member. But in Scotland they are altogether oligarchicall, so that one who is
11 most obnoxious and disagreable to the body of the town may be chosen | if he has interest enough with the magistrates, which money will procure; but no bribe will settle a mob who has once taken up a prejudice against one,

---

[v] Reading of last three words doubtful      [w] Reading doubtful

---

[71] 1 George I, st. 2, c. 38 (1716).

so that he must have at least a tollerable character in the town. It is the same way with the county elections. No one has a vote here who does not hold of the king, and has a considerable yearly rent above £600.[72] But in England every one who possesses land to the value of 40[sh], whether it hold of the king, of a subject, or be only a lease for a life or for lives, if he can swear he makes 20 sh of yearly profit from it.[73] The numbers are here much greater and 3 or 4000 will be much more formidable to him than 30 or 40.[74] Our government is therefore much more aristocraticall than that of England, and we see that when we had a seperate Parliament it really was so. The House of Commons also has the sole judgement in all controverted elections, and is on[x] them very nice and delicate, as their interest leads them to preserve them as free as can be had.[y] These laws and established

12 customs render it very difficult | and allmost impossible to introduce absolute power of the king without meeting with the strongest opposition imaginable. This of the length of the Parliaments, and the great extent of the Civill List which may bribe both the electors and the elected, is the only things which appear to be dangerous to liberty, and this too will not probably go far; it may indeed influence them so far as to obtain the passing of bad laws ⟨?but⟩ would not be sufficient to obtain any law to be passed which should evidently take away the liberty of the people. They must evidently perceive that the money they get to pass such a law will be the last they will ever receive, if they put it in the kings power to raise[z] a summ of money. They will therefore never agree to pass a law which should supersede the necessity of calling a Parliament.

Another thing which tends to secure liberty is the form of the courts of justice. The kingdom[a] ⟨?⟩. Formerly the kings courts were in the same form as the justiciary courts in Scotland before the year 1745. The judge in

13 them or president | was the bailey of the lords courts, who was not only in this manner justiciary but also factor or stuart to the baron. He both collected the rents of the estate and judged of all matters within it. The justiciary under the king were in like manner also the collectors of [of] the revenue due to the king. This connection was very naturall. The sheriff or county officer was the person to whom all fines, amercements, and compositions for crimes were payable, and these made a very considerable part of the revenue along with the feudall emoluments. No property could

---

[x] Reading doubtful   [y] Reading of last two words doubtful   [z] Reading doubtful
[a] Several illegible words deleted

---

[72] 400 pounds Scots, by Act, 1681, c. 21 (A.P.S. VIII.353, c. 87).
[73] 8 Henry VI, c. 7 (1429) gave the county franchise to those possessing a freehold worth 40 shillings a year.
[74] Dalrymple, 274: 'While there are above 30,000 voters in some particular counties in England, there are not above 3,000 voters in the whole kingdom of Scotland, freeholders and common councilmen included.'

be given from one to another either by volunt. transf. or succession without a fine to the king and such like, and as the sheriff was the collector of all those fines, it was naturall[b] to constitute him judge in them also. {The sheriffs used to keep accounts of this which they called sentence money which was given up to the king.} The Chief[c] Justiciary was the same at this time with the chief officer of the exchequer or receiver of the revenues. His power soon came by this means to be near equall to that of the kings him-

14 self from this two fold office, and he became an | object of jealousy to the king. The Parliament and the exchequer seem at this time to have had the same members, only when they considered any matters relating to the revenue they met in the exchequer chamber, the table of which was covered with a chequered cloth, from which it got the nam[am]e of *scaccarium, exchequer*.[75] The chief officer or Justiciary in this manner came not only to be the judge of causes but also the collector of the revenues, as he who gathered in the rents was appointed also to determine causes in his court. This bailey was generally some writer or such like who had but a very imperfect notion of law.[d] The Magnus Justiciarius in this manner became very powerfull, and so much on a level with the king that Edward the 1st, who could not brook a rivall, took away his power. This court had a little[e] time before three severall powers, that of judgement in criminall

15 causes, of common pleas, and | fiscall causes. But the Court of Common Pleas was seperated by John, as it was found inconvenien⟨t⟩ to have the court which tried those causes removed about with the Kings Court, as it often introduced discontinuances. Edward however took away this office entirely and divided this court into four, that of the Common Pleas; 2d, that of Kings Bench; and 3dly, that of the Exchequer; and the Court of Chancery, which was at first only an office of briefs.[76]

### Thursday. March. 10. 1763.

I had observed an other thing which greatly confirms the liberty of the subjects in England.—This was the little power of the judges in explaining, altering, or extending or correcting the meaning of the laws, and the great exactness with which they must be observed according to the literall meaning of the words, of which history affords us[f] many instances. The judiciall power in the kingdom was at first given in the very same way as it

---

[b] Replaces 'necessary'        [c] Reading doubtful        [d] The words 'This is not exact the following lecture explains it' are written vertically in the margin opposite the last two sentences        [e] 'that' interlined and deleted        [f] 'with' deleted

---

[75] T. Madox, *History and Antiquities of the Exchequer* (1711), 109. *Scaccarium* is medieval Latin for a chess-board.

[76] Briefs: the Scots term for the English writs. Cf. G. Gilbert, *Historical View of the Court of Exchequer* (1738), 7; Hume, *History*, I.411.

was in the courts of the barons and lords, by the steward or bailiey of the baronnie who collected the rents and all fines for the deciding of controversies, and all other funds of the barons dues, and at the same time was judge in all these causes.*g* So the Magnus Justiciarius in the kingdom had
16 also the fiscall power and collected and managed | the kings revenues. He was here called Magnus Justiciarius or Chief Justiciary, and in France the Mayer de Palais. This officer, having those two offices joined, came to be in time, in France at least, a greater man than the king himself. We see, as it happend in [in] France, after this office had continued for some generations in one family the authority they must have from the judiciary and fiscall power together would in that length of time be more felt and give them greater influence in the different parts of the kingdom, over the whole of which their power extended, than the king himself. We see accordingly that the Mayers de Palais during the two first races of the kings of France usurped the kingdom. This was first done by Charles Martel, and afterwards from his descendents by Hugh Capee. Edward the 1st, one of the most prudent of our kings, who seems to have known what he did as well as any one, dreading least the Great Justiciary should serve him in the same way as the Mayer de Palais had done the French kings, abolished his authority all together.[77] Before this time there had been one defalcation
17 made on the power of the Justiciary | in the time of King John. They at first had*h* the justiciary, common pleas, and fiscall causes in them,*i* but as the Justiciary attended the king in his progresses thro the kingdom to execute justice, and his court followed that of the kings, it was found necessary to seperate one of these powers from him, which was given to the Court of Common Pleas. The three powers which they possessed, or rather the three sorts of causes which they tried, are, 1, the power of judging in all civill causes betwixt man and man, principally in cases of land property, as contracts do not in an early society sustain an action; $2^{dly}$, he tried all criminall causes; $3^{dly}$, he acted in a fiscall capacity, in which case the[y] prosecutions are betwixt the sovereign and the subjects, and all demands for money, either as rent or debts of any sort betwixt them, are decided either from the king against the subjects or from the subjects against ⟨the⟩ king. All these three different parts of the judiciall power were united in the Great Justiciary.

We may observe that the form of process in criminall causes is always very different from that in civil. The process of criminall causes is always very short. The jury bring in their verdict, being all enclosed together. A triall of life and death needs but one hearing; the crime is alledged, and the
18 witnesses brought on both sides, and sentence is passed at once; | nor is

---

*g* Reading doubtful     *h* 'both' deleted     *i* Reading doubtful

[77] Gilbert, op. cit., 10–11; Hume, *History*, II.122.

there any appeal from this sentence.—But for the value of 40$^{sh}$ in England
one may be sued first before a Justice of Peace,[78] and there may demand
abatements, delays, etc. and may put of⟨f⟩ the sentence for 3 or 4 months,
and if he is not satisfied he may carry it from thence to the sheriffs court;
from thence to the Court of Common Pleas; from that again by a writ of
error to the Court of Kings Bench; and from that again to Parliament;[j]
and may in this manner delay the sentence for a very long time. We should
naturally think that the triall should be longer in a case of life and death,
and greater time allowed for the examination of the cause, as the life of a
man is a thing to him invaluable,[k] than for the pityfull sum of 40$^{sh}$. But we
see the contrary has always been the case, and the reason is plain from what
I have already observed[79] to be the foundation of punishment. The whole
of criminal law is founded on the fellow feeling we have with the resentment of the injured person. Revenge, as we[l] commonly say, is a hasty
passion: it wont wait for a delay of its gratification but demands it immediately, and the[m] prosecution dictated by our fellow feellings partakes of
19  the rapidity of the passion they were excited by. But there | does not appear
to be any thing so urgent in a demand for 40 shs. The rumour of a crime
excites the indignation of a whole corner of a country, and we are sensible
that immediate satisfaction ought to be given him; his passion demands
such gratification. But a debt does not appear to have any title to be so
eagerly prosecuted. The one demands a short trial; the other may reasonably be allowed or admit of delays from time to time. The prosecution of
civil ⟨?causes⟩ is therefore always dilatory, and is in danger of becoming
more and more so by the arts and evasions of the prosecuted. It is necessary that in civil cases there should be some time set to go thro with a
prosecution; that is, that delays and interruptions should operate a *discontinuance*. It would be very hard that if after the court was summoned
the parties should not appear or be any ways delayed, [that] the prosecutor
should be still able at any time to take up his suit where he left it. Any such
delay, when the suit is not carried[n] on in one uninterrupted            o
operates a discontinuance, and when he renews[p] his suit the whole must be
gone over again from the beginning, and all his former expences are lost.
Now, when the Justiciary Court followed the Kings Court, discontinuances
20  were | unnavoidable, as the parties could never attend the king in his
progresses. It was however no grievance in criminall causes that the court

---

[j] 'I think he said so' is interlined at this point, above a line drawn over the words 'that
again to Parliament'    [k] Reading doubtful    [l] 'generall' deleted    [m] 'satisfaction' deleted    [n] Reading doubtful    [o] Illegible word    [p] Reading doubtful

---

[78] Not the Justices of the Peace but the sheriff had a jurisdiction limited to 40 shillings:
Gilbert, op. cit., 6.
[79] ii.89–90 above.

was removed, as they are always decided by one hearing. This inconvenience was very soon perceived to require a remedy; it was therefore provided by *the Magna Charta* in King Johns time that communia placita (that is, common civill disputes) non sequuntur curiam domini regis sed in aliquo certo loco habentur,[80] and after that time they were always tried at Westminster and might be brought to it from any part of the kingdom. The criminall and fiscall powers however still continu'd joined; but Edward 1st, desirous to humble the power of which he was so jealous, [he] therefore divided the power of this officer betwixt three severall courts who had each a different set of officers.—These were the Court of Common Pleas, the Court of Exchequer, and the Court of Kings Bench.[q] Before the first of these is tried all civill causes betwixt subject and subject, ⟨?and before the second⟩ those betwixt the king and the subject for the nonpayment of any debts. Criminall causes of all sorts were brought before the Court of Kings

21 Bench; and it was also made superior to the Court of Common Pleas, | as any cause may be transferred to it by a writ of error, or what we call here an appeal. It was called the Court of Kings Bench because the king used to sit in it in person, some say till the time of Henry 5, and we certainly know he did till the time of Henry 3d, on what was called in banco regis; but now he can not sit in any court in person but must judge all caus[s]es by his officers.—The Chancery was at first no court at all, but merely an office of brieves and records; the business of the Chancellor was to record all writs and transactions that had been passed.

When Edward had thus broke the judicial power, the persons whom he appointed as judges were generally of the meanest sort of no fortune or rank, who had been bread to the knowledge of the law, and very frequently these were clergy men. I observed before[81] that at first all jurisdiction was executed precariously. Criminall causes were determined by judges merely as mediators to make up the quarrell, and civill ones either by mediators or arbitars chosen voluntarily, and in every case not with the strong hand as

22 it is when government is more establishd, | but with great hesitation, caution, and tenderness. When therefore this power was in the hands of mean persons, the        [r] of the Common Pleas, the        [s] of the Kings Bench, and the auditor of the Court of the Exche[ck]quer, being all low men who depended on the will of the king, they would be very unwilling and afraid in any shape to go beyond the meaning of the law or any ways to

[q] An oblique stroke in the MS. at this point is followed by an ampersand and what appears to be an abbreviation for 'Chancery'. These words have apparently been struck out, and the words 'in after' [reading doubtful] are interlined above them.        [r] Blank in MS.        [s] Blank in MS.

[80] 'Common pleas shall not follow the King's Court but be held in one fixed place' (art. 17).
[81] ii.95 above.

alter it;[82] and therefore in all cases brieves and writts were drawn out according to which they decided justice, and exact records of all proceedings were kept in the officina brevium. When therefore one wanted to raise suit in any of the courts of justice, the method was that the person went to the Court of Chancery and related his case to one of the clerks of the [the] Chancery who looked over all the writts and brieves to see if he could find one which should comprehend his case; for unless it agreed exactly it could be of no value. If he found one that agreed he drew one out for you, changing the names and circumstances of it but altering nothing of the form. But if there was no brief or writ in Chancery which agreed with the case, one

23 could not go to any | of the courts nor obtain any redress. The Chancery was at that time on the same footing in England as it is at this time here, merely an *officina* brevium. But there is this difference, that the Court of Session, being of late institution and formed in great part on the cannon and civil law, one may apply to it immediately, except it be in some things of mere form as serving heirs,[t] tho that also was the case here formerly.— The brief being granted was sent to the sheriff of the county wherein the person charged lived, with a writ beginning precipimus desiring him to send up to the court such a person to answer to s[h]uch a charge which had been broug⟨h⟩t against him. And this is the form at this time with very little alteration. The mean⟨n⟩ess of the judges renders them suspected both by the king and the people by the irregularity and injustice of their proceedings. And we find that they have been often tried and fined for bribery and corruption. Edward himself levi'd at one time by fines for bribery about £100,000 of the money then current,[83] which is equall to above £300000 of the present coin and in value would be then as much as

24 1000000, and above two or three years revenue at that time, so | that the bribery must have been very excessive. They were therefore orderd to judge by the strict law, and were to be tried in their proceedings by their own records, which were kept all along with great exactness, and no alteration, explanations, or amendments of any sort would be admitted, and any attempt of this sort would be punishable. This is the case to this day in many causes, and indeed is so in all where it is not taken away by the statutes of amendment, and in these a wrong spelt word or any such innacuracy destroys the whole, as these jeophels[84] or amendments are not

---

[t] Reading doubtful

---

[82] There is some confusion here, since the passage seems to refer to judicial officers like the justices of the Common Pleas and the King's Bench and the barons of the Exchequer whose adjudicating function could be said to be limited by original writs. The auditor of the Court of Exchequer (unlike the treasurer) had no judicial functions.

[83] The fines were 100,000 marks: Hume, *History*, II.68.

[84] Statutes of Jeophail (from jeo faille, I am in error) begin with 14 Edward III, st. 1, c. 6 (1340). They allow amendments of pleadings.

allowed, particularly with regard to<sup>u</sup> processes of outlawry. In jury courts
amendments are allowed of innacuracy even after the verdict is pronounced; but in appeals (or private criminall prosecutions) of all sorts, and
many other, no amendment or explanation is allowed, and this it is which
causes appeals to be so little used. There<sup>v</sup> is no remedy to be got from the
courts unless the brieves or writs in Chancery comprehend the case, and
here the words of the brief are to be adhered to exactly, or if there be any
particular statute with respect to any<sup>w</sup> cause, the words of the statute are in
25 like manner to be observ'd exactly. The exactness of the records | makes
any departure very easily perceivable. The judges therefore being at first
mean men, as the peers and higher clergy were alone accounted honourable
at that time, has given occasion to the smallness of their powers.—Another
thing which tended to support the liberty of the people and render the
proceedings in the courts very exact, was the rivalship which arose betwixt
them. The Court of Kings Bench, being superior to the Court of Com.
Pleas and having causes frequently transferred to them from that court,
came to take upon it to judge in civill causes as well as in criminall ones, not
only after a writ of error had been issued out but even immediately before
they had passed thro the Common Pleas. This they did by a fiction of a
tresspass,<sup>85</sup> that the person conceald himself and would not appear at the
court when he had been cited; a writ representing this, called a writ of
latitat, is issued<sup>x</sup> out and sent to the sheriff, desiring him to find him out.
A plea concerning land could not be put on this footing, but all those
26 disputes which arose from contracts, from | trouver and reversion, etc.,
could. Now all civill causes may be brought immediately before it. Sin⟨c⟩e
a reformation was made not very long ago in the method of their proceedings, a great<sup>y</sup> part of causes go to it immediately. There could be no method
of turning criminall into civill causes, nor could they make any evasion of
the law in that head. The Kings Bch. Court therefore incroached on the
Court of Common Pleas, but that court made no incroachment upon it.

The Exchequer however which at firs⟨t⟩ tried causes only betwixt the
king and the subjects for money due, brought in also causes betwixt the
subjects to this court. When one was sued for a debt due to the crown, he
told them that because such an one owed him so much money he could not
pay, but that if he could get payment from him he would clear the whole; on
which a writ of quominus et precipimus, in as much as such an ⟨?one⟩ owes,
etc., we order. In this manner they introduced civil causes into their court;
and as every one is some way or other debtor to the king, he can easily by

---

<sup>u</sup> 'statutes' deleted    <sup>v</sup> Illegible word deleted    <sup>w</sup> 'thing' deleted    <sup>x</sup> Read-
ing of last two words doubtful    <sup>y</sup> The last two words replace 'most'

---

<sup>85</sup> By this process, called the Bill of Middlesex, the defendant was summoned with the
allegation that he had committed a (fictitious) trespass in that county. If he failed to answer,
the writ of *latitat* was issued, alleging that he was concealing himself.

means of that debt introduce his own cause into the Court of Exchequer.—
27 The profits of these courts | depended chiefly on dues from the severall causes they tried, what we call in this country sentence money; from them also the clark and notaries derived their fees. As the whole profits of the courts thus depended on the numbers of civill causes which came before them, they would all naturally endeavour to invite every one to lay his cause before their court, by the precision, accuracy, and expedition (where agreable) of their proceedings, which emulation made a still greater care and exactness of the judges. The Chancellor was at this time only an officinarius brevium. He had also appointed him the triall of some[z] causes of lesser moment, which were called the petty bag in distinction to the others which were put into the hamper. And in these smaller causes his [his] authority first began, tho it was[a] at this time subject to the Kings Bench. But in Edward the 1st and Edward 2d,[b] and more so in the time of Edward the 3d, it was found that commerce and frequent intercourse of trade made many cases occurr to which no record or statute then in use could [not] extend,[c] which proved very detrimental and could not go long without
28 a r[r]emedy. | The Chancellor was therefore desired that if the wrong complained of agreed not with any single brief but was comprehended under any two or more, he should cause the clerk to make out a new brief in that form. By this means the Chancellor had a right of judging whether any cause had a remedy provided for it. This was at first no more than forming a new brief to the courts of justice. In this manner he was as it were the judge of the *point of law*, and the courts had only the matter of fact to examine. Many causes would however occurr in which there was no fact disputed, in which case there could be no use or necessity to carry it before the courts; the cause had been already decided and this would be to no purpose. In these cases the Chancellor could give a sufficient remedy. And in this manner it was that the equitable Court[d] of Chancery began. {But it not only considered of those which had only a point of law to be determined, but others also, especially those in which the common courts had provided no remedy.} It is not, as we are apt to apprehend it, a court to which appeals, as we call or          [e] or writs of error, can transferr a cause from the other courts, complaining of an unjust and unsatisfying sentence, for it receives
29 | none such, nor has it any connection with them. But when one wants to have his cause tried by the Court of Chancery, he relates his story to the court, representing at the same time that the courts of common law can grant him no redress.

The Chancellor as was mentioned soon began to consider those cases which the common law did not comprehend. The first thing he did in this

---

[z] Replaces 'all'    [a] 'afterwards' deleted    [b] Reading doubtful    [c] 'to' deleted
[d] The words 'and in many cases' are interlined above 'equitable Court' and deleted
[e] Blank in MS.

way was to order specifick performance of contracts. These were not sustaind by the common law; all they did was to give the pursuar damages but did not think of forcing specifick performance. This however a man was bound in honour to perform, and the Court of Chancery, which was considered as a court of concience with the Chancellor at the head who was generally a clergy man skilled in the cannon law, began to give action on this head. Anoth⟨er⟩ thing was all cases of trust and fraud. In the same manner as the common law gave no validity to contracts, neither did it

30  oblige one to perform the trust committed to him. This | was remedied by the Court of Chancery. This included also the transference of property*f* by sale, which came about that time to be carried on by lease and release; and other such methods already mentioned. 3ᵈ

*Gap of about four lines in MS.*

4ᵗʰˡʸ, the Chancellor gave validity to all wills and testaments, and all sort of successions and*g* legacies. This also gave them the power of obliging the clergy. It had been customary to leave great estates to the clergy in different parts of the kingdom. And as they were by this means likely to swallow up a great part of the lands of the kingdom, a statute was made forbidding any lands to be left in mort-main, that is, to corporations. But as the clergy had still the directions of the conciences of dying persons, they prevailed on them to leave their*h* lands to certain persons for the use of the church. The common law gave the church no satisfaction in case the person did not

31  perform his trust; but this also was sustain by the | Chancellor. These are the chief funds of all disputes, as I already mentioned. Most of them arise either from contracts; or from wills and disputed sucessions from them, for sucession ab intestato is generally altogether clear; or lastly from contracts of marriage, which is partly a contract which operates during life and parttly of a settlement to take place after death. All these*i* came to*j* be tried by the Chancellor. And in this manner he who had at first no court at all came to take a great deal of the business from the other courts.

### Friday. March. 11ᵗʰ 1763 —

In the last lecture I showed you how the liberty of the subjects was secured in England by the great accuracy and precision of the law and decisions given upon it, as well as the causes which brought this about, as well as how it came to pass that the judges in England have less strength in explaining or correcting the law than any where else—the judges at common law I mean, for the Chancellor is certainly as arbitrary a judge as

32  most. But neither is he very dangerous | to the liberty of the subject, as he

---

*f* Illegible word deleted        *g* Reading doubtful        *h* Reading doubtful
*i* 'to' deleted        *j* 'be' deleted

can not try any causes besides those which have no remedy at common law. Nor can he in any case act directly contrary to any method of proceeding laid down by the courts of common law. And from this court as from all others appeals may be carried before the House of Lords.

The first cause of the great strictness of the law is the ordinary method of proceeding in the courts, which[k] must be commenced by taking out a writ in Chancery, according to which they must form the suit and pronounce sentence without any deviation from the exact words of the brief; or if the action be founded on any particular statute, the words of the statute must be adhered to exactly. Nor can they alter or falsify any thing in the proceeding or the sentence different from the brief, as the records which[l] are kept very exactly mus⟨t⟩ bear it[m] openly. Another thing which curbs the power of the judge is that all causes must be try'd with regard to the fact by a jury. The matter of fact is left intirely to their determination.—Jurys

33  are an old institution | which formerly were in use over the greater part of the countries in Europe, tho they have now been laid aside in all countries, Britain excepted. Their origin was as follows. In the beginnings of the allodial and feudall governments, trialls were carried on in those irregular courts of the barons and suchlike, of which I have[n] given you some account,[86] before persons intirely ignorant of the law and such as could give but little attention to the minutiae of a fair trial by witnesses. In this case it became customary to bring 12 compurgatores, that is, the person prosecuted came into court with twelve others; and if he swore he was innocent and these 12 swore also that they believed him to be so, he was acquitted. This remains in some measure on what is called the action, which is a particular statute by which you can referr it to the persons oath, and if he *wages his law*, that is, swears he does not owe the money, and has 6 persons swearing that they believe he does not, then he is discharged. The temptation here has made this action ⟨to⟩ be never made use of unless where one

34  is certain the debt will | be acknowledged, to prevent unnecessary trouble. The imperfection of this method is said to have given occasion to the practise of the judiciall combat.[87] The nobles would be very highly displeased to be ousted[o] of their rights by[p] the oaths of mean persons, and at that time perjury was the most common of all crimes, and demanded therefore that they should be allowed to take the old method of referring it to what was called the judicium dei, or single combat. The 1st person who remedied these inconveniencies was Henry 2d, who of all our kings excepting Edwd. 1.s had the greatest legislative capacity. He ordered that instead

---

[k] Illegible word deleted        [l] 'appear' deleted        [m] Illegible word deleted
[n] 'been' deleted        [o] Reading doubtful        [p] 'having' deleted

---

[86] iv.119 ff. above.
[87] Kames, *Law Tracts*, I.115 ff., argues that trial by battle was replaced by compurgation, which itself gave way to jury-trial.

of the 12 compurgatores, or juratores, who were chosen by the person himself, and might be of his dependents or vassalls whom at that time he could
easily influence to swear as he pleased, instead of these the sheriff should
appoint 12 juratores who should be made acquainted with the cause, and
having considered it should give in their opinion or verdict, to which the
judge should adhere, and pronoun⟨c⟩e his sentence accordingly from the
35  law. In criminal causes they | examin'd into the fact, whether or not it be*q*
as the libell alledges, and whether all the circumstances be clearly proven
by the evidence; and in the same manner in civill, for they are used in both,
they consider whether the facts be proved or not to be on one side or t'other.

Nothing can be more carefull and exact than the English law in ascertaining the impartiality of the jurers. They must be taken from the county
where the persons live, from the neghbourhood of the land if it be a dispute
of property, and so in other cases. The persons may then challenge any of
the jurers either peremptorily or pro causa*r* (for that is the distinction). He
may challenge peremptorily, that is, capriciously, from any whim or fancy
of his without assigning any reason, 35 of the 40 jurers which attend on
every court, twelve of which make a jury.[88] He may reject the 1ˢᵗ, 2ᵈ, and
third jury offered by the judge without assigning any cause ⟨?at⟩ all to one;
or after this he can challenge a whole jury for some cause, assigning that
36  either in the whole number by the array as they stand in the pannel, | which
signifies a piece of the wainscott, a board or pane,*s* or per capita out of the
array any one for which he can assign a sufficient cause. And pretty*t* slender
cause is generally allowed. If he be the brother, particular friend, or tenent,
or dependent, or any way connected with either of the parties so that he
might be reasonably suspected of partiality ⟨?⟩; and it will be sufficient
cause for challenging the whole pannel if the sheriff be in like manner
suspected of having formed a partiality*u* thro any connection with either of
the parties. Per favorem, again, he may challenge the whole array when he
has a cause for so doing, but not such as will peremptorily throw them off,
which he referrs to the consideration of the judge.—And the same is
allowed of every particular jurer. This with many restrictions and the new
moddel which is put on it by the law is still the way in England, and seems
to be a great security of the liberty of the subject. One is tried here[89] by
a judge who holds his office for life and is therefore independent and not

*q* 'comp' deleted        *r* Replaces 'per favorem'      *s* Reading doubtful      *t* Replaces an illegible word      *u* Reading doubtful

[88] Hawkins, II.43.7. The number of peremptory challenges (without cause) was reduced
from 35 to 20 by 22 Henry VIII, c. 14 (1531).

[89] This sentence perhaps refers to Scotland, where the accused could reject up to 30 (13
is probably a mishearing) of the 45 assizers who had been cited, leaving a jury of 15: Act,
1672, c. 16 (A.P.S. VIII.80, c. 40); Sir G. Mackenzie, *Works*, II (1722), 352. But the
context seems to require reference to England.

37  under the influence of the | king, a man of great integrity and knowledge who has been bred to the law, is often one of the first men in the kingdom, who is also tied down to the strict observance of the law; and the point of fact also determined by a jury of the peers of the person to be tried, who are chosen from your neighbourhood, according to the nature of the suit, all of whom to 13 you have the power of challenging.

The chief defect is that this jury must be unanimous in their opinion, unless they would choose to be greatly harrassed and at last treated with ignominy. And in this our Scots juries, tho they do not appear to be so well contrived in other points, appear to be superior as they are not required to be unanimous. It is very hard that they should thus be obliged to declare themselves of one opinion. The best men and of the greatest integrity may differ, and each think himself altogether certain that the matter is so; this must arise from the variety of human tempers and the different lights in
38  which men see things; and yet in this case they must agree or submit | to great indignities, as being first harrassed till they declare they will not agree, and in that case are turned out of the county. As this is the case, it must be that some of them takes a false oath, and as he must go over to the opinion of the other party. In criminall cases indeed there can be no great doubt as the favourable side is always to be taken, and this is generally looked on as a rule of quasi justice, and tho the party that desires to acquit the criminall be the fewest, yet the others, when they see that there are men of integrity who think him innocent, they will readily agree to think him so. But in civill causes there can be no favourable side; no one can tell which [which] side of the jury should yield. This must often happen, and yet one side must yield unless they incline to be disgrac'd. Nothing therefore can be more dissagreable than the office of a jury man in England. The better sort therefore always avoid it, and the jurys are generally composed there, and in Ireland where the case is the same, of freeholders who possess perhaps about 40$^{sh}$ or 50$^{sh}$ per annum, and are generally of no great reputation or
39  such as can enter into the minute | consideration of the evidence. So that the English, by adhering to the old custom of the unanimity of the 12 compurgatores, in which case it was very properly required, and endeavouring to give liberty to the subject, have overthrown their chief design. But altho this disagreable part had been removd, yet the multiplicity of juries is so great, as nothing can be decided without one, ⟨?as⟩ would render it altogether insufferable to the better sort if they alone were to be admitted. But in Scotland they are on a very different footing. The number which is required to a jury is 15. Nor is unanimity required of these; it was some time ago, but has within thes⟨e⟩ 150$^v$ years gone into desuetude, but at what time I cannot pretend to say. The service therefore is not at all so

---

$^v$ 'or 160' deleted

disagreable, as one may still stand to his own opinion altho all the rest contradict it. And as juries are not here required in civill causes, they return so seldom that the better sort can, as is realy the case, be solely employed without any great hardship. Nothing however appears at first sight, or on reading an account of it, more admirably contrived for preserving liberty
40   and | freedom than this form of the English juries. And we see that the people became soon so enamoured of it that it became a matter[w] which makes an article of the Magna Charta.[90] Nemo liber, etc. Nec in eum ibimus, nec in eum mittimus nisi per legale judicium parium suorum. And this rule is still observed in all courts excepting the Chancery. The reason of their not being used in them was that when the office of Chancellor was at first erected he was not granted the power of calling a jury, since if he possessed that power he would easily form a court, which it was not intended that he should. But when it was found necessary to give him a judiciall power this was done without any regard to a jury. Justice of Peace courts also have no jury in most cases. These are the only two exceptions to the above rule in the Magna Charta. The Court of Session in Scotland never use a jury. The reason seems to be that being 15 in number they
41   considered themselves as a jury. In criminall cases also our juries | seem also to be on as good a footing, altho there is not such great liberty granted the accused person in challenging the jury, etc.

Tho the king be considered as the fountain of justice, and had originally the power of erecting courts by his own authority as he did the 4 great courts of Westminster, yet this is now taken away. Henry the 8 in like manner erected by his own patent three courts which had never been before. These were, 1st, the High Commission which tried all ecclesiasticall matters; 2dly, the Court of Star Chamber which tried criminall causes; and 3dly, the Court of Wardship which had the management of all the wards which fell to the king. The two first of these were abolished in Charles 1sts time on account of the irregularity and injustice of their proceeding.[91] The other was taken away in Charles 2ds time,[92] for when he exchanged that emolument for 1,200000 per annum the court necessarily fell to nothing.
42   He can not now however create any court without the consent of the | Parliament; nor can he judge by himself in any cause but must allow[x] the common course of justice to be followed.

There seems to be no country in which the courts are more under regulation and the authority of the judge more restricted. The form of

---

[w] Reading doubtful          [x] 'it to be taken away' deleted

---

[90] Art. 39: no free man may be taken or imprisoned or disseised or outlawed or exiled or in any way destroyed, nor will we go against him nor proceed against him except by the legal judgement of his peers or by the law of the land.
[91] 16 Charles I, cc. 10, 11 (1641).
[92] 12 Charles II, c. 24 (1660), abolishing military tenures.

proceedings as well as the accuracy of the courts depends greatly on their standing. Now the courts of England are by far more regular than those of other countries, as well as more ancient. The courts of England are much more ancient than those of France or Scotland. The Parliament of Paris[93] was instituted by Francis the 1st who was cotemporary with Henry the 8, and the Court of Session by James the 5th about the same time. As the authority of government is then strong and they have at first no precedents,[v] we see that the courts at their first institution have allways taken great liberties. They are neither tied down by the brieves nor encumbered with a jury. These courts were also instituted after the civil law came to be
43 known and to be a fashionable study; | the new courts would disdain to follow the precedents of those courts on whose ruin they had been erected, but would rather follow the rules of the civill law. The Court of Session would pay little regard to the proceedings of the old Court of Justiciary, het Parliat. of Paris to those of the bailies, and the Star Chamber to those of the other courts. The law of England is free from all such      [z] and is therefore of a peculiar nature and well worth the study of a speculative man. In some points, as those of contracts and real rights, it differs from all others. Our courts are altogether regulated either by the feudal or civil law.

New courts and new laws are as        [a] says great evills. Every court is bound only by its own practise. It takes time and repeated practise to ascertain the precise meaning of a law or to have precedents enough to determine the practise of a court. Its proceedings will be altogether loose and innacurate

*Gap of about three lines in MS.*

44                          | *Monday. March. 14*[th] *1763.*

In some former lectures I have given you an account of most of the forms of government which have existed in Europe. 1st, that of shepherds in clans, and 2[dly], that of those aristocraticall monarchys[b] which arose out of these when settled in some certain spot, which have afterwards become first of all aristocracies and afterwards democracys. The Grecians were at first in the time of the Trojan war in the first or government of clans under a chief. The Germans also were long after in that state. All Europe before the conquest of the Romans, some small parts excepted, was under the republican government. Gaul was under an aristocraticall and partly under

---

[v] Illegible word deleted        [z] Illegible word        [a] Blank in MS.        [b] Replaces 'governments'

---

[93] The Parlement de Paris in fact developed as a distinct institution during the thirteenth century, and was divided into various 'chambers' in the fourteenth. The Court of Session was founded in 1532.

a republican government, where the aristocracies were under the hereditary nobles. So also was Spain. Italy was chiefly divided into small republican governments. I showed you also how that some republics came to
have very great and extensive dominions, and that the ruin of these pro-
45 duced | monarchys far greater than those from out of the government of the
clans.—I showed you also how after the fall of the Roman Empire the
government of Europe became at first allodial and afterward feudal, and
explain'd the different sorts of government that were produced by the
overthrow of this government in France, England, Germany, etc. It still
however subsists in full vigour in Poland, Courland, etc.—This may make
a pretty generall account of the history of government in Europe. There is
only one or two more, the origin of which I shall here take notice of.

In some countries who were far from being under a proper form of civil
government there were, as I explain'd before, considerable numbers of
burrghs or towns erected; many of these took the opportunity of disorders
of the government to render themselves independent. Charles the 5<sup>th</sup>,
Emperor of Germany, was possessed at the same time of ⟨the⟩ greatest part
of all$^c$ Italy, France, Spain, and great estates in Germany. When this
46 empire was seperated under his successors, France | as I mentioned before
fell into the hands of the sucessors of Hugh Capee. Germany was siezed
[was siesed] by another familly who, assuming the title of emperors, laid
claim to Italy as annexed to the empire. Otho and his three immediate
successors accordingly made$^d$ continuall incursions into Italy, but were
frequently called back to settle disturbances which arose in their absence.
The government of Italy was therefore very weak, and could give them but
little influence over the country. This was remarkably the case in Frederick
the 1<sup>st</sup> time. The Pope and others were at great pains to raise feuds in
Germany, which obliged the emperors in Germany to recall their armies
before their enterprize was finishd. The distance of Italy from Germany
made the authority of the Germans but very weak,$^e$ so that the Italians,
who had at this time in the 14<sup>th</sup> century made as great advances in arts and
emprovement as the rest of Europe arrived to in the 16, and were consequently more independent, ⟨?tried⟩ to shake off the authority of the
47 emperors. | They possessed large populous towns, well fortified, under the
government of a town council, much in the same manner as our towns in
this country are; and now, being by their distance freed from the power of
the German emperors, who kept no governor or tributary prince in Italy,
being well provided for their own defence so that none of their neighbours
were in any shape able to subdue them or curb their power, they all set up
for themselves and ⟨?gained⟩ their own independency. In the same manner
in Germany many of what are called the free towns, taking the advantage of

---

$^c$ The last four words replace 'all'      $^d$ Replaces an illegible word      $^e$ Reading
doubtful

these disturbances, being pretty independent of all others, having a territory of their own and provided for defence by living in a walled town and being constantly in arms, found themselves a match for all the princes and other powers in their neighbourhood and therefore shook off all dependance. There is however one considerable difference betwixt the

48 Italian republicks and those free towns of | Germany such as Hamburgh, Augsburgh, etc. with respect to their manner of government. The Italians are governed intirely by a hereditary nobility. The citizens have not all an indiscriminate right of voting and determining affairs. There are as I before observed no democracys properly so called in Europe, such as were those of the old govts. The reason I have also shewn already: the people had in severalls of them these rights but as I said, finding these very troublesome they gave them up into the hands of the better sort, tho in different manners. The Venetians agreed that the Great*f* Councill for the time being, with their descendants for ever, should have the government of the city. In this manner the people in all these republicks have either tacitly or expressly given up their government to the better sort, as in Milan, Genoa, Venice, etc. At the time these recovered their liberty, hereditary nobility

49 were in high repute and fashion, and therefore flocked much to the | towns and got in many of them the chief power by their assistance and protection.—The towns of Germany on the other hand, tho they were assisted no doubt by the disturbances of the government, owed their greatness to the real power and strength which they had acquired by trade and commerce.—They freed themselves without any assistance of the nobility, and fell into the government of [a] town councils who supply themselves by cooptation; and by this means any man in Amsterdam or other such towns may arrive to the highest magistraciys. In this it is that the chief and essentiall difference betwixt these republicks consists. — — —

A confederacey or union of these together make a respublica foederata.*g* These are bound to defend, protect, and assist each other, and have a publick revenue. But each of these provinces can make laws, chuse magistrates, coin money, and even make war by itself provided it be done at its

50 own expense, for they have no title | to interfere with the publick revenue. This is the case in the United Provinces and the cantons of Switzerland. But we may observe that the union is much stronger in Holland than in the others. The reason is that the latter are much more powerfull and independant, and of themselves are better able to support themselves than the others. Every canton, as that of Bern, could be able to support itself without*h* the others which no province or town in Holland could do.*i* We see accordingly that the cantons have frequently been at variance with each other. The Protestant cantons made war on ⟨?and⟩ would totally have

*f* Replaces 'town'      *g* Illegible word deleted      *h* Replaces 'against'      *i* 'and we' deleted

ruined the popish ones had not they of their own accord desisted, but no such disorder was ever heard of in the United Provinces. They found their strength in being united whereas the others found their strength in their separation.

These comprehend all the governments which have ever existed in Europe. For Courland, Poland, and others are under the same or more strict[j] feudall government that England was in Henry 8th.

51 | We shall now consider a little the generall or publick laws which have prevaild in these governments. The 1st thing to be consider[er]d with regard to a republican govt is, what it is that determines the voice of the people, as it is that which determines the laws[k] of the people. It is a generall rule that in every society the minority must submit to the minority.[94] But it may often happen that the minority[94] who vote for the making or rejecting a law or the choosing a magistrate can not be easily and clearly determined. Thus if A, B, and C were candidates, and A had, of 100, 34, B 33, and C 33; if the majority was to carry it, A would here be chosen altho to 66 of the 100 he might be the most obnoxious of all, or perhaps in the whole. This happens often in elections in this country where that rule takes place. This is without doubt a very great grievance. It would be still more so if we should suppose a set of men who had the judicial or senatorial power directed by this rule.[95] Suppose a man was to be tried for his life, and that of

52 100, 35[96] bring him in guilty | of murther, 33 of manslaughter, and 33 of chance manly. Here altho 66 absolve him of murther he will be condemned. To prevent this it has been endeavoured to make[l] all questions bipartite in these countries. As here they would put the question, guilty of murther or not. First of all 66 would acquit him of murther. Those who had been for condemning him would in the 2d question cast the balance and cast him of manslaughter. And so in the former case of the members the first question would be, is A a fit person or not. Here A would be cast by 65,[m] and the others would depend on the share of As voters who joind them. And thus they endeavour always to reduce the vote to two contradictory votes or propositions. This is the practise at Venice. It must also sometimes happen that the assembly if it consist of 100, 40, or other equall numbers will be divided. In this case there is in[n] fact nothing determind, and in the strictest

53 sense | they allow no casting or decisive voice, and far less one joind with the deliberative one.—If the president of an assembly have only a decisive voice he is in a worse case than any of the others and his party may often be worsted tho of equall numbers. 7 out of 14 would carry it against him and

---

[j] Reading doubtful    [k] Replaces 'voice'    [l] Reading doubtful    [m] *Sic*
[n] The last three words replace 'it will'

---

[94] *Sic*. No doubt 'majority' was intended.
[95] Pufendorf, VII.2.18; Hutcheson, *System*, II.241.
[96] *Sic*. Presumably '34' was intended.

so he will be in a worse condition than the other members. But if he has this joind with a deliberative one, he has far more. No voice of this sort therefore is allowed.—The president only keeps order and regularity. If therefore the numbers be equall nothing is done. A man would not as here be acquitted, nor would he be condemned, but as neither had be⟨e⟩n carry⟨d⟩ would be brought to trial, contrary to our rules. And if this happens when a law is proposed it is neither past nor cast, but brought in again in a few days, which it could not if rejected; and this is without doubt strictly just.

54   | The next thing I shall consider is what are the respect and duties which the subjects owe to the sovereign power of whatever nature, the monarch in a monarchy, the nobles in an aristocracy, and the body of the people in a democracy; and on the other hand what are the duties the sovereign owes to his people, and the punishments to be inflicted on the infringement of these rights.—Any attempt or injury against the sovereigns person is allways punished as a very heignous crime. If this attempt is immediately against the sovereign it is accounted *high treason*. This crime however is very different in a monarchy from what it is in a republick. In a monarchy any thing that either endangers the person or derogates from the dignity of the king is accounted high treason; in a republick, whatever affects the dignity of the people as a body.—The Romans for this reason distinguish treasonable crimes into two sorts. That which was properly the law with treason was called perduellio. Laesa majestas again was any contempt[o] of

55 the magistrates or others who had dignity | and is similar to what we would call a contempt of the kings authority. The crimen perduellio was very[p] plain in a democraticall government. One was guilty of it whenever he showed animum hostilem erga rempublicam,[97] by joining, succouring, or corresponding with the enemy; when he gave up their hostages, surren-dered towns into their hands, or took away without the publick authority the life or liberty of a subject acting as a judge; levied armys without their authority; and so on. The difference chiefly consists in the respect paid to the person of the sovereign.—In a monarchy this is always looked upon as sacred and guarded by the law of treason against all attempts; and this is the case whatever the right or title of the sovereign may be. This is here any attempt to compass or bring about any injury or disgrace on the person of the sovereign, and therefore comprehen⟨ds⟩ the corrupting of his wife or

56 his sons wiv⟨es⟩, | as by that means a spurious offspring may suceed to the crown. And in generall all attempts against his life or dignity are pro-hibited, without any regard to the title by which he holds the crown. It is the interest of every sovereign that no such attempts should be permitted.

---

[o] Reading doubtful     [p] 'easily' deleted

[97] 'A hostile attitude towards the state': *D.* 48.4.11.

If tyrranncide was allowed every one would be in danger. The man who permitted it might in a few days be cut off himself, as the least stretch of authority or even an ordinary exertion of power would make him appear a tyrant in the eyes of many of his subjects. It is also necessary that all who bear arms or exercise any office of that sort in the kings name should be free from all pains and penalties. The case is quite different in republicks. Tyrannicide there is always not only permitted but commended and rewarded. One is there said to be guilty of treason quicunque injussu

57 populi bellum gessit, exercitum conscripsit, liberum | necavit, etc.[98] By this he sets himself above the authority of the people and above the laws. A murtherer tho he breaks the laws does not set himself above them, but one who by a sort of authority puts one to death plainly does. Thus the decemviri at Rome, when they infringed the priviledges of the Republick, as there was no court before which they could be called were plainly tyrants. So were Peisistratus and Nebas.[99] There was no way to get free of their authority but by assassination. Tyrranicide was therefore always allowd. But now it is all over Europe prohibited. The reason is that Holland, Switzerland, etc. are no ways comparable (tho they be very$^q$ respectable states⟨⟩) to France, England, etc. Monarchies are the prevailing government; they set the fashion and give the tone to the custom of all the others. The assassination of the greatest tyrant would now be looked upon as altogether shocking. The assassination of Oliver Cromwell would have been thought horrid and have covered the persons who executed it with

58 |shame, whereas formerly nothing was more glorious than the assassination of a tyrant. Brutus, Timoleon, and Harmodios and Aristogeiton[1] were highly celebrated for their assassinations of tyrants. The governments were mostly republican; they then gave the tone to the maners of the times and any small or single monarchy amongst them, as that of Macedon, would be obliged to comply with the generall turn. The republicks being now less numerous can not give the same tone as before, and are therefore forced to submit to the tone given by the rest. It is not any superiority of humanity or refinement of manners$^r$ above the antients which has made tyrannicide be abhorred amongst us, when at the same time it was rewarded amongst them, but merely the different state and circumstances of the times.— — —

$^q$ Reading doubtful      $^r$ 'which' deleted

[98] 'Whoever in defiance of the people has waged war, raised an army, killed a free man, etc.' Cf. *D.* 48.4.3, and Grotius, I.3.4.2.

[99] According to tradition Rome was ruled by two boards of decemviri from 451 to 449 B.C., the first being moderate, the second tyrannical. Peisistratus was tyrant of Athens for three periods between 560 and 527 B.C. Nabis was tyrant of Sparta, 207–192 B.C.

[1] Brutus was the assassin of Julius Caesar; Timoleon overthrew Dionysius II, tyrant of Syracuse, but allowed him his life; Harmodius and Aristogeiton, known as the Liberators, attempted to kill Hippias, tyrant of Athens, and his brother Hipparchus, but succeeded in killing only the latter.

## Tuesday. March. 15.$^{th}$ 1763

I endeavoured yesterday to explain some of the generall laws respecting treason. Treason is the crime which immediately attacks the being and existence of the lawfull established government. There is as I observed
59 a very | essentiall difference betwixt this crime in republicks and in monarchies. It is the interest of monarchs that the laws of treason should secure the possession of the present monarch, without rendering him answerable for every slig⟨h⟩t offence he might give them, and that the subjects should not be encouraged in two enquiries: first, that they should not enquire too minutely into the soundness of his title to the throne, or 2$^d$, into the tenor of his conduct, whatever the sovereign be who is possessed of the throne. Monarchies are therefore very unfavourable to tyrannicide as they would otherwise be very precarious.—Republicks on the other hand always favour it, have almost constantly enacted laws for its encouragement. There are severall reasons for this difference. For 1$^{st}$, one who is guilty of treason$^s$ is much more easily distinguished, as I mentioned before, and likewise their fears of treasonable persons are very different. Rebellions of the people against the sovereign, or insurrections or discontent amongst them, are what is chiefly to be feared by a monarchy. They will therefore discourage any enquiry or searching into their title or administration, or
60 any doctrine | which teaches them that the monarch ought not to possess the throne if he be not lawfully come of the family or otherwise fails in his title or his administration. That principle therefore which would maintain tyranicide as lawfull is of all others most to be discouraged, as it entirely destroys the allegiance of the people to the sovereign.—But on the contrary both these reasons plead$^t$ for it in a republican government. Treason is there very easily distinguished, and also the very thing they are afraid of is the usurpation of some of their own great men by superior art or power. This is what they chiefly dread, and they therefore encourage the slaying of such persons, as the only method of getting rid of them.—The laws of a monarchicall government for the reasons here mentioned ⟨?⟩. The laws supported Oliver Crom. no less than they did any of the lawfull sovereigns; but the laws of the republicks did never support an usurper[s].— —
61     Treason is that crime which consists in attacking | the being and existence of the government or sovereign power. This may be done in two ways. It may be done either 1$^{st}$, by the attempt of some of the$^u$ subjects to overturn by an internall change the present [and] form of government, or 2$^{dly}$, an attempt to overturn the established government by introducing a foreign enemy into the country and giving it up into their hands. The former of these is called properly perduellio and the other proditio or betraying.—

---

$^s$ The last six words replace 'a tyrant'      $^t$ Reading doubtful      $^u$ Illegible word deleted

Tarheason[2] or treason properly denotes this crime of betraying the country to an enemy from without. Both these are provided against by the laws of England.[3]— 1$^{st}$ of all,[v] attempts against the person of the sovereign to destroy or injure him. The 1$^{st}$ article of the Act of Treason therefore provides that it is treason any way to compass or imagine the death of the king,[4] and that not only when it is realy accomplished but when it is declared by any ouvert act, as forming a conspiracy against him or providing arms against him. The most atrocious attempts could not have been

62 punished if this | had not been the case. The gunpowder plot, which was an evident design to destroy the king and his nobles, could not have been punished as it was not put in execution. To have laid powder below the house of a private person would not have been death, as the attempting or conceiving the death of a private person is not considered as murther or felony, tho the same attempt when evidently directed[w] against the king is treason. In the injuries of private persons the publick enter only by sympathy, but in the case of the sovereign they punish the injuries against themselves, and for this reason injuries against the publick are always more highly punished than those of individualls.[5]— The 2$^d$ branch of this article makes it treasonable to corrupt the kings companion, that is, his wife, or his sons wife, or his eldest daughter.[6] This seems to proceed chiefly from the disgrace which is thereby incurred to the family, and this also, that it may sometimes occasion a disputed succession. Thus Edward the 5 denied

63 that Edw[x] was the son of ⟨?⟩.[7] By this | all attempts are provided against which[y] regard the person of the king or his relations, for with regard to the more distant relations the corrupting them is not treason, tho it would be a very great piece of bad manners. 3$^d$, by the 2$^d$ article it is high treason to levy war against the king openly[z] or otherwise, or even contriving or imagining the doing of it, as by entering into a conspiracy against him tho nothing is effected. This last by a wide construction is[a] constructed to come under the 1$^{st}$ article, as one who bears arms against the king is

---

[v] Reading of last two words doubtful    [w] Reading doubtful    [x] Possibly deleted
[y] Reading doubtful    [z] Reading doubtful    [a] 'extended to' deleted

---

[2] *Sic.* Presumably the French *trahison* was intended.

[3] 25 Edward III, st. 5, c. 2 (1352); Hawkins, I.17.

[4] King or queen or their eldest son.

[5] Cf. TMS II.iii.2.4: 'The design to commit a crime . . . is scarce ever punished with the same severity as the actual commission of it. The case of treason is perhaps the only exception. . . . In the punishment of treason, the sovereign resents the injuries which are immediately done to himself: in the punishment of other crimes, he resents those which are done to other men. It is his own resentment which he indulges in the one case: it is that of his subjects which by sympathy he enters into in the other.'

[6] His wife, his eldest son's wife, or his eldest daughter unmarried.

[7] This could possibly be a reference to the doubts cast by Richard III on the legitimacy of Edward V on the alleged ground that Edward IV's marriage to Elizabeth Woodville was invalid.

supposed to design his death whenever it is in his power. This also is different from the private law, as the carrying arms against a private person is not esteemed murther nor the conspiring to kill one. Under this are included the encouraging in any shape the kings enemies, the aiding, comforting, or assisting them, whether it be with arms or provisions, giving up any towns or fortresses of the kings into their hands, or refusing to give up to the king any town which may be of use to him; and this is properly called proditio in Latine.

64    | A 3ᵈ species of high treason is any attempt[8] on the kings officers when in the courts exercising their office, as the killing of the Chancellor, or the judges in the three great courts      ᵇ or in the assizes.[9] This is only when they are in court or in the exercise of their office or going to court. At an other time it is only considered in the same manner as the killing of any other man. This was established in the time of Edward the 5ᵗʰ [10] as well as the others. The wounding them even in court is not considered as treason. 4ᵗʰ, is the counterfeiting of the great or privy seal. The counterfeiting the sign manuall is an offence of a very different nature and is considered only as felony.[11] The great and privy seal are the marks of the kings authority, and the counterfeiting them is to usurp the power of the king over the subjects and is therefore justly considered as hurting his dignity and authority. 5ᵗʰ, is the *counterfeiting the kings coin*. But for this there does not appear to be so great reason. It should naturally be considered not as

65 treason, but as the crimen falsi; and for this reason it is now | generally tried as a felony, as it involves both the penalties of treason and of felony, or as a misprision.—There can be nothing to hinder any one from coining money and putting his own head and coat of arms upon it; in this there can be no crime. But such money offered does not make a lawfull tender of payment. It will pass only for the bullion that is in it. The kings coin tho ever so much debased must be accepted when tendered in payment; and the refusing it is considered as a high misdemeanour and is liable to the penalties of felony. This priviledge money coin'd by a private person could not have, so that a private person could make no benefit by coining money in his own name. The only thing which could be of any service to him would be to counterfeit the kings coin and make it of a baser standard. The coining of money can not however be properly considered as treason. The

---

ᵇ Blank in MS.

---

[8] Actual killing was required.

[9] The Act covered slaying 'the chancellor, treasurer, or the king's justices of the one bench or the other, justices in eyre, or justices of assize, and all other justices assigned to hear and determine, being in their places during their offices', but not the barons of the exchequer. Hale, I.230; Hawkins, I.17.46.

[10] Edward III.

[11] It was made high treason by 1 Mary, st. 2, c. 6; Hawkins, I.17.53.

only reason for this was the jealousy[c] the kings had of this priviledge, which was then very profitable and had not long before been possessed by many of the great lords of the kingdom. — —

66 | These are the five species of high treason established by the laws of treason under Edward 5th.[12]—There are some others which have been introducd by Henry the 8 and after him by William and Mary. Henry, having often quarrelled with the Pope, at length renounced his supremacy, and tho he did not declare himself a Protestant, acted as such and set himself up as the head of the church;[13] and to maintain his authority in these matters established the High Commission Court; and in the same manner Elizabeth afterwards was accounted as the head of the church. At this time the immoderate zeal and bigotry of the papist⟨s⟩ was an object of [as] great danger to the sovereigns of Europe who had embraced the Protestant religion. Elizabeth, Henry 8th, and Edward the 6th were in continuall danger from the plots and conspiracies of the bigotted papists, spurrd on by their priests. The Roman Catholick religion was therefore considered as one that encouraged all sorts of attempts and schemes against the sovereign. This being more than ever encouraged under the reign of

67 Mary made Elizabeth in the greater | danger. It was therefore thought necessary to inflict the penalties of treason on all those who any way encouraged it, such as the receiving of the Popes bulls and obeying their orders over the clergy;[14] being converted or converting others to this religion;[15] extolling or magnifying the Popes power to grant indulgences and otherwise as the head of the church, by writing or word of mouth;[16] bringing into the kingdom Agnus Dei's or relicts;[d][17] being educated at a popish seminary and not taking the oaths to the government in six months after return to the kingdom; the being a popish priest, or the aiding them in any way, as the receiving them into your house.[18] All these were made treasonable as being against the subsistence of the government and encouraging a religion which tended to overturn it by every possible means. Tho these laws are not put in execution for some considerable time past, yet they are still in force. Yet it were proper that they were repealed, as

[c] 'of' deleted     [d] Reading doubtful

---

[12] Edward III.
[13] 26 Henry VIII, c. 1 (Act of Supremacy, 1534).
[14] 13 Elizabeth, c. 2 (1571).
[15] 23 Elizabeth, c. 1 (1581).
[16] 5 Elizabeth, c. 1 (1563) made this a praemunire; cf. LJ(B) 84, below.
[17] This was not treason but was made a praemunire by 13 Elizabeth, c. 2.
[18] 27 Elizabeth, c. 2 (1585) made it high treason for a subject to receive popish orders, and not to return from a popish seminary within six months after a proclamation to that effect in London and take the oaths within two days. However, not to discover a popish priest to the authorities was merely punishable by fine or imprisonment. Hawkins, I.17.81.

very harmless men may be in danger from accidents of no consequence and
68 meet with great trouble, especially if he has by | any form or means offended
the government. But tho this might now be done with great propriety, any
one who reads the history of Europe at this time will see that they were alltogether reasonable at that time, considering the vast disturbances and
danger the bigotry of the papists exposed them to. Again, the long quarrels
which subsisted betwixt Charles 1ˢᵗ and his Parliament, the rebellion which
arose from them, the death of the king, and the usurpation of Oliver
Cromwell; during all this time and after the restoration of Charles 2ᵈ his
bad conduct and tyrannicall turn, and still more in the weak and silly
behaviour of his brother James, it would be naturall to enquire how far it
was lawfull to resist the power of the king. The Tudor family who immediately preceded these had (as I said)[19] been altogether absolute. This
gave the court party an opportunity of alledging, and occasioned many to
believe, that the constitutionall government of England was absolute, that
the people had no title nor could lawfully resistᵉ or limit his power in any
69 respect, | and that all the people were his subjects and servants. The other
party again alledged that he was no more than the supreme magistrate,
trusted by the people as their attorney with the management of their
affairs, and that as such he might be called to an account for his conduct;
and that if they turned him out unjustly and without sufficient cause
clearly proven it was an offence and very blameable, but still they had a
tittle to do it. The whole power of the government flowed from the people,
and that therefore they might turn out their servants when and for what
cause they pleased, and did not do any thing to which they had no title even
when they turned out one who had not done any thing amiss. A master who
turned away his servant thro mere caprice acted amiss, but he did not more
than what he might lawfully do; the same was the case, they said, betwixt
the sovereign and his subject, king and people. This was the prevailing and
favourite doctrine from the year 1640 to 1660.—But the bad conduct of
70 Cromwell and his perfidious | behaviour, as he betrayed all parties, and the
weak government of his son Richard which follow'd it, disgusted the whole
people at a republican government. The Restoration immediately followed
upon this; these principles were laid aside and the other was the fashonable
one. The Puritans or Presbyterians who favoured it became altogether
odious and were greattly oppressed, and the republican principles were
going out altogether, till theᶠ foolish and tyrannicall conduct of James
again roused them, so that he was turn'd out andᵍ the popish line for ever,
as he had been endeavouring to introduce that religion. William and Mary
were called to the throne, and then by an Act of William[20] the succession

---

ᵉ 'the' deleted        ᶠ Illegible word deleted        ᵍ Reading doubtful

[19] iv.164–5 above.        [20] 12 and 13 William III, c. 2 (Act of Settlement, 1701).

was fixt upon Queen Anne and her issue, and[h] failing her on the present family, setting asside many nearer relations as the Duke of Orleans, the King of Sardinia, and many others, passing over to them by a very wise constitution as the nearest Protestant heirs. This succession was intirely a
71  parliamentary one, and as the contrary doctrine had for some time | prevailed this new government was in danger from the prejudices which then prevailed. It was therefore thought necessary to introduce some new laws of treason, as 1st, that any one who should maintain in print or writing that the king and Parliament together had not the right to alter the sucession as they pleased should be accounted as guilty of treason; if by word of mouth, he should be liable to a premunire. 2[dly], that one who maintaind the right of the Stuart family as still subsisting should be liable to the pains of treason if in print or writing, and if by word of mouth to a premunire.[21] This law also might now be well abrogated, for tho these principles were necessary to be inforced to the support of the government at that time depending on them, [but] the government being establishd on them has fully confirmed them, and these laws can serve little other purpose than to involve innocent or harmless people in trouble.—The laws of treason before the Union were
72  very confused and absurd, making | a vast number of crimes liable to the pains of treason. Leasing making as it was called was liable to these pains, by which they meant the misrepresenting the king to the people by giving them any informations, or the people to the king, which was said to be infusing prejudices against them.—This was a great oppression as no one could then talk or write freely of the government or the ministers, and far less present to the king a bold and free memorial setting forth any grievances. But by the Union the laws of treason are the same in Scotland as in England.[22]

### Wednesday. March. 16.[th] 1763

In yesterdays lecture I gave you an account of the laws of treason in this country as established by the statute of Edward the 5.[th][23] Before that time every thing which they desired greattly to discourage was subjected to the pains of treason, as the going over to the enemies country, which was intended to subsist but for three years. That statute confined them to the five species above mentioned. These are in generall very reasonably reckond
73  | to deserve those punishments. It is altogether just that the compassing the death of the king, etc. or the corrupting his consort, etc., should be accounted treason, as these immediately tend to overturn the government and strike at its very roots. The levying war against the king or the attacking his officers in the discharge of their office are no less justly accounted so, as

[h] 'after' deleted

[21] 4 and 5 Anne, c. 8 (1705) and 6 Anne, c. 7 (1707).
[22] 7 Anne, c. 21 (1708). Mackenzie, *Laws and Customes of Scotland in Matters Criminal* (1678), VI and XXX.6.               [23] Edward III.

they would intirely overturn the foundations and prevent the execution of government. The counterfeiting the seals is also a great and atrocious injury to the government, as one by this means can falsify not only one but all or any one he pleases of the kings statutes. The 5th species, viz that of counterfeiting the coin, does not so evidently appear to be treasonable and was accounted so merely from the jealousy of the kings.—With regard to the statute which makes many severe penalties attend the encouraging the popish religion, this (as I said) needed not be continued now. The zeal of that religion is greatly abated in many points, and tho it might be reasonable to discourage it by[i] imposing double taxes or such like penalties, it can

74  hardly be reasonable | to punish as treason the weakness of any one who was so silly as to prefer the Roman Catholick to the Protestant religion. And such penalties may unwillingly involve men in great troubles. The same may be said of those brought in since the Revolution. {This indeed is seldom taken notice of as the spirit of the government is now more than ever republican.} The government is too well established to be hurt by any ones controverting the right of altering the sucession or favouring the Stuart family. And no one has been prosecuted on this head.        [24], who published a history in three volumes thro the whole of which he took it as an established principle that the king and Parliament had not the right of altering the succession, was never considered as being guilty of treason, tho without doubt it was a very great offence against the government. The punishment inflicted on treason is the highest of all, and the only one which in this country admits by law of any torture. The criminall is to be half hanged, and then before dead to be taken down, and his heart plucked out and his bowels before he is yet dead, and his ⟨?head⟩ then to ⟨be⟩ severed

75  from his body and fixed up in some pub|⟨lick⟩ place; but the mildest[25] of our manners generally mitigates this part of the punishment, allowing the criminall to be quite dead.—Besides this it is attended with forfeiture of goods and land estate, and the dower of the wife, and corruption of blood on the children, by which they are deprived not only of his estate but of every succession which would have fallen to them thro him. — —

Besides these there are many inferior offences against the king.[26] As 1st, the issuing coin or even bullion or wrought silver of a standard inferior to sterling, which by the law is punishd as felony.[27] 2d, formerly it was felony to export either coin or bullion out of the kingdom. This is now confined to coin,[28] the exportation of bullion being allowed,[29] if it be entered at the

---

[i] Illegible word deleted

[24] Blank in MS. Probably Laurence Echard, *History of England*, 3 vol., 1707–18.
[25] *Sic*. No doubt 'mildness' was intended.
[26] Hawkins, I.18.                                    [27] 7 Anne, c. 25 (1708).
[28] Exportation of coin, although still prohibited, had not been a felony since 1573: Hale, I.654–6; Hawkins, I.18.6.                    [29] 15 Charles II, c. 7 (1663).

custom house and examind before a          30. This was from a mistaken
notion called a diminishing the wealth of the kingdom. The wea⟨l⟩th of the
kingdom has by allmost ⟨?all⟩ authors after Mun been considered as consisting in the gold and silver in it. In his book called Englands          31 by
76 Foreign Trade, he endeavours to shew | the balance of trade is the only
thing which can support England, as by this means gold and silver are
brought into the kingdom, and in these allone he says the wea⟨l⟩th of the
kingdom can consist[s] as they alone are not perishable. On this doctrine of
his, which however foolish has been adopted by all suceeding writers, these
laws have been founded. For nothing in reality is more idle than such
prohibitions. The*j* exportation of bullion was allowed for the 1st time by
King William32 on the importunities of the merchants, who shewed that
the prohibition was very detrimentall to trade. The prohibition of the exportation of coin still continues but is of no effect, and the very want of it
proceeds from an erroneous constitution in our police. It was thought that
the more money there was in the kingdom the greater was the benefit. To
encourage therefore the turning of bullion into coin, the private persons
were not at any expense of the mintage, the whole of which was born by
the government;33 so that now the priviledge of coinage, so far from bring-
77 ing any profit to the king, costs him about | 14,000£ per annum. The effect
of this is that uncoined silver is always as high in its value as coined silver,
which is without doubt absurd as it should have the addition of the
expense of coinage. The pound troy of coined silver is valued at 3£ 2sh, so
that the ounce of it is worth 5sh 2d. The price of the ounce of uncoind silver
can never be under this. For if one was refused so much from any one for it
he can send it to the Mint where he will get that value for it, as the mintage
costs *him* nothing.—So that the ounce of bullion can never be below 5sh 2d,
and is in fact commonly above it. For the bullion is in many respects more
convenient than the coin as it serves the purposes of it in most cases, and
besides is more acceptable abroad, or can be wrought into plate at Rome.
So that one who is possessed of new coin finds his advantage in melting it
down, as he will get somewhat more for it. So that this constitution increases the mintage indeed, but does not increase the coin, as it gives such
78 a profit in melting new coin before it be pulled*k* down below | the nominall
value that for these twenty years or more past one has hardly seen a new
shilling which has made its way down to Scotland, as they are thrown into

*j* 'importat' deleted     *k* Reading doubtful

---

30 Blank in MS. Marked at Goldsmiths' Hall, 6 and 7 William III, c. 17 (1695), and
certified by the Mayor's Court of the City of London, 7 and 8 William III, c. 19 (1696).
   31 Blank in MS. Thomas Mun, *England's Treasure by Forraign Trade*, published by
John Mun in 1664.
   32 In fact by Charles II: Hawkins, I.18.6.
   33 18 and 19 Charles II, c. 5 (1666).

the melting pot as soon as they come from the Mint. This is also, 3^dly, accounted felony.[34] But no one has been ever punishd for it, as any one but a fool can contrive to do it in so short a time as to prevent any discovery.— 4^th, all attempts to increase the kings coin are accounted felony, as the seeking to find out the philosophers stone.[35] This does not however seem to be so reasonable as that the debasing it should.— — 5^th, is felony, any attempt against the kings councilor, the [the] raising a riot or attacking any of the kings servants,[36] {embezling the kings arms.}

The state of affairs under King John and Henry the third gave occasion to the statutes of premunire.[37] The Pope at that time frequently sent over legates into Britain who, without the consent of the king, brought over his bulls imposing heavy contributions on the clergy and even on the laiety.

79 These receivd complaints against the kings judgments | in ecclesiasticall matters, and by these bulls they carried a vast deal of money out of the kingdom, and by this means subjected it so much to the Popes authority that it was little more than a fief of the Holy See. This, long before Protestantism was thought of, made it necessary to curb his power in some respects. It was therefore made criminall to bring over the bulls of the Pope, or for any legate to enter the kin⟨g⟩dom without the kings leave, to appeal from the kings courts to the court of Rome, for the dean and cannons or chapter to refuse to admit or ordain a bishop nominated by the king. These statutes were said premunire regnum, to fortify the kingdom (against the Popes encroachments). We say now instead of that one falls under the penalties appointed by the statutes premunire regnum, that he falls under a premunire. The penalty of these, which are chiefly intended to secure the kings authority in ecclesiasticall matters, was outlawry, that is, forfeiture of goods and the want of the kings protection, by which one nor his children

80 or heirs can not sue^l | any law in any^m court, which is not the case in most crimes. The punishment of outlawry is the hig⟨h⟩est of any excepting those of treason and felony since those for heresy, witchcraft, etc. were taken away. Other misdemeanours against the king go under the name of misprisions, from the old French mespris (for mepris, the letter s being retaind by the English who seem to be fond of it, tho thrown out by the French who have a sort of dislike at it), neglect or contempt. Misprision is of two sorts, misprision of treason, and misprision not of treason.—Misprision of treason again is either positive or negative.[38] Negative misprision of treason, or contempt of the kings authority, is when one does not reveal

---

^l Reading doubtful    ^m 'other' deleted

---

[34] Forbidden, although not declared a felony, by 6 and 7 William III, c. 17 (1695).
[35] 5 Henry IV, c. 4 (1404), but repealed by 1 William and Mary, c. 30 (1689).
[36] 3 Henry VII, c. 14 (1487) and 9 Anne, c. 16 (1710).
[37] Hawkins, I.19.
[38] Ibid., I.20.

any attempts against the kings life or his consort, or any of the other sorts of treason, which comes to his knowledge.[39]— But if one receives and encourages them or any way seems to consent to it he is considered not merely as an accessory, which is the case in felony, but is punishd as being guilty of treason. Thus if one should fall into company who were talking of the right

81 of the Stuart family and | should join them, and meet then a 2$^d$ time for the same purpose, he would be considere⟨d⟩ as guilty of treason. But if one do not any ⟨?way⟩ signify his approbation of such proceedings but merely neglect to give information, he is liable not to the penalties of treason but of misprision. The approbation of a felony on the other hand does not make one guilty of it. This misprision of treason is liable to an arbitrary punishment of fine and imprisonment.—Positive misprision of treason is the counterfeiting coin not current in the country.[40] The counterfeiting of foreign coin which is current in the country by the kings proclamation is treason no less than the counterfeiting the kings own coin. But to counterfeit those which are not current by the proclamation is not treason but misprision. Misprision not of treason is of severall sorts.[41] 1$^{st}$, contempt of the kings palaces or courts. One who raises any disturbances or riots within the palace, or strikes another, is liable to the penalties of misprision, and those guilty of the latter offence lose their right hand.[42] Any disturbance

82 of the execution of justice by | interrupting the execution of justice by giving the judge bad language of any sort, these are all liable to very high penalties.—Not long ago a doctor of laws, a man of considerable rank, for an offence of this sort was obliged to walk with a paper testifying his offence fixed upon him from Temple Bar to           $^n$. And a whole court of admiralty, having given a very scurrilous paper containing a complaint against Chief Justice Willis for having tried a cause which was depending before them for$^o$ a court martial, were summoned before the court for scandalum magnatum, and obliged to beg pardon in the face of the whole court.[43]— And all such offences are subject to fine and imprisonment, and are obliged to be attoned for by begging pardon in a publick and opprobrious manner. This is the case in France in all crimes, where besides the publick punishment they ask pardon of the party offended and of God in the church before the whole congregation, doing penance for it. But in England this is required of people of character in this case only.

$^n$ Blank in MS.     $^o$ Reading doubtful

---

[39] 1 and 2 Philip and Mary, c. 10 (1554).
[40] 14 Elizabeth, c. 3 (1572). Cf. p. 430, note 37, below.
[41] Hawkins, I.21.
[42] 33 Henry VIII, c. 12 (1541) (if the king is resident at the time).
[43] A naval court martial had attempted to impeach Willis, Chief Justice of the Common Pleas, in 1746; cf. *Gentleman's Magazine*, XVI (1746), 462 ff., 598, 604; Horace Walpole, *Letters* (ed. Toynbee, 1903), II.251.

83 | $2^{d}$, is a contempt of the kings prerogative[p] in disobeying his lawfull commands; refusing to serve him, as he has a right to demand their service; or preferring a foreign court in any way, as by receiving a pension from them without the kings consent, as sovereigns are always jealous of such connections with others.[44] The same is the case when one goes out of the kingdom contrary to the kings orders; for in common cases any one has a title to go out of the kingdom without asking leave excepting peers or Members of Parliament; but the king may impose his commands on any one *ne exeat regno*; or not returning when called by a particular order under the kings privy seal or when called by a generall proclamation.

$3^{d}$, is a contempt of the kings personall government,[45] as the saying that he had broke his coronation ⟨?oath⟩, that he was a coward or a scoundrell, etc. But tresspasses of this sort have never been punished for some time past as the government is now more than ever democraticall, unless when
84 any personall reflections have been thrown out | against some individuall in the administration. And if it was to be tried it is probable the Act would be repealed altogether, as every one would in this nation dispute his liberty of censuring the administration. And the English nation think they have a right to information in politicall affairs by books and pamphlets on these subjects, which would in this case be cut off.

$4^{th}$, is contempt of the kings title, as preferring the Pretender, drinking his health, and such like; not taking the oath of allegiance which has been[q] in use of a long time, and that of supremacy and abjuration introducd after the Revolution and Reformation when lawfully tendered.[46]— The punishment of these is fine and imprisonment, incapacity of all offices, and some others, but not those of felony or outlawry.

*Friday. March. 17. 1763*

There are three branches of treason properly so called, under which all
85 these above[r] | may be reduced. $1^{st}$, the attempts of any of the subjects by unlawfull force and violence to subvert the established government. This is what was called by the Romans perduellio, which comprehends in a monarchicall government the killing or attacking the sovereign. $2^{d}$, that by which a subject of the state endeavours to betray the state to a foreign enemy, which[s] is properly called proditio. $3^{dly}$, that by which any affront is attempted to be thrown on the government, which is laesa majestas. The punishment of perduellio and proditio were very soon put upon the same

[p] Replaces 'authority' [q] The last four words replace 'supremacy introduced at'
[r] Reading doubtful [s] Reading doubtful

[44] Hawkins, I.22.
[45] *Sic.* Probably a mishearing of 'person or government'. Hawkins, I.23; and cf. LJ(B) 85–6, below.
[46] Hawkins, I.24.

footing, as they are both very heinous crimes; and both are considerably more so than the other. Under the emperors all these were mixt and blended together, so that the smallest of crimes*t* against the emperors dignity was punished in the same way as the highest treachery; uttering any contemptuous speech, or even forming a libell against the nobles, that is, his ministers, or even the throwing a stone into his palace,[47] or melting down his statues or any thing made in his honour:[48] these made one liable to the same penalties as perduellio, which was undoubtedly altogether absurd.

86    | I yesterday gave you some account of those things which are punished as treason, as well as the lesser crimes against the king; the four sorts of treason which are so by the old statute, as well as an other not altogether so reasonable. There are others which are called felonies against the king, which subject one to the penalties of felony. The other things which would be felony against the subject, *u* are also felony when committed on the king and would be prosecuted as such; these are called felonies against the king because they are considered as against him as such.—Others as I said come under less penalties.

We shall next consider *the crimes which the* sovereign may be guilty of against the subjects. The 1$^{st}$ thing to be attended to here is, who are the subjects.—The laws of different countries make great variations in this matter. In generall when the citizenship intitles one to peculiar priviledges, family descent, i.e. being desended from one who was a citizen, the number of citizens being small, gives one a probable chance of being preferred to some office or employment as their number is very large | in proportion to

87    that of the number of citizens; besides many other benefits common in small states. But in large ones, where this priviledge gives one no other advantage than that of electing or being elected out of a vast number of others, the place of ones birth generally determines whether or not he is to be accounted a citizen. In Holland, Switzerland, the Italian and other republicks, birth does not make one a citizen. One may be born of a family who have resided for some generations without having any one of the priviledges of a citizen. The numbers are here but very small, and the number of offices and other emoluments attending citizenship extremely great. One might in the same manner at Rome or Athens be born of parents*v* whose ancesstors had resided many years amongst them, and still*w* be denominated peregrinus or μετοικος.[49] At Rome it was necessary that ones father should have been a citizen; and the Athenians, who were most chary of any in bestowing this priviledge, required that both his father and mother

---

*t* Reading doubtful    *u* Replaces 'king'    *v* Replaces 'a father'    *w* Illegible word deleted

---

[47] Perhaps an inference from *D.* 48.4.5.          [48] *D.* 48.4.6.
[49] Resident alien.

88 should be Athenian citizens, or descended | from those who were. They, at least in their vigorous and flourishing state, were more chary of it than any others, in so much that when Asmyntas[50] and Philip of Macedon desired to be made citizens of Athens they could obtain none other of the priviledges of a citizen excepting that of being put on the same footing with citizens with regard to imposts and duties paid for goods, which are in most countries considerably higher on strangers than citizens, and[x] is the case in this country allso, a few instances being excepted. The reason of this was the same that has been the cause of the same measures in other states: the smallness of the number of citizens, in proportion to the power and extent of territory they possessed. The city of Athens never contained above 23 or 25000 free citizens of the military age. This number was very small compared to the extensive territory they possessed, having the property of most of the islands in the Aegean sea, besides many cities and colonies in Thrace and Asia. The revenue arising from this territory must have been very considerable, and was wholly the property of this small number, who were intituled to many benefits out of it. The⟨y⟩ had frequent distributions of money or corn; they had their children maintain'd at the publick expense
89 when | necessary in the Pironeum,[51] which was then reckoned no disgrace; the⟨y⟩ had also an allowance for their attendance on the courts and the assemblys of the people, and at last had even one to enable them to attend on the theatres. Had they been very free in communicating the citizenship, the share of the publick stock which fell in this way to each of the old citizens would have been proportionally diminished; and they therefore allways opposed the admitting of any new members into the city. Such republicks were much in the same condition as the parishes are in England, where every person who is reduced to a state of poverty has considerable allowances off the parish stock, and for this ⟨?reason⟩ no one will be admitted as a member of a parish who can not give security that his children shall not come upon it for their maintenance.[52] All small republicks therefore are very chary in communicating their priviledges; the power of electing and of being elected is no inconsiderable priviledge in a state consisting of a small number, 10 or 15000 citizens. But in a country as England where the numbers are much larger, being about 9 or 10,000000, and if we include Ireland and the plantations about 15,000000, it is no
90 great compliment to give one the right of being | elected out of so great a number. Birth therefore determines citizenship. One who has been born

[x] Replaces 'which'

---

[50] Amyntas III, king of Macedon 393–370 B.C., father of Philip, king of Macedon 359–336 B.C.
[51] For services to the community individuals could be given dining privileges in the Prytaneum (a sort of Town Hall); also war orphans were maintained at public expense.
[52] 8 and 9 William III, c. 30 (1697).

within the dominions of the state has*y* the rights of possessing lands, is capable of holding offices of trust and profit, may elect others or be himself a Member of Parliament, and all other rights of a citizen. But in Holland and Switzerland, particularly in the canton of Bern, they are remarkably chary, insomuch that they refused to comply with the King of Frances request in being made a burgess of the town. The rule at Rome was the same as in other republicks, but they were allways much more free and liberall in conferring it on those who were not born citizens. The reason of this probably was that Rome was always a much larger city than the others; we see that soon after the expulsion of the kings the number of free citizens amounted to about 100000, and as this number includes only those who were of the military age, the number of free inhabitants enclusive of slaves must have been about 800000 or 1,000000. For which reason, tho the right of voting and the others of a citizen were by law confined to those who*z* were born of citizens, yet they were very liberall in conferring them on any illustrious persons who came among them or even upon whole towns or provinces of the empire.

91  | These two are the foundations of citizenship in all countries: in the larger ones, birth within the dominions of the state; and in the smaller ones, having ones father a citizen, and in those who are still more scrupulous, both father and mother.

The dissabilities and incapacities which aliens lie under are allso very different in different countries.—In the first ages of Rome, in the kingdom of Morocco, in Turkey, and in Corea in the        [53] part of Asia, and in a word in all the barbarous nations in the four quarters of the world, a stranger who came within the territory of ⟨the⟩ kingdom was siezed and made a slave. If he belonged to a state in alliance and peace with the state into which he had come he was treated according to the footing the two nations were on in the agreement. But if he came from an unknown nation to the Roman territory, by the violence of a storm or other such like accident, and a country betwixt which and the Romans there was no alliance, he was made a slave and his goods confiscated.[54] They have probably at first belonged to the first occupant, but to prevent the scramble

92  which such unnapropriated goods occasion | they were adjudged to the fisk.[55]—Strangers and enemies were called in common by the name of hostis. The word peregrinus was introduced long after when a distinction came to be made. Cicero[56] observes that the word which now signifies an enemy anciently signified a stranger. This he, who is always at great pains to

---

*v* 'all' deleted        *z* 'had' deleted

---

[53] Blank in MS. Presumably the missing word is 'eastern'.
[54] *D.* 49.15.5.2; Montesquieu, XXI.14.
[55] Fiscus or treasury.
[56] *De Officiis*, I.37.

extoll the virtue and humanity of the old Romans, considers as a sign of their vast humanity and moderation. Our humane ancestors, says he, gave no other name to an enemy than what they gave to any stranger. But the fact realy was that they considered strangers and enemies as one and the same thing; so that we might with greater justice say that strangers had the same name as enemies.[57] And there is in fact no great difficulty in accounting for this. Two savage neighbouring nations who are in alliance will treat the members of each other with some considerable humanity. But those of other nations they have no knowledge of but what they have got when at

93   war with them. The only light they have | known them in is in that of an enemy; they have had no commerce or intercourse with them by trade, and are either presently at war with them or have been very lately, and therefore look on any one who comes amongst them as a spy, unless he has got a safe conduct from home. And on these principles it was that the crew of the Litchfield man of war were siezed and made slaves, tho the Emperor of Morocco was at peace with Britain at that time, and were[a] ransomed according to the custom of the country.[58]— But when men have a little farther progress in society and the arts[b] and improvements of it, and begin to find the benefit of having foreigners coming amongst them, who carry out what is superfluous of the product of the country and importing the superfluities of their country, which tend either to the convenience or the luxury of the country, then they will find the benefits of foreign commerce and will be induced to encourage the settling of foreign merchants amongst them. For this purpose it will be absolutely necessary to give them the protection of

94   the laws, both to their persons and their goods. | This will necessarily require that they should have the benefit of all personall actions in the same manner as the citizens, that they may have redress if they be beat or abused, and that those who should kill them should be liable to the same penalties as those who killed a citizen; otherwise they could have no security for their lives or persons, and ⟨?this⟩ is absolutely necessary if they be allowed to settle amongst the citizens. And it is no less necessary that they should have all actions which regard moveables, so that they may be enabled to make their contracts effectuall, to recover goods they have entrusted to the care of others, and such like. This is all the length aliens have come either in the ancient states or the modern ones. An alien in England has all these, which are called there personall actions, which include all those which regard moveables. Reall actions concern only land estates; of these they have none at all. They can neither purchase or

---

[a] 'ob' deleted        [b] Illegible word deleted

[57] Hume, 'Of Commerce', *Essays*, I.292, note.
[58] The Litchfield was wrecked off the Barbary coast on 29 November 1758 and the crew ransomed from the emperor for 225,000 hard dollars in April 1760. *Gentleman's Magazine* (1760), 200, 391; (1761), 359–63.

inherit lands or transmitt them to others. Neither can an alien have a lease of land for years as this is not necessary for a merchant in order to carry on
95 his business. But he may have for that purpose a lease of a | house for years. This at first was extended merely for the encouragement of merchants, but not for mechanicks or tradesmen. The English have also interpreted it in this way, and*c* in Henry the 8*ths* time, when they were more jealous than ever in this way, and looked on all such foreign tradesmen as *taking the bread out of the poors mouth*, they got a law passed that no tradesman who was an alien should be allowed to possess a house for years.[59]—There is also a distinction made betwixt an *alien enemy* and an *alien friend*, that is, an alien of a country which is at war with us and of one which is at peace. An alien friend has the priviledges above mentioned. But an allien enemy has no security without the kings protection either in person or goods, and tho he can have an action in the name of another can have none in his own name either real, personall, or mixt. An alien friend has all personall actions and mixt ones, so far as they are personall. The king of G.*d* in the beginning of this last war gave his protection to all French men who inclined to settle in that*e* country.

96 | There are two methods by which the inconveniencies of alienage can be removed: either by letters of denization from the king, or by an Act of naturallization from the Parliament. The letters of denization can make*f* him capable of purchasing lands and of transmitting them to his posterity or any heir ab intestato or testato who is also free of the country; but can not convey to him the right of inheriting from others.—The king as heir of all aliens and the person to whom all lands they purchase would belong from the moment they become possessed of them, as they are incapable of possessing, may cede from his right both during the persons life time and after his death. But he has no power in this country at least to give away the right of another. He can give away the rights of purchasing or transmitting an inheritance in any way he pleases, as that only hurts himself, but he cant give the right of inheriting to an alien, as the estate would by my alienage go to another relation. If therefore one who*g* had been a citizen has been obliged to leave the country or stay abroad on account of business, the wives of such generally return and are brought to bed at home, as they
97 could not possess any estate that falls to them, even by | an Act of denization; tho if a relation inclined to bequeath one in this condition an estate as a legacy he might inherit it, as legacys are accounted a species of purchase. But to be made inheritable and be put on a levell with other subjects

---

*c* 'have' deleted          *d* Reading doubtful; 'B' deleted          *e* Reading doubtful
Replaces 'give'          *g* 'had the' deleted

---

[59] 32 Henry VIII, c. 16 (1540) prohibited alien tradesmen from holding a house for a term of years, complaining of the detriment to Englishmen from the presence of many aliens.

an Act of Parliament is necessary, and it can do any thing. Formerly an *Act of naturallization* gave one all the rights of a citizen and made on⟨e⟩ capable of having any dignity or nobility conferred upon him. But when King William came over many of his friends in Holland came over with him, and these were frequently more about and more esteemed, as he was better acquainted with him[60] than the English, and were frequently preferred to them in honours and titles. This greatly offended the English, who took this naturall partiallity in very high hurt. And an Act of Parliament was therefore made declaring that no Act of naturallization should be passed in which it was not provided and expressly declared that the person naturallized should still continue incapable of being ever admitted as a peer into the House of Lords or of being chosen a member of the House of Commons, tho he had all the other rights above mentioned.[61] I shall observe one other peculiarity in the laws | of some countries with regard to allienage which is not the case in England.—All laws which extend property beyond the person of the possessor are of later introduction than those which constitute property, and are not at all necessary to its existence. Property naturally is connected with all those which are called the personall rights (as above mentioned) by the English law; but the power of testing is not at all necessary and has in all countries been posterior to the others. For this reason in many countries an alien can not make a will; his property goes to the king by what is called the jus albani or le droit d'albain, albain[62] being the word which signifies a foreigner. These goods have at first gone to the occupant, but to preven⟨t⟩ the confusion that ensues on such a scramble have been assigned to the king. The Elector of Saxony, now King of Poland, made a law that all those in whose nations the Saxons were capable of property should be so in Saxony, but otherwise not.[63]— This seems to be a very just retaliation. This right took place at Rome. The goods of a peregrinus who died in Rome went to the fisque.

99                    | *Monday. March. 21ˢᵗ 1763*

In the last lecture I endeavoured to explain the nature of alienage in the different countries, the reasons of those institutions, and the different dissabilities they put one under. In some countries at this day and in all barbarous nations aliens ⟨are⟩ entirely incapable of all of those rights which are possessed by the citizens, and in many in which they are allowed to possess an estate themselves they are not allowed the right of making a will. This right, as I observed formerly at great length,[64] is granted merely from the reverence and respect which we feell for the commands of the dead; it involves in it something more than what is necessary to constitute

---

60 *Sic.* Presumably 'them' was intended.        61 1 George I, st. 2, c. 4 (1714).
62 Aubaine.        63 E. Vattel, *Droit des gens*, II.8.112.        64 i.149 ff. above.

property. Piety to the dead then being the sole foundation of it, tho this may appear to be due to our friends, country-men, and relations, men are not so sensible of so great regard being due to the will or memory[h] of foreigners; and therefore in many countries where foreigners are allowed to have property, if they have no children or near relations their goods are siezed by the government by what is called the jus albani, albezani, or
100 dalbain. This is not the case in | England. The liberty of making wills is derived entirely in England from the cannon and later civill law, and being established at the time many of the laws relating to property were made, has come to be considered as an appendage of property; and is for that reason allowed to bastards which it is not in other countries. But still the aliens are incapable of inheriting or purchasing land estates. The last of these may be granted by letters of denization, but the latter only by an Act of Parliament, as the king can not, nor ever attempted to, give away to a third person the property of another. When one who is a citizen makes a bargain with another which is not allowed by law, the bargain is null and void, and the property of it returns to the proprietor. But a bargain made with an alien is neither void nor voidable; the bargain holds, but as the alien is incapable of property it is siezed by the king. This right he can give up, tho he can not take away the right of another by entituling one to inherit that which otherwise would have been his.

There is one thing more to be observed with regard to alliens, both aliens ⟨?ennemis and aliens⟩ amis, or[65] alien enemies and alien friends.—If any num-
101 ber | of aliens make depradations on the country and enter it in a hostile manner, not being authorized by the sovereign they belong to, they can not be tried as traitors. They are not subject to the king or sovereign power and owe no alegiance to him; they can not therefore be dealt with by the laws against treason; they can only be tried by the martiall laws of the country as freebooters or pirates. If they had the direction of a sovereign state who had the power of making peace or war or sending a hostile army, they would then be treatd according to the laws of war. But tho those *aliens* who commit hostilities on the kingdom can not be tried as traitors against it, yet if an alien friend who has come under the protection of the laws enters into a conspiracy or rebellion against the sovereign of the country he lives in, or corresponds with, encourages, aids, or abbetts the enemies of the country, he is liable to the pains of high treason, which are the greatest of any, as well as a subject. He is considered as equally bound to allegiance and fidelity to the sovereign as the subjects, as he has the same protection and safety from the laws. In
102 the same manner an alien enemy who | takes advantage of the kings pro-

[h] Numbers written above the words 'will' and 'memory' indicate that their order was intended to be reversed

[65] Reading of last two words doubtful. Cf. LJ(B) 90, below.

clamation and assurance of safety to those who continue within his dominions, gives any intelligence to the sovereign of his own country, enters into any conspiracy, or is guilty of any other treasonable act, is liable to the pains of treason. And in generall any one who lives under the protection of the laws is bound to the same allegiance as a subject.$=$

I come[i] now to consider the 2$^d$ part of publick law, viz the duties of the sovereign towards his subjects and the crimes he may be guil⟨t⟩y of against them. This is a question which I can not pretend to answer with such precision as the others. The nature of this branch of public law, as well as that of the law of nations, is such that we can not pretend to such precision in it as in the private laws amongst subjects, or in the other part of publick law which comprehends the duties of subjects to their sovereigns. Both of these have been frequently canvassed, and laws have regulated and courts have fairly examind and settled precedents both with regard to the duty of subject to subject and of the subject to the sovereign. Laws and the

103 proceedings of judges ascertain them; but there | is no court which can try the sovereigns themselves, no authority sovereign to the sovereign, and ⟨?which has⟩ examind and ascertaind[j] how far the actions of the sovereigns to the subject or of one sovereign to another are justifiable and how far their power extends. The precise limits have been little considered and are very difficult to ascertain to which the power of the sovereign extends. In England the exact boundaries of the kings power have been pretty well known since the Revolution; one can tell exactly what he can do. But then we are to consider that the king is not here the sovereign. The sovereign power [power] is lodged in the king and Parliament together, and no one can tell what they can not do. And in the same manner where the king is the sovereign no one can pretend to ascertain how far this power may go, as in France, Spain, Turky, etc. There are without doubt certain limits, but no one has yet considered them with the same candor and composure as ⟨a⟩ court does the private affairs of individualls. So that one who is to consider this matter must set out anew and upon his own bottom. All disputes of

104 this sort | have been decided by force and violence. If the sovereign got the better of the subjects, then they were condemned as traitors and rebells; and if the subjects have got the better of the sovereign, he is declared to be a tyrant and oppressor not to be endured. Sometimes the decision has been right and sometimes wrong, but they can never be of such weight as the decisions of a cooll and impartial court.—The three branches of the supreme power are now fully established in the hands of the sovereign; but there are still some things which must be unlawful even for the sovereign.[k] The most necessary branches of this[l] power were at first exercised precariously.

---

[i] '2$^d$' is interlined above 'come'     [j] Illegible word or words deleted     [k] 'to'
deleted     [l] 'federative' deleted

The first part of the supreme power which is exercised in society is the federative power. But as I already mentioned[66] this is altogether precarious in the beginnings of society. The majority of the state determine with regard to peace and war, but then this binds themselves only; the others are conceived to be at full liberty to carry on the war after the others have concluded peace, or to be at peace with those the others are at war with. I observd too that those who continue the war after the body of the people have made the peace are hardly ever punished, tho those ⟨?are⟩ who do
105 not | engage in the common quarrel. The reason as I said is that the motives or passions which prompt men to make peace are cool and deliberate, whereas those which prompt them to make war are hot and impetuous and hurry men to the avenging themselves on those who will not engage in the revenging the injuries or affronts they have received; and by this means it happens that the minority who desire to continue the war generally act in the same manner as the majority would were they not hindered by certain prudential reasons. This earliest branch of the supreme ⟨power⟩ is therefore at first exercised precariously, tho now it is altogether absolute, and one who continues the war after the nation⟨s⟩ have made peace is liable to be punished not only by the country against whom the injury was committed but also by the laws of his own country; and in the same manner all communication and intercourse betwixt the subjects is stopped as soon as war is declared betwixt the two nations. The judiciall power was also
106 | originally altogether precarious, and was in order of time much later of being established than the federative or executive power; and tho in many countries we cant discover a time when the sovereign had not the power of making peace and war, yet there are none in which we cannot disco⟨v⟩er certain remains and marks which plainly point out to us that this power also was precarious. There was a time when the judge was considered merely as a mediator in criminall cases and an arbiter voluntarily chosen in civill ones; tho' they have at length become absolute, so that whatever they determine must be adhered to, be it right or be it wrong, and no reference can be made from their sentence. The judges at first did not require the parties to come before them and submit to their sentence. They might instead of putting themselves on their judge and their country put themselves to the judicial combat, the triall by fire ordial or by boiling water, etc., and thus evade the sentence of the judge. Nor were they bound to
107 adhere to the sentence of the judge. They could not | indeed fight their opponents after the sentence was passed, but they might then fight their judge if they did not like his sentence,[67] and their quarrell was then turned upon him. All that was done by the sentence was to put it in their power to agree to the decision if it seemed equitable. For they had it still in their power to draw back and falsify the sentence of the judge in the

---

[66] iv.13–14, 19–20 above.          [67] Montesquieu, XXVIII.27.

same way as they had before done the claim of the opponents. The judge at this time decided all affronts or contempts done to his authority by force of arms. They asked the dissobedient persons why they did not obey their orders and then challenged and fought them. This sufficiently shews that the judicial power was then very precarious, and that mankind thought themselves bound neither to submit to the authority of the judge in appearing before him nor in adhering to his sentence; but now their authority is so establishd that no one complains, whatever injustice he may think he suffers, as they are absolute and without appeal. All resistance is unlawfull, and tho perhaps it is naturall enough to make resistance yet it is altogether prohibited,[m] in the same progress as that by which it is now un-
108 lawfull either to | continue in war or to continue correspondence after war with the enemy, after the publick have agreed to the discontinuance of war or peace.

The legislative power also comes in time to be absolute.—There is at first in the ruder periods of society no legislative power, nor for some considerable time. Tho one was ready to stand by the sentence of an arbiter chosen perhaps out of the whole body of the people, as the heads of[n] families, yet they would be altogether unwilling they should lay down laws for their conduct. He has no notion of any one having this power over him. No more than a member of a club will submit himself to the rules they may lay down, no more would a savage when he agrees to be a member of a society [would] think[o] that he was bound to obey all their regulations.— The thing which has given occasion to the establishment of laws has always been the generall or partiall institution of judges. When any nation has retaind its liberty, and property has been established amongst them, judges must soon be appointed to determine the many disputes which must occurr concerning it. A judge will to such an early nation appear very terrible. A
109 judge is now rather a comfortable than a terrible | sight as he is the source of our liberty, our independence, and our security. Savages do not feel the want of judges; and tho they must be liable to many inconveniencies on that account, yet one who has been accustomed to trust to the strength of his own arm and his own manly prowess is confident and bold to trust to it in future occasions. But for him to think that whenever he is guilty of any trespass, as he knows he has often been, there is one who has the power to call him to trial, and if the fact is proved against him to condemn him to any punishment he thinks proper, appears to[p] be altogether terrible and un-sufferable. Savages of all things hate a judge set over their heads. Of this the story of Varus recorded by Tacitus[68] is a striking instance. By all we can

[m] Illegible word deleted    [n] 'the' deleted    [o] Replaces 'that he'    [p] 'him' deleted

---

[68] Not by Tacitus but by Florus, *Epitome Rerum Romanarum*, II.30.31 ff. Montesquieu, XIX.2, also wrongly cites Tacitus in this regard.

learn of him he appears to have been a most amiable man and of very gentle
manners, so that we now can hardly conceive how it should have happened
that he should have incenced the Germans to such a height. That which
incensed them more than all the tyranny, extorsion, and oppression of the
Romans was the regular courts of justice which Varus established every
110 | where in the country, who tried and punished all offences with the same
rigour and severity as had been customary at the Roman courts. This it was
which provoked the Germans and in revenge of which they massacred the
whole Roman army. The courts of justice when established appear to a
rude people to have an authority altogether insufferable; and at the same[q]
time when property is considerably advanced judges can not be wanted.
The judge is necessary and yet is of all things the most terrible. What shall
be done in this case? The only way is to establish laws and rules which may
asertain his conduct; {This was the case at Athens, Sparta, and other
places[r] where the people demanded laws to regulate the conduct of the
judge} for when it is known in what manner he is to proceed the terror will
be in a great measure removed. Laws are in this manner posterior to the
establishment of judges. At the first establishment of judges there are no
laws; every one trusts to the naturall feeling of justice he has in his own
breast and expects to find in others. Were laws to be established in the
beginnings of society prior to the judges, they would then be a restraint
upon liberty, but when established after them they extent[69] and secure
111 ⟨?it⟩, | as they do not ascertain or restrain the actions of private persons so
much as the power and conduct of the judge over the people. In this
manner the legislative power is established, which in time, as well as the
others, grows up to be absolute; but notwithstanding that the subjects are
bound to obedienc⟨e⟩ to all these powers there are some cases in which they
may break thro them[e].

### Tuesday March. 22.

In yesterdays lecture I begun to explain the rights of the subject against
the sovereign; that is, what are the limits of the sovereign power, and in
what cases it is proper for the subjects to make resistance.—At fir⟨s⟩t all
the branches of this power were[s] extremely limited and held precariously;
even the federative power was under a precarious tenure. The judiciall
power was no less precarious, and the legislative power was at first so far
from being absolute that there was hardly any such thing. The growth of
the judicial power was what gave occasion to the institution of a legislative
power, as that first made them think of restraining the power of judicial

---

[q] 'point' deleted        [r] Reading doubtful        [s] 'all' deleted

[69] *Sic.* Presumably 'extend' was intended.

officers. Laws instituted at the beginning of a society would never be agreed
112  to; they would appear to be the greatest | restraint imaginable on the
liberty and security of the subjects; but afterwards they evidently appear to
tend to the security of the people by restraining[t] the arbitrary power of the
judges, who are then become absolute or nearly so. The legislative power
thus constituted must from the very nature and design of it be absolute
from the moment of its institution; and the other powers in time become so
also. There is now no power of resistance, whether the sentence of the
judge appear to the person to be just or not; and in the same manner there
is no remedy against a law which appears to be unjust unless it be repealed;
private persons must obey and judges give sentence agreably to it.—Those
persons who are entrusted with the severall parts of the supreme power in
the constitution must be relied on without hesitation. The authority of the
Parliament in some things, of the king and Parliament in others, and of the
king alone in some, are incontestible, and if they act amiss there is no
regular right of resisting them as sovereigns in any way. So that the limits
of the sovereign power are extremely doubtfull. The limits of the kings
power are in this country well enough known, but the king is far from
having the sovereign power. The legislative power he shares with the
113  Parliament, | who have now almost the whole of it. He is said indeed to be
the fountain of justice; which is indeed so far true that all the ordinary
judges are of his appointment; but then these judges are intirely independent of him after their constitution; nor has he in his own person any
judicial power. And besides this the House of Lords, who are the supreme
judges, are altogether independent on him either with respect to their
appointment or their proceedings. He has indeed the whole of executive or
federative power; but as the people have a power of impeaching any of his
ministers who have given him bad advice, this too is somewhat limited, tho
the king and his ministers have the disposall of peace and war in all
ordinary cases. There is no doubt then but the power of the king may be
resisted; but the question is, when is it lawfull or allowable to resist the
power of the king and Parliament. They would never have any thoughts of
making any laws which should tell us that, when they went beyond such and
such limits, the[u] people were not bound to obey them but might resist.
114  That they should do this can not be imagined. In whatever place | there is a
sovereign, from the very nature of things the power must be absolute; and
no power regularly established of calling the sovereign to account, as the
sovereign has an undoubted title to the obedience of the subjects. The
foundation of this obedience of the subjects has been often controverted.
But whatever it be, there are certain limits to the power of the sovereign,
which if he exceeds, the subject may with justice make resistance.

　　If we shall suppose with the generallity of writers on this subject (as

[t] Replaces 'securing'　　　[u] Illegible word deleted

Locke and Sidney, etc.)[70] that the government owes its origin to a voluntary contract in which the people gave over the sovereign power in its different parts, the judiciall or the legislative, to another body, and so of the executive, and promised obedience and submission to this power; even on this submission, which from what has been already explaind concerning the progress[v] of government can hardly be supposed to have ever been the case, even here the subjects must have a right of resistance. The power of the sovereign is in this case a trust reposed in him by the people; he is the great magistrate to whom they have promised obedience as long | as he rules with a midd⟨l⟩ing[w] degree of equity; but when he has abused this power in a very violent manner, for it is only a violent abuse of it which can call for such violent measures, then undoubtedly he may be resisted as he is guilty of a breach of the trust reposed in him.—When he ab[s]uses his power and does not exert[x] it for the benefit of the people for whose advantage it was given him, but turns it to the aggrandizing and exalting of himself, then he may be turned out of his office; in the same manner as a tutor who abuses to his own interest the goods of his pupil committed to his care may be turned out and another put in his room. But indeed this does not seem to be the foundation of the power[y] of the sovereign and the obedience of the people; and supposing that it had originally been the foundation of the authority of the sovereign it can not now be so; and nevertheless we find that in all ordinary cases they are bound to obey the king. Besides, this doctrine of obedience as founded on contract is confined to Britain and has never been heard of in any other country, so that there it can not be the foundation of the obedience of the people; and even here it can have | influence with a very small part of the people, such as have read Locke, etc. The far greater part have no notion of it, and nevertheless they have the same notion of the obedience due to the sovereign power, which can not proceed from any notion of contract.—Again, if the first members of the society had entered into a contract with certain persons to whom they entrusted the sovereign power, their obedience would indeed have been founded on a contract in a great measure; but this can not be the case with their posterity; they have entered into no such contract.[71] The contract of ones predecessors never binds one merely because it was his. The heir indeed is bound to pay the debts contracted by his predecessors to whom he has fallen heir, not because their promise is any way binding on him but because by possessing their money he would be *locupletior factus*

---

[v] Replaces 'power'          [w] The last two words replace 'tollerable'          [x] Reading doubtful          [y] 'of' deleted

---

[70] Locke, *Civil Government*; Algernon Sidney, *Discourses Concerning Government* (1698).

[71] Cf. Hume, 'Of the Original Contract', *Essays*, I.447.

*aliena jactura.*[72] One is not bound to personall service promised by his ancestors; their promise has no influence upon him. But if the whole hire or price of his fathers service has been paid beforehand, then he will be bound for the reason above mentiond to make restitution of the value of the part
117 not performed; | and so in all other cases. And what makes this entirely evident is that one is bound for the debts of his predecessors no more than what the estate left by them will amount to, altho it be greatly less; which overturns the old fancy of the heirs being eadem persona cum defuncto.— But to this they may answer[z] that tho one is not bound by the contract of his ancestors, nor here by any express deed of his own, yet he is bound by his [bound by his] own tacit promise. His staying in the country shews that he inclines to submit to the government established in it.[73] Hence, say they, every one who stays in the country must submit to the government. But this is a very fallacious argument. A very ingenious gentleman[74] exposed the deceit of it very clearly by the following example. If one who was carried on board of a ship when asleep was to be told that having continued afterwards on board he was bound to submit to the rules of the crew, any one would see the unreasonableness of it, as he was absolutely forced to stay on board. He had not his coming on board at his own choice, and after
118 he | was on board it was folly to tell him he might have gone away when the ocean surrounded him on all hands. Such is the case with every subject of the state. The⟨y⟩ came into the world without having the place of their birth of their own choosing, so that we may say they came asleep into the country; nor is it in the power of the greater part to leave the country without the greatest inconveniencies. So that there is here no tacit consent of the subjects. They have no idea of it, so that it can not be the foundation of their obedience.—Again, if this was the case one by leaving the country would free himself from all duty to the government; and yet we see that all nations claim the power of calling back their subjects either by proclamation or by a private mandate (as a writ of the privy seal⟨⟩⟩, and punish all those who do not obey as traitors; and in generall every one who is born under the government is considered as being bound to submit to it. Again, of all the cases where one is bound to submit to the government that of an alien comes the nearest to a voluntary or tacit contract.[75] He comes into the country not asleep but with his eyes open, inlist⟨s⟩[a] himself under the pro-
119 tection of this[b] government preferably to all others; and if the | principle of

---

[z] 'perhaps' deleted        [a] Reading doubtful        [b] Reading doubtful

---

[72] 'Enriched at the expense of another'.
[73] Cf. Locke, *Civil Government*, § 119.
[74] Hume, 'Of the Original Contract', *Essays*, I.451: 'We may as well assert, that a man, by remaining in a vessel, freely consents to the dominion of the master; though he was carried on board while asleep, and must leap into the ocean, and perish, the moment he leaves her.'          [75] Cf. Hume, 'Of the Original Contract', *Essays*, I.452.

allegiance and obedience is ever founded on contract it must be in this case. Yet we see that aliens have always been suspected by the government, and have always been laid under great dissabilities of different sorts and never have any trust or employment in the state; and yet they have shewn more strong and evident signs of an inclination to submit to the government than any others; and the obligations they are under to obedience are to those of a native subject as that of one who voluntarily enlists into the fleet compared to that of a pressed man. So that upon the whole this obedien⟨ce⟩ which every one thinks is due to the sovereign does not arise from any notion of a contract.

This principle or duty of allegiance seems to be founded on two principles. ⟨The⟩ 1st we may call the principle of authority, and the 2d the principall of common or generall interest.—With regard to the principle of authority, we see that every one naturally has a disposition to respect an established authority and superiority in others, whatever they be. The young respect the old, children respect their parents, and in generall the weak respect

120 those who excell in power and strength. Whatever be the | foundation of government this has a great effect. One is born and bred up under the authority of the magistrates; he finds them demanding the obedience of all those about him and he finds that they always submit to their authority; he finds they are far above him in the power they possess in the state; he sees they expect his obedience and he sees also the propriety of obeying and the unreasonableness of ⟨dis⟩obeying. They have a naturall superiority over him; they have more followers who are ready to support their authority over the disobedient. There is the same propriety in submitting to them as to a father, as all of those in authority are either naturally or by the will of the state who lend them their power placed far above you.— —

With regard to the other principle, every one sees that the magistrates not only support the government in generall but the security and independency of each individuall, and they see that this security can not be attained without a regular government. Every one therefor thinks it most advisable to submitt to the established government, tho perhaps he may think that it

121 is not disposed | in the best manner possible; and this too is strengthend by the naturall modesty of mankind, who are not generally inclined to think they have a title to dispute the authority of those above them. Each of these principles takes place in some degree in every government, tho one is generally predominant. The principle of authority is that which chiefly prevails in a monarchy. Respect and deference to the monarchy, the idea they have that there is a sort of sinfullness or impiety in dissobedience, and the duty they owe to him, are what chiefly influence them. No doubt but the expediency of such obedience may also have its effect on some persons. —In a republican government, particularly in a democraticall one, ⟨?utility⟩ is that which chiefly, nay allmost entirely, occasions the obedience

of the subject. He feels and is taught from his childhood to feel the ex-
cellen⟨c⟩y of the government he lives under; how much more desirable it is
to have the affairs of the state under the direction of the whole than that it
should be confined to one person; that in the one case it can hardly ever be
abused and in the other it can hardly miss of being so. This recommends the
government to the people, who are all bread to understand it. In such
122 governments the principle of authority is as it were in some measure | pre-
scribed.[76] A successfull leader, obtaining the good graces of the people, will
get every thing he can ask from them; they know ⟨no⟩ bounds in their
affections. Such persons would therefore be very dangerous in the state and
might overturn with ease the established government. This principle is
therefore discouraged, as it is in the interest of the state that no one should
be much distinguished above the others. However even here the principle
of authority has some influence in procuring the obedience of the subjects.
This respect is not indeed paid to persons, the naturall objects of it, but to
offices.—Any one who was chosen consul at Rome had great honour and
respect paid him, tho inferior to that of a hereditary sovereign. This respect
which is paid to the persons in power in every country makes the wheels of
the government go on more smoothly.—In an aristocracy the principle of
authority is the leading one, tho there is no doubt but the other has also
some effect.

In Britain the sovereign power is partly entrusted to the king, partly to
123 the people, and partly to the nobles. As it is therefore partly monarchi|call
the principle of authority takes place in a considerable degree, as also
because there is some small part of the government aristocraticall. But as
the government is in great part democraticall, by the influence of the House
of Commons, the principle of utility is also found in it. Some persons are
more directed by the one and others by the other. And to these different
principles were owing the distinctions betwixt Whig and Tory. The
principle of authority is that of the Tories, as that of utility is followd by
the Whigs. They say that as the government was established not for the
benefit of the rulers but of the people, and that therefore it is proper to
resist their power whenever they abuse it in a great degree and turn it to
their own advantages, and that they have no authority unless what they
derive from the people. This is their principle, tho they do not explain it
very distinctly, endeavouring to reconcile it to the notion of a contract. The
Torys again go on the principle of authority, tho they also make still more
124 confused work of it on the supposition of a contract. | The Tories pretend
that the kingly authority is of[c] divine institution, that the kings derive their
authority immediately from God, and that therefore it must be an impiety

[c] 'a' deleted

---

[76] *Sic.* Presumably 'proscribed' was intended.

to resist him; that he has as it were a patriarchall authority and is a sort of father to his people, and as it is unlawfull for children in any case to rebell against their father, so is it for subjects to rebell against their sovereigns.[77] These principles affect people of different casts. The bustling, spirited, active folks, who can't brook oppression and are constantly endeavouring to advance themselves, naturally join in with the democraticall part of the constitution and favour the principle of utility only, that is, the Whig interest. The calm, contented folks of no great spirit and abundant fortunes which they want to enjoy at their own ease, and dont want to be disturbd nor to disturb others, as naturally join with the Tories and found their obedience on the less generous principle of utility.[78] But whatever be the
125 foundation of the | obedience of the subjects, there are some things which it is unlawfull for the sovereign[d] to attempt and entitle the subjects to make resistance. Some certain degrees of absurdity and outrage, either in a single person or an assembly, will entirely destroy all their claim of obedience. An assembly indeed is less apt to fall into this absurdity than a single person, for tho there may be the greatest difference betwixt the behaviour of one man and another, an assembly of 4 or 500 taken out of the people will be much the same as any other 500 and will be no more liable to err. Yet even here it will sometimes happen, and from this it was that all the old aristo-cracies became democracies, the council of the nobles having incensed the people against them.—There can be no doubt that one by a certain degree of absurdity and outrage in his conduct may lose his authority altogether.
126 All agree that lunacy, nonnage,[e][79] or ideotism entirely destroy the | authority of a prince. Now there are[f] degrees of absurdity and impropriety in the conduct of a sovereign which, tho they do not equall that of lunacy or ideotism, entitle the subjects to resistance in the eyes of every unprejudiced person. Who is there that in reading the Roman history does not acknow-ledge that the conduct of Nero, Caligula, or Domitian was such as entirely took away all authority from them? No one but must enter into the designs of the people, go along with them in all their plots and conspiracys to turn them out, is rejoiced at their success, and grieves when they fail. So that even on this principle resistance must be permitted. In the principle of utility there can be still less doubt but it is lawfull. If the good of the publick is that on which the obedience ⟨?⟩, then this obedience is no longer due than it is usefull; and wherever the confusion which must arise on an

---

[d] Replaces 'subject'    [e] Numbers written above the last two words indicate that their order was intended to be reversed    [f] Illegible word or words deleted

---

[77] In TMS VI.ii.2.16 (a passage written for edition 6 of 1790) Smith writes with appro-val of 'the divine maxim of Plato, never to use violence to [one's] country no more than to his parents'.
[78] *Sic.* Presumably 'authority' was intended. Cf. Hume, 'Of the Parties of Great Britain', *Essays*, I.133-4.    [79] i.e. non-age or minority.

**127** overthrow of the | established govt. is less than the mischief of allowing it to continue, then resistance is proper and allowable. And that such cases may occur their can be no doubt. Absurdity and impropriety of conduct and great perverseness destroy obedience, whether it be due from authority or the sense of the common good.

### *Wednesday. March 23ᵈ 1763 —*

In yesterdays lecture I showed you that whatever be the principle of allegiance and obedienc⟨e⟩ of the sovereign, it must have some limits. I endeavoured also to shew that the commonly received one of a tacit contract can not be the just one. This principle must certainly be that from which the generallity of the world think themselves bound. Every morall duty must arise from some thing which mankind are conscious of. The case is the very same as in that of approbation and dissapprobation; as no one can draw a conclusion or agree to one without knowing the premises, so no

**128** one can have a notion | of any duty from a principle of which they have not at least some confused conception; for it is very seldom that one has a distinct notion of the foundation of their duties, but have merely a notion that they have such and such obligations. All have a notion of the duty of allegiance to the sovereign, and yet no one has any conception of a previous contract either tacit or express. Why do those who engage in parties and factions against the government refuse to take the oath of allegiance? If by staying in the country they come under a contract, the*g* same as if it was voluntarily entered into, what need is there of an express oath afterwards. This shews evidently that they have no notion of this tacit contract; and it is no less evident that the government do not rely on it, else why would they put this oath to them? Besides if allegiance depended on the tacit contract of the parties an express declaration against it, as well as leaving the countries, would render them altogether free from it, and an alien would be

**129** more expressly bound than any other, the quite contra|ry of which is the case. So that this tacit contract, so much talked of, is never thought of either by the governors nor the governed. The principles on which this allegiance are really founded are those of authority ⟨?and⟩ of public or generall utility. It is very difficult to define what authority is, but every one has an idea of it in his mind. Several things tend to give one an authority over others. 1ˢᵗ, superiority of age and of wisdom which is generally its concomitant. 2ᵈˡʸ, superior strength of body; and these two it is which give the old an authority and respect*h* with the young. 3ᵈ, superior fortune also gives a certain authority, caetereis paribus; and 4ᵗʰˡʸ, the effect is the same of superior antiquity when everything else is alike; an old family excites no such jealousy as an upstart does. An ancient jurisdiction and

*g* Reading doubtful      *h* Reading doubtful

power increases the authority of the person in whatever manner it be obtaind. He appears to have no more than what his father, etc. have had for time immemoriall. An office held for life gives one more respect than one
130 which is but temporary.— | A judge has more respect paid him than the mayor of a burrgh; we indeed pay a respect to him on account of his office. We know here that they[i] obtain'd their authority but as yesterday, and we know that the one must soon lay down his authority whereas the other continues for his life. The antiquity of it also adds respect to an old authority. Civill authority is for this reason never so much respected as the others, as they are hereditary. An ordinary Justice of Peace has all the power of many of the hereditary jurisdictions, yet no one thought that they were not infinitely more respected from the antiquity of the power they possessed.— For this reason a hereditary monarch has much greater power ⟨and⟩ authority than an elective one. He has a vast revenue and a great number of dependents consequent upon it which have been in his family for many generations, which gives him even greater power than that which he derives from the kingly power. This joined with the antiquity of it gives him
131 vast authority. Every one is sensible of the propriety of paying re|spect to one who is possessed of such a power, which also, being no greater than what his ancestors had, can excite envy in no one. The principle of authority goes higher here than any where else. The other principle has also its weight. Every one sees that the magistrates give security to property and strength to the laws, and that without them all must fall into confusion. It seems therefore to be his own interest and that of every one else to obey the[j] established government, when it acts with ordinary moderation and tollerable decency. Every one sees that the government has a vast authority and great influence over others so that all attempts to overturn it must be resisted, and with great vigour. And tho one may sometimes think that there are inconveniences in the government, he must see that there will be great difficulty and disturbance arise from an attempt to alter it. The persons in power will, as it is their interest, make a vigorous resistance, and he has but little reason to wish for a change. Justice is administered tho not
132 in the most perfect | manner yet tollerably well, and ones dread for himself and others in consequence of an attempt to subvert it disposes him more readily to submit to it. And indeed it will but seldom happen that one will be very sensible of the constitution he has been born and bred under; everything by custom appears to be right or at least one is but very little shocked at it. In this case and[k] in many others the principle of authority is the foundation of that of utility or common interest.

The severall parts of the supreme power were at first in the early governments altogether precarious. When now the government is become absolute in all these branches in every civilized country, there are still

---

[i] 'hold th' deleted    [j] Illegible word deleted    [k] 'all' deleted

certain cases in which the people have a right to resist the sovereign power.
Tho' every thing belongs to the sovereign, tho he is trusted with every part
of the publick government and the whole power, yet a certain gross abuse of
it must entitle the people to resist; bad conduct must necessarily deprive
them of all their authority. Childhood, lunacy, ideotism must take away all
authority and require a ⟨?new⟩ sovereign to be put in the place of the old
133 one. These interruptions cant | happen in an assembly; but a certain
degree of perverseness, absurdity, and unreasonableness, inferior indeed to
this, whether in a monarch or an assembly, as those of Caligula, etc.,
plainly establishes in the eyes of every one the right of turning them out in
the hands of the people and justifies all the measures used to that end. But
as single persons are much more liable to these absurdities than large
assemblies, so we find that revolutions on this head are much more frequent
in absolute monarchys than any where else. There are continuall revolutions
amongst the Mogulls; the Turks seldom have the same sultan (tho they
have still the same absolute government⟨⟩) above 6 or 8 years. There have
been more revolutions in Russia than in all Europe besides for some years
past. The folly of single men often incenses the people and makes it proper
and right to rebell.—An equall absurdity will have the same effect in an
aristocraticall government. The intollerable demands and severity of the
rules laid down by the Genoese with regard to their conduct to the Corsicans
justify entirely the rebellions and persevering resistance of those islanders.
134 They granted as a very great concession that | no one should be executed by
the governor informata concientia,[80] that is, without bringing him to a
triall. This being granted as a concession plainly shews the unreasonableness of the authority they required. Such cases seldom happen; and the
subjects have seldom any occasion to use these violent means, and the
encroachments of the sovereign are often overlooked as being what
the people are accustomd to.

The foundation of the allegiance of the people being a tacit contract is
not at all just, and we see accordingly that few of those limitations laid down
by writers who follow that scheme are to be found in fact in any country.—
It is a rule laid down by Mr. Locke[81] as a principle that the people have a
right to resist whenever the sovereign takes their money from them without
their consent by levying taxes to which they have not agreeed. Now we see
that in France, Spain, etc. the consent of the people is not in the least
thought of; the king imposes what taxes he pleases. It is in Britain alone
that any consent of the people is required, and God knows it is but a very
figurative metaphoricall consent which is given here. And in Scotland still
more than in England, as but very few have a vote for a Member of
135 Parliament | who give this metaphoricall consent; and yet this is not any

[80] *Informata conscientia*, 'on private information'.
[81] *Civil Government*, §§ 138–40.

where reckoned a sufficient cause of rebellion. No doubt the raising of a very exorbitant tax, as the raising as much in peace as in war, or the half or even the fifth of the wealth of the nation, would, as well as any other gross abuse of power, justify resistance in the people. But where this power is exerted with moderation, tho perhaps it is not done with the greatest propriety as it is in no country whatever, and tho not even a figurative consent is requir'd, yet they never think that they ought to resist tho they may claim the liberty of remonstrating against it.—Government was established to defend the property of the subjects, but if it come to be of a conterary tendency, yet they must agree to give up a little of their right. You must agree to repose a certain trust in them, tho if they absolutely break thro it, resistance is to be made if the consequences of it be not worse than the thing itself.[l]—

It is said also by these authors[82] that a sovereign can not alienate any part 136 of his dominions or transferr them to an other. All | that he can do is to withdraw his protection and defense from them and leave them to themselves. This is entirely agreable to the system of contracts; the people may object to the sovereign that tho they agree to be governd by him they do not agree to be under the power of one of his appointing; they agree to be subject to him but not to be at his disposall.[m] But we see that where ever government has been firmly established this is frequently done. Thus the French and Spaniards in the end of this war have agreed not only to allow us to keep the possession of some of our conquests, but also in exchange for others to yield up a vast tract of land; and they not only do not defend it but put us in the actuall possession of it, and the inhabitants thereafter become the subjects of Great Britain. This too is generally the interest of the people, as some wrongheaded people might stir them up to make a fruitless resistance to their new masters. We see that this is done not only in the making of a peace or in the course of a war, but in a much more scandalous manner, as a portion at the marriage of a daughter, or even by testament according to the good pleasure of the governors. This has been 137 often practised by France and Spain, and the Tsar | of Moscovy is also acknowledged to have this power. The feudall governments all allowed of it, and the principallities in Germany were also divided amongst the children as a private estate, the right of primogeniture not taking place till within these 150 years. This is in effect the proper rule, to observe what is actually done in these matters; in some this power is confined to the private ministry and in some extends to the whole people. It is said that the sovereign can not alter the fundamentall laws of the country: but these depend merely on the constitution of the state at that time. Thus it is said

[l] 'It' deleted    [m] Illegible word deleted

[82] e.g. Pufendorf, VIII.5.9; Cocceius, I.3.12; Hutcheson, *System*, II.297 ff.

that the French king can not alter the succession in[n] allowing it to pass by female heirs prohibited by the Salic law. But this depends merely on the circumstances of the affairs. The vast number of princes of the blood in France who are possessed of great estates, these will always oppose such a dissadvantageous alteration. But if it should happen that there were no princes of the blood nor any very great nobility, as was the case in Britain in        [83] he might no doubt alter it as he pleases, as easily as with the[o]

138 | succession of private persons. But tho the sovereign may be resisted, it cant be said that there is any regular authority for so doing. The property, life, and liberty of the subject are in some measure in his power; nor is it or can it be ascertained what abuses justify resistance. No laws, no judges, have or can ascertain this matter, nor formed any precedents whereby we may judge.— — —

With regard to governments where the supreme power is divided amongst different persons, there is no great difficulty in ascertaining when any one transgresses the limits of his power. There could be no doubt at the Revolution that the king[84] had exceeded the limitts of his power. The 1st step he took in the exercise of government, after he had engaged to do nothing without the consent of his Parliament, was to raise the customs and excise without acquainting or consulting them. They had been raised by order of the Parliament triennially. The time was then expired, and it was dreaded that if they should not be levied the merchants would bring in in that time as great a quantity of goods as would supply the country for

139 severall years. But this might have been | easily remedied by the expedient proposed by the council, viz that the officers should be continued, and keep an account with the merchants who should give bond for the customs on the goods imported in case the Parliament thought proper to continue this. But this advice he refused to comply with, and by a mere act of authority raised them thro the whole kingdom. But the affair of[p] the excise was still more scandalous an act of authority ⟨?⟩ tho unjust has still somewhat respectable; but this was not the case in the excise.[85] It had been granted by Parliament for a certain term of years during Charles reign, with a power to the managers to farm it out for a term not exceeding three years. This undoubtedly meant that they might farm it out for thre⟨e⟩ years during the time it continued to be levied. But he enterpreted it as if this meant that

[n] Reading doubtful        [o] Reading of last two words doubtful        [p] Reading doubtful

---

[83] Blank in MS. Presumably a reference to the Act of Settlement, 1701.

[84] i.e. James II. The account is based on Gilbert Burnet, *History of His Own Time*, Book IV (Edinburgh, 1753), III.7 ff.

[85] *Sic.* Presumably some words have been omitted. What Smith probably said was that the king's action in relation to the customs still had an air of respectability about it, but 'this was not the case in the excise'. Cf. 142 below.

they might let it out for three years at any time, and for this purpose forged an antedated deed which he got signed by the officers of excise as done in
140 his brothers reign, and by this littl⟨e⟩ dirty fraud he decreed the | excise for a year.

### Thursday. March. 24. 1763

I have now considered this 2ᵈ question with regard to publick law pretty nearly with all the precision it can admit of.—The sovereign power is in all governments absolute, and as soon as the govt. is firmly established becomes liable to be controuled by no regular force. In the state of hunters and shepherds it is far otherwise; but now the summa potestas is not liable to be controuled by any regular power. For if what we called the summa potestas was liable to be called to account by any man, any body of the people or the whole people, this person or body would be the summa potestas, and if this again was under the authority of another, this would be the summa potestas. So that we must always end in some body*q* who have a power liable to no controul from a regular power. The whole is trusted to them without any restriction with regard to legisle., jud., or exec. power. We are not indeed to expect that these will always be exercised with the greatest propriety.
141 Many foolish*r* laws have no doubt been made which | have been repealed the next session; many improper taxes have been imposed, the inconveniency of which was soon felt, as the hearth-money and the poll-tax; many imprudent wars have been entered into and many foolish peaces have been made by the king and his council, as that of Utrecht.[86] Now many such things may be done without intitling the people to rise in arms. A gross, flagran⟨t⟩, and palpable abuse no doubt will do it, as if they should be required to pay a tax equal to half or third of their substance. But how far the sovereign power may go with safety can not be said. We see that they may in this respect raise much higher taxes and supplys at one time than at an other. When the sovereign power is divided amongst different hands, tho it is impossible to say how far the whole sovereign power conjoind may go, it is easy to ascertain when any of those amongst whom it is divided go beyond their lawfull bounds; for this is the case whenever any one of them attempts to exercise the power which belongs to another, as if the Parliament or king should act in the legislative way without the consent of the other, if the Parliament should make war or the king endeavour to raise
142 taxes. The king can indeed remedy any unjust proceedings | of the Parliament by proroguing them.—The very definition of a perfect right opposed

*q* Reading doubtful     *r* Reading doubtful

---

[86] The peace of Utrecht, 1712 (i.e. during Queen Anne's reign) ended the war of the Spanish succession.

to the offices of humanity, etc., which are by some called imperfect rights, is one which we may compell others to perform to us by violenc⟨e⟩.—If therefore the severall parts of the governmen⟨t⟩ have a perfect right to their severall provinces, it must be supposed that they are intitled to defend themselves in them by force.—If therefore the king levies taxes which are not imposed by Parliament, he breaks the rules of the government. This was what James 2ᵈ did, and as I said above[87] without any necessity, with regard to the customs, as an easy method could have been taken to prevent all inconveniencies of a sudden importation. There was not even this excuse with regard to the excise, as it was raised chiefly from beer which the brewer could not have overstocked in any s[h]ort. It was raised in the 1ˢᵗ place by a         ˢ of law with regard to the meaning of the Act.[88] The case was precisely the same as if one should get a lease of a farm for 30 years with a power of subsetting as we call it for 3 years, and in the 30ᵗʰ year should subset part of it; that could not intitle the subtenent to any advan-

143   tage after the 30ᵗʰ year. The date was also falsified, which | is not a whit more excusable than a fo⟨r⟩gery, and subscribed by the commissioners as if in Charles time. All this was done expressly conterary to the Petition of Right,[89] which secured the Parliament in the right of levying taxes (which had been encroached on by Charles 1ˢᵗ) in a very particular manner.— Another thing which was at first little attended to was the breach of the tests. The nation, seeing that Charles 2ᵈ was likely to have no children, became extremely jealous of the bigotry, violence, and improvidence of James, of which they had had many instances. There were therefore two tests enacted,[90] the one against papists, which was brought about by all the Whig and republican party, particularly the Protes. clergy, and the other against dissenters, by the established church. These secured that no one should be admitted to any office in the government who did not take the sacramen⟨t⟩ according to the Church of England form. This was expressly levelled against the designs of James and his party as well as the dissenters; and also that no one who was a papist could serve in the army for a longer

144   time than three months unless he took the oaths of supremacy and | ab- juration. James however employed in the rebellion of the Duke of Mon- mouth severall Roman Catholick officers, as they could serve for 3 months. Finding them very serviceable he resolved to continue them; of this he acquainted theᵗ Parliament; and altho it was well known that ⟨?had⟩ he

---

ˢ Illegible word        ᵗ 'king' deleted

[87] 138 above.
[88] 12 Charles II, c. 23 (1660) had granted the excise to Charles for life, and sec. 14 allowed it to be farmed for not more than three years; for the case, see Burnet, op. cit., III.8.
[89] 3 Charles I, c. 1 (1628).
[90] 25 Charles II, c. 2 (Test Act, 1673) barred Catholics and Nonconformists from holding public office. 30 Charles II, st. 2, c. 1 (Test Act, 1678) barred them from sitting in Parlia- ment.

done it without making any mention of it, they would [have] thro their great servility have overlooked it; yet as he plainly told them that he was resolved to break thro the rules of the government they thought themselves bound to remonstrate against it.[91] He was also extremely cruel in punishing many of the state criminals. Jeffreys in one circuit executed six hundred persons after Monmouths rebellion, many of whom also, tho they had very good excuses, were compelled by force to plead guilty. In the last rebellion,[92] which threatend the government with much greater danger, there ⟨were⟩ only about 60 civil executions (tho' there were severall other military ones not altogether so justifiable) notwithstanding that there were many men of character concerned in it, and not above one or 2 in Monmouth's, which lasted only about three weeks.—By dispensing with the test, he introduced

145 many Roman Catholicks into offices; he brough⟨t⟩ | four into the Privy Council, put one at the head of the[u] Treasury, an other at that of the exchequer, etc; appointed a Roman Catholick clergy man to be Dean of Christchurch;[93] and ordered the fellows of Magdalen College to elect a Roman Catholick[94] for the master, which they refusing, as the person was not only a R. Cath. but also of a character improper for that office, he turned them out of their places, which was as evident an encroachment on property as any other action he could have been guilty of. He assumed this dispensing power not only with regard to the tests but also with regard to the penall laws. This power had been granted formerly to Charles with regard to some things of no importance, as the shape of carts and waggons, and these he quoted as precedents. The penall laws had originally been made to strengthen the kings authority in the punishing of crimes, and therefore he might be allowed to dispense with them whenever he could do without them. But that he should dispense with an Act of Parliament made plainly to restrict his power and to suppress a religion conterary to the interests of the nation could never be granted. This he did not only by dispensation to particular persons but also[v] in the progress of his govern-

146 ment suspended the laws altogether, which as it was for | an unlimited time amounted to the same thing as the abrogating them.—Another step which as much as any thing tended to bring about the Revolution was the order he issued out, which was ordered to be read by all the clergy men in the kingdom, containing a declaration of the suspension of all the penall laws. He thought they would have come the more easily into it as they had read one in the time of Charles 1st to the same effect; it however had the sanction of Parliament, which this wanted. Accordingly not above 200 clergy men in all

---

[u] 'ministry' deleted　　　　[v] 'with re' deleted

---

[91] Burnet, op. cit., III.49.　　　　　　　　　　　　[92] i.e. that of 1745.
[93] John Massey in 1686: Burnet, op. cit., III.112.
[94] Anthony Farmer: Burnet, op. cit., III.116–19.

England read it. The Archbishop of Canterbury[95] and 6 or 7 others went
and presented a remonstrance and petition drawn up in the most gentle
terms, requesting he would recall the order; but instead of listening to
them, he sent them all to the Tower. Nothing could be more alarming to
the nation than this of sending to prison 6 or 8 of the most respectable men
in the kingdom, not only for their character as clergy men but as lords of
Parliament, for doing what every subject has a right to do; and they more
especially, as they can at any time demand a private audience. Some time
after one Sharp preached a sermon against popery, which being the kings
147  religion was construed as an affront against him. He therefore | ordered the
Bishop of London to suspend him. This he told him he could not do without bringing to a fair trial; but offered at the same time to advise him to
desist, which he accordingly did. James, not satisfied with this, instituted
a court of commissioners of ecclesiasticall affairs, which he thought he
could do with safety by altering the name of the High Commission Court
which had been dissolved in the time of Charles 1$^{st}$, which court immediately sent the Bishop and Sharp to the Tower as being guilty of an
affront in dissobeying the kings authority.[96] Besides this,[w] when he saw
that the whole nation was disgusted at the encouragement he gave to
popery, he published a declaration granting liberty of concience to people
of all religions, which he had no power to do, and promising at the same
time that he would not[x] use *irresistible necessity* to oblige any one to change
his religion.[97] It was well known that he would oblidge no one to become
Protestant, so that this was no more than declaring that he would not treat
148  the Protestants with the very greatest severity; | a declaration which none
but a mad man would have thought of making in a Protestant country.
Fancying also that one great objection of the nobility against popery was
that the abbey lands which had been given to the nobility in the time of
Henry the 8$^{th}$ would be restored, he declared that every one should be
allowd to possess his lands as he did at that time, which plainly signified his
intention of introducing popery into the kingdom.—He then applied himself to the army and asked them if they approved or not of his abolishing
the test oaths. This he began to do in a single regiment, desiring that if they
were of a contrary opinion they should lay down their arms; and was surprised to find that excepting 6 or 7 men and one or two Roman Catholick
officers they all grounded their arms. This incenced him greatly and he
ordered them to take them up again, telling them that he should never

[w] Illegible word deleted        [x] Two or three illegible words deleted

---

[95] William Sancroft in 1688: Burnet, op. cit., III.174 ff.
[96] In 1686: Burnet, op. cit., III.81 ff. The Bishop and Sharp were merely suspended
from office.
[97] Burnet, op. cit., III.137: 'no invincible necessity'.

afterwards consult them on any such matters.[98] From all this we need not wonder that the whole nation deserted him and called over William in his stead. They might no doubt have passed over the whole Stuart family and 149 chosen any one they pleased for king; for as | the children of one who is guilty of treason against the government are for ever incapable of succeding to any estate, so when the sovereign is guilty of any breach of duty to his people he might well be supposed to forfeit for ever all title to the crown. But this they generously dispensed with, and passing over his son who was also a Roman Catholick and suspected as to his legitimacy, then[y] called in his daughter Mary; and in her reign[99] the kingdom was settled on Anne, and failing he⟨r⟩ issue on the family of Hanover, the nearest Protestant heirs, and a maxim established that no one of a different religion from the established one could ever fill the British throne.

*End of Volume Five of MS.*

[y] Reading doubtful

---

[98] P. Rapin, *History of England* (tr. Tindal, 1743), II.768.
[99] In fact after her death, by 12 and 13 William III, c. 2 (Act of Settlement, 1701).

| *Monday. March. 28. 1763—*

In the first of these lectures it was observed that the object of all laws in a state is either 1st, the administration of Justice in its severall parts, public or private; or 2dly, the Police of the country; or 3dly, Arms, which comprehends the state of the military force at home, that is, the management of the militias and standing army and also the manner in which these are employed, under which the laws of peace and war come to be considered. We come now to

## POLICE—

Police, the word, has been borrowed by the English immediately from the French, tho it is originally derived from the Greek πολιτεια signifying policy, politicks, or the regulation of a government in generall. It is now however generally confind to the regulation of the inferior parts of it. It comprehends in generall three things: the attention paid by the public to the cleanlyness of the roads, streets, etc; 2d, security; and thirdly, cheap-

2  ness or plenty, which is the | constant source of it. When Mr. Lamonion[1] was constituted Intendant of Paris he was told by the officers that the king required three things of him, that he was to provide for the neteté, surete, and bon marché in the city.— The two former of these are of too mean a nature, tho no doubt of considerable importance, to be the subject of a lecture.[z] The *neteté* of a country regards the regulations made in order to preserv⟨e⟩ cleanlyness of the roads, streets, etc. and prevent the bad effects of corrupting and putrifying substances. This could never be treated of in this place. The security of the people is the object of the second branch of police, that is, the preventing all crimes and disturbances which may interrupt the intercourse or destroy the peace of the society by any violent attacks. In generall the best means of bringing about this desirable end is the rigorous, severe, and exemplary execution of laws properly formd for the prevention of crimes and establishing the peace of the state.— Other

3  methods are sometimes more directly taken for this purpose— | more immediately striking at the injurious persons. Of this there is a great deal in the French towns. Every one has a marche possé or town guard who patrole in the streets and by that means intimidate villains from attempting any crimes and make the escape of a murder⟨er⟩ or robber[a] more difficult, and also give their assistance at the extinguishing of fires or other hazardous

---

[z] Replaces 'nature'        [a] 'stil' deleted

---

[1] Apparently M. d'Argenson; see p. 5 above.

accidents. This also, considering chiefly the proper regulations and form of town guards, is a subject too mean and too minute for our consideration.

We shall only observe on this head that those cities where the greatest police is exercised are not those which enjoy the greatest security. London is[b] the largest city in Europe, at least larger[c] by a third than Paris, and should therefore stand the more in need of regulations of this sort. But we find that in Paris great care is taken in this way. The collection of the statutes on this head made by De La Marre[2] makes four large folios, tho he went thro but a small part of the plan, so that the police there is a very

4 burthensome part of the law, and which can be thoroughly | understood by those only who are employed in the severall offices and courts regarding it, whereas all the statutes made concerning the police of London could be read in an hour or two. We see indeed that there is much more occasion for it: hardly a night passes in Paris without a murther or a robbery in the streets, whereas in London there are not above 3, 4, or 5 murthers in a whole year.— One should think from this that the more of police there was in any country the less was the security; but the case is that where the greatest need is, there the greatest care is taken in this manner[s]. The nature of the manner⟨s⟩ of the people and their different manner of life occasions a vast difference in this respect. In generall we may observe that the disorders in any country are more or less according to the number of retainers and dependents in it. I took notice of the great disorders and confusion of the feudall governments, which in a great measur⟨e⟩ proceeded from the numbers of retaints[3] and dependents amongst them, who, being accustomed

5 to live in ease and luxury about their patrons house, had no way to | support themselves but by rapine and violence.— We see that by the accounts collected by Mr. David Hume in ⁴ vol. of his history, in Queen Elizabeths time when the feudall government was in a declining state there were more murders committed in the kingdom within a year than we can have any notion of; and the same we see from a register of those in one county. In like manner the disorders in France seem to be owing to the vast number of servants which it is fashionable for the great to maintain. The number is indeed much less than that of the retainers[d] was 150 years ago, but is far greater than that in England, as the spirit of the feudall government is not so intirely abolished as it is here. These servants, being frequently turned off for misdemeanours and therefore without any recom-

---

  [b] 'one of' deleted　　　　[c] Numbers written above the last three words indicate that they were intended to read 'larger at least'　　　[d] 'they had' deleted

---

  [2] Nicolas de la Mare, *Traité de la Police, où l'on trouvera l'histoire de son établissement, les fonctions et les prérogatives de ses magistrats, toutes les loix et tous les règlemens qui la concernent* (Paris, 4 vol. folio, 1705–38).
  [3] *Sic.* Obviously 'retainers' was intended. Cf. iv.157 ff. above.
  [4] Blank in MS. Hume, *History*, IV.726–7.

mendation, are the most helpless set of men imaginable. Their idle and
luxuri⟨ou⟩s life in ease and plenty when with their masters renders them
altogether depraved both in mind and body, so that they neither are willing
6 nor able to support themselves by work, and have no way to live by but | by
crimes and vices. We see too that in this town (Glasgow), where each one
seldom has above one man servant, there are few or no capitall crimes
committed, and those that are, most commonly by strangers; whereas at
Edinburgh, where the resort of the nobility and gentry draws together
a vast number of servants who are frequently set adrift by their masters,
there are severall every year. Upon the whole it is the custom of having
many retainers and dependents which is the great source of all the disorders
and confusion in some cities; and we may also affirm that*e* it is not so much
the regulations of the police which preserves the security of a nation as the
custom of having in it as few servants and dependents as possible. Nothing
tends so much to corrupt and enervate and debase the mind as dependency,
and nothing gives such noble and generous notions of probity as freedom
and independency. Commerce is one great preventive of this custom. The
manufactures give the poorer sort better wages than any master can afford;
7 besides, it give⟨s⟩ the rich an op|portunity of spending their fortunes with
fewer servants, which they never fail of embracing. Hence it is that the
common people of England who are alltogether free and independent are
the honestest of their rank any where to be met with. The gentry and
nobility of France are no doubt as good a set of men as those of England or
other countries, but the commonalty as being more subjected are much less
honest and fair in their dealings. The gentry of Scotland are no worse than
those of England, but the common people being considerably more oppressed have much less of probity, liberality, [and] and amiable qualities*f*
in their tempers than those of England.

The third thing which is the object of police is the proper means of
introducing plenty and abundance into the country, that is, the cheapness
of goods of all sorts. For these terms plenty and cheapness are in a manner
8 synonimous, as cheapness is a nec⟨e⟩ssary consequence of plenty. Thus | we
see that water,*g* which is absolutely necessary for the support of mankind,
by its abundance costs nothing but the uptaking, whereas diamonds and
other jewels, of which one can hardly say what they serve for, give an
immen⟨s⟩e price.[5] In order to consider the means proper to produce
opulence it will be proper to consider what opulence and plenty consist in,
or what are those things which ought to abound in a nation. To this it will

*e* 'the' deleted     *f* The last three words replace 'generality'     *g* 'one' deleted

[5] For the contrast between the plentifulness and cheapness of water and the scarcity
and dearness of diamonds see John Law, *Money and Trade Considered* (1705), I.4, and
Harris, I.3.

also be previously[h] necessary to consider what are the naturall wants and demands of mankind. Man has received from the bounty of nature reason and ingenuity, art, contrivan⟨c⟩e, and capacity of improvement far superior to that which she has bestowed on any of the other animalls, but is at the same time in a much more helpless and[i] destitute condition with regard to the support and comfort of his life.[6] All other animalls find their food in the state they desire it, and that which is best suited to their severall natures, and few other necessaries do they stand in need of.— | But man, of a more delicate frame and more feeble constitution, meet⟨s⟩ with nothing so adapted to his use that it does not stand in need of improvement and preparation to fit it for his use. All other animalls are content with their food in the state it is producd by nature, and have no conception that it would be improved by cookery or rendered more agreable or more nourishing by a sauce. It appears indeed from the practise of some savage nations that the human stomach can digest food in its naturall and unprepared state, and that too even of the animall kind; but this does not seem to be the way most agreable or beneficial to him. As soon as he applies fire to the preparation of his food he finds the beneficial effects of the change it produces. The food thus prepared he soon relishes as more agreable, and finds by experience that it more easily submits to the operation of his feeble and puny stomach than the coarse and unprepared, which at first after this he disrelishes and afterwards looks upon as loathsome. For we see that tho the stomachs of savage⟨s⟩ | can make a shift to conquer a quantity of undressed victualls, they are not at all so adapted for it. Diseases arising from indigestion and crudities are nowhere so frequent as amongst the savage nations, and we are surprised to find melancholy and hypochondriack disorders more prevalent amongst them than any where else. Want of air, exercise, and labour to carry of⟨f⟩ superfluous humours can not be the cause of it amongst them, as they are here. The only reason that can be assigned for them is the effects of raw, unprepared, and indigestible foods.

The naturall temperature of the air is altogether adapted to the condition of the other animalls, who seem to feel very little inconvenience from the severall vicissitudes of the weather. But even this soft and subtl⟨e⟩ fluid is too severe for his tender and delicate frame. One should imagine that this subtle and fleeting element would not submit to any change from his hands, but he[j] even forms to himself around his body a sort of a new atmosphere, more soft, warm, | and comfortable than that of the common circumambient air. For this purpose he furnishes himself with cloaths which he wraps round his body, and builds himself a house to extend this atmosphere

[h] Numbers written above the last seven words indicate that they were intended to read 'Previously to this it will also be'    [i] 'dependent' deleted    [j] Replaces 'even'

[6] Cf. Hume, *Treatise of Human Nature*, III.ii.2 (ed. Selby-Bigge, 484).

to some greater distance around him. These are contrivances which none of the other animalls perceive the need of, but men can hardly subsist without them. Even those who live in a country where the benign influence of the sun makes it unnecessary to defend their bodies against the chillness of the air such as is found in other countries, are necessitated to use other preventives, without which the heat would crack their tender skins and render them incapable of supporting the winds and rains. For this they anoint and soften their skins with oil and grease, and stain their skins with various dies which as it were tann them and render them callous and able to endure the scorching sun, the piercing winds, and the chill, battering rain. But
12 these necessities can be supplied without great difficulty | in some tollerable manner and by the industry of each individuall. The savages who do not apply themselves to different trades can each of them supply themselves with food, with cloaths, and with lodging. The fruits of the earth spontaneously produced, with the flesh of the animalls he takes by the chase, supply him with food which he can easily prepare. A few skins, stitched perhaps together with a few thongs of the same, supply him with raiment, and a few poles stuck in the ground and covered over with skins or matts afford him a shelter in the night or in the inclemencies of the weather.— The same temper and inclinations which prompted him to make these improvements push him to still greater refinements. This way of life appears[k] rude and slovenly and can no longer satisfy him; he seeks after
13 more elegant nicities and refinement.— Man alone of all animalls | on this globe is the only one who regards the differences of things which no way affect their real substance or give them no superior advantage in supplying the wants of nature. Even colour, the most flimsy and superficiall of all distinctions, becomes an object of his regard. Hence it is that diamonds, rubys, saphires, emerallds and other jewels have at all times been distinguished from the more[7] peb⟨b⟩les of less splendid hues. Figure also is a distinction which is of no small weight in directing the choice of man in many of his pursuits. A sort of uniformity mixd at the same time with a certain degree of variety gives him a certain pleasure,[8] as we see in the construction of a house or building which pleases when neither dully uniform nor its parts altogether angular. When the parts of the figure bear a certain proportion to one an other without any breaks ⟨?or⟩ gaps this is also pleasing; and lastly, we find a pleasure in beholding an object which to these adds that other quality of being easily and distinctly comprehended on the first sight.[9] From the 1st of these arises the preference give to

[k] 'ever' deleted

---

[7] 'ordinary' deleted. Probably 'the more' should also have been deleted.
[8] Cf. Hutcheson, *Inquiry concerning Beauty*, II.iii.
[9] Cf. ibid., VIII.ii.2.

14          | *Gap of one line in MS.*

From the 2$^d$ it is that the gentle bendings of curvilineall figures are gener-
all⟨y⟩ prefer[e]red to [to] the abrupt and irregular angles of some, and almost
all righttened ones. From the 3$^d$ it is that the constantly varying direction
of the circle, which at the same time is [at the same time] allways similar
and easily conceived, is preferred to the more$^l$ varied figures of the elipse,
parabola, and hyperbola, and the Archimedean spirall, which last far
exceeds it in variety, as it is more easily conceved than these, whose nature
can not at first sight be understood. Hence also it is that polygons of above
8 sides are never admitted into architecture, as they are either not at all
comprehended or put one to the trouble of counting.— Imitation also
greatly attracts the attention, and that when it is altogether disjoined from
the other sources of liking.$^m$ Of this we have a remarkable example in the
Dutch paintings which please merely by the resemblance they have to
15 other objects, tho these objects be | in themselves no ways beautiful.[10] A
picture of a dunghill or a flitch of bacon will catch our eye, and be very
agreable; we wonder how the variations of the tints and stains of the colours
can represent the risings and fallings, the protuberances and the inequali-
ties of those solid bodies, when laid on a board altogether smooth and
plain.—$^n$ Rarity also gives a preference to things otherwise equall, and
makes things of no value be considerably esteemed. Tis from this principally that the gems get their value; the preparations of paste or glass which
are now made in Europe come in a very small degree short of the real ones
but are far less valued. We are told likewise that the savage nations to
which they have been given in barter for reall ones of less size, run off as
soon as they have receiv'd them, highlly pleased with the exchange but
affraid least the Europeans should endeavour again to recover them. Hence
pinchbeck, which equalls gold in its colour, is noways so highly esteemed;
16 and that preparation of tin and other metalls which | in$^o$ England goes by
the name of French plate is noways esteemed, tho it comes little short
of the splendor of silver.

    These four distinctions of colour, form, variety or rarity, and imitation
seem to be the foundation of all the minute and, to more thoughtfull
persons, frivolous distinctions and preferenc⟨e⟩s in things otherwise equall,
which give in the pursuit more distress and uneasieness to mankind than

---

$^l$ Illegible word deleted      $^m$ Reading doubtful      $^n$ 'Vari' deleted      $^o$ 'bright-
ness' deleted

---

[10] Cf. *Imitative Arts,* 5–7: 'A painted cloth, the work of some laborious Dutch artist, so
curiously shaded and coloured as to represent the pile and softness of a woollen one, might
derive some merit from its resemblance even to the sorry carpet which now lies before me.
The copy might, and probably would, in this case, be of much greater value than the
original. . . . In Painting, the imitation frequently pleases, though the original object be
indifferent, or even offensive.'

all the others, and to gratify which a thousand arts have been invented. {And whose prosecution leads men into customs with regard to food, cloathing, and lodging which have no relation to convenience and are often conterary to the ends proposed to be supplied by those[p] things, which makes us dress and eat and lodge in a way not always adapted to ease, health and conveniency, and warmth.—} Indeed to supply the wants of *meat, drink,* cloathing, and lodging allmost the whole of the arts and sciences have been invented and improved.— Agriculture multiplies the materialls on which the severall artificeres are imployed, but[q] chiefly those things which are fit for food as of these their is the greatest consumption. The forrest supplies us with [with] trees and planks for building, and from the plain we have wool, flax, cotton, and by the cultivation of the mu⟨l⟩- berry tree, silk for cloathing, besides indigo, woad, madder, and 100 other plants employed in dying the above substances.— It would be impossible to enumerate all the artists who join their labours in improving on these

17 ori|ginall productions and prepare them for use. The butcher, the miller, the baker, the brewer, the cook, the confectioner, etc., etc., etc., etc. all give their labour to prepare the various products of the earth for food to man. How many artists are employed to prepare those things with which the shops of the uphorsterrer, the draper, the mercer and cloth-seller ⟨?⟩, to clip the wool, pick it, sort it, spin, comb,[r] twist, weave, scour, dye, etc. the wool, and a hundred other operators engaged on each different com- modities? How many artists concur to furnish the various commodities to be met with in the grocers, chiefly for the food of man. The carpenter, the wright, the carver in wood, etc. all contribute their aid[s] allong with the mason, bricklayer, et⟨c⟩. to build or to furnish our dwellings. The artificers in brass and iron, copper, etc. all bestow their labour in preparing house- hold utensils of various sorts or tools for the other artificers. Commerce and traffick and all the arts of the ship builder, etc., etc., and the mariner and

18 the | assiduous industry of the merchant, tend to the same end. They import into one country the supperfluities of another in food and raiment, carrying out in return others of the same sort in which they abound.— Geometry, arithmetick, and writing have all been invented originally to facilitate the operation of the severall arts. Writing and arithmetick have been invented to record and set in a clear light the severall transactions of the merchant and trades man, and geometry has been originally invented (either to measure out the earth and divide it amongst the inhabitants or) to assist the workman in the fashioning of those pieces of art which require more acccurate mensuration. All most all laws[t] and regulations tend t[t]o the encouragement of these arts, which provide for those things which

---

[p] Illegible word deleted     [q] Reading doubtful     [r] Numbers written above the last two words indicate that their order was intended to be reversed     [s] Reading of last two words doubtful     [t] Replaces an illegible word

⟨?we⟩ look upon as the objects of the labour of the vulgar alone, meat, drink, and cloathing. Even law and government have these as their finall end and ultimate object. They give the inhabitants of the country liberty
19 and security in the cultivate the[11] | land which they possess in safety, and their benign influence gives room and opportunity for the improvement of all the various arts and sciences. They maintain the rich in the possession of their wea⟨l⟩th against the violence and rapacity of the poor, and by that means preserve that usefull inequality in the fortunes of mankind which naturally and necessarily arises from the various degrees of capacity, industry, and diligence in the different individualls. They protect the subjects against the danger of the unjust attacks of foreign incroaching enemies, and leave men at leisure to cultivate the arts, and give them room to pursue what is called the conveniencies of life. Even wisdom and virtue in all its branches derive their lustre and beauty with regard to utility merely[u] from their tendency to provide for the security of mankind in these conveniencies. Laws and government are their principall business in a publick view, and their end must be the same in every individuall.
20 Probity, honesty, and entegrity of dealing tend all to the main[12] | of the severall persons, and encourage them by that means in their severall occupations. The superior wisdom of the good and knowing man directs others in the management of his affairs, and spurs them on to imitate and emulate his industry and activity. Their valour protects them from the attacks of the foreign and the inroads of the domestick foes, and their generosity relieves us by their assistance when the schemes fail that have been laid for the attaining of these necessities and conveniencies of life. Nor can these virtues be ever more usefull to the state than when being put into practise they by example spur men on to the like industry. So that in a certain view of things all the arts, the science⟨s⟩, law and government, wisdom, and even virtue itself tend all to this one thing, the providing meat, drink, rayment, and lodging for men, which are commonly reckoned
21 the meanest of[v] employments and fit for the pursuit | of none but the lowest and meanest of the people. All the severall arts and businesses in life tend to render the conveniencies and necessaries of life more attainable.— We see accordingly that an ordinary day-laybourer, whom he false account[13] to live in a most simple manner, has more of the conveniencies and luxuries of life than an Indian[14] prince at the head of 1000 naked savages. His c⟨o⟩arse blue woolen coat has been the labour of perhaps 100 artificers,

[u] Reading doubtful    [v] 'of' deleted

---

[11] *Sic.* Presumably something like 'in the cultivation of the' was intended.
[12] *Sic.* Probably 'maintenance' was intended.
[13] *Sic.* Presumably something like 'we falsely account' was intended: cf. 25 below.
[14] i.e. American Indian. Cf. Locke, *Civil Government*, § 41.

the shearer, the picker, the sorter, the comber, the spinner, etc. as well as
the weaver and fuller whose loom and mill alone have more of art in them
than all the things employed about the court of a savage prince; besides
the ship which brought the dies and other materials together from distant
regions, and all the workmen, wrights, carpenters, coopers,[w] smiths, etc.
which have been employed to fit her out to sea and the hands which have
navigated her.[15] The iron tool with which he works, how many hands has it
22 gone thro.— The miner, the quarrier, the breaker, | the smelter, the forger,
the maker of the charcoall to smelt it,[x] the smith, etc. have had a hand in
the forming it. How many have been required to furnish out the coarse
linnen shirt which [which] he wears;[16] the[y] tanned and dressed-leather-
shoes; his bed which he rest⟨s⟩ in; the grate at which he dresses his victuals;
the coals he burns, which have been brought by a long land sea carriage;
his knives[z] and forks; his plates of pewter or earthen ware; and the various
workmen who have been necessary to prepare his bread, his beer, and other
food; besides the glass of which his windows are composed, production
⟨of⟩ which required vast labour to bring it to its[a] present perfection,
which at the same time excludes the wind and rain and admitts[b] the light,
a commodity without which this country would scarcely be habitable, at
least by the present effeminate and puny set of mortals. So that to supply
23 this poor labourer | about 1000 have given their joint assistance. He enjoys
far greater convenience than an Indian prince, tho inferiorer indeed to
⟨?that⟩ of the princes or nobles of Europe, but far greater than the others.
And perhaps the condition and ease of a prince does not [perhaps] so far
exceed that of the labourer here describe⟨d⟩, as his does that of a savage
chief. It may not indeed seem wonderful that the great man who has 1000
dependents and tenen[e]ts and servants who are oppressed that he may
live in luzury and affluen⟨c⟩e, that the moneyd man and man of rank,
should be so very affluent, when the [when the] merchant, the poor, and
the needy all give their assistance to his support. It need not, I say, seem
surprising that these should far exceed the greatest man amongst a whole
tribe of savages. But that the poor day labourer or indigent farmer should
24 be more at his ease, notwithstanding all | oppression and tyranny, should
be more at his own ease than the savage, does not appear so probable.
Amongst the savages there are no landlords nor usurers, no tax gather⟨er⟩s,
so that every one has the full fruits of his own labours, and should therefore
injoy the greatest abundan⟨c⟩e; but the case is far otherwise.— — — —

---

[w] Reading doubtful      [x] 'the forger' deleted      [y] 'coarse' deleted      [z] Reading doubtful      [a] The last three words replace 'them to'      [b] Replaces 'excludes'

---

[15] Cf. Mandeville, I ('A Search into the Nature of Society'), 356–7.
[16] Cf. ibid., I (Remark P), 169.

*Tuesday. March. 29. 1763*

In yesterdays lecture I endeavour'd to explain the causes which prompt man to industry and are peculiar to him of all the animalls, the naturall feebleness of his frame and his desires of elegance and refinement. These wants a solitary savage can supply in some manner, but not in that which is reckoned absolutely necessary in every country where government has been some time established. I shewed you also how the far greater parts of the arts and sciences have been invented and improved to supply three great wants of mankind, or subservient to these three ends,[c] food, cloaths, and lodging; how that mankind are far better provided in all the neces-

25 saries and conveniences of life[d] | in a civilized than in a savage state; that plenty and opulence is far greater. The unassisted industry of a savage can not any way procure him those things which are now become necessary to the meanest artist. We may see this odds in comparing the way of life of an ordinary day-labourer in England or Holland to that of a savage prince, who has the lives and liberties of a thousand or 10000 naked savages at his disposall. It appears evident that this man, whom we falsly account to live in a simple and plain manner, is far better supplied than the monarch himself. Every part of his cloathing, utensils, and food has been produced by the joint labour of an infinite number of hands, and these again required a vast number to provide them in tools for their respective employments.[e] So that this labourer could not be provided in this simple manner (as we call it) without the concurrence of some 1000 hands. His life indeed is

26 simple when compared to the luxury and profusion | of an European grandee. But perhaps the affluence and luxury of the richest does not so far exceed the plenty and abundance of an industrious farmer as this latter does the unprovided and unnesisted manner of life of the most respected savage. It need not seem strange that the man of fortune should so far exceed in the conveniencies and ease of his life the rude and indigent savage. The labour and time of the poor is in civilized countries sacrificed to the maintaining the rich in ease and luxury. The landlord is maintaind in idleness and luxury by the labour of his tenents, who cultivate the land for him as well as for themselves. The moneyd man is supported by his exactions from the industrious merchant and the needy who are obliged to support him in ease by a return for the use of his money. But every savage has the full enjoyment of the fruits of his own labours; there are there no landlords, no usurers, no tax gatherers. We should expect therefore that the savage should be much better provided than the dependent poor man who labours both for himself and for others. But the case is far otherwise. The

---

[c] The last six words are interlined, a caret apparently referring to them being placed between the words 'supply' and 'three' in the preceding phrase        [d] 'than' deleted
[e] The words 'It will not indeed seem to', followed by three or four illegible words, are deleted at this point

27 indigence of a savage is far greater than that | of the meanest citizen of any thing that deserves the name of a civilized nation. There is an other consideration which increases the difficulty in accounting for this. If we should suppose that labour was equally proportioned to each, the difficulty would cease. That is, if we should suppose that of the 10,000 whose labour is necessary to the support of one individuall, each was maintaind by the labour of the rest, there would here be the reciprocall proportion of the labour of 1 to 10000 and 10000 to 1, so that every one would have the labour of one bestowed upon him. But in no civilized state this is the case. Of 10,000 families which are supported by each other, 100 perhaps labour not at all and do nothing to the common support. The others have them to maintain besides themselves, and besides ⟨?those⟩ who labour have a far less share of ease, convenience, and abundance than those who work not at all. The rich and opulent merchant who does nothing but give a few directions, lives in far greater state and luxury and ease and plenty of all the conveniencies and delicacies of life than his clerks, who do all the business. They too, excepting their confinement, are in a state of ease and plenty far

28 superior to that | of the artizan by whose labour these commodities were furnished. The labour of this man too is pretty tollerable; he works under cover protected from the inclemency in the weather, and has his livelyhood in no uncomfortable way if we compare him with the poor labourer. He has all the inconveniencies of the soil and the season to struggle with, is continually exposed to the inclemency of the weather and the most severe labour at the same time. Thus he who as it were supports the whole frame of society and furnishes the means of the convenience and ease of all the rest is himself possessed of a very small share and is buried in obscurity. He bears on his shoulders the whole of mankind, and unable to sustain the load is buried by the weight of it and thrust down into the lowest parts of the earth, from whence he supports all the rest. In what manner then shall we account for the great share he and the lowest of the people have of the conveniencies of life. The division of labour amongst different hands can alone account for this.[17] Let us consider the effects this will have on one

29 | particular branch of business, and from thence we may judge on the effect and from the effe[t]cts it will have on the whole. We shall take for this purpose an instance frivolous indeed, but which will sufficiently illustrate it; this is pin-making. If we should suppose that one man should dig the ore in the mine, break and melt, smelt it, and prepare the furnaces, and forge the brass into bars, draw these out into wire, cut this wire, form the head and etc., etc., he would hardly be able to form a pin in a years time. As therefore it must be that the workman gets the price of his labour, and we should value the labour of a man in a year at £a6, each pin would in this case cost about £6.—If we should suppose that the greatest part of the work

[17] Cf. Mandeville, II (Dialogue 6), 284.

is done to his hand, and the brass given him drawn into wire, and that he performs all the severall operations requisite to form it into pins, he would not be able to make above 20 pins a day, and as the value of the labour per diem with the ⟨?addition⟩ of the price of the brass and wearing$^f$ of tools will amount to about 20$^d$, he could not afford to sell his pins at less than 1$^d$ each.

30 The pin-maker | now divides this work betwixt a great many hands; one cutts the wire, another sharps$^g$ the one end for receiving the head, 3 or 4 are employed in making the head, one puts it on[e], another forms the point, another gild⟨s⟩ and another papers them. So that in the making of *a pin* there are about 18 persons employed.[18] These in a day will make about 36000 pins, and this comes to the same thing as if each one made about 2000. So that by this means the work is greatly$^h$ increased, and he can afford both to increase the workmans wages [and can] and to sell the commodities cheaper, so that instead of 6 pounds, or 20 pence for one, he can now sell some dozens for a halfpenny. The case is the same in all other mechanicall arts.

The labour of the farmer is intirely seperated from that of the manu-facturer. The farmer has his part and the manufacturer his. How many different hands and seperate businesses are there betwixt the grazier who feeds the sheep or the raiser of the flax, and the smoother and presser of the woolen or he who glazes and finishes the linnen. Agriculture however does not admit of this$^i$ seperation of employment in the same degree as the manufactures of wool or lint or iron work. The same man must often be the

31 plower | of the land, sower, harrower, reaper and thresher of the corn (tho here there may be some distinctions). But the difference of the seasons at which these different works are carried on makes it impossible for one to make a livelyhood by any one of these. The thresher, the millar, as they can work equally at all times of the year; the husbandman may also be greatly relieved when the different parts of the work necessary to$^j$ provide his instruments are done by other hands, when plow wrights, cart and waggon wrights, smiths who do the iron work of these, are seperated from the others. But still the impracticability of seperating the labour in so great a degree as it is done in the manufactures renders it impossible that the im-provements in agriculture should ever keep pace with those in the manu-factures. Tho an oppulent state will no doubt far exceed a poorer one both in the culture of the ground and the goodness and cheapness of its manu-factures, yet this will not be so remarkable in the produce of the soil as the handycraft trades. Thus the corn of France is generally as good in every

$^f$ Reading doubtful          $^g$ Reading doubtful          $^h$ 'diminished' deleted
$^i$ 'of' deleted          $^j$ 'carry' deleted

---

[18] Cf. *Encyclopédie* (vol. V, 1755), s.v. *Épingle*, where eighteen successive operations are minutely described. Cf. also E. Chambers, *Cyclopaedia* (1728), s.v. Pin, where twenty-five workmen are said to be successively employed.

respect and as cheap as that of England; but the toys, the buttons, buck⟨l⟩es,
32 knives, etc., etc. of the latter far exceed | those of the other in neatness,
strength of work, and cheapness. When these improvements have been
made, each branch of trade will afford enough both to support the oppu-
lence and give considerable profit of the great men, and sufficiently reward
the industry of the labourer. Every trade can afford something[k] for those
who do not work, and give enough to the industrious. Thus to take the
same frivolous example as before, if we should suppose that the pin makers
can furnish 1000 pins in the day, that these (including the price of the
mettall which is about 20$^d$ per pound, out of which many thousand pins
may be made) can be sold at the rate of 3 halfpence per 100. The whole
thousand will then be worth 15$^d$, of which the artizan can afford 3 to his
master and have 12 as the price of his labour, or may give him 200 and
retain 800 to himself, for it is the same thing whether we suppose each[l] one
to have the commodity he works in or the value of his share. If we should
again suppose that the pin maker can so contrive it that each man shall
make 2000 per diem, and that he sells these at 1$^d$ per 100, 20$^d$ will be the
value of the whole. The master may here have 5 for his share and can
33 | afford the artizan 15$^d$. The price of the work will here be less, the publick
will be far better supplied, and the artizan will be far better rewarded. The
work now costs but very little. The brass wire is about 20$^d$ per pound, and
after it has been made into pins, of which severall thousands may be made
from a pound, it costs no more than 2$^{sh.}$ 6$^d$, so that the price of the work of
a lib. of pins is no more than 10$^d$. In this manner the price of labour comes
to be dear while at the same time work is cheap, and these two things, which
in the eyes of the vulgar appear altogether incompatible, are in this evidently very consistent, as the improvement of arts renders things so much
easier done that a great wage can be afforded to the artizan and the goods
still be at a low price. That state is opulent where the necessaries and conveniencies of life are easily come at, whatever otherwise be its condition,
and nothing else can deserve the name of opulence but this comeattible-
ness. That is, a state is opulent when by no great pains and a proper
34 | application of industry these things may be easily obtaind; and this whether
money or other things of that sort abound or not. Industry and well applied
labour must always improve the productions, and an opulent state can
always afford commodities more reasonably than a poor one. And if it ever[m]
happens that of two states, whereof[n] one is opulent and the other poor,
the former loses any branch of its trade by being undersold by the other
who can afford it at a less price, the opulence of the former can never be the
cause of it. We must look for it somewhere else. It must proceed from some
improper inconveniencies that that branch of business has imprudently

[k] Replaces 'sufficient'    [l] Replaces an illegible word    [m] Reading of last two
words doubtful    [n] Reading doubtful

been laid under by oppresive and insupportable taxes or excise, or from the insolence and oppression of the officers, still more insupportable than any tax, or the excessive price of the necessaries of life from some particular cause. As a rich merchant can always afford to under-sell a poor one, so can a rich nation one of less wealth. In Holland where the artizans are as well

35 paid as any where | one can purchase goods for exportation cheaper than any where else, tho for home consumption they are pretty dear; which difference is intirely owing to the taxes and excise laid on them in the latter case, which are not in the former. The masters having greater stocks in the severall works can° divide the work amongst the greater number of hands; by this means they get it better done and can afford it cheaper. By the division of the work, 10, 20, or 40 times the quantity of work is done which is done when the hands are fewer, and the more highly the work is divided the cheaper it will always be. We see accordingly, tho it is not generally imagined, that the price of allmost all commodities has fallen since the Revolution, of linnen and woolen cloth, of all sorts of wares and manufactures, notwithstanding the supposed abundance of money. The only things which have rose in their prices are grass and in consequence of it butcher meat, for a particular reason.[19] In the Mogulls country, where every art and manufacture is carried to the greatest perfection, every thing of the necessaries of life can be purchased for much less money than here. There,

36 cottons | of different sorts, and silks, which in their different sorts serve much better as cloathing than our linnen and woolen, are far cheaper, and were it not for the high taxes which are laid upon them (notwithstanding the great carriage), which are sometimes 4 or 5 times the value of them at this distance, we should be cloathed by the labour of the Mogulls in their cottons and silks, which would be cheaper and better than any thing of our own produce. These taxes alone support our manufacturers.^p

We are not to judge whether labour be cheap or dear by the moneyd price of it, but by the quantity of the necessaries of life which may be got by the fruits of it. We are told that at Bengal 2^d or there abouts is the hire of a man for a day; but we are not to conclude from thence that labour is cheaper than in this country. Labour may be as highly rewarded in that country by 1^d as at London by 1^sh or 1^sh 6^d, as the penny there will purchase as much of the necessaries of life as 1 shill. will do in this country. The conveniencies

37 of life are more | comeattible, and this low moneyd price of labour takes place, conterary to the commonly received notions, notwithstanding that money is there in great abundan⟨c⟩e. The money'd price of labour seldom rises in the same proportion as the improvements of industry and arts advances. Gold and silver being found usefull in the exchange of com-

---

° 'afford' deleted     ^p 'We' deleted

---

[19] See 95–6 below.

modities, the multiplying of them in a country adds no doubt to its wea⟨l⟩th. But they can not be so easily multiplied as other commodities. A man who cultivates one*q* acre, by cultivating two or a certain method of treating that one, can be almost certain of doubling his stock of corn; but he has no such certainty that by applying double industry to the mine he shall multiply in the same proportion the quantity of gold and silver. The same addition of industry applied to the one and the other is much more certain of multiplying corn or other produce than of multiplying gold; and as I shall show hereafter, every other trade is rather more profitable than the working of gold mines.

38 | This increase of the stock of commodities, and the cheapness of work arising*r* from the division of work, has three causes.—1$^{st}$, the dexterity which it occasions in the workmen; 2$^{dly}$, the saving of time lost in passing from one piece of work to an other; and 3$^{dly}$, the invention of machines which it occasions. The 1$^{st}$ of the increase of dexterity from this division of work is immense, the*s* work being reduced to the most simple operations, and one man being employed constantly in one of these acquires an amaxing dexterity in it and can do many times the quantity of work that another can. A country smith who works occasionall⟨y⟩ at all sorts of works, locks, ploughs, grates,*t* hinges, etc. and employs himself sometimes in spare hours in making of nails, may make in a day at most 1500; whereas a nail smith of 15 years old who has wrought at nothing else will make 3 or 4000. And a smith who has never perhaps made nails, tho he has been employed in all sorts of work, wont make above 2 or 300, and then but very in-

39 different. And this great odds there is, altho this of | nail making be not one of the most simple operations even in the way it is practised. The odds in needle or pin-making, which are reduced to the simplest operations, is far greater. The rapidity with which some of these operations are performed by those who have been long habituated to them is altogether wonderfull and inconcivable to those who have not been accustomed to the like.

2$^{d}$, the saving of time by this division of labour is very considerable. It is altogether evident that there must be a loss of time in some cases where the work is to be performed at different places. A weaver who cultivates a farm must lose a good deal of time in passing from the ground to his loom. But altho the different branches of business are carried on in the same work house, there is still a considerable loss. He saunters and rests himself betwixt the one and the other; one can hardly apply their mind to any work at once; they find a sort of listlesness and innactivity at the beginning, and this makes them apt to saunter betwixt them.—A man of spirit when hard

40 pushed will pass | quickly from one work to another and apply to each with equall vigour. But even a man of spirit must be hard pushed before he will

---

*q* Replaces 'two'          *r* Four or five illegible words deleted          *s* 'labou' deleted
*t* Reading doubtful

do this, otherwise even he will saunter betwixt them. This is one great reason why country work men who cant apply themselves to any particular branch[20]—where a smith cant make his livelyhood by locks or nails but must work at all different sorts and with all different tools; where a wright cant live by making chairs and tables only, or cant use the axe[u] only, but now must *plaine*, then saw, then hew with the hatchet, then with the adse, afterwards work with the chisel—contract a certain indolence and sauntering disposition altogether different from the activity of a town workman, besides the want of dexterity.

The invention of machines vastly increases the quantity of work which is done. This is evident in the most simple operations. A plow with 2 men and three horses will till more ground than twenty men could dig with the spade. A wind or water mill directed by the miller will do more work than 8 men with hand-mills, and this too with great ease, whereas the handmill

41 was reckoned the hardest labour | a man could be put to, and[v] therefore none were employed in it but those who had been guilty of some capitall crime. But the handmill was far from being a contemptible machine, and had required a good deal of ingenuity in the invention. How far superior was this to the rubbing of the corn betwixt two rough stones, a method practised[w] not only in the savage countries but by the inhabitants of the remote parts of this country. When one is employed constantly on one thing his mind will naturally be employed in devising the most proper means of improving it. It was probably a farmer who first invented the plow, tho the plough wright perhaps, having been accustomed to think on it ⟨?⟩. And there is none of the inventions of that machine so mysterious that one or other of these could not have been the inventor of it. The drill plow, the most ingenious of any, was the invention of a farmer. A slave who had been set to rub corn into pouder betwixt two hard and rough stones was probably the person who first thought of facilitating the labour by

42 supporting | one of the stones on a spindle and turning it round by a horizontall crank. He too might improve it by means of the feeder and hopper, and with the assistance of the mill-wright might adapt the trundle, etc. by means of which and the hole in the upper stone the feeder and hopper supplied it with grain. The wheel wright also, by an effort of thought and after long experien⟨ce⟩, might contrive the cog wheel which, turne[n]d by a verticall winch, facilitated the labour exceedingly as it gave the man a superior power over it. But the man who[x] first thought of applying a stream of water and still more the blast of the wind to turn this, by an outer wheel in place of a crank, was neither a millar nor a mill-wright but a

---

[u] Reading doubtful; 'of' deleted　　　　[v] Illegible word deleted　　　　[w] 'by' deleted
[x] The last three words replace 'it was a philosopher'

---

[20] Cf. ii.40 above.

philosopher, one of those men who, tho they work at nothing themselves, yet by observing all are enabled by this extended way of thinking to apply
43 things together to produce effects to which they seem noway adapted. | To apply a power of a$^y$ sort which has been used in that way before is what many, nay any, are capable of who are much employed in that way; but to apply powers which have never been used in that way and seem altogether unfit must be the work of one of these generall observers whom we call philosophers. The fire engine which raises water by a power which appears hardly applicable to such an effect, tho it has been improved no doubt by artists who have observed, was the invention of an ingenious philosopher; and such without doubt was the inventor of wind and water mills.$^z$

Philosophy itself becomes a seperate trade and in time like all others sub-divided into various provinces: we have a mechanical, a chymicall, an astronomicall, a metaphysicall, a theologicall, and an ethical philosopher. This division improves it as well as all other trades. The philosophers, having each there peculiar business, do [do] more work upon the whole and in each branch than formerly.

44     | This division of work is not however the effect of any human policy, but is the necessary consequen⟨c⟩e of a naturall disposition altogether peculiar to men, viz the disposition to truck, barter, and exchange; and as this dis-position is peculiar to man, so is the consequence of it, the division of work betwixt different persons acting in concert. It is observed that the hounds in a chace$^a$ turn the hare towards one [one] another, and in this manner are helpfull to each other and divide the labour, but this does not arise from any contract, as is evident since they generally quarrell about her after she is killed; no one ever saw them make any agreement giving one bone for another, nor make any signs by which they declared, This is mine and that is thine.—Dogs draw all the attention of others by their fawning and flattering. Man too some times uses this art, when no others will do, of gaining what he wants by fawnin⟨g⟩ and adulation. But this is but seldom
45 the case; he commonly falls upon other expedients. | The other animalls live intirely independent of others. And some times indeed when in danger its cries may draw the attention of man or other animalls; but this rarely is the case, and there seems to be no more provision made by nature in such cases than there is for one who is shipwrecked in the midst of the sea. The propagation of the kind and the preservation of the species goes on not-withstanding. Man continually standing in need of the assistance of others, must fall upon some means to procure their help. This he does not merely by coaxing and courting; he does not expect it unless he can turn it to your advantage or make it appear to be so. Mere love is not sufficient for it, till he applies in some way to your self love. A bargain does this in the easiest

---

$^v$ Reading of last two words doubtful     $^z$ 'P' deleted     $^a$ Reading doubtful; illegible word deleted

manner. When you apply to a brewer or butcher for [for] beer or for beef
you do not explain to him how much you stand in need of these, but how
much it would be your[21] interest to allow you to have them for a certain
46 | price. You do not adress his humanity, but his self-love.—Beggars are the
only persons who depend on charity for their subsistence; neither do they
do so alltogether. For what by their supplications they have got from one,
they exchange for something else they more want. They give their old
cloaths to one for lodging, the mony they have got to another for bread, and
thus even they make use of bargain and exchange. This bartering and
trucking spirit is the cause of the seperation of trades and the improvements
in arts. A savage who supports himself by hunting, having made some more
arrows than he had occasion for, gives them in a present to some of his
companions, who in return give him some of the venison they have catched;
and he at last finding that by making arrows and giving them to his neighbour, as he happens to make them better than ordinary, he can get more
venison than by his own hunting, he lays it aside unless it be for his diver-
47 sion, and becomes an arrow-maker. | In the same manner one who makes
coverings for huts becomes altogether a maker of coverings, another a
smith, another a tanner, etc. Thus it is that the certainty of being able to
exchange the surplus produce of their labours in one trade induces them to
seperate themselves into different trades and apply their talents to one
alone.[22]

It is not the difference of naturall parts and genius (which if there be any
is but very small), as is generally supposed,[23] that occasions this seperation
of trades, as this seperation of trades by the different views it gives one that
occasions the diversity of genius. No two persons[b] can be more different in
their genius as a philosopher and a porter, but there does not seem to have
been ⟨?any⟩ originall difference betwixt them. For the 5 or 6 first years of
their lives there was hardly any apparent difference; their companions
looked upon them as persons of pretty much the same stamp. No wisdom
48 and ingenuity appeared in the one superior to | that of the other. From
about that time a difference was thought to be perceivd in them. Their
manner of life began then to affect them, and without doubt had it not been
for this they would have continued the same. The difference of employment occasions the difference of genius; and we see accordingly that
amongst savages, where there is very little diversity of employment, there
is hardly any diversity of temper or genius.

This disposition to truck, barter, and exchange[c] does not only give
occasion to the diversity of employment, but also makes it usefull. Many

---

*b* Replaces 'trades'          *c* Illegible word deleted

---

[21] *Sic.* Presumably 'his' was intended.
[22] Cf. Mandeville, II (Dialogue 6), 335–6, 421.          [23] e.g. by Harris, I.11.

animalls who are confessedly of the same species and are of very different
genius make no advantage of it, as they want this disposition. The philosopher and the porter do not differ so much in their naturall genius as the
differen⟨t⟩ sorts of dogs. Yet these are noways useful. The swiftness of the
greyhound, the streng⟨t⟩h and sagacity of the mastiff, and the docil⟨i⟩ty of
49 the sheep dog, as they do not occasion a divisi|on of work, no way ease the
labour of the species. Each works for himself. But even the philosopher and
the porter are mutually beneficiall to each other. The porter assist⟨s⟩ the
philosopher not only by carrying to him what he wants; but by his assistance in packing, carrying, and unpacking the goods which fill the shop⟨s⟩
and ware houses of the merchants he makes every thing the philosopher
byes come so much cheaper than if a less diligent workman had been
employed. The philosopher again benefits the porter not only as being
occasionally a customer, but by the improvements he makes in the different
arts. Every one who burns coalls or eats bread is benefitted by the philosopher who invented the fire engine or the corn mill; and those who do not
invent any engines or improve upon them are beneficiall as they preserve[d]
the knowledge of the idea       [e] others, or as they form plans of improvement for other sciences.

50                    | *Wednesday. March. 30. 1763.*

                    continues to illustrate former, etc.—

In yesterdays lecture I shewed you how the division of labour increases
the opulence of a nation, which may be justly said to arise from it. If ten
men can work in a day 40 times as much as a man by himself, every one does
then[f] 4 times what he would by himself; consequently he can afford to sell
his good 1/4 part cheaper than formerly; that is, he can exchange the
superfluous produce of his labour for a fourth of the former value. In some
the encrease is far greater; in the instance already mentiond, a man who
should perform all the operations of mining, smelting, forging, splitting,
heading, etc. would hardly fournist[24] ten pins in a year, and if his maintenance be valued at 6£, which is very moderate for such an injenious man,
he could not sell a pin for less than ten shills. But if by having the wire
ready made (as the pin-makers generally have it from Sweden), by which
the work has been divided betwixt 5 or 6, the miner, the smelter, etc., and
he makes another, if by this means he should be able to make[g] 10 pins in a
51 day, he will then in one day do | what was formerly a years work, that is,
365 times the former, or to use round numbers 300. If again the pin maker

---

[d] Reading doubtful      [e] Illegible word      [f] 'about' deleted      [g] Reading
doubtful

---

[24] *Sic*. No doubt 'fournish' was intended.

by dividing the work amongst 18 different hands, as it is where well
carry'd on, can have work done by the whole, even the slowest which is the
forming of the head, to the amount of 2000 pins per man, this is 200 times
what was done in the former, and multiplying this into 800,[25] the former
number, we have 60,000 times as much work done as when it was all done
by one man. So that here he can afford his pins for $\dfrac{1}{60000}$ of what he did at
first and have as much to himself. And if he should sell them a little dearer,
as will be easily allowed, he will have a considerable profit and the work will
be cheaper. Thus it is that labour becomes dearer when at the same time
work is cheaper; and these two things, which are vulgarily reckond incompatible, are not only altogether compatible but allmost necessarily
connected. Labour is not dear or cheap according to the moneyed price
payd for it. If $1^{far}$ or $1^d$ can get a great quantity of the necessarys of life, a
52  farthing or $1^d$ is high wages, that is, if for the moneyd price | of his labour
he can get a great deal of goods or provisions. A Mogull for $1/2^d$ can get
more rice than a man can eat in a day, while the West-Indian labourer can
hardly lay by any thing out of $2^{sh}$ $6^d$ or $3^{sh}$ per diem, which is his wages.
The price of labour is not here so great as in the former case. The opulence
of a state depends on the proportion betwixt the moneyd price of labour
and that of the commodities to be purchased by it. If it can purchase
a great quantity then it is opulent; if a small then it is poor.

I shewed how the division of labour[h] increases the work performed from
three causes: dexterity acquired by doing one simple thing, the saving of
time, and the invention of machines which is occasioned by it. In the
instance above mentioned a man can do in one sence 60000 or at the other
6000 times as much by this acquired dexterity.[26]—The same appears by
another instance mentioned, wher⟨e⟩ the man who makes nothing but nails

[h] Replaces 'work'

---

[25] *Sic*. Probably '300' was intended.

[26] If, as seems probable, the two figures in this sentence relate to the illustration on 50–1
above, the second figure would appear to be wrong. In this illustration Smith assumes (a)
that if all the parts of the pin were made *ab initio* by one man working alone, he could at
the best produce ten pins per year; and (b) that if the wire were provided to him ready-
made, he could produce 3,000 pins per year. When the division of labour is introduced,
Smith assumes that each man becomes able in effect to produce 600,000 pins per year.
This is 60,000 times as many as the man working alone could produce on assumption (a),
and 200 times as many as he could produce on assumption (b). Cf. the similar calculation in
ED 6–8, below, where Smith assumes (a) that the man working alone *ab initio* could produce only one pin per year (cf. 29 above); and (b) that if the wire were provided to him
ready-made, he could produce 6,000 pins per year (cf. 29 above). When the division of
labour is introduced, and each man becomes capable (as before) of producing 600,000 pins
per year, this is correctly stated by Smith (ED 7–8) to amount to 600,000 times the former
output 'upon the first supposition' (i.e. upon assumption (a)), and 100 times the output
'upon the second' (i.e. upon assumption (b)).

53 can do more work by three times than one who has | wrought with all the
tools of the smith but has not particularly applied to nail-making but only
as a by work, and 100 times what one will do who never has tried it. The
odds here is not nearly so great by the division of labour as in button, pin,
or tile making. The operation is here still pretty complex; he blows the
fire, heats the iron and mends the fire, and changes his position and his
tools severall times, which prevents his ever acquiring that perfect dexterity which the workmen in the other trades do whose work is constantly
one and the same simple operation. The advantage gaind in point of time
was explained by the instance of the weaver and the wright, and this it is
which occasions the slothfullness of the country labourer.—That the
originall invention of machines is owing to the division of labour is not to be
doubted. One whose thoughts all center on one piece of work will be at
pains to contrive how to do this in the cleverest and easiest manner. The
inventions of the mill or the plow are so old that no history gives an[an]y
54 account of them. | But if we go into the work house of any manufacturer in
the new works at Sheffiel⟨d⟩, Manchester, or Birmingham, or even some
towns in Scotland, and enquire concerning the machines, they will tell you
that such or such an one was invented by some common workman. — —

    No human prudence is requisite to make this division. We are told
indeed that Sesostris[27] made a law that every one should for ever adhere to
his fathers possession,[28] and the same rule has been made in other eastern
countries. The reason of this constitution was that they feared lest, every
one endeavouring to advance himself into what we call a gentlemanny
character, the lower trades should be deserted. But in this generall scramble
for preeminence, when some get up others must necessarily fall undermost,
and these may supply the lower[i] trades as well as any others. The naturall
course of things will in this manner either give or leave[j] enough of hands
to the lower professions; and if things be allowed to take their naturall
55 course there is no great danger that any branch | of trade should be either
over or under stocked with hands. The constitution of Sesostris also did not
endeavour to introduce it but to preserve the division of trades, which he
without reason was afraid would not be maintaind by the causes which had
produced it. I shewed also how the disposition to truck, barter, and exchange is the foundation of this division.—Twas thus that a savage, finding
he could by making arrows and disposing of them obtain more venison
than by hunting,[k] became an arrow maker. The certainty of disposing of the
su⟨r⟩plus produce of his labour in this way is what ena⟨b⟩led men to
seperate into diffrenet[l] trades of ev⟨e⟩ry sort. This disposition is the

---

[i] Reading doubtful     [j] Reading of last three words doubtful     [k] 'which' deleted
[l] *Sic*

---

[27] Cf. p. 192, note 23, above.
[28] *Sic*. No doubt 'profession' was intended.

ocasion (as I said⟨⟩) of the difference of genius rather than the vice versa. Dogs and others more various make no benefit by their variety of disposition. It is the certainty that his produce will enable him to purchase all that he may want which enables one to seperate himself to one business; a shoe maker for his shoes can get every thing he wants. The whole produce
56 is as it were brought into the common stock,*m* and thence*n* arises | the benefit of it, as ever⟨y⟩thing*o* can then be purchased for every thing if it be good of its sort.*p*

If we should enquire into the principle in the human mind on which this disposition of trucking is founded, it is clearly the naturall inclination every one has to persuade. The offering of a shilling, which to us appears to have so plain and simple a meaning, is in reality offering an argument to persuade one to do so and so as it is for his interest. Men always endeavour to persuade others to be of their opinion even when the matter is of no consequence to them. If one advances any thing concerning China or the *more distant moon* which contradicts what you imagine to be true, you immediately try to persuade him to alter his opinion. And in this manner every one is practising oratory on others thro the whole of his life.—You are uneasy whenever one differs from you, and you endeavour to persuade ⟨?him⟩ to be of your mind; or if you do not it is a certain degree of self command, and to this every one is breeding thro their whole lives. In this
57 manner they acquire a certain dexterity and | adress in managing their affairs, or in other words in managing of men; and this is altogether the practise of every man in the most ordinary affairs.—This being the constant employment or trade of every man, in the same manner as the artizans invent simple methods of doing their work, so will each one here*q* endeavour to do this work in the simplest manner. That is bartering, by which they adress themselves to the self interest of the person and seldom fail immediately to gain their end. The brutes have no notion of this; the dogs, as I mentiond, by having the same object in their view sometimes unite their labours, but never from contract. The same is seen still more strongly in the manner in which the monkeys rob an orchard at the Cape of Good Hope.—But after they have very ingeniously conveyd away the apples, as they have no contract they fight (even unto death) and leave after many dead upon the spot.[29] They have no other way of gaining their end but by

*m* Reading doubtful      *n* Illegible word deleted      *o* Reading doubtful
*p* 'I' deleted      *q* Reading doubtful

[29] The way in which baboons rob orchards at the Cape of Good Hope is described in Peter Kolben (or Kolb), *The Present State of the Cape of Good Hope* (German edn., 1719; English edn., London, 1731). Kolben's account will be found on pp. 121–2 of vol. II of the English edn. (bound together with vol. I but separately paginated). The baboons, according to Kolben, 'keep up a Sort of Dicipline among themselves, and go about every Thing with a surprising Cunning and Fore-cast' (121). According to Smith's account, the monkeys ('as they have no contract') fight over the division of the spoils (cf. LJ(B) 222, below) and

gaining ones favour by fawning and flattering. Men when nec⟨e⟩ssitated do so also, but[r] generally apply to the stronger string[30] of self interest.

58 | In treating of opulence I shall consider:

1st ⎱ The rule of exchange, or what it is which regulates the price of
   ⎰ commodities.—

2 ⎱ Money as ⎱ 1st The measure by which we compute the value of
  ⎰          ⎰    commodities (as measure of value⟨⟩)
             ⎰ 2d The common instrument of commerce or exchange.

3dly ⎱ The causes of the slow progress of opulence, and the causes which
     ⎰ retarded it, which are of two sorts:
        1st Those which affect the improvement of agriculture
        2   Those which affect the improvement of manufactures.

4th   Taxes or ⎱ as no part of pu⟨b⟩lick law so much connects with
      publick   ⎰ opulence or has such an influence upon it; as ill con-
      revenue   ⎰ trived laws relating to commerce and taxes have been one
      great drawback upon opulence.— — —

5th   The effects of commerce, both good and bad, and the naturall
      remedies of the latter[e].—

      1st Of the Price of Commodities.—

There are properly speaking two sorts of price on commodities, which tho they appear unconnected are nevertheless very closely connected.— Let us consider what it is that will induce a man to apply all his art and industry to some particular branch of business. In the first place he must be certain that by disposing of the surplus produce of his labour he will be
59 able to procure a livelyhood. Thus before one would turn | an arrow maker he must be certain that by disposing of his arrows he will be able to support himself in the necessaries of life. He must undoubtedly have as much as will be sufficient to maintain him during the time in which he[s] labours. But besides this he must have 2dly a compensation for the time he has bestowed in learning any trade. There are some trades which need no apprentice-ship. A boy going about errands or otherwise employed sees as much of the ordinary work of a day laybourer in ploughing, ditching, mowing, etc. as must enable him, as soon as he comes to have strength, to do the work

---

[r] Reading doubtful          [s] Illegible word deleted

---

some are usually killed. Kolben's explanation of the subsequent fighting is very different. It is supposed, he says, that 'they punish Neglect of Duty in the Watch with Death: For when any of the Troop are shot or taken before the Cry is given, there is heard a mighty quarrelling Noise among 'em, when they get back to the Hills; and now and then some of 'em are found torn to Pieces in the Way; and Those are judg'd to have had the Watch' (122).

[30] *Sic.* Probably 'spring' was intended.

himself, and has in this manner no time lost. But a smith, a taylor, or a weaver can not learn their trade of themselves all at once. They must be content for some time to learn of a master, and during this time they must be satisfied to work to no profit either to themselves, their master, or any one else. They will in this time destroy or spoil a good deal of materialls before they can do the work in any tollerable manner; for these also he must recompense his master, which occasions an apprentice fee. During all this time he can do nothing to his own maintenance, but must be maintaind by

60 his parents. Now | the life of a young man when he leaves his apprentice-ship is worth at most but about 10 or 12 years purchase. His wages there-fore afterwards must be such as will not only maintain him, but will in ten or 12 years time repay him this expence of his education.[31] For this reason the longer the apprenticeship is the higher will be the wages of it. If a trade be learned by an apprenticeship, the wages will be lower than those of one which is not acquired in less than seven years. Less of human life then remains to compensate the expence of the education; if the apprenticeship be 7 years there are but 5 of the 12 remaining; and besides this the expence of the education is so much the greater. He must not only be able to maintain himself in the same manner as a day labourer, but also to make up the expence of his education. So that wages must differ according to the expence of the education requisite. Besides this other trades require some previous instruction in other arts. A smith may do well enough though he

61 can neither read nor write, and may by | practise learn perfectly the use of his tools, tho he be not in the least acquainted with the mechanic principles on which these operations depend. But a watch maker must read and write, must understand arithmetick, a little of geometry, trigonometry, and astronomy. A weaver may in this manner by the time he is 16 or 17 be a proficient in his trade, whereas a watch maker[t] will be 22 or 23 before he can be any way skilled in his art. He must therefore be highly rewarded of not being compensated before his death. Others have not only a tedious education which gives them the risque of dying ere their education is repayed, but have likeways the hazard that though they shall live never so long, they shall never make any thing by it. Thus in the study of the law not one out of 20 ever are in a way to get back the money they have laid out. Few have abilities and knowledge sufficient to make themselves any way eminent or distinguished or usefull to the peopl⟨e⟩. The ten or twelve

62 | therefore who come into business must have wage⟨s⟩ not only to compensate the expence of their education, which is very great[u] as a man must be 30 years or thereabouts before he can be of any service as a lawyer, but also the risque of not being ever able to make any thing by it. The temptation to

[t] The last three words replace an illegible word     [u] 'but also' deleted

[31] R. Cantillon, *Essai sur la nature du commerce en général* (1755), 23–4.

engage in this or any other of the liberall arts is rather the respect, credit, and emin⟨en⟩ce it gives one than the profit of it.³² Even in England where they are more highly rewarded than any where else, if we should compute them according to the same rule as that of a smith or other artizan they would be still rather too low. But the honour and credit which attends on them is to be considered as a part of the wages and a share of the reward. This is therefore the rule of the naturall price of labour. When the wages are so proportiond as that they are exactly sufficient to maintain the person, to recompense the expence of education, the risque of dying before this is
63 made up, | and the hazard that tho one lives he shall never be able to beccome any way serviceeable, they are then at their naturall rate, and the temptation is great enough to induce any one to apply to it. If the wages are lower than this they are below their naturall rate and there is no temp-tationᵛ to induce any one to apply to it; and e contra if they be *higher than* this.

### Tuesday. April. 5ᵗʰ 1763 —

Having given an account of the nature of opulence and the things in which the riches of a state might consist, I proceeded to shew that this was greatly promoted by the division of labour, which took its rise from the disposition to truck, etc., as well as the means by which it produced that effect.—We may observe on this head that as the division of labour is occasioned [by]ʷ immediately by the market one has for his commodities, by which he is enabled to exchange one thing for every thing, so is this division greater or less according to the market. If there was no market
64 every one would be obliged to exercise every trade in the propor|tion in which he stood in need of it. If the market be small he can't produce much of any commodity. If there are but 10 persons who will purchase it he must not produce as much as will supply 100, otherwise he would reap no benefit by it; far less will he be induced to bring about the great increase which follows on the farther improvement of this division. The being of a market first occasioned the division[ed] of labour, and the greatness of it is what puts it in ones power to divide it much. A wright in the country is a cart-wright, a house-carpenter, a square wright or cabinet maker, and a carver in wood, each of which in a town makes a seperate business. A mer-chant in Glasgow or Aberdeen who deals in linnen will have in his ware-house Irish, Scots, and Hamburgh linnens, but at London there are seperate dealers in each of these. The greatness of the market enables one to lay out his whole stock not only on one commodity but on one species of a

---

ᵛ Illegible word deleted       ʷ 'the' deleted

---

³² Cf. Mandeville, II (Dialogue 6), 342-3.

commodity and one assortment of it. This also lessens his corresspondence
65 and gives | him less trouble; besides that as he deals in^x a large quantity he
will get them cheaper and consequently can get the higher profit. Hence
as commerce becomes more and more extensive the division of labour
becomes more and more perfect.^y From this also we may see the necessity
of a safe and easy conveyance betwixt the different places from whence the
commodities are carried. If there is no conveyance of this sort the labour
of the person will not be extended beyond the parish in which he lives. If
the roads are infested by robbers the commodities will bear a higher price
on account of the risque. If the roads are bad in winter the commerce is then
greatly retarded, if not altogether stopped. A horse in a bad road in winter
will take 4 times the time he took before to carry his loading of equall
quantity, that is, will carry 1/4 of the goods he formerly did, whereas when
they are good, winter and summer makes no odds. And hence we see that
the turnpikes of England have within these 30 or 40 years increased the
66 opulence of the inland parts. | This may shew us also the vast benefit of
water^z carriage thro the country. Four or 5 men will navigate a vessel
betwixt Scotland and England, Norway, etc. which may contain perhaps
200 tons. The whole expense of the carriage is the tear and wear of the ship
and the wages of these men backwards and forwards, that is, if we suppose
she returns empty; but if she returns loaded this will be born in half by the
2^d cargo. If we should suppose that this should be carried by land the
expence is far greater. If a waggon carries 5 tons, it will be requisite to have
40 wag. for 200 t. Each of these have 6 or 8 horses^a with 2 men. The
expense here will be much greater. The tear and wear is much the same, but
the wages is much higher, besides that the ship does it in a much shorter
time. Land carriage therefore obstructs the^b supply of goods and the greatness of the market. Hence also we may see the great benefit of commerce,
not as it brings in money into the country, which is but a fancifull advantage,
but as it promotes industry,^c manufactures, and opulence and plenty made
by it at home.
67    | I had begun also to treat of the prices of commodities. There are in
every species of goods two seperate prices to be considered, the natural and
the market price. The 1^st is that which is necessary ⟨?to induce⟩ one to
apply to a particular business. Thus one would not become a hackney-
writer unless he had a prospect of maintaining himself and recompensing
the expense of education. Maintenan⟨ce⟩ is the first thing necessary to be
afforded by every business. But if this trade gives no more than bare
maintenance this will not induce any one to enter into it. I perhaps having
by some accident fallen into some strange out-of-the-way business, may by
dint of application make a miserable lively hood of it, but if this be all, the

---

^x Reading doubtful     ^y 'and so this' deleted     ^z Replaces 'land'     ^a Replaces 'men'     ^b 'com' deleted     ^c Replaces an illegible word

trade will end in me. No one will apply to ⟨it⟩ if it be one which requires any education, as by being a day-labourer he can get his maintenance without any previous education and with much greater certainty. Most businesses require some education; there is then the expense of food, cloaths, and lodging, in which I have been maintaind during that time by my parents, which as well as an apprentice fee is to be laid to the charge of this business.

68 There is here a stock which must be repayd by any*d* trade, not | only in principall but with the interest and profit which I might have made of it. This must also be done in a reasonable time, that the risque of dying before this is repayed may be counterballanced. Many trades also require[s] not only the knowledge of the method of handling the tools of that trade, but also of severall other branches of learning. The liberall professions of law and physick must*e* also be recompensed for the chance there is that the person, tho he live, will make nothing of it. This is the case in many other arts besides the liberall ones. Thus in the business of mining for the precious metalls, if we consider the expence of the work and the risque there is of not getting any of the metall and losing their labour either in prosecuting the old veins or discovering new ones, we will find the price of silver is noways extravagant. If we take an equall number of people employed in working of mines and of raising corn, we will find that on the whole the latter are as abundantly rewarded as the others for the expence they are at and the risque they run*f* of never getting in their money. If we take a

69 hundered persons who | cultivate corn with the same number of hands and the same expence as 100 others*g* ⟨who⟩ work in mines, we will find the profits of the first not to be the least. Of the 100, perhaps 75 make nothing at all. The remaining 25 must therefore be equall in*h* their profits to all that should have*i* made the profits of the 100.—Tho some therefore raise great fortunes others have nothing at all, and on the whole the estates made by the 100 are not more than the moderate fortunes raised by each of the 100 farmers. So that we may perhaps justly apply here a saying used in a very different sense, that there is not a worse trade in the world than a gold finder. If mining should give no greater profits than were sufficient to maintain the labourers in it, this would tempt no one to engage in it. Three fourths of those who do lose all their labour; the others must therefore be so great as equall what should have maintaind the whole number.— These are the circumstances which regulate the naturall price, and when it is equall to all these there is sufficient temptation to induc⟨e⟩ people to engage in it.

70 | The market price often differs considerably from this, and is regulated by other circumstances. When goods are brought to the market we seldom enquire what profits the person will have if he get such or such a p⟨r⟩ice.

---

*d* Reading doubtful    *e* Reading doubtful    *f* Reading doubtful    *g* 'cultiva' deleted    *h* Replaces 'to'    *i* The last two words replace 'was'

Other circumstances determine what he shall have. These are$^j$ 1$^{st}$, the demand or need for it (whether this be real or capricious⟨⟩); 2$^{dly}$, the abundance of it in proportion to this demand; and 3$^{dly}$, the wea⟨l⟩th of the demand, or demanders.

    1$^{st}$, a thing of no use, as ⟨a⟩ lump of clay, brought into the market will give no price, as no one demands it. If it be usefull the price will be regulated according to the demand, as$^k$ this use is generall or not, and the plenty there is to supply it. A thing which is hardly of any use, yet if the quantity be not sufficient to supply the demand, will give a high price; hence the great price of diamonds. Precious metalls, which are certainly not so usefull as gold, bear a far greater price, partly on this account. Abundance on the other hand such as does more than supply all possible

71 demands, | renders water of no price at all and other things of a price the next thing to nothing. The scarcity on the other hand raises the price immoderately.—This also depends on the other circumstance, viz the riche[r]s or poverty of the demand. We are told that a merchant and a traveller, whose tombs are still to be seen, meeting in the desarts of Arabia, the merchant, in want of water, gave the travellerr 10000 crowns for one cruise of water. This price, however necessitated, he could not have given had he had only 100 crowns about him. If there is less than is sufficient to supply the demand, the parties contend who shall have it. The case is here the very same as at an auction. If there be two persons equally in fancy with any thing and equally earnest to have it, they will bid equally according to their abilities, whether their$^l$ desire for it be reasonable or unreasonable. The richest however will always get it as he is best able to bid high⟨e⟩st. The price is in this manner regulated by the demand and the

72 quantity there is to | supply this demand; and whenever the quantity is not sufficient the price will be regulated by the fortunes of those who are the purchasers.—So that in some things where the demand is little the price is still high, as there is not enough to answer even this small demand. The demand for water exceeds that for any thing else whatever, but as the abundance is more than sufficient to answer all the possible demands water bears no price; whilst other things of no real value whose use we can hardly conceive, yet being but in very small quantities bear an immence price as becoming only the purchase of a few. This is the case with jewels and precious stones. The famous Pits diamond[33] would not have been purchased for £250000 had there not been a prince so vain and proud, as well as rich, as Lewis 12 of France. The other sovereigns of Europe would not

---

   $^j$ Illegible word deleted    $^k$ Reading doubtful    $^l$ 'reaso' deleted

---

   [33] The Pitt or Regent diamond, bought for £20,000 by Thomas Pitt, Governor of Madras, and subsequently in 1717 sold for £80,000 according to one account, or £135,000 according to another, to the Duke of Orleans, Regent of France during the minority of Louis XV.

have given so much, so that perhaps £50000 would have been the highest price it would have given. And had such an one been brought into Europe[m]
73 150 years before it would | not have drawn nearly so high a price. There was then not near so much wealth in any European nation. The price would not only have been less in the money paid for it, for that is nothing to the purpose, but for the reall wealth which could have been purchased by it. Every thing is dearer or cheaper according as the quantity of it makes it the purchase of the rich or of the poor. Diamonds, antiques, medalls, and such like are only the purchase of those who are extremely rich. Golden vessels of all sorts, being very scarce, become the purchase of those only who are vastly rich. Silver work, being in greater plenty, can not be disposed of intirely to those who are immensely rich; those of more moderate fortunes become purchasers and the price[n] accordingly falls, being regulated by the fortunes of the majority of the purchasers. Bread and beer, being
74 produced in | great quantities and being necessary likewise to all, become the purchase of the whole people (the nobles can not consume the whole); that is, become[s] the purchase of those of whom 99 in a hundred are of the poorer sort, for not above 1 in 100 has what we call a gentlemany fortune. The price of these commodities therefore is regulated by the abilities of the populace. This must depend on the price of labour, or to speak more properly the price of labour must depend on the quantity and price of the corn which is their support.—When therefore corn is cheap labour will be cheap; also when it is dear labour will likewise be so. Tho this is said to be contrary to experience in this count⟨r⟩y, it does not any way contradict the generall rule that when corn is low priced or ⟨?high⟩ priced labour will accompany it.

These therefor are the circumstances which regulate the price of com-
75 modities in exchange betwixt | the buyer and the seller.—Corn and beer are nec⟨e⟩ssary for the rich, but as all others must have them the price is not regulated by the rich. The quantity is so great as that it can not be made use of by the rich;[o] if the raisers of it have a mind to dispose of the whole they must sell to the poor, that is, to 99 of 100, and must be spread amongst the whole. The meanest of the people become able to purchase it, and they being the majority the price they can afford is that which regulates it. When the quantity of any of these is small the price rises proportionably, as the corn in this case becomes the purchase of those only who have great fortunes, the lower sort being obliged to live on turnips or other roots. Thus is it that water and bread rise so high in the time of a famine or siege.

These two different prices, which appear at first sight to be noway connected nor to have the least dependance on each other, are very intimately
76 related, tho the circumstances | which regulate them appear also independent. For if the market price be so high as to be more than sufficient to

---

[m] Replaces 'the country'         [n] Replaces 'value'         [o] Illegible word deleted

make up the naturall price, and answers all those things for which every tradesman has a demand (as above mentiond), this will appear to be a vastly profitable trade and all will croud into it with expectations of making a fortune. As the number of hands increases so will the quantity of work done, and consequently it will become the purchase of a lower rank of men and fall down to its naturall price.[b] For plenty and cheapness are one and the same.[q] If the paintings equall to those of Raphaels had been in great abundance they would not as now sell for £10000 but perhaps for £10. If a business be such that any one who applys to it makes mony by it, every father and mother will bread his son to it, and the price will soon be reduced to the naturall one. If the trade by this or any other means becomes overstocked, and instead of the great price for this work they do

77 not get even the | price ordinary in other trades, then no one will enter into it, and many who have engaged ⟨in⟩ it will learn some other, even when far advanced in life, rather than continue at so unprofitable a business in which the labourers do not even get their due reward. The quantity of goods made immediately diminishes and the price[s] rises up to the naturall one, in the same manner as when it is above the naturall price all rush into it, the quantity increases, and the price again comes down. The quantity of diamonds being very small, they are the purchase only of the richest people; but if by any industry their quantity could be multiplied, and instead of 100 pound, which is more than is in all Britain, 100000 pounds could be brought into the kingdom every year, they would become the purchase of the lowest people and a diamond would be bought for a shilling.—It is evident therefore that the market and naturall price of

78 commodities are | very strictly connected.— —

I observed that where grain is cheap, there wages will be cheap also; on the other hand where corn is at high price, there labour will be dear. The price of labour ought in this manner to rise or fall with that of corn.—The cheaper the labourer can subsist the greater will his profit be, as he will have the more above his maintenance. And if corn was to be cheap for a considerable time, all would apply themselves to that business where they got the highest wages, tho the corn was cheap. The[r] work done would also be increased. When meal is cheap the reward given is really greater, tho the price be very small. The price will therefore fall to the naturall rate; and on the conterary when meal is dear, for instance at double the ordinary price, then the same money reward is but in reality one half of what it was formerly.

79 A labourer who earned 1[sh] per day has in reality but a 6[d] when | the price of provisions is doubled.—The price of labour therefore should rise. But we are told that it is found by experience that in a dear year labour is

---

[b] At this point the following words are struck out: 'But if in such a case as this the trade should happen to be overstocked'    [q] This sentence is interlined above the first eight of the deleted words referred to in the previous footnote    [r] Reading doubtful

cheap and in a cheap year labour is dear. But this observation is in a great measure false, as there is only one sort ⟨of⟩ labour in which it holds, viz that of meniall servants. In all other sorts of labour the rule holds that when provisions are cheap labour is so, and *e contra*. But here this is not the case. Every one abhors naturally the subjected and mean condition of a meniall servant, liable[s] to[t] the caprice and extravagance of a master; he will work for days wages much more willingly than become your servant. When therefore the naturall and market price of[u] labour do not regulate each other[v] in an instant, as they never can, a man who before could not main-
80 tain himself by his industry finds when commodities become cheap that | he can easily do it. He eagerly runs out of service, where he gets less than he can by his labour in the manufactures, where[w] the price keeps up for some time above the naturall one. The maid servant who had been employed at spinning sets up for herself, tho before she could not have lived by her own labour. All therefore withdraw from service, and they will also do more work for themselves than they did when in service. The price of labour would of consequence fall in some time to its naturall standard. We see as a sign that labour of other sorts is cheap at the time when corn is so, that tho one pays more to a servant who spinns in the house yet the spinning out of the house is cheaper than before. In the same manner these prices do not regulate themselves at once when provisions are dear. Necessity obliges all to croud into service to get the bread which the price of other labour will
81 not afford them. But if the deart⟨h⟩ | or the cheapness was to continue over[x] severall years the prices would then regulate themselves; in the dearth, labour would be dear, and in the cheap season, cheap.— — — — —

### *Wednesday.*
### *April. 6ᵗʰ 1763 —*

The market price as I observed sinks or rises in the same manner as the naturall one, being intimately connected with it, altho the circumstances which regulate the naturall price seem to be noways connected with those which regulate the market price, viz the greatness of the demand, the quantity there is to answer this demand, and the riches or poverty of the demandants. Whenever the quantity of the goods is not altogether sufficient to supply all possible demands, those goods will bear a certain price which
82 will be regulated according to the fortunes of those who | make the demand, or bidders for them.—Those things which are scarcest bear the highest price, as they become the purchase of the richest persons who can afford to bid highest. They alone purchase diamonds, rubies, and all manufactures

[s] Reading doubtful          [t] The last two words replace 'and'          [u] 'commodities or of' deleted          [v] The last two words replace 'themselves'          [w] Reading doubtful
[x] Reading doubtful

which by the work required are scarce, tho of no great additionall reall
worth, and in generall all productions whether of art or of nature which are
scarce and ill to be come at. But if more of these things was produced
whether by art or nature, altho they be of no real value or a small, yet they
would become the purchase of the middling ranks. If again there be something which all stand in need of in some degree, and not enough to supply
all possible demands, tho more than the richest sort or the middling sort
can consume, these will bear a price, but must necessarily become the
purchase of the common people, and be regulated by them as the great
majority, being 99 of each 100.—The price of corn therefore depends on the
83 price they get for their labour; or more properly, as I | said, the p⟨r⟩ice of
their labour depends on the price of corn. For corn is one of those things
which all demand, but as there is not such plenty as we might fall upon a
shift to consume, it bears a price; this must be regulated by what the people,
the great majority of the purchasers, can afford. If corn be high so will
labour, and e contrâ. As the concourse into any trade where the wages are
too high brings it down, and if it be overstocked the desertion of the hands
occasions a diminution of the quantity and raises the price at least to the
naturall height. The market and naturall price therefore naturally coincide,
unless they be hindered by some bad police. If more money is made by it
than recompence⟨s⟩ the labourer in every shape all run into it, the quantity
done is increased, it becomes the purchase of inferior people; this sinks the
price perhaps below the naturall one, on which many quit that trad⟨e⟩ and
the price again rises.

84    | Whatever policy tends to raise the market price above the naturall one
diminishes publick opulence and naturall wea⟨l⟩th of the state. For
dearness and scarcity, abundance and cheapness, are we may say synoni-
mous terms. For whatever abounds much will be sold to the inferior
people, whereas what is scarce will be sold to those only of superior fortune,
and the quantity will consequently be small. So far therefore as any thing is
a convenience or necessary of life and tends to the happiness of mankind,
so far is the dearness detrimentall as it confines[v] the necessary to a few and
diminishes the happiness of the inferior sort. Whatever therefore raises or
keeps up the price of them diminishes the opulence and happiness and ease
of the country. As far as watches are a conveniency of life, the taxes which
raise there price diminish[es] the generall and nationall opulence[z] by con-
85 fining them to | fewer hands. Hence it is evident that all taxes on industry
must diminish the national opulence as they raise the market price of the
commodities. Thus the tax on leather occasions shous to be much dearer,
and we see accordingly that there is no part of dress of the dearth of which
the country people complain so much. And tho they being absolutely
necessary are still worn by all, yet the dearness we may say confines them to

---

[v] Reading doubtful        [z] 'of' deleted

fewer persons, as they are much more sparing and saving of them. The tax
on salt and small-beer have the same effect. Strong liquors are allmost a
nec⟨e⟩ssary in every nation. Man is a carefull animall, has many wants and
necessities, and is in continuall care and anxiety for his support. This he
prevents in some shape by laws and government, which protect every one
and make their livelyhood easier come at. Strong liquors are an expedient
86 to the same purpose which all nations have fallen upon, and | they are
therefore become allmost necessaries of life, and when used in moderation
probably conduce to health. Whatever taxes raise*a* their price diminish
opulence in this point. It is said indeed that taxes on those liquors prevent
drunkeness, but the conterary is probably the case. By raising their price
they make them an object of their desire, and such as good-fellowship
requires them to press on their guests. We see accordingly that in Spain
and France, where all liquors are very cheap, there is less drunkeness than
in this country. We may see also that this is the case here. A gentleman
drunk with ale is a sight never to be seen, whereas one drunk with wine is
not so uncommon. One will never press his friend to drink a glass of ale, as
he never imagines that he will scruple him that. But good fellowship
requires that he should press him to drink wine, which costs him all he can
well afford.

87 | In the same manner also as all *monopo*lies raise the pric⟨e⟩ of com-
modities they must be detrimentall to the opulence of the nation. In this
manner the Hudsons Bay Company, having the sole priviledg⟨e⟩ of importing furrs, render the opulence of the nation less as far as they are a
necessary or conveniency of life. The company will always bring in less of
them than if the trade was free. What they bring in also is sold higher;
fewer persons therefore are supplied with them. The manufactures are also
worse supplied with them if necessary and are consequently the higher
priced. All such companys prevent a free concurrence, which brings down
the price of every thing to its naturall height. A few persons can never make
this concurrence, and these few can easily lay their heads together and join
88 in bringing in a small quantity and selling it very high, | which would be
prevented by a free concurrence. For if any trade is overprofitable all
throng into it till they bring it to the naturall price, that is, the maintenance
of the person and the recompence of the risque he runs; that is, what is
sufficient to maintain the person according to his rank and station. As all
companies such as the East Indian, Turky, and Hudsons Bay diminish the
opulence with regard to these commodities, so do all corporations, which
tho formerly very usefull are now a publick nuisance.[34] Such are those of
butchers, brewers, bakers, etc., etc. They prevent a concourse and by that

*a* Reading doubtful

[34] Cf. ii.34-41 above.

means raise the price of these commodities. And accordingly there is generally a magistrate who settles the price of all these commodities. But as there is no corporation of the dealers in cloth there is no one who regulates
89 the price of it. It is found absolutely necessary in the others. The | corporation produces but a small quantity and take⟨s⟩ a great price for it; this gives them the same profit, and at less trouble[b] than if they had made a greater quantity. It is the same thing to a baker whether he makes £50 by making 1000 or 100000 loaves in the year. And when there are few in any branch of business they can easily agree amongst themselves to do this. There is therefore a magistrate or clerk of the market appointed who regulates the price of this[c] according to that of corn or oats in the neighbourhood. This expedient, tho necessary where corporations are allowed, does not answer the end of a plentifull market in any shape so well as that of allowing a free concurrence. A considerable profit must be allowed on each branch above the naturall price else no one will engage in it. Thus we are
90 told that          [35] occasioned a most grievous famine at Antioch | by endeavouring to give plenty by appointing a low price of corn, which being a little too low made all who had corn to transport it to other places. The assizer therefore fixes the price generally considerably above the naturall price; if he fixes it below, it will make a most intollerable scarcity. All succh commodities are therefore very dear. A baker, whose trade is very soon[d] learnt, is a very profitable business, and so is that of a brewer; this would be remedied by a free concurrence. Every discouragement to industry therefore hurts opulence in the nation. This is the case with all the revenues on commodities, as that on salt. The price of the work is the same, but to this must be added the tax, principall and interest, and the expense of collecting it. Salt therefore as a necessary of life becomes dearer, and the consumption of it, if not excluded[e] from some, is greatly lessend.—Not only
91 | does every thing hinder the opulence which raises the market price above the naturall, but every thing which tends to sink it below, tho from a different cause. Nothing can do this but a *bounty* given by the publick on some branch of manufacture or exportation of som⟨e⟩ commodity. Thus there is a bounty in this country in all coarse linnen at less than a shilling per yard,[36] the greatest part of which is made for exportation. This bounty is about 3ᵈ per yard. Now if we suppose the cloth to be worth 6ᵈ, the publick pays about 1/4 part of the price. So that the foreign merchant can get for 1/4 part less than would have been a sufficient price to the workman if no bounty had been attending the making it. In the same manner there is a bounty of 5

---

[b] Replaces 'expence'     [c] Reading doubtful     [d] Reading doubtful     [e] Reading doubtful

---

[35] Blank in MS. Probably the Emperor Julian: Ammianus Marcellinus, XXII.14.1; Libanius, *Orations*, I.126 and XVIII.195; Julian, *Misopogon*, 369c.
[36] The bounty varied from ½d. to 1½d. per yard: 29 George II, c. 15 (1756).

shillings per quarter on all corn exported when it is above 30 or 35 shil.,[37] which is the ordinary price. So that here also the publick pays an eight part of the price, and thence it can be sold 1/8 cheaper to the foreign merchant than otherwise it could have been afforded. This therefore makes the price

92 of corn lower | and causes more purchasers for it, or what is the same thing causes the purchasers to take greater quantities. This encourages the raising of corn and makes in this manner an artificiall abundance. This also is hurtfull to the opulence of the nation by overturning the naturall balance of industry. The industrious people naturally apply themselves to the different branches of trade just in proportion to the demand that is for those commodities. Whatever breaks this naturall balance by giving either an extraordinary discouragement by taxes and duties, or [by] an extraordinary encouragement by bounties or otherwise, tends to hurt the naturall[38] opulence. When any branch of trade has a bounty on it all croud into it, and work not so much with expectation of answering a great demand but from a desire of making a fortune by this*f* bounty, and proportion their work to it rather than to the demand. When things are left to their naturall course, according as the demand is, the quantity made is greater or less in each

93 commodity. | As far as you encourage by bounty you make the quantity greater than the publick has a demand for, and consequently sink the price below what is necessary to encourage the labourers at an other time. In order to make the produce greater in this branch, you call away as many hands from other employments as you add to this.—The number of hands employed in*g* business depends on the stored ⟨stock⟩ in the kingdom, and in every particular branch on the stored stock of the employers. Many goods produce nothing for a great while. The grower, the spinner, the dresser of flax have no immediate profit. The flax must pass thro a vast number of hands ere it can bring any price. All these must be maintaind by the stor'd stock of the manufacturer, as they gain nothing of themselves. This stored stock thro the kingdom, tho it may be continually increasing, does not readily alter at any particular time.—The quantity of money may rise or

94 fall but | the stored stock which can afford the labourers food, cloaths, and lodging continues much the same, and it is in proportion to it that the number of hands is regulated. Whenever therefore you call more hands than are naturally engaged in it to any particular business, you sink inde⟨e⟩d the price of that commodity to the foreign merchant, but you raise the price or perhaps of all others proportionably at home. There is then no concurrence in those branches equall to what there was formerly. The manufacturer in each branch requires a particular stock. The man

---

*f* Illegible word deleted	*g* Illegible word deleted

---

[37] In fact 48 shillings: 1 William and Mary, c. 12 (1688).
[38] *Sic.* Probably 'national' was intended.

who employs 5 or 6 weavers must have a certain stock as he can not sell the produce of their labour from day to day; one who has 25 or 100 requires proportionably a greater stored stock to enable him to want his money perhaps for 3, 4, 5, or 6 months. This stock is limited by the quantity of food,

95 cloaths, and other necessaries which the | manufacturer can afford them. A certain number can therefore be employed in each branch. When therefore you increase the number in one branch you necessarily diminish those in others. The price of that commodity fall⟨s⟩, but those of all or some others rise[s]. We see that the bounty on corn has sunk the price of it continually, the necessary consequence of which was that the rent of corn farms should sink also. The rent of a farm intended to produce 1000 qur of corn must be less when corn is low priced than when it is high, the 1000 qurs not being worth so much as formerly. This bounty however was at first laied[h] on[i] to raise the rents of the corn farms. The landholders were told that by giving them a ready vent for their corn it would enable them to bear the land tax without any hurt.[j] This it did indeed for some time by causin⟨g⟩ a great deal of waste ground to be taken into tillage, and other ground greatly improved. But this effect has been long since answered, as

96 the ground in most places of the country is as far improved | in the raising of corn as it can well be. It has consequently for some time diminished the quantity of grass below what it was formerly, and below the naturall quantity. More ground has been turnd into corn and consequently less has been left for the production of grass. The quantity of grass being diminished the price of it necessarily rises, and along with it the price of butcher meat which must depend on it. And we see that the price of butcher meat is much greater in the richest parts of England and Ireland than it is here, proportionally to the difference of opulence. Thus tho corn becomes cheaper, another commodity no less usefull rises in its price. The price of hay must also rise as well as that of pasture grass. The quarter of corn formerly gave 40 or 45 shill., but has now been found to be about 30 or 35, so that it has fallen about 1/8. The load of hay gives now 20 or 23 sh, which is double of its former price. This was partly owing to the fall of corn and partly to other causes. The maintenance of horses is therefore | become

97 much higher. If this extended to saddle horses only the grievance would not be intollerable. But as horses are necessary for the facilitating of land carriage thro the [the] kingdom, by raising this maintenance the expense of transportation is increased and the inland commerce of the kingdom greatly embarrassed. The market of commodities becomes more confined and the concurrence is lessend, which necessarily lessens opulence or plenty. So that the best police would be to leave every thing to its naturall course, without any bounty or an⟨y⟩ discouragement.[k]

---

[h] Reading doubtful　　　　[i] 'a' apparently deleted　　　　[j] Replaces an illegible word
[k] 'We' deleted

We come now to the 2ᵈ thing proposed, viz money, and 1ˢᵗ we are to consider it as the measure of values. At first when men dealt in a few species of goods, any species might be the common measure of the value of the rest. Thus if they dealt in corn, sheep, and black-cattle they might have an
98 account that so many measures of corn were equall in value to 1 sheep | or two,¹ and thence again that 4 sheep were of equall value with an ox. These relative values would be easily remembered. But if we should suppose that they dealt in 100 different commodities, not to say 100,000 as there is in this and many other countries, every one will there be compared to 99 others and have as many different values, so that there will be in all 9900 values to be remembered. This puts them on fixing on some particular commodity as the common standard, for in that case there will be only 99 different values to be remembered. This common measure has always been that with which they were best acquainted. In Gre⟨e⟩ce cattle were the most generally used commodity, and this was for some time the measure. In Homer every thing is valued as worth so many oxen; the arms of Glaucus were worth 100 oxen and those of Diomede worth 9.³⁹ Italy again, being a hilly country, was more stored with sheep; they therefore were the measure of value, as [were] they were amongst the Tuscans; and in generall they
99 would compare all others | with that commodity with which they were best acquainted. But it would soon be found that one ox was not of equall value with an other; besides the difference of size and age there are many other varieties. Hence every wise man when he had dealt some time in merchandize would attempt to form a better measure. They wanted a more certain and accurate measure of value than cattle could be, of which equall quantities should have equall values. This in the same country is pretty nearly the case with all metalls, but more expecially with gold and silver, as the quantity of alloy in them is much more easily ascertaind than the temper or quality on which depends the value of iron or brass, and with far greater accuracy, tho that can not be done even here with the utmost facility or precision.ᵐ

These metalls are the only commodities whose value is the same in proportion to the quantity, and the proportion of which can be easily ascertaind. They have accordingly in all countries been found to be much better
100 measures of | value than cattle or sheep, and have therefore been used as such sooner or later. In the same manner as they changed the naturall measures of length into artificiall ones, so did they those of value. All measures were originally taken from the human body; a fathom was measured by the stretch of a mans arms, a yard was the half of this, a span an inch or digit, a foot a pace, etc. These natu⟨rall⟩ⁿ measures could not

---

¹ Reading of last four words doubtful        ᵐ 'T' deleted        ⁿ Reading doubtful

³⁹ *Iliad*, vi.236; Pufendorf, V.5.1.

long satisfy them, as these would vary greatly, not only in different men but even in the same one at different times and in different tempers. Prudent men therefore contrived, and the publick established, artificiall yards, fathoms, feet, inches, etc. which should be the measures of all different lengths. For the same reason they converted the originall and naturall measures of value into others not so naturall, but more convenient than any of those naturally used by men in the ruder[o] ages of society.

101                          | *Thursday.*

*April. 7. 1763.*

Money as I observed now serves two severall purposes. It is first the measure of value. Every one tells you that the goods he has to sell are worth so many pounds, shillings, etc., as believing you know this as a measure. It is also the instrument of commerce, or medium of exchange and permutation. A shoe maker who has a mind to bye beef or bread does not offer shoes to the butcher, but converts or exchanges his shoes for money, and this again he exchanges for bread or beef. By means of money he brings his goods to market and purchases what he wants himself. I had begun to shew you how the[p] metalls gold and silver came to be the measure of value, for it was from thence that they came to be the instrument of commerce. When the things in commerce are so numerous that people can not easily remember the respective values, they find it necessary, as I observed, to have some common measure of the value of all. This as I observed is the commodity with which they are most familiar, whatever that be—sheep, or

102 oxen, or any other.—When men deal | either to a small extent or in commodities of a small value, the naturall and innaccurate measures will be sufficient. In measures of length this is the case. One who should sell a few yards of coarse cloth of no great value would not be greatly a looser if he lost an inch or two on each yard by the inaccuracy of the measures, as that of a fathom measured by a mans sp⟨r⟩ead arms. These naturall measures taken from the human body are by no means accurate, varying in different persons. When therefore they dealt to a great extent, or in valuable commodities, they would naturally fall upon more accurate measure⟨s⟩ which should be more certainly ascertaind; hence artificiall feet, yards, spans, paces, inches, etc. For in these more extensive exchanges a small innaccuracy often repeated will produce a great loss on the whole.—All wise men would see the necessity of this to prevent frauds and rogueries. The same was the case with regard to the measures of value, as soon as men came to be more carefull of their bargains. The naturall measures of sheep or oxen would not answer their purpose; a more precise measure was

---

[o] Reading doubtful          [p] Reading doubtful

103 requisite, | the value of which could always be ascertain'd by its quantity. Metalls in generall are of this sort; one pound of iron or copper is pretty much of the same value as another, but in gold and silver particularly, as their fine⟨ne⟩ss is most certain[ed] and easily ascertain'd. Hence all people have used them in this manner, and came to say that such a commodity was worth so many pounds or talents of gold or silver instead of so many sheep or oxen, in the same manner as they used*q* the artificiall instead of the natural fathom.—Hence also it came to be accounted the instrument of commerce. It is absolutely necessary that a market should be had in which to buy and sell commodity⟨s⟩ of all sorts. Cattle from severall circumstances ceased to be fitted for this purpose. It had answered it very well in the age of shepherds. Every one had then cattle or sheep; he could take as many as he inclined for any commodity. They made an addition to his

104 flock or herd and cost him nothing in | maintenance, as*r* the whole face of the earth was then one common pasture. Cattle would therefore be the most acceptable thing to every one and what every one would offer. But when land was divided amongst different proprietors, the great part of which was also employed in raising of corn, this could no longer be the case. Every one could then maintain only a certain number of cattle. Besides, there were many who could not keep cattle without a great expence, having no ground or but very little. The worker in brass or the dresser of leather could have his goods lye by him as long as he pleased at no expence; but the maintenance of an ox would be more perhaps than he could easily afford. Cattle therefore could no longer be this common measure. But it was absolutely necessary that they should have some

105 common measure and instrument of exchange | in their stead. A weaver who wanted bread or beef of a baker or butcher could not always get them for his cloath, and they again wanting smith work could not get it for their commodities.—I want your goods but you do not want mine. We are both wanters perhaps but not of each others goods. So that there can be no exchange betwixt us unless we have some common instrument of traffick. Cattle were now laid aside. The most naturall and proper thing they could fall upon was the metall⟨s⟩, and of these gold and silver have severall advantages over the others. But any of them is pretty accurate, and we see accordingly that for a long time in the beginning of the Roman state copper was the measure of value and generall instrument of exchange, as iron was at Lacedaemon;[40] the poverty of those state⟨s⟩ was such that gold and silver were not introduced till the later times. The precious metalls are however [been] generally the instrument of commerce. A certain weight of them has always a certain value. The keeping a quantity of gold or silver

*q* Reading doubtful          *r* Reading doubtful

[40] Sparta. Plutarch, *Life of Lycurgus*, 9; cf. Pliny, *Historia Naturalis*, XXXIII.13.43.

106 by one costs him nothing. The⟨y⟩ lose nothing | by it, which is not the case with the other metalls; and gold above all others is least corruptible. A[s] great value$^s$ goes into little room, that is, a small quantity goes a great length in purchasing the necessaries of life, on account of their scarcity and beauty. Their value is not as Mr. Locke⁴¹ imagines founded on an agreement of men to put it$^t$ upon them; they have what we may call a naturall value, and would bear a high ⟨?one⟩ considered merely as a commodity, tho not used as the instrument of exchange. Their beauty is undoubtedly superior to that of the other$^u$ mettalls; gold takes a finer polish than any other, and silver next to it. Besides this all instruments except those for cutting could be better ⟨?if made⟩ of the⟨m⟩ than of any other metalls; all houshould utensils, as plates, spoons, kettles, etc., et⟨c⟩. [all] with a few exceptions would be the better if made of gold or silver. As therefore they are the most beautifull, and if we except iron the most usefull, and are also the scarcest, they would naturally bear a high value and exchange for a great

107 quantity of other commodities. Their scarcity | also fitted them for being the instrument of commerce. They therefrom have the higher price, and have therefore a great value in a small bulk by which means they are easily transported. A small quantity of silver is more easily carried about than the same value of coarse linnen or other commodity, and considerably more than iron or copper. And from thence it is that in some towns in Sweden they are obliged to carry the mony they intend to lay in their winter$^v$ provisions with to the market in a wheell barrow. As they had been already used as the measure$^w$ of value they were the more easily admitted in this way also. Every one values his own commodities in this way; whatever they be, bread, beer, or cloth, he will tell you they are worth so many pounds or shillings. No one could have any objections to accept of them, as he measured his goods by them and so also did all those he had to deall with.

    In this manner money came to be the instrument of commerce, and all

108 exchange, from being carried on by the intervention of cattle, was | carried on by the intervention of these metalls. In order to render$^x$ them the more proper for this purpose it is necessary to ascertain two things, their weight and their fine⟨ne⟩ss. The first of these is the easiest, but even it does not want its difficulties. A balance, tho a simple machine, was not soon invented, and the Roman statera which preceded it was liable to many and great innaccuracies unless in very well skilled hands. And besides this the weighing of such valuable commodities as gold required great care and attention as well as a nice balance, and this is one great hindrance in the

---

$^s$ The last two words replace 'small quantity'    $^t$ Reading doubtful    $^u$ 'valu' deleted    $^v$ Replaces 'month'    $^w$ Replaces 'instrument'    $^x$ Replaces 'ascertain'

---

⁴¹ *Civil Government*, § 50.

exchange of them. The fineness again is a matter still more difficult to be known; the alloy may be mixt both in silver and gold so as that the good coin can hardly be distinguished from the bad. This can not be known but by the hydrostaticall bance[42] and not even then with great accuracy if the alloy be of lead.—The quantity being therefore not easily ascertaind without great hindrance, the exchange and the assaying being so difficult that

109 | that is generally a trade by itself, some method was requisite to answer both of these ends that might ascertain both the quantity and fine⟨ne⟩ss of this common measure of value and instrument of commerce which was found to be so usefull. Coinage answered both of these ends. The publick finding how much money facilitated exchange and promoted commerce, which as it inriched the nation was also highly beneficiall to the government, besides that they greatly facilitated the payment of taxes, etc., it was therefore their interest to put it on the best footing. They therefore took upon them to coin money of gold and silver and put a stamp upon it, which tho it neither added to nor diminish'd the value gave every one who saw it the publick faith that it was of such a weight[43] and such a fine⟨ne⟩ss. The first thing in all probability which would be ascertaind by coinage would be the fine⟨ne⟩ss, which was most difficult to be discovered[y] befor the art of milling or stamping the edges was invented, and that of fitting the stamp precisely to

110 the size of the metall, so | that the first coin would be much[z] of the same nature as the Spanish ingots or pieces of eight, the stamp of which ascertains only the value as to the fine⟨ne⟩ss. The weighing, tho difficultly done with accuracy, was yet what any ordinary man was capable of. Coin however becomes most perfect when both the fine⟨ne⟩ss and the quantity are ascertaind; payments can then be made by the tail[44] instead of weight, which in small summs is much more expeditious. The names of silver coins and of nominall summs of gold or silver wer⟨e⟩ regulated at first by the names of the w⟨e⟩ight of certain quantities of silver, as silver was generally the standard.[45] There must be but one standard as no one thing can have two values; and as silver is more frequently used it came to be the standard. The person who wants to bye a thing of small value in the market can not give out gold; the daily expense[a] will not allow of it. He first exchanges his gold into silver, and then changes his silver for the commodity he

111 stands in need of. | A certain number of pieces of coin were concev'd to be in every weight. The French livre was originally the pound troys or libra[b] of silver. This pound was that used at the city of Troy in       [46], a place of

---

  [y] 'and the other' deleted        [z] Reading doubtful        [a] Reading doubtful
  [b] Replaces an illegible word

---

  [42] Reading doubtful. No doubt 'balance' was intended.
  [43] Aristotle, *Politics*, 1257[a]38–41, quoted in Pufendorf, V.1.12.
  [44] By tale: i.e. by number, as distinguished from by weight.
  [45] Harris, I.28; cf. II.1, note.        [46] Blank in MS. Troyes in Champagne.

great resort to the merchants of all countries.—The pound English was originally a pound of silver, Tower weight, which was somewhat less than the Troy pound, and seems to have been the same with the Roman.

We may observe that tho the measures of value constantly decrease, the measures of quantity are always increasing. The English pound is but little more than 1/3 of what it was in the time of Edward 1st. The French livre is now but of ten pence value, which before in the time of Charlemagne was about 72 times that some,ᶜ being a full Troy pound. So that the measures of value have been continually shrinking. The government have found their interest in diminishing the measures of value, but have not had the same
112 interest in diminishing the measure⟨s⟩ of quantity. The dealers in | commodities would find profit by contracting these measures, but as the publick have no advantage in this there is generally a magistrate appointed to regulate and oversee the measures. And as the dealers generally contract them, these magistrates go to the safest side and rather increase them; and this has made them to grow in most countries. Our measures of length, our foot, yard, pace, et⟨c⟩. are all borrowd from the Roman, but are respectively considerably larger.

The case has been the same with respect to our wet measures and our weights. The standard of the pound in the city of Troy was that used over all Europe; this too was considerably larger, to wit by half an ounce, than the Tower or Roman weight. This weight also has been laid aside in all commodities, unless gold and silver, and has been succeded by another
113 called the avoirdupois weig⟨h⟩t, which according | to the meaning of the name is sometimes calld heavy weight. The causeᵈ of the introduction of this was that it had been customary to give the byer the cast of ballancing; and as this was an uncertain thing the merchants modified it to 3 ounces, and the pound came to consist of 15 oz instead of 12. But as this number would not divide so conveniently as the number twelve, as it divided only by 3 and 5, they added another ounce which made it 16, but at the same time lessend the ounce so that the avoirdupois weight is about 14 troy ounces. The measure of weight has thus been increasing, and so have all measures of quantity, tho the measure⟨s⟩ of value have diminished. The pound Easterling, or that used in the Hanse towns, was agreed upon as the standard in England of weight, and this was what was called a pound of money. But the present pound is but about one third of it. The poundᵉ troy contains 62 shillings, but as the troy pound was somewhat larger the difference is not entirely so great.⁴⁷
114 | The necessities or frauds of the government have been the occasion of this shrinking in the measures of value. It was necessary that the govern-

ᶜ *Sic*    ᵈ Reading doubtful    ᵉ Replaces 'ounce'

⁴⁷ Harris, I.31.

ment should be at the trouble and expence of coinage; no other could find their interest in it. The stamp gives it no additionall value; it merely ascertains the value. The government found it their interest to be at that expence, as money facilitated taxes and the intercourse by commerce, which as it enriched the people was beneficial to the government. A private man had no motive to undertake it. He might put his stamp upon it, as he may do still, but this will not be of any service. Besides, no one man would have such generall credit as that his word would be taken for the quantity or fine⟨ne⟩ss of the mettall. It was necessary therefore to ordain that no other should coin money besides the government, for tho the government might be honest there was great danger that a private man, as the temptation was great, might falsify the publick money, putting more alloy into it. So that the coining of money in the manner of the publick was to be

115 considered as a fraud of the most heinous nature and a great | affront on the government. But as faith was put in the king *f* government it was also necessary that all should be oblidged to accept of them. You must accept of the kings coin under the value and denomination that is put upon it, and to refuse it is an affront to the government which is liable to severall penalties. The offer of money must be considere⟨d⟩ as a legall tender of payment, and it was necessary that it should be so, that whether a creditor accepted of it or not the offer of the payment in this coin should be considered as freeing him from all trouble and disquietude from the government. Any one[n]*g* may issue money in his own name and if it be accepted it is well; but no one is obliged to accept of it as a legall tender of payment. The power and authority of the government amongst a barbarous and unobserving people would easily pass upon them coin of a less value; and they were often tempted also to endeavour in this manner to debase its standard by giving the same quantity of silver a larger proportion of alloy,

116 and this in the language of the Mint is | called raising the coin, as it raises the value of the quantity of silver. If out of 4 oz, which is nearly equall to 20 sh, you should coin 40 by adding more*h* alloy, you debase the standard one half and double the value, as two oz then have the value of one p. sterl. This was often their interest ⟨?where⟩ they had but £1,000,000 in the Treasury and had occasion for 2 millions to pay off their debts, fullfill their contracts, and pay soldiers and mariners. They coin this one million into 2, debasing its standard and making the new coin resemble the old as nearly as possible; and by this means, in⁴⁸ appears, they discharge all their debts. This does well enough for some time. And thus a temporary interest of the government by this fraud diminishes the measures of value.—But like all other frauds it is merely a temporary temptation, and in the whole is

*f* Illegible word          *g* Reading doubtful          *h* Reading of last two words doubtful

⁴⁸ *Sic.* Presumably 'it' was intended.

a loss to those who practise it. The government of England being the freeest, and the people most upon the watch, the coin is sunk not quite 1/3

117 of the value; in France it is reduced to less than 1/70, and more or less | in all others; in Scotland to 1/36, as the Scots^i pound was originally the pound troy. For as the Scots had the greatest intercourse with the French, their coin generally [their coin generally] kept pace with it till the time of James the 6th [time], since which it has been on the same footing with the English, which has not been altered. But still the coin is on a precarious footing, being under the management of the king and Privy Councill, as the Parliament can not legally intermeddle.— — — — —

### Friday. April. 8^th 1763.

Money has been shewn to be extremely necessary as an instrument of commerce. It by that means promotes the exchange of commodities; this exchange again promotes the industry of the people and facilitates and encourages the division of labour. It is indeed a very naturall invention, and has accordingly been used by all nations who have come to a tollerable

118 degree of improvement. The Europeans, | on their first going into China, Me[e]xico, Peru, and all the eastern countries, found metalls used as the instruments of commerce, and they had the publick stamp upon them, which is all that is requisite to constitute money.

I pointed out the reasons also which brought^j the coin below the originall standard in point of weight, for in point of purity it is at present as high as ever. This has been brought about by the temporary and fraudulent views of the government, who found their interest at times to diminish the coin by adding a greater quantity of alloy, in order to pay off their various debts with a small quantity of silver and gold. I shall by and by shem[49] some other effects of these operation⟨s⟩ on the coin; one which always happens is the diminishing of the nominall value of the coin. This in England is about 1/3; the pound of silver being not quite four oz instead of its^k value, as the pound weight of silver is divided into 63^sh 6^d so that £1.00^sh 08 is 4 oz. {The gold coin has kept pace pretty nearly with it, being now about 46 guineas and a half in the pound.}

119 | The effects of this operation is very prejudiciall to commerce. The great benefit of money is to give a plain, clear, and ready measure of value and medium of exchange for all commodities; but this is considerably disturbed by this means. Measures tho somewhat inconvenient should never be altered; tho your yard be of an inconvenient length, it is better to allow it to continue so; any alteration[s] always occasions an embarrassment of

---

^i Reading doubtful     ^j Replaces 'debased'     ^k Reading doubtful

---

[49] *Sic.* No doubt 'shew' was intended.

business. The former standards do not any longer agree and a new calculation is requisite$^l$ which take⟨s⟩ some time to become familiar to us. The
case is the same with regard to the measures of value. When any alteration
is made one does not readily know how much of the new coin is equall to a
certain value; this necessarily embarrasses commerce. The merchant wont
sell but for a very high price, being affraid of losing, and the purchaser for
the same reason will not give but a very low one[s]. And as both stand off in
120  this manner, the merchant choosing rather to keep up | his goods than to
sell them too low, a stagnation must necessarily follow in the exchange of
commodities; and money in some measure ceases to answer its end as a
measure of value. It is also productive of a great deal of fraud. For in the 1$^{st}$
place, the creditors of the government are cheated of their money; if the
coin be one half less they have but one half of the value that was given to the
government, tho they have in appearance the whole. To screen$^m$ themselves
also it is necessary that all debts in the kin⟨g⟩dom should be paid by this
money in the same manner as by$^n$ the old money. So that all the creditors
in the kingdom are in this manner defrauded of their just debts. This for
some time keeps up the value of the coin and hinders the price of commodities from rising in the same manner as the money has been debased;
but afterwards it rises to the proper height if not prevented. Money serves
for two purposes, it pays debts and$^o$ purchases$^p$ commodities. The first of
these purposes it answers tho debased, as the coin can not be refused tho
sunk one half in its value. When one carries it to market, especially | to a
121  forreign one, he finds that it will not indeed purchase above what ten
shillings formerly purchased for 20 of the new ones; but at the same time he
can discharge his debts as easily as before. And by this means the pound,
which is worth in reality but ten shillings, keeps up at the value of 18 or 20.
All workmen are pay'd by the new coin; the weaver, the mason, etc. all pay
their tradesmen in this coin, besides 200000 or 400000 soldiers, an immense number of officers of excise, messenger⟨s⟩, and of police are all
payed in this coin.$^q$ Their wages are in reallity greatly diminished, as they
are paid according to the denomination put upon the coin and not its real
value. And as the lower class are those who regulate the price of all sorts of
necessaries,$^{50}$ and as they can not now afford the same price as formerly,
[and] they must therefore be sold for what they can give. And in this manner
the stocks of the people being less, the commodities must fall to a less price
also. Soon however the prices of commodities will rise as much as the
122  nominall value of the coin | has risen and the reall one diminished. But this

---

$^l$ 'and new calculations' deleted        $^m$ Reading doubtful        $^n$ The last seven
words replace 'also as well as'        $^o$ Illegible word deleted        $^p$ Replaces 'exchanges'
$^q$ The words 'N.B. France' are written vertically in the margin at about this point

---

$^{50}$ 73-4 above.

will not happen till the journeymen and mechanicks and labourers, finding that their wages can not support them, gradually raise them to be proportionable to the diminution of the coin, and become able to give their former value; and this will generally happen in a few months. The sovereign would for this reason soon lose more than he had gaind by thus raising of the money. He makes the augmentation when the money is in his treasury, and by that means pays his debts by a smaller value. But afterward as his revenues are to be raised, when the money is thus raised in value tho no higher in denomination he would lose immensely, as the money when given out would not go so far by one half as formerly.—A diminution therefore becomes necessary and always follows the augmentation. If out of four oz you$^r$ coin 40 shillings, the value of every thing is nominally$^s$

123 doubled; 10 sh become a pound, 1/2 crown a cro[n]wn, etc. | This is frequently done in France by crying up the mark. The mark their as here containd 2/3 of the pound, ⟨?which⟩ in England is equall to ab⟨o⟩ut 42 shil. This in France was some time$^t$ ⟨?ago⟩ divided into 28 livres; this was at once raised to 40, from thence to 60, and that without any new coinage but merely by an order declaring that the mark should contain so many livres; and afterwards at once from 60 to 120.$^{51}$ But immediately after these augmentations are issued a diminution is expected. The augmentation is made when the treasury is full, and the government gains by it; and the diminution being made before the revenues are raised prevents in some measure the loss. This alteration is of no less bad consequence than the former. The standard is by this means perpetually fluctuating, and by that means commerce is retarded. As the augmentation injured the creditor, so this injures the debtor, who ought rather to be favoured. For instead of 10

124 shillings which he owed when | money was cried up he is obliged to pay 15 or 16. But this is not so much felt as the other, as it is generally brought on by degrees and the people forewarned of the time they are to take place. But this can not entirely prevent them, as the time of the debtors payment may not perhaps come till after the diminution has taken place. The debtors therefor suffer, tho not so much as the creditors do by an augmentation, and it comes on all on a sudden and makes a fraud in every contract which is then existing.

In most countries there are three sorts of coin: gold, silver, and copper. 'Tis only the silver and gold which one is obliged to accept of in payment. We need not take any copper above the lowest exchange, that is above 1, 6 pence.—It may even sometimes be a hardship to be obliged to take silver,

---

$^r$ Reading doubtful  $^s$ Reading doubtful  $^t$ The last two words replace 'at first'

---

$^{51}$ Cf. ii.81 above.

as the banks have[u] frequently endeavour'd to perplex by making payment
125 in sixpences; but they ought not to be indulged in | trifling in business. A
certain proportion betwixt these coins must necessarily be ascertaind, and
this in all well ordered states is not          [v] by the caprice of the government but by the market price of gold and silver. If gold brings in the market
16 times as much as the same quantity of silver, then gold and silver coin
ought to be as 16:1; if the value of gold be 14 times or 15 times that of
silver, then gold and silver coin ought to be as 14 or 15:1. For this reason
the value of gold keeps pace with that of silver, and their[w] relative value
frequently alters according to demand. The guinea, which is now worth
21$^{sh}$, was formerly worth 22, but was at first cryed down to 21$^{sh}$ 6$^d$ and
afterwards to 21$^{sh}$; and before that had been worth only 20$^{sh}$.[52] Gold is said
to be worth more in England than in the rest of Europe, being here 16 times
the worth of the same weight of silver and in other countries but about 14 or
15 times the value of silver. And hence it is that our silver coin immediately
dissappears. We have here 46½ guineas from the pound of gold, and 63$^{sh}$ 6$^d$
126 from the pound of silver; the proportion is | therefore nearly as 16:1; in
other countries it is as 14:1. As the silver therefore is of less value than
gold, there is profit in carrying it abroad as soon as it comes from the Mint,
as 16 pound of silver will purchase only one pound of gold in this kingdom
but will procure somewhat more in other countries. One who carries silver
abroad gets more gold than he would at home, and bringing the gold back
he gets more silver than he could abroad, and by this means can constantly
increase his stock; and hence it is that our gold coin continually increases
tho the silver diminishes, by this small mistake in the relative proportion of
gold and silver. A proposall was made in Parliament to have remedied this,
but as it was found to be extremely troublesome it was laid aside. The false
shillings which are issued at an other place and are worth not above 10$^d$ are
for this reason overlooked by the government. They supply the nation with
coin, save them the trouble and expence of coinage, and prevent this
inconveniency of the exportation of the silver, as this can no longer be
profitable.
127     | The intention of money as an instrument of commerce is to circulate
goods nec⟨e⟩ssary for men,[x] and food, cloaths, and lodging. The greater
part of the food, cloaths, etc. which is laid out to procure this circulation,
the less of food, cloaths, and lodging is there in the country, and the people

---

[u] Reading doubtful      [v] Illegible word      [w] Reading doubtful      [x] Reading
doubtful

---

[52] Guineas were worth 20 shillings when first coined in 1663, then moved to 21 shillings,
then 21 shillings 6 pence. 7 and 8 William III, c. 19 (1696) provided that a guinea should
not be taken at more than 22 shillings, but in 1699 the House of Commons resolved that
the Act did not oblige anyone to accept guineas at 22 shillings, after which they fell to
21 sh. 6d. The maximum was reduced to 21 sh. by proclamation of 22 December 1717.

are so much the worse fed, cloathd, and lodged, caet. paribus. So that the nation, instead of having receivd an addition to its wealth by the increase of the medium of circulation, is realy increased in poverty, caet. paribus. For it is not this money which makes the opulence of a nation, but the plenty of fodd,ᵛ cloaths, and lodging which is circulated.—For if we suppose the whole worth of the money and commodities in Scotland to be 20 mills (no matter whether it be more or less⟨)⟩, if of this one million is necessary to circulate the rest, then 19 mills are left to feed, cloath, etc. the inhabitants. If 2 mills be necessary to the purpose, which from the bank accounts is nearly the case, then there is only 18 millions to f., c., l. the people. So that

128 in the one case as many people as are supported by one million are | laid aside to support circulation, and ⟨in⟩ the later case as much as 2 m. can afford of f., c., l. The smaller the quantity necessary to circulate the stock of f., c., l., the stock remaining is so much the greater. It is so much dead stock which increases not the opulence of the nation, as it neither fs., c., nor lodges any one, but just serves merely to circulate these things and bring them to a market. The more that is employed in this shape, the less is there of the convenienci⟨e⟩s of life to be had in the country. The high roads may in one sense be said to bear more grass and corn than any other ground of equall bulk, as by facilitating carriage they cause all the other ground to be more improved and encourage cultivation, by which means a greater quantity of corn and grass is producd. But of themselves they produce nothing. Now if by any means you could contrive to employ less ground in

129 them by straightening them or contracting | their breadth without interrupting the communication, so as to be able to plow up 1/2 of them, you would have so much more ground in culture and consequently so much more would be produced, viz a quantity equall to what is produced by 1/2 of the road. Much spare ground producing nothing would be turnd to produce grass and corn, etc. from whence food and cloathing would be produced to the people. Tis in the same manner that money increases opulence. Tis not in money that opulence consists, any more than on the high ways that the corn grows; it consists in the abundance of the necessarys and conveniences of life and the industry of the people; money is only beneficiall in circulating of these. It is evident therefore that the less of the wealth and stock of the nation is employed in this manner, the more will there be of commodities and necessarys in the nation. Any contrivance which would tend to lessen

130 the stock employed in | circulating the rest would tend to increase publick opulence. Paper money is an expedient of this sort. Two millions or thereabouts are necessary to carry on the circulation in Scotland; some say only 1 million, but the accounts of the banks show that it is nearer to two millions. If the stock therefore or wea⟨l⟩th of a nation be 20 millions there are still 18 to be circulated.— — —

ᵛ *Sic*

If now we should suppose that the 6 great banking companies in Scotland should at once issue notes to the amount of 2 mills. These are given out to the merchants who have bank credit. Of the 2 mills of money in the circulation we shall suppose each bank keeps £50000 by them to answer any emergency of demand. The whole six will therefore have 300000 pounds by them. And there will be £1700000 of gold and silver and 2 mills of paper money to carry on the circulation; in all 3700000, so that the money for circulation is nearly doubled. For the paper (as is now the case⟨⟩) is as readily accepted of as the gold or silver, and can be exchanged for it on going to the bank which issued them. But notwithstanding of this the real

131 wealth of no one is increased. If a | merchant have bank credit, and being worth £1000 take out £1000 of notes from them, I have still but £1000 of wea⟨l⟩th in my possession. The circulation in the kingdom depends on the wea⟨l⟩th of the byers; a man of £10000 will circulate 20 times as much as one of 500, and he five times as much as one of £100 pr annum. Every wise man is sensible that his wealth is not increased by this money, and tho some fools may spend more, thinking they have got an addition to their wea⟨l⟩th, the prudent part which is to be supposed the majority will spend in the same manner as before. The exchange or circulation will therefore be pretty much the same as before (as the majority generally act with common sense in this matter), and the same quantity of money will carry it on. The two millions which were sufficient before still[z] answer all the demands. The country can consume no more, and whatever is above that overflows. The whole of the £3,700,000 can[a] not be consumed in the kingdom; some part will therefore be sent abroad. Paper money can not be sent abroad as it will not be receivd but at a very high discount, the credit of the bank not extending so far. The paper money being at first given out [to merchants]

132 on cash account | to the merchants, who give a bill equall to the money they take out, a merchant has by this means[s] perhaps 1000 pounds more than he had of his own. This he can not employ altogether at home as the country will not consume it; the paper can not be sent abroad; he therefore employs his coined money in forreign countrys, where it is exchanged for goods of different sorts. The quantity of goods brought home being in this manner increased, more hands must be employd in manufacturing them. Two mills carry on the circulation, and £300000 supply the banks; so that there are goods brought into the country to the ammount of £1,700000, which being wrought and manufactured feed, cloath, lodge, and employ a part of the inhabitants, as it is sent abroad for some thing that may be food, cloathing, etc. The people, it is true, consume this within the year; but at the same time they produce more by their industry, which enables the merchants to bring against the next year a greater quantity of goods to feed, cloath, and employ the people. We see accordingly that since the institution

[z] Reading doubtful        [a] Reading doubtful

of banks in Scotland the trade and manufactures have been gradually
increasing so[53]

133      | All industry is employed, and has and will be to the end of the world, in
increasing and multiplying the objects of human desire; that is, equally
goods and money: goods as the end and money as the mean⟨s⟩. But these
do not increase equally. Which is most easily and certainly multiplied, gold
or corn. Gold finding is altogether uncertain. One may go to Peru or the
Andes or Appening mountains and not add a guinea to the present stock.
Corn, tho not so profitable as gold mines some times are, is more certain
and hardly ever fails when set about. And as therefore corn and indeed all
other commodities and manufactures are more easily multiplyed than gold,
goods will increase in a greater proportion than money, which will therefore rise[b] in its price and they fall. In a nation of savages, as our Saxon
ancestors or the present North Americans, mony has an immense price and
134   is only possessed by the richest[c] sort as bein⟨g⟩ | vastly rare[d] and will
purchase an immense quantity of goods. All the gold or silver they have
must be the produce of their own country, and they have no commerce.
Their skill to find it out and seperate it from the ore can be very small;
those arts require more improvement. The arts of[e] working gold and silver
and seperating them from the ore are not to be expected from them. They
fave[54] not the art of working and fining them so as to give them that
admirable lustre which makes them the object of desire and a friend[f] of
vanity amongst mankind. They are therefore scar⟨c⟩e and of g⟨r⟩eat value.
—When mankind are more improv'd, all the mines are carefully wrought,
and commerce brings in abundance of them, and they sink in their value.
This has been the case. From the fall of the Roman Empire till ⟨the⟩
135   discovery of the Span. West Indies prices continuall⟨y⟩ rose, since | which
they have fallen, unless at the Revolution when they rose for some time.

---

[b] Replaces 'fall'      [c] Reading doubtful      [d] Reading doubtful      [e] Illegible
word deleted      [f] Reading doubtful

---

[53] The word 'so' falls at the end of the last line of 132, and there is no full point after it.
132 is the last (recto) page of a gathering which the student has numbered 33; and 133, on
which the text is resumed, is the first page of a gathering which the student has numbered
40. It seems quite likely that six gatherings numbered 34–39, containing material corresponding to the passages in LJ(B) 246–53, below, of which there is no counterpart in LJ(A),
were omitted from the bound volume, presumably by accident. There is no *comparable*
discontinuity in the numbering of the gatherings anywhere else in the MS. It is true that
the number of the last gathering in vol. iii is 126, whereas the first gathering in vol. iv has
been numbered 129. But this discontinuity was clearly deliberate: as stated above (p. *10*),
the reporter evidently intended to write up some additional material at the end of vol. iii,
on a number of blank leaves which he instructed the binder to insert.
[54] *Sic.* No doubt 'have' was intended.

## Tuesday April. 12. 1763

This system,[55] so different from that I have been endeavouring to explain, had been hinted at by preceding writers, but Mr. Mun was the first who formed it into a regular system.[56]— Many writers have since adopted it. Mr. Locke has likewise followed it, and made it indeed have somewhat more of a philosophicall air and the appearance of probability by some amendments. He allowed that other commodities as corn, cloth, cattle, etc. were part of the wealth of a nation, but affirmed at the same time that they make but a small or at least an insignificant part of it as being perishable, whereas gold and silver by their durableness became a reall part[g] of wealth, on a stock of which the nation might rely in all emergencies and by which it would be supported in plenty and opulence.[57] But it is evident on the

136 slightest attention that the | perishable quality of all other commodities is so far from making them inferior[h] to gold and silver, which can not be consumed, that the very thing which ⟨?makes⟩ them to be of greater real worth is their consumptib⟨il⟩ity. 'Tis this which[i] gives them their value in the country; and it is even of no consequence whether the thing thus consumed be of home or of foreign produce. The consumption being great occasions a greater quantity to be made. If it be made at home, there is a greater quantity to be made by the people, and thus encourages industry and manufactures. If it be a foreign production, then a greater quantity of some other produce must be raised at home in order to supply the demand by being exchanged for it. The consumption encouraging industry promotes opulence, as every one who is industrious in his way produces[j] more than he can destroy or consume himself. Cash (*or something in the* place of it) we will find makes the smallest part of the riches of a country. The highest computation of the cash in Great Britain makes it not above 30 mills; it is | probably less, but can not be more by no computation. This

137 must in every light be but a very small part of the nationall opulence. For as one proof of this, the nationall debt is now about 120 or 130 mills. This must not be a very great burden as the interest of it is paid so easily, which it could not be if the nationall opulence was no more than 30 mills, as it would be a 5th or 6th part of the whole, which could not be raised. 30 mills must undoubtedly bear a very small proportion to the stock or opulence of

---

[g] Replaces an illegible word    [h] Replaces 'liable'    [i] 'whi' deleted    [j] Reading doubtful

---

[55] i.e. the theory or hypothesis that the opulence of a nation consists in, or can be measured by, its stock of gold and silver. This principle was in all probability discussed and criticized (along the lines of the account in LJ(B) 251–3, below) in the passages missing before 133.

[56] *England's Treasure by Forraign Trade* (1664).

[57] This account of Locke's views on this matter is probably based—although not very soundly based—on *Civil Government*, §§ 46–50.

the country. If we suppose that in G. Britain there are 10 mills of inhabitants, and that each of these consumes to the value of 10£ per annum, the consumption amounts in all to 1000000.[k] Nor is this computation at all extravagant. For if we consider the immoderate consumption of the wealthy, which could hardly be conceivd to be so great if we did not see it, this will

138 abundantly make up for the others who consume | less. The consumption of children is not nearly so great; but few grown consume less than 10£, and the luxury of the rich affords the greater quantity for the poor by increasing the production. The pay of a soldier is 9 per ann., and he has besides this kept as his arrears nearly[l] 3£ for cloaths and lodging, so that his pay[m] consumption amounts to 12£. Others indeed sometimes consume less than this, but the luxury of others fully equalls it. The consumption therefor amounts to 100 mills. The stock which can afford this must ⟨be⟩ far larger. For we can hardly imagine that the stock yields above 10 per cent by the industry of the people. For it is out of this stored stock that all the industrious people are maintain'd till their work be brought to market. The stock therefore which produced this must be about 1000 mills. In this light it is easy to conceive how 20 mills could be spared in the kingdom for the

139 extraordinary | expenses of the war. But if the stock was only 30 mills, we can hardly imagine that they could have spared two thirds of the stock without the greates⟨t⟩ disturbance. Nor could even 1/5 or 1/6 have been dispensed with; but if the stock be 1000 mills it is no great diminution. In this case the cash is but a small part of the stock. The land tax, when imposed[n] in King Williams time, when it was supposed to be 4:h in the pound or 1/5 of the rent, amounted to 2,500,000 in England alone; if this was 1/5, the produce of the rent would be 12½ mills. But it is well known that in most counties the rentalls were given in so much below the real rent, that even then it was not above 2 shillings in the pound. But even in those counties where a just rentall was given in, the land is so much improvd (especially since the bounty on corn was given, which *has* had the good effect of causing the country to be well cultivated) that it will not be above

140 1/3[o] of the rent; | and on the whole it is a sufficient allowance if we say that this which is called 4:h is equall to two shills in the pound of the reall rent, and hence the rent would be about 25 mills. The rent of the land in England can not be computed at above 1/3 of the produce; it is not in reality so much. In this country indeed, in all the low parts of it, where the rents are at the highest as they generally are at a rack-rent, it will be in that proportion. But as England is a more opulent country the reward of the farmer must be the higher. A man who can not subsist and is at the point of starving will accept of any bargain which will give him a subsistence, however poor. But one who has a stock which alone could maintain him for some

years will not accept of one which is not at least tollerably profitable; and
as this is the case with many of the farmers in England the rent is seldom so
high. But granting that it was 1/3 of the produce, the produce must be
141 worth 75$^p$ mills. If we | should set apart for the seed necessary to maintain
the crop, and the expence of keeping up the stock of cattle, and all others,
15 mills, which is certainly more than is nec⟨e⟩ssary, there remains 60 for
the annuall consumption, in cattle, corn, and other produce of the ground.
For this 75 millions is the value of the coarse and rough produce of the
ground, without any manufacturing; of the grain from the thresher, of the
wool from the shearer, of the flax from the puller, and of the cattle from
the feeder. Now it is very strange if all the industry bestowed upon the corn
to turn it into bread and beer, and the wool and flax to work them into cloths
of all the various sorts, does not make them worth 40 millions more, that is,
in all 100, so that here the$^q$ produce[58] cannot be much under 1000 mills.$^r$ If
again we suppose that every one over head has a 6pence pr. day, which is
not too much on the whole, he will need *two pence* of this for bread and
142 | beer, 2$^d$ for butcher meat, and the remaining 2$^d$ for other nec⟨e⟩ssaries as
cloaths, lodging, etc. This ⟨is⟩ much about soldiers pay, without there
arrears which is about £9 per ann., and this being taken over head make⟨s⟩
99,000,000$^s$ £, or we may say 100 mills, for anual consumption in the nation.
So that every shape the cash amounting to 30 mills bears a very small
proportion to the stock of the whole kingdom of G.B. But it is probably
still less than 30 mills. The only method we have to judge of the quantity of
money requisite to carry on the circulation is the$^t$ ammount of the rent of
land estates. This according to the computation of the land tax is but 12½
mills in the half year. The landholders in fact pay all the others. They pay
off the rents to clear a mortgage or pay the steward; they again pay the
shopkeeper or baker or butcher; and they again pay the great dealer whether
at home or abroad who supplies them with goods, or other correspondents.
143 So that the land rent circulates thro the country and pays all the | nation.
It is collected in the hands of the tenents, and is paid out again by the landlords who receive it from them. Hence it is that before the term of payment
there is a great scarcity of money, but afterwards there is great plenty, and
the other terms of payment generally come soon after. Before this term the
tenents have been collecting it together, and after that time it is soon diffused thro the kingdom. It must therefore amount at least to £12,500000.
It is true the whole is not assembled in the hands of the tenants, and if you
should allow as much more for the other transactions, which is more than
can be wanted$^u$ in that time, it will not be above 25 mills. We cant shew

---

$^p$ Replaces an illegible figure          $^q$ Illegible word deleted          $^r$ 'I' deleted
$^s$ Replaces '99,900,000'          $^t$ 'value' deleted          $^u$ Reading doubtful

---

[58] *Sic.* Possibly something like 'the stock which produced this' was intended.

where there is any more employed or to be found at one time, and to shew that more is employed at different times proves nothing. Twelve and 1/2 mills are absolutely necessary for the circulation, and if we consider that of
144 this and the other 12½ allowed to carry on trade in the absence | of it,[v] a great part, tho not so much as in this country, consists in bank notes, the computation of 28 or even of 20 mills is sufficient; and the[w] part of the wealth of the kingdom which is in cash is but a very small one compared to the whole stock.

Money therefore can not be that in which the opulence of the state con-sist⟨s⟩. If it had, then the supplies necessary to the war could not have been raised, being 2/3 of the whole stock; but when we compute it at 1000 mills we need not be surprised that it was so little felt. They observe indeed in favours of this system that every one endeavours, when he leaves trade, to sell off his stock and turn it into money; money is the great thing he has in view and desire⟨s⟩ to have in a considerable quantity. But it is not because he will be any thing the richer on that account, not for the money itself,
145 but that he may | have it in his power to command goods of all the sorts he may want with the greater certainty, from the baker, the butcher, the wine merchant, the clothier, etc. To one[x] of these he can give £150 and purchase goods for it more easily than he could have done for a quantity of linnen cloth which they did not want. He can in the same manne⟨r⟩ purchase a land estate with much greater ease, or an annuity. The workman to whom he gives £150 gives him to the amount of 50 or £70 of stuff, 50 he has to his workmen, and the rest he has to himself; and this he could not have done in any other manner than by money. He desires to live at ease and leisure and for this end he desires money, not for its own sake but as it procures him means of a comfortable subsistence. Even the miser, who appear places[59] the greatest esteem on the money itself, pleases himself not with the money
146 itself but with the consideration that he has what may be a mean⟨s⟩ | of abundance when he pleases to employ it as such, and that he is above want or danger of being reduced to necessity. Money is not the ultimate object[y] of any mans desires. But as we generally look no farther than money, and commonly say *we want money*, they have been of opinion that the great quantity of money should be the view of a nation also. This system has occasioned many errors in the practise of this and other nations {which are partly inneffectuall and partly prejudiciall, as they tend to increase that—} in endeavouring to raise the quantity of money, which can be of no service farther than as a medium of circulation; and whatever is above that is a

[v] '20 mills' deleted      [w] Reading doubtful      [x] Reading doubtful      [y] Re-places 'and'

[59] 'appear' is interlined. Probably it was intended to substitute 'appears to place' for 'places'.

dead stock,[60] which had it been sent abroad would have given returns which would have increased the industry and wealth of the nation.

One of these hurtfull regulations which has been practised by many countries is the prohibition on the exportation of coin and bullion. It is, as I before observed, still felony against the king to export coin,[61] and this prohibition formerly extended to bullion also. 'Till the reign of King
147 William there were in Britain two sorts of money, | the milled and the unmilled money. The first of these was not liable to be clipped nor impared (as the art of      *z*, now often practised, was not then known). The other was very much injured in this manner, and reduced in its value perhaps 1/8 part. This raised a great outcry, for which indeed there was*a* some reason as one had not the value which the coin ought to have born, and great confusion was like to have ensued. On this the Parliament came to the general*b* resolution of calling in all the clipped coin, and giving out the same nominall value of the just weight and standard. This was accordingly done, and the recoinage together with the loss on the clipped money cost the nation 2 millions. The next thing to be done, after having thus supplied the nation with money, was to prevent its being carried abroad; for which purpose[s] the old laws were revived making it felony to export it, and as a naturall consequence of that regulation it was made capitall also to export bullion. This latter regulation was however soon repealed, and bullion was
148 allowed to be exported under | certain regulations and directions.[62] This the merchants found absolutely necessary, as otherwise no foreign trade could have been carried on, and therefore petitioned and obtained that it should be abrogated. The prevailing notion however was that the greater quantity of current specie there was in the country, so much the better; they thought they could never have enough of it. For this reason the coinage of bullion was encouraged, being thought to increase its value. For which purpose the mintage was made to cost nothing,[63] and any one who carried to the Mint a pound of ⟨gold⟩ got out the whole, without any charges, in $44\frac{1}{2}$ guineas, or a pound of silver in 63 shill., paying nothing but a few shillings to the servants who gave it to him, and even this was also*c* forbidden.—It was imagined that the making it into money increased publick opulence; but a guinea or a shilling is in fact worth no more than the worth of the quantity of bullion equall to the metall contain in it.
149 Hence it came that coind gold can never bear a greater price | than the un-coined ingot of equall weight. For if it was but a sixpence in the pound higher, one would send it to the Mint and turn it into coin; and hence*d* the

---

*z* Blank in MS.        *a* Replaces 'is'        *b* Reading doubtful        *c* Reading of last
two words doubtful        *d* 'it' deleted

---

[60] Harris, I.51.
[62] 15 Charles II, c. 7 (1663).

[61] Not so: Hale, I.655; cf. p. 299 above.
[63] 18 and 19 Charles II, c. 5 (1666).

uncoin'd gold must always be at least equall to the coined. It is generally
even above it, as being fitter for exportation and not liable to the danger of
incurring any penalty. And as ingots are worse to be got than coin'd*e*
metall, notwithstanding of the penalty[64] attending it ⟨a⟩ great part of the
coin is put into the melting pot, and unless one be an arrant fool it is impossible he can be discovered, as it can be done in an instant. If one is
known to have got so much money from the bank, it is nobodies business to
enquire nor can they learn how he has disposed of it. For tho it be missing
he cant be obliged to tell where he disposed of it. In this manner these
regulations are in a great measure inneffectuall. They are however prejudiciall as far as they take effect, for they endeavour to throw more into the
channell of circulation than is naturally proper. This can never go above
that which is nec⟨e⟩ssary for the circulation, nor sink far below it. There
150  can be no fear of want of money, for if their be too little it will | soon be
supplied by the exportation of goods, and if too great it will be sent abroad
for goods either in specie or melted down. And their is one peculiar conveniency in gold and silver, that being melted down they lose hardly any
thing; silver very little and gold nothing at all, being the most fix'd of all
metalls tho 20 times melted. The coinage being performd for nothing
encourages the melting and exportation of coin as well as bullion. But if a
small duty was imposed on the minting of money, this would soon be prevented. An oz of silver or gold when coind is better adapted for exchange
than before, and the*f* coinage is at some charge; it being therefore of more
value, it is reasonable that it should have a higher price; and the Master of
the Mint might give out the pound of gold not into $44\frac{1}{2}$ guineas, but might
turn the gold which uncoind is worth $44\frac{1}{2}$ guineas into 45. There would
then be no temptation to melt or export the coin. The Master of the Mint*g*
should not however be allowed to take any price he inclined for the coinage,
151  for it is necessary that he should be the only coiner | and have a monopoly
of the coinage. It is therefore necessary that here, as in all other monopolies,
there should be a fixed or assized price. By this means the £14000[65] which
is expended annually on the coinage might be saved and laid out to some
other purpose. In this manner the prohibition on the exportation is in a
great part inneffectual. It is however in some measure effectuall, and where
it is, it not only raises the prices of commodities at home but makes them
trade at a dissadvantage. Portugall has little or nothing else to give in
exchange for our corn and other goods but money. If therefore the exportation of it be prohibited by high penalties, the Portugese merchant

---

*e* 'silver' deleted     *f* Reading of last two words doubtful     *g* Replaces 'bank'

---

[64] 6 and 7 William III, c. 17 (1695).
[65] Reading doubtful. The figure might possibly be '64000', but it is given as 'about
fourteen thousand' in LJ(B) 260, below.

who byes any commodities must pay not only the naturall price and what is requisite for the expense of transportation, but must also give a price on account of the risque the English merchant runns in getting it out of the country.[66] Every one who has been there knows the difficulty of getting money out of the country; allmost[h] all those who are not merchants must be employed in carrying it aboard a ship in their pockets, one by one. If this

152 prohibition was taken off, more of the gold and silver | might be carried out of the kingdom, but then more goods would be brought in, and that in a greater price than the difference of the money, as the dissadvantage they at present bye[i] under would be taken off. They being necessitated to have foreign goods, as they get them cheeper than their own, are[j] brought by this means to sell cheep and bye dear. The ballance of trade being thus against them they must pay the rest by cash, and if a prohibition be put on the exportation of coin or mettalls the price must be still raised higher, and more money paid for less goods.— —

2$^{dly}$, every unnecessary accumulation of wealth can serve no good purpose whatever. It is so much dead stock, which brings nothing into the country, hinders the produce at home, and prevents exportation. The money being increased, the prices of goods and of labour must increase proportionably, and industry will be at a stand, as they can not afford to sell cheep and will be undersold by all other nations. There can be no sale abroad; and as all others work cheaper, the goods ⟨of⟩ other countries will be brought in; and if they be prohibited will be smuggled, as no prohibition

153 | will prevent it when their is a great profit. Money will indeed go out of the kingdom in this manner; but still if their be supplies, as the Spanish and Portugese American mines, the mony may still be dammed up to an unnaturall height even altho as much goes out as comes in, as a dam in a river will raise the waters altho as much (after it comes to the head⟨⟩) runs over as comes to it. By this means the price of labour will still continue to be unnaturally high, so that all others will undersell them and their manufactures will not even be sufficient to supply themselves, as others can do it cheeper.[67] Tho the Spanish wool be absolutely necessary, as far as ⟨has⟩ yet been found, to[k] the working of fine cloth, yet none has ever been exported from Spain. The quality which we have fondly attributed to our wool, that no cloth could be made without it and that if we could keep it at home we should have all the cloathin⟨g⟩ trade, seems to be realy the case with the

154 Spanish wool. Yet they have never manufactu⟨re⟩d | any for sale. The greatness of the moneyd price of all commodities make[i]s it impossible for them

---

[h] 'all' deleted    [i] Reading doubtful    [j] Illegible word deleted    [k] 'supp' deleted

---

[66] Cf. John Law, *Money and Trade Considered* (1705), II.25.
[67] Cf. Hume, 'Of the Balance of Trade', *Essays*, I.333–4.

to serve other countries, and they are even supplied by the goods of other countries smuggled in upon them.—This seems to be one great cause[s] amongst many others of the misery of Spain and Portugal. It dimi⟨ni⟩shes their industry, lessens the stock, and destroys opulence.

3ᵈˡʸ, another bad consequence of this system is improper and absurd encouragement of some trades or branches of trades, and the oppression or prohibition of others. For as some trades*ˡ* seem to have a ballance, these must draw money from the kingdom and*ᵐ* diminish the wealth of the kingdom. These were therefore hurtfull and were restraind. Others in which the ballance being for us mony must be brought into the kingdom, were encouraged with great care. The French trade was for this reason discouraged in every branch, for as they have all the productions and manufactures which we have they have no occasions for ours, and besides, having some of both which we[e] have not, money must be sent for these.—
155 | The Portugese again, having none of their own of those which we have, and few besides, pay us all in money, and were therefore much encouraged. They by this means supply us almost solely with fruits and wines, which are not only dearer, as being from a country of less industry and at a greater distance, but are of an inferior quality. The French trade would however be much more beneficiall, as they would afford us much more goods and of greater variety to be wrought up by the industry of the people.

*Wednesday April 13. 1763*

I began yesterday to give some account of those bad*ⁿ* practicall effects which proceeded from that system or theory which placed the opulence of a nation on its coin and money. The first of these was the regulations concerning coin and bullion with regard to exportation. It was thought that to accumulate money and to accumulate wea⟨l⟩th was one and the same thing. Every method would therefore be taken to bring into the country all
156 | the money which could be got and to prevent any from going out of it. With this view the Spaniards, having discovered the silver mines in Peru and not knowing of those of Brazil, imagining they had the whole silver at their disposal, [and] thought that if they could keep it at home to themselves alone they would grow not only the most powerfull but the most wealthy kingdom in Europe. They, therefore, and the Portugese afterwards on the same plan, prohibited the exportation of gold and silver. This as I said is in a great measure ineffectuall as the balance of trade, which is against them, must go out in gold and silver. The goods the⟨y⟩ want are likewise all bought at a dissadvantage. The Portugese merchant who byes of an English one pays not only for the price of the goods but also for the

*ˡ* 'or branches' interlined and deleted     *ᵐ* Reading doubtful     *ⁿ* Reading of last two words doubtful

risque he runns in getting out the money, 3, 4, 5, or perhaps ten per cent. The English merchant, when he has got the price, runns a risque of never getting ⟨?⟩ and therefore takes⁰ something more of the merchant as an

157 | insurance against this risque. In as far as they are effectual they are also prejudiciall. They damn up money to ⟨an⟩ unnatural height, and tho it goes out the damn still keeps it up, as an equall quantity comes in. This being more than is necessary for circulation lies as dead stock upon their hands, and when by any means it is forced into the channell of circulation it can produce no other effect than that of raising every thing to a price unnaturally high. If this damn was bored,ᵖ gold going out of these kingdoms would soon bring things to their naturall price; the gold and silver would be less, but the godds⁶⁸ would be brought in in greater abundance and at a lower rate. The channel of circulation is by this damm kept quite full, and all goods and all labour are so excessively dear that nothing can be made for the forreign market. Nothing was ever seen in any country which came from Spain but what was the naturall produce of the country. {Spain is the finest sheep country in the world, being all sandy hills covered with an excellent

158 herbage.} They have wool without which | no broad cloth can be made in Europe, and yet no one ever saw Spanish broad cloth in the market; nor is any other thing else to be met with. The only things to be met with of Spanish growth are their fruits and their wines, which are allmost the ⟨?only⟩ naturall productions of that fine country. The only other production we meet with is Spanish steel, which is of a peculiarly excellent quality, but the quantity of it is but very inconsiderable. Regulations were allso made in Britain in King Will.s time; these I have already mentiond, as well as the bad consequences of them with reggard to the melting down and exportation of coin and the method by which it might be remedied. But all attempts of this kind must be idle as the channel of circulation can never contain above a certain quantity.

It has also produced many other bad effects with regard to the regulations of trade and commerce. As money was the only wealth of the kingdom, all those trades were con⟨si⟩dered as pernicious which carried money out of the kingdom, and those again which brought in money were reckond

159 | highly beneficial. The French trade was therefore discouraged as it was thought to carry wealth out of the kingdom, they having most of the manufactures as well as all the productions we have, and severall manufactures and naturall productions which we have not. They have wine, which we have not, and the species of lint of which the finest cambricks are made will not grow in this country. As therefore our importation from France exceeds our exportation to it, the balance must be paid in money, and therefore

---

⁰ Reading doubtful      ᵖ Reading doubtful

---

⁶⁸ *Sic.* No doubt 'goods' was intended.

(according to this notion) such a trade was to be discouraged. The French trade is therefore allmost intirely locked up from us by high duties on many comm⟨o⟩dities, which amount to the same thing as a prohibition, and express prohibitions on others, as on cambricks, proceeding partly from this consideration and partly from the mutuall enmity and jealousy of the nations, from which they can never be pleased in being supplied by each other[s].[69] A free commerce on a fair consideration must appear to be
160 advantageous | on both sides. We see that it must be so betwixt individualls, unless one of them be a fool and makes a bargain plainly ruinous; but betwixt prudent men it must always be advantageous. For the very cause of the exchange must be that you need my goods more than I need them, and that I need yours more than you do yourself; and if the bargain be managed with ordinary prudence it must be profitable to both. It is the same thing with regard to nations. The exchange must always be profitable if they act with prudence, and as the number of the prudent will be pretty much the same on both sides, and this will be the far greater part, the benefit will be mutual. For it is evident that the other nation stands more in need of it than the other does of its own, and this must be the case on both sides. Thus to take an instance, tho most unlikely: if claret was not of mo⟨r⟩e value here than in Franc⟨e⟩, or the money he sends for it is here, he could have no temptation to send out for it. He would not import it if he did not get more here than he gave in France. Perhaps he will give 1000 pound in France
161 for what will here be | worth £1100. This gold is sent out of the nation, but it is returnd in a larger[q] quantity of wine, which adds to the opulence of the nation. 'Tis true indeed that the gold lasts for a long time and the claret is very soon consumed, but this makes no odds. For to what purpose do all those things which a nation possesses serve? To no other but the maintaining the people? And how is ⟨it⟩ that this end is answered? By being consumed. It is the *consumptibility* of a thing which makes it usefull. To what purpose does industry serve but to produce the greatest quantity of these necessaries. It is no[r] matter therefore what the time be in which they are consumd, whether 3, 30, or 300 years. Commercy and industry ar⟨e⟩ more promoted by the former than the latter. The business of commerce and indust⟨r⟩y is to produce the greatest quantity of the necessaries of life for the consumption of the nation, or exchanging one commodity for another which is more wanted. It is on the power of this exchange that the division of labour depends, which as has been shewn to the satisfaction of the whole of you is the great foundation of opulence, as it occasions the
162 | production of a greater quantity of the severall things wrought in. The production of the necessaries of life is the sole benefit of industry. If you do

[q] Reading doubtful      [r] Reading of last two words doubtful

[69] Cf. Hume, 'Of the Jealousy of Trade', *Essays*, I.345 ff.

not use them, what is the benefit of the greatest abundance. What would be the advantage of employing a number of hands and cherishing the cultivation of the arts. The whole benefit of wea⟨l⟩th and industry is that you either employ a greater number or give those already employed a more comfortable subsistence, and there is no trade which, carried on properly, will not answer this end. There is requisite for this end a certain quantity of money to promote the circu⟨la⟩tion of the rest. To what purpose would it serve to keep this gold at home. The channel of circulation is always of itself sufficiently filled. If it becomes scrimp, money will soon be poured into it on all hands from other nations; or the plate at home will be melted down and turnd into coin. If it is too full, it must sink by exportation to foreign countries and the melting pot. So that it can neither be filled above,

163 nor can it fall below, the just propor|tion to the goods. Now if it be at the proper              *s* as it ordinarily ⟨is⟩, wherefore or*t* how would you or could you add any more to it. 30 mills answers all the purposes of it; why should any more be added. It is universally acknowledged that to prohibit any branch of exportation altogether is hurtfull to that branch of manufactures or improvement. If this be ⟨the⟩ case, as there is no question it is, it must be prejudiciall to hinder the exportation to any one country, as so much the less will be produced as was nec⟨e⟩ssary to supply that country, and this loss is the greatest when the country to which the exportation is prohibited is that to which the exportation and traffick is most profitable. If it be prejudiciall to prohibit the exportation to the richest and best country, it must also be prejudiciall to prohibit the exchange of this commodity for the best and most profitable the country affords. The prohibition of the exportation of cloth and corn is no*u* doubt prejudicial, and

164 therefore to prohibit the | exportation to France must be so also, as the corn and cloth which would be raised to go there is no longer necessary; and if you should prohibit the exportation of it for claret, all the industry necessary to raise cloth and corn to purchase the wine. They may say here, Ay, we should allow you to send corn or cloth for claret, but it is gold which ye send. But there is no difference whether it be gold or whether it be corn. The one is nowise preferable to the other. This money if kept at home is very prejudicial to industry, and might be sent abroad directly to France for wine,*v* or may be sent first to Brazil for gold, or which is the same thing to Portugall where it has been already brought and afterwards sent for claret to France. For it is all one whether the goods be sent or the money receiv'd for them. So that if you stop the importation of claret, you stop the manufactures which would be sent to Spain no less effectually than by a direct prohibition. These prohibitions hurt ourselves more than they do the French. All these national jealousy⟨s⟩ which prompt them to spite and

---

*s* Illegible word          *t* Illegible word deleted          *u* Illegible word deleted
*v* Replaces 'gold an'

165 ill-will each other, and refuse to be supplied by them in any | convenience of life, must lessen the exchange of commodities, hurt the division of labour, and diminish the opulence of both. All commerce with France is now in a manner prohibited; the[w] nations are deprived of the benefit of the mutuall exchanges which would be made betwixt them. Both are by this means impoverished, but Britain being the richer country of the two is most impoverished. For in all traffick which is fairly carried on both parties must improve their fortunes, but if the one be rich and the other poor the rich for many reasons will mend his fortune more than the other.—On the other hand the trade to Portugal is greatly encouraged, as the ballance being much in our favours money must be got by it. But to what purpose does the money serve, if it be more than the exchange demands. If it be kept at home it is hurtfull, and must therefore be sent abroad or some other way turnd out of the channell of circulation.—The exchange with Portugall is also much inferior and consequently less profitable by[x] a free trade than
166 a free trade to Portugall[70] | would be. Portugall contains about 2 mills of men; France on the other hand contains about 20 mills. The exchanges which would be made to France would probably be 100 times those made to Portugall, and a free trade to it would therefore excite much greater industry than one to Portugall. For 20 millions in a society, in the same manner as a company of manufacturers, will produce 100 times more goods to be exchanged than a poorer and less numerous one of 2 mill. France indeed is poorer than England or even the low parts ⟨of⟩ Scotland, but compared with Spain or Portugall is immensely rich, and all manufactures are found in it in much greater abundance. For one exchange that is made to Portugall 100 would be made to France, and the industry which would be excited by a free trade to both would be in the same proportion. By our prohibiting French wines we are supplied intirely by the Portugese at a higher price and in inferior quality than we would be from France. I mentioned this instance as it is one of the least importance in[y] appearance.
167 | But it will be said that wine is merely a superfluity; but it is[z] not more so than pepper, sugar, tea, coffee, tobacco, dying stuffs, drugs, etc., and there is nothing more absurd in desiring to have good wine for our money than any other commodity.

No nation can be ruined by the ballance of trade being against them. If we look into Gees book[71] we find that trade to all the nations of Europe had a ballance against us excepting Spain, Portugall, and Ireland, besides the American plantations, for the West Indian islands had a vast ballance

---

[w] Reading doubtful        [x] Reading doubtful        [y] Reading doubtful        [z] 'no more' deleted

---

[70] *Sic.* Probably 'France' was intended.
[71] Joshua Gee, *The Trade and Navigation of Great-Britain Considered* (1729).

against us. This he represents as threatening us with immediate ruin; and
as Swift[72] imagined that in six or seven years there would not be a shill. or
a guinea left in Ireland, notwithstanding of which Ireland is improving very
fast, so he seems to have imagined that England would be utterly ruined in
a short time if some stop was not put to this destructive and ruinous
forreign trade. This indeed has been the cry, that the forreign trade would
168  be the ruin | of England, ever since the time of Ch. 2ᵈ, and notwithstanding
of this the nation has continually improved in riches, in strength, and
opulence; and money when wanted is raised in greater abundance and with
greater facility now than ever. The greatest summ that was raised by Queen
Annes ministers, who were very clever ones, did not exceed 6 millions. Mr.
Pelham raised in one year 10 mills. and Mr. Pit 23,[73] and with greater ease
than it had ever been done before. We complaind that navigation was
ruind, but we find the number of ships and our strength in every shap⟨e⟩ᵃ
is increasing. The case is the same in other countries: France, Holland,
Italy have all complaind that the ballance of trade would ruin them, and
yet they are continually improving. No nation can ever be ruind by this.
The same thing ruins nations as individualls, viz their consumption being
greater than their produce. If the nation produce to the value of 90 millions
and consume an hundred, such a nation can not long subsist.
169     | 3ᵈ, another bad effect of this system, not indeed so prejudiciall as the
former as it has affected the theory more than the practise, is the notions
with regard to forreign and home expence. It was a rule that necessarily
followed from this, that nothing spent at home could diminish public or
nationall opulence. From hence {Sir John Mandeville, author of the Fable
of the Bees.[74]—} formed his theory that private vices were publick benefits.
It was thought that no luxury nor folly whatever, not the greatest extravagance imaginable, if laid out on comodities of home production could in
the leastᵇ be prejudiciall: many were even beneficiall; that if we kept out all
other goods, let one spend as much as he pleased, the nation was as rich as
before; the money is not sent abroad to France or Holland but is still at
home. It is the same as the right hand paying the left, in which case the man

ᵃ Reading doubtful      ᵇ Reading doubtful

---

[72] Jonathan Swift, *A Short View of the State of Ireland* (1727–8: *Prose Works*, ed. H.
Davis, vol. XII, 1955, 9–10). Cf. Hume, *Essays*, I. 332.
[73] Henry Pelham was First Lord of the Treasury between 1743 and 1754, during which
period the most money was voted in 1748 (including £3,640,350 for the Navy and
£4,261,575 for the Army). William Pitt, later first Earl of Chatham, was in effective power
as Secretary of State between 1756 and 1761, during which period the highest sum voted
was £19,616,119 for war charges in 1760 (J. Sinclair, *History of the Public Revenue of the
British Empire*, 2nd edn., 1790, III.58–69).
[74] *The Fable of the Bees; or, Private Vices Public Benefits* (1714) was written by Bernard
Mandeville, who was quite unconnected with Sir John Mandeville, author of a fourteenth-
century book of travels.

cant grow poorer; so here the money being still amongst the subjects the nation can not. But we will find that every one who spends his stock in this manner must diminish opulence by the same quantity. For tho the money is in the kin⟨g⟩dom, the stock is diminished just so much. If I am worth £1000 and spend it all on follies and extravagances, there is still a thousand
170　pound in | the kin⟨g⟩dom, but there is 1000 £s worth of less stock. The whole is destroyed and nothing is producd in return. But if I send it out to a merchant who employs it in trade, a farmer or land holder who employs by this means a greater number of hands and cultivates the ground to better purpose, these will by this means make of it £75 profit per annum, of which they give me £50 and have still 25 to themselves. The money is in this manner of service in industry and opulence. I, who*c* now live on £50, as I am idle man can do ⟨?little⟩ good, but then I do no harm. My stock is employed, and more industry and wea⟨l⟩th is produced. If I was also industrious and produced goods also, no doubt I would be of an advantage. But if I consume the £1000 without any thing being produced by ⟨?⟩ the country is poorer to the value of £1000. To make this the more evident, let us suppose that my father leaves me goods, cattle at pasture, beer in his cellars, cloth, linnen, etc., etc. in his ware room, and all the things I can want, so that I can live within myself to the value of £1000; and that I with some others as idle as myself eat and drink, tear and wear, the cattle*d* and
171　[and] beer, cloth and linnen, etc. so as to destroy | it all by the years end, there is plainly here a diminution of £1000 for which nothing is produced

*End of Volume Six of MS.*

*c* Reading of last two words doubtful　　　*d* Reading doubtful

# LECTURES ON JURISPRUDENCE

## REPORT DATED 1766

# JURIS PRUDENCE

*or*

*Notes from the Lectures on Justice, Police, Revenue, and Arms delivered in the University of Glasgow*

*by*

**Adam Smith** Professor of Moral Philosophy.

MDCCLXVI.

# | *Juris Prudence*

## INTRODUCTION

Jurisprudence is that science which inquires into the general principles which ought to be the foundation of the laws of all nations. Grotius seems to have been the first who attempted to give the world any thing like a regular system of natural jurisprudence, and his treatise on the laws of war and peace, with all its imperfections, is perhaps at this day the most compleat work on this subject.[1] It is a sort of casuistical book for sovereigns and states determining in what cases war may justly be made and how far it may be carried on. As states have no common sovereign and are with respect to one another in a state of nature, war is their only method of redressing injuries. He determines war to be lawfull in every case where the state receives an injury which would be redress'd | by an equitable civil magistrate.[2] This naturaly led him to inquire into the constitution of states, and the principles of civil laws; into the rights of sovereigns and subjects; into the nature of crimes, contracts, property, and whatever else was the object of law, so that the two first books of his treatise, which are upon this subject, are a compleat system of jurisprudence.

The next writer of note after Grotius was Mr. Hobbes. He had conceived an utter abhorrence of the ecclesiastics; and the bigottry of his times gave him occasion to think that the subjection of the consciences of men to ecclesiastic authority was the cause of the dissensions and civil wars that happened in England during the times of Charles the 1st and of Cromwell. In opposition to them he endeavoured to establish a system of morals by which the consciences of men might be subjected to the civil power, and which represented the will of the magistrate as the only proper rule of conduct. Before the establishment of civil society mankind according to him were in a state of war; and in order to avoid the ills of a natural state, men enter'd into contract to obey one common sovereign who should determine all disputes. Obedience to his will according to him constituted civil government, | without which there could be no virtue, and consequently it too was the foundation and essence of virtue.

[1] Cf. TMS VII.iv.37 (the last paragraph of the book): '. . . natural jurisprudence, or a theory of the general principles which ought to run through and be the foundation of the laws of all nations. . . . Grotius seems to have been the first who attempted to give the world any thing like a system of those principles which ought to run through, and be the foundation of the laws of all nations; and his treatise of the laws of war and peace, with all its imperfections, is perhaps at this day the most complete work that has yet been given upon this subject.'

[2] Grotius, II.i.2.

The divines thought themselves obliged to oppose this pernicious doctrine concerning virtue, and attacked it by endeavouring to shew that a state of nature was not a state of war but that society might subsist, tho' not in so harmonious a manner, without civil institutions. They endeavoured to shew that man in this state has certain rights belonging to him, such as a right to his body, to the fruits of his labour, and the fullfilling of contracts. With this design Puffendorf wrote his large treatise.[3] The sole intention of the first part of it is to confute Hobbes, tho' it in reality serves no purpose to treat of the laws which would take place in a state of nature, or by what means succession to property was carried on, as there is no such state existing.

The next who wrote on this subject was the Baron de Cocceii, a Prussian.
4 | There are five volumes in folio of his works published,[4] many of which are very ingenious and distinct, especially those which treat of laws. In the last volume he gives an account of some German systems.

Besides these there are no systems of note upon this subject.

*Remainder of 4 left blank in MS.*

5      | Jurisprudence is the theory of the general principles of law and government.

The four great objects of law are Justice, Police, Revenue, and Arms.

The object of Justice is the security from injury, and it is the foundation of civil government.

The objects of Police are the cheapness of commodities, public security, and cleanliness, if the two last were not too minute for a lecture of this kind. Under this head we will consider the opulence of a state.

It is likewise necessary that the magistrate who bestows his time and labour in the business of the state should be compensated for it. For this purpose and for defraying the expences of government some fund must be raised. Hence the origine of Revenue. The subject of consideration under this head will be the proper means of levying revenue, which must come from the people by taxes, duties, etca. In general whatever revenue can be raised most insensibly from the people ought to be preferr'd, and in the sequel it is proposed to be shewn how far the laws of Brittain and of other
6 European | nations are calculated for this purpose.

As the best police cannot give security unless the government can defend themselves from forreign injuries and attacks, the fourth thing appointed by law is for this purpose, and under this head will be shewn the different

---

[3] *De Iure Naturae et Gentium* (1672), especially II.2.6 ff., attacking Hobbes's *De Cive* (1642) and *Leviathan* (1651).

[4] *Henrici de Cocceii Grotius Illustratus* (4 vol. folio, 1744–52), together with his son's commentary *Samuelis de Cocceii Introductio ad Henrici de Cocceii Grotium Illustratum* (1 vol. folio, 1748).

species of Arms with their advantages and dissadvantages, the constitution of standing armies, militias, etca.

After these will be considered the laws of nations, under which are comprehended the demands which one independent society may have upon another, the priviledges of aliens, and proper grounds for making war.

# Part 1st. Of *Justice*

The end of justice is to secure from injury. A man may be injured in several respects.

1st, as a man

$2^{dly}$, as a member of a family

$3^{dly}$, as a member of a state.

As a man, he may be injured in his body, reputation, or estate.

As a member of a family, he may be injured as a father, as a son, as a

7 husband or wife, as a master or servant, as a guardian or pupil. | For the two last are to be considered in a family relation, till such time as the pupil can take care of himself.

As a member of a state, a magistrate may be injured by dissobedience or a subject by oppression, etca.

A man may be injured 1st, in his body by wounding, maiming, murthering, or by infringing his liberty.

$2^{dly}$, in his reputation, either by falsely representing him as a proper object of resentment or punishment as by calling him a thief or robber, or by depreciating his real worth, and endeavouring to degrade him below the level of his profession. A physician's character is injured when we endeavour to perswade the world he kills his patients instead of curing them, for by such a report he loses his business. We do not however injure a man when we do not give him all the praise that is due to his merit. We do not injure Sir Isaac Newton or Mr. Pope, when we say that Sir Isaac was no better philosopher than Descartes or that Mr. Pope was no better poet than the ordinary ones of his own time. By these expressions we do not bestow on them all the praise that they deserve, yet we do them no injury, for we do not throw them below the ordinary rank of men in their own professions.

8 | These rights which a man has to the preservation of his body and reputation from injury are called natural. Or as the civilians express them *iura hominum naturalia*.

$3^{dly}$, a man may be injured in his estate. His rights to his estate are called acquired or *iura adventitia* and are of two kinds, real and personal.

A real right is that whose object is a real thing and which can be claimed *a quocumque possessore*. Such are all possessions, houses, furniture.

Personal rights are such as can be claimed by a law-suit from a particular person, but not *a quocumque possessore*. Such are all debts and contracts, the payment or performance of which can be demanded only from one person. If I buy a horse and have him delivered to me, tho' the former owner sell him to another, I can claim him a quocumque possessore; but if he was not delivered to me, I can only pursue the seller.

Real rights are of four kinds, Property, Servitudes, Pledges, and Exclusive Priviledges.

Property is our possessions of every kind which if any way lost, or taken from us by stealth or violence, may be redemanded a quocumque possessore.

9 | Servitudes are burthens upon the property of another. Thus I may have a liberty of passing thro' a field belonging to another which lyes between me and the high way, or if my neighbour have plenty of water in his fields and I have none in mine for my cattle, I may have a right to drive them to his. Such burthens on the property of another are called servitudes. These rights were originally personal, but the trouble and expence of numerous lawsuits in order to get possession of them, when the adjacent property which was burthened with them passed thro' a number of hands, induced legislators to make them real, and claimable a quocumque possessore. Afterwards the property was transferred with these servitudes upon it.

Pledges, which include all pawns and mortgages, are securities for something else to which we have a right. The laws of most civilized nations have considered them as real rights, and give a [a] liberty to claim them as such.

Exclusive priviledges are such as that of a book-seller to vend a book for a certain number of years, and to hinder any other person from doing it during that period. These rights are for the most part creatures of the civil
10 law, tho' some few of them are natural, | as in a state of hunters even before the origin of civil government if a man has started a hare and pursued her for sometime, he has an exclusive priviledge to hunt her, by which he can hinder any other to come in upon her with a fresh pack of hounds.

An heir has also an exclusive priviledge of hindering any person to take possession of the inheritance left him while he is deliberating whither or not it will be for his interest to take possession of it and pay off the debts with which it is burthened.

Personal rights are of three kinds as they arise from Contract, Quasi Contract, or Delinquencey.

The foundation of contract is the reasonable expectation which the person who promises raises in the person to whom he binds himself; of which the satisfaction may be extorted by force.

Quasi contract is the right which one has to a compensation for necessary trouble and expence about another man's affairs. If a person finds a watch in the high-way he has a claim to a reward and to the defraying of his expences in finding out the owner. If a man lend me a sum of money[5] he has a right not only to the sum, but to interest also.

11   | Delinquencey is founded upon damage done to any person, whither thro' malice or culpable negligence. A person has a right to claim these only from a certain person.

The objects of these seven rights make up the whole of a man's estate.

The origin of natural rights is quite evident. That a person has a right to have his body free from injury, and his liberty free from infringement unless there be a proper cause, no body doubts. But acquired rights such as property require more explanation. Property and civil government very much depend on one another. The preservation of property and the inequality of possession first formed it, and the state of property must always vary with the form of government. The civilians begin with considering government and then treat of property and other rights. Others[6] who have written on this subject begin with the latter and then consider family and civil government. There are several advantages peculiar to each of these methods, tho' that of the civil law seems upon the whole preferable.

12                 | *Of Public Jurisprudence*

There are two principles which induce men to enter into a civil society, which we shall call the principles of authority and utility. At the head of every small society or association of men we find a person of superiour abilities; in a warlike society he is a man of superiour strength, and in a polished one of superior mental capacity. Age and a long possession of power have also a tendencey to strengthen authority. Age is naturaly in our imagination connected with wisdom and experience; and a continuance in power bestows a kind of right to the exercise of it. But superior wealth still more than any of these qualities contributes to conferr authority. This proceeds not from any dependance that the poor have upon the rich, for in general the poor are independent, and support themselves by their labour, yet tho' they expect no benefit from them they have a strong propensity to pay them respect. This principle is fully explained in the Theory of moral Sentiments, where it is shewn that it arises from our sympathy with

13 our superiours being greater | than that with our equals or inferiors: we admire their happy situation, enter into it with pleasure, and endeavour to promote it.

Among the great, as superior abilities of body and mind are not so easily judged of by others, it is more convenient, as it is more common, to give

---

    [5] Loan, being the result of agreement, is a contract, not a quasi-contract. Smith may have been misled by Hutcheson, *System*, II.82–3, where 'advances upon hazard' are treated as quasi-contractual.

    [6] Notably Hutcheson, *M.P.*, Books II and III, and *System*, Books II and III. LJ(A) follows Hutcheson's order of treatment.

the preference to riches. It is evident that an old family, that is, one which has been long distinguished, by it's wealth has more authority than any other. An upstart is always dissagreable; we envy his superiority over us[7] and think ourselves ⟨as⟩ well entitled to wealth as he. If I am told that a man's grandfather was very poor and dependent on my family, I will grudge very much to see his grandson in a station above me and will not be much disposed to submit to his authority. Superiour age, superior abilities of body and of mind, ancient family, and superiour wealth seem to be the four things that give one man authority over another.

The second principle which induces men to obey the civil magistrate is utility. Every one is sensible of the necessity of this principle to preserve
14 justice and peace in the society. | By civil institutions, the poorest may get redress of injuries from the wealthiest and most powerfull, and tho' there may be some irregularities in particular cases, as undoubtedly there are, yet we submit to them to avoid greater evils. It is the sense of public utility, more than of private, which influences men to obedience. It may sometimes be for my interest to dissobey, and to wish government over-turned. But I am sensible that other men are of a different opinion from me and would not assist me in the enterprize. I therefore submit to it's decision for the good of the whole.

If government has been of a long standing in a country and if it be supported by proper revenues, and be at the same time in the hands of a man of great abilities, authority is then in perfection.

In all governments both these principles take place in some degree, but in a monarchy the principle of authority prevails, and in a democracey that of utility. In Brittain, which is a mixed government, the faction's formed sometime ago under the names of Whig and Tory were influenced by these principles; the former submitted to government on account of it's utility
15 and the advantages which they | derived from it, while the latter pretended that it was of divine institution, and to offend against it was equally criminal as for a child to rebell against it's parent. Men in general follow these principles according to their natural dispositions. In a man of a bold, daring, and bustling turn the principle of utility is predominant, and a peaceable, easy turn of mind usually is pleased with a tame submission to superiority.

It has been a common doctrine in this country that contract is the foundation of allegeance to the civil magistrate. But that this is not the case will appear from the following reasons.

In the first place, the doctrine of an original contract is peculiar to Great Brittain, yet government takes place where it was never thought of, which is even the case with the greater part of people in this country. Ask a

---

[7] Cf. TMS I.ii.5.1: 'An upstart, though of the greatest merit, is generally disagreeable, and a sentiment of envy commonly prevents us from heartily sympathizing with his joy.'

common porter or day-labourer why he obeys the civil magistrate, he will tell you that it is right to do so, that he sees others do it, that he would be punished if he refused to do it, or perhaps that it is a sin against God not to do it. But you will never hear him mention a contract as the foundation of his obedience.

16    2$^{dly}$, when certain powers of government were | at first entrusted to certain persons upon certain conditions, it is true that the obedience of these who entrusted it might be founded on a contract, but their posterity have nothing to do with it, they are not conscious of it, and therefore cannot be bound by it. It may indeed be said that by remaining in the country you tacitly consent to the contract and are bound by it. But how can you avoid staying in it? You were not consulted whether you should be born in it or not. And how can you get out of it? Most people know no other language nor country, are poor, and obliged to stay not far from the place where they were born to labour for a subsistance. They cannot therefore be said to give any consent to a contract, tho' they may have the strongest sense of obedience. To say that by staying in a country a man agrees to a contract of obedience to government, is just the same with carrying a man into a ship and after he is at a distance from land to tell him that by being in the shop[8] he has contracted to obey the master. The foundation of a duty cannot be a principle with which mankind is entirely unacquainted. They must have some idea however confused of the principle upon which they act.

17    | But again, upon the supposition of an original contract, by leaving the state you expressly declare that you will no longer continue a subject of it and are freed from the obligation which you owed it, yet every state claims it's own subjects and punishes them for such practices, which would be the highest injustice if their living in the country implies a consent to a former agreement. Again, if there be such a thing as an original contract, aliens who come into a country preferring it to others give the most express consent to it, yet a state always suspects aliens as retaining a prejudice in favour of their mother country, and they are never so much depended upon as freeborn subjects. So much is the English law influenced by this principle, that no alien can hold a place under the government, even tho' he should be naturalized by Act of Parliament.[9] Besides if such a contract were supposed, why should the state require an oath of allegiance whenever a man enters on any office, for if they supposed a previous contract, what occasion is there for renewing it. Breach of allegiance or high treason is a much greater crime and more severely punished in all nations than breach of contract, in which no more but fullfillment is required. They must

18  therefore be on a different footing. | The less can by no means involve in it

8 Copyist's error for 'ship'.
9 1 George I, st. 2, c. 4 (1714).

the greater contract. Contract is not therefore the principle of obedience to civil government, but the principles of authority and utility formerly explained.

We shall now endeavour to explain the nature of government, it's different forms, what circumstances gave occasion for it, and by what it is maintained.

The forms of government however various may not improperly be reduced to these three, Monarchical, Aristocratical, and Democratical. These may be blended in a great number of ways, and we usually denominate the government from that one which prevails.

Monarchical government is where the supreme power and authority is vested in one, who can do what he pleases, make peace and war, impose taxes, and the like.

Aristocratical government is where a certain order of people in the state, either of the richest, or of certain families, have it in their power to choose magistrates, who are to have the management of the state.

Democratical government is where the management of affaires belongs to the whole body of the people together.

19   | These two last forms may be called republican, and then the division of government is into monarchical and republican.

To acquire proper notions of government it is necessary to consider the first form of it, and observe how the other forms arose out of it.

In a nation of hunters there is properly no government at all. The society consists of a few independent families, who live in the same village and speak the same language, and have agreed among themselves to keep together for their mutual safety. But they have no authority one over another. The whole society interests itself in any offence. If possible they make it up between the parties, if not they banish from their society, kill, or deliver up to the resentment of the injured, him who has committed the crime. But this is no regular government. For tho' there may be some among them who are much respected, and have great influence in their determinations, yet he never can do any thing without the consent of the whole.

Thus among hunters there is no regular government; they live according to the laws of nature.

20   | The appropriation of herds and flocks, which introduced an inequality of fortune, was that which first gave rise to regular government. Till there be property there can be no government, the very end of which is to secure wealth, and to defend the rich from the poor. In this age of shepherds if one man possessed 500 oxen, and another had none at all, unless there were some government to secure them to him, he would not be allowed to possess them. This inequality of fortune, making a distinction between the

rich and the poor, gave the former much influence over the latter, for they who had no flocks or herds must have depended on those who had them, because they could not now gain a subsistence from hunting as the rich had made the game, now become tame, their own property. They therefore who had appropriated a number of flocks and herds, necessarily came to have great influence over the rest; and accordingly we find in the Old Testament that Abraham, Lot, and the other patriarchs were like little petty princes. It is to ⟨be⟩ observed that this inequality of fortune in a nation of shepherds occasioned greater influence than in any period after
21 that. Even at present, a man may spend a great estate | and yet acquire no dependents. Arts and manufactures are increased by it, but it may make very few persons dependent. In a nation of shepherds it is quite otherways. They have no possible means of spending their property, having no domestic luxury, but by giving it in presants to the poor, and by this means they attain such influence over them as to make them in a manner their slaves.

We come now to explain how one man came to have more authority than the rest and how chieftans were introduced. A nation consists of many families who have met together and agreed to live with one another. At their public meetings there will always be one of superiour influence to the rest, who will in a great measure direct and govern their resolutions, which is all the authority of a chieftan in a barbarous country. As the chieftan is the leader of the nation, his son naturaly becomes the chief of the young people, and on the death of his father succeeds to his authority. Thus chieftanship becomes hereditary. This power of chieftanship comes in the progress of society to be increased by a variety of circumstances. The
22 number of presants which he receives encrease his fortune | and consequently his authority. For amongst barbarous nations no body goes to the chieftan, or makes any application for his interest, without something in his hand. In a civilized nation the man who gives the presant is superior to the person who receives it. But in a barbarous nation the case is directly opposite.

We shall now consider the different powers which naturaly belong to government, how they are distributed, and what is their progress in the first periods of society.

The powers of government are three, to wit, the Legislative, which makes laws for the public good. The Judicial, or that which obliges private persons to obey these laws, and punishes those who dissobey. The Executive, or as some call it, the Federal power, to which belongs the making war and peace.

All these powers in the original form of government belonged to the whole body of the people. It was indeed long before the legislative power was introduced, as it is the highest exertion of government to make laws
23 and lay down rules | to bind not only ourselves, but also our posterity, and

those who never gave any consent to the making them. As for the judicial power, when two persons quarrell'd between themselves the whole society naturaly interposed, and when they could not make up matters turned them out of the society. During this early age crimes were few, and it was long before the punishment was made equal to the crime.

Cowardice and treason were the first crimes punished. For cowardice among hunters is considered as treason, because when they went out in small numbers, if their enemy attacked them, and some of their party deserted them, the rest might suffer by it, and therefore they who deserted were punished for treason.

The priest generally inflicted the punishment as it were by the command of the gods, so weak at that time was government. The power of making peace and war in like manner belonged to the people, and all the heads of families were consulted about it.

Tho' the judicial power which concerns individuals was long precarious, 24 the society first interposing as friends, and then as arbitrators, | the executive power came very soon to be exerted absolutely. When any private quarrell happens concerning the property of this cow, or of that ox, society is not immediately concerned. But it is deeply interested in making peace and war. In the age of shepherds this power is absolutely exerted. In Great Brittain we can observe vestiges of the precariousness of the judicial power, but none of the executive. When a criminal was brought to trial, he was asked how he would chuse that his cause should be decided, whither by combat, the ordeal trial, or the laws of his country. The society only obliged him not to disturb them in the decision. In England the question still remains, tho' the answer is not now arbitrary. It was very common in the ruder ages to demand a trial by dipping their hand in boiling water, by means of which almost every one was found innocent, tho' now scarce any one would escape by this means. When people were constantly exposed to the weather boiling water could have little effect upon them, tho' now, 25 when we are quite covered, it must have a contrary effect. | This choice of trial shews the weakness of the judicial laws. We find that the judicial combat continued in England as late as the days of Q. Elizabeth. It has now worn out gradually and insensibly, without so much as a law or a rule of court made against it.

In the periods of hunters and fishers and in that of shepherds, as was before observed, crimes are few; small crimes passed without any notice. In these ages no contraversies arose from interpretations of testaments, settlements, contracts, which render our law-suits so numerous. For these were unknown among them. When these took place and difficult[10] trades began to be practised contraversies became more frequent. But as men were generally employed in some branch of trade or another, without great

---

[10] Possibly copyist's error for 'different'.

detriment to themselves they could not spare time to wait upon them. All causes must be left undecided, which would be productive of every inconvenience, or they must fall upon some other method more suitable to the several members of society. The natural means they would fall upon 26 | would be to chuse some of their number to whom all causes should be referred. The chieftan who was before this distinguishd by his superior influence, when this comes to be the case would preserve his wonted precedence and would naturaly be one of those who were chosen for this purpose. A certain number would be chosen to sit along with him, and in the first ages of society this number was always considerable. They would be afraid to trust matters of importance to a few, and accordingly we find that at Athens there were 500 judges at the same time. By this means the chieftan would still further encrease his authority, and the government would appear in some degree monarchical. But this is only in appearance, for the final decision is still in the whole body of the people, and the government is realy democratical.

The power of making peace and war, as was before observed, was at first lodged in the whole body of the people. But when society advanced, towns 27 were fortified, magazines prepared, stocks of money got together, | generals and officers appointed, the whole body of the people could not attend to deliberations of this kind. This province would either fall to the court of justice, or there would be another sett of people appointed for this purpose, tho' it would naturally at first fall to the court of justice. This is properly called the senatorial power, which at Rome took care of the public revenue, public buildings, and the like. But afterwards at Rome the court of justice and the senatorial one became quite distinct. The same may be said of the areopagite court at Athens.

We shall now make some observations on nations in the two first periods of society. These *viz.* of hunters and shepherds.

In a nation of hunters and fishers few people can live together, for in a short time any considerable number would destroy all the game in the country, and consequently would want a means of subsistance. Twenty or thirty families are the most that can live together, and these make up a village, but as they live together for their mutual defence and to assist one 28 another, their villages are not far distant from each other. | When any controversie happens between persons of different villages, it is decided by a general assembly of both villages. As each particular village has it's own leader, so there is one who is the leader of the whole nation. The nation consists of an alliance of the different villages, and the chieftans have great influence on their resolutions, especially among shepherds. In no age is antiquity of family more respected than in this. The principle of authority operates very strongly, and they have the liveliest sense of utility in the maintenance of law and government.

The difference of the conduct of these nations in peace and war is worth our observation.

The exploits of hunters, tho' brave and gallant, are never very considerable. As few of them can march together, so their number seldom exceeds 200 men, and even these cannot be supported above 14 days. There is therefore very little danger from a nation of hunters. Our colonies are 29 much affraid of them without any just grounds. | They may indeed give them some trouble by their inroads and excursions, but can never be very formidable. On the other hand a much greater number of shepherds can live together. There may be a thousand families in the same village. The Arabs and Tartars who have always been shepherds have on many occasions made the most dreadfull havoc. A Tartar chief is extremely formidable, and when one of them gets the better of another, there always happens the most dreadfull and violent revolutions. They take their whole flocks and herds into the field along with them, and whoever is overcome loses both his people and wealth. The victorious nation follows it's flocks, and pursues it's conquest, and if it comes into a cultivated country with such numbers of men, it is quite irresistable. It was in this manner that Mahomet ravaged all Asia.[11]

There is a very great difference betwixt barbarous nations and those that are a little civilized. Where the land is not divided, and the people live in hutts which they carry about with them, they can have no attachment to 30 the soil, | as all their property consists in living goods which they can easily carry about with them. On this account barbarous nations are always disposed to quit their country. Thus we find such migrations among the Helvetii, Tuetones, and Cimbrians. The Huns, who dwelt for a long time on the north side of the Chinese Wall, drove out the Astrogoths on the other side of the Palus Maeotis, they again the Wisigoths, etca.

Having considered the original principles of government, and it's progress in the first ages of society, having found it in general to be democratical, we come now to consider how republic⟨an⟩ governments were introduced. It is to be observed in general, that the situation of a country, and the degree of improvement of which it is susceptible, not only in the cultivation of the land but in other branches of trade, is favourable to the introduction of a republican government.

There is little probability that any such government will ever be introduced into Tartary or Arabia, because the situation of their country is such 31 that it cannot be improved. | The most part of these is hills and deserts which cannot be cultivated, and is only fit for pasturage. Besides they are generaly dry, and have not any considerable rivers. The contrary of this is the case in these countries where republican governments have been established, and particularly in Greece. Two thirds of Attica are surrounded

[11] Probably reporter's error for 'Arabia'. Cf. LJ(A) iv.40, above.

by sea, and the other side by a ridge of high mountains. By this means they have a communication with their neighbouring countries by sea and at the same ⟨time⟩ are secured from the inroads of their neighbours. Most of the European countries have most part of the same advantages. They are divided by rivers and branches of the sea, and are naturaly fit for the cultivation of the soil and other arts. We shall now see how favourable this is to the reception of a republican government. We may suppose the progress of government in Attica in the infancey of the society to have been much the same with that in Tartary and the other countries we have mentioned, and we find in reality that at the time of the Trojan war it was

32 much in the same situation, | for then there was little or no cultivation of the ground, and cattle was the principle part of their property. All the contests about property in Homer regard cattle. Here as in every other country in the same period the influence of the chieftan over his own vassals was very considerable. A people inhabiting such a country, when the division of land came to take place and the cultivation of it to be generally practised, would naturaly dispose of the surplus of their product among their neighbours, and this would be a spur to their industry. But at the same time it would be a temptation to their neighbours to make inroads upon them. They must therefore fall upon some method to secure themselves from danger, and to preserve what it formerly cost them so much trouble to procure. It would be more easy to fortify a town in a convenient place than to fortify the frontiers of the whole country, and accordingly this was the method they fell upon. They built fortified towns in the most convenient places, and whenever they were invaded took shelter in them with their flocks and moveable goods, and here they cultivated the arts and

33 sciences. | Agreable to this we find that Theseus fortified Athens and made the people of Attica carry into it all their goods, which not only increased his power over them, but also the authority of that state above others. When people agreed in this manner to live in towns, the chieftans of the several clans would soon lose their authority, and the government would turn republican, because their revenue was small and could not make them so conspicuous and distinguished above others as to retain them in dependance. The citizens gradually increase in riches, and coming nearer the level of the chieftan, become [his] jealous of his authority. Accordingly we find that Theseus himself was turned out; after this nine regents were sett up who were at first to have authority for life but were afterwards continued only for ten years; thus Athens, and in like manner all the Greek states, came from a chieftanship to something like monarchy and from thence to aristocracey. In general, as was before observed, the revenue becomes insufficient to support the authority of a number of chieftans, but a few getting into their hands superiour wealth form an aristocracey.

34    | It is to be observed that there is a considerable difference between the

ancient and modern aristocracies. In the modern republics of Venice, Milan, etca the government of the state is entirely in the hands of the hereditary nobility, who are possessed of all the three powers of government. Both in modern and ancient aristocracies the people had the choice of those in authority, but the difference is this, that only the nobility could be elected in modern times. The institution of slavery is the cause of this difference. When the freemen had all their work done by slaves, they had it in their power to attend on publick deliberations. But when the ground came to be cultivated by freemen, the lower sort could not have it in their power to attend, but consulting their interest they would endeavour to avoid it. Agreable to this we find that at Venice the populace desired to be free of it. In the same manner the towns in Holland voluntarily gave it up to the town council, which was in consequence of this vested with the whole

35 power. | Nothing like this happened in the republics of Greece and Rome. In the early ages of these states, tho' the populace had the whole power, they were called aristocracies, because they always chose their magistrates from among the nobility. They were not indeed hindered by any express law to do otherwise, but it was customary to do so, because the lower classes were maintained by the fortunes of the rich, and thereby became dependent on them, and gave their vote for him whose bounty they shared. The nobility might differ among themselves about elections, but would never propose the election of plebeians. Thus the influence of the nobility was the law, and not any express prohibition.

At Athens, Solon enacted that none of the lower of the four classes into which the people were divided should be elected. But afterwards magistrates were elected out of all classes, and the government became democratical.

At Rome, it was long before the power of being elected extended to the

36 whole body of the people. After | decemvirs were appointed the power of the people began to encroach more and more upon the nobles, and still more when they got military tribunes elected. The cause of this was the improvement of arts and manufactures. When a man becomes capable of spending on domestic luxury what formerly supported an hundred retainers, his power and influence naturaly decrease. Besides, the great usually had every trade exercised by their own slaves, and therefore the taylors and shoemakers being no longer dependant on them would not give them their votes. The popular leaders then endeavoured to get laws passed by which they might be allowed to be elected magistrates. It was long before the generality even of the plebeians would consent to this, because they thought it dissagreable to have their equals so far above them. In process of time, however, they got it enacted that there should be in authority an equal number of patricians and plebeians. *Viz.* a consul chosen out of each.

37   We have shewn how republics arose, | and how they again became

democratical; we are next to shew how this liberty was lost, and monarchy or something like it was introduced.

Considering these states in the situation above described, as possessed of their towns and a small territory in the adjacent country, they must either confine themselves within their ancient boundaries, or enlarge their territory by conquest: they must either be what may not improperly be called a defensive republic or a conquering one. The Grecian states are a good example of the former and Rome and Carthage of the latter. We are to shew how each of these lost their liberty, and first how the defensive states lost theirs.

When a country arrives at a certain degree of refinement it becomes less fit for war. When the arts arrive at a certain degree of improvement, the number of the people encreases, yet that of fighting men becomes less. In a state of shepherds the whole nation can go out to war, and even when it becomes more refined, and the division of labour takes place, and every one 38 is possessed of a small farm, they can send out a great number. | In such an age their champaigns are always in summer, and from seedtime till harvest their young men have nothing ado but to serve in them. The whole business at home can be performed by the old men and woemen, and even these have sometimes beat the enemy in the absence of their soldiers. In a state where arts are carried on, and which consists chiefly of manufacturers, there cannot be sent out such numbers, because if a weaver or taylor be called away nothing is done in his absence. Scarce one in an hundered can be spared from Brittain and Holland. Of an hundered inhabitants fifty are woemen, and of fifty men, twenty five are unfit for war. In the last war Brittain could not spare so many, as any one almost may be convinced, if he reflect whether among his acquaintances he missed one out of twenty five. According to this principle, Athens tho' a small state could once send out 30000 fighting men, which made a very considerable figure. But after the improvement of arts they could not send out more than 10000, which was quite inconsiderable. Brittain, notwithstanding the politeness and refinement at which it has arrived, on account of the largeness of it's territories 39 | can still send out a very formidable army. But a small state necessarily declines. However there is one advantage attending slavery in a small republic, which seems to be it's only advantage, that it retards their declension. At Rome and Athens the arts were carried on by slaves, and the Lacedemonians went so far as not to allow any freeman to be brought up to mechanic employments, because they imagined that they hurt the body. Accordingly we find that at the battle of Chaeronea, when the Athenians were come to a considerable degree of politeness, they were able to send out great numbers of men, purely on this account that all trades were carried on by slaves. We may observe that in the Italian republics, where slavery did not take place, they soon lost their liberty. When in consequence of the improvement of arts a state has become opulent, it must be reckoned a great hardship to go out to war, whereas among our ancestors it was thought no inconvenience to take the field. A knight {*eques*} was no more than a horseman, and a footsoldier was a gentleman. They were inured to hardships at home, and therefore a champaign appeared no way dreadfull. But

40 when opulence and luxury encreased | the rich would not take the field but on the most urgent account, and therefore it became necessary to employ mercenaries and the dregs of the people to serve in war. Such persons could never be trusted in war unless reduced to the form of a standing army, and subjected to rigid discipline, because their private interest was but little concerned and therefore without such treatment they could not be expected to be very resolute in their undertakings. Gentlemen may carry on a war without much discipline. But this a mob can never do. As the citizens in Greece thought it below them to bear arms, and entrusted the republic to mercenaries, their military force was diminished and consequently a means was provided for the fall of the government. Another cause of their declension was the improvement of the art of war, which rendered every thing precarious. In early ages it was very difficult to take a city, as it could only be done by a long blocade. The siege of Troy lasted ten years, and Athens once could withstand for two years a siege both by land and sea. In modern times the beseigers have an advantage over the beseiged and a good

41 engineer can force almost any town to surrender in six weeks. | But it was not so once. Phillip of Macedon made great improvements in this art, which at last occasioned the dissolution of all the Greek governments and their subjection to forreign powers. Rome stood out much longer than Greece, because the number of it's citizens was daily increasing. At Rome any person might be made a citizen, as this was of little advantage. But at Athens the right of citizenship was given to very few, as it was itself a little estate. However Rome itself, after opulence and luxury encreased, shared the fate of other republics, tho' the event was brought about in a different manner. Till the time of Marius, the better sort of freemen went out to the field. Marius was the first that recruited ⟨?⟩.[12] He gathered the freed slaves into his army, and established a rigid military discipline. That army which before had consisted of gentlemen was now made up of runaway slaves and the lowest of the people. With such an army Marius conquered and kept in awe the provinces. He had the disposal of all offices and posts in this army. Every one among them owed his rise to him and was consequently depen-

42 dant upon him. | Whenever such a general was affronted he would naturaly apply to his army for relief, who would easily be induced to side with their general against their own nation. This was the very expedient that Marius fell upon. By the influence of Sylla he was, in his absence, banished from Rome, and a price sett upon him. Marius applied to his army, who were

[12] Cf. the corresponding passage in LJ(A) iv.88, above.

determined at all events to follow him, marched to Rome when Sylla was abroad on an expedition against Mithridates, took possession of the government, and vanquished Sylla's party. Marius died soon after, and Sylla having conquered Mithridates returned to Rome, and in his turn beat the Marian party, changed the government into a monarchy, and made himself perpetual Dictator, tho' he afterwards had the generosity and magnanimity to resign it. About thirty or forty years afterwards the same thing happened between Caesar and Pompey. Caesar as well as Sylla got himself made perpetual Dictator, but had not enough of public spirit to resign it. His veteran troops which were settled in Italy, mindfull of the

43 favours which he conferred upon them, after his death | gathered about Octavius his adopted son and invested him with the supreme authority. Much the same thing happened in our own country with respect to Oliver Cromwell. When the Parliament became jealous of this man, and disbanded the army, he applied to them, in a manner indeed more canting than that of the Roman generals, and got the Parliament turned out and a new one appointed more suitable to his mind, with the whole authority vested in himself.

Thus we have seen how small republics, whether conquering or defensive, came at length to a dissolution, from the improvements in mechanic arts, commerce, and the arts of war. We are next to consider what form of government succeeded the republican.

When small republics were conquered by another state, monarchy, or whatever other government pleased the conquerors, was established, tho' they generally followed the model of their own country. The Athenians always established democracey, and the Spartans aristocracey. The Romans indeed more prudently divided their conquests into provinces

44 which were governed pretty absolutely | by persons appointed by ⟨the⟩ Senate for that purpose. The case is somewhat different when a state is conquered by it's own subjects. Both the nature of the action and the instruments by which it is performed require a military monarchy, or a monarchy supported by military force, because it is as necessary to keep them in awe as to conquer them. This was the form of government that was established in Rome during the time of the emperors; these emperors took the whole executive power into their own hands, they made peace and war as they thought proper, and even named the magistrates, either immediately themselves, or by means of a Senate of their own appointment. They did not however alter any institutions of the civil law. Right and wrong were decided as formerly. Cromwell did the same in our own country: he kept the state in awe by an insignificant army, but he allowed the judge to determine right and wrong as formerly. Nay, he made such improvements in the civil law, by taking away wardships, etca, that the first thing the Parliament of Charles II$^d$ did was to confirm many of Cromwell's laws.

45 | The Roman authors tell us that justice was never better administered than under the worst of the emperors, Domitian and Nero. It is the interest of all new administrators to make few alterations in what the generality of people are much concerned and have been long accustomed to. They will more easily go into any thing else, when they are indulged in this. It was particularly the interest of the emperors to keep up the ancient system of laws, and accordingly we find that all consuls who misbehaved in their respective provinces were severely punished. It was not so under the Republic; the most scandalous crimes were committed by governours, as we learn from Cicero's Orations.[13]

A military government allows the strictest administration of justice. No body indeed can have a fair trial where the emperor is immediately concerned, then he will do as he pleases. But where he is in no way interested, it is his interest to adhere to the ancient laws.

It is to be observed that there was a very great difference between the military government established at Rome and these that were established in Asia. At Rome the conquerors and conquered were the same people. 46 The conquerors themselves | were sensible of the good effects of these laws, and were so far from being willing to abrogate them that they made improvements upon them. It is not so with the Asiatic governments, tho' they are purely military. Turky, Persia, and the other countries were conquered by Tartars, Arabians, and other barbarous nations, who had no regular system of laws and were entirely ignorant of their good effects. They established in all public offices their own people who were entirely ignorant of all the duties of them. A Turkish bashaw or other inferior officer is decisive judge of every thing, and is as absolute in his own jurisdiction as the signior. Life and fortune are altogether precarious, when they thus depend on the caprice of the lowest magistrate. A more miserable and oppressive government cannot be imagined.

We have considered how the dissolution of small states was brought about, and what form of government succeeded them, by what means an imperial government was introduced into conquering republics, and what kind of administration this was. We come now to shew how this military monarchy came to share that fated dissolution that awaits every state and constitution whatever.

47 In the time of the imperial governments at Rome | they had arrived at a considerable degree of improvement both in arts and commerce. In proportion as people become acquainted with these, and their consequence domestic luxury, they become less fond of going out to war, and besides the government finds that it would hurt it's revenue ⟨?to send out⟩ those employed in manufactures. If barbarous nations be in the neighbourhood, they can employ them as soldiers at an easier rate, and at the same time not

[13] Particularly the two speeches *Against Verres*.

hurt their own industry. Sensible of these things, the Romans recruited their armies in Germany, Brittain, and the northern barbarous countries which bordered on the Roman Empire. They had the liberty of recruiting in these countries, in the same manner that the Dutch did in Scotland before the beginning of the last war. After they had gone on for sometime in this practice, they would find for several reasons that it would be much easier to make a bargain with the chieftans of these barbarous nations whom they employed, and give him so much money to lead out a number of men to this or that expedition. Supposing then an institution of this kind. The barbarous chieftan, at the head of his own men, possessed the whole military authority of the people for whom he fought, and whenever the government in the least offended him, he could turn his arms against
48 those who employed him, and make himself master of their country. | We find that all the western provinces were taken possession of much in this manner. After they had by their practice given such invitations to the inroads of barbarians, we find that most of the Roman provinces were infested by them. In this country the Romans built a wall and kept garrisons to secure their province from the pillagers of the north. The garrisons which secured this station were called away to the defence of Gaul which at that time was also infested. The historians tell us that the Brittains then got leave to shake off the Roman yoke, but it could be no advantage to the Romans to give any country in Brittain it's liberty, and it was no favour done it to have no protection from Rome, which the province in reality wanted to have continued. The Romans undoubtedly meant that they should take the trouble of defending themselves, as they were for sometime to be otherwise employed. The Brittains, however, did not like the proposal but resolved to invite over a body of Saxons to their relief. Accordingly Hengist and Hursa came over with a considerable army, which was frequently recruited, entirely drove out the Romans,[14] and finding themselves masters of the whole country took possession of it, and founded the
49 Saxon Heptarchy. In this manner fell the western Empire of Europe | and military monarchy came to ruin. We find in the last hundered and fifty years of the Roman Empire this custom of recruiting in barbarous nations carried on, and many of their chieftans had greatly raised themselves. Patricius Aelias[15] under Honorious and many others acquired great power. In the same manner all the Asiatic governments were dissolved. Their soldiers were hired from Tartary. Arts and manufactures were carried on; the people made more by their trades than by going to war. The East India trade which Italy and some other nations carried on by the Red Sea had rendered them very opulent. Every nation as well as Rome was

[14] Probably reporter's error for 'Britons' or 'Picts and Scots': cf. LJ(A) iv.102, above.
[15] i.e. the *patricius* Aetius, who was in fact later than the reign of Honorius, when Stilicho held power. Cf. LJ(A) iv.101–4, above.

willing to make a bargain with the neighbouring barbarous princes to
defend them, and this proved the ruin of the government.

Having now considered all the ancient forms of government of which we
have any distinct accounts, we shew next what form succeeded the fall of
the Roman Empire, and give an account of the origin of the modern
governments of Europe.

The government which succeeded this period was not altogether unlike
the Tartar constitution formerly mentioned, tho' the Germans and others,
who upon the fall of the Roman Empire took possession of the western
50 countries, had better notions of property | and were a little more accus-
tomed to the division of lands. The king and the other chieftans after they
had become conquerors of the country would naturaly for their own purposes take possession of a great part of it. They would distribute it among
their vassalls and dependants as they thought proper, and would leave but
a very inconsiderable share to the ancient inhabitants. They did not however
extirpate them entirely, but still paid them some little regard. Among the
Franks who took possession of Gaul, the person who killed a Frank paid
only five times the fine which was payable for killing one of the old inhabitants. As these nations were almost lawless, and under no authority,
depredations were continually committed up and down the country and all
kinds of commerce stopped.

In consequence of this arose the allodial government, which introduced
an inequality of fortune. All these chieftans held their lands allodialy without any burthen of cess, wardship, etca. One of these great lords was
51 possessed of almost a county,[a] | but as he was unable himself to reap any
advantage from so much of it he found it necessary to parcell it out among
vassals, who either paid a certain annuity, attended him in war, or performed some service of this nature. By this means his incomes became so
great that, as there was then no domestick luxury, he could not consume
them in any way but by maintaining a great number of retainers about
his house. These were another species of dependants, who increased his
authority and secured domestic peace. For they kept the tenants in awe,
and were kept in awe by the tenants. So great was the authority of these
lords, that if any one claimed a debt from any of their vassals, the king had
no power to send a messenger into the lords dominions to force payment.
He could only apply to the lord, and desire him to do justice. To them also
lay the last result[16] in judging of all manner of property under their own
jurisdiction, the power of life and death, of coining money, and of making
bye laws and regulations in their own territories. But besides this power of
government which in a great measure was betwixt the king and the great

[a] Originally 'country' and then apparently emended

[16] Presumably copyist's error for 'resort'.

52 lords, if there had been no other | the balance would not have been properly
kept. But besides the allodial lords there was a great number of free
people, who were allowed to consult about justice in their own spheres.
Every county was divided into hundereds, and subdivided into tens. Each
of these had their respective court, *vizt* the decemary[17] court, the hundered
court. Over those was placed the Wittenagemot or assembly of the whole
people. Appeals were brought from the ten to the hundered, and from it to
⟨the⟩ county court. An appeal could be brought to the kings court in case
the inferiour court denied justice by refusing to hear a cause, or if it was
protracted by unreasonable delays. Appeals were also sometimes carried to
the Wittenagemott, which was made up of the king, allodial lords, alder-
men or earls, bishops, abbots, etca. This was the first form of government
in the west of Europe, after the downfall of the Roman Empire.

We are next to shew how the allodial government was overturned, and
the feudal system introduced.

53   As these great lords were continually making war upon one another, | in
order to secure the attendance of their tenants they gave them leases of the
lands which they possessed from year to year, which afterwards for the
same reasons came to be held for life. When they were about to engage in
any very hazardous enterprize, that, in case of the worst consequences,
the families of their vassals who went along with them might not be left
destitute and that they might still be more encouraged to follow them, they
extended this right to the life of the son and grandson; as it was thought
cruel to turn out an old possessor, the right became at last hereditary, and
was called feuda. The feudal tenant was bound to certain offices, but
service in war was the chief thing required, and if the heir was not able to
perform it he was obliged to appoint one in his place. It was in this manner
that wardships were introduced. When the heir female succeeded, the
feudal baron had a right to marry her to whomever he pleased, because it
was thought reasonable that he should have a vassal of his own chusing.
The prima seizin was another emolument of the master. When the father
died the son had no right to the estate till he publickly declared his willing-
54 ness to accept of it. | And on this account the lord sometimes had the estate
in his own hand and enjoyed the profits of it for sometime. The heir paid a
sum to get it back, which was called relief. There was still another emolument belonging to the lord, called escheat, that is, after the estate became
hereditary, if there was no heir of the family to succeed, it returned to the
lord. The same thing happened if the heir fail'd of performing the services for
which he had the tenure. There were besides these some small sums due to the
superior on redeeming his son when taken prisoner, or on knighting him,[18]

[17] Reporter's or copyist's error for 'decennary'.
[18] This should read 'on redeeming him when taken prisoner, or on the knighting of his son'. See Dalrymple, 52; and cf. LJ(A) iv.131, above.

and on the marriage of his daughter and some such occasions. The same causes that made allodial lords give away their lands to their vassals on leases which afterwards became hereditary, made the king give away the greater part of his lands to be held feudaly, and what a tenant possessed in feu was much the same with real property. They were indeed subject to the above mentioned emoluments, but they possessed their lands for themselves and posterity. Feudal property may in some respects be inferiour to allodial, but the difference is so inconsiderable that allodial lops[b] soon
55 became to be held feudaly. | About the tenth century all estates came to be held feudaly, and the allodial lords, that they might enjoy the kings protection, exchanged their rights for a feudal tenure.

It is to be observed that these historians who give an account of the origin of feudal laws from the usurpation of the nobility are quite mistaken. They say that the nobility wanted to have these lands which they held at pleasure of the king to be hereditary, that it might not be in his power to turn them out, and that the feudal law was introduced on account of the diminution of the kings power. But it was actualy the contrary; it was on account of the encrease of his power, and it required great influence in the king to make the lords hold their lands feudaly. The best proof of this is that William the Conqueror changed all the allodial lordships in England into feudal tenures and Malcolm Kenmure did the same in Scotland.

The introduction of the feudal system into all Europe took away every
56 thing like popular government. | The popular courts were all removed. Neither decemary, hundered, nor county courts were allowed. All public affairs were managed by the king and the great feudal lords. No commoners, none but hereditary lords had a right to sit in Parliament. These great lords who held immediately of the king were considered as his companions, pares convivii comites. They advised concerning public affairs and nothing of importance could be done without them. The consent of the majority was to be obtained before any law could be passed, and it was necessary to have them called together. The barons or inferior lords observed the same method in their jurisdictions, and they who held [them] of them were called pares curiae baronis. It was likewise necessary that they should be consulted, as they too were in arms. The baron could neither go to war nor make a law without the consent of the majority. Nothing could be done in the kingdom without almost universal consent, and thus they fell into a kind of aristocracey with the king at the head of it.

Besides these orders of men of which we have taken notice, there were
57 two others | which in that period were held in the utmost contempt. The first was that of the villains {villani} who plowed the ground and were adscripti glebae. The second order was the inhabitants of borroughs who were much in the same state of villainage with the former or but a little

---

[b] Contraction for 'lordships'

beyond it. As the boroughs were much under the influence of the lord who gave them protection, it was the kings interest to weaken as much as possible this interest and to favour their liberty. Henry II^d carried this so far that if a slave escaped to a borrough and lived there peaceably a year and day, he became free. He gave them many other priviledges, but what secured them most was the power of forming themselves into corporations upon paying a certain sum to the king. They held of him in capite, and at first every man paid his proportion to the king, but afterwards the borrough paid the sum and levied it as it seem'd proper to itself. By this means as the number of inhabitants encreased the burthen became lighter, and the borroughs became opulent and very considerable. In the reign of King John a law was made that if a lord married his ward to a burgher he only forfeited his wardship.[19]

58 | Thus we have considered the several orders of men of which the whole kingdom then consisted. We shall next show how each of them got a share in the government and what share of it was allotted to each of them. Every person who had an estate, great or small, had a right to sit in the kings court and to consult and advise with him about public matters. In the reign of William Rufus 700 sat in Parliament; in Henry III^ds time it was enacted that the smaller barons, who could not afford to attend in Parliament, should send a representative. These representatives were considered as lords and sat in the same house with them. In the same manner borroughs came to have representatives in Parliament, because they themselves were become opulent and powerfull and the king found it his interest to give them some weight so as to lessen the authority of the peers.

It became necessary to have their consent as well as that of the barons before any law was passed. These representatives of the borroughs sat in a house by themselves, and the smaller barons, being far from the level of the great lords with whom they sat and not much superior to the Commons, soon joined them. The kings revenues were then on many occasions in-
59 sufficient for his demands; they consisted chieffly | 1st, of the royal demesnes, 2^dly, knights services, III^dly, feudal emoluments such as wardships, 4^thly, fines, amercements, compositions, for crimes, etc, 5^thly, all waff goods, *res nullius*, etc. These were the principal sources of the kings revenue. But these were by no means sufficient to supply the encreasing expences of government. The two bodies of the commoners when joined made a very considerable figure, and the greater part of the subsidies came from them. The king excused the smaller barons from a constant attendance and called them or not as he pleased. When he did call them he issued a writ summoning them, and from this was the origin of creating peers by writ or patent, which is the only way of doing it at present.

Having shewn how the House of Commons became considerable, we

[19] Not John but Henry III: 20 Henry III, c. 6 (Statute of Merton, 1236).

shall next shew how the nobilitys power decreased and the government turned arbitrary. In all the courts of Europe the power of the nobility declined from the common causes, the improvements in arts and commerce. When a man could spend his fortune in domestic luxury he was obliged to dismiss his retainers. By their antient rustic hospitality they could more easily maintain 1000 retainers than at present lodge one lord for a night. Richard Earl of Warwick, who was stiled Make-King, maintained every day forty thousand people besides tenants, but when luxury took place he was unable to do this. Thus the power of the nobility was diminished, and 60 that too before the House of Commons had established it's authority. | And thus the king became arbitrary. Under the House of Tudor the government was quite arbitrary, the nobility were ruined, and the borroughs lost their power.

It might be expected that the sovereign also should have lost his authority by the improvement of arts and commerce, but a little attention will convince us that the case must have been quite opposite. A man possessed of forty thousand pounds a year, while no other body can spend above a hundered, cannot be affected by the encrease of luxury. This is precisely the case of the king. He is possessed of a million while none of his subjects can spend above 30 or 40 thousand pounds, and therefore he can spend it in no other way but by maintaining a great number of people. Luxury must therefore sink the authority of the nobility whose estates are small in proportion to that of the king, and as his continues unaffected his power must become absolute. Tho' this was the case in most nations of Europe, yet in Germany it was quite otherways. The monarchy there was elective and consequently never could have so much authority. The country is much larger than any other in Europe, and at the dissolution of the feudal government the nobility, who were possessed of considerable fortunes already, got more in proportion than the rest; thus their estates rose so high above those that were immediately below them, that it was impossible for them to 61 spend them in luxury, | and therefore they were able to keep a considerable number of retainers. Thus in Germany the power of the nobility was preserved, while in England it was utterly destroyed and the king rendered absolute.

We have now shewn how the government of England turned absolute; we shall next consider how liberty was restored, and what security the British have for the possession of it. The Act[20] of Henry VII[th] allowing the nobility to dispose of their estates had already placed them entirely on a level with the Commons. Elizabeth, who always affected popularity, was continually unwilling to impose taxes on her subjects. In order to supply her exigences she sold the royal demesnes, as she knew that none of her offspring was to succeed her. Her successors therefore standing in need of

[20] 4 Henry VII, c. 24 (1490); Dalrymple, 136.

frequent supplies were obliged to make application to Parliaments. The Commons were now become very considerable, as they represented the whole body of the people, and as they knew the king could not want, they never granted him any thing without in some degree infringing his priviledges. At one time they obtained freedom of speech, at another they got it enacted that their concurrence should be necessary to every law. The king on account of his urgent necessities was forced to grant whatever they

62 asked | and thus the authority of the Parliament established itself. A peculiar advantage which Brittain enjoyed after the accession of James Ist was that as the dominions of Brittain were every way bounded by the sea, there was no need for a standing army and consequently the king had no power by which he could overawe either people or Parliament. The 120000[21] P$^{ds}$ a year which was settled upon the king at that time[22] might have secured his independencey, had not the bad oeconomy of Charles II$^d$ rendered him as indigent as any of his predecessors. His successor was still more dependant and was forced to quit the throne and the kingdom altogether. This brought in a new family which as the royal demesnes were entirely alienated depended wholly upon taxes, and were obliged to court the people for them. Ever since, the kings revenue tho' much greater than it was then depends so much on the concurrence of the Parliament that it never can endanger the liberty of the nation. The revenue at present consists chiefly of three branches, to *wit. 1st*, the Civil List, which is entirely consumed in the maintenance of the royal family and can give the king no influence, nor hurt the liberty of the subject. *II$^{dly}$*, the annual land and malt taxes, which depend entirely on the Parliament. *III$^{dly}$*, the funds mortgaged for paying of the public debts, such as the taxes on salt, beer, malt, etc, levied by the

63 officers of custom and excise. | These the king can by no means touch; they are paid to the Court of Exchequer, which is generally managed by people of interest and integrity who possess their offices for life and are quite independent of the king. Even they can pay nothing but to those appointed by Parliament, and must have the discharge of the public creditor. The surplus of the mortgages[23] goes into what is called the sinking fund for paying the public debt ⟨?which⟩ secures the government in the present family, because if a revolution were to happen the public creditors, who are men of interest, would lose both principal and interest. Thus the nation is quite secure in the management of the public revenue, and in this manner a rational system of liberty has been introduced into Brittain. The Parliament consists of about 200 peers and 500 commoners. The Commons in a great measure manage all public affairs, as no money bill can take its rise except in that House. Here is a happy mixture of all the

---

[21] Reporter's or copyist's error for '1,200,000'.
[22] i.e. at the Restoration.
[23] For a less abbreviated and more accurate account, see LJ(A) iv.174–6, above.

different forms of government properly restrained and a perfect security to liberty and property.

There are still some other securities to liberty. The judges appointed for the administration of justice are fixed for life, and quite independent of the king. Again, the king's ministers are liable to impeachment by the House of 64 Commons for maladministration and the king cannot pardon[24] them. | The Habeas Corpus Act, by which the arbitrary measures of the king to detain a person in prison as long as he pleased is restrained, and by which the judge who refuses to bring a prisoner to his trial if desired within forty days is rendered incapable of any office, is another security to the liberty of the subject. The method of election, and placing the power of judging concerning all elections in the hands of the Commons, are also securities to liberty. All these established customs render it impossible for the king to attempt any thing absolute.

Besides all these, the establishment of the courts of justice is another security to liberty. We shall therefore consider the origin of these courts, the history of them, and their present state.

In England, and indeed in all Europe, after the feudal law was introduced, the kingdom was governed and justice administered in the same manner as by a baron in his jurisdiction. As a steward managed all affairs in the county belonging to the lord, so the Grand Justiciary had the management of all in the kingdom. He appointed sherriffs and other inferior officers. He was himself a great lord, and by the authority of his office, in every country but 65 England he became as powerfull as the king. | But Edward the first saw the danger and got it prevented. All kinds of law, criminal or civil, were determined by the Justiciary or King's Court which always attended the king; these delays and adjournments in civil suits, to which this court always attending the king must have been liable, gave occasion for seperating common causes from the Kings Court, and fixing for them at Westminster a Court of Common Pleas. Criminal causes have always a more speedy determination. One would indeed think that when a person's life is at stake, the debate should be longer than in any other case. But resentment is roused in these cases and precipitates to punish. It is a matter of no moment to the spectator how a triffling matter of cash be determined, but it is by no means so in criminal cases. When common pleas were taken away, the criminal and fiscal powers were connected and the power and authority of the Great Justiciary little diminished. Afterwards Edward Ist divided the business of the Justiciary into three different courts *vizt*

The Court of King's Bench
The Court of Exchequer
The Court of Common Pleas

[24] i.e. stay the proceedings by pardon. Cf. LJ(A) v.6–7, above.

In the last all civil suits were tried. In the first all criminal ones, and to it lay the appeal from the Court of Common Pleas; it was called King's
66 Bench | because the king then frequently sat upon it, tho' this cannot now be done, as it is improper that the king should judge of breaches of the kings peace. The Court of Exchequer judged in all affairs between the king and his subjects, the debts due by either of them to the other, and whatever regarded the revenue. The Court of Chancery was originally no court at all. The Chancellor was no more than a keeper of breives or writs according to which justice was done. What gave occasion to the keeping of these breives shall now be considered.

Edward Ist abolished the power of the Grand Justiciary. He employed mean persons to be judges, generally clergyman. As the decision depended on such persons their jurisdictions would be exercised very precariously, and accordingly we find that in both [in] criminal and civil cases they interposed with hesitation, in the former as mediators and in the latter as arbitrators, and accordingly they would be unwilling to give justice in these cases where they had no precedent from the Court of Justiciary. On this account all the breives by which the Court of Justiciary determined were kept. To keep these seems to have been originaly the office of Chancellor. If a person had a law-suit, he went to the clerk of the Court of Chancery
67 who examined the breives | and if he found one that comprehended your case justice was done accordingly, but if one could not be found you could not have justice. Thus we find that the Chancellor was not a judge originaly. In Scotland the office of the English Chancellor is lodged in the Court of Session. In England a brief was sent from the Chancellor to the sherriff by which he was obliged to appear before the kings judges. Judges then, from the irregularity and inaccuracey of their proceedings, gave great jealousie to the king, and on this account many severe sentences went out against them. £10000[25] has at one time been levied from the judges on account of corruption. They were therefore tied down strictly to the Chancery breives, and always bound by their records in such a manner that they could not be in the least amended, not so much as a word wrong spell'd rectified. This precision still remains in some cases, where not taken away by the statutes of amendment. A meer orthographical blunder, tho' evidently so, has in many cases made the whole of no effect. The judges were therefore tied down to the precise words of the brief, or if there was a statute to the words of it. This was the origin and jurisdiction of the Court of Chancery.

During the improvement of the law of England there arose rivalships
68 among the several courts. | We shall therefore shew how each of them began to extend it's power and encroach ⟨?on⟩ the priviledges of another, and how the Court of Chancery encreased it's influence. The Court of King's Bench, which judged criminal causes and every breach of the

[25] The fines were actually 100,000 marks: see LJ(A) v.23, above.

king's peace, was the first that assumed immediately, and previously to an appeal, to judge in civil causes, and to encroach on the jurisdiction of the Court of Common Pleas, by what is called a writ of error, that is, they supposed the person to be guilty of a trespass. For example, when a man owed 10£ and did not come to pay it at the time appointed, an order went out from the Kings Bench to examine and find him out, supposing that he intended to conceal himself, and they punished him for this trespass.[26] At present an action on contract can come immediately before the Kings Bench. In this manner it was that this court extended it's power, and being supreme over all, none could encroach upon it.

The Court of Exchequer brought in civil causes to be tried immediately by them, in the following manner: suppose a man owed a sum of money to the king, which it is the business of the court to take care of, and the man
69 cannot pay unless his debtors first pay him. The court took upon them | to sue this other man by what is called the quo minus, that is, by what he is rendered less able to pay the king. As the debts of the king were many, and as the profits of the judges arose from sentence money, which was more or less according to the business of the court, they eagerly grasped at this extension of their power. All the courts endeavoured, by the speediness of their determinations and accuracey of their proceedings, to encourage prosecutors to come before them.

In what manner the Chancellor came to attain his equitable jurisdiction shall be taken notice of in the next place. After the improvement of arts and commerce, which gave occasion to many law suits unheard of before, people suffered a great deal by the imperfections of law. Edward III[d27] found that there were a great many injuries to which no brief nor court statute extended, and therefore the Parliament allowed that if a person applied to the clerk of Chancery and found there was no brief that could give him any remedy, the clerk should look for some breives of a similar nature and out of them compose a new one by which the complainer might have redress. In this manner the Chancery prescribed rules to the other courts. But as they appointed the brieffs and manner of proceeding this was
70 putting an end to the affair, | for there was no occasion to go to any other court, and the Chancery got these affairs into its own hands. There could be no appeal brought from the Courts of Kings Bench or of Common Pleas to that of Chancery, but they applied to it for what the common law could not redress. The Chancellor in this manner obtained the power of judging in all cases of equity, and is applied to in the greater part of civil cases. The chief of which are 1st, the specific performance of contracts. By the common law if a person was bound by contract to deliver a piece of ground,

---

[26] The process is that of a Bill of Middlesex, not of writ of error. See p. 280, note 85, above.
[27] In fact Edward I: 13 Edward I, c. 24 (Statute of Westminster II, 1285, the *in consimili casu* clause). Cf. LJ(A) v.27, above.

and afterwards refused to do it, he was only obliged to pay damages, but not to perform it specifically. The Chancery, which was not considered as a court of conscience, enjoined the specific performance of it. $2^{dly}$, the Chancery gave redress for all incests,[28] and frauds in trust when the common law could not. As the leaving lands to the church deprived the king of the emoluments arising from them, an Act was passed against it. The clergy ordered that they should be left to certain persons who would dispose of them for the benefit of the church, and if they did not perform it, then as it
71 was a fraud in trust | the Chancellor allowed the bishop to see it done. In like manner, when persons in the state of affairs at that time were obliged to alienate their estates to persons that had no concern in them, the Chancellor caused them to be restored. Wills, legacies, and things of this sort also fell under the equitable decision of the Chancellor.

It will be proper when we are treating of courts to enquire into the origin of juries. In the begining of the allodial government, when the several courts had arrived at a very small degree of improvement and before they had experience to examine thoroughly into matters, when any person was brought before them on an action depending on his oath he was obliged to bring twelve compurgators to swear that the oath was just. There are remains of this at present in actions of debt, where if the person can bring in a certain number of persons to swear that his oath is just he gains the suit. It is to be observed that the imperfection of this way of trying was one of the great causes that gave origin to the judicial combat. A nobleman, or indeed any man of spirit, who was eluded of his right by a
72 sett of perjured fellows, would rather choose to combat it in the field | and appeal to the judgement of God than leave his cause to them. Henry II[d] first instituted that the sherriff and a certain number of persons who had opportunity to be best acquainted with the crime should have the whole affair laid before them, and that the person should be judged by their sentence. The law of England, always the friend of liberty, deserves praise in no instance more than in the carefull provision of impartial juries. They who are chosen must be near the place where the crime was committed, that they may have an opportunity of being acquainted with it. A great part of the jury may be laid aside by the pannel. He can lay aside 30 of their number, and he can challenge them either per capita, that is, any single juryman, or any number of them, if he suspect the sherriff of partiality. There may be many small causes for suspicion of partiality, and of the relevancey of these the court is judge. Nothing can be a greater security for life, liberty, and property than this institution. The judges are men of integrity, quite independent, holding their offices for life, but are tied down
73 by the law. | The jurymen are your neighbours who are to judge of a fact upon which your life depends. They too can be laid aside for several

[28] Possibly reporter's or copyist's error for 'deceits'.

reasons. The laws of England with regard to juries are only defective in
one point, in which they differ from the laws of Scotland. In England the
whole jury must be unanimous, which renders the office of a juryman a very
dissagreable service. A case may appear to you more clear than it does to
me, and may realy be different from what it appears to either of us, and yet
there is a necessity for our agreement, and of consequence a necessity that
one of us should swear contrary to our conscience. In criminal causes there
is little danger; people are generally disposed to favour innocence and to
preserve life. But in civil cases people are not so much troubled; they are
not so much disposed to favour, and many of them are exceedingly doubtfull. People of fashion are not fond of meddling in a jury attended with such
inconveniences, and therefore only the meaner sort of people attend the
judge. A great man would not choose to be so often called and returned,
and perhaps treated in such a manner as no gentleman would choose to be.

74 | In this case the law providing for security has done too much. In this
country, where unanimity is not required, the service is not so dissagreable.
Tho' a person differ from the majority, he may stand by his opinion and is
not forced to comply, and the people of the highest rank are willing to be
jurors. In the actions which come before the Court of Chancery no jury is
required, and the Court of Session in Scotland has taken them away in civil
causes.

Besides the courts that have been mentioned, there were several others
erected by the kings patent. Henry VIII$^{th}$ erected three, the Court of High
Commission which sat upon ecclesiastics, the Court of Star Chamber which
takes in any thing less than death, and the Court of Wardship which took
care of the king's interest in these emoluments. This last was taken away by
Charles II$^d$, who accepted a sum for the whole. It is now understood that
the king cannot erect a court without consent of Parliament. In no other
country of Europe is the law so accurrate as in England because it has not
been of so long standing. The Parliament of Paris was only erected about

75 the time of Henry VIII$^{th}$ of England. | The British Parliament consists of
a great number of men, and these of great dignity. All new courts disdain to
follow the rules that were formerly established. All new courts are a great
evil, because their power at first is not precisely determined and therefore
their decisions must be loose and inacurrate.

Thus we have considered the origin of government
1. Among a nation of savages
2. Among a nation of shepherds
3. The government of small clans with chieftans. The manner in which
aristocracies arose, the fall of little republics, conquering or defensive, and
lastly the different forms of government that arose in Europe after the
dissolution of arbitrary government.

*Last line of 75 and whole of 76 left blank in MS.*

77    |*c* We shall next consider the origin of the little republics in Europe, and consider the rights of sovereign*d* and subject.

First, of the origin of these republics. In some countries the provinces which were far from the seat of government sometimes became independant, as was the case in a good part of Germany and France during the time of Charlemagne. Hugh Capet who was Chief Justiciary got the government into his hands, but took only the tittle of King o' France. The Pope, by raising disturbances in Germany, for a long time hindered the Emperor Otho from taking possession of Italy. But when he got possession of it, on account of it's distance he could not retain it. Every little town formed itself into a republic, with a council of it's own chusing at it's head. Some towns in Germany being well fortified, such as Hamburgh, assumed the same priviledges, and still in some measure retains them. The Italian towns are governed by a hereditary nobility, tho' the ancient republics were perfectly democratical. In Venice the people freely gave up the government, as they also did in Holland, because they could not support the

78    trouble which it gave them. The Dutch and | Swiss republics are formed into a respublica foederata, and on this depends their strength.

We shall make some remarks on the manner of voting in these republics. When there are 100 votes and three candidates, it is possible that the person who is most odious may be elected. If $A$, $B$, and $C$ be candidates there may be 34 votes for $A$, and 33 for $B$, and as many for $C$. Thus tho' there are 66 votes against $A$ he carries it. This must be still more the case when a criminal is brought before this assembly. For 34 may think him guilty of murther, 33 of man slaughter, and 33 of chance medley, yet he must suffer for murther. To prevent this, in some of these republics they always bring the question to a simple state, is he guilty of murther or not? If there be 3 candidates, they put a previous vote, by which they exclude one of the candidates. In their Senates the president never has a deliberative vote, but only a decisive one, because they will allow no member to have two votes. When there is an equality on both sides, nothing can be done, and therefore the business is not rejected but referred to another meeting.

We shall now consider what duty is owing to the sovereign, and what is the proper punishment of dissobedience. Every attempt to overturn this

79    power | is in every nation considered as the greatest crime and is called high treason. It is to be observed that there is a great difference between treason in monarchies and treason in republics. In the one it is an attempt

---

*c* At the top left-hand corner of 77, outside the frame containing the text, there is written 'A'. Cf. 'B', 'C', and 'D' at 82, 87, 88, and 93 below. The letters were evidently intended to come at intervals of five pages.        *d* Originally 'sovereigns' and then apparently emended

on the king's person and in the other on the liberties of the people, from whence we may see how the maxim of assassination came to be established in republics, and not in monarchies. It is the interest of monarchies that the person in authority be defended whatever his tittle or conduct be, and that no person be allowed to enquire into them. The laws of monarchy are therefore unfavourable to the assassination of tyrants. In a republic the definition of a tyrant is quite clear. He is one who deprives the people of their liberty, levies armies and taxes, and puts the citizens to death as he pleases. This man cannot be brought to a court of justice and therefore assassination is reckoned just and equitable. The present republican governments in Europe, indeed, do not encourage this maxim, because monarchies now sett the fashion, and ⟨?other⟩ government⟨s⟩ copy their pattern. According to our present notions Oliver Cromwell's assassination is most opprobrious, but it would have appeared otherwise when the republics of Greece and Rome sett the fashion.

Having thus taken notice of this difference between monarchical and republican governments, we shall next consider the crimes reckoned treason.

80   | There are three kinds of treason, or attacks upon the essence of government. 1st, *perduellio*, or an attempt to subvert the established government by force or rebellion. 2$^{dly}$, *proditio*, or the joining the enemy, delivering up to him forts, hostages, etc., or the refusing to deliver up garrisons, etc. to the government when they demand them. This is called high treason. 3$^{dly}$, *laesa majestas*, or an insult on the authority of the magistrate, which is not so heinous a crime as the two former. These were the kinds of treason among the Romans. Under the emperors these were blended, and a breach of the smallest, even in so triffling a manner as throwing a stone at the emperor's statue, was punished with death. Under Honorious, a conspiracey against any of the emperors ministers was high treason.[29]

The crimes accounted treason by the English law are the following. 1st, killing the king, wishing$^e$ his death, or providing arms against him with every attempt of this kind are punished capitally. The gun powder plot was never executed, yet the conspirators were put to death. Had they intended only the death of some other person they would not have been executed. 2$^{dly}$, corrupting the king's wife or oldest daughter, because these are
81 affronts to the king, | and may introduce a spurious offspring to the crown. If it be a younger daughter the crime is not so great. 3$^{dly}$, levying a force against the king, aiding his enemies, etc. 4$^{thly}$, attempting the life of the Chancellor or judge of$^f$ assize when sitting in court; at another time it is

---

$^e$ A second hand, probably eighteenth-century, has underlined 'wishing' and has written 'compassing' beside it in the margin      $^f$ Last two words added in margin by a second (probably eighteenth-century) hand

---

[29] *C.* 9.8.5.

only felony. Edward Ist, however, made the meer wounding of them not [not] treason.[30] 5$^{thly}$, counterfeiting the king's great or privy seal, which is accounted an usurpation of the government, because by them the acts of government are carried on. 6$^{thly}$, counterfeiting of the king's coin, tho' this should not properly be treason, because it is no attempt on the essence of government. This crime is no more than forgery and is usually punished as such. These were the branches of treason before the Reformation. At this period Henry VIII$^{th}$ declared himself head of the church, assumed the sovereignty in ecclesiastical affairs as a part of his prerogative, and established for this purpose the Court of High Commission to judge of ecclesiastics, which was abolished by Mary and restored by Elizabeth. As there was some danger then from the popish party the Catholic religion was considered as influenceing the being of government, and therefore it was
82 declared |$^g$ high treason to bring in any bull of the Pope, Agnus Dei, or whatever might support his authority, to support popish seminaries, or conceal popish priests. This law, however proper then, should now be repealed, as there is no more occasion for it; no notice would now be taken of entertaining a popish priest.

During the Civil War and usurpation of Cromwell it became a question how far it is lawfull to resist the power of government. The court party believed the king to be absolute, and the popular doctrine was that the king is only a steward and may be turned out at the pleasure of the people. After the Restoration the court party got the better, and the other party become odious. At the Revolution the Stewart family were set aside, for excellent reasons, and the succession established in the present family. By this the court party was turned out, and began to influence the dispositions of the people. It was therefore enacted that whoever should speak against the present succession should be guilty of treason.[31] This is now altogether unecessary, because the government is now so well established that there is no reason to take notice of those who write or speak against it.

In Scotland the laws were very confused with regard to treason; pre-
83 judiceing the people against the king or the king against the people | were made high treason. But by the Union they are made the same with those of England. These are the laws of Brittain with respect to treason, and they subject the person who breaks them to the highest penalties. He is half hanged and then his entrails are taken out, he forfeits his estate, his wife's dowry,[32] etc., and corrupts his blood so that his children cannot succeed.

$^g$ At the top right-hand corner of 82, outside the frame containing the text, there is written 'B'. See textual note $^c$ to 77 above.

---

[30] Under 25 Edward III, st. 5, c. 2, it was high treason to take, but not merely to attempt, the life of a judge on the bench.

[31] In fact only writing was treason; cf. LJ(A) v.71, above.

[32] i.e. his wife forfeits her dower.

Besides these there are other offences against the crown which do not subject to the pains of high treason, but to those of felony. *1st*, the making of coin below the standard and the exportation of coin. From the notion that opulence consists in money, the Parliament resolved that every one might have bullion coined without any expence of mintage. Thus coined money was never below the value of bullion, and therefore there was a temptation to melt it down. This occasioned the Act declaring this practice felony. $2^{dly}$, any attempt to encrease the coin, as by the philosophers stone, was made felony. $3^{dly}$, destroying the kings armour is also felony.[33] $4^{thly}$, any attempt against the king's officers is also felony, and in general whatever is felony against another person is felony against the king. If his pocket were picked it would be felony against him, as it is against any private

84 gentleman, | but the former offences are committed against him as king.

There are some other small offences which may be done to the king which do not amount to felony but incurr what is called a premunire. This is necessary to explain. In the reigns of King John and Henry III$^d$ England was entirely under the dominion of the Pope; his legate brought over bulls, and raised contributions as he pleased, and long before the Reformation it was necessary to defend the king's liberty against the Pope. The king sometimes appointed one to a benefice, and the Pope another, and the Pope's candidate was often preferr'd. A law was therefore made forbidding any bull to be brought from Rome, or any appeal to be carried thither, and subjecting every person who refused to ordain the king's presentee to the penalties of premunire-regem, *i e* to fortify the king against the Pope. The penalty was forfeiture of goods and outlawry. After Henry VIII$^{th}$ was declared head of the church by the Pope, it was made a premunire to attack the king's prerogative with regard to ecclesiastical matters.[34]

Beside these there are other offences called misprisions of treason and

85 ⟨?these⟩ are either positive or negative. | Positive misprision[35] of treason is the not revealing an attempt against the king's person, his oldest daughter, or the heir of the kingdom. In like manner it is felony if you do not reveal any notice you receive of conspiracies and rebellions. Negative misprision[36] is the counterfeiting of forreign coin current in the kingdom, such as Portuguese gold, but it is not felony to counterfeit French or Dutch money because they are not current here.[37]

In the last place, there are offences against the king called contempts, which are fourfold. 1st, contempt of the kings court or palaces; a riot committed in any of these is a great indignity offered to the sovereign. Riots in

[33] 31 Elizabeth, c. 4 (1589).    [34] 5 Elizabeth, c. 1 (1563); Hawkins, I.19.23.
[35] In fact negative misprision: Hawkins, I.20.
[36] In fact positive misprision.
[37] Forging foreign coin current by consent of the crown was high treason by 1 Mary, sess. 2, c. 6 (1553), and forging foreign coin not current here was misprision of treason by 14 Elizabeth, c. 3 (1572).

courts of justice are also severly punished, because there persons are often provoked, and if the law were not strict they wou'd disturb the court. $2^{dly}$, contempt of the king's prerogative, such as dissobeying the king when lawfully called, going out of the kingdom when in office without his leave, refusing to come after a summons under the privy seal, accepting a pension from a forreign prince without the king's permission, even in a man of letters. $3^{dly}$, contempt of the kings person and government (of

86 which many are guilty), as by saying he is indolent or cowardly, | that he has broken the coronation oath, or to speak disrepectfully of his ministers. These are never regarded at present, because the government is so well established that writing and speaking cannot affect it. $4^{thly}$, contempt of the kings tittle, by denying it, or preferring the Pretenders to it, by drinking the Pretenders health, or refuseing to take the oaths of alledgiance and abjuration. All these subject to imprisonment or fining but not to the penalties of treason, felony, premunire, nor outlawry.

Having considered the offences of the subject against the sovereign, we shall next treat of the crimes which the sovereign may commit against the subject. But first it is proper to consider who are subjects of a state.

The laws of different countries vary much with regard to those to whom the right of citizenship belongs. In most of the Swiss republics nothing gives the right of citizenship[h] but to be born of a citizen. In Rome a family might be peregrina for four or five generations. At Athens no man was a citizen unless both father and mother were Athenians. It is to be observed that the Athenians were particularly sparing in giving the right of citizenship because it entitled them to very great priviledges. Even kings were denied that honour. All they did when they wanted to bestow a favour on a

87 neighbouring king was to free him |[i] from taxes on imports. This they did to Amyntas, father of Phillip, King of Macedon. As aliens paid higher duties than natives, it was no small priviledge to have these removed. After the defeat of the Persians their forces amounted to 25000 men, there country was well cultivated, many cities in Asia paid them tribute. In consequence of this, the people were entitled to attendance on the court of justice, to have their children educated at the publick expence, to have certain distributions of money among them, with many other emoluments. If the number of citizens encreased these priviledges would not be so valuable, and therefore they were very jealous of it. As whoever comes into a parish in England must give a bond not to be burthensome to it, so ⟨?in⟩ all little republics where the number of freemen are small and election in the hands of a few, citizenship is of great importance. But in a large city

---

[h] The last twelve words, which are interlined, are written in different ink and apparently by a different (eighteenth-century) hand. A mark of omission has been made after 'belongs' in the ink of the original text.          [i] At the top left-hand corner of 87, outside the frame containing the text, there is written 'C'. See textual note [c] to 77 above.

such as Rome it was a very small compliment, and accordingly they made whole provinces citizens at once. In Brittain, one born within the kingdom is under the protection of the laws, can purchase lands, and if of the established religion can be elected to any office. In great estates[38] the place of birth makes a citizen, and in small ones the being born of parents who are citizens.

88   |[j] In like manner the incapacity of being a citizen is different in different countries. By the old laws of Rome, and of every barbarous nation, the goods of every person who came within their territories were confiscated, and he himself became a slave to the first person who happened upon him. By a law of Pomponius, if he came from a nation at peace with Rome he was treated as the law prescribed. In barbarous countries they have but one word to signify a stranger and an enemy. At Rome every stranger was hostis, as they considered all nations as their enemies, and the person who came from them as a spy. The Leitchfield man o' war was shipwreck'd on the Emperor of Morocco's dominions, and because we had no league with him the whole crew were made slaves. Our sovereign so far complied with the custom of the place as to ransom them. When they found the advantages of exporting their own goods, and importing those of others, they would naturally allow those who traffick'd with them to be in a state of safety, both with respect to his person and goods, and would allow him an action if injured in either. This is the state of aliens in most of the countries of Europe at present. In Brittain an alien cannot purchase nor inherit land

89   property, nor maintain a real action. | He cannot make a will because it is the greatest extension of property and is founded on piety and affection to the dead, which an alien can have but few opportunities of deserving. By a particular statute an alien merchant, but not a tradesman, may have a lease of a house. This arises from a whimsical principle that it would discourage our own tradesmen to allow forreigners to settle among them. This is the state of aliens in most countries.

In Brittain the manner of obtaining citizenship is twofold. *1st*, by letters of denization, which is a part of the kings prerogative. $2^{dly}$, by a bill of naturalization, which is an Act of Parliament. By the former an alien is capacitated to purchase lands and to transmit them to posterity if subjects of Great Brittain, but he cannot inherit, because as the king is heir of aliens he may transferr his own right but cannot take away the right of the person who ought to succeed. A denizen alien may inherit an estate bequeathed to him, but to be capable of inheriting in all respects an Act of naturalization is necessary, by which he has a right to all the priviledges of a free-

---

[j] At the top right-hand corner of 88 there is written 'C', presumably a mistaken repetition of 'C' on 87. See textual note [c] to 77 above.

---

[38] i.e. states.

born subject. When King William came to the throne naturalized aliens
90 were made peers. | As many Dutch families came over with him it was
natural to suppose that he would favour them with every priviledge. The
English, offended at this partiality, made an Act declaring that there should
be no Act of Parliament for the future by which they should be allowed such
emoluments. As in most countries they are ⟨not⟩ allowed the right of trans-
mitting lands, it was ⟨?not⟩ necessary that they should have an action for
it. Neither in England nor in Germany are aliens allowed to make a will.[39]
In Saxony there was made a very equitable law that aliens from countries
where they were allowed no priviledges should be allowed none among
them. In Rome it was the right of citizens only to make a will.

It is to be observed with respect to aliens, that they are aliens amis, or
aliens ennemie. If a number of the latter should make war upon the king or
injure him, they cannot be prosecuted for high treason, because he is not
their lawfull sovereign and they owe no alledgiance to him. If the laws of
nations do not protect them they must be dealt with by martial law. Aliens
however who live in the country are protected by the laws, and as they thus
own alledgiance to the king they may be prosecuted for treason, and
punished accordingly. Whatever makes a freeborn subject guilty of treason
91 | makes an alien ami guilty of it. An alien ennemie, that is, one who comes
from a country at war with us, if he give information to his natural sovereign is also guilty of treason.

Having thus considered who are properly the subjects of a state, we
come now to treat of the crimes of the sovereign against the subject, or the
limitations of his power.

On this branch of public law it is impossible to speak with any degree of
precision. The duties of one subject to another are sufficiently ascertained
by the laws of every country and the courts of justice, but there are no
judges to determine when sovereigns do wrong. To suppose a sovereign
subject to judgement, supposes another sovereign. In England it can be
exactly ascertained when the king encroaches on the priviledges of the
people, or they on that of the king, but none can say how far the supreme
power of king and Parliament may go. In like manner where the absolute
power of sovereignty is lodged in a single person, none can tell what he may
not do, with accuracey. God is the only judge of sovereigns, and we cannot
say how he will determine. All decisions on this subject have been made by
the prevailing party, and never cooly by a court of justice, and can give us
no light into the subject. Our best notions of it will arise from considering
the several powers of government and their progress.

92 | In the beginning of society all the powers of government are exercised
precariously. The majority may make war but cannot force the minority to
it. Tho' this power was the first that was exerted absolutely. The judicial

[39] Alien friends in England could make wills.

power was much longer executed precariously than the foederative. In every country the judges once only interposed as mediators, and sometimes the pannel had his choice to referr his cause to the judge or to God, by combat, hot water, and nay, if the sentence of the judge did not please the pannel, he might challenge the judge to fight him in the court. In time however it became absolute. The legislative power was absolute whenever it was introduced, but it did not exist in the beginnings of society. It arose from the growth of judicial power. When the judicial power became absolute, the very sight of a judge was terrible as life, liberty, and property depended on him. Tacitus tells us that Quintillius Varus, having conquered a part of the Germans, wanted to civilize them by erecting courts of justice, but this so irritated them that they massacred him and his whole army. To a rude people a judge is the most terrible sight in the world. When property was extended it therefore became necessary to restrain their arbitrary decisions

93 by appointing strict rules which they must follow. |*k* Thus the legislative power was introduced as a restraint upon the judicial. In Brittain the king has the absolute executive and judicial power. However the Commons may impeach his ministers, and the judges whom he appoints are afterwards independent of him. The legislative power is absolute in the king and Parliament. There are however certain abuses which no doubt make resistance in some cases lawful on whatever principle government be founded.

Suppose that government is founded on contract and that these powers are entrusted to persons who grossly abuse them, it is evident that resistance is lawfull, because the original contract is now broken. But we shewed before[40] that government was founded on the principles of utility and authority. We also shewed that the principle of authority is more prevalent in a monarchy, and that of utility in a democracey, from their frequent attendance on public meetings and courts of justice. In such a government as this last, as the principle of authority is as it were prescribed,[41] popular leaders are prevented from acquiring too great power, because they are not allowed to continue in office till they acquire any great ascendancey. But still there is a respect paid to certain offices, whoever be the person that exercises them. In Brittain both principles take place.

94 | Whatever be the principle of alledgiance, a right of resistance must undoubtedly be lawfull, because no authority is altogether unlimited. Absurdity of conduct may deprive an assembly of it's influence, as well as a private person. An imprudent conduct will take away all sense of authority. The folly and cruelty of the Roman emperors make the impartial reader go along with the conspiracies formed against them.

*k* At the top left-hand corner of 93 there is written 'D'. See textual note *c* to 77 above.

[40] 12 ff. above.   [41] Reporter's or copyist's error for 'proscribed'.

It is to be observed that the right of resistance is more frequently exerted in absolute monarchies than in any other, because one man is more apt to fall into imprudent measures than a number. In Turky eight or ten years seldom pass without a change of government. The same degree of ill usage will justify resistance to a Senate or body of men. It must be allowed that resistance is in some cases lawfull, but its excessively difficult to say what an absolute sovereign may do or may not do, and there are different opinions concerning it. Mr. Locke says that when a sovereign raises taxes against the will of the people resistance is lawfull, but there is no country besides England where the people have any vote in the matter. In France the kings edict is all that is necessary, and even in Brittain it is but a very figurative consent that we have, for the number of voters is nothing to that

95 of the people. | Exorbitant taxes no doubt justify resistance, for no people will allow the half of their property to be taken from them; but tho' the highest propriety be not observed, if they have any degree of moderation people will not complain. No government is quite perfect, but it is better to submitt to some inconveniences than make attempts against it. Some other writers alledge that the king cannot alienate any part of his dominions. This notion is founded on the principle of the original contract, by which indeed, tho' a people were willing to submitt to one government, they will not have one of anothers choosing. This doctrine is however groundless. In France and Spain great part of the dominions have been given to the kings children as a portion without any complaint. When Florida was put into our hands,[42] they never made any opposition. The King of Spain and Czaar of Moscovy can even alter the succession as they please. This was in general the case in all feudal jurisdictions; they were divisible at the pleasure of the lord. It was but lately that the right of primogeniture took place in the principalities of Germany.

It is alledged that the King of France cannot alter the Salic law by which daughters cannot succeed to the crown. This law was owing to the power of the princes of the blood, who would not allow the succession to go past themselves. | But if France had been as destitute of nobility as Brittain was

96 at the accession of the present family, the Salic law might have been altered as easily as any other law. It is hard to determine what a monarch may or may not do.

But when the summa potestas is divided as it is in Brittain, if the king do any thing, which ought to be consented to by the Parliament, without their permission, they have a right to oppose him.

The nature of a parliamentary right supposes that it may be defended by force, else it is no right at all. If the king impose taxes or continue them after the time is expired, he is guilty of breach of priviledge.

[42] As a result of the Peace of Fontainebleau, 3 November 1762, confirmed in the Peace of Paris, 10 February 1763. See Introduction, p. *8*.

James II$^d$ attempted some impositions of this sort upon importation. In the Petition of Right, it is expressly appointed that the taxes shall not continue a moment after the time determined by Act of Parliament. When the Parliament saw the crown going to James II who was a Roman Catholick they appointed two tests, to witt, an abjuration of the Pope, and the oath of supremacey, and that every person within 3 months after his acceptance of any office should take the sacrament after the form prescribed by the Church of England. K. James employed Roman Catholics both in the army and Privy Council, and besides appointed persons entirely un-
97  qualified | to the Treasury and broke in upon the priviledges of the universities. He also assumed a power of dispensing with the laws in cases where he himself was no way concerned. Some of the bishops, merely for doing what every British subject has a right to do, to witt, remonstrating against such proceedings, were sent to the Tower. Nothing could more alarm the nation than this attack upon the bishops. One Sharp preached against popery, the religion of the king, upon which the Bishop of London was ordered to suspend him. But he only cautioned him against such practices. The king, not pleased with this, created a Court of High Commission, which had been long abrogated and discharged ever after to be erected, and summoned both the Bishop and Sharp to appear before it. The king, perceiving the disgust of the people and thinking it proceeded from the fear of those possessed of abbay lands, lest they should be taken from them, and from a fear of a change in the religion of the country, he declared that he would grant liberty of conscience to all and retain every one in the possession of the church lands. This plainly shewed his intention
98  to change | the religion of the country, which is the most difficult thing in the world. It is necessary before a religion be changed that the opinions of the people be changed, as was done by Luther, Calvin, John Knox, and others before the Reformation. K. James then applied to the army, but found they by no means sympathized with him. He in return told them that he would never any more bring down his sentiments to theirs, nor consult them on any occasion. It was no wonder that by such practices the Revolution was brought about, and the family sett aside, for the whole nation was disposed to favour the Prince of Orange. They might justly have passed by the whole family, but they generously dispensed with the rigorous law which corrupts the blood with the forfeiture of the estate, and bestowed the crown on his two Protestant daughters. Their brother, on account of the suspicions of his being a papist, as he had been educated in that religion, was rejected. The present family being the nearest Protestant heirs was by Act of Parliament settled in the government, and it was enacted that no prince unless a Protestant shall sit on the throne of Brittain. Thus K. James, on account of his encroachments on the body politic, was
99  with all justice and equity in the world | opposed and rejected.

Thus we have considered man as a member of a state.

As ecclesiastics and laymen are two grand divisions of men in a state, under this head too might be considered ecclesiastic law, and the respective rights of these two [two] bodies of men. Here too we might consider military law, which arises from considering the state as divided into two bodies, civil and military. But these are forreign to our purpose.

---

*Remainder of 99 and whole of 100 left blank in MS.*

101                    | *Domestic Law.*

We come now to consider man as a member of a family, and in doing this we must consider the threefold relation which subsists in a family. These, to witt, between Husband and Wife, Parent and Child, Master and Servant. 1st of these we shall consider husband and wife.

In every species of animals the connection between the sexes is just as much as is necessary for the propagation and support of the species. Quadrupeds whenever the female impregnates have no farther desire for each other. The support of the young is no burthen to the female, and there is no occasion for the assistance of the male. Among birds some such thing as marriage seems to take place. They continue the objects of desire to each other, their connection remains for a considerable time, and they jointly support the young. But whenever the young can shift for themselves all further inclination ceases.

102        In the human species | woemen by their milk are not capable of providing long for their children. The assistance of the husband is therefore necessary for their sustenance, and this ought to make marriage perpetual. In countries however where Christianity is not established, the husband possesses an unlimited power of divorce, and is not accountable for his conduct. In ancient Rome, tho' they had the power of doing it, yet it was thought contrary to good manners.[43]

We may observe an utility in this constitution of our nature, that children have so long a dependance upon their parents, to bring down their passions to theirs, and thus be trained up at length to become usefull members of society. Every child gets this piece of education, even under the most worthless parent.

On this subject it is proposed to consider the duties of each of the two parties during their union, how this union should be[*l*] begun and ended, and what are the particular rights and priviledges of each.

The first duty is fidelity of the wife to the husband; breach of chastity is the greatest of offences. Spurious children may be introduced into the

103 family and come to the succession instead of lawfull ones. | This real utility however is not the proper foundation of the crime. The indignation of the public against the wife arises from their sympathy with the jealousy of the husband, and accordingly they are disposed to resent and punish it. The sentiment of jealousy is not chiefly founded, or rather not at all, upon the idea of a spurious offspring. It is not from the particular act that the

---

*l* Interlined, in different ink and apparently by a different hand

43 Montesquieu, XVI.16.

jealousy arises, but he considers her infedility as an entire alienation of that preference to all other persons which she owes him. This is the real idea he has of it, as may appear from the following consideration. The idea we have of a father does not arise from the voluptuous act which gave occasion to our existence, for this idea is partly loathsome, partly ridiculous. The real idea that a son has of a father is the director of his infancey, the supporter of his helplessness, his guardian, pattern, and protector; these are the proper filial sentiments. The fathers idea of a son is of one that depends upon him, and was bred up in his house, or at his expence, by which connection there should grow up an affection towards him. But a spurious offspring is dissagreable from the resentment that arises against the mother's infidelity.

104    | In these countries where the manners of the people are rude and un-cultivated there is no such thing as jealousy. Every child that is born is considered as their own. The foundation of jealousy is that delicacey which attends the sentiment of love, and it is more or less in different countries in proportion to the rudeness of their manners. In general, wherever there is little regard paid to the sex infidelity is little regarded, and there will be the greatest looseness of manners. Agreable to this we find that Menelaus expressed his resentment against Paris, not against Helen, and this not for debauching her but for carrying her away. In the Odyssey[44] she talks before her husband of that action without reserve. In Sparta it was common for them to borrow and lend their wives. When manners became more refined, jealousy began and rose at length to such a height that wives were shut up, as they are among the Turks at this day. As mankind became more refined, the same fondness which made them shut up woemen made them allow them liberties. In the latter ages of Greece woemen were allowed to go any where. This same fondness carried to a high degree gives as great a licence as when infidelity was disregarded. In no barbarous country is there more licentiousness than in France. Thus we may observe the pre-judice of manners, with respect to woemen, in the different periods of

105    society. | Tho' there was little or no regard paid to woemen in the first state of society as objects of pleasure, yet there never was more regard paid them as rational creatures. In North America, the woemen are consulted con-cerning the carrying on of war, and in every important undertaking.[45] The respect paid to woemen in modern times is very small. They are only put to no trouble for spoiling of their beauty. A man will not exempt his friend from a laborious piece of business, but he will spare his mistress. When the infedility of the wife is considered as an injury to the husband, it is neces-sary that unmarried woemen should be laid under restraints, that when married they may be accustomed to them. Hence the origin of punishment for fornication.

[44] iv.261 ff.          [45] Lafitau, *Mœurs des sauvages amériquains* (1724), I.477.

We come now to consider how this union is begun. As the duty after marriage is quite different from what it was before, it is necessary that there should be some ceremony at the commencement of it. This differs in different countries, but in general is connected with religion, as it is supposed to make the greatest impression. In the infancey of society, though marriage seemed intended to be perpetual, yet the husband had an unlimited power of divorce, tho' it was reckoned indecent to exercise it, unless 106 for an enormous crime. | The reason was that the government durst intermeddle little with private affairs, and far less with matters in private families. For the security of government they endeavoured by all means to strengthen the power of the husband and make him as absolute as possible. In ancient Rome, the husband was sovereign lord of life and death in all matters belonging to his own family.

In Rome three kinds of marriages took place.[46] 1st, by Conferriation,[47] a religious ceremony.

$2^{dly}$, by Exemption,[m] when the husband bought his wife.

$3^{dly}$, by Use. If he had lived with her a year and day, she was his by prescription, and he could divorce her.

The power of divorce extended to the wife after female succession took place; a woman possessed of a great fortune, who lived happily before marriage and had so much in her own power, would not encline to give it 107 all to her husband. | The lawyers therefore invented a new kind of marriage in favour of heiresses, which was called the deductio domi[48] or marriage by contract. Certain terms were agreed on between the parties, and then the husband came and carried her home. To prevent prescription taking place, she went away three or four days every year, which according to the form of the contract secured her fortune. Thus the wife became equally independent with the husband, and had equally the power of divorce. As the marriage was founded upon the consent of both parties, it was reasonable that the dissent of either party should dissolve it.

This form of marriage is pretty similar to the present, with this material difference, however, that it did not legitimate the children, nor preserve the honour of the woemen.[49] The Roman form caused great disorders. When the parties seperated, which was often the case, they married others, and very often the woemen went thro' five or six husbands. This so cor-

---

[m] Emended in the margin by a second (probably eighteenth-century) hand to 'Coemption'

---

[46] Heineccius, I.10.1.

[47] Reporter's or copyist's error for 'Confarreation'.

[48] *Deductio in domum*, a ceremony evidencing the parties' consent to the marriage, but never itself a legal requirement. Cf. LJ(A) iii.8–9, above.

[49] In fact it was as much a legal marriage, whose issue was legitimate, as the *manus* marriage. Cf. LJ(A) iii.9, above.

rupted their morals that about the end of the monarchy there was scarce
108 a great man that was not cuckolded. | The disorder came to such a height
that after the establishment of Christianity, the power of divorce was
restrained unless for certain causes. Among the Scythian nations which
settled in the west of Europe, divorce was taken away altogether. In
Burgundy, however, the power of the husband was very great. By a law
there, if a man abused his wife he was liable to a fine, but if the wife mis-
behaved she was put to death.

As in general only flagrant crimes were taken notice of by the civil court,
small ones went into the hands of the ecclesiastics, and that first gave
occasion to their great power. When the civil court gave no redress for
breach of contract, the ecclesiastics punished the offender for perjury, and
when any difference happened betwixt man and wife they made them
suffer penance for it. Afterwards the power of divorce was taken away
unless for adultery, and when the one was afraid of bodily harm from the
other. Even this last was not a perfect divorce, for neither of the parties
109 was allowed to marry again, but only a seperation *a mensa et toro*. | The
causes of a perfect divorce, after which they were allowed to marry again,
were these three. 1st, if they were within the degrees of consanguinity,[50] the
marriage was made null, unless they had a dispensation from the Pope; $2^d$,
precontract with any other woman; $3^d$, frigidity in a man, and incapacity
in a woman.

The ecclesiastics brought in other alterations besides these with regard to
marriage. It is to be observed that the laws made by men are not altogether
favourable to woemen. They considered the infidelity in the husband and
wife were equally punished. He had no more power to divorce than she.
Adultery, saevitia, and metus were considered as causes of seperation but
not of divorce.[51]

The cannon law when it took place was dictated by ecclesiastics, who on
most occasions copied the Roman law, as they were the only persons that
understood Latin, and among whom the remains of literature were preserved. At first even the ecclesiastic law required no ceremonies at marriage.
As the ceremonies of conferriation[52] and exemption[53] had gone into
desuetude in the latter times of the Roman law, when the only thing that
110 | was required was the deductio domi, so by the ecclesiastic law for a long
time a contract of any kind made a marriage, whether a contract in praesenti or in futuro. Contract in praesenti is when I say, I take you for a wife,
or, I take you for a husband. Contract in futuro is when they say, I will do
it. Either of these contracts might be proved either by evidence or by oath,

[50] i.e. the prohibited degrees of consanguinity.
[51] The meaning of this very condensed paragraph will be clearer if a comparison is made
with the corresponding passage in LJ(A) iii.13, above.
[52] Reporter's or copyist's error for 'confarreation'.
[53] Reporter's or copyist's error for 'coemption'.

if they declared themselves married persons, or that they were to be so. Pope Innocent III[d] enacted that all marriages should be performed in facie ecclesiae, but tho' this was considered as the only decent marriage, yet others were often in use and in some cases were valid. If a person was married in futuro, and afterwards in facie ecclesiae, and the first wife made no opposition till after the banns were out, the first marriage was null. If it was contractu presenti[54] the second was null. This was the case in England till the late Marriage Act.

If a contract in futuro can be proved, or if the man refuse his oath, the marriage is in some countries considered as valid. The contract in presenti
111 is every where valid especially if they cohabit afterwards. | All these institutions are derived from the canon law, which made the breach of them liable to church censures as ours does.

An Act of Parliament only makes a divorce in England, the infidelity of the wife will not do it. In Scotland it is much more easily done.

Protestants never carried matters so far as the canon law, for the clergy married themselves. Besides, love which was formerly a ridiculous passion became more grave and respectable. As a proof of this it is worth our observation that no ancient tragedy turned on love, whereas now it is more respectable and influences all the public entertainments. This can be accounted for only by the changes of mankind.

The species of marriage of which we have been treating took place only in Rome and in the Christian countries, with a few others, for in many countries they took as many wives as they were able to maintain. This naturaly leads us to consider the origin of polygamy.

It is to ⟨be⟩ observed that tho' voluntary divorce be attended with in-conveniences, yet it is not altogether contrary to the principle of justice
112 that a man should | put away his wife and take another for less reasons than adultery, because they make them quite unhappy together, tho' either of them might live very well elswhere. The same is the case with polygamy. If a woman consents to be one of five or twenty or more wives, and the laws allows it, there is no injury done her, she meets with the treatment which she might naturaly expect. The ancient Jewish and Oriental laws tolerated polygamy, but tho' it and voluntary divorce be not altogether contrary to justice, it must always be a very bad policy where they are established or allowed.

Polygamy excites the most violent jealousy, by which domestic peace is destroyed. The wives are all rivals and enemies. Besides, the children are ill taken care of, and the wife complains that her children are not used as they ought, because she measures the affection of the father by her own, between which there is no proportion, as he[55] is divided among 40 or 50

---

[54] The last two words are probably a copyist's error for 'contract *in praesenti*'.

[55] Presumably reporter's or copyist's error for 'his'.

children and hers only among 4 or 5. Where polygamy takes place, there must both be a jealousy of love and a jealousy of interest, and consequently a want of tranquillity. It may be said that in the seraglios of the eastern monarchs there is the greatest peace, but this is owing to the most im-

113 perious discipline. | When rebells are subdued their humility is remarkable. In Africa we find the most horrid disorders, their discipline not being severe enough. It is the greatest misery to the woemen that they are entirely shut up and can enjoy no company but that of the eunuchs, which they detest. The man too who has the seraglio is by no means happy, tho' apparently so. He too must be jealous, and on account of the inequality betwixt him and them he can have no entertainment at his own house, no opportunity of social improvements. You must never mention his wife to a Turk, she can never be seen by men, not even by her physician, as Tourne-fort tells us. This gravity and reserve of the husband must have a bad effect upon the manners of the country; as the men have no trust nor dependance upon each other, they cannot form into parties, and therefore the government must always be arbitrary, of which they have a model in their own houses, where there is little parental and less conjugal affection. Besides all this, it tends to depopulate the species; the greater part of men can get no wives, and many of them are castrated to take care of the seraglio. It is indeed alledged that there are more woemen born than men. Montesquieu says that at Bantam in the East Indies there are 10 woemen

114 born for 1 man. | Dutch authors say that on the coast of Guinea there are 50 to one. The account from Japan is better attested, where it is said there are 11 woemen to 9 men. Where this is the case, if the fact be true, it would be an inconvenience if polygamy did not take place.

By strict examination, we find that in Europe there is little difference. The general computation is that there are 13 men to 12 woemen, or 17 to 16, which as men are more exposed to dangers than woemen makes the number about equal. Now if there be no difference in Europe, we have reason to conclude that there is not any difference in any other place. The laws of nature are the same every where, the laws of gravity and attraction the same, and why not the laws of generation. In some of the forementioned places there may indeed be more woemen than men. In places where the seat of religion is and where the court sits, and consequently the opulent live, there must be more woemen, because the rich only have seraglio's and they purchase the woemen from other places, so that there is a constant import of woemen from these countries in which polygamy does not take place. Polygamy takes place under despotic governments. When a country is conquered by savages they indulge themselves in all manner of brutality,

115 and this among the rest | as there is no established law to the contrary. It never took place in ancient Carthage or Rome, tho' it takes place in Turky. In every country freedom puts out polygamy. There is nothing that free

men will less submitt to than a monopoly of this kind. But despotism is always favourable to polygamy. Montesquieu observes still further in favour of polygamy, that in some countries woemen are marriageable at 8 or 9, and are old and withered at 30.[56] When they have their beauty they cannot have much understanding, and when it encreases their beauty is gone, and consequently they cannot long be agreable companions, and therefore a husband had need of more than one. It may be their custom, indeed, to deflower infants, but the fact is not well attested. Cleopatra was 36 when taken by Augustus, yet she was with child; Constantia bore a child at 54. But tho' [But tho'] the fact[57] were true, it is not reasonable that polygamy should take place, but only voluntary divorce. If woemen were only usefull 10 or 12 years it might be reasonable to take another, but not a number at the same time.

116  Wherever polygamy takes place there can be no hereditary nobility. It is difficult to make the right of primogeniture take place where | there are so many wives, several of whom bring forth nearly at the same time. Where there are so many children they cannot all have the affection of the parent, and it is only by this means that any of them can establish themselves. Where the children are numerous affection diminishes. I may regard 4 or 5 children who are connected with my friend, but if there are 100 in the same relation they are little regarded.[58] Now hereditary nobility is the great security of the people's liberty. Being in every corner of the country, whenever the subjects are oppressed they fly to him as their head. In eastern countries there is no such thing. Every man is almost an upstart, and the royal family alone is regarded. The families of the bashaws after their death mix with the vulgar.

Wherever there is a hereditary nobility the country cannot easily be conquered, or rather not at all. They may be beat once or twice, but they still recover under their natural heads. Eastern countries, for this very reason that they want these, make feeble resistance against forreign invaders.

117  | Polygamy is exceedingly hurtfull to the populousness of a nation. An hundred woemen married to an hundred men will have more children than the same number married to two or three. It may indeed be said that in China, about the mouth of the Ganges, and in Egypt they are populous notwithstanding polygamy. In these countries there are regulations regarding populousness, and some other circumstances contribute to it such as the remarkable fertility of the soil.

Thus we see marriage is of two kinds, vizt polygamy or monogamy, of

---

[56] Probably copyist's error for '20'. The MS. entry suggests that he hesitated between the two.

[57] i.e. the supposed fact that girls are old at 20.

[58] The meaning of this sentence will be clearer if a comparison is made with the corresponding passage in LJ(A) iii.42, above.

which the latter is of three kinds: 1st, when the husband can divorce the wife at pleasure, $2^{dly}$, when the power of divorce is equally in their power, and $3^{dly}$, when it is in the power of the civil magistrate entirely.

Where polygamy is allowed, the wife is entirely in the power of the husband; he may divorce her, or dispose of her as he pleases.

The laws concerning monogamy differ according to the species of it. That kind where the contract or agreement is indissoluble but by the civil magistrate is the most convenient. By this indeed nothing but what is very
118 dissagreable to society is the occasion of divorce. | But it is always better that the marriage tye should be too strait, than that it should be too loose. The unlimited power of divorce in the latter ages of the Republic[59] was productive of the most disorderly consequences, the prevention of which sufficiently attones for any hardships it may occasion. When both parties have the power of divorce they can have no mutual trust nor dependance upon each other, but their interests are quite seperate.

We come now to consider what interest the husband has in the property of the wife, or the wife in that of the husband, according to the different species of marriage.

Where polygamy takes place the wife, being in absolute slavery, has no interest at all in the husbands property and is only entitled to an aliment after his death. When the husband only has the power of divorce the property of the wife becomes his, as much as his own. When they have the power of divorce in the hands of both, whatever portion the wife brings is secured, and the husband can have no more ado with it but to manage it.
119 | When he dies the wife has no more share of the husband's property than was agreed upon by the contract. In the species of monogamy when divorce is in the hand of the magistrate, the right of the husband extends not so far as formerly, but that of the wife extends further, as she is more independent of him than in any other species. If a wife has a land estate, the husband receives the rents which are at his absolute disposal. If the wife die and leave a son, the husband is the natural guardian of it, and is entitled to a courtesie of the life rent of his wife's estate.

In England the husband can dispose of all chattels real in his lifetime, but if he do not dispose of them in his lifetime they go to the wife, not to the heir, at his death.

All chattels personal he can dispose of as he pleases. Debts on bonds are the same with chattels real; if the husband demands payment of the debt he can dispose of the money as he pleases, but if he do not claim it in his lifetime it goes to his wife after his death. If the wife die first all chattels real and debts on bond go to her relations, if the husband have not already disposed of them. If the husband die first the wife has a third part of his
120 land estate,[60] | whether there be children or not. This is considered as her

---

[59] Of Rome.                                                    [60] For her life.

dowry.[61] In England she has a compleat third of all,[62] but in Scotland she has only a third of all bills, money, moveables, and bygone rents. Bonds bearing interest go to the children.

In Scotland the husband can sell his wife's land with her own consent, but she must first be examined before a court and declare that it was with her own consent, and then her executors[n] cannot claim it. Both in Scotland and in England, no bond granted by the wife is binding upon the husband unless it be granted for the necessaries of life. In this respect she is considered as a servant, for if a servant buys provision in his name he is obliged to pay them. In Scotland the husband may have a writ of inhibition to prevent the wife from contracting debts in his name. In England any verbal notice that he will not be accountable for them is sufficient. If they be seperated, he is not even obliged to pay what she purchases for her aliment.

We come now to consider what persons are capable of contracting 121 marriage. | Betwixt ascendants and descendants marriage is prohibited in infinitum. Nothing can be more shocking to nature than for a mother to marry her son. By this the mother becomes inferiour to her son, and on account of the inequality of their ages the ends of marriage are seldom accomplished. Therefore it is never tolerated unless where superstition takes place. In like manner a marriage between a father and a daughter is incestuous. It is however to be observed that this is not so contrary to nature as the former, because the father still is superiour when he is husband, and accordingly we find that many barbarous nations tolerated this. But still it is unatural that the father, the guardian and instructor of the daughter, should turn her lover and marry her. Besides, a mother can never look agreably on a daughter who will probably supply her place. Nothing can be more destructive of domestic happiness.

For the same reasons, the uncle and niece or the aunt and nephew never marry. At Rome and Carthage, indeed, they used sometimes to give a dispensation to the uncle and niece, but never to the aunt and nephew.

122    The marriage of collaterals, such as brother and sister, | seems to have been prohibited chiefly from political views, because they are bred up together, and would be in danger of mutual corruption unless properly restrained. The same reason lay against a marriage between cousins in these ages when they were brought up in the same house.

At Athens a man might marry his sister consanguinea but not his sister

---

[n] A later hand has, in pencil, underlined this word and inserted the emendation 'heirs' in the margin

---

[61] Her dower.
[62] A life interest in a third of the land and a third of the movables if there are children or half the movables if there are no children of the marriage.

uteral.⁰ Many eminent men married in this manner, thus Cimon married his father's daughter Elpinice.⁶³

By the law of England, the wife of the deceased grand-uncle can marry her husbands grand nephew, it being above four degrees.

Affinity by the Christian law is considered as the same with consanguinity. The wife's sister is considered as the husband's sister and the wife's aunt as the husband's aunt. It is to be observed that the rules of affinity are rather rules of police than of nature, for it is not contrary to nature that a man should marry his wife's sister. In many countries of the East Indies this kind of marriage takes place, because they think that the wife's sister will probably make the best mother in law to her sisters children. But it may be answered to this, that it entirely hinders all intercourse between the sister and her brother in laws family, and that it might be expected that she would answer this purpose by living in his house unmarried with no children of her own. | The cannon and civil law reckoned affinity⁶⁴ differently. The civil law counted brothers and sisters as one degree removed from the common stock, and cousins german two. The canon law counted how far the persons were asunder. Brothers were two degrees, the father being one and either of the brothers another. In the same manner cousins german were four degrees. The canon counted both sides from the stock and the civil law only one. When the one says the second degree was prohibited from marriage, and the other the fourth, they both mean cousins german. The Pope often dispensed with these laws, and by that means extended his authority and promoted his interest.

Having now considered all the different species of marriage, we come to consider the effects of the want of it. The effect of marriage is to legitimate the children. We must therefore consider the difference of legitimate and illegitimate. Legitimation gives the children inheritable blood, so that they can succeed to their father and his relations. An illegitimate child has no inheritable blood, and therefore cannot succeed to his father intestato, because it is unknown who is his father, nor to his mother, because no child succeeds that is not lawfully begotten. As a bastard can succeed to no body, so no body can succeed to him, as he is not related to any human creature. | If he die intestate without children, his wife has one half of his moveables and one third of his land estate, and the rest goes to the king, but if he has children, the wife has a third of all. The king is still considered as *ultimus haeres.*

---

⁰ A much later hand has, in pencil, struck out the letters 'al' and inserted 'ine' above them

---

⁶³ Cornelius Nepos, V.1.2; cited by Montesquieu, V.5.
⁶⁴ Presumably 'consanguinity' was intended. Civil law and canon law have been interchanged in the account which follows, the actual position being the opposite of what is stated. Cf. p. 166, note 72, above.

In Scotland there is a further inconvenience attending it. As the king is the heir of bastards, a bastard is incapable of making a testament. Because it would cut the king out of his right. The king can, however, grant him letters of legitimation which make him capable of testating, because as the right of succession belongs to the king he may dispose of it as he pleases. However, this or any thing less than an Act of Parliament cannot give him inheritable blood, but an Act of the whole legislature can do any thing.

The canon and civil law restore to blood a person born out of wedlock in the following ways:

1st, per subsequens matrimonium, or marrying the woman that had the children. As concubines were numerous, it was enacted that whoever married his concubine legitimated her children. This Justinian afterwards made perpetual.

2$^{\text{dly}}$, per oblationem curiae. When the children were willing to execute certain parish offices, as deacons,[65] etc, tho' this entitled them only to succeed to the father and not to his relations.

125    | 3$^{\text{dly}}$, per adrogationem. As for example one Roman could adopt the son of another, and the son accept of him as a father. They had it in their power to adrogate any freeman; bastards were considered as freemen and if they were willing to accept might be adrogated as such.

4$^{\text{thly}}$, per ⟨re⟩scriptum principis, which was much the same with letters of legitimation.

5$^{\text{thly}}$, per testamentum, by which they probably succeeded only to their fathers estate.

The canon law introduced the subsequens matrimonium into all countries but England. The English clergy were then unpopular by joining with the king against the barons, and therefore in England the subsequens matrimonium never could legitimate.

That subsequens matrimonium might legitimate, the canon law made some restrictions which did not take place at Rome. Bastards of adulterous persons could not succeed, those, to wit, of a woman who has a husband alive, or of a concubine to a man whose wife is alive, tho' they should marry afterwards. Incestuous children also could not succeed, unless legitimated by a dispensation from the Pope. Thus we have seen the dissabilities and incapacities of illegitimate children, which can only have an

126  effect where monogamy prevails, and indeed these alone | hinder polygamy from gaining ground in any country, because if bastards were allowed to succeed men would hardly subject themselves to the inconveniences of lawfull marriage. To have a wife entirely in their power and to take others when they please would be more convenient.

*Three lines left blank in MS.*

[65] Decurions, municipal officials; cf. LJ(A) iii.73, above.

We come now to consider the history of parentage, being the second relation in which we were to consider man as a member of a family.

The authority of the father over his children, both with respect to liberty and property, was at first absolute. He was at liberty to choose whether he would bring up his children or not. And it was accounted no injustice to refuse to do it. The law hinders the doing injuries to others, but there can be no fixed laws for acts of benevolence.[66] All that the law prohibited was immediately putting them to death, but he might expose them if he pleased. Even with us a father is not obliged to ransom a son who is taken captive, but may do it or not as he pleases. In the same manner anciently

127 a father might choose whether he would ransom his son | from starving, from wild beasts, and the like. Tho' some regulations were made in Rome concerning this, they were never well kept, and the practice was not abolished till the establishment of Christianity. In China, at present, where polygamy takes place, they are often obliged to expose them and generally drown them. As the father had it entirely in his power to bring up his son or not, he had an absolute jurisdiction over him if he did bring him up. At Rome the father had the ius vitae et necis, et vendendi. Besides, whatever the son acquired belonged to the father, and if he married his children were considered as members of the grand father's family. This power of the father over his son was very soon lessened. The son was connected with the mother's relations, and the uncle, whom on some occasions he was to succeed, would naturaly look after the person who was to be his heir. By a law of Numa-Pompilius, if a son was married it was no longer in the father's power to sell him. The Twelve Tables indeed mention this priviledge of the father, but it is probable it was only those who married without their

128 father's consent. In like manner the ius vitae et necis went out. | The father only put in execution the laws of his country for capital crimes. He could take the power out of the hands of the magistrate and condemn his son to punishment himself, but he could not free his son if he was accused by the laws of his country. This shews that the patria potestas was not altogether absolute. This power of the father weaken'd by degrees, and at last went out altogether. The father only pronounced the sentence as it was dictated to him by the civil magistrate, as he himself might have gone wrong in some forms, and by that means rendered the whole null. It is much the same with the gentlemen in this country, who have it in their power to seize the goods of their tenants when in debt, without any form of law. As they are ignorant how it ought to be done, they are obliged as well as others to apply for authority to the civil court, tho' they are vested with the power of doing it themselves.

The power of the father with respect to the property of the son soon went out likewise. We find that very early, by a law of Marcianus, the

[66] Cf. TMS II.ii.1.3–5.

fathers were obliged to provide proper wives for their sons, and to bestow proper portions upon ⟨them⟩, and if they refused the government was to see
129  it done. | This shews that the property after marriage must have been their own. The law seems and has[67] been made because the wife brought a fortune along with her, and therefore it was but reasonable that the husband should also have some property independent of his father. It must therefore only have been the property of unmarried children over which the parent had any power, and this is not unreasonable. The authority of the father was not arbitrary at Rome, for we often find men accused there for not taking proper care of their children, which could hardly have been the case if they could have put them to death.

Julius Caesar, and after him Augustus, were the first that gave to sons property independent of their fathers. At first they kept as their own whatever they took in war, or the peculium castrense, afterwards whatever they acquired by the liberal and mechanic arts. This was extended by Adrian, and afterwards by Justinian, to every thing, unless what they got from their fathers. All donations and legacies were entirely at their own disposal.

We also find the power of the father in dissinheriting them limited. There were only certain cases in which it was in his power.

130    | After the fall of the Roman Empire, the power of the father over the son, as well as over the wife, was softened. The father came to have over the son, while he continued in the family with him, an authority much the same with that a father has among us, that, to witt, of taking care of his morals. But when out of the family he was not so immediately concerned about him. The father has this particular priviledge with respect to his son, that he can become tutor to him without surety, and is not accountable, as every other tutor is, for negligence and omission. This is the natural authority the father has over the son. The father is obliged to bring up his children, and the children in case of old age or infirmity to maintain the father.

We now come to consider the history of law with regard to masters and servants, which was the third relation in which we proposed to consider ⟨?man as a member of a⟩ family.

We have found that the same principle which gave the husband authority over the wife also gave the father authority over the son. As the power of
131  the husband was softened by means of his wife's friends | with whom she was connected and to whom she could complain, so that of the father was softened by the same means. But it was not so with the servants; they had no body to whom they could complain, they had no connection with any person, and having none to take their part they necessarily fell into a state of slavery. Accordingly we find that the master had the power of life and

---

[67] The last two words are probably a copyist's error for 'to have'. He first wrote '& have' and then altered 'have' to 'has'.

death over them, quite different from the ius vitae et necis over the wife and children, which was restricted to criminal cases; the power over the servants was perfectly arbitrary. Besides, as the master had the disposal of his liberty, a slave could have no property. Whatever he has or can acquire belongs to his master. No contract of the slave could bind the master, however, unless the laws found a tacit consent of the master implied. A slave can only acquire for his master. If I promised a slave 10£ I am obliged to pay it to the master. But besides these disadvantages there are many others to which the ancient Greek and Roman slaves, as well as our Negroes, were liable, tho' less attended to.

132    | 1st. They were hindered from marriage. They may cohabit with a woman but cannot marry, because the union between two slaves subsists no longer than the master pleases. If the female slave does not breed he may give her to another or sell her. Among our slaves in the West Indies there is no such thing as a lasting union. The female slaves are all prostitutes, and suffer no degradation by it.

2$^d$. But slavery is attended with still greater evils than these, for a slave who is a polytheist is properly under the protection of no religion. He has no god any more than liberty and property. The polytheistic religion consists of a great number of local deities. Every place has it's own divinity. The slaves belong not to the country, and therefore it's gods are no way concerned about them. Besides, a heathen can never approach a deity empty handed. The slaves had nothing to offer and therefore could expect no favour from them. These slaves who were employed about the temples were the only ones who could have any tittle to the protection of the gods.

133 The master prayed for them | but it was in the same manner that he prayed for his cattle. Every person is superstitious in proportion to the precariousness of his life, liberty, or property, and to their ignorance. Gamesters and savages are remarkably so. It is then a very great hardship that a slave, who is addicted to superstition from both these causes, should be deprived of that which is so well fitted to sooth the natural feelings of the human breast. The religion, therefore, which discovered one God who governed all things would naturaly be very acceptable to slaves. Accordingly we find that the Jewish religion, which, tho' well fitted for defending itself, is of all others the worst adapted to the making of converts, because they could never be of the stock of Abraham from whom the Messiah was to come, could not be on a level with the Jews but only proselytes of the gate, and were obliged to abstain from many kinds of food, with all these disadvantages made great progress among the Roman slaves. When Christianity was introduced, which was attended with none of these disadvantages, it made the most rapid progress among the slaves.

134    | We are apt to imagine that slavery is quite extirpated because we know nothing of it in this part of the world, but even at present it is almost

universal. A small part of the west of Europe is the only portion of the globe that is free from it, and is nothing in comparison with the vast continents where it still prevails. We shall endeavour to shew how it was abolished in this quarter and for what reasons it has continued in other parts and probably will continue.

It is to be observed that slavery takes place in all societies at their begining, and proceeds from that tyranic disposition which may almost be said to be natural to mankind. Whatever form of government was established, it was a part of its constitution that slavery should be continued. In a free government the members would never make a law so hurtfull to their interest, as they might think the abolishing of slavery would be. In ⟨a⟩ monarchy there is a better chance for it's being abolished, because one 135 single person is lawgiver | and the law will not extend to him nor diminish his power, tho' it may diminish that of his vassals. In a despotic government slaves may be better treated than in a free government, where every law is made by their masters, who will never pass any thing prejudicial to themselves. A monarch is more ready to be influenced to do something humanely for them; when Augustus was visiting Vidius Pollio, one of the slaves who had accidentaly broken a platter threw himself down before Augustus imploring his protection, that he might not be cut in pieces and thrown into the fish pond. Augustus was so shocked with this that he immediately manumitted all Pollio's slaves, tho' Pollio no doubt relished not the behaviour of his guest. In the reigns of Adrian and Antoninus, when monarchy had taken place, there were several laws made in favour of slaves, but never one in the times of the Republic. Slavery, then, may be gradualy softened under a monarch, but not entirely abolished, because 136 | no one person whatever can have so much authority as to take away at once the most considerable part of the nation's property, because this would occasion a general insurrection.

In an opulent country the slaves are always ill treated, because the number of slaves exceeds the number of freemen and it requires the most rigid discipline to keep them in order. If a freeman was killed in a house[68] all the slaves were put to death. Several authors tell us that in the nighttime at Rome, nothing was to be heard but the cries of slaves whom their masters were punishing. Ovid tells us that the slave who kept the gate was chained to it, and the slaves who manured the ground were chained together lest they should run away, and what was more cruel, when an old slave was incapable for work he was turned out to die on an island near the city kept for that purpose.

137 | Slavery is more tolerable in a barbarous than in a civilized society. In an uncultivated country the poverty of the people makes the number of the slaves any one can keep quite inconsiderable, and therefore their discipline

[68] His own house.

will not be so rigid as where they are numerous. Besides, in a barbarous country the master labours himself as well as the slave and therefore they are more nearly on a levell. In the early periods of Rome the slave worked with his master and ate with him, and the only punishment in case of misbehaviour was the carrying a cross stick thro' the town or village.

In Jamaica and Barbadoes, where slaves are numerous and objects of jealousy, punishments even for slight offences are very shocking. But in North America they are treated with the greatest mildness and humanity.

Thus we have shewn that slavery is more severe in proportion to the culture of society. Freedom and opulence contribute to the misery of the slaves. The perfection of freedom is their greatest bondage. And as they are the most numerous part of mankind, no human person will wish for liberty
138 | in a country where this institution is established.

It is almost needless to prove that slavery is a bad institution even for freemen. A freemen who works for days wages will work far more in proportion than a slave in proportion to the expence that is necessary for maintaining and bringing him up. In ancient Italy an estate managed by slaves, in the most fertile country, yielded to the master only one sixth of the produce, whereas a landlord even in our barren country receives a third and the tenants live much better. Slaves cultivate only for themselves, the surplus goes to the master, and therefore they are careless about cultivating the ground to the best advantage. A freeman keeps as his own whatever is above his rent and therefore has a motive to industry. Our colonies would be much better cultivated by freemen.

That slavery is a dissadvantage appears from the state of colliers and salters in our own country. They have indeed priviledges which slaves have not. Their property after maintenance is their own, they cannot be
139 sold but along with the work, they enjoy marriage | and religion, but they have not their liberty altogether, and it would certainly be an advantage to the master that they were free. The common wages of a day labourer is between six and eight pence. That of a collier is half a crown. If they were free their prices would fall. At Newcastle the wages exceed not 10$^d$ or a shilling, yet colliers often leave our coalworks where they have half a crown a day, and run there tho' they have less wages, where they have liberty.

There is still one inconvenience more that attends slavery, that it diminishes the number of freemen even to a degree beyond imagination, for every slave takes up the room of a freeman. The inequality of fortune seemed at first a misfortune and laws were made against it. £10 per *ann.* is reckoned the necessary expence of one man. A landed gentlemen who has £10,000 per *ann.* spends what would maintain a 1000 men. At first sight we are apt to conceive him a monster who eats up the food of so many, but if we attend to it he is realy usefull, and he eats or wears no more than the rest; £10 serves him too, and his £10,000 maintains a thousand people who

are employed in refining his £10 by an infinity of ways so as to make it
140 worth the whole. | This gives room for all kinds of manufactures. When
slaves are employed to sift as it were this 10£ out of the 10,000£, one must
be a taylor, another a weaver, a third a smith, and thus each takes up a
freeman's place.

We come now to account for the abolition of slavery in this part of the
world. The slaves in this and the neighbouring countries were those who
cultivated the ground and were what was called adscripti glebae, and could
only be sold along with the land. As they had nothing but their maintenance for their labour, the ground was but badly cultivated. To remedy
this dissadvantage tenants by stillbow[69] were introduced; they had no
stock themselves, and therefore the landlord gave them cattle and the
implements for plowing, which they resigned at the end of the lease. At
harvest the crop was equally divided between the landlord and tenant.
This was the first species of free tenants, who were plainly emancipated
villains. After this custom had continued for a long time the tenants picked
up so much as enabled them to make a bargain with the landlord to give
141 him a certain sum | for a lease of so many years; and whatever the ground
should produce, they would take their venture. This is plainly an advantage
to the landlord: the ground every year is better cultivated, he is at no
expence, and the half of the product[70] was better to the tenants than any
sum they would give. By the feudal law, the lord had an absolute sway
over his vassals. In peace he was the administrator of justice, and they were
obliged to follow him in war. When government became a little better
established, the sovereign did all he could to lessen this influence, which on
some occasions was dangerous to himself and hindered people from applying to him for justice. As therefore the ancient villains were tenants at will,
were obliged to perform certain duties to their master, and were entirely
at his disposal, a law was made taking away all their burthens but that of
being tenants at will, and at last their priviledge was extended and they
became copyholders.

Another cause of the abolition of slavery was the influence of the clergy,
but by no means the spirit of Christianity, for our planters are all Chris-
tians. Whatever diminished the power of the nobles over their inferiours
142 |encreased the power of the ecclesiastics. As the clergy are generaly more in
favour with the common people than the nobility, they would do all they
could to have their priviledges extended, especially as they might have
expectations of reaping benefit by it. Accordingly we find that Pope
Innocent the III$^d$ encouraged all landlords to emancipate their slaves. Thus
the influence of the clergy combining with that of the king hastened the

---

[69] Reporter's or copyist's error for 'steelbow'.
[70] i.e. the half formerly handed over to the landlord and now kept by the tenant in
addition to the other half.

abolition of slavery in the west of Europe. Agreable to this we find that in countries where neither the king nor the church were very powerfull slavery still prevails. In Bohemia, Hungary, and these countries where the sovereign is elective and consequently never could have great authority, and besides, where the church never had any great influence, servitude still remains, because the court is by no means powerfull enough to emancipate the slaves of the nobility.

To shew by what means slaves are acquired, to consider the state of domestic servants in our own country, together with mentioning a certain 143 particular state of families, | will be all that is to be said on this head respecting man as a member of a family.

Slaves may be acquired five different ways. 1st, captives in war in almost every country are slaves; if the conqueror does not kill them, he has a right to make them slaves. $2^{dly}$, as captives become slaves, having no body to deliver them, so their children become slaves also. $3^{dly}$, persons guilty of certain crimes were made slaves, sometimes to the person injured, sometimes to the public. $4^{thly}$, debtors in the ancient state of the Roman Republic were made slaves. If they could not pay their debt it was thought reasonable they should work for it. This still takes place in all countries where slavery is established. $5^{thly}$, there is a sort of voluntary slavery when an indigent citizen sells himself to be the slave of another person. When a person sells himself to another for any sum, by the laws of slavery this very sum becomes the property of the person who bought him. But when a person was in debt and obliged to become a slave for it, he would not 144 perhaps choose to be his creditor's slave | for fear of ill usage, and would therefore sell himself to another person, on condition that he would pay his debt. The citizens of Rome were often in debt, and by that means became entirely dependent upon their superiours. Many of them had no means of subsistance but what they received from candidates for their votes, and as this was by no means sufficient for that purpose, they often borrowed from them to whom they gave their votes, who were ready enough to lend that they might secure them entirely to their interest. By this means they could not give their vote to any other person, unless he paid what they owed to their creditors, which few would be willing to do, as for the most part they owed more than the value of their votes.

In the middle age of the Republic, these two last methods of acquiring slaves were prohibited by express laws, the first by what was called cessio bonorum, and the latter by a law prohibiting any freeman to sell himself.

The slavery in the West Indies took place contrary to law. When that country was conquered by Spain, Isabella and Ferdinand were at the greatest pains to prevent the Indians from falling into a state of servitude, 145 | their intention being to make settlements, to trade with them and to instruct them. But Columbus and Cortez were far from the law, and obeyed not their orders but reduced them to slavery, which in a manner instituted itself among them.

We come now to consider the state of servants. A Negroe in this country is a ⟨?free⟩ man.[71] If you have a Negroe servant stolen from you, you can have no action for the price, but only for damages sustained by the loss of your servant. In like manner if a Negroe is killed, the person who does it is guilty of murder. But tho a Negroe servant is intitled to the priviledges of a freeman while here, you can oblige him to return to America and keep him as formerly.[72] It is not from Christianity but from the laws of this country that he enjoys freedom, because there is no such thing as slavery among us.

The greatest dependants among us are menial servants {inter menia[73]} who are bound from one term to another. They have almost the same priviledges with their master, liberty, wages, etca. The master has a right to correct his servant moderately, and if he should die under his correction

146 it is not murther, unless it was done with an offensive weapon | or with forethought and without provocation.[74] A servant can acquire property for his master either when he acts by his express authority, or when a tacit consent is implied. If a servant buys or sells goods in his master's name, his master has room for an action in case of none payment or of non delivery. As there is a peculiar connection between master and servant, they can be vindicated in many cases where any other person would be found guilty. If either master or servant kill any other person in defence of each other, it is justifiable homicide.[75] If a master dies before the term, the executors are obliged to pay up the whole of the servant's wages, and to maintain him besides.

Apprentices are much in the same way with servants, only with this difference that the master receives a fee with the apprentice and is obliged to teach him a trade, and if he refuse to do it he may be pursued for damages and loss of time.

We come now to consider the particular state of families.

[71] This remark was probably occasioned by a judgement of Lord Chancellor Henley (later Lord Northington) in 1762 (2 Eden 126), reiterating the maxim that a man becomes free as soon as he sets foot in England. This had been affirmed by Lord Chief Justice Holt in 1706 (2 Salkeld 666), but had since been challenged (see next note).

[72] The word 'altered', written in a different ink and hand, appears in the margin at about this point. In 1729 Sir Philip Yorke, attorney-general, and Charles Talbot, solicitor-general, gave an opinion that a slave coming to the British Isles from the West Indies did not become free and could be compelled by his master to return to the plantations (reported in Morison's *Dictionary of Decisions*, 14547). The first part of this opinion was disapproved by Lord Chancellor Henley (see previous note). The second part was finally overruled by Lord Mansfield in *Sommersett's Case* in 1772 (Howell's *State Trials*, XX.1), which was followed by the Scottish Court of Session in *Knight* v. *Wedderburn* in 1778 (Morison's *Dictionary of Decisions*, 14545).

[73] Presumably *moenia*, though 'menial' is not in fact so derived.

[74] Hawkins, I.29.5.                                    [75] Hale, I.40.2.

When a father dies leaving his children young, it is necessary that they should be taken care off. Even in the times of exposition, when an infant 147 was sometime kept it was thought cruel to put him to death. | The child was destitute, there were then no hospitals or places of charity, it must therefore be put into the custody of some person. The nearest relation by the father's side was he whom the law fixed upon. In an early age the maintenance of the child was all that was to be taken care of, for there were no estates to manage, and the mother went back to her father's family. This guardianship terminated when the child was about 13 or 14 years of age, at which time it was capable in that age to shift for it self.[76]

But when men came to be possessed of estates, tho' he might be supposed capable of shifting for himself about that age, yet he could not be capable of managing an estate. Now it became necessary to retain him in pupillarity more than 14 years. By praetorian law, at that age he was allowed to choose his guardians or curators. A curator can do nothing without the consent of the pupil; a guardian can act without his consent, but is accountable to his pupil for whatever he does during his minority. At first lunatics and ideots were almost the only persons who had guardians, and on account of it's being disgracefull to have one, it was generaly declined. Afterwards the law made invalid all acts of the pupil till he was 21, without the consent 148 of his curators. As the nearest relation by the father's son[77] | is often next heir, it was reckoned improper to trust the person of the son with him. The English law carried this so far that if an estate was left to the son in ⟨?the⟩ father's lifetime he was not trusted with him. By our law the care of the estate is entrusted to the next heir, as he will probably take best care of it, and the heir to a more remote relation, who will take best care of him, as he cannot be benefited by his death.

We will now mention some offences in families with their peculiar punishments.

Infidelity of the wife to the husband is punished with the greatest ignominy. In the husband, it never was punished with death, nor in the woman unless where the greatest jealousy prevails. It would be thought ridiculous in our country to bring a woman to the scaffold for adultery.

Forcible marriages and rapes are generally punished with death.[78]

Bigamy as it dishonours the former wife is punished capitally.[79] As there is the closest connection betwixt persons in a family, if the wife kills[p] the

---

[p] The copyist wrote 'punishes' and this has been emended by a second (eighteenth-century) hand to 'kills'

---

[76] In Roman law *tutela impuberum* for boys not in the power of a paterfamilias ended at fourteen years when they became adults and had full legal capacity. Later, curators (an office first developed for insane persons and prodigals) were appointed for those over fourteen and under twenty-five years of age, who were known as minors rather than pupils.

[77] Reporter's or copyist's error for 'side'.

[78] Hawkins, I.41,42.                                    [79] 1 James I, c. 11 (1603).

husband it is considered as a sort of petty treason, and the punishment by the English law is burning alive.[80]

The same is the punishment if a servant kills his[81] master, or makes an attempt upon him.

Thus we have finished all that is to be said with regard to man considered as a member of a family.

[80] Hawkins, I.32; II.48.6.

[81] Her master, since the statement applies to a servant woman who kills (but not one who merely attempts), and not to a manservant.

149                              | *Private Law.*

We formerly explained the nature of rights and divided them into natural
and acquired. The former need no explanation; the latter are divided into
real and personal. Real rights are property, servitude, pledge, and exclusive
priviledge. We are first to treat of property.

Property is acquired five ways. 1st, by occupation, or the taking possession of what formerly belonged to no body. 2$^d$, by accession, when a man
has a right to one thing in consequence of another, as of a horse's shoes
along with the horse. 3$^d$, by prescription, which is a right to a thing belonging to another arising from long and uninterrupted possession. 4, by
succession to our ancestors or any other person, whither by a will or
without one. 5$^{th}$, by voluntary transferrence, when one man delivers over
his right to another.

We shall first treat of occupation, the laws of which vary according to the
periods of human society. The four stages of society are hunting, pasturage,
farming, and commerce. If a number of persons were shipwrecked on a
desart island their first sustenance would be from the fruits which the soil
naturaly produced, and the wild beasts which they could kill. As these
could not at all times be sufficient, they come at last to tame some of the
wild-beasts that they might always have them at hand. In process of time
even these would not be sufficient, and as they saw the earth naturally
produce considerable quantities of vegetables of it's own accord they would
150 think of cultivating it so that it might produce more of them. | Hence
agriculture, which requires a good deal of refinement before it could become
the prevailing employment of a country. There is only one exception to
this order, to witt, some North American nations cultivate a little piece of
ground, tho' they have no notion of keeping flocks. The age of commerce
naturaly succeeds that of agriculture. As men could now confine themselves to one species of labour, they would naturaly exchange the surplus
of their own commodity for that of another of which they stood in need.
According to these stages occupation must vary.

Occupation seems to be well founded when the spectator can go along
with my possession of the object, and approve me when I defend my
possession by force. If I have gathered some wild fruit it will appear
reasonable to the spectator that I should dispose of it as I please.

The first thing that requires notice in occupation among hunters is what
constitutes it and when it begins, whether it be on the discovery of the wild
beast or after it is actualy in possession. Lawyers have varied on this head;
some give a part to the person who has formerly wounded a wild beast, tho'
⟨he⟩ have given up the chace, and others do not. All agree that it is a

breach of property to break in on the chace of a wild beast which another has started, tho' some are of opinion that if another should wound the beast in it's flight he is entitled to a share, as he rendered the taking it more easy upon the whole. Among savages property begins and ends with possession, and they seem scarce to have any idea of any thing as their own which is not about their own bodies.

151     Among shepherds the idea of property is further extended. Not only what they carry about with them | but also what they have deposited in their hovels is their own. They consider their cattle as their own while they have a habit of returning to them. When the generality of beasts are occupied, they consider them as their own even after they have lost the habit of returning home, and they may be claimed for a certain time after they have strayed. But property receives its greatest extension from agriculture. When it first became necessary to cultivate the earth, no person had any property in it, and the little plot which was dressed near their hovels would be common to the whole village, and the fruits would be equally divided among the individuals. There are the remains of a common land property in our own country at this day. In many places there is a piece of ground belonging equally to several persons, and after harvest cattle are in many places allowed to feed where they please. Private property in land never begins till a division be made from common agreement, which is generally when cities begin to be built, as every one would choose that his house, which is a permanent object, should be entirely his own. Moveable property may be occupied in the very first beginings of society, but lands cannot be occupied without an actual division. An Arab or a Tartar will drive his flocks over an immense country without supposing a single grain of sand in it his own.

152     By the laws of many countries there are some things, however, that cannot be occupied by any private person. | Treasure and derelict goods by the laws of Brittain belong to the king. This arises from that natural influence of superiours which draws every thing to itself that it can without a violation of the most manifest rules of justice. In like manner seas and rivers cannot be occupied by any private person; unless particularly specified in your charter, you cannot take large fishes in a river running thro' your own estate. A sea surrounded by several nations cannot be occupied by any one, but all must have a part of the jurisdiction, but any nation may hinder another from fishing in it's bays or approaching it's coasts with vessells of war.

    The right of accession is not so much founded in it's utility as in the impropriety of not joining it to that object on which it has a dependance. The milk of a cow I have purchased may not be of great value, but it is very improper that another person should have a right to bring up his calf upon it. The most important accessions are in land property. Land property is founded on division or an assignation by the society to a particular person of a right to sow and plant a certain piece of ground. In consequence of this right he must also have a right to whatever it produces, trees, fruit, minerals, etca. Alluvians made by any river naturaly | belong to the proprietor of the adjacent territory, but when the additions are very large, as is often the case in low countries, the government claims them, and the proprietor of the adjacent estate must purchase it before he possess it.

The principal dispute concerning accession is, when does the principal belong to me and the accession to another, or if they be mixed to whom does the whole belong? It is a maxim in law that no person be a gainer by anothers loss. If a man build a house by mistake upon my ground, tho' the materials be his, it is but reasonable that I should have the house or be indemnified for my loss. In generall the accession follows the principal, tho' in some cases, as where the workmanship is of more value than the materials, *substantia cedet formae*. The lawyers were however unwilling directly to contradict their general and established maxim, and therefore evaded it by giving the principal to the proprietor of the accession when it became a new species, that is, when it received a new form and a new name. This however was liable to exceptions. A picture and the board on which it was painted were in Latin of the same species; each was a tabula, and therefore the picture by this amendment still belonged to the proprietor of an insignificant board. The most general rule with regard to accessions is this. When the thing can be reduced to it's primitive form without lessening it's value or without any great loss to the proprietor of the accession, | the proprietor of the principal may justly claim it, but when this cannot be done the law justly favours the proprietor of the accession, and obliges him only to content the original proprietor for his property.

Prescription is founded on the supposed attachment of the possessor to what he has long been possessed of, and the supposed detachment of affection in the old possessor to what has been long out of his possession. There are four things requisite to form a right by prescription. 1st, bona fides, for if a person be sensible that his right to a thing is bad it is no injury to deprive him of it, and the indifferent spectator can easily go along with the depriving him of the possession. 2$^d$, iustus titulus, by which is not meant a tittle just in all respects, for this is of itself sufficient without any thing else, but a iustus titulus signifies some reasonable foundation that the person has to think a thing his own, such as ⟨a⟩ charter of some kind. If he claims a right without any such tittle no impartial spectator can enter into his sentiments. 3$^d$, uninterrupted possession is also necessary to prescription, for if the property have often been claimed of him the former possessor has not derelinquished his right. 4$^{th}$, the time is only to be reckoned when there was a person to claim the property, and therefore the longest uninterrupted | possession when the proprietor was a minor, a lunatic, or in banishment can give no right.

A iustus titulus is a proof of bona fides, and bona fides is requisite to a iustus titulus. By the Roman law bona fides was only required at the first taking possession, and tho' afterwards you found a fault in your title prescription took place. Nature has fixed no period for prescription, and accordingly it varies according to the stability of property in a country. At Rome, ⟨im⟩moveables once prescribed in two years, but afterwards more was required. In our country a feudal lord who continualy had claims upon his neighbour could scarce be brought to admit any law of this nature. He was willing to revive a claim tho' as old as the days of Noah. And when at last they fixed on a period they made it as long as possible, to witt, forty years. Among the Romans it is to ⟨be⟩ observed that if any ones possession was interrupted during the time required for prescription by an enemy coming into the country, he had to begin a new again. By the English law nothing can interrupt prescription but a claim of the old possessor. Kings seldom ever allow their claims to prescribe, at least they account no length of uninterrupted possession sufficient to do it. However, immemorial possession will ever carry this along with it.

Succession is either legal or testamentary. By legal succession is meant that the law should distribute the goods of the deceased to those whom it is to be presumed the person himself would have chosen that they should be 156 given, | according to some lawyers. But this supposes that testamentary succession, or a distribution of the goods according to the will of the deceased, was previous to legal succession, which is contrary to experience. In a rude period a man had scarce the full property of his goods during his lifetime, and therefore it cannot be supposed that then he should have had a power to dispose of them after his death. In all nations the relations of the dead person succeeded long before there was any such thing as a testament. The Twelve Tables at Rome, and the laws of Solon at Athens, seem first to have introduced testamentary succession, but long before this there was legal succession in both countries. The claim of the heir of blood is always thought the preferable one, but this claim is never founded on the presumed will of the deceased. If we consider succession in the earlyest times we shall find that it is more founded on the connection of goods than of persons. As the father and sons lived together and were joint acquirers of any property they had, when the father died the children had a joint right to the goods not so much on account of their relation to the father as on account of the labour they had bestowed on acquiring them. The mother and the children would therefore continue in possession. Among the Romans the wife was considered as a daughter and had her share accordingly. If any of the children were settled out of the family or were emancipated, they had no share in the succession, because they ceased to co-157 operate with the rest in acquiring the goods. | It may be observed that when families in this manner lived together it was necessary to prohibit marriages of cousins. When wives, sons, and grandsons lived in the same house, if all succeeded equally it was called succession secundum capita, but if the grandsons succeeded only to his father's part it was secundum stirpes. If a man had three sons who were all dead, but the oldest had left behind him one son, the second two, and ⟨the⟩ third three, by the former rule on the death of their grandfather each would have a sixth, but by the latter the son of the oldest would have a third alone, the two sons of the second a third between them, and the three sons of the third a third among them. The grandsons were as it were the representatives of their father. The right of representation is the same with the successio secundum stirpes. Among the Romans the right of representation was introduced in favour of the strong and in prejudice of the weak, but in Brittain is the contrary.[82] Among the Romans a son could not succeed to the mother when she died, because as she was considered as a daughter of the family every thing she had belonged to the husband; if the husband died first, the wife shared with her children and then went home to her father's house and succeeded anew to her father. But in times of more refinement under the emperors, the mother could succeed to the son and the son to the mother. Anciently when a son died no person succeeded to him because he and every thing he had belonged to his father. Caesar first made a law that a son might possess as his own | whatever he got in war, or acquired by the liberal arts.

158

Three classes of men may succeed, ascendants, descendants, and collaterals, as these in an upper line may succeed to those in a lower, these in a lower to those in an upper line, or those of the same line to one another. Collateral succession at first extended only to the nearest in blood, and if he refused it the goods belonged to the public,[83] but afterwards the praetor extended it to the seventh in blood.[84] When a brother died and another succeeded, it was in consequence of their connection with the father, who is the common stock, and therefore succession of ascendants must have been prior to that of collaterals. But the right of descendants is stronger than either of these, because the son's claim on the father is evidently more strong than that of the father on the son. The principles of succession then in moveables are founded on the community of goods which took place anciently in families.

The different state of families in our country makes a considerable difference betwixt our law and that of the Romans. The wife is among us a much more considerable person than a daughter and accordingly succeeds to more. When the husband dies, the goods are supposed to be divided into three equal parts, one of which is supposed to belong to the

---

[82] The meaning of this sentence will be clearer if a comparison is made with the corresponding passage in LJ(A) i.98, above.
[83] To the gens, or members of the deceased's clan: Twelve Tables, V.5.
[84] Heineccius, III.5.5.

deceased husband, one to the wife and one to the children; there is however this difference, that the husband can dispose of his part by testament which the wife cannot. A forisfamiliated son is not in the same condition with an emancipated son among the Romans. He can succeed with his brothers.

159 Only if he has got | a portion, he must bring it into the common stock at his father's death. Grand children do not succeed in place of their deceased father as among the Romans. The English law however admits of representation, and it preferrs ascendants if males to collaterals.

We come now to treat of indivisable inheritance, which was introduced by the feudal law. When the nations that conquered the Roman Empire settled in the west of Europe an inequality of fortune necessarily ensued. As the great had no way of spending their fortunes but by hospitality, they necessarily acquired prodigious influence over their vassals. They gave out their lands merely as a maintenance to their dependants, and it is observable that the Saxon-word farm signifies victuals. The chieftans from their influence were the sole administrators of justice in their own territories. It was the interest of government to authorize this jurisdiction as it was the only method of preserving peace, and as the superiour was the leader both in peace and war. So lately as in the year 1745 this power remained in the Highlands of Scotland, and some gentlemen could bring several hundereds of men into the field. As these lords had no other way to dispose of their lands, they gave some of them as munera, which were revocable at their pleasure, and others they gave as beneficia, which continued during life and returned to the lord after their decease.

160 The benefices of the clergy seem to have been | on this foundation and have retained the name. By this means the lords secured the fidelity of their vassals. As benefices were for life the property of them naturaly came to be extended to the son of the deceased tenant, and by degrees the tenures became hereditary and were called feudal. Thus the tenant became more independant. When any chieftan died and left his son a minor, the king appointed a leader to the vassals during the minority, and appropriated the profits and emoluments arising from the lands to his own use. When a female succeeded, the lord had the power of disposing of her in marriage, as it was reasonable that he should name the husband who was to be his own vassal. As the lord was guardian of the heir male, it was also thought unreasonable that he should marry without his consent. As the feudal lord possessed the lands during a minority, before the minor could recover his estate he was obliged to pay what is called a relief. This was introduced by the court of the king or lord, before which the minor was obliged to swear fealty before he could recover his estate. He was also obliged to promise homage to his superiour before he could enter on possession. Thus they held their lands of the superiour for military service, homage, fealty, wardship, marriage, relief, etca. Allodial estates were free from all such

services, but as it was for security of property to hold of some great man
161 | who could protect the proprietor from violence, the generality of estates
became feudal. For the same reason men possessed of great estates paid
feu and swore fealty to the sovereign.

It appears from this that it must have been a very difficult matter to
secure property, especially if it was small, in those early times, and therefore nothing could have a worse consequence than the division of estates.
The consequences of dividing the kingdom of France were sufficiently
experienced, and the case would have been still worse in private estates.
However, on account of the opposition from the rest of the sons it was long
before the right of primogeniture or the indivisibility of estates could be
introduced, and in Germany it did not fully take place before the last
century. But as the circumstances necessarily required it, estates were at
last made indivisible, and since a single person was to be preferred the
oldest son would naturaly be the person. This legal preference must be
given for some quality that is altogether indisputable. If it were to be
given to wisdom or valour there might be great disputes, but among
brothers there can be no*q* contest who is the oldest. In the beginings of
society age itself is very much respected, and to this day among the Tartars
the king is not succeeded by his son, but by that one of the royal family
who is oldest.

162 | Primogeniture when introduced would naturaly occasion succession by
representation, for the following reason. The younger brothers at first
would think it hard that their older brother should be preferr'd to them,
and if he died they would still think it harder that his son, an infant, should
come in before them. Accordingly in many places this has been disputed
in single combat. Bruce and Baliol disputed on this account. According to
our notions Baliol had the best right for he was descended from the oldest
daughter, tho' Bruce was a step nearer the common stock. The difficulty of
introducing this at first gave rise to a new species of succession, by which
when a father died his estate went to his eldest son, but if he died while his
children were minors, or if he died while his father was alive, his brother,
not his son's, succeeded. This was attended with one inconvenience, that on
the death of the youngest his sons were preferred to those of the other
brothers. By the Roman law a grandson succeeded only to his father's part;
he might succeed as a son but not as an oldest son. The brothers naturaly
thought that they were nearer the father than any grandson he could have,
but as this was a hardship to the brother's claim so it was also a hardship to
cut of*r* the reasonable expectation which the grandson had if his father
had lived. This last circumstance after gave occasion to lineal succession.

163 | When this difficulty is got over there is little dispute about collateral
succession. In feudal lordships a woman could not succeed, as she was

*q* Inserted by a second (eighteenth-century) hand      *r* *Sic*

incapable of performing military services, but they could succeed to lands where there was required any other kind of service.

Of fiefs there are two kinds, masculine and feminine. France, to the crown of which no woman can succeed, is an instance of the former, and England of the latter.

There are some niceties whimsical enough in the Scotch law with regard to succession of collatorals.[85] If the second brother has an estate and dies it goes to the third and not to the oldest, who is supposed to have been sufficiently provided for. Conquest on the contrary ascends, but it does not go to the oldest but to the immediately older brother. By the English law the old brother excludes the whole blood from one half of the estate by conquest, in other countries the preference is not so great.

We must observe that the right of primogeniture hinders agriculture. If the whole estate were divided among the sons, each one would improve his own part better than one can improve the whole. Besides, tenants never cultivate a farm so well as if it were their own property. Primogeniture is
164 also hurtfull to the family, for while it provides for one | it suffers all the rest in a few generations to be reduced to beggary. In succession to a monarchy, however, it has one evident advantage, that it prevents all dangerous rivalships among the brothers.

There are some other kinds of succession that take place, or have taken place in several countries. Thus in some countries the youngest son succeeds to the father. There is something like this among our tenants to this day; the older sons as they grow up are provided for, and the youngest remaining with the father succeeds to him.

So much for legal succession. We come next to testamentary. It is to be observed that there is no extension of property so great as this, and therefore it was long before it could be introduced; it was very natural to give a man a right to dispose of his property while he lived, but a testament supposes him to dispose of a right when properly speaking he can have none himself. He cannot be said to transferr his right, for the heir has no right in consequence of the testament till after the testator himself have none. Puffendorf whimsicaly accounts for this from the immortality of the soul. At Rome the right of making testaments was introduced gradually. At first it was only allowed, and that too after the consent of the fellow citizens was asked and obtained, to childless people. This was much the same with
165 adopting children. | When a person died and wanted to leave his estate to a son in exile, he would naturaly request his neighbours not to take it from him after his own death. This request would be regarded, not so much on account of its being his will as from a kind of piety for the dead. We naturaly find a pleasure in remembering the last words of a friend and in executing his last injunctions. The solemnity of the occasion deeply impresses the

[85] Stair, III.4.33. Conquest was land acquired otherwise than by inheritance.

mind. Besides, we enter as it were into his dead body, and conceive what our living souls would feel if they were joined with his body,[86] and how much we would be distressed to see our last injunctions not performed. Such sentiments naturaly enclined men to extend property a little farther than a man's lifetime.

This seems to have been the foundation of testamentary succession. It was a sort of impiety not to comply with the father's desire, tho' it was no injury to deprive the heir of the estate as there was no law established in his favour, and as his being in exile cut off all reasonable expectation of succeeding. The injury is conceived to be done to the dead person, as we enter into what would be his sentiments were he to live again.

It is to be observed that this practice is a considerable refinement in
166 humanity, and never was practised in a rude nation. | Before the Twelve Tables no Roman had a right to make a will. Our Saxon ancestors had no right to dispose of their lands by testament, and in the history of the Old Testament we hear of no such practice. Piety for the dead could take place only with regard to the immediate successor, and therefore at first the right of making testaments extended no further, unless in case the person in whose favour it was made should refuse to succeed, in which case another might be appointed. This was a further extent of the right. Again, if a man died and left his sisters son heir to him, that the estate might not go to forreign relations the testator was allowed to say that if the pupil die at a certain age the estate shall go to such another person. This was called popular succession.[87] Thus property was still further extended.

The greatest of all extensions of property is that by entails. To give a man power over his property after his death is very considerable, but it is nothing to an extension of this power to the end of the world. In the beginings of society the state of families is very different from what it is at present. As the wife was subject to the husband, and at the best only on the footing of a daughter, she seldom made any addition to the husband's estate unless by her own industry. But when female succession took place,
167 and woemen came to be possessed of fortunes, | they would not marry without a previous capitulation by which they insured themselves of good usage, and stipulated that some part of their fortune should go to their relations after their death. By this arose a new species of marriage from agreement which rendered the parties equally independant. This great alteration in domestic affairs would naturally at first be complained off, and as the ultimate cause of it was the succession of females they would endeavour to prevent their opulence. On this account a law was made at

---

[86] Cf. TMS I.i.i.13: our imagined idea of the feelings of the dead arises 'from our lodging, if I may be allowed to say so, our own living souls in their inanimated bodies'.

[87] Pupillary substitution: cf. LJ(A) i.154, above.

Rome bringing matters to their ancient footing, called the Vaccinianˢ law. To elude this law a fide⟨i⟩ com⟨m⟩issum was invented, by which, when a man had a mind to leave his estate to a person whom the law would not allow, ⟨?he left it to another person⟩ and took his solemn promise that he would transferr it to the person for whom he intended it. Augustus made a law obliging the trustee always to restore it, and appointed a fide⟨i⟩ commissaryᵗ praetor for that purpose. The person for[88] whom the estate was left was called haeres fiduciarius, and the person to whom it was to be restored was called fide⟨i⟩ commissarius. Thus property was extended beyond the first successor, and when this step was gained they easily advanced further and introduced entails.

Entails were first introduced into the modern law by the ecclesiastics, whose education made them acquainted with the Roman customs. As they were the preachers of this doctrine they naturaly became the explainers and executors of wills, till Theodosius Valentinus[89] took it from them. | In England William the Conqueror restored it to the ecclesiastics.

168

By the customs of our country a man if he leave a wife and children can dispose only of a third by testament, and if he leave a wife without children only a half. Lands after the introduction of the feudal system could only be disposed ⟨of⟩ by testament in the same way with military services, by the consent of the superiour. Originally in England there were no entails by will but by tenure. A man held an estate for himself and his heirs, but if he had no heirs he could not alienate it, it returned to the superiour. But if he had heirs he could alienate it, and thus the lord was deprived of his right of reversion. A law was afterwards made to secure this.

Upon the whole nothing can be more absurd than perpetual entails. In them the principals of testamentary succession can by no means take place. Piety to the dead can only take place when their memory is fresh in the minds of men. A power to dispose of estates for ever is manifestly absurd. The earth and the fulness of it belongs to every generation, and the preceeding one can have no right to bind it up from posterity. Such extension of property is quite unnatural. The insensible progress of entails was owing to their not knowing | how far the right of the dead might extend, if they had any at all. The utmost extent of entails should be to those who are alive at the person's death, for he can have no affection to those who are unborn.

169

---

ˢ Emended in pencil by a later hand to 'Voconian'      ᵗ The copyist wrote 'commissary'; 'fide' has been added in the margin by another hand

---

[88] Reporter's or copyist's error for 'to'.

[89] No doubt Theodosius and Valentinian, emperors respectively of the eastern and western Roman Empire in the early fifth century, are intended. But if the reference is to the ruling of the Fourth Council of Carthage in 398 (cf. p. 68 above), that was in the reign of their predecessors, Arcadius and Honorius.

Entails are dissadvantageous to the improvement of the country, and these lands where they have never taken place are always best cultivated. Heirs of entailed estates have it not in their view to cultivate lands and often they are not able to do it. A man who buys land has this entirely in view and in general the new purchase⟨r⟩s are the best cultivaters.

In voluntary transferrance two things are required:

1st, a declaration of the intention both of the person who transferrs and of him to whom it is transferr'd.

2$^d$, the actual delivery of the thing.

In most cases the first of these is not binding without the latter because there is no right without possession. If a man indeed have borrowed a thing and afterwards purchase it there is no need of delivery, for it is already in his possession. Before possession you can have no right to the thing, tho' you may have a right to make the man keep his promise or contract. If I buy a horse from a man and before delivery he sell him to a third person, I cannot demand the horse from the possessor but only from the person who sold him. | But if he has been delivered I can claim him from any person. Property therefore cannot be transferred without tradition or delivery. Grotius indeed justly observes that in the transferrance of a pledge there is no need of delivery, because in this case the thing is already in the man's possession. In France, if a man declare his purpose to make a donation, and die before delivery, the donation goes to the heir. This was also a custom among the Wisigoths.

In transferring the property of lands and other large objects, what gives possession is not so easy to determine. As there cannot be an actual delivery, in our country a symbolical delivery is used. An ear or sheaf of corn signifies the whole field, a stone and turf the estate to the center of the earth, and the keys of the door, the house. By the Scotch law if there be a transferrance of several estates the purchaser must be infeft in each; by the English law infeftment in one serves for all when done in presence of the county court. In Scotland it must be done on the land; it is enough in England if it be done in view of it. Besides delivery, a charter or writing shewing on what terms the transferrence was made is also requisite for security. Till the custom was abolished by a late statute, no vassal or possessor had a right of alienating his estate without the consent | of the superiour, as he held it for military service. It was requisite that the estate should be resigned to the superiour, who resigned it to the purchaser, as it was proper that his vassal should be of his own chusing. Afterwards however it became necessary to accept of creditors, and this was often used as a handle to elude the law. The seller gave a bond for a sum of borrowed money without any mention that it was a sale, by which means the lands were adjudged to the creditor, and the lord was obliged to accept of him as his vassal. In like manner, as the tenant was liable to oppression from a new superiour the lord could not dispose of his estate without consent of his vassal. If therefore either of them alienated any part of their estates without the others consent his right was forfeited.

The duty of vassals to their lords continued [in] longer in Scotland than in England, which may be accounted for from the difference of their government, for that ⟨of⟩ England all along favoured democracey, and that of Scotland aristocracey. After society was fully established there was no occasion for mutual consent, because the tenant was protected by law, whatever the lord was.

In the time of the civil wars a new sort of delivery took place. When a person transferred his estate to another for his own use it was not affected by forfeiture. The person to whom it was transferred was considered as the bailliff, and took possession in the others name.

172 | The second species of real rights is servitudes, or burthens which one man has on the property of another. These rights were at first personal, as they were entered into by a contract between the persons. It is necessary that I should have a road to the market town. If a man's estate lye between me and it, I must bargain with him for the priviledge of a road thro' it. This contract produces only a personal right, tho' I should bind him not to sell this estate without the burthen. But here was an inconveniencey, for if the land were sold and the new proprietor refused the road, I could not sue him on a personal right upon the former proprietor. Before I can come at the new purchaser I must pursue the person from whom I had the right, who must pursue him to whom he sold it. If the land has gone thro' several hands this is very tedious and inconvenient. The law, to remedy this, made servitudes real rights, demandable a quocumque possessore. Servitudes were rusticae, such as the right of a road to the town, or to the river, and of feeding so many cows on another man's pasture grounds; or urbanae, such as the right of leaning the beams of my house on your gabel, the right of obliging him who is proprietor of the under story to make his wall strong enough to support mine, and the like. These are all naturaly personal rights and are only made real by lawyers. Life rents on estates and many other things are also servitudes, and are properly personal. Feudal burthens

173 were only persons rights | and therefore every new vassal must renew his homage and the promise of fealty.

In the begining of the feudal law, if the proprietor did not perform his duty in every article he forfeited his feu. In like manner, if the tenant encroached on his lord's grounds what he had feued returned to the superiour. The right of the vassal is founded on the charter of the superiour, and every article of it must be fullfilled, and every new possessor must renew the obligation. When tenants became independant and had a real property they were said to have the dominium directum, not the dominium utile.[90]

90 *Directum* and *utile* should be transposed.

Pledges and mortgages are certain securities for the payment of debts. At first they could not be claimed as real rights, tho' afterwards the law considered them as such. Pledges properly regard moveable subjects and mortgages immoveable. If a pledge be not redeemed at a certain time it is forfeited. As people in bad circumstances are naturaly slothfull, the negligence of debtors among the Romans gave occasion to the Lex Com⟨m⟩issaria by which the creditor was impowered to seize the pledge and return the overplus if there was any. By the English law, if no day be named the pledge falls to the pawntaker on the death of the pawner.[91] In immoveables lands are mortgaged but not delivered, and in case of failure they are forfeited. The Roman law and ours are much the same on this head. If payment be not made within some few months after demand, the creditor adjudges the land for the whole sum and the penalty incurred, but his property is not secure without long possession, for the proprietor has a
174 power of redeeming it | within a reasonable time. But as upon redemption much trouble must be occasioned in examining old accompts and the like, the law has made 20 years the stated time in England for redeeming mortgages.

Hypothecs are another kind of pledges realy arising from contract, but made real rights by the civil law. By them anciently the landlord was impowered to detain the furniture and whole stock of the tenant if he turned bankrupt, and could claim them a quocumque possessore. This arose from the practice of keeping tenants by steelbow, by which the whole stock in the farm was the landlords. At present the landlord has only a right of preference, and we have not so many hypothecs as the Romans had. All pledges are naturally personal rights, and are only made real by the civil law.

Exclusive priviledges are the last division of real rights. Among these is the right of inheritance, which is not a creature of the civil law but arises from nature. The heir, previous to any other person, has a priviledge of demanding what belonged to the deceased, and after he is admitted heir it is his real property. Again, if a person start a wild beast he has an exclusive priviledge of pursuing, and whatever person comes in upon the chace is liable to punishment not ⟨?for breach of property but⟩ because he breaks in upon his exclusive priviledge.[92] In the year 1701 an English man-of-war engaged with a French merchant fleet under convoy which was just about to fall into their hands, when a Scotch privateer came and carried off the prize. A lawsuit commenced and the Scotch privateer was declared guilty
175 of breach of property. | But upon strict inquiry we shall find that it was only breach of privilege.

Tho' these and some other exclusive priviledges arise from nature, they

[91] M. Bacon, *New Abridgement of the Law*, s.v. Bailment, I.239.
[92] Cf. LJ(A) i.28–9, above.

are generaly the creatures of the civil law. Such are monopolies and all priviledges of corporations, which tho' they might once be conducive to the interest of the country are now prejudicial to it. The riches of a country consist in the plenty and cheapness of provisions, but their effect is to make every thing dear. When a number of butchers have the sole priviledge of selling meat, they may agree to make the price what they please, and we must buy from them whether it be good or bad. Even this priviledge is not of advantage to the butchers themselves, because the other trades are also formed into corporations, and if they sell beef dear they must buy bread dear. But the great loss is to the public, to whom all things are rendered less comeatible, and all sorts of work worse done. Towns are not well inhabited and the suburbs are encreased. The priviledge however of vending a new book or a new machine for 14 years has not so bad a tendencey. It is a proper and adequate reward for merit. A right to servitudes and exclusive priviledges, it is to be observed, may be acquired by prescription.

So much for the different kinds of real rights. We proceed now to personal rights, which arise either from contract, quasicontract, or delinquencey.

### Of Contract

That obligation to performance which arises from contract is founded on the reasonable expectation produced by a promise, which considerably 176 differs from a mere declaration of intention. | Tho' I say I have a mind to do such a thing for you, yet on account of some occurrences do not do it, I am not guilty of breach of promise. A promise is a declaration of your desire that the person for whom you promise should depend on you for the performance of it. Of consequence the promise produces an obligation, and the breach of it is an injury.

Breach of contract is naturaly the slightest of all injuries because we naturaly depend more on what we possess than what is in the hands of others. A man robbed of five pounds thinks himself much more injured than if he had lost five pounds by a contract. Accordingly in rude ages crimes of all kinds, except those that disturb the public peace, are slightly punished, and society is far advanced before a contract can sustain action or the [or the] breach of it be redressed. The causes of this were the little importance of contracts in these times, and the uncertainty of language.

The first contracts that sustained action would be those where the damage done was very great, and where there could be no doubt but the person once intended to perform. Accordingly among the ancients promises entered into with great solemnity first sustained action. Among them no stipulation could be made unless the contractors were personaly present, and no promissary note in writing was binding.

As no promises by the Roman law sustained action without a stipulation, so by the English a consideration or cause for the promise was at first 177 necessary to make it obligatory. | It was thought contrary to good manners to insist on a promise. If a man promised with his daughter a certain sum, there is a consideration and therefore he was obliged to perform it. But if he promised it with any other man's daughter it was sine causa, and unless she was a relation could not sustain action. If I made you a promise it did not sustain action, but if I again promised not to forget my former promise, the latter promise was obligatory, and the former was the consideration that made it so.[93]

By the civil law the first promises that sustained action were those entered into in presence of a court where there could be no doubt of the intention, and accordingly recognizance of every promise was taken before some court. A recognizance is when the debtor comes before a court with the creditor, and acknowledges that he owes him a certain sum; a copy of this acknowledgement was given to the creditor and another lodged in the hands of the clerk, and whenever the creditor produced this, if it was found to correspond to the other, he might pursue for his money. Afterwards a recognizance before the magistrate of a staple town served the purpose.[94]

The next contracts that sustained action were the contractus reales, or those which were entered into by the delivery of a thing to be returned itself, or in species, or in value. These are of four kinds, the mutuum, commodatum, depositum, and pignus.

The mutuum is when I lend any thing to be returned in value, as money. This soon sustained action.

178    | Commodatum is when the thing itself is to be restored, as a borrowed horse.

Depositum is when a thing is committed to anothers care, but not to his use.

Pignus is a security for debt.

All these sustained action before the consensual[u] contracts, which are also four, to witt, buying and selling, letting and hireing, partnership, and commission. In buying, if the contract be not fullfilled you lose your earnest money. Letting and hireing once comprehended leases, days wages, building, and almost every thing with regard to society. If the contract of commission was performed gratuitously it could not at first sustain any action. But if a reward was given it was nearly the same with the commodatum.

[u] Originally 'consential' and emended by a second (eighteenth-century) hand to 'consensual'

---

[93] Never quite English law, although attempts were being made to modify the doctrine of consideration in this direction before it was reasserted in *Rann* v. *Hughes* (1778), 7 T.R. 30n.
[94] M. Bacon, *New Abridgement of the Law*, s.v. Execution, II.330–2.

If a small price be paid for the loan of a thing it becomes letting and hireing. The mutuum does not inferr interest, and in a bond unless the interest be specified it will carry none.

Besides these there was in the Roman law what was called a pactum nudum, when there was a bare promise without any consideration, which produced an exception or defence against the action of the pursuer. As contracts deprive men of that liberty which every man wishes to enjoy, a very small defence sett them free. Originally no[95] contracts were sued before any court but the ecclesiastic, but they came gradually to civil courts. The common[96] law, which judged from principles of honour and

179 virtue, | obliged men to perform even these promises that were made gratuitously. This was imitated by the civil law, and by our law if a promise be clearly proven he who promises must perform it. In general the law gave only action for damages till the Court of Chancery was introduced. It is indeed the natural idea of ⟨a⟩ court to redress injuries, and accordingly if a person refused to perform his contract he was only obliged to pay the loss which the other had sustained. But the Court of Chancery forced the person to a performance of the agreement.

Nothing can be more different than the present and ancient state of contracts. Execrations and the most solemn ceremonies were scarce thought sufficient to secure the performance of a contract; drinking blood and water mixed, bleeding one another, promising before the altar, breaking a straw, and a number of other ceremonies to impress the mind, were invented; at present almost any thing will make a contract obligatory.

There are some questions concerning contracts much agitated by lawyers, especially one in the case when the coin happens to be debased. ⟨?If⟩ I borrow £100 when the coin is 4 oz. the pound, and it be afterwards debased to 2 oz., whether should I pay £100 of the new coin or 200£. When the government makes any alteration in the coin it is to answer some urgent necessity. In 1703[97] the crown of France had a demand for 10 million and

180 could raise only five. They cried up the coin and paid the 10 with five. | As the government allows private persons to pay with the new coin, the injury is not great. The debasement of the coin cheapens for sometime all commodities and provisions, as all are paid in the new coin, and therefore the uses of money may be served by the new as well as the old coin.

Quasi contract is founded on the duty of restitution. If you find a watch on the way, you are obliged to restore it by the right of property, because a man loses not property with possession. But if you and I balance accompts, and you pay me a sum which both think due, but you afterwards find you

---

[95] This is an exaggeration.

[96] Reporter's or copyist's error for 'canon'.

[97] The last digit is not clear and might be '5'. The date is given as 1701 in the corresponding passage in LJ(A) ii.81, above, but it seems likely (as there noted) that the reference is in fact to the recoinage of 1709.

did not owe that sum, how will you claim it? You cannot ask it as your property, for you alienated that sum, nor can you claim it by contract, for there never was one made between us, yet it is evident that I am a gainer by your loss and therefore restitution is due.

In the same manner if a man was called away by a sudden order of the state without leaving an attorney to manage a law suit that he had going on, and a friend undertakes this office without commission, as the defence is necessary and the undertaking it prudent, restitution of his expences are due. On the same principle were founded the actiones contrariae of the Roman law. If you lent me a horse which had cost me extraordinary expences, by the contract commodate you could redemand your horse in

181 the same ⟨?condition⟩ in which you lent him, but I could claim | my extraordinary expences by an actio contraria.

The same principle takes place in many other cases. If a person borrows money and gets three of his acquaintances sureties for him jointly and severally, and if he turn bankrupt, the creditor pursues the ablest surety, who has a claim by the duty of restitution on the other two for their thirds. The Scotch law carries this still farther.[98] If a bankrupt had two estates, and two creditors *A* and *B*. *A* has a security on both estates, *B* has security only on the best. *A* has a liberty of drawing his money from either estate he pleases, and draws from that on which *B* has his security. As *B* in this case is cut out, the law obliges *A* to give up his security on the other estate to *B*. The same was the case in the Roman-law with regard to tutory.

We come now to the third kind of personal rights, those, to witt, ex delicto.

Delicts are of two kinds, as they arise ex dolo when there is a blameable intention, or ex culpa when they are done thro' a culpable negligence.

Injury naturaly excites the resentment of the spectator, and the punishment of the offender is reasonable as far as the indifferent spectator can go along with it. This is the natural measure of punishment. It is to be observed that our first approbation of punishment is not founded upon the

182 regard | to public utility which is commonly taken to be the foundation of it. It is our sympathy with the resentment of the sufferer which is the real principle. That it cannot be utility is manifest from the following example. Wool in England was conceived to be the source of public opulence, and it was made a capital crime to export that commodity. Yet tho' wool was exported as formerly and men were convinced that the practice was pernicious, no jury, no evidence, could be got against the offenders. The exportation of wool is naturaly no crime, and men could not be brought to consider it as punishable with death. In the same manner if a centinel be

---

[98] Kames, *Essays upon Several Subjects in Law* (1732), II ('*Beneficium cedendarum actionum*'); Kames, *Principles of Equity* (1760), I.1.2.1; Erskine, II.12.29.

put to death for leaving his post, tho' the punishment be just and the injury that might have ensued be very great, yet mankind can never enter into this punishment as if he had been a thief or a robber.

Resentment not only prompts to punishment but points out the manner of it. Our resentment is not gratified unless the offender be punished for the particular offence done ourselves, and unless he be made sensible that it is for that action. A crime is always the violation of some right, natural or acquired, real or personal. The non performance of a contract indeed is not a crime, unless it be thro' some fraudulent intention.

183    The greatest crime that can be done against any person | is murther, of which the natural punishment is death, not as a compensation but a reasonable retaliation. In every civilized nation death has been the punishment of the murther⟨er⟩, but in barbarous nations a pecuniary compensation was accepted of, because then government was weak and durst not meddle in the quarrells of individuals unless in the way of mediation. In the age of hunters particularly, there was little more than the name of authority, and a man of superiour influence can do no more than perswade the parties to an agreement. When one man killed another the whole society met and advised the one party to give and the other to take a compensation. In America when one member of a family kills another the society does not intermeddle with them, as this cannot hurt the peace of the society. They only take notice of it when one family attacks another. It was long before the government could call a man before them and tell him what he must do, because it was long before people would submitt to such absolute authority. In the laws of all nations we have the remains of this ancient state of weakness.

When government became more powerfull, the murtherer was not only
184  obliged to make a compensation to the relations of the slain, | but likewise to the publick, who were put to the trouble of lending him their protection on that occasion, against the revenge of those who were concerned. This was the state of criminal law among the Germans at the declension of the Roman Empire.

The Germans were much farther advanced than the Americans at this day. Tho' they seldom punished with death yet they seemed to make the punishment in some measure proportioned to the crime. A price was sett on every person according to his station. There was one price paid for killing the king, and another for killing a slave. The compensation was proportioned to the dignity of the person and of his relations. What was paid to the prince for interposition was increased and diminished in the same proportion. It was a higher fine to kill a man belonging to a lord than one belonging to a little baron. To disturb the kings peace subjected to [to] a greater fine than to disturb the peace of a baron or lord. If the injurer refused to pay the compensation he was left to the resentment of the injured, and if

he was not able to pay it he was obliged to implore the assistance of his friends. As the compensation was not adequate to the offence, the government after it acquired strength took this additional compensation to itself, as the price of the offenders freedom. From this the sovereign acquired the
185 right of pardoning criminals, | for naturaly he has no more right to pardon a crime than to discharge an unpaid debt.

Anciently a crime was considered in two lights, as committed against the family injured and against the peace. The government had the exclusive right of punishing those who had disturbed the peace and killed any of the kings vassals. The compensation to the government was afterwards changed into a capital punishment. After the king's pardon the offender was free, and the relation had no right to pursue him. In England the offender can be punished for the relation as well as for the king. When an appeal is made to the king he cannot pardon. But appeals are seldom or never used, as it is difficult to bring them about. If a man was murthered no body but the wife could pursue for an appeal, or if she was accessory, the legal heir. Any mistake in the process, such as a word wrong spelled, stopped the procedure, for the statute of amendment, which permitted courts to overlook errors, did not extend to appeals. Appeals in former times were often made in cases of maiming, hurting, etca.

There are several kinds of murther by the English law. The word originaly signified stealth as the crime was usually committed in private. Afterwards
186 felony and[99] killing of every kind was called murther and | compensation made for it accordingly. Murther arises either from malice propense, or from sudden provocation, or from chance per infortunium. Of these the first alone is properly called murther. The second is manslaughter, and the last chance medley, which is often excusable and often justifiable. Murther committed se defendendo is when two persons quarrel, and the one is obliged to kill the other for his own safety. This is excusable, not justifiable homicide. Justifiable homicide is of two kinds. 1st. In defence ⟨of⟩ one's person, goods, or house. It differs from homicide se defendendo in this, that there is no quarrel, but an attack on the highway or in a man's own house. $2^d$. Homicide is justifiable in support of a constable or officer of justice.

These are the different species of murther and homicide; we shall next shew what is the nature of each. When a person lyes in wait for another and kills him it is plainly murther. It is the same when a man kills another without provocation. By the English law there is no provocation without a blow, no words or menaces are sufficient. However, if a man give you a blow and you return it and kill him it is not murther but manslaughter.
187 If a man be shooting at tame fowl or doing any other criminal action | and without intending it kill a man, it is murther. Wherever there is any

---

[99] The last two words are perhaps a copyist's error for 'felonious'.

appearance of malice or forethought, it is murther. If a person kills another in the afternoon for some provocation received in the forenoon, it is murther. But if he has only retired a few steps and returned to do it immediately, it is not murther but manslaughter. Homicide se defendendo is not punishable if there was no possibility of escape, but if a man had time to retire and draw his sword it is punishable because he might have escaped. The Scotch law makes no distinction between manslaughter and murther. In England manslaughter was introduced by what is called benefit of clergy. When civil government encreased in authority, the punishments of crimes were made more severe that the peace might be less disturbed. The clergy pled that this was not agreable to the word of God, and as they derived their authority from Jesus Christ and the Pope they would answer before no civil judicatory. They pretended that the scripture did not consider any crime where there was no malice or forethought as murther, and this they proved from Deuteronomy XIX^{th}. When any ⟨?such⟩ person therefore had committed a crime, the bishop had a power to claim him and take him out of the hands of the secular power. If a person could get 12 persons to swear for him he was acquitted; if not, the bishop judged whither

188   he was corrigible or not. | If he was incorrigible he was degraded. The bishop could claim in this manner all clergy and beadles, wardens, or other persons who had any connection with the church. But the civil courts after allowed him only to claim those that could read, as this was^{v} more immediately connected with the office of the clergy. Queen Ann afterwards extended the priviledges aris[is]ing from benefit of clergy with regard to manslaughter to all equally.

For chance medley a man forfeits his goods, but he has the power of suing for them again and of obtaining pardon. In justifiable homicide a man must plead not guilty of any thing the court can meddle ⟨with⟩, and if he can bring in his evidence he is not arraigned.

Our resentment naturaly falls upon inanimate as well as animate objects, and in many places the sword or instrument that had killed any person was considered as excrable, and accordingly was destroyed, particularly among the Athenians.

By the English law if a man fell from a house[1] and was killed, the house[1] was forfeited by the law of deodand. Deodand signifies to be given to the devil, by the same sort of metaphor that the scripture uses where it is said he blessed God in his heart, that is, he cursed him. Afterwards the clergy applied deodands to charitable uses. If a man was killed by an object at rest, only the part by which he was killed was forfeited. If he was killed

---

^{v} Inserted by a second (eighteenth-century) hand

---

[1] Probably copyist's error for 'horse'. Cf. LJ(A) ii.120, above.

⟨?falling⟩ from the wheel of a waggon standing, only that wheel was deodand, but if the waggon was in motion the whole team was forfeited. It was long questioned if a ship was forfeited by a man being killed in it 189 |but as mariners are so much exposed it was thought hard that it should.

A person may also be injured in his body by demembration, mutilation, assault and battery, or restraint on his liberty. Maiming and mutilation originaly by the Roman law were compensated for in the same way with murther, and if the person was incapable with the assistance of his friends to pay the compensation he was given over to the person maimed, to be maimed in the same manner, as we are acquainted by the Salic law which gives us the form of their procedure. In the same manner all hurts among many nations, particularly among the Lombards, were compounded for; they paid so much for a tooth, so much more if it was a foretooth, so much for two teeth, but, what is very remarkable, tho' twenty were knocked out the injured person could claim no more than the price of three. They had a precise sum for every member of the body. Among the Romans, if a man could not pay his composition, he was obliged to make satisfaction by the law of retaliation; he received as many blows as he gave. An eye went for an eye, and a tooth for a tooth. This custom continued long, and is in general reasonable, but in some cases it is not proper. If a man got his arm broken in wrestling, it was hard that anothers should be broken for it in cold blood. In some cases it was impracticable, as when a man causes an abortion in a woman, he could not be punished in the same manner. This custom by 190 degrees went out, and pecuniary fines | according to the circumstances of him who was to pay them were introduced, and the praetor at Rome caused them to be received, but in some countries it continued longer and there are remains of it in Holland to this day. When a person was maimed in any member that rendered him incapable of military service the punishment was more severe.

By the Coventry Act, maiming in the face from malice or forethought was punished with death. The reason of this was that Sir John Coventry had spoken impertinently against the king in Parliament. The Prince of Wales[2] with some others, probably not without the king's permission, laid wait for him and cut his ears and his face. The Parliament immediately enacted that maiming in the face from forethought should be punishable with death. There was never one, however, executed upon this law but one Cook, who lay in wait to murder his brother, but did not get it executed, only he maimed him in the face. He was therefore by the Coventry Act found guilty of deliberate malice. He pled that his intention was to murther, not to maim, but the court from the instrument he used found that he intended to maim as well as murder.

A man may also be injured by assault and battery. When a person is put

[2] In fact Charles II's natural son, the Duke of Monmouth. Cf. LJ(A) ii.124–5, above.

to bodily fear it is assault, and when he is actualy beat it is battery. Originaly no assault by words subjected to punishment, unless there was likewise a shaking of the fist, drawing an instrument or something of this kind; 191 | a composition was the first punishment for these crimes, but now it is fine and imprisonment.

A man may further be injured in his body by restraining his liberty, therefore the laws of every country are particularly carefull of securing it. No magistrate in this country has an arbitrary power of imprisonment. It is indeed reasonable that he should have it in his power to imprison when there is ground of suspicion, tho' an innocent man may sometimes suffer a little by it. Nothing is more difficult than perfectly to secure liberty. If the person can bring some circumstances to alleviate the suspicion, he may be sett at liberty upon bail, unless it be a capital crime. If the bail be not sufficient it is unjust in the magistrate to accept of it. But if it be, he is punishable if he do not. If a person be wrongously kept in prison beyond the time when he ought to have been tried, he has so much a day according to his station. In England, if a person be confined the day after the assizes, 40 days after he may have the benefit of the Habeas Corpus Act, that is, he may be carried to London at his own expence, but if he cannot afford this he must wait till the next assizes. In Scotland, there is no occasion for the Habeas Corpus Act. A person may be tried by the sherriff if he pleases, and at any rate can be carried to Edinburgh to the Kings Court. All this is for the security of liberty in free governments, but in despotic governments the will of the magistrate is law.

192	| It is to be observed with respect to what is done thro' fear, that a bond given from this principle is not binding. No obligation is valid unless the person acted voluntar⟨il⟩y. However, if a person is threatned to be pursued and gives a bond to avoid it, the bond is valid, and the fear is not considered as a metus injustus.

A rape or forcible marriage is capital, because the woman is so dishonoured that no other punishment can be a sufficient retaliation. Tho' forcible marriage be forbidden by law, yet if the woman afterwards consent the friends can have no appeal, yet the king may pursue it.

A man may be injured in his reputation, by affronts, by words, and by writings. An affront in company is a real injury; if the affront be offered in words it is a verbal injury, if in writing it is a written injury. In all these the law gives redress. Affronts by the old law were punished in the same manner with assault and battery. Affronts in company are most atrocious crimes. The triffling fine of five or ten pounds is by no means an adequate compensation for them. Where the law denies justice we are naturaly led to take it ourselves. This introduced dueling in Europe, which brings along with it an additional injury. I must not only receive a box on the ear, but I am obliged to expose my life or become altogether odious. It is to be observed that in

193 Socrates time | the affront of giving the lie was little thought of. He does it himself without any ceremony.

Verbal injuries are redressed both by ancient and modern laws. When a person is accused by words it sustains a process before a court of justice. If he be accused of forgery, theft, or any crime, as he may be subjected to great dammages he is entitled to sufficient redress. In the same manner if a person's right or tittle be slandered he suffers an injury. If I say you have no more right to your own house than I have, it is an injury, as it may excite those who have pretended tittles. Tho' it be true, this is only an alleviation and will not secure me from a prosecution. There are some offences that are only prosecuted in spiritual courts, as if a person call a woman a whore.

Written injuries are subjected to severer punishments than verbal ones, as they are more deliberate malice. Abusive words in a lybel give a process tho' the same words would not if spoken. Lybels and satyres are punished according to the nature of the government. In aristocratical governments they are punished severely. Little petty princes may be quite destroyed by abusive lybels, whereas kings and ministers of state in a free country, being far out of their reach, cannot be hurt by them. In governments and in Rome for a long time they were not punished.[3] Augustus at last revived
194 the law, subjecting the authors to a capital punishment. | In general people of circumstances take no notice of such lybels, unless it be absolutely necessary to clear themselves of some crime.

A person may be injured in his estate, real or personal. With regard to his real estate he may be injured either in his moveables or immoveables. In his immoveables[w] he may be injured by arsine or forcible entry. Arsine is wilfull fire raising, either in the house of another or in our own, so as to affect that of another. By the Roman, English, and Scotch law this is punished capitally. If the fire be occasioned by negligence no punishment is inflicted. Forcible entry is the violently putting a man out of his estate. The laws are so strict on this head that the person outed may retake his own by violence.[4] This was occasioned by the feudal customs, by which it was very common for barons and their vassals to deprive one another of their possessions, and this was the only way ⟨that⟩ then could be fallen on to get it restored. Afterwards it was enacted that if any person could prove that he was violent⟨ly⟩ disspossessed his estate should be restored.[5] But if the violent possessor had kept it three years, the old possessor must prove not only that he was disspossessed by violence, but that he has a real right to it, before it be restored.

    [w] The copyist wrote 'moveables' and a second (eighteenth-century) hand has inserted 'imm'

---

[3] Something has evidently been omitted from this sentence. Cf. LJ(A) ii.142–3, above.
[4] Hawkins, I.64.1.
[5] 5 Richard II, c. 7 (1381); 15 Richard II, c. 2 (1391); 8 Henry VI, c. 9 (1429).

A man may be injured in his moveables three ways, by theft, robbery, and piracey. Theft is the clandestinely taking away the property of another. This crime does not naturaly excite that degree of resentment which prompts to capital punishment, and for a long time it was not punished with 195 death. | By the old Roman law the thief was obliged to restore what he had taken, and to add to it as much more; if he stole a sheep he restored two. There was however a peculiar distinction between the fur manifestus and fur nec manifestus. The former as he was taken with the goods about him paid quadruple, and the latter only double the value of things stolen. This they borrowed, it is said, from the Lacedemonians, who taught their youth to steal and hide well as they thought it improved them in that cunning which is necessary in war. However, the Lacedemonians never encouraged the stealing the property of another. In their feasts nothing was prepared for their young men, and it was expected that they should purloin from the tables of their fathers what was sufficient for themselves. To steal such triffles as a crust of bread was indulged, but nothing else. The real reason of their punishing the fur manifestus more severely than another was that barbarous nations punish crimes according to the degree of resentment they excite, and when the thief was catched in the act their resentment was very high, and consequently disposed them to punish him severly. Since the 13$^{th}$ century this crime has been punished capitaly. The vassals of great lords were continually making incursions into the neighbouring territories and carrying off bootty. When government came to be established, it naturaly punished most severely these crimes to which men had the 196 greatest propensity, | and consequently endeavoured to restrain this practice. The Emperor Barbarossa first made this crime capital, and he was followed by all civilized nations, tho' undoubtedly the punishment is too great, for a thief is but a petty mean creature and does not excite a very high degree of resentment. He seems to be in some degree below this passion. By the old Scotch law theft in a landed gentleman was considered as treason, because the gentry were considered as the abutters and assistants of thieves and vagrants, and as they made war on one another, which looked like an usurpation of soveraignty, they were considered as guilty of treason. By the English law any theft below a shilling was punished with the pillory, and above that with death. In Scotland it requires a much greater sum. Nothing is theft with us but what belongs to particular persons. The man who stole deer in a forrest or pidgeons at a distance from a pidgeon house could not be punished till by a late statute.[6] Housebreaking indeed, tho' there was not the value of a shilling carried off, was punished capitaly. Such punishments, however necessary once, are certainly now too severe. Government was$^{x}$ at first weak and could not punish crimes, but was

---

$^{x}$ Inserted by a second (eighteenth-century) hand

$^{6}$ Probably 24 George II, c. 34 (1751), applying to Scotland.

obliged to interpose in these cases in which the interest of society was concerned. But when it acquired more strength it made punishments severe
197 that it might | restrict the licentiousness of manners which lax discipline
had introduced. Accordingly we find that the laws of the 12 Tables made
almost every crime capital. In Europe after the custom of compensations
went out, they punished every thing as treason. Theft in a landed man, a
servant killing his master, a curate his bishop, or a husband his wife[7] were
all petty treason. Afterwards only crimes respecting the state were considered as treason, and this crime came by degrees to it's proper extent.

Robbery, as it puts a man to the greatest bodily fear, is subjected to the
greatest punishment; no occasion can save the robber, even tho' he should
cover the injury by pretending to buy a man's goods after he has forced
him to sell them to him.[8]

Piracey is punished still more severly.

A man may be injured in his personal estate by fraud or forgery. The
natural punishment of the dolus malus is not death, but some sort of
ignominy such as the pillory. Some frauds, however, on account of the
facility and security with which they may be committed and the loss which
they occasion, are justly subjected to capital punishment. When an insured
ship, for instance, is cast away, it is difficult to prove that it was done by
fraud. But if she be insured to the full value there is a great temptation to
cast her away, and therefore the law, in order to intimidate the merchant,
198 |make death the punishment. It was a question whether a ship ought to be
insured for her value at the port whence she setts out, or at the port to
which she is bound, and it was determined that it should be at the port
where she setts out. If a Glasgow merchant sends out a ship with 3000£'s
worth of goods for Virginia, they are worth more than 4000£ when they
arrive there. And if the merchant were allowed to insure for this last sum he
would have a great temptation to make shipwreck of her. He can expect no
more when he is at the expence of taking his goods to Virginia; he may meet
with bad debtors and he can lose nothing by the insurers. In the same
manner it was anciently capital to steal any thing from the plow,[9] as it was
so much exposed.

In England a bankrupt may have a discharge on surrendering himself
and all his effects, but as he has it in his power to defraud his creditors, if he
does not give up all he has he is punishable by death.[10]

Forgery is also punished capitally, and nobody complains that this
punishment is too severe, because when contracts sustain action property
can never be secure unless the forgeing of false ones be restrained. However,

[7] Should be 'a wife her husband'.
[8] Hawkins, I.34.10.
[9] Sir G. Mackenzie, *Laws and Customes of Scotland in Matters Criminal* (1678), I.19.9,
citing Act, 1587, c. 82 (A.P.S. III.460).
[10] 5 George II, c. 30 (1732); Hawkins, I.57.

the forgery of every deed is not capital, but only the forgery of deeds payable to the bearer on demand, because any forgery of a deed regarding the conveyance of land may easily be discovered before any dammage be done.

199 | Perjury is not punished capitaly.

As there are several ways of acquiring personal rights, so there are several ways in which they expire. First, by payment of what is due by contract or quasi contract, because the fullfillment of the obligation satisfies the other party. Secondly, by discharge or acquittance, even tho' the debt be not paid. This also takes place with regard to crimes, for when the king or the injured person choose to drop prosecution or to give a pardon the person is free. Thirdly, by prescription. If a debt be not claimed within a certain time the debtor is free. This is very reasonable, for if a debt be not claimed for a long time the negligence of the debtor is encouraged. By the Scotch law, if he call for neither principal nor interest of a bond for forty years, it very justly prescribes. No body of common prudence would neglect any part of his affairs for forty years, if ever he intended to meddle with them again. According to strict law, if the interest be demanded in the $39^{th}$ year the capital does not prescribe. Crimes likewise prescribe, and it is reasonable that they should, whether they be punished from a sympathy with the resentment of the sufferer, or from public utility, or to satisfy the public. Resentment wears out in a few years,

200 | and a person who has behaved well for twenty years, the time fixed on by our law, cannot be very dangerous to the public. Appeals by the English law prescribe in one year, but an indictment does not prescribe so soon, because the king prosecutes for public security and not to gratify private resentment and therefore the law favours his claim. At any rate it would be unreasonable to prosecute a man for a crime committed 40 years ago, because he may now be a quite different man from what he was then. Besides, the thing is quite forgotten and the end of punishing and public example is entirely lost. Treason itself prescribes in a few years. From a resentment in law, however, if sentence have actualy ⟨been⟩ passed upon a person, and he have made his escape, he may be executed on his former sentence. The escape is considered as a new crime. However, this is not very natural, and if a man live quietly after his return he is seldom troubled. We had an instance of an earl who had been sentenced in 1715 and had returned to his native country and lived peaceably in it till the year 1745, when he again joined the rebels and was executed on his former sentence. Dr. Cameron suffered in Scotland in the same manner. In every country, if a person return after twenty years he is not troubled; it would be thought invidious in the officers of justice to meddle with him.

Some general observations on the criminal law is all that remains on this subject.

201    | Resentment seems best to account for the punishment of crimes. If a person fires a pistol down a street, tho' he do no harm, public utility requires that he should be punished. But such crimes are by the laws of every country more slightly punished than if some mischief had ensued. The reason is plain. Resentment never rises to any great pitch unless some injury be actualy done. Some things that are in themselves criminal are not punished unless some bad consequence follow. A man meets with little resentment for riding an unruly horse in the market place, but if he kill any body resentment is very high. For the same reason deodands, tho' inanimate objects, are accounted execrable. In many cases the resentment falls upon the very member of the body which perpetrated the action. Resentment is on the whole a very indiscriminating principle and pays little attention to the disposition of the mind.

Certain persons are not to be considered as objects of punishment, such as ideots, madmen, and children. We are not so much shocked by an action done by a madman as one done by another person. We think binding the only punishment adequate to their crimes.

This is all we intended on the injuries that may be done to a man as a man.

Having now considered man as a member of a state, as a member of a family, and as a man, we proceed to Police, 2$^d$ division of jurisprudence.

*Whole of 202 left blank in MS.*

203

# | *Juris-prudence*

## Part II.

### Of Police

Police is the second general division of jurisprudence. The name is French, and is originaly derived from the Greek πολιτεια, which properly signified the policey of civil government, but now it only means the regulation of the inferiour parts of government, *viz.* cleanliness, security, and cheapness or plenty. The two former, to witt, the proper method of carrying dirt from the streets, and the execution of justice, so far as it regards regulations for preventing crimes or the method of keeping a city guard, tho' usefull, are too mean to be considered in a general discourse of this kind. An observation or two before we proceed to the third particular is all that is necessary.

We observe then, that in cities where there is most police and the greatest number of regulations concerning it, there is not always the greatest security. In Paris the regulations concerning police are so numerous as not 204 to be comprehended in several volumes. | In London there are only two or three simple regulations. Yet in Paris scarce a night passes without somebody being killed, while in London, which is a larger city, there are scarce three or four in a year. On this account one would be apt to think that the more police there is the less security, but this is not the cause. In England as well as in France, during the time of the feudal government and as late as Queen Elizabeth's reign, great numbers of retainers were kept idle about the noblemen's houses, to keep the tenants in awe. These retainers, when turned out, had no other way of getting their subsistance but by committing robberies and living on plunder, which occasioned the greatest disorder. A remain of the feudal manners, still preserved in France, gives occasion to the difference. The nobility at Paris keep far more menial servants than ours, who are often turned out on their own account or thro' the caprice of their masters, and, being in the most indigent circumstances, are forced to committ the most dreadfull crimes. In Glasgow, where almost no body has more than one servant, there are fewer capital crimes than in Edinburgh. In Glasgow there is not one in several years, but not a year passes in Edinburgh without some such disorders. Upon this principle, therefore, it is not so much the police that prevents the commission of crimes as the having as few persons as possible to live upon others. Nothing tends so much to corrupt mankind as dependencey, while independencey 205 still encreases the honesty of the people. | The establishment of commerce and manufactures, which brings about this independencey, is the best police for preventing crimes. The common people have better wages in this way than in any other, and in consequence of this a general probity of manners takes place thro' the whole country. No body will be so mad as to expose himself upon the highway, when he can make better bread in an honest and industrious manner. The nobility of Paris and London are no doubt much upon a level, but the common people of the former, being much more dependent, are not to be compared with these of the latter, and for the same reason the commonality in Scotland differ from these in England, tho' the nobility too are much upon a level.

Thus far for the two first particulars which come under the general division of police. In the following part of this discourse we are to confine ourselves to the consideration of cheapness or plenty, or, which is the same thing, the most proper way of procuring wealth and abundance. Cheapness
206 is in fact the same thing with plenty. | It is only on account of the plenty of water that it is so cheap as to be got for the lifting, and on account of the scarcity of diamonds (for their real use seems not yet to be discovered) that they are so dear. To ascertain the most proper method of obtaining these conveniences, it will be necessary to shew first wherein opulence consists, and still previous to this we must consider what are the natural wants of mankind which are to be supplied; and if we differ from common opinions we shall at least give the reasons for our non-conformity.

Nature produces for every animal every thing that is sufficient to support it without having recourse to the improvement of the original production. Food, cloaths, and lodging are all the wants of any animal whatever, and most of the animal creation are sufficiently provided for by nature in all these wants to which their condition is liable. Such is the delicacey of man alone, that no object is produced to his liking. He finds that in every thing there is need of improvement. Tho' the practice of savages shews that his
207 food needs no preparation, | yet being acquainted with fire he finds that it can be rendered more wholesome and easily digested, and thereby may preserve him from many diseases which are very violent among them. But it is not only his food that requires this improvement. His puny constitution is hurt also by the intemperate of the air he breathes in, which tho' not very capable of improvement must be brought to a proper temperament for his body and an artificial atmosphere prepared for this purpose. The human skin cannot endure the inclemencies of the weather, and even in these countries where the air is warmer than the natural warmth of the constitution, and where they have no need of cloaths, it must be stained and painted to be able to endure the hardships of the sun and rain. In general, however, the necessities of man are not so great but that they can be supplied by the unassisted labour of the individual. All the above

necessities every one can provide for himself, such as animals and fruits for his food, and skins for his cloathing.

208    As the delicacey of a man's body requires much greater provision | than that of any other animal, the same or rather the much greater delicacey of his mind requires a still greater provision, to which all the different arts ⟨are⟩ subservient. Man is the only animal who is possessed of such a nicety that the very colour of an object hurts him. Among different objects a different division or arrangement of them pleases. The taste of beauty, which consists chiefly in the three following particulars, proper variety, easy connection, and simple order, is the cause of all this niceness. Nothing without variety pleases us: a long uniform wall is a dissagreable object. Too much variety, such as the crowded objects of a parterre, is also dissagreable. Uniformity tires the mind; too much variety, too far encreased, occasions an overgreat dissipation of it. Easy connection also renders objects agreable; when we see no reason for the contiguity of the parts, when they are without any natural connection, when they have neither a proper resemblance nor contrast, they never fail of being dissagreable. If simplicity of order be not observed, so as that the whole may be easily comprehended, it hurts the delicacey of our taste.

209    | Again, imitation and painting render objects more agreable. To see upon a plain, trees, forrests, and other such representations is an agreable surprize to the mind. Variety of objects also renders them agreable. What we are every day accustomed to does but very indifferently affect us. Gems and diamonds are on this account much esteemed by us. In like manner our pinchbeck and many of our toys were so much valued by the Indians, that in bartering their jewels and diamonds for them they thought they had made by much the better bargain.

These qualities, which are the ground of preference and which give occasion to pleasure and pain, are the cause of many insignificant demands which we by no means stand in need of. The whole industry of human life is employed not in procuring the supply of our three humble necessities, food, cloaths, and lodging, but in procuring the conveniences of it according to the nicety and [and] delicacey of our taste. To improve and multiply the materials which are the principal objects of our necessities, gives occasion to all the variety of the arts.

210    | Agriculture, of which the principal object is the supply of food, introduces not only the tilling of the ground, but also the planting of trees, the producing of flax, hemp, and inumerable other things of a similar kind. By these again are introduced different manufactures, which are so very capable of improvement. The mettals dug from the bowells of the earth furnish materials for tools, by which many of these arts are practised. Commerce and navigation are also subservient to the same purposes by collecting the produce of these several arts. By these again other subsidiary

⟨arts⟩ are occasioned. Writing, to record the multitude of transactions, and geometry, which serves many usefull purposes. Law and government, too, seem to propose no other object but this, they secure the individual who has enlarged his property, that he may peaceably enjoy the fruits of it. By law and government all the different arts flourish, and that inequality of fortune to which they give occasion is sufficiently preserved. By law and government domestic peace is enjoyed and security from the forreign invader. Wisdom and virtue too derive their lustre from supplying these

211 necessities. | For as the establishment of law and government is the highest effort of human prudence and wisdom, the causes cannot have a different influence from what the effects have. Besides, it is by the wisdom and probity of those with whom we live that a propriety of conduct is pointed out to us, and the proper means of attaining it. Their valour defends us, their benevolence supplies us, the hungry is fed, the naked is cloathed, by the exertion of these divine qualities. Thus according to the above representation, all things are subservient to supplying our threefold necessities.

In an uncivilized nation, and where labour is undivided, every thing is provided for that the natural wants of mankind require; yet when the nation is cultivated and labour divided a more liberal provision is allotted them; and it is on this account that a common day labourer in Brittain has more luxury in his way of living than an Indian sovereign. The woolen coat he wears requires very considerable preperations; the wool gatherer, the dresser, the spinster, the dyer, the weaver, the taylor, and many more must all be employed befor the labourer is cloathed. The tools by which all this is effectuated employ a still greater number of artists, the loom maker, miln wright, ropemaker, not to mention the bricklayer, the treefeller, the

212 miner, the smelter, | the forger, the smith, etc. Besides his dress, consider also his houshold furniture, his coarse linens, his shoes, his coals dug out of the earth or brought by sea, his kitchen utensils and different plates, those that are employed in providing his bread and beer, the sower, the brewer, the reaper, the baker, his glass windows and the art required in preparing ⟨?them⟩, without which our northern climate could hardly be inhabited. When we examine the conveniences of the day labourer, we find that even in his easy simple manner he cannot be accomodated without the assistance of a great number, and yet this is nothing compared with the luxury of the nobility. An European prince, however, does not so far exceed a commoner as the latter does the chief of a savage nation. It is easy to conceive how the rich can be so well provided for, as they can direct so many hands to serve their purposes. They are supported by the industry of the peasant. In a savage nation every one enjoys the whole fruit of his own labour, yet their indigence is greater than any where.

It is the division of labour which encreases the opulence of a country.

213 | In a civilized society, tho' there is indeed a division of labour there is no

equal division, for there are a good many who work none at all. The division of opulence is not according to the work. The opulence of the merchant is greater than that of all his clerks, tho' he works less; and they again have six times more than an equal number of artizans, who are more employed. The artizan who works at his ease within doors has far more than the poor labourer who trudges up and down without intermission. Thus he who, as it were, bears the burthen of society has the fewest advantages.

We shall next shew how this division of labour occasions a multiplication of the product, or, which is the same thing, how opulence arises from it. In order to this let us observe the effect of the division of labour in some manufactures. If all the parts of a pin were made by one man, if the same person dug the ore, ⟨s⟩melted it, and split the wire, it would take him a whole year to make one pin, and this pin must therefore be sold at the expence of his maintenance for that time, which taking ⟨it⟩ at$^y$ a moderate computation would at least be six pounds for a pin. If the labour is so far divided that the wire is ready made, he will not make above 20 per day, which allowing 10 pence for wages makes the pin twopence.[11] The pin maker therefore divides the labour among a great number of different

**214** persons, | the cutting, pointing, heading, and gilding are all seperate professions. Two or three are employed in making the head, one or two in putting it on, and so on, to the putting them in the paper, being in all eighteen. By this division every one can with great ease make 2000 a day. The same is the case in the linen and woolen manufactures. Some arts, however, there are which will not admit of this division, and therefore they cannot keep pace with other manufactures and arts. Such are farming and grazing. This is entirely owing to the returns of the seasons, by which one man can only be for a short time employed in any one operation. In countries where the season⟨s⟩ do not make such alterations it is otherwise. In France the corn is better and cheaper than in England. But our toys, which have no dependance on the climate and in which labour can be divided, are far superiour to those of France.

When labour is thus divided, and so much done by one man in proportion, the surplus above their maintenance is considerable, which each man can exchange for a fourth of what he could have done if he had finished it alone.[12] By this means the commodity becomes far cheaper, and

---

$^y$ The copyist first wrote 'it' and then emended to 'at'

---

[11] An allowance is apparently being made here for the price of the wire; cf. the similar calculation in LJ(A) vi.29, above.

[12] This sentence, the meaning of which is a little obscure when it is considered in isolation, is probably best regarded as an attempt by the reporter to summarize the over-all conclusions to be drawn from a set of numerical illustrations similar to those given in LJ(A) vi.32–3, above, and in ED 10–11, below.

the labour dearer. It is to be observed that the price of labour by no means
215 determines the opulence of society. | It is only when a little labour can
procure abundance. On this account a rich nation, when it's manufactures
are greatly improven, may have an advantage over a poor one by under-
selling it. The cotton and other commodities from China would undersell
any made with us, were it not for the long carriage and other taxes that are
laid upon them.

We must not judge of the dearness of labour by the money or coin that is
paid for it. One penny in some places will purchase as much as eighteen-
pence in others. In the country of the Mogul, where the days wages are only
twopence, labour is better rewarded than in some of our sugar islands,
where men are almost starving with four or five shillings a day. Coin therefore can be no proper estimate. Further, tho' human labour be employed
both in the multiplication of commodities and of money, yet the chance of
success is not equal. A farmer by the proper cultivation of an acre is sure of
encrease, but the miner may work again and again without success. Commodities must therefore multiply in greater proportion than gold and
silver.

But again, the quantity of work which is done by the division of labour is
much encreased by the three following articles, first, encrease of dexterity,
secondly, the saving of time lost in passing from one species of labour to
216 another, | and thirdly, the invention of machinery. Of these in order.

1st. When any kind of labour is reduced to a simple operation, a fre-
quencey of action insensibly fits men to a dexterity in accomplishing it. A
country smith not accustomed to make nails will work very hard for 3 or
400 a day, and these too very bad. But a boy used to it will easily make
2000, and these incomparably better; yet the improvement of dexterity in
this very complex manufacture can never be equal to that in others. A nail
maker changes postures, blows the bellows, changes tools, etca. and therefore the quantity produced cannot be so great as in manufactures of pins
and buttons, where the work is reduced to simple operations.

2$^{dly}$. There is always sometime lost in passing from one species of labour
to another, even when they are pretty much connected. When a person has
been reading he must rest a little before he begin to write. This is still more
the case with the country weaver, who is possessed of a little farm; he must
saunter a little when he goes from one to the other. This in general is the
case with the country labourers; they are always the greatest saunterers, the
217 country employments of sowing, | reaping, threshing being so different.
They naturaly acquire a habit of indolence and are seldom very dextrous.
By fixing every man to his own operation, and preventing the shifting from
one piece of labour to another, the quantity of work must be greatly
encreased.

3$^{dly}$. The quantity of work is greatly encreased by the invention of machines. Two men and three horses will do more in a day with the plow than 20 men without it. The miller and his servant will do more with the water miln than a dozen with the hand miln, tho' it too be a machine. The division of labour no doubt first gave occasion to the invention of machines. If a man's business in life is the performance of two or three things, the bent of his mind will be to find out the cleverest way of doing it, but when the force of his mind is divided it cannot be expected that he should be so successfull. We have not nor cannot have any compleat history of the invention of machines, because most of them are at first imperfect, and receive gradual improvements and encrease of powers from those who use them. It was probably a farmer who made the original plow, tho' the improvements might be owing to some other. Some miserable slave who had perhaps been employed for a long time in grinding corn between two stones probably first found out the method of supporting the upper stone 218 | by a spindle. A miln wright perhaps found out the way of turning the spindle with the hand. But he who contrived that the outer wheel should go by water was a philosopher, whose business it is to do nothing, but observe every thing. They must have extensive views of things, who as in this case bring in the assistance of new powers not formerly applied. Whether he was an artizan, or whatever he was who first executed this, he must have been a philosopher; fire machines, wind and water-milns, were the invention of philosophers, whose dexterity too is encreased by a division of labour. They all divide themselves, according to the different branches, into the mechanical, moral, political, chymical philosophers. Thus we have shewn how the quantity of labour is encreased by machines.

We have already shewn that the division of labour is the immediate cause of opulence. We shall next consider what gives occasion to the division of labour, or from what principles in our nature it can best be accounted for. We cannot imagine this to be an effect of human prudence. It was indeed made a law by Sesostratis[13] that every man should follow the employment of his father. But this is by no means suitable to the dis-219 positions of human nature | and can never long take place. Every one is fond of being a gentleman, be his father what he would. They who are strongest and in the bustle of society have got above the weak, must have as many under as to defend them in their station; from necessary causes, therefore, there must be as many in the lower stations as there is occasion for. There must be as many up as down, and no division can be over-stretched. But it is not this which gives occasion to the division of labour. It flows from a direct propensity in human nature for one man to barter with another, which is common to all men and known to no other animal. No body ever saw a dog, the most sagacious animal, exchange a bone with his companion for another. Two greyhounds, indeed, in runing down a

[13] Reporter's or copyist's error for 'Sesostris'.

hare, seem to have something like compact or agreement betwixt them, but this is nothing else but a concurrence of the same passions. If an animal intends to truck, as it were, or gain any thing from man, it is by it's fondness and kindness. Man, in the same manner, works on the selflove of his fellows, by setting before them a sufficient temptation to get what he wants; the language of this disposition is, give me what I want, and you shall have what you want. It is not from benevolence, as the dogs, but from selflove
220 that man expects any thing. | The brewer and the baker serve us not from benevolence but from selflove. No man but a beggar depends on benevolence, and even they would die in a week were their entire dependance upon it.

By this disposition to barter and exchange the surplus of ones labour for that of other people, in a nation of hunters, if any one has a talent for making bows and arrows better than his neighbours he will at first make presents of them, and in return get presents of their game. By continuing this practice he will live better than before and will have no occasion to provide for himself, as the surplus of his own labour does it more effectualy.

This disposition to barter is by no means founded upon different genius and talents. It is doubtfull if there be any such difference at all; at least it is far less than we are aware of. Genius is more the effect of the division of labour than the latter is of it. The difference between a porter and a philosopher in the first four or five years of their life is properly speaking none at all. When they come to be employed in different occupations, their views widen and differ by degrees. As every one has this natural disposition
221 to truck and barter | by which he provides for himself, there is no need for such different endowments, and accordingly among savages there is always the greatest uniformity of character. In other animals of the same species we find a much greater difference than betwixt the philosopher and porter antecedent to custom. The mastiff and spaniel have quite different powers, but tho' these animals are possessed of talents they cannot, as it were, bring them into the common stock and exchange their productions, and therefore their different talents are of no use to them.

It is quite otherwise among mankind; they can exchange their several productions according to their quantity or quality. The philosopher and the porter are both of advantage to each other. The porter is of use in carrying burthens for the philosopher, and in his turn he burns his coals cheaper by the philosopher's invention of the fire machine. Thus we have shewn that different genius is not the foundation of this disposition to barter, which is the cause of the division of labour. The real foundation of it is that principle to perswade which so much prevails in human nature. When any arguments are offered to perswade, it is always expected that they should have their proper effect. If a person asserts any thing about the
222 moon, tho' it should not be true, | he will feel a kind of uneasiness in being

contradicted, and would be very glad that the person he is endeavouring to perswade should be of the same way of thinking with himself. We ought then mainly to cultivate the power of perswasion, and indeed we do so without intending it. Since a whole life is spent in the exercise of it, a ready method of bargaining with each other must undoubtedly be attained. As was before observed, no animal can do this but by gaining the favour of those whom they would perswade. Sometimes, indeed, animals seem to act in concert, but there never is any thing like bargain among them. Monkeys when they rob a garden throw the fruit from one to another till they deposit it in the hoard, but there is always a scramble about the division of the booty, and usually some of them are killed.

From all that has been said we may observe that the division of labour must always be proportioned to the extent of commerce. If ten people only want a certain commodity, the manufacture of it will never be so divided as if a thousand wanted it. Again, the division of labour, in order to opulence, becomes always more perfect by the easy method of conveyance in a country. If the road be infested with robbers, if it be deep and con-
223 veyance not easy, the progress of commerce must be stopped. | Since the mending of roads in England 40 or 50 years ago, its opulence has increased extremely. Water carriage is another convenience, as by it 300 ton can be conveyed at the expence of the tare and wear of the vessel and the wages of 5 or 6 men, and that too in a shorter time than by 100 waggons, which will take 6 horses and a man each. Thus the division of labour is the great cause of the increase of public opulence, which is always proportioned to the industry of the people, and not to the quantity of gold and silver as is foolishly imagined, and the industry of the people is always proportioned to the division of labour.

Having thus shewn what gives occasion to public opulence, in farther considering this subject we propose to consider:

1st. What circumstances regulate the price of commodities.

2$^{\text{dly}}$. Money in two different views, first as the measure of value and then as the instrument of commerce.

3$^{\text{dly}}$. The history of commerce, in which shall be taken notice of the causes of the slow progress of opulence both in ancient and modern times,
224 | which causes shall be shewn either to affect agriculture or arts and manufactures. Lastly, the effects of a commercial spirit on the government, temper, and manners of a people, whether good or bad, and the proper remedies. Of these in order.

Of every commodity there are two different prices, which tho' apparently independent will be found to have a necessary connection, viz. the natural price and the market price. Both of these are regulated by certain circumstances. When men are induced to a certain species of industry rather than any other, they must make as much by the employment as will maintain them while they are employed. An arrow maker must be sure to exchange as much surplus product as will maintain him during as long time as he took to make them. But upon this principle in the different trades there must be a considerable difference, because some trades, such as these of the taylor and weaver, are not learned by casual observation and a little experience, like that of the day-labourer, but take a great deal of time and

225 pains | before they are acquired. When a person begins them, for a considerable time his work is of no use to his master or any other person, and therefore his master must be compensated both for what maintains him and for what he spoils. When he comes to exercise his trade, he must be repaid what he has laid out, both of expences and of apprentice fee. And as his life is not worth above 10 or 12 years purchase at most, his wages must be high on account of the risque he runs of not having the whole made up. But again, there are many arts which require more extensive knowledge than is to be got during the time of an apprenticeship. A blacksmith and weaver may learn their business well enough without any previous knowledge of mathematics. But a watch maker must be acquainted with several sciences in order to understand his business well, such as arithmetic, geometry, and astronomy with regard to the equation of time, and their wages must be high in order to compensate the additional expence. In general, this is the case in all the liberal arts, because after they have spent a long time in their education it is ten to one if ever they make any thing by it. Their wages therefore must be higher in proportion to the expence they

226 have been at, | the risk of not living long enough, and the risk of not having dexterity enough to manage their business. Among the lawyers there is not one among twenty that attains such knowledge and dexterity in his business as enables him to get back the expences of his education, and many of them never make the price of their gown, as we say. The fees of lawyers are so far from being extravagant, as they are generally thought, that they are rather low in proportion. It is the eminence of the profession, and not the money made by it, that is the temptation for applying to it, and the dignity of that rank is to be considered as a part of what is made by it.

   In the same manner we shall find that the price of gold and silver is not extravagant if we consider it in this view, for in a gold or silver mine there is a great chance of missing it altogether. If we suppose an equal number of men employed in raising corn and digging silver, the former will make more than the latter, because perhaps of forty or fifty employed in a mine only twenty make any thing at all. Some of the rest may indeed make fortunes, but every cornman succeeds in his undertakings, so that upon the whole

227 there is more made this way than the other. | It is the ideal acquisition which is the principal temptation in a mine. A man then has the natural price of his labour when it is sufficient to maintain him during the time of labour, to defray the expence of education, and to compensate the risk of

not living long enough and of not succeeding in the business. When a man has this, there is sufficient encouragement to the labourer and the commodity will be cultivated in proportion to the demand.

The market price of goods is regulated by quite other circumstances. When a buyer comes to the market, he never asks of the seller what expences he has been at in producing them. The regulation of the market price of goods depends on the three following articles:

1st. The demand or need for the commodity. There is no demand for a thing of little use; it is not a rational object of desire.

2$^{dly}$. The abundance or scarceity of the commodity in proportion to the need of it. If the commodity be scarce, the price is raised, but if the quantity be more than is sufficient to supply the demand, the price falls. Thus it 228 is that diamonds and other precious stones are dear, | while iron, which is much more usefull, is so many times cheaper, tho' this depends principally on the last cause, *viz.*

3$^{dly}$. The riches or poverty of those who demand. When there is not enough produced to serve every body, the fortune of the bidders is the only regulation of the price.

The story which is told of the merchant and the carrier in the desarts of Arabia is an evidence of this. The merchant gave 10,000 ducats for a certain quantity of water. His fortune here regulated the price, for if he had not had them, he could not have given them, and if his fortune had been less, the water would have been cheaper. When the commodity is scarce, the seller must be content with that degree of wealth which they have who buy it. The case is much the same as in an auction; if two persons have an equal fondness for a book, he whose fortune is largest will carry it. Hence things that are very rare go always to rich countries. The King of France only could purchase that large diamond of so many thousand pounds value. Upon this principle every thing is dearer or cheaper according as it is the purchase of a higher or lower sett of people.

Utensils of gold are comeatible only by persons in certain circumstances. 229 These of silver fall to another sett of people | and their prices are regulated by what the majority can give. The prices of corn and beer are regulated by what all the world can give, and on this account the wages of the daylabourer have a great influence upon the price of corn. When the price of corn rises, wages rise also, and vice versa. When the quantity of corn falls short, as in a sea voyage, it always occasions a famine and then the price becomes enormous. Corn then becomes the purchase of a higher sett of people, and the lower must live on turneeps and potatoes.

Thus we have considered the two prices, the natural and the market price, which every commodity is supposed to have. We observed before that however seemingly independant they appear to be, they are necessarily connected. This will appear from the following considerations. If the market price of any commodity is very great, and the labour very highly rewarded, the market is prodigiously crouded with it, greater quantities of it are produced, and it can be sold to the inferiour ranks of people. If for every ten diamonds there were ten thousand, they would become the purchase of every body, because they would become very cheap, and would sink to their natural price. Again, when the market is overstocked and there is not enough got for the labour of the manufacture, no body will bind to it; they cannot have a subsistence by it, because the market price falls then

230 below the natural price. | It is alledged that as the price of corn sink⟨s⟩, the wages of the labourer should sink, as he is then better rewarded. It is true that if provisions were long cheap, as more people would flock to this labour where the wages are high, thro' this concurrence of labour the wages would come down. But we find that when the price of corn is doubled the wages continue the same as before, because the labourers have no other way to turn themselves. The same is the case with menial servants.

From the above we may observe that whatever police tends to raise the market price above the natural, tends to diminish public opulence. Dearness and scarceity are in effect the same thing. When commodities are in abundance, they can be sold to the inferiour ranks of people, who can afford to give less for them, but not if they are scarce. So far therefore as goods are a conveniencey to the society, the society lives less happy when only the few can possess them. Whatever therefore keeps goods above their natural price for a permanencey, diminishes ⟨a⟩ nations opulence. Such are:

231 | 1st. All taxes upon industry, upon leather, and upon shoes, which people grudge most, upon salt, beer, or whatever is the strong drink of the country, for no country wants some kind of it. Man is an anxious animal and must have his care swept off by something that can exhilarate the spirits. It is alledged that this tax upon beer is an artificial security against drunkeness, but if we attend to it, ⟨?we shall find⟩ that it by no means prevents it. In countries where strong liquors are cheap, as in France and Spain, the people are generally sober. But in northern countries, where they are dear, they do not get drunk with beer but with spirituous liquors. No body presses his friend to a glass of beer unless he choose it.

2$^{\text{dly}}$. Monopolies also destroy public opulence. The price of the monopolized goods is raised above what is sufficient for encourageing the labour. When only a certain person or persons have the liberty of importing a commodity, there is less of it imported than would otherwise be: the price of it is therefore higher, and fewer people supported by it. It is the concurrence of different labourer[er]s which always brings down the price. In

232 monopolies such as the Hudson's Bay and East India companies | the people engaged in them make the price what they please.

3$^{\text{dly}}$. Exclusive priviledges of corporations have the same effect. The butchers and bakers raise the price of their goods as they please, because

none but their own corporation is allowed to sell in the market, and therefore their meat must be taken, whether good or not. On this account there is
always required a magistrate to fix the prices. For any free commodity,
such as broad cloth, there is no occasion for this, but it is necessary with
bakers, who may agree among themselves to make the quantity and price
what they please. Even a magistrate is not a good enough expedient for this,
as he must always settle the price at the outside, else the remedy must be
worse than the disease, for no body would apply to these businesses and
a famine would ensue. On this account bakers and brewers have always
profitable trades.

As what rises the market price above the natural one diminishes public
opulence, so what brings it down below it has the same effect.

It is only upon manufactures to be exported that this can usualy be done
by any law or regulation, such as the bounty allowed by the government
233 upon coarse linen, by which it becomes exportable | when under 12 pence
a yard. The public paying a great part of the price, it can be sold cheaper to
forreigners than what is sufficient for encourageing the labour. In the same
manner, by the bounty of five shillings upon the quarter of corn when sold
under 40 shillings, as the public pays an eight part of the price, it can be
sold just so much cheaper at a forreign market. By this bounty the commodity is rendered more comeatible, and a greater quantity of it produced,
but then it breaks what may be called the natural balance of industry. The
disposition to apply to the production of that commodity is not proportioned to the natural cause of the demand, but to both that and the annexed
bounty. But[14] has not only this effect with regard to the particular commodity, but likewise people are called from other productions which are less
encouraged, and thus the balance of industry is broken.

Again, after the ages of hunting and fishing, in which provisions were
the immediate produce of their labour, when manufactures were introduced, nothing could be produced without a great deal of time. It was a
long time before the weaver could carry to the market the cloth which he
bought in flax. Every trade therefore requires a stock of food, cloaths, and
lodging to carry it on.

234    | Suppose then, as is realy the case in every country, that there is in store a
stock of food, cloaths, and lodging, the number of people that are employed
must be in proportion to it. If the price of one commodity is sunk below it's
natural price, while another is above it, there is a smaller quantity of the
stored stock left to support the whole, on account of the natural connection
of all trades in the stock. By allowing bounties to me[15] you take away the
stock from the rest. This has been the real consequence of the corn bounty.

The price of corn being sunk, the rent of the farms sinks also, yet the
bounty upon corn, which was laid on at the time of the taxes, was

---

[14] *Sic.* Presumably copyist's error for 'It'.          [15] Probably copyist's error for 'one'.

intended to raise the rent, and had the effect for sometime, because the tenants were assured of a price for their corn both at home and abroad. But tho' the effects of the bounty encourageing agriculture brought down the price of corn, yet it raised the grass-farms, for the more corn the less grass.

The price of grass being raised, butcher's meat, in consequence of its dependance upon it, must be raised also. So that if the price of corn is diminished, the price of other commodities is necessarily raised. The price of corn has indeed fallen from 42 to 35, but the price of hay has risen from 25 to near 50 shillings. | As the price of hay has risen, horses are not so easily kept, and therefore the price of carriage has risen also. But whatever encreases the price of carriage diminishes plenty in the market. Upon the whole, therefore, it is by far the best police to leave things to their natural course, and allow no bounties, nor impose taxes on commodities. Thus we have shewn what circumstances regulate the price of commodities, which was the first thing proposed.

We come now to the second particular, to consider money, first as the measure of value and then as the medium of permutation or exchange.

When people deal in many species of goods, one of them must be considered as the measure of value. Suppose there were only three commodities, sheep, corn, and oxen, we can easily remember them comparatively. But if we have a hundered different commodities, there are ninety nine values of each arising from a comparison with each of the rest. As these cannot easily be remembered, men naturaly fall upon one of them to be a common standard with which they compare all the rest. This will naturaly at first be the commodity with which they are best acquainted. Accordingly we find that black cattle and sheep were the standard in Homer's time. | The armour of one of his heroes was worth nine oxen, and that of another worth an hundred. Black cattle was the common standard in ancient Greece. In Italy, and particularly in Tuscany, every thing was compared with sheep, as this was their principal commodity. This is what may be called the natural measure of value.

In like manner there were natural measures of quantity, such as fathoms, cubits, inches, taken from the proportions of the human body, once in use with every nation. But by a little observation they found that one man's arm was longer or shorter than anothers, and that one was not to be compared with the other, and therefore wise men who attended to these things would endeavour to fix upon some more accurate measure, that equal quantities might be of equal values. This method became absolutely necessary when people came to deal in many commodities and in great quantities of them. Tho' an inch was altogether inconsiderable when their dealings were confined to a few yards, more accuracey was required when they came to deal in some thousands. We find, in countries where their

237 dealings are small, the remains of this inaccurracey. | The cast of the balance is nothing thought of in their coarse commodities.

Since, then, there must of necessity be a common standard of which equal quantities should be of equal values, mettals in general seemed best to answer this purpose, and of these the value of gold and silver could best be ascertained. The temper of steel cannot be precisely known, but what degree of alloy is in gold and silver can be exactly found out. Gold and silver were therefore fixed upon as the most exact standard to compare goods with, and were therefore considered as the most proper measure of value.

In consequence of gold and silver becoming the measure of value, it came also to be the instrument of commerce. It soon became necessary that goods should be carried to market, and they could never be cleverly exchanged unless the measure of value was also the instrument of commerce. In the age of shepherds it might be no great inconvenience that cattle should be the medium of exchange, as the expence of maintaining them was nothing, the whole country being considered as one great common. But when lands came to be divided and the division of labour introduced, this custom would be productive of very considerable inconveniences. The butcher and shoemaker might at times have no use for one another's com-

238 modities. | The farmer very often cannot maintain upon his ground a cow more than he has; it would be a very great hardship on a Glasgow merchant to give him a cow for one of his commodities. To remedy this, these materials which were before considered as the measure of value came also to be the instrument of exchange. Gold and silver had all advantages; they can be kept without expence, they do not waste, and they are very portable. Gold and silver however do not derive their whole utility from being the medium of exchange. Tho' they never had been used as money, they are more valuable than any other mettals. They have a superiour beauty, are capable of a finer polish, and are more proper for making any instrument except these with an edge. For all these reasons gold and silver came to be the proper measure of value and the instrument of exchange. But in order to render them more proper for these purposes, it was necessary that both their weight and their fineness should be ascertained. At first their balances were not very accurate and therefore frauds were easily committed; however, this was remedied by degrees.

239 | But common business would not allow of the experiments which are necessary to fix precisely the degree of fineness; tho' with a great quantity of alloy, they are to appearance good. It was necessary therefore, to facilitate exchange, that they should fall upon some expedient to ascertain with accuracey both weight and fineness. Coinage most effectualy secures both these. The public, finding how much it would tend to facilitate commerce, put a stamp upon certain pieces, that whoever saw them might have the

public faith that they were of a certain weight and fineness; and this would be what was at first marked upon the coin, as being of most importance.

Accordingly the coins of every country appear to have been[16] the names of the weights corresponding to them, and they contained the denomination they expressed. The British pound sterling seems originaly to have been a pound weight of pure silver. As gold could be easily exchanged into silver, the latter came always to be the standard or measure of value. As there cannot be two standards, and in the greater part of purchases silver is necessary, we never say a man is worth so many guineas, but always pounds.

240   It is to be observed that the measure of | quantity has always encreased, while that of value has decreased. The British pound has now decreased to less than a third of its original value, which was sixty three shillings, while the measure of quantity has considerably encreased. The reason is that the interest of the government requires this. It is the interest of the baker and the brewer to make the measure of quantity as little as possible, and therefore there are inspectors appointed who, when it is brought down, always settle it a little farther up. All our measures which were taken from the Roman foot, fathom, and inch, are now a great deal more. In like manner what was called Troy weight, from Troy, a town in Champaigne where then the greatest commerce was carried on, gave rise to a heavier weight, because there was usualy given the cast of the balance along with it, and as this render'd dealings inaccurate, it was necessary that this cast of the balance should be determined. Accordingly, averdupois (avoir du poise) or heavy weight was settled at 13 ounces, but as this was a number not easily divided, it was settled at 16, the ounces being made proportioned to it.

Thus the measure of quantity has been encreasing. We shall next shew how the coin decreased.

241   | When the government takes the coinage into its own hands, the expences naturaly fall upon it, and if any private man coins, he must lessen the value or have nothing but his labour for his pains; and besides, as no man's authority can be so great as to make his coin pass in common payments, he must forge the stamp of the government. As the government took the task upon themselves, they would endeavour, in order to prevent frauds, to prevent counterfeiting the king's coin and encroaching on his prerogative. Besides, as the public faith was engaged, it was necessary to prevent all kinds of fraud, because it was likewise necessary that people should be obliged to receive the coin according to its denomination, and that if any refused it after a legal tender of payment was made, the debtor should be free and the creditor guilty of felony.[17]

In rude and barbarous periods the government was laid under many

---

[16] Probably copyist's error for 'borne'.

[17] In fact to refuse legal tender was never a felony. Cf. the formulation in LJ(A) vi.115, above.

temptations to debase the coin or, according to the Mint language, to raise it. When, for instance, on any important occasion, such as paying of debts, or of soldiers, it has occasion for two millions, but has no more than one, it calls in the coin of the country and, mixing with it a greater quantity of alloy, makes it come out 2 millions, as like as possible to what it was before.

242 Many operations of this kind have | [have] been performed in every country. But England, from the freedom which it has almost uninterruptedly enjoyed, has been less troubled with this than any other nation. There it has only fallen to one third. But in many other countries it is not a fiftieth of its original value.

The inconveniences of such practices are very great. The debasement of the coin hinders commerce or at least greatly embarrasses it. A new calculation must be made, how much of the new coin must be given for so much of the old. People are disposed to keep their goods from the market, as they know not what they will get for them. Thus a stagnation of commerce is occasioned. Besides, the debasing of the coin takes away the public faith. No body will lend any sum to the government, or bargain with it, as he perhaps may be paid with one half of it. As there is a fraud committed by the government, every subject must be allowed to do the same and pay his debts with the new money, which is less than he owed. This scheme, however, serves the purpose for some small time, on the following account. The use of money is twofold, for the payment of debts and the purchasing of commodities. When the coin is debased, a debt of twenty shillings is

243 then paid with ten, but if the new coin be carried to a forreign market | it will give nothing but the old value. All day labourers are paid in the new coin. The necessities of life must be sold at what the greater part of people can give, and consequently their price will for sometime be diminished. However, the king himself loses much, tho' he gains in the meantime. His doubling it is no doubt a present advantage, but it necessarily diminishes his revenue, because all his taxes are paid in the new coin. To prevent this loss the French, and indeed all other nations on the like occasion, when they double the money by edict without recoinage, make the augmentation after the money is called in and before it goes out, and a diminution is made before next term of payment.[18] A diminution has always a worse effect than an augmentation. An augmentation injures the creditor, a diminution the debtor, who should always be favoured. If I bind for ten pounds and be obliged to pay fifteen, common industry must be excessively embarrassed.

The coins of most countries are either of copper, silver, or gold. We are obliged even to receive payment in sixpences, which sometimes is the occasion of confusion and loss of time. The different coins are regulated

[18] Augmentation was by increasing, and diminution by decreasing, the number of livres (money of account, not actual coins) in a coin of given weight. Cf. LJ(A) ii.81 and vi.123, above.

not by the caprice of the government, but by the market price of gold and silver, and according to this the proportion of gold and silver ⟨is⟩ settled.

244 | This proportion sometimes varies a little. The guineas sometime ago were valued at 22 shillings, and at other times they have been at 20. The gold rises more in proportion in Brittain than any where else, and as it makes the silver of somewhat less value it is the cause of a real inconvenience. As silver buys more gold abroad than at home, by sending abroad silver they bring gold in return, which buys more silver here than it does abroad. By this means a kind of trade is made of it, the gold coin encreasing and the value[19] diminishing. Sometime ago a proposal was given in to remedy this, but it was thought so complex a case that they resolved for that time not to meddle with it. We have shewn what rendered money the measure of value, but it is to be observed that labour, not money, is the true measure of value. National opulence consists therefore in the quantity of goods and the facility of barter. This shall next be considered.

The more money that is necessary to circulate the goods of any country, the more is the quantity of goods diminished. Suppose that the whole 245 stock of Scotland in corn, cattle, money, etca. | amounts to 20 millions, and if one million in cash is necessary to carry on the circulation, there will be in the country only 19 millions of food, cloaths, and lodging, and the people have less by one million than they would have if there were no occasion for this expedient of money. It is therefore evident that the poverty of any country encreases as the money encreases, money being a dead stock in itself, supplying no convenience of life. Money in this respect may be compared to the high roads of a country, which bear neither corn nor grass themselves but circulate all the corn and grass in the country. If we could find any way to save the ground taken up by highways, we would encrease considerably the quantity of commodities and have more to carry to the market. In the same manner as ⟨?the value of⟩ a piece of ground does not lye in the number of highways that run thro' it, so the riches of a country does not consist in the quantity of money employed to circulate commerce, but in the great abundance of the necessaries of life. If we could therefore fall on a method to send the half of our money abroad to be converted into goods, and at the same time supply the channel of circulation at home, we 246 would greatly encrease the wealth of the country. | Hence the beneficial effects of the erection of banks and paper credit. It is easy to shew that the erection of banks is of advantage to the commerce of a country. Suppose as above that the whole stock of Scotland amounted to 20 millions, and that 2 millions are employed in the circulation of it, the other 18 are in commodities. If then the banks in Scotland issued out notes to the value of 2 millions, and reserved among them 300,000£ to answer immediate demands, there would be one million seven hundered thousand pounds

---

[19] Reporter's or copyist's error for 'silver'.

circulating in cash, and 2 millions of paper money besides. The natural
circulation however is 2 million, and the channel will receive no more.
What is over will be sent abroad to bring home materials for food, cloaths,
and lodging. That this has a tendencey to enrich a nation may be seen at
first sight, for whatever commodities are imported, just so much is added
to the opulence of the country.[20] The only objection against paper money is
that it drains the country of gold and silver, that bank notes will not circulate in a forreign mercat, and that forreign commodities must be paid in
247 specie. This is no doubt the case. | But if we consider attentively we will
find that this is no real hurt to a country. The opulence of a nation does not
consist in the quantity of coin but in the abundance of the commodities
which are necessary for life, and whatever tends to encrease these tends so
far to encrease the riches of a country.

Money is fit for none of the necessaries of life; it cannot of itself afford
either food, cloaths, or lodging, but must be exchanged for commodities fit
for these purposes. If all the coin of the nation were exported and our commodities proportionably encreased, it might be recalled on any sudden
emergencey sooner than any one could well imagine. Goods will always
bring in money, and as long as the stock of commodities in any nation
encreases, they have it in their power to augment the quantity of coin, if
thought necessary, by exporting their stock to forreign countries. This
reasoning is confirmed by matter of fact. We find that the commerce of
every nation in Europe has been prodigiously encreased by the erection of
banks. In this country every body is sensible of their good effects, and our
American colonies, where most of the commerce is carried on by paper
circulation, are in a most flourishing condition.

248     | What first gave occasion to the establishment of banks was to facilitate
the transferrence of money. This at this day is the only design of the bank
at Amsterdam. When commerce is carried to a high pitch, the delivery of
gold and silver consumes a great deal of time. When a great merchant had
ten or 20 thousand pound to give away, he would take almost a week to
count it out in guineas and shillings. A bank bill prevents all this trouble.
Before the erection of the bank[s] at Amsterdam, the method the merchants
fell upon to lessen the trouble of counting out great quantities of cash was
to keep certain sums put up in bags to answer immediate demands. In this
case you must either trust the honesty of the merchant or you must take
the trouble of counting it over. If you trusted his fidelity, frequent frauds
would be committed; if not, your trouble was not lessened. The inconveniences arising from this gave occasion to the erection of that bank, of
which the whole transaction is this: you deposit a certain sum of money
there, and the bank gives you a bill to that extent. This money is secure,

[20] There is no direct counterpart in LJ(A) of most of the material between this point
and the end of the first paragraph on 253 below. Cf. p. 380 above.

249  and you never call for it, because the bill will generally | sell above par, and
     it is therefore an advantage to yourself to let it ly. The bank has no office for
     payment, because there is seldom any payment demanded. In this manner
     the bank of Amsterdam has a good effect in facilitating commerce, and it's
     notes circulate only there. The credit of that city is not in the least en-
     dangered by the bank. In 1701,[21] when the French army was at Utrecht,
     a sudden demand was made upon it, and all Holland was alarmed with the
     expected fatal consequences, but no danger ensued. Before this a suspicion
     prevailed that the bankers had fallen into a custom of trading with the
     money, but at that time it was found that a great quantity of the money had
     been scorched by a fire that happened in the neighbourhood about 50 years
     before that. This plainly shewed that there was no ground for the sus-
     picion, and the credit of the bank remained unhurt. It has been affirmed by
     some that the bank of Amsterdam has always money in its stores to the
     amount of 80 or 90 millions. But this has lately been shown by an ingenious
     gentleman to be false, from a comparison of the trade of London and
     Amsterdam.[22]

250      | The constitution of the banks in Brittain differs widely from that in
     Amsterdam. Here there is only about a sixth part of the stock kept in
     readiness for answering demands, and the rest is employed in trade.
     Originaly they were on the same footing with the Amsterdam bank, but
     the directors taking liberty to send out money, they gradually came to their
     present situation.

         The ruin of a bank would not be so dangerous as is commonly imagined.
     Suppose all the money in Scotland was issued by one bank and that it
     became bankrupt, a very few individuals would be ruined by it, but not
     many, because the quantity of cash or paper that people have in their hands
     bears no proportion to their wealth. Neither would the wealth of the whole
     country be much hurt by it, because the 100 part of the riches of a country
     does not consist in money. The only method to prevent the bad conse-
     quence arising from the ruin of banks is to give monopolies to none, but to
     encourage the erection of as many as possible. When several are established
     in a country, a mutual jealousy prevails, they are continualy making un-
     expected runs on one another. This puts them on their guard and obliges
     them to provide themselves against such demands. Was there but one bank
251  in Scotland it would perhaps be a little more enterprizing | as it would have
     no rival, and by mismanagement might become bankrupt, but a number
     puts this beyond all danger. Even tho' one did break, every individual
     ⟨would⟩ have very few of it's notes. From all these considerations it is

---

[21] In fact 1672.

[22] Nicholas Magens, *The Universal Merchant* (London, 1753), 32–3. Cf. also the same
author's *Farther Explanations of some Particular Subjects . . . contained in the Universal
Merchant* (London, 1756), 24–7.

manifest that banks are beneficial to the commerce of a country, and that it is a bad police to restrain them.

Several political writers have published treatises to shew the pernicious nature of banks and paper money. Mun, a London merchant, published one with this intention,[23] in answer to a book that had been written on the opposite before. He affirms that as England is drained of it's money it must go to ruin. The circulation of paper banishes gold and silver from the country. All other goods which we have in our possession, being spent upon our subsistence, gradually diminish, and must at last come to an end. Money never decays, a stock of it will last for ever, and by keeping up great quantities of it in the country we shall insure our riches as long as the world stands. This reasoning was in these days thought very satisfactory. But from what has been said before concerning the nature of public opulence, it appears evidently absurd.

252     | Sometime after that, Mr. Gee, likewise a merchant, wrote with the

---

[23] Mun did not in fact publish any treatise with the intention of showing 'the pernicious nature of banks and paper money'. Smith has evidently been rather badly misreported in this passage, of which there is unfortunately no counterpart in LJ(A). In order to reconstruct Smith's actual argument, the best starting-point is his own summary of this section of the Lectures in ED 35–6, below. Under the general heading of money as an instrument of commerce, or medium of exchange, his aim is to make three separate but closely related points: first, that the greater the amount of the precious metals necessary to circulate the goods of a country, the smaller will be the amount of food, clothing, and housing in the country; second, that any contrivances (e.g. banks and paper money) which can enable the goods of a country to be circulated with a smaller quantity of the precious metals will be very advantageous to the country; and third, that national opulence neither consists in nor depends upon the quantity of the precious metals in the country, and that no kind of preference ought to be given to this species of goods above any other. Under this third subheading, Smith sets out to deal in particular with what he calls in ED 'the bad effects of the contrary opinion both in speculation and practice'. In the passage in the Lectures to which the present note refers, Smith is evidently embarking upon his discussion of 'the bad effects of the contrary opinion' *in speculation*—i.e., roughly, in economic theory. He probably began this discussion by reminding his class of a point he had made a little earlier under the second subheading (246–7 above), to the effect that those writers (Hume and Harris, for example) who objected to paper money on the ground that it drained the country of gold and silver were implicitly adopting (at any rate up to a point) the notion that opulence consists in and depends upon the quantity of the precious metals. He may then have gone on to say that the same notion, in more explicit form, lay behind the advocacy by earlier writers like Mun of measures to attract 'treasure' by means of foreign trade. Unfortunately the reporter apparently lost the thread, and attributed to Mun, quite incorrectly, the idea that banks and paper money were pernicious—together with the idea that 'money never decays', which Smith usually in fact attributed to Locke. On this interpretation, the passages which follow the present one fall neatly into place. Gee's book, which was concerned, as Mun's had been, with the relation between the balance of trade and the quantity of 'treasure' in a country, comes up next for consideration. Then, by way of a reply to Mun and Gee, Smith outlines and commends Hume's famous theory of the specie-flow mechanism in international trade—although not without a critical backward glance, in the last sentence of the relevant paragraph, at Hume's ideas about paper money. The next paragraph (marking the point at which the text of LJ(A) resumes) is perhaps best considered as a digression; and the following one, dealing specifically with Locke's 'money never decays' idea, is self-explanatory.

same intention.[24] He endeavours to shew that England would soon be ruined by trade with forreign countries; by the exchange he calculates that the balance is always against us, and consequently that in almost all our commercial dealings with other nations we are losers. As they drain us of our money, we must soon come to ruin.[25] The absurdity of this is likewise evident from former considerations, and we find that tho' no stop was put to the manner of carrying on forreign commerce by any regulations, the nation has prodigiously encreased in riches, and is still encreasing. He proposed indeed some regulations to prevent our ruin from this quarter, which if the government had been foolish ⟨?enough⟩ to have complied with, they would more probably have impoverished the nation.

Mr. Hume published some essays shewing the absurdity of these and other such doctrines.[26] He proves very ingeniously that money must always bear[s] a certain proportion to the quantity of commodities in every country, that wherever money is accumulated beyond the proportion of commodities in any country the price of goods will necessarily rise, that this country will be undersold at the forreign market and consequently the

253 money | must depart into other nations; but on the contrary whenever the quantity of money falls below the proportion of goods the price of goods diminishes, the country undersells others in forreign marketts and consequently money returns in great plenty. Thus money and goods will keep near about a certain level in every country.[27] Mr. Hume's reasoning is exceedingly ingenious. He seems however to have gone a little into the notion that public opulence consists in money, which was considered above.[28]

We may observe upon this that human industry always multiplies goods and money together, tho' not always in the same proportion. The labour of men will always be employed in produceing whatever is the object of human desire, and things will encrease in proportion as it is in the power of man to cultivate them. Corn and other commodities of that kind must always be produced in greater abundance than gold, precious stones, and the like, because they are more within the reach of human industry. Almost any part of the surface of the earth may by proper culture be made capable

[24] Joshua Gee, *The Trade and Navigation of Great-Britain Considered* (1729). Gee's intention, of course, was *not* to show 'the pernicious nature of banks and paper money'. See previous note.

[25] Cf. op. cit., 'Conclusion' (separately paginated), 16: 'A Nation may gain vast Riches by Trade and Commerce, or for Want of due Regard and Attention may be drained of them. I am the more willing to mention this, because I am afraid that the present Circumstances of ours carries out more Riches than it brings home.'

[26] Smith is probably referring here not only to Hume's essay 'Of the Balance of Trade', which contains the argument he is about to describe, but also to the essays 'Of Money' and 'Of the Jealousy of Trade'.

[27] 'Of the Balance of Trade', *Essays*, I.333–4.

[28] The reference is probably to those places in his essays where Hume argues against paper money. Cf. *Essays*, I.311–12 ('Of Money') and I.337–8 ('Of the Balance of Trade').

of produceing corn, but gold is not to be found every where, and even
254 where it is to be found it lies concealed in the bowells of the earth, | and to
produce a small quantity of it long time and much labour are requisite. For
these reasons money never encreases in proportion to the increase of goods,
and consequently money will be sold at a cheaper rate in proportion as
a country becomes opulent. In savage nations money gives a vast price
because savages have no money but ⟨?what⟩ they acquire by plunder, for
they have not that knowledge which is necessary for produceing money in
their own country. But when a nation arrives at a certain degree of improvement in the arts, it's value diminishes; then they begin to search the mines
and manufacture it themselves. From the fall of the Roman Empire to the
discovery of the West Indies, the value of money was very high and continualy encreasing. Since that latter period it's value has decreased considerably.

Mr. Locke, too, published a treatise to show the pernicious consequences
of allowing the nation to be drained of money. His notions were likewise
founded upon the idea that public opulence consists in money, tho' he
treats the matter in a more philosophical light than the rest.

He affirms with Mr. Mun that if there is no money in a nation it must
255 soon come to ruin, | that all commodities are soon spent, but money lasts
for ever. Upon the whole we may observe on this subject that the reason
why our riches do not consist in money, but commodities, is that money
cannot be used for any of the purposes of life, but that commodities are
fitted for our subsistence. The consumptibility, if we may use the word, of
goods is the great cause of human industry, and an industrious people will
always produce more than they consume. It is easy to shew how small
a proportion the cash in every country bears to the public opulence. It is
generally supposed that there are 30 millions of money circulating in
Brittain, but the annual consumption amounts to much more than a 100
millions, for, computing the inhabitants of the island at 10 millions, and
allowing 10 pounds per annum for the subsistence of each person, which is
by much too little, the whole annual consumption amounts to that sum. So
it appears that the circulating cash bears but a small proportion to the
whole opulence of the country.[29] It is probable however that there are not
30 millions in Brittain, and in that case the proportion will be still less.

It is said by some who support the notion that the riches of a country
consists in money, that when a person retires from trade he turns his
256 stock immediately into cash. | It is plain, however, that the reason of this is

[29] The reporter has missed the point here, as a reference back to LJ(A) vi.138 will show.
The comparison which Smith is making is *not* between the 30 millions of money and an
'annual consumption' estimated at upwards of 100 millions, but between the 30 millions of
money and the value of the 'stock' which may be conceived to have produced this 'annual
consumption'—approximately 1,000 millions, according to Smith's account as reported in
LJ(A).

that as money is the instrument of commerce, a man can change it for the necessaries and elegancies of life more easily than any thing else. Even the miser who locks up his gold in his chest has this end in view. No man in his senses hoards up money for it's own sake, but he considers that by keeping money always by him he has it in his power to supply at once all the necessities of himself and his family. This opinion that riches consist in money, as it is absurd in speculation, so it has given occasion to many prejudicial errors in practice, some of which are the following.

It was owing to these tenets that the government prohibited the exportation of coin.[z] Which prohibition has been extremely hurtfull to the commerce of the country, because whatever quantity of money there is in any country above what is sufficient for the circulation is merely a dead stock.

In King William's time there were two species of coin, milled and unmilled. The unmilled was frequently clipped by different persons in it's circulation. This occasioned frequent disorders among the people, and therefore the Parliament ordered all the clipt money to be brought into the

257 Mint, and the government was at the expence of recoining it, | which operation cost them about 2 millions. As they had been at this expence, they thought it just and proper to prohibit the exportation of money for the future. The merchants however complained of this hardship, and were then allowed to export money to a small extent. The great complaint, however, was always scarceity of money. In order to remedy this, the government established a common office for coining money where every one might get their gold and silver turned into coin without any expence. The consequence of this was that as coin was of no more value than bullion a great deal of coin was melted down and exported. To prevent this it was rendered felony to melt coin, but it is so simple an operation, and so easily gone about, that the law was easily eluded. The immediate effect of this regulation was that more coin was exported than ever. This might have been easily prevented by fixing a certain price upon the coinage of bullion, or by ordaining the Master of the Mint to be paid by the persons who brought their money to be coined. But such a regulation was never thought of. Any regulation of the above kind is very absurd, for there is no fear if things be left to their free course that any nation will want money sufficient for the circulation of their commodities, and every prohibition of exporta-

258 tion is always ineffectuall, | and very often occasions the exportation of more than otherwise would be. Suppose for instance the Portuguese prohibited from exporting their money by a capital punishment. As they have few goods to give in exchange for ours, their forreign trade must cease; or if they attempt to smuggle, the British merchant must lay such a price upon

[z] The copyist wrote 'corn'. This has been emended, both in the text and in the margin, by a second (probably eighteenth-century) hand, to 'coin'.

his goods as will be sufficient to reward him for the risk he runs of being detected, and the Portuguese merchant, being obliged to buy his goods too dear, must be a loser. In general, every prohibition of this kind[a] hurts the commerce of a country. Every unecessary accumulation of money is a dead stock which might be employed in enriching the nation by forreign commerce. It likewise raises the price of goods, and makes the country undersold at forreign markets.

It is to be observed that prohibiting the exportation of money is realy one great cause of the poverty of Spain and Portugal. When they got possession of the mines of Mexico and Peru, they thought they could command all Europe by the continual supplies which they received from thence, if they could keep the money among them, and therefore they prohibited the exportation of it. But this had a quite contrary effect, for when money is, as it were, dammed up to an unatural height, and there is more than the circulation requires, the consequences are very unfavourable to the country.
259 | For it is impossible that the exportation of gold and silver can be wholly stopped, as the balance of trade must be against them, that is, they must buy more than they sell, and it is indispensibly necessary that this balance be paid in money. Every commodity rises to an extravagant height. The Portuguese pay for English cloth, additional to the natural price of it, the expence and risk of carrying it there, for no body ever saw a Spanish or Portuguese ship in a British harbour. All the goods sent to these countries are carried by ourselves and consigned to the British factors, to be disposed of by them. But besides the carriage and insurance, the British merchant must be paid for the risk of having his money seized in Portugal in consequence of the prohibition. All risk of forfeiture or penalty must ly upon the goods. This has a miserable effect upon the domestic industry of these countries, and has put a stop to their manufactures. No body ever saw a piece of Spanish cloth in any other country, yet they have the best materials in the world and, with the same art that we have, might monopolize the trade of Europe. It drew the attention of the nations who trade with them in these commodities, when a general on a certain occasion presented to
260 His Majesty | the regiment of which he had the command cloathed in the manufactures of Spain. In general they export no manufactured commodities, swords and armour excepted, as they have confessedly the best steel in the world, but only the spontaneous productions of the country such as fruits and wines.

Regulations of a similar nature were made in Brittain in King William's time. Money was thought to constitute opulence, and therefore the accumulation of it commanded the whole of the public attention. They coined all money brought in for nothing, and the expences of coinage, which amounted to about fourteen thousand pounds, were entirely thrown away; and,

---

[a] The copyist apparently began to write 'sort' and then overwrote 'kind'

besides, great encouragement was given to exportation, because, as gold and silver were coined for nothing, coined money could never be dearer than bullion. As the exportation of bullion was free they melted down the coin and sent it abroad. At present there is a great temptation to such practices, for an oz. of pure silver at mint price is exactly valued at 5 sh. 2ᵈ, but bullion is often bought at 5 sh. 6ᵈ. As nothing is lost in melting, here is a profit of 4ᵈ per oz. It is on this account that we seldom or never see a new shilling, and it is one of the causes that silver is so scarce in proportion to gold.

261      | The idea of publick opulence consisting in money has been productive of other bad effects. Upon this principle most pernicious regulations have been established. These species of commerce which drain us of our money are thought disadvantageous and these which increase it beneficial; therefore the former are prohibited and the latter encouraged. As France is thought to produce more of the elegancies of life than this country, and as we take much from them and they need little from us, the balance of trade is against us, and therefore almost all our trade with France is prohibited by great taxes and duties on importation. On the other hand, as Spain and Portugal take more of our commodities than we of theirs, the balance is in our favours, and this trade is not only allowed but encouraged. The absurdity of these regulations will appear on the least reflection.

All commerce that is carried on betwixt any two countries must necessarily be advantageous to both. The very intention of commerce is to exchange your own commodities for others which you think will be more convenient for you. When two men trade between themselves it is un-
262 doubtedly for the advantage of both. | The one has perhaps more of one species of commodities than he has occasion for, he therefore exchanges a certain quantity of it with the other, for another commodity that will be more usefull to him. The other agrees to the bargain on the same account, and in this manner the mutual commerce is advantageous to both. The case is exactly the same betwixt any two nations. The goods which the English merchants want to import from France are certainly more valuable to them than what they give for them. Our very desire to purchase them shews that we have more use for them than either the money or the commodities which we give for them. It may be said indeed that money lasts for ever, but that claret and cambrics are soon consumed. This is true. But what is the intention of industry if it be not to produce these things which are capable of being used, and are conduceive to the convenience and comfort of human life? Unless we use the produce of our industry, unless we can subsist more people in a better way, what avails it? Besides, if we have money to spend upon forreign commodities, what purpose serves it
263 | to keep it in the country? If the circulation of commodities require it, there will be none to spare; and if the channel of circulation be full, no more

is necessary. And if only a certain sum be necessary for that purpose, why throw more into it?

Again, by prohibiting the exportation of goods to forreign mercats, the industry of the country is greatly discouraged. It is a very great motive to industry that people have it in their power to exchange the produce of their labour for what they please, and wherever there is any restraint on people in this respect they will not be so vigorous in improving manufactures. If we be prohibited to send corn and cloth to France, that industry is stopped which raises corn and prepares cloth for the French market. It may be said indeed that if we were allowed to trade with France we would not exchange our commodities with theirs, but our money, and thus human industry is by no means discouraged. But if we attend to it we shall find that it comes to the same thing at last. By hindering people to dispose of their money as they think proper, you discourage these manufactures by which this money 264 is gained. All jealousies therefore between different nations, | and prejudices of this kind, are extremely hurtfull[b] to commerce and limit public opulence. This is always the case betwixt France and us in the time of a war.

In general we may observe that these jealousies and prohibitions are most hurtfull to the richest nations, and that in proportion as a free commerce would be advantageous. When a rich man and a poor man deal with one another, both of them will encrease their riches, if they deal prudently, but the rich man's stock will encrease in a greater proportion than the poor man's. In like manner, when a rich and a poor nation engage in trade the rich nation will have the greatest advantage, and therefore the prohibition of this commerce is most hurtfull to it of the two. All our trade with France is prohibited by the high duties imposed on every French commodity imported. It would however have been better police to encourage our trade with France. If any forreign commerce is to be prohibited, it ought to be that with Spain and Portugal. This would have been much more advantageous to England. France is much more populous, a more extensive country, farther advanced in arts and manufactures of every kind, and the 265 industry which a commerce | with that country would have exerted[30] at home would have been much greater. Twenty millions of people perhaps in a great society, working as it were to one anothers hands, from the nature of the division of labour before explained would produce a thousand times more goods than another society consisting only of 2 or 3 millions. It were happy, therefore, both for this country and for France, that all national prejudices were rooted out, and a free and uninterrupted commerce established. It may be observed in general that we never heard of any

---

[b] Inserted by a second (probably eighteenth-century) hand

[30] Probably copyist's error for 'excited'.

nation ruined by this balance of trade. When Gee published his book, the balance with all nations were against us, except Spain and Portugal. It was then thought that in a few years we would be reduced to an absolute state of poverty. This indeed has been the cry of all political writers since the time of Charles II$^d$. Notwithstanding all this we find ourselves far richer than before, and when there is$^c$ occasion for it we can raise much more money than ever has been done. A late Minister of State levied in one year 23 millions with greater ease than Lord Godolphin could levy 6 in Q. Ann's time.

266   | The French and Dutch writer's, embraceing the same principle, frequently alarmed their country with the same groundless terror, but they still continue to flourish.

It is to be observed that the poverty of a nation can never proceed from forreign trade if carried on with wisdom and prudence. The poverty of a nation proceeds from much the same causes with these which render an individual poor.

When a man consumes more than he gains by his industry, he must impoverish himself unless he has some other way of subsistence. In the same manner, if a nation consume more than it produces, poverty is inevitable. If its annual produce be 90 millions and it's annual consumption an 100, then it spends, eats and drinks, tears, wears, 10 millions more than it produces, and it's stock of opulence must gradualy ⟨?come⟩ to nothing.

There is still another bad effect proceeding from that absurd notion that national opulence consists in money. It is commonly imagined that whatever people spend in their own country cannot diminish public opulence,

267 if you take care of exports and imports. | This is the foundation of Dr. Mandevilles system that private vices are public benefits. What is spent at home is all spent among ourselves, none of it goes out of the country. But it is evident that when any man tears and wears and spends his stock, without employing himself in any species of industry, the nation is at the end of the year so much the poorer by it. If he spend only the interest of the money he does no harm, as the capital still remains and is employed in promoting industry, but if he spend the capital the whole is gone. To illustrate this let us make a supposition, that my father at his death, instead of a thousand pounds in cash, leaves me the necessaries and conveniences of life to the same value, which is precisely the same as if he left it in money because I afterwards purchase them in money. I get a number of idle folks about me and eat, drink, tear and wear, till the whole is consumed. By this I not only reduce myself to want, but certainly rob the public stock of a 1000 pounds, as it is spent and nothing produced for it. As a farther illustration of the hurt which the public receives from such practices, let us suppose that this island was invaded by a numerous band of Tartars, a

---

$^c$ 'no' deleted

people who are still in the state of shepherds, a people who lead a roving
268 life and have little or no idea of industry. | Here they would find all com-
modities for the taking, they would put on fine cloaths, eat, drink, tear and
wear every thing they laid their hands upon. The consequence would be
that from the highest degree of opulence the whole country would be
reduced to the lowest pitch of misery and brought back to its ancient state.
The 30 millions of money would probably remain for sometime. But all the
necessaries of life would be consumed. This shews the absurdity of that
opinion that no home consumption can hurt the opulence of a country.

Upon this principle that no public expence employed at home can be
hurtfull, a war in Germany is thought a dreadfull calamity, as it drains the
country of money, and a land war is always thought more prejudicial than a
sea one for the same reason. But upon reflection we will find that it is the
same thing to the nation how or where its stock be spent. If I purchase
a thousand pounds worth of French wines and drink them all when they
come home, the country is 2000 pounds poorer, because both the goods and
money are gone. If I spend a 1000 pounds worth of goods at home upon
myself, the country is only deprived of 1000 pounds, as the money still
remains. But in maintaining an army in a distant war it is the same thing
whether we pay them in goods or money, because the consumption is the
269 same at any rate. | Perhaps it is the better police to pay them in money, as
goods are better fitted for the purposes of life at home. For the same reason
there is no difference between land and sea wars, as is commonly imagined.

From the above considerations it appears that Brittain should by all
means be made a free port, that there should be no interruptions of any
kind made to forreign trade, that if it were possible to defray the expences of
government by any other method, all duties, customs, and excise should be
abolished, and that free commerce and liberty of exchange should be
allowed with all nations and for all things.

But still further, and on the same principles as above, an apology is made
for the public debt. Say they, tho' we ⟨owe⟩ at present above 100 millions,
we owe it to ourselves, or at least very little of it to forreigners. It is just the
right hand owing the left, and on the whole can be little or no disadvantage.
But ⟨it⟩ is to be considered that the interest of this 100 millions is paid by
industrious people, and given to support idle people who are employed in
gathering it. Thus industry is taxed to support idleness. If the debt had not
been contracted, by prudence and oeconomy the nation would have been
much richer than at present. Their industry would not be hurt by the
270 oppression of these idle people who live upon it. | Instead of the brewer
paying taxes which are often improper, the stock might have been lent out
to such industrious people as would have made 6 or 7 per cent. by it, and
have given better interest than the government does. This stock would
then have been employed for the country⟨'s⟩ wellfare. When there are such

heavy taxes to pay, every merchant must carry on less trade than he would otherwise do; he has his taxes to pay before he sell any of his commodities. This narrows as it were his stock, and hinders his trade from being so extensive as it otherwise would be. To stop this clamour Sir Robert Walpole endeavoured to shew that the public debt was no inconvenience, tho' it is to be supposed that a man of his abilities saw the contrary himself.[31]

The last bad effect that shall be taken notice of is the notion of Mr. Law, a Scotch merchant. He thought that national opulence consists in money, and that the value of gold and silver is arbitrary and depends on constitution and agreement. He imagined that the idea of value might be brought to paper, and it preferred to money. If this could be done, he thought it would be a great convenience, as the government then might do

271 what it pleased, | raise armies, pay soldiers, and be at any expense whatever. Mr. Law proposed his scheme to the Scotch Parliament in 1701.[32] It was rejected, and he went over to France, where his project was relish'd by the Duke of Orleans. In this book[33] he agrees with the forementioned writers that, the balance of trade being against a nation, it must soon be drained of its money. In order to turn the balance of trade in our favours, he proposed to the Scotch Parliament the following scheme.

As there was little gold or silver in this country, he thought they might fall upon some other method of creating money independent of it, to witt, by paper. On this account he proposed the erecting of a land bank at Edinburgh, in which it is to be observed he falls into many blunders concerning tenures and the nature of property. At this bank they were to keep by them only 20 or 30 thousand pounds to answer small demands, and to give out notes for land. For 2 acres of arable land they were to issue out a note of equal value, and if any extraordinary demand was made upon them, they would pay so much of it in money and so much in land. By this means in a very short time the whole land of Scotland would go from hand

272 to hand, | as a 20 shilling note does. As this project never was executed, it is hard to say what the consequence might have been; it is however obviously liable to the following inconveniences. Taking the land rent of Scotland at 5 million per annum, tho' it be much more, at 20 years purchase it amounts to an 100 millions; there would then be just so much currency in the country, and if one million was then necessary for circulation there would just be 99 millions for no purpose, as none of it could go abroad. They would not have been able to maintain one man more than formerly, as their

---

[31] This was alleged against Walpole (later Lord Orford) by Hume, 'Of Public Credit', *Essays*, I.362, note 2 (a passage omitted in editions after 1768).

[32] In fact 1705. The date in the text is that of Law's *Proposals and Reasons for Constituting a Council of Trade in Scotland* (now attributed to William Paterson).

[33] *Money and Trade Considered; with a Proposal for Supplying the Nation with Money* (1705), especially ch. VII.

food, cloaths, and lodging would not have been encreased, and every commodity would have risen to 99 times it's present value.

Mr. Law, not meeting with the encouragement he expected, went over to France in the year[s] 1714 and, as was before mentioned, found favour with the Duke of Orleans, then Regent,[34] and got liberty to erect a bank there, which at first was only to the extent of 6 millions of livres[35] or 3200£ sterling. From this beginning he carried it on to a very great height, issued out many notes, and in a short time engrossed the whole circulation of

273 France. | As Mr. Law's notes were received in payment of the revenue, this contributed to the success of the scheme. This too had a greater effect in France than it could have had here, considering the number of taxes and the manner in which they are levied. By this and other circumstances his notes were always at par with gold and silver, especially as they were making continual changes in their coin. About that time 28 livres, which were equal to 8 ounces of pure silver, were raised to 60, and as a diminution of coin is always the consequent of a sudden rise,[36] this was daily expected. Mr. Law made his notes payable in what was called the money of the day. Instead of promising to pay his notes, as we would say, in pounds sterling, he did it in crowns and half crowns, which was a very proper method to make them par with gold and silver. Suppose that our coin were raised to double, a half crown would become a crown, and so in this manner the bank notes and money would rise and fall together.[37]

274 | As Law wanted to make his notes above par, he fell upon the following scheme. He issued out his bank notes payable in livres turnois,[38] by which, when the coin came to be diminished, he would not be obliged to pay above one half. The coin was not received in the market or elsewhere, as the diminution was still expected and did not come for sometime. This favoured his design and kept the notes above par, by which the credit of his bank was established. The next step Mr. Law fell upon was the relieving of the public debts, which amounted to 200 millions.[39] As he saw the diminution must needs come, he took another method to keep up his notes. He got a grant of the exclusive priviledge of trading to Canada, and established the Mississippi Company. To this he joined the African, the Turky, and the East India companies. He also farmed the tobacco and all the public revenues of

[34] In fact the Duke became Regent on the death of Louis XIV on 1 September 1715.
[35] P. Du Verney, *Examen du livre intitulé Réflexions politiques sur les finances et le commerce* (1740), I.207 ff.
[36] Cf. 243 above.
[37] The pound, like the French livre, was then not a particular coin but a money of account, and its value could be changed by altering the amount of silver coined in twenty shillings.
[38] The *livre tournois* was the livre (of 20 sous) minted at Tours.
[39] The figure should probably be 2,000 millions, which is near to that given by Dutot, *Réflexions politiques sur les finances et le commerce* (1738), in E. Daire, ed., *Économistes financiers du XVIIIᵉ siècle* (1843), 806.

275 France at 12 millions,[40] | for in France the whole revenue is farmed by one man, who undertakes it and levies it without excisemen, and the farmers there are the richest in the country, and must be skilled in the finances and public revenues. Mr. Law undertook this, and having the whole trade of the country monopolized, it was difficult to say what profits he would make.

He wanted to lend the government 80 or 90 millions, which he could easily do by issuing notes to that value, but then he saw that they would soon return upon him. To prevent this his invention was sett on work, and we shall see how far he succeeded. As the company he erected seemed to be in a very flourishing condition, shares were purchased in it at a very considerable rate. He opened a subscription to it at 500 livres, so that a navy ticket or billet d'etat purchased a share into it, which raised them to a par as they had for a long time been far below it. The government of France was never in such a miserable condition as then. The interest of the money

276 which should have paid the billets d'etat | was seized upon for other purposes. Never was monarch more degraded than Lewis XIV[th]. After the Treaty of Utrecht he had occasion to borrow 8 millions of livres from Holland, and not only to give them his bond for 32 millions but to get some merchants to be security for him.[41] Since that was the case, we need not be surprized that the billets d'etat sold at great discount, as they bore no interest and it was quite uncertain when they would be paid. Law published a declaration that one of these, which was granted for 500 livres, should purchase a share in the company, and thus they came again to par. The people still continuing in great expectations of profit, he in a few days opened a new subscription at 5000 livres, and afterwards another at 10000. At this time he was enabled to lend the government 1600 millions of livres at 3 per cent.[42] Had he stopt here it is probable that he would have answered all engagements, but his future proceedings ruined all. It was impossible that the value of shares could long continue at such a high rate.

277 | He thought, however, that it was necessary to do all that he could to keep them up, as the whole fortunes of many people were in the bank. He had issued out notes to double the circulation of the country, which raised the price of every thing to an enormous pitch, and consequently the exchange was against France in all forreign trade. This was principaly occasioned by his opening an office to purchase 500 livres shares at 9000 livres,[43] which obliged him to issue out many notes. People of prudence who were concerned opposed this scheme, and indeed it was the first thing that made his bank lose credit and occasioned it's dissolution. As he was not obliged to pay the capital sums, only the annual dividend of 200 livres

[40] Du Verney, op. cit., I.249, gives the figure as 52 millions.
[41] Cf. Dutot, op. cit., 805.
[42] Du Verney, op. cit., I.250, 273, 289.                    [43] Ibid., I.280–1.

arising from the profits, he might have let them fall to their original 500 without any great loss but that of reputation. But his buying up the shares occasioned his issuing out so many notes that they must of necessity return upon him. This was so much the case that he was obliged to open offices in different parts of Paris for the payment of them. When in this manner oppressed, he was making continual changes on the coin, in order to dissuade people from returning on the bank, and disgust them at gold

278 and silver.[44] | He cried up gold, but as coin cannot be kept much above the level of the mettal, when it was so much depreciated it was not taken. If a person had 20,000 guineas, as he was affraid that the coin would not continue at that value, he went to the bank and got it exchanged for notes. The same consideration prevented them from returning upon the bank, as they would there be paid in coin. By this means he not only prevented his notes from coming upon him, but filled his coffers with almost all the gold in the country. In order to accomplish this part of his scheme more perfectly, he most arbitrarily published an edict prohibiting any persons from keeping by them gold or silver beyond a certain sum.[45] He also took away the severe penalties that were in force against the exportation of coin, and every person was allowed to export money free from duty.[46] By this means much of it went to Holland. He reasoned with himself, some instrument of exchange is necessary. Paper, gold, and silver at present are the medium. If gold and silver be utterly exported, paper only remains, and may be ren-

279 dered the sole instrument of commerce. | This he thought he had done effectualy when by an edict he had swept a part into his coffers, and cleared the country of the remainder. They would therefore be obliged to take paper. At last, however, after a great number of expedients he found it was impracticable. By paying out great sums he kept off ruin for some months, but at last published an edict that all bank notes were to be paid only in one half; and indeed if he had stood to this, as some imagined he might have done, it would have been far better than to have suffered the after consequences. Upon this edict the credit of the bank was entirely broken, and the bank notes all on a sudden sunk to nothing.[47]

This ruined an immense number of people. Brittain can never be much hurt by the breaking of a bank, because few people keep notes by them to any value.[48] A man worth 40,000£ will scarce ever have 500£ of notes by him. But the breaking of this bank in France occasioned the most dreadfull confusion. The greatest part of people had their whole fortunes in notes and were reduced to a state of beggary. The only people who were safe were the stockjobbers who had sold out in time, or with their bank notes had

280 purchased all the valuable goods and a great deal of land, tho' | [tho'] at the highest prices. These made immense fortunes by it.

[44] Ibid., I.316.        [45] Ibid., I.335.        [46] Ibid., I.320–1.
[47] Ibid., II.6–8.        [48] Cf. 250 above.

The South Sea scheme in our own country was nothing to this. No body was under any obligations of going into it, the government had no share in it, and the loss was but a triffle in comparison. The clamour which Laws last edict made caused it soon to be rescinded, and the notes were again declared to be paid at value. But the bank never recovered it's credit, and this had no effect. However, by raising the coin and other expedients he kept it from May to October, and then[49] was obliged to leave France, which with difficulty he accomplished; his goods were confiscated and he died soon after.[50]

This amazing scheme was founded on these two principles, that public opulence consists in money, and that the value of money is arbitrary, founded upon the common consent of mankind. Consistent with these principles he thought he might easily encrease the public opulence if he could annex the idea of money to paper, and the government could never be at any loss to produce any effect that money could do.

This scheme of Mr. Laws was by no means contemptible; he realy
281 believed in it | and was the dupe of it himself. It was thought he had provided well for himself, but it was found to be otherways. If the Duke of Orleans had lived only a few days longer, it was agreed upon that he was to have been reestablished. After his death it was not thought expedient to have it put in execution.

This scheme of Laws was imitated all over Europe. It gave occasion to the South Sea Company in England, which turned out at last a meer fraud, and, could it have been carried to as great an extent as Laws, would have been productive of the same consequences. It was erected in the latter end of Q. Ann's reign, and the intention of it was to carry on a trade to the South-Seas. For this purpose they bought up the greater part of the debts of the nation. Their stock however was not great, and the profits which could be expected from it were very inconsiderable, the expectations of the people were never greatly raised, and it's fall was not very prejudicial to the nation.

We have only two things further to mention relating to the price of commodities, to witt, interest and exchange.

It is commonly supposed that the premium of interest depends upon the
282 value of gold and silver.[51] | The value of these are regulated by their quantity, for as the quantity encreases the value diminishes, and as the quantity decreases the value rises. If we attend to it, however, we shall find that the premium of interest is regulated by the quantity of stock. About the

[49] In December 1720.
[50] In fact not until 1729.
[51] This view, which was held by many writers in the seventeenth and eighteenth centuries (including Locke, Law, and Montesquieu), had been attacked by Hume, 'Of Interest', *Essays*, I.320 ff.

time of the discovery of the West Indies, it is to be observed that common interest was at 10 or 12 per cent, and since that time it has gradualy diminished. The plain reason is this. Under the feudal constitution there could be very little accumulation of stock, which will appear from considering the situation of these three orders of men which made up the whole body of the people, the peasants, the landlords, and the merchants. The peasants had leases which depended upon the caprice of their masters. They could never encrease in wealth because the landlord was ready to squeeze it all from them, and therefore they had no motive to acquire it. As little could the landlords encrease their wealth as they lived so indolent a life and were involved in perpetual wars. The merchants again were oppressed by all ranks, and were not able to secure the produce of their 283 industry from rapine and violence. | Thus there could be little accumulation of wealth at all. But after the fall of the feudal government, these obstacles to industry were removed and the stock of commodities began gradualy to encrease. We may further observe that what one trade lends to another is not so much to be considered as money, as commodities. No doubt it is generaly money which one man delivers another in loan. But then it is immediately turned into stock, and thus the quantity of stock enables you to make a greater number of loans.

The price of interest is entirely regulated by this circumstance. If there be few who have it in their power to lend money, and a great number of people who want to borrow it, the price of interest must be high. But if the quantity of stock on hand be so great as to enable a great number to lend, it must fall proportionably.

Exchange is a method invented by merchants to facilitate the payment of money at a distance. Suppose I owe 100£ to a merchant at London, I apply to a banker in Glasgow for a bill upon another merchant in London, payable to my creditor. For this I must not only give the banker £100 but I must 284 also reward him for his trouble. | This reward is called the price or premium of exchange. Between Glasgow and London it is sometimes at 2 per cent, sometimes more, sometimes less. Between London and Glasgow again it is sometimes 4 or 5 per cent below par, and between Glasgow and the West India colonies it is often at 50 per cent below par. The value of exchange is always regulated by the risk of sending money between two places. It is often, however, greater than the risk can be supposed to be, and this is owing to paper circulation. Between Glasgow and London one can easily get £100 carried for 15 or 16 sh$^s$, but as paper in Scotland makes a great part of the currencey, and as there is an inconveniencey in getting bank notes exchanged for gold and silver, a merchant chooses rather to pay 2 per cent than take the trouble of changeing the notes for cash and sending the money. This too is the cause of the high price of exchange between

Virginia and Glasgow. In the American colonies the currencey is paper,
and their notes are 40 or 50 per cent below par because the funds are not
285 sufficient. In every exchange you must pay the price, | the risk, some profit
to the banker, and so much for the degradation of money in notes. This is
the cause of the rise of exchange. Whenever it rises beyond the price of
insurance, it is owing to the money of one country being lower than that of
another. This was the cause of the high price of exchange between France
and Holland about the time of the Mississippi Company. It was then at
80 or 90 per cent. All the money had been expelled from France by the
scheme of Mr. Law, and the whole circulation was paper, and the credit of
the bank had fallen. All these reasons conspired to raise the exchange to
such an enormous pitch.

We come now to the next thing proposed, to examine the causes of the
slow progress of opulence.

When one considers the effects of the division of labour, what an immediate tendencey it has to improve the arts, it appears somewhat sur-
prizing that every nation should continue so long in a poor and indigent
state as we find it does. The causes of this may be considered under these
two heads, first, natural impediments, and secondly, the oppression of
civil government.

286 A rude and barbarous people are ignorant | of the effects of the division of
labour, and it is long before one person, by continualy working at different
things, can produce any more than is necessary for his daily subsistence.
Before labour can be divided some accumulation of stock is necessary. A
poor man with no stock can never begin a manufacture. Before a man can
commence farmer he must at least have laid in a years provision, because he
does not receive the fruits of his labour till the end of the season. Agreably
to this, in a nation of hunters or shepherds no person can quit the common
trade in which he is employed, and which affords him daily subsistence,
till he have some stock to maintain him and begin the new trade. Every one
knows how difficult it is, even in a refined society, to raise one's self to
moderate circumstances. It is still more difficult to raise one's self by these
trades which require no art nor ingenuity. A porter or day labourer must
continue poor for ever. In the beginings of society this is still more difficult.
Bare subsistence is almost all that a savage can procure, and having no
stock to begin upon, nothing to maintain him but what is produced by the
287 exertion of his own strength, | it is no wonder that he continues long in an
indigent state. The meanest labourer in a polished society has in many
respects an advantage over a savage. He has more assistance in his labour;
he has only one particular thing to do, which by assiduity he attains a
facility in performing; he has also machines and instruments which greatly
assist him. An Indian has not so much as a pick-ax, a spade, or a shovel,

nor any thing else but his own labour. This is one great cause of the slow progress of opulence in every country; till some stock be produced there can be no division of labour, and before a division of labour take place there can be very little accumulation of stock.

The other cause that was assigned was the nature of civil government. In the infancey of society, as has been often observed, government must be weak and feeble, and it is long before it's authority can protect the industry of individuals from the rapacity of their neighbours. When people find themselves every moment in danger of being robbed of all they possess, they have no motive to be industrious. There could be little accumulation of stock, because the indolent, which would be the greatest number, would 288 live upon the industrious, and spend whatever | they produced. When the power of government becomes so great as to defend the produce of industry, another obstacle arises from a different quarter. Among neighbouring nations in a barbarous state there are perpetual wars, one continualy invading and plundering the other, and tho' private property be secured from the violence of neighbours, it is in danger from hostile invasions. In this manner it is next to impossible that any accumulation of stock can be made. It is observable that among savage nations there are always more violent convulsions than among those farther advanced in refinement. Among the Tartars and Arabs, great bands of barbarians are always roaming from one place to another in quest of plunder, and they pillage every country as they go along. Thus large tracts of country are often laid waste and all the effects carried away: Germany too was in the same condition about the fall of the Roman Empire. Nothing can be more an obstacle to the progress of opulence.

We shall next consider the effect of oppressive measures, first with regard to agriculture, and then with regard to commerce.

289    | Agriculture is of all other arts the most beneficent to society, and whatever tends to retard its improvement is extremely prejudicial to the public interest. The produce of agriculture is much greater than that of any other manufacture. The rents of the whole lands in England amount to about 24 millions, and as the rent is generaly about a third of the produce, the whole annual produce of the lands must be about 72 millions. This is much more than the produce of either the linen or woolen manufactures; for as the annual consumption is computed to be about 100 millions, if you deduce from this the 72 millions, the produce of agriculture, there will remain only 28 millions for all the other manufactures of the nation. Whatever measures, therefore, discourage the [the] improvement of this art are extremely prejudicial to the progress of opulence.

One great hindrance to the progress of agriculture is the throwing great tracts of land into the hands of single persons. If any man's estate be more than he is able to cultivate, a part of it is in a manner lost. When a nation of

savages takes possession of a country, the great and powerfull divide the
290 | [the] whole lands among them, and leave none for the lower ranks of
people. In this manner the Celtae, and afterwards the Saxons, took
possession of our own island.

When land is divided in great portions among the powerfull, it is cultivated by slaves, which is a very unprofitable method of cultivation. The
labour of a slave proceeds from no other motive but the dread of punishment, and if he could escape this he would work none at all. Should he
exert himself in the most extraordinary manner, he cannot have the least
expectations of any reward, and as all the produce of his labour goes to his
master, he has no encouragement to industry. A young slave may perhaps
exert himself a little at first, in order to attain his masters favour, but he
soon finds that it is all in vain, and that, be his behaviour what it will, he
will always meet with the same severe treatment. When lands, therefore,
are cultivated by slaves, they cannot be greatly improven, as they have no
motive to industry.

A cultivation of the same kind is that by villains. The landlord gave a
291 man a piece of ground | to cultivate, allowing him to maintain himself by
it, and obliging him to restore whatever was over his own maintenance.
This was equally unfavourable to the progress of agriculture, because the
villains, who were a kind of slaves, had no motive to industry but their own
maintenance. This objection lyes equaly against all cultivation by slaves.
Some of the West India islands have indeed been cultivated by slaves, and
have been greatly improven, but they might have been cultivated by freemen at less expence; and had not the profits of sugar been very great, the
planters could not have supported the expence of slaves, but their profits
have been so enormous that all the extraordinary expence of slave cultivation has vanished before it. In the northern colonies they employ few
slaves, and tho' they are in a very flourishing condition in these colonies,
the lands are generaly cultivated by the proprietors, which is the most
favourable method to the progress of agriculture. A tenant of the best kind
has always a rent to pay, and therefore has much less to lay out on improve-
292 ments. When a country sends out a colony, it may hinder a large | tract of
land to be occupied by a single person. But when savages take possession of
a country, they are subject to no laws, the strongest man takes possession
of most ground, and therefore among them agriculture cannot be quickly
promoted.

After villains went out, as was explained before,[52] tenants by steel bow
succeeded. The landlord gave a farm with a stock to a villain, which were
restored with half of the produce at the end of the year to the landlord.
But as the tenant had no stock nor, tho' he had, any encouragement to lay it
out on improvements, this method always was unfavourable to agriculture.

[52] 140–1 above.

For the same reason that tythes, by depriving the farmer of a tenth of his produce, hinder improvement, this, tho' in a higher degree, was a hindrance, because the tenant was deprived of one half of the produce. A great part of France is still cultivated by tenants of steel bow, and it is said that it still remains in some parts of the Highlands of Scotland.

The next species of cultivation was that by tenants, such as we have at
293 present. | Some of the tenants by steel bow, by extreme pinching and cunning, got a small stock laid up and offered their masters a fixed rent for the ground. Thus in progress of time the present method of cultivation was introduced, tho' it was long liable to inconveniences. If the landlord sold his land the new proprietor was not bound to the terms of agreement, and the tenant was often turned out of his farm. The landlord too invented a method to get rid of the tenant when he pleased by selling the estate to another, on whom he had a back bond to make him return the estate whenever the tenants were turned out. As the tenants were continualy in danger of being turned out, they had no motive to improve the ground. This takes place to this day in every country of Europe except Brittain. In Scotland contracts of this kind were rendered real rights in the reign of James III[d]53 and in England in that of Henry VII[th].54

294 Besides these there were several other impediments | to the progress of agriculture. At first all rents were paid in kind, by which, in a dear year, the tenants were in danger of being ruined. A diminution of produce seldom hurts the tenant who pays his rent in money, because the price of corn rises in proportion to its scarceity. Society however is considerably advanced before money comes to be the whole instrument of commerce.

Another embarrassment was that the feudal lords sometimes allowed the king to levy subsidies from their tenants, which greatly discouraged their industry. Besides all, under the tyranny of the feudal aristocracey the landlords had nothing to stop them from squeezing their tenants and raising the rents of their lands as high as they pleased. England is better secured in this respect than any country, because every one who hold but 40s/ a year for life has a vote for a Member of Parliament, by which, if he rent a farm, he is secure from oppression.

Several circumstances concurred to continue the engrossment of lands.
295 The right of primogeniture | was pretty early established and hinderd estates from being divided. The institution of entails is to this day attended with the same bad consequences. The embarrassment too of the feudal law in transferring property detarded the progress of agriculture. Any quantity of any other commodity may be bought or sold in an instant, but in purchasing 4 or 5 acres of land a great deal ⟨of⟩ time must be spent in examining the progress of writts and getting your right legally constituted. This tends

53 In fact James II, Act, 1449, c. 18 (A.P.S. II.35, c. 6).
54 In 1498 or 1499: A. Fitzherbert, *New Natura Brevium*, 220 H.

greatly to the engrossment of lands and consequently stops their improvement.

If all the forms in buying lands were abolished, every person almost who had got a little money would be ready to lay it out on land, and the land by passing thro' the different hands would be much better improved. There is no natural reason why a 1000 acres should not be as easily purchased as a 1000 yards of cloth. The keeping land out of the market always hinders its improvement. A merchant who buys a little piece of land has it in his eye to improve it and make the most of it he can. Great and ancient families have seldom either stock or inclination to improve their estates, except a small piece of pleasure ground about their house.

296 | There are many errors in the police of almost every country, which have contributed greatly to stop the progress of agriculture. Our fathers, finding themselves once in every two or three years subject to the most grievous dearths, to escape that calamity prohibited the exportation of corn. This is still the police of the greater part of Europe, and it is the cause of all that dearth it is intended to prevent. In a plentifull year the corn of Spain, tho' the most fertile country in the world, is not worth the cutting down. They suffer it to lye rotting on the ground, because they would get nothing for it. The cause of this is not the indolence of the people, as is commonly imagined. The fact is, the farmer, finding he cannot dispose of his corn this year, will not risk a crop next year, but turns his grounds to grass. Next year a famine ensues, and he sows more than can be disposed of for the following season. It is to be observed that this was one great cause of the depopulation of ancient Italy. Exportation of corn was prohibited by severe 297 penalties, and the importation of it encouraged | by high premiums. So that the Italian farmers had no encouragement to industry, not being sure of a market. In the latter times of the republic the emperors tried several methods of promoting the cultivation of the country, but being ignorant that the real cause of their want was the immense quantity of corn daily imported from Egypt and other parts of Africa, all their endeavours were ineffectuall. Caligula and Claudius gave their soldiers land for nothing, upon condition that they would cultivate it. But as the soldiers had no other motive, very inconsiderable improvements were made. Virgil too published his Georgicks to bring the cultivation of land into fashion, but all was in vain. Forreign corn was always sold cheaper than their own could be raised. Agreabley to this we find Cato, in the 3$^d$ Book of Cicero's Offices,[55] preferring pasturage of any kind to farming. The kings of Spain have also done all in their power to promote the improvement of land. Phillip IV$^{th}$ went to the plow himself in order to sett the fashion. He did every thing for the farmers except bringing them a good market. He conferred the tittles of nobility upon several farmers. He very absurdly endeavoured to oppress

[55] In fact *De Officiis*, II.89.

298 manufacturers | with heavy taxes in order to force them to the country. He thought that in proportion as the inhabitants of towns became more numerous, these in the country decreased. This notion was highly ridiculous, for the populousness of a town is the very cause of the populousness of the country, because it gives greater encouragement to industry. Every man in a town must be fed by another in the country, and it is always a sign that the country is improving when men go to town. There are no parts of the country so well inhabited nor so well cultivated as those which lye in the neighbourhood of populous cities. All these causes have hindered and still hinder the improvement of agriculture, the most important branch of industry.

We may observe that the greater number of manufacturers there are in any country, agriculture is the more improved, and the causes which prevent the progress of these re-act, as it were, upon agriculture. It is easy to shew that the free export and import of corn is favourable to agriculture. In England the country has been better stored with corn, and the price of it has gradualy sunk, since the exportation of it was permitted. The bounty on exportation does harm in other respects, but it increases the quantity of
299 corn. | In Holland corn is cheaper and plentyer than any where else, and a dearth is there unknown. That country is, as it were, the magazine of corn for a great part of Europe. This is entirely owing to the free export and import they enjoy. If no improper regulations took place, any country of Europe might do more than maintain itself with all sorts of grain.

The slow progress of arts and commerce is owing to causes of a like kind. In all places where slavery took place the manufactures were carried on by slaves. It is impossible that they can be so well carried on by slaves as by freemen, because they can have no motive to labour but the dread of punishment, and can never invent any machine for facilitating their business. Freemen who have a stock of their own can get any thing accomplished which they think may be expedient for carrying on labour. If a carpenter think that a plane will serve his purpose better than a knife, he may go to a smith and get it made; but if a slave make any such proposal he is called a lazy rascal, and no experiments are made to give him ease. At present the Turks and Hungarians work mines of the same kind, situated upon opposite sides of the same range of mountains, but the Hungarians
300 make a great deal more of them than the Turks, because | they employ freemen while the Turks employ slaves. When the Hungarians meet with any obstacle every invention is on work to find out some easy way of surmounting it, but the Turks think of no other expedient but to sett a greater number of slaves to work.[56] In the ancient world, as the arts were all carried on by slaves, no machinery could be invented, because they had no stock. After the fall of the Roman Empire, too, this was the case all over Europe.

[56] Montesquieu, XV.8.

In a rude society nothing is honourable but war. In the Odyssey, Ulysses is sometimes asked, by way of affront, whether he be a pirate or a merchant.[57] At that time a merchant was reckoned odious and despicable. But a pirate or robber, as he was a man of military bravery, was treated with honour. We may observe that these principles of the human mind which are most beneficial to society are by no means marked by nature as the most honourable. Hunger, thirst, and the passion for sex are the great supports of the human species. Yet almost every expression of these excites contempt.[58] In the same manner, that principle in the mind which prompts to truck, barter, and exchange, tho' it is the great foundation of arts, com-
301 merce, and the division of labour, | yet it is not marked with any thing amiable. To perform any thing, or to give any thing, without a reward is always generous and noble, but to barter one thing for another is mean. The plain reason for this is that these principles are so strongly implanted by nature that they have no occasion for that additional force which the weaker principles need.

In rude ages this contempt rises to the highest pitch, and even in a refined society it is not utterly extinguished. In this country a small retailer is even in some degree odious at this day. When the trade of a merchant or mechanic was thus depreciated in the beginings of society, no wonder that it was confined to the lowest ranks of people. Even when emancipated slaves began to practise these trades, it was impossible that much stock could accumulate in their hands, for the government oppressed them severely, and they were obliged to pay licences for their liberty of trading. In Dooms-day-Book we have an account of all the different traders in every county, how many of them were under the king, and how many under such a bishop, and what acknowledgements they were obliged to pay for their liberty of trading.
302 | This mean and despicable idea which they had of merchants greatly obstructed the progress of commerce. The merchant is, as it were, the mean between the manufacturer and the consumer. The weaver must not go to the market himself, there must be somebody to do this for him. This person must be possessed of a considerable stock, to buy up the commodity and maintain the manufacturer. But when merchants were so despicable and laid under so great taxations for liberty of trade, they could never amass that degree of stock which is necessary for making the division of labour and improving manufactures.

The only persons in these days who made any money by trade were the Jews, who, as they were considered as vagabonds, had no liberty of purchasing lands, and had no other way to dispose of themselves but by becoming mechanics or merchants. Their character could not be spoiled by merchandize because they could not be more odious than their religion

---

[57] Cf. p. 224 above.                          [58] Cf. TMS I.ii.1.1–2.

made them. Even they were grievously oppressed and consequently the progress of opulence greatly retarded.

303    Another thing which greatly retarded commerce | was the imperfection of the law with regard to contracts, which were the last species of rights that sustained action, for originaly the law gave no redress for any but those concluded on the spot. At present all considerable commerce is carried on by commissions, and unless these sustained action little could be done. The first action on contracts extended only to the moveable goods of the contractor, neither his lands nor his person could be touched. His goods were often very inconsiderable, and probity is none of the most prevalent virtues among a rude people. It is commerce that introduces probity and punctuality.

Another obstacle to the improvement of commerce was the difficulty of conveyance from one place to another. The country was then filled with retainers, a species of idle people who depended on the lords, whose violence and disorders rendered the going from one place to another very difficult. Besides, there were then no good highways. The want of navigable rivers in many places were also an inconvenience. This is still the case in Asia and other eastern countries; all inland commerce is carried on by great caravans, consisting of several thousands, for mutual defence, with 

304  waggons, etca. | In our own country a man made his testament before he sett out from Edinburgh to Aberdeen, and it was still more dangerous to go to forreign countries. The laws of every country to aliens and strangers are far from being favourable. It is difficult, or rather impossible, for them to obtain satisfaction. After this was a little remedied, still conveyance by sea remained difficult. Piracey was an honourable occupation. Men were ignorant of navigation and exposed to dangers on this account. The price of all these risks was laid upon the goods, and by this means they were so much raised above the natural price that the improvement of commerce was greatly retarded.

Another piece of police which was thought a wise institution by our forefathers had the same effect. This was the fairs and markets all over Europe. Till the sixteenth century all commerce was carried on by fairs. The fairs of Bartholomew, of Leipsic, of Troy in Champaigne, and even of Glasgow, are much talked of in antiquity. These were the most centrical places and best fitted for carrying on business. All linen and black cattle were brought in from the country to these assignations or trysts, and, least 

305  the purchaser should be dissappointed, | they were all brought on a certain day and were not allowed to be sold on any other day. Forestallers,[59] who went up and down the country buying up commodities, were severely punished, as this was a temptation not to bring them to the market. This might be necessary when it was not safe to go any where alone, but tho'

[59] i.e. people who buy up goods in order to profit by their enhanced price.

you make no fairs, buyers and sellers will find a way to each other. Easy conveyance and other conveniences of trafficking will be of more advantage than the bringing them to a fixed market and thereby confining buying and selling to a certain season. All fairs, however necessary they then were, are now real nusances. It is absurd to preserve in people a regard for their old customs when the causes of them are removed.

Another obstacle to commerce was staple towns, which had the exclusive priviledge of selling a certain commodity within that district. Calais, when it belonged to the English, was long the staple for wool. As men were obliged to carry their wool to such a distance, it's price was very high. It was however a very great advantage to any town to have the staple, and therefore the king gave it to that town with which he was best pleased, and

306 took it away whenever it dissobliged him. | Staple-towns had all the dissadvantages of fairs and markets with this additional one, that the staple commodity could be sold at no fair nor market except one. By this the liberty of exchange, and consequently the division of labour, was diminished.

All taxes upon exportation and importation of goods also hinder commerce. Merchants at first were in so contemptible a state that the law, as it were, abandoned them, and it was no matter what they obliged them to pay. They however must lay the tax upon their goods, their price is raised, fewer of them are bought, manufactures are discouraged, and the division of labour hindered.

All monopolies and exclusive priviledges of corporations, for whatever good ends they were at first instituted, have the same bad effect. In like manner the statute of apprenticeship, which was originaly an imposition on government, has a bad tendencey. It was imagined that the cause of so much bad cloth was that the weaver had not been properly educated, and therefore they made a statute[60] that he should serve a seven years apprenticeship before he pretended to make any. But this is by no means a

307 sufficient security against bad cloth. | You yourself cannot inspect a large piece of cloth, this must be left to the stampmaster, whose credit must be depended upon. Above all other causes the giving bounties for one commodity, and the discourageing another, diminishes the concurrence of opulence and hurts the natural state of commerce.

Before we treat of the effects of police upon the manners of a people, we propose to consider taxes or revenue, which is in reality one of the causes that the progress of opulence has been so slow.

In the beginings of society all public offices were performed by the magistrate without any reward, and he was fully satisfied with the eminence of his station. This is the case among the Tartars, Arabs, and Hottentots even to this day. Voluntary presants only are accepted, which have always

[60] 4 and 5 Philip and Mary, c. 5, sec. 22 (1558).

a bad effect, but cannot be prevented while one is willing to give and another to receive. It was in this manner too that the governours of the Roman provinces got their revenues. When government becomes so complex as to take up the whole attention of the public magistrate he must undoubtedly have some reward, and if this be not given him by the public he will fall upon some more dangerous method of obtaining it. Few will be so generous as to exact nothing. When applications are made, every one must bring his presant and the man who pays best will be best heard.

308 | When government is a little farther advanced, magazines must be provided, ships built, palaces and other public buildings erected and kept up, and consequently a public revenue levied; at first indeed among the Romans there was no revenue levied for carrying on war, because the soldiers required no pay. In savage nations this is always the case; every one of the Athenians went out to war at his own expence. The same was the case with our feudal lords; the burthen of going to war was connected with the duty of the tenant or vassal. Such a practice cannot be of long duration, and accordingly we find that it ceased at Rome and was the great cause of the dissolution of that republic.

The governours of provinces made such grievous exactions from the people that they alienated their affections, so that they gave no assistance in defending the state when it stood in need of assistance.

After the appropriation of land property, a portion óf lands was commonly assigned for the maintenance of government. The free states of Greece had land set apart for this purpose, and we find Aristotle[61] giving his opinion that private property should surround the royal lands, because those who were near a city were always for war, because they were sure of

309 defence, and as the enemy would first come upon these lands | which were near the boundaries. In all ⟨?barbarous⟩ countries we find lands appropriated to the purposes of sovereignty, and therefore little occasion for taxes and customs. We shall shew that this is a bad police, and one cause of the slow progress of opulence.

Let us conceive what an immense tract of land would be required to support the British government. The annual expence of it in times of peace amounts to 3 millions, the whole land rents amounts to 24 millions; therefore the government must have an $8^{th}$ part in it's own hands. If we conceive further how such a tract of land would be cultivated, the quantity requisite would be prodigious. Allow it but to be half as well cultivated as the rest, which for many reasons would not be the case, the government would have in its hands a $4^{th}$ of the whole country. By this therefore the stock of the country would be greatly diminished and fewer people maintained. After government becomes expensive, it is the worst possible method to support it by a land rent. We may observe that the government in a civilized

[61] Cf. p. 22 above.

country is much more expensive than in a barbarous one; and when we say that one government is more expensive than another, it is the same as if we said that the one country is farther advanced in improvement than another. To say that the government is expensive and the people not oppressed | is to say that the people are rich. There are many expences necessary in a civilized country for which there is no occasion in one that is barbarous. Armies, fleets, fortified places and public buildings, judges and officers of the revenue must be supported, and if they be neglected disorder will ensue. A land rent to serve all these purposes would be the most improper thing in the world.

All taxes may be considered under two divisions, to witt, taxes upon possessions, and taxes upon consumptions. These are the two ways of making the subjects contribute to the support of government. The land-tax is of the former kind, and all taxes upon commodities of the latter.

Possessions are of three kinds, to witt, land, stock, and money. It is easy to levy a tax upon land because it is evident what quantity every one possesses, but it is very difficult to lay a tax upon stock or money without very arbitrary proceedings. It is a hardship upon a man in trade to oblige him to shew his books, which is the only way in which we can know how much he is worth. It is a breach of liberty, and may be productive of very bad consequences by ruining his credit. The circumstances of people in trade are at sometimes far worse than at others. But if on account of this difficulty you were to tax land, | and neither tax money nor stock, ye would do a piece of very great injustice. But tho' it be a difficult thing to tax money or stock without being oppressive, yet this method is used in several countries. In France, for example, in order to ascertain the circumstances of the subject, every bill is assigned and all business transacted in presence of a public notary and entered into his books, so that land, stock, and money are there all taxed in the same manner. Of these three only land is taxed in England, because to tax the other two has some appearance of despotism, and would greatly enrage a free people. Excepting the land tax, our taxes are generaly upon commodities, and in these there is a much greater inequality than in the taxes on land possession. The consumptions of people are not always according to what they possess, but in proportion to their liberality. When taxes are laid upon commodities, their prices must rise, the concurrence of tradesmen must be prevented, an artificial dearth occasioned, less industry excited, and a smaller quantity of goods produced. Taxes upon land possessions have this great advantage, that they are levied without any great expence. The whole land tax of England does not cost the government above 8 or 10,000 pounds. | Collectors are chosen by the gentlemen of the county, and are obliged to produce proper security for their carrying safely to the exchequer the money which they collect. The taxes of customs and excise, which produce such immense sums, are almost eaten up by the legions of officers that are employed in collecting them. These officers must have supervisors over them to examine their proceedings. The supervisors have over them collectors, who are under the commissioners, who have to account to the exchequer. To support these officers there must be levied a great deal more than the government requires, which is a manifest dissadvantage.

Another advantage of a land tax is that it does not tend to raise the price of commodities, as it is not paid in proportion to the corn and cattle, but in proportion to the rent. If the tenant pay the tax he pays just so much less rent. Excise raises the price of commodities and makes fewer people able to carry on business. If a man purchase a 1000£ worth of tobacco he has an 100£ of tax to pay, and therefore cannot deal to such an extent as he would otherwise do. Thus as it requires greater stock to carry on trade, the dealers must be fewer and the rich have, as it were, a monopoly against the poor.

313 | It was observed before that in England, from a kind of delicacey with regard to examining into the circumstances of particular persons, which is apparently an infringement upon liberty, no tax is laid upon stock or money, but all upon consumptions. Whatever advantages this method may have, there is evidently in it an inequality. The landlord who pays his annual land tax pays also a great part of the taxes on consumptions. On this account the landed interest complains first of a war, thinking the burthen of it falls upon them. While on the other hand the moneyed men are gainers, and therefore oppose them. This perhaps occasions the continuance of what is called the Tory interest. Taxes upon possessions are naturaly equal, but those upon consumptions naturaly unequal, as they are sometimes paid by the merchant, sometimes by the consumer, and sometimes by the importer, who must be repaid it by the consumer. In Holland all goods are deposited in a public warehouse, one key of which is kept by the commissioner of the customs and another by the owner of the goods. If the goods are exported no tax is advanced, but if they go into the country the consumer pays down the price to the merchant and the custom to the commissioner. This method is much the same with the famous excise

314 scheme | of Sir Robert Walpole, which was at last his ruin. It was to this effect, that a general excise should be established, and all goods imported deposited in a public warehouse, and the tax should only be paid upon the inland sale of them. Tho' this scheme be liable to inconveniences, such as subjecting the owner to anxiety from not having his goods entirely in his own power, yet it is plainly this which gives the Dutch so great an advantage over all the other nations of Europe. The Dutch are in a manner the carriers of the other Europeans; they bring corn from the Baltic and these places where it is cheap, and wines from these places where there has been a good vintage, and keep them by them till they hear of a dearth, and then export them to the places where it is. But in England the moment you

bring the commodities to the country, you must pay the tax and sell them where you please. Thus the merchant may lye out of his interest for a long time, and therefore must sell his commodities dearer. The Dutch, having no tax to pay but upon inland sale, are enabled to sell cheaper than the English or any other nation.

Taxes on consumptions have however some advantage over those on
315 possessions. | They are not felt, being paid imperceptibly, but a person possessed of a 1000£ of land-rent feels very sensibly an 100£ going from him. The taxes on consumptions are not so much murmured against, because they are laid upon the merchant, who lays them on the price of goods, and thus they are insensibly paid by the people. When we buy a pound of tea we do not reflect that the most part of the price is a duty paid to the government, and therefore pay it contentedly as tho' it were only the natural price of the commodity. In the same manner when an additional tax is laid upon beer the price of it must be raised, but the mob do not directly vent their malice against the government, who are the proper objects of it, but upon the brewers, as they confound the tax price with the natural one. Taxes upon consumptions, therefore, which are paid by the merchant, seem most to favour liberty, and will always be favoured by this government. In Holland they buy a hogshead of wine and first pay the price to the merchant, and then so much to the officers of excise, as it were to get leave to drink it. We in reality do the very same thing, but as we do
316 not feel it immediately we | imagine it all one price, and never reflect that we might drink port wine below sixpence a bottle were it not for the duty.

Taxes on consumptions have still another advantage over those on possessions. If a person be possessed of a land rent of an hundred pounds per annum, and this estate be valued at a high rate, he perhaps pays 20£ to the government. The collector must be paid at a certain time of the year, and few people have so much self command as to lay up money to be ready. He has therefore 20£ to borrow to answer his present demands. When next payment comes, he has not only the tax to pay but also the interest of the money borrowed the former year. He begins to encumber his estate, and thus upon examination it will be found that many landholders have been ruined. The best method of preventing this is to make the tenant pay the land tax in part payment of his rent. The taxes on consumptions are not liable to this inconvenience. When a person finds that he is spending too much on the elegancies of life, he can immediately diminish his consumption. Taxes upon consumptions are therefore more eligible than taxes upon possessions, as they have not so great a tendencey to ruin the circumstances of individuals.
317    It is to be observed that taxes both on consumptions | and possessions are more or less advantageous to industry according to the manner in which they are levied. The land tax in England is permanent and uniform

and does not rise with the rent, which is regulated by the improvement of the land. Notwithstanding modern improvements it is the same that it was formerly. In France the tax rises proportionably to the rent, which is a great discouragement to the land-holder. It has much the same effect with the tythes in England. When we know that the produce is to be divided with those who lay out nothing, it hinders us from laying out what we would otherwise do upon the improvement of our lands. We are better financeers than the French, as we have also the advantage of them in the following particulars.

In the method of levying our customs we have an advantage over the French. Our customs are all paid at once by the merchants, and goods, after their entry in the custom house books, may be carried by a permit thro' any part of the country without molestation and expence, except some triffles upon tolls, etca. In France a duty is paid at the end of almost every town they go into, equal, if not greater, to what is paid by us at first. Inland industry is embarrassed by theirs, and only forreign trade by ours.

318   We have another advantage in levying our taxes by commission while theirs are levied by farm, by which means | not one half of what they raise goes into the hands of the government. In England the whole expence of levying above 7 millions does not come to 300,000£. In France 24 millions are levyed every year, and not above 12 goes to the expence of the government, the rest goes for defraying the expence of levying it and for the profit of the farmer. In England no excise officers are requisite but at the seaports, except a few up and down the country. The profits of the farmers in France would pay the expence of them all. In the collecting of our excise there is a regular subordination of officers who have their fixed salaries and nothing more. But in France the highest bidder has the place, and as the man who undertakes it must advance the sum at a certain time, and runs a risk of not getting it up, he deserves a very high profit. Besides, in an auction of this kind there are few bidders, as none are capable of undertaking the office but those who are brought up to business, and are possessed both of a great stock and credit, and can produce good security. When there are few bidders they can easily enter into an association among themselves and have the whole at a very easy rate. Upon the whole we may observe that the English are the best financeers in Europe, and their taxes are levied with more propriety than those of any country whatever.

319   | Upon this subject it is in general to be observed that taxes upon exportation are much more hurtfull than those upon importation. When the inhabitants of a country are in a manner prohibited by high taxes from exporting the produce of their industry, they are confined to home consumption and their motives to industry are diminished. Taxes upon importation, on the contrary, encourage the manufacturing of these particular commodities. The tax upon Hamburgh linen, for example, hinders

the importation of great quantities of it and causes more linen to be manufactured at home. In general, however, all taxes upon importation are
hurtfull in this respect, that they divert the industry of the country to an
unatural channel. The more stock there is employed in one way, there is the
less to be employed in another; but the effects of taxes upon exportation are
still more pernicious.

This is one great cause of the poverty of Spain. They have imposed a
high tax on the exportation of every commodity, and think that by this
means the taxes are paid by forreigners, whereas, if they were to impose a
tax on importation, it would be paid by their own subjects, not reflecting
that by bringing a burthen on the exportation of commodities they so far
confine the consumption of them and diminish industry.

To conclude all that is to be said of taxes, we may observe that the
common prejudice that wealth consists in money has not been in this
320 respect so hurtfull as might have been imagined, | and has even given
occasions to regulations not very inconvenient. These nations to whom we
give more goods than we receive, generaly send us manufactured goods;
these on the contrary from whom we receive more goods than we give, or
with respect to whom the balance is in our favour, generaly send us unmanufactured goods. To Russia for example we send fine linen and other
manufactured goods, and for a small quantity of these receive in return
great quantities of unmanufactured goods. This kind of trade is very
advantageous, because goods in an unmanufactured and rude state afford
employment and maintenance to a great number of persons. It is merely
from the absurd notion that wealth consists in money, that the British
encourage most these branches of forreign trade where the balance is paid
in money.

There are still some other species of taxes, but as their nature is much the
same it is unecessary to mention them. Having thus given a general view of
taxes, it will not be improper here, on account of their connection, to consider the nature of stocks and the causes of their rising and falling.

Soon after the Revolution, on account of the necessities of government,
it was necessary to borrow money from subjects, generaly at a higher rate
than common interest, to be repaid in a few years. The funds allotted for
payment of this interest were taxes on certain commodities. These taxes
were at first laid on for a certain number of years, according to the term for
which the money was borrowed. But when by various arts of government
321 these loans came to be perpetual, | the taxes came of course to be perpetual,
and thus the funds were mortgaged. Tho' they were made perpetual when
money could no longer be borrowed upon them, yet they were still redeemable upon paying up the money borrowed on them. When these taxes were
laid on, nothing would have shocked people more than to have thought that
they were to be perpetual. But their progress was so insensible that it was

never murmured at. What shocks at first will soon become easy from custom, which sanctifies every thing. Thus ⟨?these⟩ taxes were first laid on, and thus they came to the situation in which they are at present.

When a sum of money is lent to a private person, the creditor can come upon the debtor when he pleases for both capital and interest, but it is not on this footing that the government borrows money; they give you a right to a perpetual annuity of 3 or 4 per cent, but not to redemand your capital. It seems very odd at first sight that the creditor should consent to such an inconvenience as that his money should never be paid up, but this is realy his advantage. If you lend to the government a 1000£ in time of war, as they have immediate use for it they will perhaps be obliged to give you 5 per cent of interest, and when peace comes they continue your annuity. You have it in your power to dispose of your annuity, and as your money is perfectly secure, and interest is paid by no private person with so much

322 punctuality as by the government, | you may very often sell the annuity of your 1000£ at 1100 or more. The government, finding that these annuities sold above par, and for the same reason that people were much disposed to subscribe to the government funds, they resolved, as the funds were still redeemable, to take the advantage by paying up the sums borrowed at 5 per cent and borrowing money at a lower rate. This made the contractors with the government to be on their guard, and as they saw their design, they would not lend them any more money without at least some part of the interest should be irredeemable, perhaps 2 per cent of the 4 they were to receive. In every fund therefore there was a part irredeemable, which made them continue to sell above par.

In the reigns of King William, Q. Ann, and in the begining of that of K. George the Ist, the funds rose and fell according to the credit of the government, as there was still some risk of a revolution. Of late, tho' there be no danger of a revolution, even in the times of peace stocks are sometimes at 10, 20, and even 50 per cent below par, and sometimes as much above it. No body can suspect any risk of losing that money by change of government. How then comes it that stocks are thus every day fluctuating without any visible cause? How comes it that good or bad news have such an influence on the rising and falling of stocks? The real cause is as follows.

323 Every misfortune in war makes peace to be at a greater | distance, and every fortunate occurrance seems to favour it's approach. When war continues, the necessities of government must be supplied, more money levied, and new subscriptions opened for these purposes. As in war the interest must necessarily rise, every one is eager to be in the new subscription, and they who have annuities find that it will be for their advantage to sell out of the old stocks in prospect of a higher interest. The number of sellers therefore increases with the prospect of a war, and consequently stocks fall. On the other hand, whenever there is a prospect of

peace, as there are no expectations that new subscriptions will be opened, they who have annuities are not fond of selling them, and therefore, the number of sellers decreasing, stocks must rise. In time of war, every one who has any stock runs to have it in the hands of the government, as it cannot be so advantageously employed any where else, as they got interest perhaps at 7 or 8 per cent, of which two or three perhaps is redeemable,[62] and frequently a lottery ticket into the bargain. A person who has an annuity only at 3 per cent will do all he can to sell it, that he may employ his stock to greater advantage, and for this reason will often sell it below par, and consequently stocks must necessarily fall.

But in time of war, for the following reasons, even the new subscriptions come to sell below par.

324 As there are a great many stockholders who are merchants, and who keep their stocks in the hands of the government | that they may be ready to sell out on any sudden demand and take the advantage of a good bargain when it casts up, and as these chances occurr most frequently in time of war, they have often occasion to sell out, and thus more stock runs to the market and the new subscriptions sink[s] below par.

But further, in time of war, as was observed before, stock cannot be so advantageously employed, and every body is tempted to subscribe. Even those whose circumstances are but very inconsiderable, subscribe for great sums in hopes that stocks will rise and that they may sell out before the time of delivery to great advantage; but when things do not answer their expectations, and they are forced to sell out one way or another to support their credit, they are often obliged to sell below par. In this manner the new subscriptions may fall. Stockjobbers that are well acquainted with their business observe particularly when a number of indigent persons are in the subscriptions, and as they are soon obliged to sell out, and consequently stocks fall, it is their proper time to purchase them.

The practice of stockjobbing, or the buying stocks by time, has too on all occasions a very considerable influence on the rise and fall of stocks. The method in which this practice is carried on is as follows. A man who has not perhaps 1000£ in the world subscribes for 100,000£, which is to be delivered
325 at several fixed times and in certain portions. | He therefore hopes to get these several portions sold out to great advantage by the rising of the stocks before they fall due. But as any thing he is worth would go if the stocks should fall, he uses all means to make them rise. He spreads reports at Change Alley that victories are gained, that peace is to be concluded, etca. On the other hand they who want to purchase a stock, and want that it should fall, propogate such reports as will sink the stocks as low as possible, such as that war will continue, that new subscriptions are thought on, etca. It is owing to this that in time of war our newspapers are so filled with

[62] Reporter's or copyist's error for 'irredeemable'.

invasions and schemes that never were thought of. In the language of Change Alley the buyer is called the bull and the seller the bear, and as the bulls or bears predominate stocks rise or fall.

This practice of buying stocks by time is prohibited by the government, and accordingly, tho' they should not deliver up the stocks they have engaged for, the law gives no redress.[63] There is no natural reason why 1000£ in the stocks should not be delivered or the delivery of it enforced, as well as 1000£ worth of goods. But after the South Sea scheme this was thought upon as an expedient to prevent such practices, tho' it proved ineffectual. In the same manner all laws against gaming never hinder it, and tho' there is no redress for a sum above 5£,[64] yet all the great sums that are

326 lost are punctualy paid. | Persons who game must keep their credit, else no body will deal with them. It is quite the same in stockjobbing. They who do not keep their credit will soon be turned out, and in the language of Change Alley be called lame duck. It is unecessary here to give any account of particular funds, as they are all of the same nature and the security equal. If the interest of any sum of money be not paid by the funds allotted for that purpose, it is paid out of the sinking fund, which is the surplus of all the rest. There is perhaps some little difference in the facility of payment, but this is by no means considerable and merits not our attention.

In[65] remains now that we consider the last division of police, and shew the influence of commerce on the manners of a people.

Whenever commerce is introduced into any country, probity and punctuality always accompany it. These virtues in a rude and barbarous country are almost unknown. Of all the nations in Europe, the Dutch, the most commercial, are the most faithfull to their word. The English are more so than the Scotch, but much inferiour to the Dutch, and in the remote parts of this country they ⟨are⟩ far less so than in the commercial parts of it. This is not at all to be imputed to national character, as some pretend.

327 | There is no natural reason why an Englishman or a Scotchman should not be as punctual in performing agreements as a Dutchman. It is far more reduceable to self interest, that general principle which regulates the actions of every man, and which leads men to act in a certain manner from views of advantage, and is as deeply implanted in an Englishman as a Dutchman. A dealer is afraid of losing his character, and is scrupulous in observing every engagement. When a person makes perhaps 20 contracts in a day, he cannot gain so much by endeavouring to impose on his neighbours, as the very appearance of a cheat would make him lose. Where people seldom deal with one another, we find that they are somewhat disposed to cheat,

---

[63] 7 George II, c. 8 (1734).

[64] 9 Anne, c. 14 (1710) allowed the loser of more than £10 who paid to recover from the winner.

[65] Presumably copyist's error for 'It'.

because they can gain more by a smart trick than they can lose by the injury which it does their character. They whom we call politicians are not the most remarkable men in the world for probity and punctuality. Ambassadors from different nations are still less so: they are praised for any little advantage they can take, and pique themselves a good deal on this degree of refinement. The reason of this is that nations treat with one another not above twice or thrice in a century, and they may gain more by one piece of fraud than ⟨lose⟩ by having a bad character. France has had this character with us ever since the reign of Lewis XIV*th*, yet it has never in the least hurt either its interest or splendour.

328    But if states were obliged to treat once or twice | a day, as merchants do, it would be necessary to be more precise in order to preserve their character. Wherever dealings are frequent, a man does not expect to gain so much by any one contract as by probity and punctuality in the whole, and a prudent dealer, who is sensible of his real interest, would rather chuse to lose what he has a right to than give any ground for suspicion. Every thing of this kind is ⟨as⟩ odious as it is rare. When the greater part of people are merchants they always bring probity and punctuality into fashion, and these therefore are the principal virtues of a commercial nation.

There are some inconveniences, however, arising from a commercial spirit. The first we shall mention is that it confines the views of men. Where the division of labour is brought to perfection, every man has only a simple operation to perform. To this his whole attention is confined, and few ideas pass in his mind but what have an immediate connection with it. When the mind is employed about a variety of objects it is some how expanded and enlarged, and on this account a country artist is generally acknowledged to have a range of thoughts much above a city one. The former is perhaps a joiner, a house carpenter, and a cabinet maker all in one, and his attention must of course be employed about a number of objects of very different kinds. |

329 The latter is perhaps only a cabinet maker. That particular kind of work employs all his thoughts, and as he had not an opportunity of comparing a number of objects, his views of things beyond his own trade are by no means so extensive as those of the former. This must be much more the case when a person's whole attention is bestowed on the $17^{th}$ part of a pin[66] or the $80^{th}$ part of a button, so far divided are these manufactures. It is remarkable that in every commercial nation the low people are exceedingly stupid. The Dutch vulgar are eminently so, and the English are more so than the Scotch. The rule is general, in towns they are not so intelligent as in the country, nor in a rich country as in a poor one.

Another inconvenience attending commerce is that education is greatly neglected. In rich and commercial nations the division of labour, having reduced all trades to very simple operations, affords an opportunity of

[66] Cf. 213–14 above.

employing children very young. In this country[67] indeed, where the division of labour is not far advanced, even the meanest porter can read and write, because the price of education is cheap, and a parent can employ his child no other way at 6 or 7 years of age. This however is not the case in the commercial parts of England. A boy of 6 or 7 years of age at Briming-

330 ham can gain his 3 pence | or sixpence a day, and parents find it to be their interest to set them soon to work. Thus their education is neglected. The education which low people's children receive is not indeed at any rate considerable; however, it does them an immense deal of service, and the want of it is certainly one of their greatest misfortunes. By it they learn to read, and this gives them the benefit of religion, which is a great advantage, not only considered in a pious sense, but as it affords them subject for thought and speculation. From this we may observe the benefit of country schools, and, however much neglected, must acknowledge them to be an excellent institution. But besides this want of education, there is another great loss which attends the putting boys too soon to work. The boy begins to find that his father is obliged to him, and therefore throws off his authority. When he is grown up he has no ideas with which he can amuse himself. When he is away from his work he must therefore betake himself to drunkeness and riot. Accordingly we find that in the commercial parts of England, the tradesmen are for the most part in this despicable condition: their work thro' half the week is sufficient to maintain them, and thro' want of education they have no amusement for the other but riot and debauchery. So it may very justly be said that the people who cloath the whole world are in rags themselves.

331 | Another bad effect of commerce is that it sinks the courage of mankind, and tends to extinguish martial spirit. In all commercial countries the division of labour is infinite, and every ones thoughts are employed about one particular thing. In great trading towns, for example, the linen merchants are of several kinds, for the dealing in Hamburgh and Irish linens are quite distinct professions. Some of the lawyers attend at King's Bench, some at the Court of Common Pleas, and others at the Chauncery. Each of them is in a great measure unacquainted with the business of his neighbour. In the same manner war comes to be a trade also. A man has then time to study only one branch of business, and it would be a great dissadvantage to oblige every one to learn the military art and keep himself in the practice of it. The defence of the country is therefore committed to a certain sett of men who have nothing else ado; and among the bulk of the people military courage diminishes. By having their minds constantly employed on the arts of luxury, they grow effeminate and dastardly.

This is confirmed by universal experience. In the year 1745 four or 5 thousand naked unarmed Highlanders took possession of the improved

Scotland.

parts of this country without any opposition from the unwarlike inhabitants. 332 | They penetrated into England and alarmed the whole nation, and had they not been opposed by a standing army they would have seized the throne with little difficulty. 200 years ago such an attempt would have rouzed the spirit of the nation. Our ancestors were brave and warlike, their minds were not enervated by cultivating arts and commerce, and they were already[68] with spirit and vigor to resist the most formidable foe. It is for the same reason too that an army of 4 or 500 Europeans have often penetrated into the Mogul's country, and that the most numerous armies of the Chinese have always been overthrown by the Tartars. In these countries the division of labour and luxury have arrived at a very high pitch, they have no standing army, and the people are all intent on the arts of peace. Holland, were its barriers removed, would be an easy prey. In the beginning of this century the standing army of the Dutch was beat in the field, and the rest of the inhabitants, instead of rising in arms to defend themselves, formed a design of deserting their country and settling in the East Indies.[69] A commercial country may be formidable abroad, and may defend itself by fleets and standing armies, but when they are overcome and the enemy penetrates into the country, the conquest is easy. The same obser- 333 vation may be made with respect to Rome and Carthage. | The Carthaginians were often victorious abroad, but when the war was carried into their own country they had no share with the Romans. These are the dissadvantages of a commercial spirit. The minds of men are contracted and rendered incapable of elevation, education is despised or at least neglected, and heroic spirit is almost utterly extinguished. To remedy these defects would be an object worthy of serious attention.

Thus we have finished the three first great objects of law, to witt, Justice, Police, and Revenue. We proceed now to treat of Arms, the fourth part of the general division of jurisprudence.

*Remainder of 333 left blank in MS.*

[68] Reporter's or copyist's error for 'all ready'.
[69] In fact 1672: Hume, *History of Great Britain* (1757), II.226.

334                                | *of Arms.*

In the begining of society the defence of the state required no police, nor particular provision for it. The whole body of the people rose up to oppose any attempt that was made against them, and he who was chief in time of peace naturaly preserved his influence in time of war. But after the division of labour took place, it became necessary that some should stay at home to be employed in agriculture and other arts, while the rest went out to war. After the appropriation of lands and the distinction of ranks were in some measure introduced, the cultivation of the ground would naturaly fall to the meanest rank. The less laborious but more honourable employment of military service would be claimed by the highest order. Accordingly we find that this was the practice of all nations in their primitive state. The Roman equites or knights were originaly horsemen in the army, and no slaves or those who did not pay taxes ever went out to war. In like manner, among our ancestors only they who held by what was called knight's service were employed in the defence of the state, and the ancient villains were never considered as a part of the national force. When the state was thus defended by men of honour who would do their duty from this
335 principle, | there was no occasion for discipline. But when arts and manufactures encreased and were thought worthy of attention, and men found that they could rise in dignity by applying to them, and it became inconvenient for the rich to go out to war, from a principle of avarice, these arts which were at first despised by the active and ambitious soon came to claim their whole attention. The merchant who can make 2 or 3000£ at home will not incline to go out to war. But it was an amusement to an ancient knight who had nothing else ado. When the improvement of arts and manufactures was thought an object deserving the attention of the higher ranks, the defence of the state naturaly became the province of the lower, because the rich can never be forced to do any thing but what they please. In Rome, after the knights gave over serving in the army, the lowest of the people went in their stead, and in our own country, after the feudal militia went out, another of the lowest ranks succeeded. This therefore is the progress of military service in every country. Among a nation of hunters and shepherds, and even when a nation is advanced to agriculture, the whole body goes out together to make war. When arts and manufactures begin to advance the whole cannot go out, and as these arts are laborious and not very lucrative, for the reasons formerly adduced, the highest go out. After that, when arts and commerce are still farther advanced and begin to be very lucrative, it falls to the meanest to defend the
336 state.[70] This is our present condition in Great Brittain. | When the whole

[70] Cf. Hutcheson, *M.P.*, III.8.5.

body went out together there could be no occasion for military discipline, they being all as it were upon the same level, and as their common cause was so well discerned it was quite unecessary. When the highest orders went out, a principle of honour would supply the place of discipline. But when this office fell upon the lowest order, the most severe and rigid discipline became necessary, and accordingly we find that it has been introduced into all standing armies. In general it is necessary that they should be kept under such authority as to be more afraid of their general and officers than of the enemy. It is the fear of their officers and of the rigid penalties of the martial law which is the chief cause of their good behaviour, and it is to this principle that we owe their valiant actions. In the late war 800 Prussians defended a pass a whole day against several thousands of Austrians, and at night in their retreat deserted almost to a man. What could be the foundation of this courage? It was not a principle of honour, nor love to their country, nor a regard to their officers, for these would still have detained them; it was nothing but the dread of their officers, who were hanging as it were over their heads, and whom they durst not dissobey. This, by the bye, shows the governableness of our nature, and may also shew how much that manly courage we so much boast of depends upon external circumstances. We may further observe how far this principle of fear may be carried. If a bold, fierce, and tyrannic adjutant be succeeded by one of a mild and
337 gentle disposition, the ideas of terror are conveyed with the coat, | and it is sometime before it be perceived that he is not so terrible as the other. In this manner standing armies came to be introduced, and where there are none the country is an easy prey to its enemies. The only thing to be observed concerning them is that they should be raised in the most convenient way and with as little hurt as possible to the country. However much standing armys may be exclaimed against, in a certain period of society they must be introduced. A militia commanded by landed gentlemen in possession of the public offices of the nation can never have any prospect of sacrifising the liberties of the country for any person whatever. Such a militia would no doubt be the best security against the standing army of another nation.

Standing armies are of two kinds. The first is when the government gives offices to particular persons and so much for every man they levy. From such a standing army as this, which is the model of our own, there is less danger than from the second kind, when the government makes a slump bargain with a general to lead out a certain number of troops for their assistance, which is the model of the standing armies in some little states of Italy. They make a bargain with some chieftan in these parts where the arts have not yet reached, and as the officers are all dependent on him, and he independent of the state, his employers lye at his mercy. But a standing army like ours is not so apt to turn their arms against the government, because the officers are men of honour and have great connections in the country.

338 | Yet on some occasions a standing army has proved dangerous to the liberties of the people, when that question concerning the power of the sovereign came to be disputed, as has been the case in our own country, because the standing army generaly takes the side of the king. The principle of the soldier is to obey his leader, and as the king appointed him and pays him it is to him that he thinks he owes his service. This would never be the case if a proper militia were established. In Sweden, where it takes place, they are in no danger. Thus far concerning standing armies. It is needless to enter into any account of their pay and other circumstances.

Having considered the laws of nature as we proposed, as they regard Justice, Police, Revenue, and Arms, we shall proceed to the last part of our plan, which is to consider the Law of Nations, or the claims which one nation may have upon another.

*Remainder of 338 left blank in MS.*

339              | *of the Laws of Nations*

It is to be observed that the rules which nations ought to observe or do observe with one another cannot be treated so accurately as private or public law. We find the rules of property pretty exactly established in every nation. The extent of the sovereigns power, as well as the duty of the subject, so far as justice is concerned, are pretty uniform every where. But with respect to the laws of nations, we can scarce mention any one regulation which is established with the common consent of all nations,[71] and observed as such at all times. This must necessarily be the case, for where there is no supreme legislative power nor judge to settle differences, we may always expect uncertainty and irregularity.

The laws of nations are such as take place either in peace or war. Those that take place in times of peace have been formerly explained, where it was shewn with respect to aliens that they are entitled to security as to their persons and effects, but that they have no power to make a will, but all goes to the sovereign at their death.[72]

The laws or rules observed in time of war shall be considered in the following order.

1st. What is a just cause of war, or according to the Latin phrase, quando liceat bellare.

340   | 2$^{\text{dly}}$. What it is lawful for one nation to do to another in time of war, or quantum liceat in bello, and upon this head we shall consider the differences between the ancient and modern governments and the great modifications of the latter.

3$^{\text{dly}}$. What is due to neutral nations from the belligerant powers.

4$^{\text{thly}}$. The rights of ambassadors between different nations.

1st. Quando liceat bellare? In general whatever is the foundation of a proper law suit before a court of justice may be a just occasion of war.[73] The foundation of a law-suit is the violation of some perfect right whose performance may be extorted by force, and is so extorted in a rude society, but in modern times is decided by the magistrate, lest the society should be disturbed by every one taking justice at his own hands. When one nation encroaches on the property of another, or puts to death the subjects of another, imprisons them or refuses them justice when injured, the sovereign is bound to demand satisfaction for the offence, as it is the intention of the government to protect it's several members from forreign enemies, and if redress be refused there is a foundation for war. In the same manner breach of contract, as when a debt is due by one nation to another, and

341 payment refused, is a very just | occasion of war. If, for example, the King

---

[71] Grotius, I.1.14.                              [72] 88–90 above.
[73] Grotius, II.1.2; Hutcheson, *M.P.*, II.15.6 and *System*, II.350 ff.

of Prussia should refuse to pay the money advanced for him by the British nation in the time of the last war:[74] a declaration of war against him would be just and reasonable. Every offence of the sovereign of one country against the sovereign of another, or of the sovereign against the subject, or of the subject of one country against the subject of another, without giving reasonable satisfaction, may be the cause of a war. There seems to be only one exception to the general rule that every thing that is the subject of a law suit may be a cause of war, and that is with respect to quasi contracts. In this case indeed it is difficult to determine whether a war would be reasonable or not, and we find no instance of a war declared upon the violation of this right. It must be allowed that the introduction of quasi contract was the highest stretch of equity, and except in the Roman law[75] it was never perfected nor introduced. In England, if you repair a man's house in his absence you must trust to him for the payment of it, for you have no action by law. In the same manner, if a Russian do a piece of service to an English merchant, which if he had not done, the merchant would have suffered extremely, and afterwards demand satisfaction for his trouble, if he be refused it and apply to the courts of justice they will tell him that he must depend on the honour of the merchant for payment. Excepting this, every thing which is the foundation of a proper law suit will also make war just and reasonable.

342   | Quantum liceat ⟨in⟩ bello? How far a nation may push the resentment of an injury against the nation which has injured them, is not easy to determine. The practice of ancient and modern nations differs extremely. In general, when an injury is clearly and distinctly done or when it is plainly intended, and satisfaction refused, resentment is necessary and just. There are a few cases in which it is lawful even without satisfaction being demanded. If a robber was plainly intending to kill you, it would be quite lawfull in you to do all you could to prevent him. The injury is plain. In the same manner, when one nation seems to be conspiring against another, tho' it may have done no real injury, it is necessary that it should be obliged to declare its intentions and to give security when this demand would not subject it to inconveniences. Tho' this satisfaction be not demanded, when the King of Prussia saw his dominions about to be overwhelmed by the Elector of Saxony and the Queen of Hungary,[76] it was quite right in him to be beforehand with them and to take possession of their territories, and nothing would have been more absurd than for him to have told them that he was going to attack them. On the other hand, if it be only a debt that is due, it would be as unreasonable to go to war without demanding satis-

---

[74] An annual subsidy of £670,000 was granted to Frederick the Great from April 1758, but it was withheld by Bute in 1762, on account of disagreement with Frederick's policy.

[75] *Negotiorum gestio*, looking after another's affairs without his authority, gave one a right of action for expenses: *Inst.* 3.27.1.

[76] In 1756, at the beginning of the Seven Years War.

faction, and it is only upon the dilatory and evasive manner of giving satisfaction that a war in this case becomes lawfull. But to consider a little

343 more particularly what is lawfull | in war, suppose a subject of any government is injured, they who have injured him become natural objects of resentment, and also the government which protects him if it refuse satisfaction, but the greater part of the nation is perfectly innocent and knows nothing about the affair. In the late war with France not one out of twenty, either of the French or us, knew any thing of the offences done. Upon what principle or foundation of justice therefore do we take their goods from them, and distress them in all possible ways? This can by no means be founded upon justice and equity properly so called; it must be upon necessity, which indeed in this case is a part of justice. Mr. Hutchinson indeed very ingeniously accounts for this,[77] but if we examine his opinion thoroughly we shall find that he has not built his reasoning on a proper foundation. Every nation, says he, maintains and supports the government for it's own good. If the government commit any offence against a neighbouring soveraign or subject, and it's own people continue to support and protect it, as it were, in it, they thereby become accessary and liable to punishment along with (it). As by the Roman law,[78] if any of these slaves which every private person kept for his own advantage had done any damage to another, one of these two things was to be done, he must either keep the

344 slave no longer, or pay the damnage. | In like manner a nation must either allow itself to be liable for the damnages, or give up the government altogether. It is to be observed that in this reasoning, tho' excessively ingenious, the cases are not in the smallest degree parallel. A man can do with his slave as he pleases, he can either put him away or pay what damages he has occasioned, but a nation in most cases can neither do the one nor the other. A government is often maintained, not for the nation's preservation, but it's own. It was never the doctrine of any public law that the subjects had a right to dispose of the sovereign, not even in England, where his right has been so much contested. How then comes it that a nation should be guilty of an injury which was not in it's power. The real cause why the whole nation is thought a reasonable object of resentment is that we do not feel for those at a distance as we do for those near us. We have been injured by France, our resentment rises against the whole nation instead of the government, and they, thro' a blind indiscriminating faculty natural to mankind, become the objects of an unreasonable resentment. In a war between France and us, a Dane would naturaly enter into the same sentiments that we do, and would involve together without distinction both the guilty and the innocent. | This is however quite con-

345 trary to the rules of justice observed with regard to our own subjects. We

[77] Hutcheson, *M.P.*, III.9.4; *System*, II.355 ff.
[78] The principle of noxal surrender: *Inst.* 4.8.

would rather chuse that 10 guilty persons should escape than that one innocent person should suffer.

Another cause is that it is often very difficult to get satisfaction from a subject or from a sovereign that may have offended. They are generaly in the heart of the country and perfectly well secured. If we could get at them, no doubt they would be the first objects of our resentment, but as this is impossible we must make reprizals some other way. We have suffered unjustly on account of our connections, let them also suffer unjustly on account of theirs. In war there must always be the greatest injustice but it is inevitable.

The practice of ancient and modern nations differs widely with regard to the length to which the outrages of war may be carried. Barbarians, if they do not kill these taken in war, may dispose of them as they please. As all who made war were considered as robbers and violators of the peace of society, such punishments were by no means thought inadequate. Even among the Romans, if the battering-ram had once struck the walls no agreement nor capitulation was allowed, but every thing fell into the hands of the con-
346 querors, | and they were at liberty to use it as they pleased. So much was this the case in Cicero's time that he represents it as the greatest stretch of humanity that a capitulation was allowed after the ram had once struck the walls.[79] But tho' force and fraud were in former periods the great virtues of war, modern manners have come to a greater degree of refinement, both with respect to persons and effects. Captives in war are now by no means made slaves or liable to oppression. An officer is sett free upon his parole or word of honour; and in the war between France and us, they generaly treated our wounded prisoners better than their own wounded soldiers.[80] Indeed there is no nation that pushes this point of gallantry farther than we do. When the sixpence a day which was allowed the French prisoners at Edinburgh and elsewhere, was thought insufficient to maintain them on account of the diminution it sustained before it came to their hands by subcontracts, etc., a collection of 10,000£ was generously made for them. In general, prisoners of war are now as well treated as other people.

In the same manner cartel-treaties,[81] by which soldiers and sailors are
347 valued at so much | and exchanged at the end of every campaign, the nation which has lost most prisoners paying the balance, is an evidence of our refinement in humanity. In the late war indeed, we refused to enter into any such treaty with France for sailors, and by this wise regulation soon unman'd their navy, as we took a great many more than they. It was the want of humanity, no doubt, which rendered ancient towns so obstinate, for it was better to sustain the most terrible hardships than to surrender.

[79] *De Officiis*, I.11.35, cited by Grotius, III.11.14.
[80] See, e.g., *Gentleman's Magazine*, January 1759, 42.
[81] Cf. Hume, 'Of the Populousness of Ancient Nations', *Essays*, I.402.

But now the besieged know very well how they will be treated before they capitulate, and will run no great risk before they do so.[82]

This superiour degree of humanity was introduced during the time of popery. We never find it among the Greeks and Romans, notwithstanding all their attainments. The Pope was considered as the common father of Christendom, the clergy were under his subjection, and he had intercourse by his legates with all the courts of Europe. By this they were more nearly connected, and he obliged them to treat one another with more humanity. The Holy War too, which at that time was undertaken by most of the princes in Europe, made them turn their arms against all those of a different

348 religion, who they thought | deserved to be treated in the most cruel manner. But when they came to be engaged in a war among themselves, as they had all been on one side in that common cause, and as they thought that Christians should not be treated in the same manner with infidells, a greater degree of humanity was introduced. From those causes moderns behave differently from the ancients with regard to the persons of prisoners.

It is more from motives of policey than humanity that the effects of enemies are secured. When a French army invades Germany, the general makes a law that all the people who will live quietly and do not rise against him shall be secure in their persons and possessions, and he will punish a soldier as severely for injuring the peasants of his enemys country as those of his own. But this is not the case in a sea war. An admiral seizes and plunders all the merchant ships he can get. Many of the merchants have done as little harm as the peasants. Why then this distinction? It is the interest of the general not to rob the peasants, because it would be difficult to march an army carrying all it's provisions thro' the country of an enemy.

349 But by engageing them to stay | he is supplyed without any other expedient. By this means war is so far from being a dissadvantage in a well cultivated country that many get rich by it. When the Neitherlands is the seat of war all the peasants grow rich, for they pay no rent when the enemy are in the country, and provisions sell at a high rate. This is indeed at the expence of the landlords and better sort of people, who are generaly ruined on such occasions. This is so much the case that all the poor people who are abroad, whenever they hear of a war, will not stay from their native country. It is quite otherways in a sea war. Every ship carrys it's own provisions and has no dependance for them upon the ships which it meets.

Another cause of modern refinement is that courtesy, or rather gallantry, which takes place between hostile nations, by which even ambassadors are kept at their several courts.

Anciently it was the greatest gallantry to kill the general of an army,[83] but nothing could make a person more infamous at present than such a

[82] Grotius, III.12.8; Hume, loc. cit.
[83] Grotius, III.4.18.

practice. When the King of France[84] in person besieged a certain castle, the governour sent to know in what part of the camp the king lodged, that he might not canonade it. The King of Prussia indeed did not grant the princes

350 of Saxony this request, when they | informed him where the royal tent stood, but this was because he was assured that the chief magazine was there. Now if there be any in a nation who have injured more than others, they are the king and generals. How comes it then that it is not now thought lawfull to kill them as well as formerly. The plain reason is that monarchies, whose interest it always is to shew respect to those in authority, set the example at present, but republics, whose interest lyes in adopting the opposite maxim, formerly led the fashion.[85]

The same policey which makes us not so apt to go to war makes us also more favourable than formerly after an entire conquest. Anciently an enemy forfeited all his possessions, and was disposed of at the pleasure of the conquerors. It was on this account that the Romans had often to people a country anew and send out colonies. It is not so now. A conquered country in a manner only changes masters. They may be subjected to new taxes and other regulations, but need no new people. The conqueror generaly allows them the possession of their religion and laws, which is a practice much better than the ancient. Modern armies too are less irratated at one another because fire arms keep them at a greater distance.[86] When they always fought sword in hand their rage and fury were raised to the highest pitch, and as they were mixed with one another the slaughter was vastly greater.

351 | 3$^d$, we are next to shew what is due to neutral nations from the belligerant powers.[87]

The rule of justice with respect to neutral nations is that as they have offended no party they should suffer no injury. In a war between France and England, the Dutch should have the liberty of trading to both countries as in the time of peace, as they have injured neither party. Unless when they carry contraband goods or are going to a town that is besieged, they can trade to any part of the country without molestation. A neutral bottom will not however protect the goods of the enemy, nor does the hostility of the bottom, so to speak, forfeit the goods of the neutral power.

There is some difference between the practice of ancient and modern nations with respect to the ius postliminii, or the recovery of what was lost.[88] The maxim in time of war anciently was, we are always in the right, and our enemies always in the wrong. Whatever is taken from the enemy is justly taken, whatever is taken from us is unjustly taken. On this account if a

---

[84] Louis XIV: A. M. Ramsay, *Histoire de Henri de la Tour d'Auvergne, Vicomte de Turenne* (1735), I.416.

[85] Cf. 79 above.

[86] Hume, *Essays*, I.401.

[87] Hutcheson, *M.P.*, III.9.5; *System*, II.357 ff.

[88] Grotius, III.6.3; III.9.15.

Carthaginian had sold to a Roman a Roman ship taken in war, the former owner, whenever he had an opportunity, took it back, as on the above
352 principle | it was unjustly taken from him. Now it is quite otherways. We consider every thing done in war as just and equitable, and neither demand nor would take back any captures made in it. If an English ship be taken by the French and sold to the Dutch, and come to a British harbour, the former owner pretends no claim to her, for he had lost all hopes of it when it had gone into the possession of the enemy.

It is to be observed that there is a very great difference in the conduct of belligerant nations towards one that is neutral, in a land-war from what ⟨it⟩ is in a sea war, which is more the effect of policey than humanity. When an army retreats and the conqueror pursues into a neutral nation, unless it have power to hold out both, it becomes the seat of war, as is often the case, and little or no satisfaction is given for damages. But in a sea war, a ship taken from the most inconsiderable neutral power is always restored. The reason commonly assigned, that it injures their commerce more to take their ships than any thing else, is unsatisfactory, for a land war hurts commerce more than it does. The real reason is that a small country has it not in its power to assert it's neutrality in a land war, but the smallest is able to do it in a sea war. A small fort can oblige ⟨?ships⟩ of the greatest nation to respect the neutrality of it's harbour.

353 | 4. We are in the last place to consider the rights of ambassadors between different nations.

When nations came to have a great deal of business one with another, it was found necessary to send messengers betwixt them, who were the first ambassadors. Anciently, as there was little commerce carried on between different nations, ambassadors were only sent on particular occasions and were what we now call ambassadors extraordinary, who returned home after their business was transacted. We find nothing like resident ambassadors in Rome or Greece; their whole office was on particular occasions to conclude peace, make alliances, etca. The first time that resident ambassador's were employed was in the begining of the 17$^{th}$ century, by Ferdinand, King of Spain. Even the word ambassador comes from the Spanish verb ambassare, to send.[89] The Pope indeed from the earliest times had residents, or legates, at all the courts of Europe. The very same reason that makes embassies now so frequent induced the Pope formerly to fall upon this method. He had business in all the countries of Europe and a great part of his revenue was collected from them, and as they were con-
354 tinualy attempting to infringe the right he claimed, | he found it necessary to have a person constantly residing at their courts to see that his priviledges were preserved. The Pope from this custom derived several advantages. When commerce was introduced into Europe, and the

---

[89] Wicquefort, *L'Ambassadeur et ses fonctions* (1681), 4.

priviledges of every country, with the duties payable on goods in another, were settled, the merchants of one country had constant claims on those of another; they themselves were strangers in these countries, and would very readily be injured and oftener think themselves so. It became necessary therefore to have one of their countrymen constantly residing at the courts of different nations to protect the rights of his fellow subjects. Anciently, as was observed, there was little intercourse with different nations and therefore no occasion for resident ambassadors; but now, as there is something almost every day to adjust betwixt dealers, it is necessary that there should be some person of weight and authority who has access to the court, to prevent any occasion of quarrel betwixt them. We have already observed that it was Ferdinand of Spain who established this practice. At first it gave great jealousy to the neighbouring nations to keep ambassadors residing at their courts. He indeed pretended to have no right to do this, but by sending an ambassador upon a certain occasion, and starting different questions, he found means of keeping him there. This practice was soon imitated, and it immediately became the universal custom of the European princes, and

355 was so far from being taken amiss that it was | reckoned a great affront not to send one. Grotius, whose opinions are founded on the practice of ancient nations, declares against resident ambassadors and calls them resident spies.[90] But if he had lived in the present age, he would have found that extensive commerce renders it impossible to preserve peace a month, unless grievances be redressed by a man of authority who knows the customs of the country and is capable of explaining what injuries are realy done. The custom of sending ambassadors preserves peace and, by giving intelligence, prevents one country from being invaded by another without timeous notice. When any kind of dispute happens, and the ambassador is recalled, you can have intelligence by your communication with other courts, your ambassador there being informed, for ambassadors in general are acquainted with all the business in Europe.

Though one country might attain some kind of pre-eminence by the influence and assiduity of it's ambassador, no attention was for a long time given to it, and that balance of power which has of late been so much talked of was never then heard of. Every sovereign had enough to do within his own dominions and could bestow little attention on forreign powers. Before the institution of residents they could have little intelligence. But ever since the begining of the 16th century the nations of Europe were divided into two great alliances. On the one hand were England, Holland,

356 Hungary, Muscovy, etca. | On the other France, Spain, Prussia, Denmark, Sweden, etca. In this manner a kind of alliance was kept up, sometimes one leaving the one side and another joining it, as at present Prussia is with

---

[90] Grotius, II.18.3, criticizes ambassadors; Cocceius's note ad loc., quoting Wicquefort, refers to their role as spies.

England and Hungary on the other side. A system of this kind was established in Italy about ⟨the⟩ 15$^{th}$ century among the great families there. The
resident ambassadors of these nations hinder any one country from domi-
neering over another either by sea or land, and are formed into a kind of
council not unlike that of the Amphictyons in ancient Greece. They have
power to advise and consult concerning matters but not to determine any,
and by combining together can threaten any one country pretending to
superiority or making an unreasonable demand. Post offices too are of
great importance for procuring intelligence, as communication is open
thro' all these countries both in peace and war, which makes commerce
easy and gives notice of every movement.

An ambassador's person must be sacred and not subject to any of the
courts of justice in the country where he resides.[91] If he contract debts or
do any injury, a complaint must be made to his country. When the Dutch
arrested the Russian ambassador in the year 1718, it was complained off as
a violation of the laws of nations.[92] The goods which an ambassador buys
are not subject to any custom. As a sovereign would be exempted from
357 taxes, so must his ambassador who represents him. | When an ambassador
makes any attempt to disturb the peace by entering into conspiracies or the
like, he may be imprisoned. By way of compliment, and to keep up the
dignity of an ambassador, his house is considered as an asylum for offenders. He must be cautious however of this priviledge, and extend his
authority only to the protection of debtors and small delinquents, for the
right will be broken thro' if he harbour those guilty of capital crimes. The
servants of ambassadors, too, are entitled to some considerable priviledges.
If indeed they have contracted debts they may be arrested, but this is never
done voluntarily.

All the words that signify these persons employed by one court at
another are derived from the Spanish language. The Spanish court was
then the most ceremonious in the world, and Spanish dress was every where
affected. As ambassadors were obliged to keep up much ceremony, they
were hindered in the prosecution of their business. A man that has to
negociate matters of the highest importance could not allow so much time
to be spent in the endless ceremony of paying and returning visits. Envoys
were therefore sent, to whom less ceremony was due, and who could be
addressed on any occasion. Their dignity, too, soon advanced and in-
358 capacitated them to transact business. | As they continued for sometime,
they were called resident ambassadors ordinary, being of an inferiour order
to the ambassadors extraordinary. Below this rank is the minister, who

[91] Hutcheson, *M.P.*, III.10.2; *System*, II.367.
[92] As Cannan (279) notes, this is probably a conflation of three cases. The Dutch arrested
the Swedish minister in 1717; the English arrested the Russian ambassador for debt in
1708; and the French arrested the Spanish ambassador in 1718.

resides in the country on account of his own business, and has power to transact any little business of the country to which he belongs.

A consul is a particular magistrate who is a judge of all matters relating to the merchants of his own country, and takes care to do them justice in these places where it may not be very accurately administered.

These are the names and offices of the several persons employed in the forreign affaires of the nation, occasioned by the introduction of commerce, and now become absolutely necessary.

Thus we have considered both the laws of nature and the laws of nations.

FINIS.d

d Two pages are left blank before the Index appears. Both they and the pages of the Index are unnumbered.

# INDEX[93]

## A.

---

[93] This index forms part of the 1766 Report. The references are to the pages of the MS.
[94] Copyist's error for 328, 9, 31, 2 (i.e. 328–9, 331–2).

[95] Error for 'Jus postliminii 351–2'.

# APPENDIX

# INTRODUCTION

THE first of the three documents in this Appendix was discovered by Professor W. R. Scott and published by him with annotations and comments, under the title 'An Early Draft of Part of *The Wealth of Nations*', in his *Adam Smith as Student and Professor*.[1] The circumstances of his discovery of ED, and the physical characteristics of the document, are fully described by Scott in this work,[2] and only one point needs to be added here. Scott identified the handwriting with that of the College scribe who wrote in 1762 a report of a committee on the powers of the Rector and Principal.[3] We can confirm his judgement in that identification, and can add a further identification with a manuscript written in 1759. This is a revision of TMS, intended for inclusion in edition 2, and in the hand of the same amanuensis.[4]

The other two documents are fragments on the division of labour (FA and FB), which were also discovered by Scott ('amongst letters which belonged to Adam Smith')[5] and published by him—in facsimile, and without annotations or extensive comments—in *Adam Smith as Student and Professor*.[6] In physical appearance, FA consists of a single folio sheet of four pages (each page measuring 203 × 315 mm.), with the text extending almost, but not quite, to the bottom of the last page. FB consists of a single folio sheet of the same size and format, with the text covering rather more than two and one-half pages. The two documents were evidently written in the same hand, and have the same watermark. This watermark seems to be the same as that found in ED, but the hand is different.

ED, it would appear, represented a preliminary and rather tentative attempt by Smith to translate the 'economic' material in his Jurisprudence lectures into book form—an attempt which he probably made at some time shortly before April 1763. The origin of FA and FB is perhaps not quite so certain, but it seems implausible to assign them, as Scott did,[7] to Smith's Edinburgh period. It is much more likely, we feel, that they were in fact written in the 1760s. Our judgement on these matters is based on the argumentation in an article by R. L. Meek and A. S. Skinner, which contains an exhaustive survey of the relationships between ED, FA, FB, LJ(A), LJ(B), and WN, and to which the interested reader is referred.[8]

The principles adopted in the transcription of ED, FA, and FB are the same (*mutatis mutandis*) as those adopted above in the case of LJ(A) and LJ(B).

[1] Scott, 317–56.
[2] Ibid., 317–22.
[3] Ibid., 318.
[4] It was enclosed by Smith with Letter 40 addressed to Sir Gilbert Elliot, dated 10 Oct. 1759.
[5] Scott, 57.
[6] Ibid., 379–85.
[7] Ibid., 57–9, and see also the captions to the facsimile reproductions on 379–85, each of which begins 'Very early economic work of Adam Smith, one of the Edinburgh Lectures.'
[8] 'The Development of Adam Smith's Ideas on the Division of Labour', *Economic Journal*, lxxxiii (1973).

1 | Chap. 2.

Of the nature and causes of public opulence.

The unassisted labour of a solitary individual, it is evident, is altogether unable to provide for him such food, such cloaths, and such lodging, as not only the luxury of the great but as the natural appetites of the meanest peasant are, in every civilized society, supposed to require. Observe in what manner a common day labourer in Britain or in Holland is accommodated with all these, and you will be sensible that his luxury is much superior to that of many an Indian prince, the absolute master of the lives and liberties of a thousand naked savages. The woolen coat which covers the day labourer, as coarse and rough[a] as it may appear to be, could not be produced without the joint labour of a multitude of artists. The shepherd, the grazier, the clipper, the sorter of the wool, the picker, the comber, the dyer, the scribbler, the spinner, the weaver, the fuller, the dresser, must all join their different arts in order to make out this very homely production. Not to mention the merchants and carriers, who transport the materials from one of those artists to another, who often lives in a very distant country; how many other artists are employed in producing the tools even of the very meanest of

2 these. I shall say nothing of so very complex a machine as the loom of | the weaver or as the mill of the fuller; much less of the immense commerce and navigation, the ship building, the sail-making, the rope-making, necessary to bring together the different drugs made use of by the dyer, which often come from the remotest corners of the world; but consider only what a variety of labour is necessary to produce that very simple machine, the sheers of the clipper. The miner, the builder of the furnace for smelting the ore, the burner of the charcoal to be made use of in that operation, the feller of the timber of which that charcoal is made, the brickmaker, the bricklayer, the smelter, the mill wright, the forger, the smith, must all club their different industries in order to produce them. If we[b] were to examine in the same manner all the other parts of his dress and household furniture, the coarse linnen shirt which he wears next his skin, the shoes which cover his feet, the bed which he lyes in and all the different parts which compose it, the kitchen grate at which he prepares his victuals, the coals which he makes use of for that purpose, dugg from the bowels of the earth, and brought to him, perhaps, by a long sea and a long land-carriage, all the other utensils of his kitchin, all the furniture of his table, the knives and forks, the delft or pewter plates upon which he serves up and divides his victuals, the many hands who are employed in preparing his bread and his beer, the plowman, the sower of the corn, the reaper, the thresher, the maltster, the miller, the brewer, the baker, with all the other artists who supply each of them with the tools of their respective

3 trades, the glass window which lets in the heat and the | light and keeps out the wind and the rain, and all the knowledge and art which were requisite for

---

[a] Replaces 'rough', possibly mis-spelt     [b] 'exam' deleted

preparing that beautiful and happy invention, without which these northern parts of the world could scarce have been made habitable, at least by that effeminate and delicate race of mortals who dwell in them at present: If we examine, I say, all those different conveniencies and luxuries with which he is accomodated and consider what a variety of labours is employed about each of them, we shall be sensible that without the assistance and cooperation of many thousands the very meanest person in civilized society could not be provided for, even in, what we very falsely imagine, the easy and simple manner in which he is commonly accomodated. Compared, indeed, with the yet more extravagant luxury of the great, his accomodation must no doubt appear extremely simple and easy; and yet, perhaps, it may be true that the accomodation of a European prince does not so much exceed that of an industrious and frugal peasant, as the accomodation of this last exceeds that of the chief of a savage nation in North America.

It cannot be very difficult to explain how it comes about that the rich and the powerful should, in a civilized society, be better provided with the conveniencies and necessaries of life than it is possible for any person to provide himself in a savage and solitary state.[c] It is very easy to conceive that the person who can at all times direct the labours of thousands to his own purposes, should be better provided with whatever he has occasion for than he who depends upon his own industry only. But how it comes about that the labourer | and the peasant should likewise be better provided is not perhaps so easily understood. In a civilized society the poor provide both for themselves and for the enormous luxury of their superiors. The rent which goes to support the vanity of the slothful landlord is all earned[d] by the industry of the peasant. The monied man indulges himself in every sort of ignoble and sordid sensuality, at the expence of the merchant and the trades man to whom he lends out his stock at interest. All the indolent and frivolous retainers upon a court are, in the same manner, fed, cloathed, and lodged by the labour of those who pay the taxes which support them. Among savages, on the contrary, every individual enjoys the whole produce of his own industry. There are among them no landlords, no usurers, no taxgatherers. We might naturally expect, therefore, if experience did not demonstrate the contrary, that every individual among them should have a much greater affluence of the necessaries and conveniencies of life than can be possessed by the inferior ranks of people in a civilized society.

What considerably increases this difficulty is the consideration that the labour of an hundred, or of an hundred thousand men, should seem to bear the same proportion to the support of an hundred or of an hundred thousand, which the labour of one bears to the support of one man. Supposing therefore that the produce of the labour of the multitude was to be equally and fairly divided, each individual, we should expect, could be little better provided for than the single person who laboured alone. But with regard to the produce of the labour of a great society there is never any such thing as a fair | and equal division. In a society of an hundred thousand families, there will perhaps be one hundred who don't labour at all, and who yet, either by violence or by the more orderly oppression of law, employ a greater part of the labour of the society than any other

---

[c] 'to provide himself' deleted        [d] Replaces 'earned', possibly mis-spelt

ten thousand in it. The division of what remains, too, after this enormous defalcation, is by no means made in proportion to the labour of each individual. On the contrary those who labour most get least. The opulent merchant, who spends a great part of his time in luxury and entertainments, enjoys a much greater proportion of the profits of his traffic than all the clerks and accountants who do the business. These last, again, enjoying a great deal of leisure and suffering scarce any other hardship besides the confinement of attendance, enjoy a much greater share of the produce than three times an equal number of artizans, who, under their direction, labour much more severely and assiduously. The artizan, again, tho he works generally under cover, protected from the injuries of the weather, at his ease and assisted by the conveniency of innumerable machines, enjoys a much greater share than the poor labourer who has the soil and the seasons to struggle with, and who, while he affords the materials for supplying the luxury of all the other members of the common wealth, and bears, as it were, upon his shoulders the whole fabric of human society, seems himself to be pressed down below ground by the weight, and to be buried out of sight in the lowest foundations of the building. In the midst of so much oppressive inequality, in what manner

6 shall we account for the superior affluence and abundance | commonly possessed even by this lowest and most despised member of civilized society, compared with what the most respected and active savage can attain to.

The division of labour, by which each individual confines himself to a particular branch of business, can alone account for that superior opulence which takes place in civilized societies, and which, notwithstanding the inequality of property, extends itself to the lowest member of the community. Let us consider the effects of this division of labour as it takes place in some particular manufactures, and we shall from thence more easily be enabled to explain in what manner it operates in the general business of society. Thus, to give a very frivolous instance, if all the parts of a pin were to be made by one man, if the same person was to dig the mettal out of the mine, seperate it from the ore, forge it, split it into small rods, then spin these rods into wire, and last of all make that wire into pins, a man perhaps could with his utmost industry scarce make a pin in a year. The price of a pin, therefore, must in this case at least have been equal to the maintenance of a man for a year. Let this be supposed equal to six pounds sterling, a miserable allowance for a person of so much ingenuity, the price of a single pin must have been six pounds sterling. Supposing that the wire was furnished to him ready made, as at present, even in this case, I imagine, one man could with his utmost dilligence scarce make twenty pins in a day, which, allowing three hundred working days in the year, will amount to six thousand pins in the year; an immense increase!*  His maintainance for a day therefore must be

7 charged upon those twenty pins. Let us suppose this maintainance equal | to ten pence, a most liberal allowance compared with the foregoing, there must be a half penny of this charged upon each pin over and above the price of the wire and the profite of the merchant, which would make the price of a pin about a penny: a price which appears as nothing compared with the foregoing, but which is still extravagant compared with that which actually takes place. For the pin-maker, in

* The last twenty-one words are written in the margin

preparing this small superfluity, very properly takes care to divide the labour among a great number of persons. One man straightens the wire, another cuts it, a third points it, a fourth grinds it at the top for receiving the head, three or four people are employed about making the head, to put it on is the business of a particular person, to guild the pins is the occupation of another, it is even a trade by itself to put them in the paper. When this small operation is in this manner divided among about eighteen persons, these eighteen will perhaps among them make upwards of thirty six thousand pins in a day. Each person, therefore, making an eighteenth part of thirty six thousand pins, may be considered as making two thousand pins a day, and supposing three hundred working days in the year, each person may be considered as making six hundred thousand pins in the year, that is, each person produces six hundred thousand times the quantity of work which he was capable of producing when he had the whole machinery and materials to provide for himself, as upon the first supposition; and one hundred times the quantity of work which he was capable of producing when the
8   wire was | afforded him ready made, as upon the second. The yearly maintainance, therefore, of each person is to be charged not upon one pin as by the first supposition, nor upon six thousand as by the second, but upon six hundred thousand pins. The master of the work, therefore, can both afford to increase the wages of the labourer, and yet sell the commodity at a vastly lower rate than before: and pins instead of being sold at six pounds a piece as upon the first supposition, or at twelve pence a dozen as upon the second, are commonly sold at several dozens for a half penny.

The division of labour has the same effect in all the other arts as in this frivolous manufacture, and occasions in the same manner an immense multiplication of the productions of each. In every opulent society, the farmer is nothing but a farmer, the manufacturer nothing but a manufacturer. The labour which is necessary to produce any one compleat manufacture is divided among a vast number of hands. How many different people are employed in each branch of the linnen and woollen manufactures, from the growers of the flax and the wool to the dyers and dressers of the cloth, or the bleachers and smoothers of the linnen! The nature of agriculture, indeed, does not admit of so many subdivisions of labour, nor of such an entire seperation of one business from another, as commonly takes place in manufactures. It is impossible to seperate so entirely the business of the grazier from that of the corn farmer, as the trade of the carpenter is com
9   monly seperated from that of the smith. | The spinner is always a different person from the weaver. But the plowman, the harrower, the sower of the seed, and the reaper of the corn are often the same. The occasions for their different labours returning with the different seasons of the year, make it impossible for one man to be entirely employed on any one of those different occupations. With regard even to agriculture, however, in well cultivated countries the businesses of the thresher and the ditcher, as they can do their work through the whole year, are often considered as compleat trades, distinct and seperated from all others. It is the same case with the plow-wright and the makers of all the other instruments of agriculture, the forgers of the scythe and reaping hook, the wheel wright, the cart and waggon maker. It is this impossibility, however, of making so compleat and entire a seperation of all the different branches of labour employed in agriculture

which must forever hinder the improvement of this art from keeping pace with
the improvements of manufactures. The most opulent nation will commonly
excell all its' neighbours in agriculture as well as in manufactures; but it will
always be more distinguished by its superiority in the latter than in the former,
tho' the former may be of much greater value. The corn of France is fully as good
and in the provinces where it grows rather cheaper than that of England, at least
during ordinary seasons. But the toys of England, their watches, their cutlery
10  ware, their locks and hinges of doors, their buckles | and buttons, are in accuracy,
solidity, and perfection of work out of all comparison superior to those of France,
and cheaper too in the same degree of goodness.*ƒ*

It is the immense multiplication of the productions of all the different arts, in
consequence of the division of labour, which, notwithstanding the great inequali-
ties of property, occasions in all civilized societies that universal opulence which
extends itself to the lowest ranks of the people. So great a quantity of every thing
is produced that there is enough both to gratify the slothful and oppressive profusion of the great, and at the same time abundantly to supply the wants of the
artizan and the peasant. Each man performs so great a quantity of that work
which peculiarly belongs to him that he can both afford something to those who
do not labour at all, and at the same time have as much behind as will enable him,
by exchanging it for the productions of other arts, to supply himself with all the
necessaries and conveniencies which he stands in need of. Let us suppose, for
example, to return to the frivolous instance which I formerly gave, that pins may
be valued at a penny the hundred, which is nearly the price of some particular
sorts of them. The pinmaker who, according to the forgoing supposition, could
be considered as making two thousand pins a day, produces work to the value of
twenty pence. Let five pence be allowed for the price of the wire, the wear of the
tools, and the profits of the master of the work, there remain fifteen pence for the
11  wages of the artizan, with | which he can purchase all the necessaries and con-
veniencies of life. The case here is the same as if he gave five hundred pins to his
master for affording him the wire, the tools, and the employment, and kept
fifteen hundred to himself, in order to be exchanged for the productions of the
other arts which he had occasion for. For it is the same thing, with regard to
opulence, whether we consider a person as possessed of a particular merchandize,
or of the value of a particular merchandize. Let us suppose that by still further
divisions of labour and improvements of art a pin-maker could be made to produce four thousand pins a day. In this case, tho' pins were to be valued one fourth
less, and to be sold for three farthings the hundred, the artizan would produce
work to the value of thirty pence a day. His master might have ten pence, or the
value of thirteen hundred and thirty three pins, for his profits and expences, and
the artizan retain twenty pence, or the value of two thousand six hundred and
sixty seven pins, for his wages. The price of the work would be diminished,
and the wages of the labourer increased; the public would be better supplyed and
the workmen more amply rewarded. I do not mean that the profits are divided

---

*ƒ* As the MS. originally stood, the first twenty words of the next paragraph ('It is the
immense multiplication . . . the division of labour') followed on immediately after 'the
same degree of goodness.' These twenty words were deleted, and then rewritten so as to
form the opening of a new paragraph.

in fact precisely in the above manner, but that they may be divided in such manner.[g]

It is in this manner that in an opulent and commercial society labour becomes dear and work cheap, and those two events, which vulgar prejudices and superficial reflection are apt to consider as altogether incompatible, are found by 12 experience to be perfectly consistent. | The high price of labour is to be considered not meerly as a proof of the general opulence of society which can afford to pay well all those whom it employs; it is to be regarded as what constitutes the essence of public opulence, or as the very thing in which public opulence properly consists. That state is properly opulent in which opulence is easily come at, or in which a little labour, properly and judiciously employed, is capable of procuring any man a great abundance of all the necessaries and conveniencies of life. Nothing else, it is evident, can render it general, or diffuse it universally through all the members of the society. National opulence is the opulence of the whole people, which nothing but the great reward of labour, and consequently the great facility of acquiring, can give occasion to. As this labour however is applied with great skill and judgement, as it is supported by the concurrence and united force of a great society, and over and above all this, as it is assisted by innumerable machines, it produces a much greater effect and performs a much greater quantity of work than in proportion to the superiority of its reward. The more opulent therefore the society, labour will always be so much the dearer and work so much the cheaper, and if some opulent countries have lost several of their manufactures and some branches of their commerce by having been undersold in foreign markets by the traders and artizans of poorer countries, who were contented with less profit and smaller wages, this will rarely be found to have been 13 meerly the effect of the opulence of the one country and the poverty of | the other. Some other cause, we may be assured, must have concurred. The rich country must have been guilty of some great error in its police. It must either have oppressed that particular branch of commerce or manufacture by improper customs and excises, or by the licensed insulence[h] of the officers of revenue, frequently more vexatious than all the taxes which they levey. Or by taxing, and thereby raising the prices of the necessaries of life, it must have increased the difficulty of subsistance, and thereby have screwed up the price of labour to an unnatural height, far beyond what the opulence of the society could of its own accord have raised it to. Where no error of this kind has been committed, as among individuals a rich merchant can always undersell and a rich manufacturer underwork a poor one, so among great societies a rich nation must always in every competition of commerce and manufactures have an equal or superior advantage over a poor one.

This immense increase of the quantity of work performed, in consequence of the division of labour, is owing to three different circumstances. First, to the increase of dexterity in every particular workman; secondly, to the saving of the time which is lost in passing from one species of work to another; and last of all, to the invention of innumerable machines, which facilitate labour and enable one workman to do the business of many.

The improvement of the dexterity of the workmen greatly increases the

---

[g] The last sentence is written in the margin          [h] Sic

quantity of the work performed; and the division of labour, by reducing the work which every man has to perform to a very simple operation, and by making the

14　performance of that operation the sole business | of his life, necessarily improves to the highest degree the dexterity of the workman. A smith, who has rarely or never had occasion to make nails, tho accustomed to use his hammer in a hundred other operations which one would think not very different, can, I am informed, with his utmost dilligence scarce make two or three hundred nails in a day, and these too excessively bad. A country smith who shoes horses, mends locks and hinges of doors, makes and mends spades, shovels, and all the other instruments of agriculture, when he has no particular piece of work upon his hands commonly employs his time in making nails. Such a person can, when he exerts himself, make about a thousand nails a day, and those too pretty good. I have seen a boy of nineteen years of age, who had done nothing else all his life but made nails, who in twelve hours could make two thousand three hundred nails, that is, about eight times the work of the first, and more than double the work of the second. The making of a nail, however, is by no means one of the simplest operations. The same person mends the fire, blows the bellows, heats the iron, [i] forges every part of the nail, and in forging the head is obliged to change his tools, which occasions a considerable loss of time; notwithstanding all this, a good workman will make very near four nails in a minute. [j] The different operations into which the making of a pin or of a mettal button is subdivided are all of them much more simple, and the dexterity acquired by the person, the sole business of whose life is to perform

15　them, is out of all proportion | greater. The rapidity with which some of the operations of those manufactures are performed far exceeds what the human hand could, by those who had never seen them, be supposed capable of acquiring.

The advantage, too, which is gained by saving the time commonly lost in passing from one species of work to another is very considerable, and much greater than what we should at first be apt to imagine. It is impossible to pass very quickly from some businesses to others, which are carried on in distant places and with quite different tools. A country weaver who likewise cultivates a small farm must lose a good deal of time in passing from his loom to the field and from the field to his loom. Where the two businesses can be carried on in the same work house, the loss of time is no doubt much less. It is even here, however, very considerable. A man commonly saunters a little in turning his hand from one sort of employment to a quite different ⟨?one⟩. When he first begins the new work he is seldome very keen or hearty. His mind does not go with it, and he for some time rather triffles than applies to good purpose. A man of great spirit and activity, when he is hard pushed upon some particular occasion, will pass with the greatest rapidity from one sort of work to another through a great variety of businesses. Even a

16　man of spirit and activity, however, must be hard pushed before | he can do this. In the ordinary course of business, when he passes from one thing to another he will saunter and trifle, tho' not undoubtedly in the same degree, yet in the same manner as an idle fellow. This habit of sauntering and of indolent, careless application, which is naturally or rather necessarily contracted by every country workman, who is obliged to change his work and his tools every half hour, and to

---

[i] 'and' deleted　　　[j] The last fifteen words are written in the margin

apply his hand in twenty different manners almost every day in his life, renders him almost always very slothful and lazy, and incapable, even upon the most pressing occasions, of any vigourous application. Independent therefore of his want of the most perfect dexterity this cause alone must always make the quantity of the work which he performs extremely inconsiderable.

Every body must be sensible how much labour is abridged and facilitated by the application of proper machinery. By means of the plough[k] two men, with the assistance of three horses, will cultivate more ground than twenty could do with the spade. A miller and his servant, with a wind or water mill, will at their ease grind more corn than eight men could do, with the severest labour, by hand mills. To grind corn in a hand mill was the severest work to which the antients commonly applied their slaves, and to which they seldome condemned them unless[l] when they had been guilty of some very great fault. A hand mill, however, is a very ingenuous[m] machine which greatly facilitates labour, and by which a
17 great deal of more work can | be performed than when the corn is either to be beat in a mortar, or with the bare hand, unassisted by any machinery, to be rubbed into pouder between two hard stones, as is the practice not only of all barbarous nations but of some remote provinces in this country. It was the division of labour which probably gave occasion to the invention of the greater part of those machines, by which labour is so much facilitated and abridged. When the whole force of the mind is directed to one particular object, as in consequence of the division of labour it must be, the mind is more likely to discover the easiest methods of attaining that object than when its attention is dissipated among a great variety of things. He was probably a farmer who first invented the original, rude form of the plough. The improvements which were afterwards made upon it might be owing sometimes to the ingenuity of the plow wright when that business had become a particular occupation, and sometimes to that of the farmer. Scarce any of them are so complex as to exceed what might be expected from the capacity of the latter. The drill plow, the most ingenious of any, was the invention of a farmer. Some miserable slave, condemned to grind corn between two stones by the meer strength of his arms, pretty much in the same manner as painters bray their colours at present, was probably the first who thought of supporting the upper stone by a spindle and of turning it round by a crank or
18 handle which moved | horizontally, according to what seems to have been the original, rude form of hand mills. He who first thought of making the spindle pass quite through the under millstone, which is at rest, of uniting it with a trundle, and of turning round that trundle by means of a cog wheel, which was itself turned round by a winch or handle, according to the present form of hand mills, was probably a mill wright, or a person whose principal or sole business it was, in consequence of the still further division of labour, to prepare that original, rude machine which it does not exceed the capacity of a common slave to have invented. Great advantages were gained by this improvement. The whole machinery being thus placed below the under millstone, the top of the upper one was left free for the conveniencies of the hopper, the feeder and shoe, and the crank or handle, which turned the cog wheel, moving in a circle perpendicular to

---

[k] Replaces 'plow'          [l] Replaces 'but'          [m] *Sic*

the horizon, the strength of the human body could be applied to it with much more advantage than to any crank which was to be turned round in a circle parallel to the horizon. These different improvements were probably not all of them the inventions of one man, but the successive discoveries of time and experience, and of the ingenuity of many different artists. Some of the more simple of them, such as the feeder and the shoe, might be the contrivances of the miller. But the more complex, such as the cog wheel and the trundle, were
19 probably the inventions of the millwright. They bear |[n] the most evident marks of the ingenuity of a very intelligent artist. He who first thought of substituting, in the room of the crank or handle, an outer wheel which was to be turned round by a stream of water, and much more, he who first thought of employing a stream of wind for the same purpose, was probably no work man of any kind, but a philosopher or meer man of speculation; one of those people whose trade it is not to do any thing but to observe every thing, and who are upon that account capable of combining together the powers of the most opposite and distant objects. To apply in the most advantagious manner those powers which are allready known and which have already been applyed to a particular purpose, does not exceed the capacity of an ingenious artist. But to think of the application of new powers, which are altogether unknown and which have never before been applied to any similar purpose, belongs to those only who have a greater range of thought and more extensive views of things than naturally fall to the share of a meer artist. When an artist makes any such discovery he showes himself to be not a meer artist but a real philosopher, whatever may be his nominal profession. It was a real philosopher only who could invent the fire engine, and first form the idea of producing so great an effect by a power in nature which had never before been thought of. Many inferior artists, employed in the fabric of this wonderful
20 machine, | may afterwards discover more happy methods of applying that power than those first made use of by its illustrious inventer. It must have been a philosopher who, in the same manner, first invented those now common and therefore disregarded machines, wind and water mills. Many inferior artists may have afterwards improved them. Philosophy or speculation, in the progress of society, naturally becomes, like every other employment, the sole occupation of a particular class of citizens. Like every other trade it is subdivided into many different branches, and we have mechanical, chymical, astronomical, physical, metaphysical, moral, political, commercial, and critical philosophers. In philosophy as in every other business this subdivision of employment improves dexterity and saves time. Each individual is more expert at his particular branch. More work is done upon the whole and the quantity of science is considerably increased by it.

This division of labour from which so many advantages result is originally the effect of no human wisdom which forsees and intends that general opulence to which it gives occasion. It is the necessary tho very slow and gradual consequence of a certain principle or propensity in human nature, which has in view
21 no such extensive utility. This is a propensity, common to all men, | and to be found in no other race of animals, a propensity to truck, barter, and exchange one

[n] 'in them' deleted

thing for another. That this propensity is common to all men is sufficiently obvious. And it is equally so that it is to be found in no other race of animals, which seem to be acquainted neither with this nor with any other species of contract. Two greyhounds, in running down the same hare, have sometimes the appearance of acting in some sort of concert. Each turns her towards his companion, or endeavours to intercept her when his companion turns her towards himself. This however is not the effect of any contract, but arises meerly from their passions happening at that instant to concurr in the same object. No body ever[y] saw a dog make a fair and deliberate exchange of one bone for another with another dog. No body ever saw one animal by its gestures and natural cries signify to another, 'This is mine, that yours; I am willing to give this for that.' When an animal wants to obtain something either of a man or of another animal, it has no other means of persuasion but to gain the kindness and favour of those whose service it stands in need of. A puppy fawns upon its dam, and a spaniel
22 endeavours, by a thousand attractions, | to engage the attention of its master who is at dinner, when it wants to be fed by him. Man sometimes uses the same arts with his bretheren, and when he has no other means of engaging them to act according to his inclinations endeavours by every fawning attention to obtain their goodwill. He has not time, however, to do this upon every occasion. So necessitous is his natural situation that he stands at all times in need of the co-operation and assistance of great multitudes, while his whole life is scarce sufficient to gain the friendship of a few persons. In every other race of animals each individual is almost entirely independent, and in its ordinary and natural state has occasion for the assistance of no other living creature. When any uncommon misfortune befals it, its piteous and doleful cries will sometimes engage its fellows, and sometimes prevail even upon man, to relieve it. When such assistance, however, becomes indispensibly necessary, the creature must generally lay its account with perishing for want of it. Such occasions can in the common course of things occur but seldom, and nature, with her usual oeconomy, has not thought proper to make any particular provision for them, any more than she has
23 made for the relief of man | when he is ship wrecked in the middle of the ocean. Her great purpose, the continuance and propogation of each species,[1] she has thought, was not likely to be interrupted by such uncommon and extraordinary accidents. But tho' an animal when once it has grown up to maturity stands but seldom in need of the assistance of its fellows, a man has almost constant occasion for the help of his bretheren, and it is in vain for him to expect it from their benevolence only. He will be much more likely to prevail if he can interest their self love in his favour, and show them that it is for their own advantage to do for him what he requires of them. Whoever offers to another a bargain of any kind proposes to do this. 'Give me that which I want and you shall have this which you want', is the plain meaning of every such offer. It is in this manner that we obtain from one another by far the greater and more important part of those good offices which we stand in need of. It is not from the benevolence of the butcher, the brewer, and the baker that we expect our dinner, but from their regard to their

---

[1] In TMS II.ii.3.5 Smith writes of 'the two great purposes of nature, the support of the individual, and the propagation of the species'.

own interest. We address ourselves not to their humanity but to their self love,
24 and never talk to them of our own necessities but of their advantages. | Nobody
but a beggar chuses[o] to depend chiefly upon the benevolence of his fellow citizens.
Even a beggar does not depend upon it entirely. If he did he would perish in a
week. The charity of well disposed people, indeed, may supply him perhaps with
the whole fund of his subsistence. But tho' this principle ultimately provides him
with all the necessaries of life which he has occasion for, it neither does nor can
provide him with them as he has occasion for them. The greater part of his
occasional wants are supplied in the same manner as those of other people, by
treaty, by barter, and by purchase. With the money which one man gives him he
purchases food. The old cloaths which another bestows upon him he exchanges
for other old cloaths which suit him better, or for lodging or for food, or for
money, with which he can buy either food, cloaths, or lodging as he has occasion.

As it is in this manner, by barter and exchange, that we obtain from one another
the greater part of those mutual good offices which we stand in need of, so it is
this same trucking disposition which originally gives occasion to that division of
labour upon which is founded the whole opulence of civilized societies. Among a
25 nation of hunters or | shepherds a particular savage is observed to make bows and
arrows with more readiness and dexterity than any other person. He sometimes
exchanges them for venison or for cattle with[p] his companions, and by degrees
comes to find that he can in this manner procure[q] more venison and more cattle
than if he himself went to the field to hunt them. From a regard to his own
interest and ease, therefore, it grows to be his chief business to make bows and
arrows; and he becomes in this manner a kind of armourer. Another excells in
making the frames and covers of their little huts or moveable houses. He is
accustomed in this way to be of use to those of his own tribe, who reward him in
the same manner with cattle and with venison, till at length he finds it for his
interest to dedicate himself entirely to this employment, and he becomes a sort
of house carpenter. In the same manner, a third becomes a smith; a fourth a
tanner or dresser of hydes and skins, the principal part of the cloathing of savages;
and thus the certainty of being able to exchange all that part of the produce of
his own labour which he himself has no occasion for, for such parts of the produce
of other mens labours as he has occasion for, enables every man to apply himself
26 to a particular occupation and | to cultivate and bring to perfection whatever
natural genius or talent he may possess for that particular species of business.

In reality the difference of natural talents in different men is perhaps much less
than we are aware of, and the very different genius which appears to distinguish
men of different professions when grown up to maturity is not, perhaps, so much
the cause as the effect of the division of labour. What two men can be more
different than a philosopher and a common porter? This difference, however,
seems to arise not so much from nature as from habit, custom, and education.
When they came into the world, and for the first five or six years of their existence,
they were perhaps pretty much alike, and neither their parents nor their play
fellows could observe any remarkable distinction. About that age, or soon after,
they come to be employed in very different occupations. The difference of what

[o] Replaces 'chooses'    [p] 'some of' deleted    [q] Replaces 'procure', possibly
mis-spelt

we call genius[r] comes then to be taken notice of, and widens by degrees, till at last the vanity of the philosopher is scarce willing to acknowledge any resemblance. But without the disposition to truck, barter, and exchange, every man must have procured for himself every necessary of life which he wanted. Every 27 man must have employed himself in every thing. All must have had the | same work to do and the same duties to perform, and there could ha've been no such difference of employment as could alone give occasion to any great difference of character. It is upon this account that a much greater uniformity of character is to be observed among savages than among civilized nations. Among the former there is scarce any division of labour and consequently no remarkable difference of employments; whereas among the latter there is an almost infinite variety of occupations, of which the respective duties bear scarce any resemblance to one another. What a perfect uniformity of character do we find in all the heroes described by Ossian? And what a variety of manners, on the contrary, in those who are celebrated by Homer? Ossian plainly describes the exploits of a nation of hunters,[2] while Homer paints the actions of two nations who, tho' far from being perfectly civilized, were yet much advanced beyond the age of shepherds, who cultivated lands, who built cities, and among whom he mentions many different trades and occupations, such as masons, carpenters, smiths, merchants, soothsayers, priests, physicians.[s] It is this disposition to truck, barter, and exchange 28 which not only gives occasion | to that difference of genius and talents, so remarkable among men of different professions, but which renders that difference usefull. There are many tribes of animals, which are all confessedly of the same species, upon whom nature seems to have stampt a much more remarkable distinction of genius and disposition than any which takes place among men, antecedent to custom and education. By nature a philosopher is not, in genius and disposition, half so different from a porter as a mastiff is from a greyhound, or a greyhound from a spaniel, or this last from a sheep dog. Those different tribes of animals, however, tho' all of the same species, are of scarce any use to one another. The strength of the mastiff is not in the least supported, either by the swiftness of the greyhound, or by the sagacity of the spaniel, or by the docility of the sheep dog. The effects of those different geniuses and talents, for want of the power or disposition to barter and exchange, cannot be brought into a common stock, and do not in the least contribute to the better accomodation of the species. Each animal is still obliged to support and defend itself seperately and independently, and derives no sort of advantage from that variety of talents with which nature has distinguished its fellows. Among men, on the contrary, the most dissimilar geniuses are of use to one another, the different produces of their 29 different talents being brought, as | it were, into a common stock by the general disposition to truck, barter, and exchange. A porter is of use to a philosopher, not

---

[r] 'between them' deleted          [s] The words 'a new paragraph' are written in the margin at this point

---

[2] Cf. Hugh Blair, *Critical Dissertation on the Poems of Ossian* (1763), 17: 'Throughout Ossian's poems, we plainly find ourselves in the first of these periods of society; during which, hunting was the chief employment of men, and the principal method of their procuring subsistence.'

only by sometimes carrying a burden for him, but by facilitating almost every trade and manufacture whose productions the philosopher can have occasion for. Whatever we buy from any shop or ware-house comes cheaper to us by means of those poor despised labourers, who in all great towns have set themselves aside for the particular occupation of carrying goods from one place to another, of packing and unpacking them, and who in consequence have acquired extraordinary strength, dexterity, and readiness in this sort of business. Every thing would be dearer if before it was exposed to sale it had been carried, packt, and unpackt by hands less able and less dexterous, who for an equal quantity of work would have taken more time, and must consequently have required more wages, which must have been charged upon the goods. The philosopher on the other hand is of use to the porter, not only by being sometimes an occasional customer, as well as any other man who is not a porter, but in many other respects. If the speculations of the philosopher have been turned towards the improvement of the mechanic arts, the benefit of them may evidently descend to the meanest of the people. Whoever burns coals has them at a better bargain by means of the

30 inventor of the fire engine. | Whoever eats bread receives a much greater advantage of the same kind from the inventors and improvers of wind and water mills. Even the speculations of those who neither invent nor improve any thing are not altogether useless. They serve at least to keep alive and deliver down to posterity the inventions and improvements which had been made before them. They explain the grounds and reasons upon which those discoveries were founded, and do not allow the quantity of usefull knowledge to diminish. In opulent and commercial societies, besides, to think or to reason comes to be, like every other employment, a particular business, which is carried on by a very few people, who furnish the public with all the thought and reason possessed by the vast multitudes that labour. Let any ordinary person make a fair review of all the knowledge which he possesses concerning any subject that does not fall within the limits of his particular occupation, and he will find that almost every thing he knows has been acquired at second hand, from books, from the literary instructions which he may have received in his youth, or from the occasional conversations which he may have had with men of learning. A very small part of it only, he will find, has been the produce of his own observations or reflections. All the rest has been purchased, in the same manner as his shoes or his stockings, from those whose business it is to make up and prepare for the market that particular species of goods. It is in this manner that he has acquired all his

31 general ideas concerning the great subjects of | religion, morals, and government, concerning his own happiness or that of his country. His whole system concerning each of those important objects will almost always be found to have been originally the produce of the industry of other people, from whom either he himself or those who have had the care of his education have procured it in the same manner as any other commodity, by barter and exchange for some part of the produce of their own labour.

## Contents of the following chapters.

Chap. 3ᵈ Of the rule of exchanging, or of the circumstances which regulate the prices of commodities. Treats of

1$^{mo}$ The price which is requisite to induce the labourer to apply himself to any particular species of industry, which must be sufficient 1$^{st}$ to maintain him; 2$^{dly}$ to indemnify him for the expence of his education to that particular business; 3$^{dly}$ to compensate him for the risk he may run, either of not living long enough to receive this indemnification, or of not succeeding in the trade, let him live ever so long. Price of country labour. Of handicraft work. Of ingenious arts. Of the liberal professions. Profits of silver mines.

2$^{do}$ The price which is fixed by the market, and which is regulated 1$^{st}$ by the
32 need or demand for any particular commodity; 2$^{dly}$ by the | abundance or scarcity of the commodity in proportion to that need or demand; and 3$^{dly}$ by the riches or poverty of the demandants.

3$^{tio}$ The connection between those two prices. That the market price can never, for any considerable time, be either above or below that price which is sufficient to encourage the labourer, unless there is some great error in the public police, which prevents the concurrence of labour when the price is too high, or forces a greater concurrence than is natural when the price is too low.

4$^{to}$ That as national or public opulence consists in the cheapness of commodities in proportion to the wages of labour, whatever tends to raise their price above what is precisely necessary to encourage the labourer tends to diminish national or public opulence. Of excises and other taxes upon industry. Of monopolies.

5$^{to}$ That there is in every country what may be called a natural balance of industry, or a disposition in the people to apply to each species of work pre-⟨c⟩isely in proportion to the demand for that work. That whatever tends to break this balance tends to hurt national or public opulence; whether it be by giving
33 extraordinary discouragement to some sorts of industry | or extraordinary encouragement to others. Of the French kings edict against planting new vineyeards, and of some equally absurd laws of other nations. Of bounties either upon the exportation or manufacture of certain goods. That they tend to render, indeed, such goods cheaper, the public paying a part of the price, but all others dearer; and upon the whole to enhance the price of commodities. Of the bounty upon corn. That it has sunk the price of corn, and thereby tends to lower the rents of corn farms. That by diminishing the number,$^t$ it tends to raise the rent of grass farms,$^u$ to raise the price of butcher meat, the price of hay, the expence of keeping horses, and consequently the price of carriage, which must, so far, embarrass the whole inland commerce of the country.

Chap. 4$^{th}$ Of money, it's nature, origin, and history, considered first as the measure of value, and secondly as the instrument of commerce.

Under the first head I have little to say that is very new or particular; except a general history of the coins of France, England, and Scotland; the different changes they have undergone; their causes and effects. And except some observations upon what may be called the money prices of commodities. That human
34 industry being at all times equally employed to multiply both | silver and commodities, and it being more in human power to multiply commodities than to multiply silver, the quantity of the former should naturally be expected to increase in a much greater proportion than that of the latter, and that

$^t$ 'of grass farms' deleted        $^u$ The last five words replace 'the rent of such farms'

consequently the money prices of commodities should at all times be continually sinking. That, however, things do not exactly correspond to this expectation. That in times of great barbarism and ignorance the money prices of such commodities as are in those times to be had are always extremely low, and for what reason. That they rise gradually till the society arives at a certain pitch of civility and improvement; and that in its further progress from this improved state to still greater opulence and improvement, those prices sink gradually again. That the money prices of commodities have in general been sinking in England for near a century past, and would have sunk much more had they not been artificially kept up by improper taxes and excises, and by some unjust monopolies. That the cheapness of commodities in China and the Moguls empire is the necessary effect of the immense opulence of those countries, notwithstanding their great abundance of gold and silver.

Under the second head, after explaining the use and necessity of a general
35 instrument | of commerce, or medium of exchange, and the way in which the precious metals come naturally to be made use of as such, I endeavour to show

I$^{mo}$ That as the sole use of money is to circulate commodities, that is, food, cloaths, and the conveniences of lodging, or domestic accomodation, and that as money itself is neither food, cloaths, nor lodging, the larger the proportion which that part of the stock of any nation which is converted into money bears to the whole, the less food, cloaths, and lodging there must be in that nation; which must, therefore, be so much the worse fed, cloathed, and lodged, and consequently so much the poorer and less powerful. That money, serving only to circulate commodities, is so much dead stock which produces nothing, and which may very properly be compared to a high road, which, while it helps to circulate the produce of all the grass and corn in the country, and thereby indirectly contributes to the raising of both, produces itself neither grass nor corn.

2$^{do}$ That whatever contrivance can enable any nation to circulate the produce of its industry with a smaller quantity of money than would otherwise be necessary, must be extremely advantagious; because the quantity of money saved may
36 be exchanged abroad for commodities, by means | of which a greater number of people can be fed, cloathed, lodged, maintained, and employed, the profit upon whose industry will still further increase the public opulence. That banks and bank notes are contrivances of this sort. They enable us, as it were, to plough up our high roads, by affording us a sort of communication through the air by which we do our business equally well. That, therefore, to confine them by monopolies, or any other restraints, except such as are necessary to prevent frauds and abuses, must obstruct the progress of public opulence. History of banking, ancient and modern.

3$^{tio}$ That national opulence, or the effect of national opulence, either at home or abroad, neither consists in nor depends upon the quantity of money, or even of gold and silver, that is in the country; and that no sort of preference is due to this species of goods above any other. The bad effects of the contrary opinion both in speculation and practice.

In speculation it has given occasion to the systems of Mun and Gee, of Mandeville who built upon them, and of Mr. Hume who endeavoured to refute them.

In practice it has given occasion

1$^{mo}$ To the prohibition which takes place in some countries of exporting either coin or | bullion. A prohibition which, very happily, is always in a great measure ineffectual; and which, so far as it is effectual, necessarily tends to impoverish the country. First, because whatever gold and silver there is in any country, over and above what is sufficient to circulate the produce of its industry, is so much dead stock, which is of no use at all: whereas, if allowed to go abroad, it would naturally be exchanged for what would feed, cloath, maintain, and employ a greater number of people, whose industry would increase real national opulence by multiplying the conveniences and necessaries of life. Secondly, because this unnecessary accumulation of gold and silver renders those metals cheap in proportion to other commodities, and consequently raises the money price of every thing. This stops all industry, the peasants, manufacturers, and traders of such a country being necessarily undersold, both at home and abroad, by the traders of other countries in which the money prices of things are lower. The misery of Spain and Portugal, owing, in part, for many other causes concur, to this prohibition.

2$^{do}$ To the unreasonable restraints imposed upon certain branches of commerce, and to the unreasonable encouragement given to others; | upon pretence that the one drains us of our money, we sending abroad money and getting home only goods which we consume; and that the other enriches us, we sending abroad only goods and getting home hard cash. The meanness, vulgarity, and folly of both these conceptions. First, that every branch of commerce which one nation can regularly carry on with another is, and necessarily must be, advantagious to both, each exchanging that which it has less need of for that which it has more need of, each giving what is of less value in its own country for what is of more value in the same country; each therefore increasing its own real opulence, and consequently its own power of feeding, cloathing, maintaining, and employing people. Secondly, that whatever tends to restrain the liberty of exchanging one thing for another tends to discourage industry, and to obstruct the division of labour which is the foundation of the opulence of society. It is allowed that all prohibitions of exportation discourage industry; but a prohibition of importation must have the same effect, since it is the same thing whether you forbid me to exchange my wares at the place where I can exchange them to most advantage, or for the goods for which I can exchange them to most advantage. If you prohibit the importation of French | claret, for example, you discourage all that industry of which the produce would have been exchanged for French claret. Whether that industry would have been exercised in making a piece of broad cloth, or in bringing gold from the Brazils, is of no consequence to national opulence. If that cloth is$^v$ more than the home consumption requires, it must go abroad; and if that gold is more than the channel of home circulation requires, or can receive, for these are the same, it must go abroad in the same manner, and be exchanged for something to be consumed at home, and why not for good claret? Thirdly, that the produce of every species of industry which is not either destroyed by some misfortune, or taken from us by an enemy, is, must, and ought to be consumed at home, either in substance or in what it is exchanged for, after

$^v$ Replaces 'was'

one, two, three, or three hundred exchanges: and that this is so far from either taking away or diminishing the national profit upon industry, that it is the very circumstance which renders all industry profitable to the nation; since it is only by means of this home consumption that more people can be maintained and employed, or those maintained and employed before be maintained and employed more agreably, or that the nation can in any respect better its circum-
40 stances. Fourthly, that no | nation ever was ruined by what is called the ballance of trade being against them, but by the excess of their annual consumption above the annual produce of their industry, which would necessarily ruin them tho' they had no foreign trade at all. Fifthly, that no nation whose industry and opulence are entire can be long in want of money; goods commanding money even more necessarily than money commands goods. Sixthly, that all extraordinary encouragement given to any one branch of commerce breaks the natural balance of industry in commerce as well as in manufactures, and, so far, obstructs the progress of opulence. Of the British trade to France and Portugal. That a free trade to France would tend infinitely more to enrich Great Britain than a free trade to Portugal, because France, on account of its superior opulence having more to give, would take more from us, and exchanging to a much greater value and in a much greater variety of ways, would encourage more industry in Great Britain and give occasion to more subdivisions of labour; and that it is only passion and national prejudice which ever made any body think otherwise. The British merchant.

3$^{tio}$ The notion that national opulence consists in money has given occasion to
41 the | current and pernicious opinion that we can never hurt ourselves by any expence incurred at home; because the money, being all spent among ourselves, does not go out of the country; and that what one loses another gets. That the difference with regard to the diminution of public opulence, when a stock of the conveniences and necessaries of life is wasted uselessly at home, and when either these or the money which purchases these is sent abroad to be wasted in the same manner, is extremely inconsiderable. Useless sea wars very near as destructive to public opulence as useless land wars.

4$^{to}$ The notion that national opulence consisted in or depended upon money, joined to another false notion that the value put upon the precious metals was a matter of institution and agreement, gave occasion to the famous system of Mr. Law. That gentleman imagined that by proper measures the inhabitants of a particular country might gradually be induced to affix the idea of a certain value to a certain paper currency, in the same manner as they affix it at present to a certain sum of money, and even to prefer the paper to the money; and that if this was once fairly brought about, the government, which had the issuing of this
42 paper, might excite what industry, raise and pay what | armies, and fit out what fleets they thought proper, without being at any other expence but that of building a paper mill. The vanity of both these imaginations, together with the history and analysis of the principal operations of this system. South Sea scheme.

Chap. 5$^{th}$ Concerning the causes of the slow progress of opulence.

Those causes of two kinds. First, natural impediments; and, secondly, oppressive or injudicious government.

The original poverty and ignorance of mankind the natural impediments to the progress of opulence. That it is easier for a nation, in the same manner as for an individual, to raise itself from a moderate degree of wealth to the highest opulence, than to acquire this moderate degree of wealth; money, according to the proverb, begetting money, among nations as among individuals. The extreme difficulty of beginning accumulation and the many accidents to which it is exposed. The slowness and difficulty with which those things, which now appear the most simple inventions, were originally found out. That a nation is not always in a condition to imitate and copy the inventions and improvements of its more wealthy neighbours; the application of these frequently requiring a stock with which it is not furnished.

43 The oppressive and injudicious governments to which mankind are almost always subject, but more especially in the rude beginnings of | society, greatly increase those natural impediments, which of themselves are not easily surmounted. The oppression and errors of government affect either $1^{mo}$ agriculture; or $2^{do}$ arts and commerce.

$1^{mo}$ The great importance of agriculture and how much the value of its annual produce exceeds that of any other art. That the cultivation of land depends upon the proportion which the stock of those who cultivate it$^w$ bears to the quantity of land to be cultivated. That consequently whatever tends to prevent the accumulation of stock in the hands of the cultivators, or to discourage them from continuing this species of industry after they have accumulated some stock in this manner, must tend to retard the progress of agriculture.

That the chiefs of an independent nation which settles in any country, either by conquest or otherwise, as soon as the idea of private property in land is introduced never leave any part of the land vacant, but constantly, from that greediness which is natural to man, seize much greater tracts of it to themselves than they have either strength or stock to cultivate. From the same greediness and rapacity, being$^x$ unwilling to divide the profites of this land with any freeman, what they cannot or will not cultivate by their own strength they endeavour to cultivate by the strength of slaves, whom they either conquer in war or purchase in some other way, and in whose hands no stock ever can accumulate.

## Of the cultivation by slaves.

44 That land can never be cultivated to the best | advantage by slaves, the work which is done by slaves always coming dearer than that which is done by freemen. Of the scanty produce and great expence of the slave cultivation among the antient Greeks and Romans. Of villenage as it took place among our Saxon and Norman ancestors; of the adscripti glebae in Germany and Poland, and the rustici in Russia, and those who work in the coal and salt works of Scotland. That the high cultivation of Barbadoes, and of some other sugar and tobacco colonies, notwithstanding that in them the labour is performed almost entirely by slaves, is owing to this circumstance, that the cultivation of tobacco and sugar is engrossed, the one almost entirely by the English, the other by the English and French, who thus enjoying a sort of monopoly against all the rest of the world,

---

$^w$ 'for their own benefite' deleted        $^x$ 'the' deleted

indemnify themselves by the exorbitancy of their profites for their expensive and thriftless method of cultivation. The great expence of slave cultivation in the sugar plantations. The yet more exorbitant profites of the planter. That the planters in the more northern colonies, cultivating chiefly wheat and Indian corn, by which they can expect no such exorbitant returns, find it not for their interest to employ many slaves, and yet Pensilvania, the Jerseys, and some of the provinces of New England are much richer and more populous than Virginia, notwithstanding that tobacco is by its ordinary high price a more profitable cultivation.

45     | Of the cultivation of the antient metayers, or tenants by steelbow.[y]

That through the whole of that very small corner of the world in which slavery has, by a concurrence of different causes, been abolished, what naturally and almost necessarily came after the cultivation by slaves was that by the antient metayers or tenants by steelbow. To these at the commencement of the lease a certain number of cattle were delivered by the lord, to be returned in equal number and goodness at the expiration of it. With these cattle the tenant was to cultivate the land, and the lord and he were to divide the produce between them, each chusing a sheaff in his turn when the corn was cut down and set up in sheaffs on the field. That land could never be improved to the best advantage by such tenants. $1^{st}$, because stock could not, without the greatest difficulty, accumulate in their hands; and $2^{dly}$, because if it did accumulate they would never lay it out in the improvement of the land, since the lord, who laid out nothing, was to divide the profites with them. That the greater part of the lands in the western parts of Europe, the only corner of the world in which slavery has ever been abolished, particular⟨l⟩y about five sixth parts of the lands in France, are still cultivated by tenants of this kind.

Of the cultivation by farmers properly so called.

46     | That to those metayers or tenants by steelbow succeeded, in some few places, farmers properly so called, or tenants who had a lease of their lands either for life or during a term of years, for a rent certain to be paid at first in kind and afterwards in money. That those tenants seem to have been originally metayers, in whose hands, notwithstanding many oppressions, some property had accumulated, and who were thereby enabled to stock their own farms, and consequently to offer a contract of this kind to their lords. That such farmers, having some little stock of their own, and not being liable to have their rents immediately raised upon them, might be both able and willing to make some improvements. That they still, however, laboured under many inabilities and discouragements. That a lease of lands, being a transaction founded upon contract, originally and naturally begot only a personal right in the tenant, which, tho it was good against the lessor and his heirs, was not good against a purchaser. That, therefore, if a tenant made any such improvement of his lands as greatly increased their value, he was sure of being turned out[z] of his lease, either by a real or by a sham

---

[y] The following note is written in the margin at this point: 'The first of these expressions is French; the second, Scotch. This species of lease having been long disused in England, and even in all the tollerably cultivated parts of Scotland. I know no English word for it at present.'     [z] The last two words replace an illegible word

purchaser. Of the statutes of England and Scotland by which leases were first secured against purchasers, and that this police is almost peculiar to Great
47 Britain. Of the many other discouragements which tenants laboured under. | Of the disadvantages of a rent paid in kind, and of the difficulties which attended the first introduction of money rents. Of leases from year to year, or at will.ᵃ Of the arbitrary services with which all sorts of tenants were all over Europe long burdened at the will of the landlord. Of the laws by which these were restrained or abolished in some countries, of the political reasons of those laws, and how far these services are still due in many countries. Of purveyance. Of the arbitrary and exorbitant tallages to which tenants of all kinds were liable, and how far these still subsist in many countries. Of the taille in France and its effects upon agriculture. Of the advantage which agriculture derives in England from the law which gives certain lease holders a right of voting for Members of Parliament, which thereby establishes a mutual dependance between the landlord and the tenant, and makes the former, if he has any regard to his interest in the county, very cautious of attempting to raise his rents, or of demanding any other oppressive exactions of the latter. The superior liberty of the English above the Scots.

That the original engrossment of lands by the chiefs of the nations has been perpetuated in Europe by three different causes. First, by the obstruction which the antient feudal government gave to the alienation of land, which, notwith-
48 standing the almost | entire extinction of that government, is still every where embarrassed by many unnecessary forms, not requisite in the transference of any other property, how valuable soever. Secondly, by entails and other perpetuities. Thirdly, by the right of primogeniture. The reasons of the rapid progress of opulence in those colonies in which this engrossment of lands has been in some measure prevented, and in which the greater part of lands are cultivated not by farmers but by proprietors. Of the British North American colonies.

Of other discouragements to the cultivation of lands. Of tythes. Of the prohibition of the exportation of corn according to the antient police of almost every part of Europe. That sometime after the full establishment of the power of the Romans, a prohibition of this kind, together with the distributions which were annually made by the government of Sicilian, Egyptian, and African corn at a very low price to the people, and which must have had the same effect to discourage home cultivation as a bounty upon importation, gave occasion to the depopulation of antient Italy, and to the saying of old Cato, 'Qui cuidam querenti quid maxime prodesset in re familiari? Bene pascere, respondit. Quid proximum? Satis bene pascere. Quid tertium? Male pascere. Quid quartum? Arare.' Cicero, de off. lib. 2ᵈ at the end.³

2ᵈᵒ        of

---

ᵃ The last nine words are written in the margin

---

³ 'Who, when asked what was the most profitable aspect of land-owning, replied "Raising cattle well." "What next?" "Raising cattle adequately." "What comes third?" "Raising cattle badly." "What comes fourth?" "Raising crops." ' Smith is quoting from memory. The actual text of Cicero (*De Officiis*, II.89) differs slightly in words but not in meaning.

# FIRST FRAGMENT ON THE DIVISION OF LABOUR

1 | who, for an equal quantity of work, would have taken more time and consequently[a] have required more wages, which must have been charged upon the goods. The philosopher, on the other hand, is of use to the porter; not only by being sometimes an occasional customer, like any other man who is not a porter, but in many other respects. If the speculations of the philosopher have been turned towards the improvement of the mechanic arts, the benefit of them may evidently descend to the meanest of the people. Whoever burns coals has them at a better bargain by means of the inventer of the fire-engine. Whoever eats bread receives a much greater advantage of the same kind from the inventers and improvers of wind and water mills. Even the speculations of those who neither invent nor improve any thing are not altogether useless. They serve, at least, to keep alive and deliver down to posterity the inventions and improvements which have been made before them. They explain the grounds and reasons upon which those discoveries were founded and do not suffer the quantity of useful science to diminish.

As it is the power of[b] exchanging[c] which[d] gives occasion to the division of labour, so the extent of this division will always be in proportion to the extent of that power.[e] Every species of industry will be carried on in a more or less perfect manner, that is, will be more or less accurately subdivided into[f] the different

2 branches according to[g] which it is capable of being split, in proportion | to the extent of the market, which is evidently the same thing with the power of exchanging. When the market is very small it is altogether impossible that there can be that separation of one employment from another which naturally takes place when it is more extensive. In a country village, for example, it is altogether impossible that there should be such a trade as that of a porter. All the burdens which, in such a situation, there can be any occasion to carry from one house to another would not give full employment to a man for a week in the year. Such a[h] business can scarce be[i] perfectly separated from all others in a pretty large market town. For the same reason, in all the small villages which are at a great distance from any market town, each family must bake their own bread and brew their own beer, to their own great expence and inconveniency,[j] by the interruption which is thereby given to their respective employments, and by being obliged, on this account, to maintain[k] a greater number of servants than would otherwise be necessary. In mountainous and desart countries,[l] such as the greater part of the Highlands of Scotland, we cannot expect to find, in the same manner,[m] even a smith,[n] a carpenter, or a mason within less than twenty or thirty miles of another smith,[o] carpenter, or mason. The scattered families who live at ten or fifteen

[a] 'would' deleted    [b] 'bartering and' deleted    [c] 'which one thing for another' deleted    [d] 'originally' deleted    [e] 'The lar greater the market, the larger the commerce' deleted    [f] Replaces 'into according to'    [g] The last two words replace 'into'    [h] 'buss' deleted    [i] 'there' deleted    [j] 'being obliged upon this account, not only frequently' deleted    [k] 'on this account' deleted    [l] 'in the same manner' deleted    [m] The last four words replace 'such as'    [n] 'or' deleted    [o] 'or another' deleted

miles distance from the nearest of any[p] of those three[q] artisans, must learn to perform themselves a great number of little pieces of work for which, in more populous countries, they would readily have recourse to one or other of them,[r] whom they now can afford to send for[s] only upon very extraordinary occasions.[t]

3 | In a savage tribe of North Americans, who are generally hunters, the greatest number who can subsist easily together seldom exceeds one hundred or[u] one hundred and fifty persons.[v] Each village is at so great a distance from every other, and it is so very difficult and dangerous to travel the country, that there is scarce any intercourse between the different[w] villages[x] even of the same nation except what war and mutual defence give occasion to. In such a country it is impossible that any one employment should be entirely separated from every other. One man, etc:[y] One man may excel all his companions in some particular piece of dexterity, but it is impossible that he can be wholly employed in it, for want of a market to take off and exchange for other commodities the greater part of the goods which he would, in this case, necessarily produce. Hence the poverty which must necessarily take place in such a society. In a tribe of Tartars, or wild Arabs, who are generally shepherds, a greater number can live conveniently in one place. They do not depend upon the precarious accidents of the chace for subsistence, but upon the milk and flesh of their herds and flocks, who graze in the fields adjoining to the village. The Hottentots near the Cape of Good-hope are the most barbarous nation of shepherds that is known in the world. One of their villages or Kraals, however, is said generally to consist of upwards of five hundred persons. A Hord of Tartars frequently consists of five, six, or even ten times that number. As among such nations, therefore, tho' they have scarce any foreign commerce, the home market is somewhat[z] more extensive, we may expect to find something like the beginning of the division of labour.[a] Even in each village of Hottentots, therefore, according to Mr. Kolben,[1] there are[b] such[c] trades as those of a smith, a taylor, and even a phisician, and the persons who

4 exercise them, tho' they | are not entirely, are principally supported by those respective employments, by which too they are greatly distinguished from the rest of their fellow citizens. Among the Tartars and Arabs we find the faint

---

[p] Replaces 'either'		[q] Replaces 'two'		[r] Replaces 'those workmen'
[s] 'at much trouble and expence' deleted		[t] 'It is the same | thing with the mason' deleted		[u] 'one hundred and fifty men two hundred' deleted		[v] 'They live' deleted		[w] The last two words replace 'one'		[x] 'and another' deleted		[y] The words 'One man, etc:' and the three sentences which precede them are written in the margin. Indicators show that the three sentences are intended to replace the following passage, which has been deleted: 'In a tribe of ['savage' deleted] hunters who perhaps do not among them make above a hundred or a hundred and fifty persons and who have no regular commerce or intercourse of any kind with any other tribe, except such as mutual hostility and war may give occasion to, it is scarce possible that any one employment of any kind should be compleatly separated from every other.'		[z] Replaces 'a good deal'		[a] 'We find' deleted		[b] Replaces 'is'		[c] 'a' deleted

---

[1] Peter Kolben (or Kolb), *The Present State of the Cape of Good Hope* (German edn., 1719; English edn., London, 1731). Smith's comments on the Hottentots in this section of the fragment were probably derived from p. 216 of vol. I of the English edn. (population of kraals); ch. xix *passim* (the smith and the tailor); and ch. xxv *passim* (the physician).

commencements[d] of a still[e] greater variety of employments. The Hottentots, therefore, may be regarded as a richer nation than the North Americans, and the Tartars and Arabs as[f] richer than the Hottentots. The compleat division of labour, however, is posteriour to the invention even of agriculture. By means of agriculture the same quantity of ground[g] not only produces corn but is made capable of supporting a much greater number of cattle than before. A much greater number of people, therefore, may easily subsist in the same place. The home market, in consequence,[h] becomes much more extensive. The smith, the mason, the carpenter, the weaver, and the taylor soon find it for their interest not to trouble themselves with cultivating the ground, but to exchange with the farmer the produces of their several employments[i] for the corn and cattle which they have occasion for. The farmer too very[j] soon comes to find it equally for his interest not to interrupt his own business with[k] making cloaths for his family, with building or repairing his own house, with mending or making the different instruments of his trade, or the different parts of his houshold furniture, but to call in the assistance of other workmen for each of those purposes whom he rewards with corn and with cattle.[l]

---

[d] 'in the same manner' deleted            [e] Replaces 'much'            [f] Replaces 'much'
[g] 'is made to support far' deleted            [h] The last two words replace 'therefore'
[i] 'with' deleted            [j] The last two words replace 'too'            [k] Replaces 'in order to'
[l] The last thirteen words replace 'for each of these purposes'

# SECOND FRAGMENT ON THE DIVISION OF LABOUR

1 | or ten men, and sailing from the port of Leith, will frequently in three days, generally in six days, carry two hundred tuns of goods to the same market. Eight or ten men, therefore, by the help of water carriage, can transport, in a much shorter time, a greater quantity of goods from Edinburgh to London than sixty six narrow wheeled waggons drawn by three hundred and ninety six horses and attended by a hundred and thirty two men: or than forty broad wheeled waggons drawn by three hundred and twenty horses and attended by eighty men. Upon two hundred tuns of goods, therefore, which are carried by the cheapest land carriage from Edinburgh to London there must be charged the maintenance of eighty men for three weeks, both the maintenance and what, tho' less than the maintenance, is however of very great value, the tear and wear of three hundred and twenty horses as well as of forty waggons. Whereas upon two hundred tuns of goods carried between the same markets by water carriages, there is to be charged only the maintenance of eight or ten men for about a fortnight and the tear and wear of a ship of two hundred tuns burden. If there was no other communication, therefore, between Edinburgh and London but by land, as no goods could be transported from the one place to the other except such whose price was very high in proportion to their weight,[m] there could not be the hundredth part of the commerce which is at present carried on between them, nor, in consequence, the hundredth part of the encouragement which they at present mutually give to each other's industry. There could be very little[n] commerce of any kind between the distant parts of the world. How few goods are so precious as to bear the
2 expence of land carriage between London and Canton in China, | which at present carry on so extensive a commerce with one another and give consequently so much mutual encouragement to each other's industry? The first improvements, therefore, in arts and industry are always made in those places where the conveniency of water carriage affords the most extensive market to the produce of every sort of[o] labour. In our North American colonies the plantations have constantly followed either the sea coast or the banks of the navigable rivers, and have scarce any where extended themselves to any considerable distance from both. What James the sixth of Scotland said of the county of Fife, of which the inland parts were at that time very ill while the sea coast was extremely well cultivated, that it was like a coarse woollen coat edged with gold lace, might[p] still be said[q] of the greater part of our North American colonies.[r] The countries in the world which appear to have been first civilised are those which ly round the coast of the Mediterranean Sea. That sea,[s] by far the greatest inlet that is known in the world, having no tides nor consequently any waves except such as are caused by the wind only, was by the smoothness of its surface as well as by the

---

[m] The last twenty-five words are written in the margin    [n] The last two words replace 'scarce any'    [o] 'industry' deleted    [p] Replaces 'is'    [q] The last two words replace 'true'    [r] 'the most favoured by nature perhaps of any country in the world the countries in the world perhaps the most favoured by nature' deleted    [s] 'the gre' deleted

multitude of its islands and the proximity of its opposite coasts[t] extremely favourable to the infant navigation of the world, when from the[u] want of the compass men were[v] afraid to quit the coast, and from the imperfection of the art of shipbuilding to abandon themselves to the boisterous waves of the ocean. Egypt, of all the countries upon the coast of the Mediterranean, seems to have

3   been the first | in which either agriculture or manufactures were[w] cultivated or improved to any considerable degree.[x] Upper Egypt scarce extends[y] itself any where above five or six miles from the Nile; and in lower Egypt that great river, etc:[z] breaks itself into a great many different canals which with the assistance of a little art afforded, as in Holland at present, a communication by water carriage not only between all the great towns but between all the considerable villages and between almost all the farm houses in the country. The greatness and easiness of their inland navigation and commerce, therefore, seem to have been evidently the causes of the early improvement of Egypt.[a] Agriculture and manufactures too seem to have been of very great antiquity in some of the maritime provinces of China and in the province of Bengal in the East Indies. All[b] these are countries very much of the same nature with Egypt, cut by innumerable canals which afford them an immense inland navigation.

[t] 'was' deleted        [u] The last two words replace 'men for'        [v] The last two words replace 'were' and an indecipherable word which is deleted above the line        [w] Replaces 'seem to have been'        [x] 'In lower Egypt the Nile' deleted        [y] The first few words of this sentence originally read 'In upper Egypt the country scarce extends'. 'In' and 'the country' have been deleted, and 'upper' emended to 'Upper'.        [z] This sentence is written in the margin        [a] 'They seem to have been the only people in the world who never ventured from', followed by eight or nine indecipherable words, deleted        [b] Replaces 'both'

# Index of Roman Law and Medieval Law Sources

# Index of Acts of the English and United Kingdom Parliaments

# Index of Acts of the Parliaments of Scotland[1]

# Index of Legal Cases

[1] English reported cases are found either in *The English Reports* (176 vol., Edinburgh–London, 1900–30) or Howell's *State Trials* (34 vol., London, 1809–28).

[2] Scots reported cases are found in W. M. Morison's *Decisions of the Court of Session in the form of a Dictionary* (38 vol. with continuous pagination, Edinburgh, 1811).

# Index of Authorities[1]

(Cited in Introduction, Text, and Notes)

[1] ASL indicates that *an* edition of the work (or the collected works of the author) was in Smith's library, as reported in J. Bonar's *A Catalogue of the Library of Adam Smith*, 2nd ed., London, 1932, or H. Mizuta's *Adam Smith's Library* (with a check-list of the whole library), Cambridge, 1967. Q indicates that an edition of the work was bought for Glasgow University Library when Smith was Quaestor, according to the Quaestor's accounts printed in W. R. Scott's *Adam Smith as Student and Professor*, pp. 179–84.

Abu'l Ghasi (Husain), *Shajarat al Atrak*: Eng. trans. *The Genealogical History of the Tatars*, in *A General History of the Turks, Moguls and Tatars with a description of the countries they inhabit, made English from the French* (2 vol., London, 1729–30), 216
*Acts and Ordinances of the Interregnum, 1642–1660*, ed. C. H. Firth and R. S. Rait (3 vol., London, 1911), 237
Afranius in *Comicorum Romanorum Fragmenta*, ed. O. Ribbeck (Lipsiae, 1898), 180
Ammianus Marcellinus, 364 (ASL)
Aristotle, *Nicomachean Ethics*, 88 (ASL)
— *Politics*, 22, 192, 371, 530 (ASL)

Bacon, M., *A New Abridgement of the Law* (5 vol., London, 1736–66), 80, 471, 473 (Q)
Bible, 116, 118, 166, 167, 180, 205, 478 (ASL)
Bielfeld, Baron J. F. von, *Institutions politiques* (2 vol., La Haye, 1760), 5, 230 (ASL)
Blair, H., *A Critical Dissertation on the Poems of Ossian, the Son of Fingal* (1763), 573
Bolingbroke, Lord (Henry St. John), *Remarks on the History of England, from the Minutes of Mr Oldcastle* (1730–1), in *Works* (4 vol., Philadelphia, 1841), 270 (ASL)
Bosman, W., *A New and Accurate Description of the Coast of Guinea, containing a particular account of the rise, progress and present condition of all the European settlements upon that coast* (London, 1705), 154
Bouquet, P., *Le Droit public de France, éclairci par les monumens de l'antiquité* (Paris, 1756), 52, 251, 252, 253
Burnet, G., *History of His Own Time* (1724; 6 vol., Edinburgh, 1753), 118, 325, 327, 328, 329 (ASL)

Caesar, *De Bello Gallico*, 218 (ASL)
Callis, R., *Reading on Sewers* (2nd ed., London, 1685), 26
Cannan, E. (ed.), *Lectures on Justice, Police, Revenue and Arms delivered in the University of Glasgow by Adam Smith* (Oxford, 1896), 5, 6, 7, 8, 553
Cantillon, R., *Essai sur la nature du commerce en général* (1755), 354 (ASL)
Chambers, E., *Cyclopaedia, or an Universal Dictionary of Arts and Sciences* (1728; 4th ed., London, 1741), 342 (ASL)
Charlevoix, P.-F.-X. de, *Histoire et description générale de la Nouvelle France, avec le Journal historique d'un voyage fait par l'ordre du Roi dans l'Amérique septentrionnale* (3 vol., Paris, 1744), 21, 106, 201 (ASL)
Cicero, *Ad Atticum*, 196 (ASL)
— *Ad Quintum Fratrem*, 196 (ASL)
— *De Finibus*, 41, 67 (ASL)
— *De Officiis*, 174, 197, 306, 525, 548, 581 (ASL)
— *In Verrem*, 414 (ASL)
Cocceii, Baron H. de, *Grotius Illustratus, seu commentarii ad Hugonis Grotii de jure belli et pacis libros tres* (4 vol., Wratislaviae, 1744–52), 398, 552 (ASL)
Cocceii, Baron S. de, *Introductio ad Henrici L. B. de Cocceii Grotium Illustratum continens dissertationes proemiales XII* (Halae, 1748), 28, 36, 39, 324, 398 (ASL)

# General Index